An Infantile Disorder?
The Crisis and Decline
of the New Left

NIGEL YOUNG
School of Peace Studies
University of Bradford

An Infantile Disorder?
The Crisis and Decline
of the New Left

Westview Press
Boulder, Colorado

Published in 1977
in the United States of America by
Westview Press, Inc.
1898 Flatiron Court
Boulder, Colorado 80301
Frederick A. Praeger, Publisher
and Editorial Director
Printed in Great Britain
© Nigel Young 1977

Library of Congress Cataloging in Publication Data

Young, Nigel.

An infantile disorder.

Bibliography: p.
Includes index.
1. Radicalism—United States.   2. Radicalism.
I. Title.
HN90.R3Y68   320.5'3   76-30272
ISBN 0-89158-549-4

Contents

Preface   ix
Acknowledgments   x
Chronology   xi
Introduction   1

1 Convergence and Breakthrough
The blocs begin to crumble   8
Consensus and utopia   9
The convergent orthodoxies   10
Cold War and the critique of bureaucracy   13
Beyond the blocs   15
Theory and language   16
An end of politics?   18
Alienation and control   19
Back to utopia   21
Sociology and the New Left   21

2 The New Left: A Core Identity
Forces and movements for change   24
The bomb generation   27
Direct action spreads   29
Outside the national frame   33
Radical pacifism   34
Morality and political rebellion   36
Theory and practice   38
Let the people decide   43
Living the revolution   44
Participatory democracy   46

3 A New Radicalism
The movement crystallizes   51
The central themes of the movement   55

The communalist vision 57
Contra-culture 58
The birth of radical community 60
'There's a Change Gonna Come': the counter-institutions 61
The dynamics of radicalization 63

4 After Reformism: The Dilemmas of Extra-Parliamentarism
The liberal disenchantment and the origins of anti-politics 66
From pressure group to extra-parliamentary opposition:
CND in Britain 70
Organizing the excluded: SDS and power at the grassroots 78
The Democratic Party and the crisis of black reform 82
Electoral interludes: the temptations of re-alignment and
coalition 85
Outside the system: Syndicalism revisited 89
Anti-parliamentarism and the rejection of the State 92
Organizing the counter-democracy 96

5 The Problem of Agency
In quest of proletariat 99
A black proletariat? 104
A new class: 'Students as niggers' 108

6 Black Movements in Crisis
Blackness and integration 114
Black Power and the grassroots 117
'A slice of Whitey's pie' 120
The Black Panthers 126

7 In Search of Ideology
Marxism and the ideological vacuum 130
The New Left as Anarchist revival 133
Marxism, Revisionism and Anarchism 138

8 The New Left in Britain: 1956–70
A false start 144
CND: decline and fall 148
The Communist Party's role 153
After CND 157

9 Vietnam and Alignment
Non-alignment and internationalism: the third way 163
Pacifism and national liberation 168

The New Left and the Vietnam war   174
Indo-China solidarity in Britain   179
Anti-imperialism and anti-America   182
The Third World trap: 'thinking with the blood'   186

10 SDS in Flux   189

11 Annus Mirabilis: 1968
Point of no return   205
Tet   209
Memphis   210
Columbia   212
May 1968: France   215
Prague summer   218
'Czechago': the National Democratic Convention demonstrations   221

12 Turn Towards Violence
Nonviolence in crisis   223
The great divide   230
The problem of self-defence   238
From confrontation to terror   244

13 Revolution and the New Left
Theories of insurgence   254
The urban guerillas   259
Modern revolution: violent and nonviolent   266
Weatherman   275

14 Provocation: Response and Repression
Confrontation and reaction   283
Provoking counter-revolution   286
Repression and the New Left   290

15 The New Left and the Old
Waiting in the wings   298
The Old Left counter-attacks   302
The Old Left takes over   308
Progressive Labor: killing the goose   314
Back to square one   322

16 A Crisis of Identity
A movement loses itself   324
Crisis of the counter-institutions   331
Participatory democracy and after   336

One-dimensional tolerance   341
Emasculation by the media   346
The music dies   353

17 Picking up the Threads
Reconnections   360
Sexism and liberation   367
Post-scarcity radicalism   376

Appendix: Leninism, militarism, and peasant revolution   385
Notes   391
Select Bibliography   477
Index   480

Preface

Shortly after the Russian revolution, Lenin wrote a stern attack on those who identified either the 1917 events, or the process of 'socialist transformation' elsewhere, with expressive spontaneity and freedom, which he identified as a 'children's disease' – in particular he selected the libertarian socialist oppositionists – both within Russia itself, and outside, where the Communist organizations were forming, as 'left-wing communists', engaging in romantic, extra-parliamentary, revolutionism – an 'infantile disorder', preventing disciplined party action.[1] Lenin's organizational discipline and doctrinal severity survived as the major legacy of 1917, and stamped itself on the international left movements for nearly fifty years. But less than half a century later, latter-day Leninists were confronting what they perceived as a renewal of infantile leftism.

This new 'Infantile Disorder', a *new* left, in many ways a counterpart to the earlier oppositional communists, was radical, extra-parliamentary, and libertarian – both young and disordered – and often, too, incurably romantic. But this time, whilst the influence of Leninism (to which in part the new radicalism had initially reacted) had a hand in the new movement's crisis and destruction, it had no chance of channelling its increasingly chaotic energies, or organizing its disparate constituencies, into new parties as it had largely succeeded in doing in 1920.

Acknowledgments

To Antonia and Phyllis Young for irreplaceable help throughout the writing of this book; to Gillian Lucas and Dr Samuel Okufor for initial research help; to Howard Clarke, Laurens Otter, Keith Paton, Victor Anderson, Dave Wellman, Bob Overy, Jeff Lustig and to other friends and students who have heard or read and commented on various points in relation to earlier versions of this book, and also made bibliographical suggestions; to several editors of *Peace News* over more than fifteen years, for working out some of the connections made here, for allowing me space in that time to work some of them out for myself in print, and for their comments on various parts of an earlier draft of this book; and to Sandra Bates, Hazel Downing, John Tsimba, Margaret Wright, Francis Hanley, François Demunck and others for help in preparing the final manuscript and index.

Chronology

Dates of relevant events, periodicals, organizations, etc., with abbreviations used in text.

1953		First Russian nuclear tests.
1954		Pacific H-Bomb Tests by USA/UK.
		A. J. Muste's Third Camp Proposals. His pamphlet seized and burned.
		Supreme Court decision on desegregation (USA).
1955	*1 Dec.*	Montgomery, Alabama; bus-boycott begins with Rosa Park's direct action
		M. L. King emerges as leader.
		First anti-civil-defence protests (New York).
1956		Publication of:

Marcuse's *Eros and Civilisation*
Fromm's *Sane Society*
First English translation of Camus's *L'Homme Révolté (The Rebel)*
Colin Wilson's *The Outsider*
C. Wright Mills's *Power Elite*
Paul Goodman's *Growing Up Absurd*
W. Whyte's *Organisation Man.*

Osborne's *Look Back in Anger* at the Royal Court Theatre.

Mar.   *Liberation* magazine founded by Muste, Dellinger, Lynd, Goodman and others, and in Britain *Peace News* (PN) splits from *Peace Pledge Union* (PPU) and publishes independently.

UK conscription phased out (ends May 1957).

Feb.   Revelations about Stalin at 20th Communist Party Congress (Russia).

June   Revolts occur in Poland and Hungary. Soviet troops repress workers' rising in Budapest (November). China supports Russian action.

	Oct.	England, France and Israel invade Egypt.
		Mass demonstrations against Suez venture (London).
		IRA renews armed hostilities against British in Ireland.
1957	*Jan.*	Southern Christian Leadership Conference (SCLC) formed.
		Agitation against US tests in Britain and America.
		Committee for Nonviolent Action (CNVA) formed in USA.
	May	*New Reasoner* published by ex-communists (UK) after anti-Stalinist gatherings.
	June	Committee for a Sane nuclear policy (SANE) formed in USA.
		Direct Action Committee (DAC) against Nuclear War formed, UK.
	Aug.	Nonviolent action at Atomic Energy Commission (AEC), Nevada.
		Allen Ginsberg's *Howl*, Jack Kerouac's *On The Road*, and other 'Beat' literature published.
	Oct.	*Universities and Left Review* (ULR) published in England.
	Nov.	British H-Bomb test at Christmas Island; Steele's voyage.
1958	*Feb.*	Campaign for Nuclear Disarmament (CND) founded in London, followed by sit-down in Downing Street.
		Mills's *Causes of World War III* published.
	Easter	DAC/CND first Aldermaston March.
		Action versus US tests; Cheyenne sit-down; voyage of *Golden Rule* and *Phoenix* to testing areas.
	May	Mass CND Lobby of Parliament; May Day Confrontations in St Pancras.
		SLATE student party organized at the University of California, Berkeley.
	Aug./ Sept.	South Bank building strike; *Newsletter* activity (UK).
		Race riots in Notting Hill (London).
		Sino-Soviet support for National Liberation movements.
	Dec.	Direct action at North Pickenham and other USAF bases, Norfolk.
1959	*Jan.*	Castro's revolution in Cuba; opposition to HUAC (House Unamerican Activities Committee) grows.
		Student Peace Union (SPU) formed in Chicago, actively supported by Young People's Socialist League (YPSL) (Third Camp) and Student League for Industrial Democracy (SLID).
		Studies on the Left, founded at Wisconsin.

		SLID changes name to Students for a Democratic Society (SDS) under leadership of Haber.
		Growth of CND in England.
		Robert Williams arms local National Association for the Advancement of Coloured People (NAACP) in Monro, North Carolina.
		Fred Moore's anti-military vigil (Berkeley).
1960	*Jan.*	*ULR/New Reasoner* merge to become *New Left Review* (NLR), UK.
		St Pancras rent strike (London).
	Feb.	Sit-ins at Greensborough, North Carolina, begin: 50,000 in wave of sit-ins; militant phase of civil rights movement.
	March	Sharpeville shootings in South Africa triggers growth of anti-apartheid movement in UK.
	Apr.	Student Nonviolent Co-ordinating Committee (SNCC: Snick) formed, by Bob Moses, Bob Parris, John Lewis and others.
	Easter	Aldermaston march becomes mass-demonstration. Anti-HUAC demonstrations (San Francisco).
	May	C. Wright Mills publishes *Listen Yankee*.
	June	SDS officially founded as an independent organization.
		New University Thought published in Chicago.
		Councils of correspondence formed in US.
	Summer	Fair Play for Cuba Committee founded.
		Committee of 100 formed in England by Russell for civil disobedience, and other direct action against French Sahara Tests.
		San Francisco to Moscow March (CNVA) 1960–1.
	Fall	Purge of Communists from SANE following Senator Dodd's allegations.
	Oct.	CND resolution carried at Labour Party Conference, Scarborough (UK)
		International Socialism formed from Trotskyist coalition.
		Opposition to Polaris Nuclear Bases (Scotland) and demonstrations in USA.
1961	*Feb.*	USA severs contact with Cuba. Death of Mills.
		First Committee mass sit-down in London, over 4,000 take part.
		Growing opposition to nuclear testing (including Russian tests) in Britain and US; active opposition to fall-out shelter programme (summer) and civil defence also. Large marches in many European countries against nuclear weapons.

March	Peace Corps formed (USA).
Apr.	Large Easter March (UK).
	Bay of Pigs invasion.
	Second mass sit down against nuclear war in London, over 800 arrests.
Spring	SNCC begins voter registration drive at McComb, Mississippi and community organizing in South.
May	Freedom rides with Congress of Racial Equality (CORE) begin.
Aug.	Berlin Wall built – tension grows.
Sept.	Robert Williams calls for arming of black people for self-defence, flees to Cuba, then China.
	Liberation publishes Williams's debate with King.
	W. E. B. Du Bois clubs formed.
	Bay of Pigs affair.
	Anarchy magazine published (UK).
	USA and Russia resume H-Bomb Tests.
	Committee of 100 reaches its peak; leaders arrested.
	Mass sit-down in London (17 Sept.).
	Russell imprisoned; public order act invoked. Over 15,000 take part.
Oct.	Mass CND lobby on Berlin issue.
Nov.	Women Strike for Peace (WSP) formed.
Dec.	Raids on Committee of 100 offices; five charged with secrets offences, conspiracy, etc. Committee of 100 demonstrations at Wethersfield and throughout Britain, over 10,000 take part.
1962 *Feb.*	Student SANE splits – over 5,000 join SPU march (Washington), opposing E/W testing.
	World Peace Brigade actions, including Sahara protests against French testing.
Apr.	150,000 at Easter rally of CND.
	Committee of 100 trial begins, London.
May	CNVA voyage.
June	Port Huron Statement (SDS). *Root and Branch* magazine (Berkeley). Albany, Georgia, demonstrations.
July	Immigration act passed (UK).
	Bad Godesberg conference of SPD (Germany) sees defeat of radical left policies.
	Sino-Soviet split. Student SANE disbands after refusal to expel communists.
Sept.	PL (Progressive Labor (Maoist)) splits from Communist Party. Hazard, Kentucky, miner's strike.
22 Oct.	Cuban missile crisis; demonstrations.
	Russell resigns from Committee of 100.
Oct.–Nov.	US peace candidates (Stuart Hughes's campaign).

	Dec.	Harrington's *Other America* published; first community projects (SDS) and Hazard strike, involves SDS members.
1963		Campaign for Social Justice formed in Ireland. 'America and the New Era' statement (SDS) and Education Research Action Project (ERAP).
	Apr.	'Spies for Peace' on Aldermaston march. *Pacem in Terris* encyclical.
	May	Massive civil disobedience demonstrations in Birmingham, Alabama, led by MLK. Voter registration drive in South (US) organized. Council of Federated Organizations (COFO) formed; First Mississippi Freedom Summer—Freedom Ballot.
	June	Greek royal visit demonstrations (London).
	Aug.	March on Washington; 250,000 call for 'jobs and freedom now'. King's 'I have a dream' speech; church bombings.
	Fall	Songs of Bob Dylan, Beatles, etc., gain wide audience.
	Nov.	Diem overthrown by Vietnamese Buddhists' demonstrations. Baez refuses war taxes.
		Leary and Alpert dismissed on drugs charge.
		Kennedy assassination.
1964		SPU dissolved. 'War on Poverty'.
		Sheraton Palace demonstration, San Francisco.
		Du Bois clubs become nationwide organization.
	Feb.	500,000 in School boycotts (New York and Chicago). May Second Movement (M2M) formed: more trips to Cuba.
		'Northern' and 'Southern' Student movements active. Harassment of Civil Rights Workers.
	Mar.	Malcolm X leaves Muslims, denounces civil rights movement and liberal establishment.
		Committee of 100 sit down at Ruislip USAF base.
	June	800 volunteers in Second (COFO) Mississippi Freedom Summer; volunteers killed.
	July	Harlem riots: Civil Rights Act.
		Fanon's *Wretched of the Earth* published in English. Marcuse's *One-Dimensional Man* published.
	Aug.	Mississippi Freedom Democratic Party (MFDP) formed.
		Delegation rejected by Democratic Party convention at Atlantic City.
		Gulf of Tonkin incident. N. Vietnam shelled.
	Sept. –Oct.	Start of Free Speech Movement (FSM), Berkeley, continuous actions Oct.–Dec.
	Dec.	Mass sit-in at University of California (Sproul Hall).

1965 *Feb.*   Malcolm X killed.
Vietnam war escalates – North Vietnam bombed.
Mar.   Selma, Alabama: March to Montgomery. Vietnam teach-ins begin at Michigan, then Berkeley.
SDS Vietnam War marches, supported by CNVA and War Resisters (WRL), 25,000 take part.
Apr.   Anti-US slogans on CND march (UK).
USA invades Dominican Republic.
Free Universities founded.
June   Julian Bond's election in Georgia. Following MFDP challenge. First Black Panther Party (BPP) formed in Alabama (Lowndes County Freedom Organization) by SNCC.
Free Speech Movement starts in Berlin (Free University).
Apr.   Provos formed in Amsterdam; Ken Kesey's 'Merry Pranksters'.
Berkeley Barb and *Los Angeles Free Press* begin publication.
Spring   SDS grows rapidly – 100 chapters.
May   Vietnam Day Committee (VDC) active in Berkeley, 2-day teach-in.
Delano Grape strike spreads (California).
Summer   SDS Assembly of Unrepresented People in Washington: 350 arrests.
Carl Oglesby president of SDS.
SDS drops exclusionism clause: PL becomes a 'party'.
Aug.   Watts riots (L.A.). Voting Rights Act.
Troop train demonstrations at Oakland, California.
Oct.   International Days of Protest (USA). Immolations protesting Vietnam war. Draft cards burnt.
Nov.   Oakland Army-Terminal March (VDC).
CND adopts anti-Vietnam war platform.
'New Politics' group forms; Norman Morrison's death.
Dec.   SANE march against the war.
1966 *Jan.*   SNCC denounces war and initiates anti-war platform and draft resistance programme: 'We won't go' groups.
Hayden, Lynd and Aptheker visit North Vietnam.
SDS student power and draft resistance strategies announced. Draft unions, draft cards burnt, anti-war sit-ins (Chicago). Palomares nuclear accident.
Mar.   Julian Bond refused seat. Lowndes County Freedom Organization.

Apr. Stokeley Carmichael ousts John Lewis as Chairman of SNCC. Meredith shot.

June Meredith Mississippi march.

SNCC launches 'Black Power' slogan; first black power conference. Carmichael starts speaking tours.

PL enters SDS; student power strategies.

SNCC expels whites.

Black Panthers formed (BPP) by Newton and Seale; Black rebellions in northern ghettoes.

Marcuse's influence grows with publication of his essay on 'Repressive Tolerance'.

Summer The 'Fort Hood Three' army dissenters court martialled. King leads Chicago marches.

San Francisco Diggers active; free food distribution.

Growth of underground press in America. *It* and *Oz* in Britain.

July Labour Government gives general support to US Vietnam policy. Demonstrations in London against bombings.

Radical Student Alliance (RSA) formed.

Fall Draft-call exceeds 40,000 per month. 'We won't go' campaign (USA).

Community organizing in Notting Hill (London).

Nov. Unrest at LSE grows, boycott of lectures.

BIT and Release formed in London.

Scheer's electoral campaign for congress gets 45 per cent vote (California). 'Rubin for Mayor' in Berkeley.

Ultra-feminist 'Scum' manifesto (Valerie Solanas).

Dec. Anti-imperialist position adopted by SDS.

1967 *Feb.* 'The Resistance' formed in California, becomes national.

Mar. LSE (London School of Economics) occupied for six days.

Bloom and Adelstein suspended.

Apr. 1,500 draft cards returned or burned. Draft arrests: Coffin, Spock and Goodman (on trial in December).

Anti-war actions at universities. Opposition to DOW Chemical Company, the CIA and Reserve Officers Training Corps' (ROTC) Spring mobilization formed: largest marches since 1965. 500,000 take part. 'Revolutionary Contingent'.

Discontent with Labour Left grows.

May 'May Day Manifesto' published (England) at London Conference.

Civil Rights Association (CRA) founded (Northern Ireland).

Black Panthers demonstrate at Sacramento State Capital. Muhamed Ali refuses induction.

Haight-Ashbury Community; San Francisco 'Be-in'.

Summer First Vietnam Summer.

Debray's *Revolution in the Revolution* published.

July Dialectics of Liberation Conference at Round House (London), Carmichael, Marcuse, Laing and Goodman etc., attend.

Sept. Newark black power conference – 1,100 delegates present.

Huey Newton jailed for murder, urban violence in Detroit and Newark; Carmichael visits Cuba.

Eldridge Cleaver's *Soul on Ice* published.

Rap Brown succeeds Carmichael as SNCC secretary.

5000 attend New Politics convention (NCNP) in Chicago. First Women's Liberation groups.

Death of A. J. Muste.

Anti-university of London.

Oct. Dellinger takes leadership of Mobilization Committees. Stop the Draft Week (STDW) in Oakland and New York, blockade of induction centres; 2,000 draft cards turned in. GI coffee houses started.

Student mobilization at Pentagon: 50,000 in march on Pentagon confront National Guard; Yippees active.

Catonsville 9 destroy draft files.

Riots in Berlin follow killing of student demonstrator. Movement towards humanization in Czechoslovakia gathers momentum.

Peace and Freedom Party (PFP) active in California.

Dec. First Grosvenor Square confrontation (London), Guevara killed, Bolivia. Vietnam Solidarity Committee (VSC) founded.

1968 *Jan.* Tet Offensive. Vietnam Solidarity Campaign active in UK.

2,000 draft cards returned, USA.

Poor People's Campaign begins (Memphis and Washington). Resurrection City.

Feb. Orangeburg 'Massacre' USA. Arrests of Seale and others (BPP). Siege of Hue and Khe Sanh (Vietnam). Further immigration curbs by Labour government. Eugene McCarthy's campaign for president gains groundswell support, on peace platform.

Mar. Peace and Freedom Party enters coalition with Black Panthers, organises nationally. Kerner Commission. LBJ stands down; Bobby Kennedy campaign.

	March 22nd Movement formed in France. RSA active in Britain; RSSF (Revolutionary Socialist Students Federation) formed. VSC demonstration in England attracts 10,000 marchers.
Apr.	Memphis, M. L. King assassinated – nationwide rioting. 'Poor Peoples Campaign'. Columbia university occupation. Unrest at the Sorbonne (France). Bobby Hutton killed. Hornsey, Guildford and Essex student occupations (UK). Hilliard and Cleaver charged.
Easter	Militant demonstrations in most European cities. Paris peace talks start. Strasbourg Situationists. Rudi Dutschke almost assassinated. Anti-Springer demonstrations, in Germany and after CND's Easter March (London).
2–24	France, events develop;
May	Paris confrontations, General Strike. Arts Labs movement grows in Britain. *Black Dwarf* published.
June	French factory occupations end. SDS convention deeply split; struggle with Maoists emerges. Bobby Kennedy killed. Warhol shot. *Socialist Worker* published (UK). Street fighting in Berkeley, Boston and New York.
July	VSC demonstration (London). Spock convicted.
July & *Aug.*	Civil war in Biafra (Nigeria). Pro-Dubček forces growing in Prague.
Aug.	Soviet invasion of Czechoslovakia. Carmichael splits from SNCC: Cleaver's presidential candidacy. Fort Hood stockade, GI protests. Chicago 'riots'; demonstrations; police riots and repression (Democratic Convention).
Sept.	Newton sentenced; Black Panthers under attack, clash with police. SNCC merges with Black Panthers. Cleaver flees to Algeria. Women's Liberation movement grows rapidly (USA).
Oct.	Third Vietnam solidarity demonstration (England); Revolutionary Socialist Students Federation (RSSF) active. LSE occupied again. Bombing of N. Vietnam ceases. Civil Rights Association (CRA) march in Northern Ireland; police attack demonstrators (Londonderry).

Abbie Hoffman's *Revolution for the Hell of it* published. GI March (San Francisco).

Legalize marijuana campaigns. Black Power salute at Olympics.

Sit-ins begin at Bristol, Hull and Birmingham Universities.

Nov. Squatting Campaign begins (London), Hyde Park concerts.

Nixon becomes president. More stockade revolts.

San Francisco State College strike and occupation.

Dec. Revolutionary youth movement (RYM) faction opposes PL/WSA (Worker Student Alliance) in SDS; 600 attend council meeting. Raids on Panthers.

1969 People's Democracy (PD) formed (Northern Ireland); 144 Piccadilly Squat (London).

Jan. Suicide of Jan Palach.

Apr. Earth Day.

Moratorium continues.

Apr./ Police raids on BPP HQ's.

June High School rebellions (USA).

May People's Park conflict in Berkeley reaches climax.

Woodstock Festival.

Berrigan and others burn thousands of draft records.

Women's Liberation Movement spreads to Europe.

National Convention of the Left (England) sponsored by May Day Manifesto group.

Schools Action Union (SAU) formed.

Stop the Seventies Tour (STST) demonstrations begin (England).

June SDS convention: three major splinters form: Marxist–Leninists predominate, Weathermen and RYM II emerge; bombings spread.

July Carmichael resigns from Panthers; Seale purges BPP.

Third World Strike at Berkeley.

Native Americans occupy Alcatraz.

Sept. Chicago 8 Conspiracy Trial begins.

Oct./ Anti-war rebellions at army bases; Vietnam Mora-

Nov. torium, half a million involved.

Police offensive against Panthers.

New Mobilization emerges, with mass support.

RYM II convention at Atlanta; 'Venceremos' brigade.

Washington demonstrations.

Dec. Days of Rage in Chicago: Weatherman War Council.

Fred Hampton killed.

David Hilliard arrested: all Panther leaders now in prison, dead or abroad.

1970   Orange Free State proclaimed in Amsterdam: Kabouters active, win election victories.

IRA splits: provisionals begin terror offensives.

Feb.   Day After demonstrations following Chicago sentences. SDS disintegrates. Student mobilization grows. Large conference at Cleveland: Panther protests.

Cambodia nationwide demonstrations mainly sponsored by the 'New Mobe'. Kent State killings; Jackson killings.

Revival of draft resistance: union of National Draft Opposition.

Mar. Weatherman communiqués: Town House explosion.
April 'New Mobe' coalition dissolves. SWP growing (USA).
Sept. Escape of Timothy Leary. *Easy Rider* released; Manson murders.

'Angry Brigade' explosion in Britain; Warwick University crisis.

Dutschke expelled from Britain; first Women's Liberation conference (UK).

Changes in Selective Service Laws (USA).

Soledad brothers affair: Angela Davis flees.

Reich's *Greening of America* published.

'Angry Brigade' bombings and arrests (UK).

1971   IRA offensive Northern Ireland.

Tupamaros (Argentina). Black September and Al Fatah actions.

Newton splits with Panthers and Cleaver on issue of militarism.

USA's withdrawal from Vietnam accelerates – bombing intensifies.

Pentagon papers published.

Operation Omega leaves Britain for East Pakistan/ Bangladesh.

Ink and *Seven Days* published (UK).

1972   North Vietnamese offensive; invasion into South Vietnam, siege of An Loc, Kon Tum and Quang Tri produce heaviest casualties yet.

First Greenpeace voyage to French testing area; Greenpeace formed in UK.

McGovern campaign; Watergate burglary.

Re-election of Nixon.

Death of Paul Goodman.

Lakey's *Strategy* and *Manifesto* for nonviolent revolution appear.

Night Assembly Bill and Angry brigade trial (UK).

Concert for Bangladesh (New York).

Spare Rib and *Undercurrents* published.

1973 *Jan.*   Vietnam 'ceasefire'; US withdrawal completed.
Bobby Seale's mayoral candidacy (Oakland).
Symbionese Liberation Army (SLA) kills Marcus Foster.
OZ ceases publication in Britain.

1974   Watergate revelations (USA). More SLA shootings.
Community Levy for Alternative Projects (CLAP) and Windsor Free Festival (UK).
Anti-Fascist confrontations.
Friends of the Earth (FOE) Active.
British withdrawal from Northern Ireland campaign and Troops Out group, active.

Introduction

This study of the New Left (NL) in crisis, deals with it not as a set of organizations or of personalities, or even of ideas, although each of these has a place in it, but rather as a social movement. The main purpose of the study is to provide an alternative perspective on the Western NL as distinct from currently established right-wing and left-wing versions.[1] The intention is to challenge both these accepted definitions of what the NL is or was, and their view of how it developed its major problems.

Movement theorists have argued in relation to the NL that its history and its theory must arise from the participants, from the movement itself, and not in abstraction.[2] In following this advice, and in adding personal judgments and impressions drawn from my own involvement in many of the movements described, I have sought to avoid the inherited and accepted definitions, and to aid re-evaluation. I have tried initially (in chapters 1, 2 and 3) to define the NL from within: what the movement was in and for itself, at first, before the media got hold of it, critics re-defined it and told it what it was or should be, and the more parasitic theorists latched on to it. Thus my approach attempts to interpret an NL in terms of a movement's own evolving history and logic, rather than only as a creature of 'external' history, or as a response to state or international pressures – or even as the historical vehicle of certain definite ideas and theories, or group interests.

In its period of growth, the American movement, far more than the British, created its own history rather than reacting to somebody else's, and thus its own events are judged to be of more critical importance. In the second and third chapters, in order to elaborate a core 'New Left identity', a number of projects and events are specifically selected, not in order to describe or analyse them in detail, but in order to see the way in which the major themes and characteristics of the earlier NL are illustrated by them: Aldermaston and the Committee of 100 in England; SNCC up to the 1965 Selma/Montgomery march; the 1964

Free Speech Movement at Berkeley; the SDS community projects. Thereafter the approach, though not chronological, is fundamentally developmental; analytical chapters and reviews of ideas are placed in juxtaposition to the main historical stages of the Movement.

A number of attempts have been made at a simple periodization of the development of the NL: Elinor Langer, writing in 1974,[3] discerned two principal stages in the American movement: 'a first stage that was fresh, American, vigorous', and full of promise and potential, and a second stage that became 'sectarian, irrelevant and self-destructive'. Teodori, writing in 1969, saw basically three stages: the first marked by the moral commitment, individual concern and personal witness of the peace and civil rights movements, and the free speech issue; the second being collective and community oriented, based on participatory democracy and organizing projects (1963–7); the third as engaged in a struggle for power in the more specifically political senses.[4] O'Brien, writing two years later, broadly accepted the first two stages in Teodori's scheme – emphasizing liberal issues and direct action in the first stage, and radical organizing and participatory democracy in the second, up to 1967. In the third stage he stresses the shift of the anti-war movement towards an anti-imperialist stance (1965–8) and with it the development of mass protest, and he also notes a fourth stage closer to the 'power' stage of Teodori. In this final stage, domestic revolution, black power and draft resistance begin a basic challenge to the state, and lead on to the guerilla (or pseudo-guerilla) activity of 1968–70.[5]

The problem with all such attempts is that in fact these stages overlap and are intertwined with each other (and with the growing counter-culture). As the NL is multi-centred, and with a tendency to sudden trends and changes, no simple periodization is adequate; it is a movement of movements. Thus this study is intended to be neither definitive nor comprehensive, but focuses on three specific aspects of the NL mainly in Britain and America. First, the relationship of the new radicalism to an 'Old' Left in each changing context; second, the transition of the movement through several distinguishable phases of crisis – especially, for example, the evolution from nonviolence to physical or armed violence, in the years 1964–8; and, third, the relation between external (especially international) factors and internal ('movement') transformations, especially the Vietnam war and the events and happenings of 1968 (chapter 11).[6]

On the whole the earlier period of the NL (which includes the important 'trial-run' English experiences of 1958–63 as an essential ingredient) has tended to be neglected by later writers; in the American context O'Brien, for example, claims that 'as a coherent movement the NL may be said to have existed only from 1965–9'.[7] Unfortunately, in order to concentrate on the later period of crisis and decline, in this study too, the early mainstream period of the movement tends to receive a more perfunctory treatment than it deserves. This reflects merely the exigencies of space rather than an estimate of the intrinsic importance of the pre-1965 phase.

Throughout the 1960s the term 'Movement' was used in America to cover a whole variety of activities including SNCC, the freedom rides, the peace movement, black power, the student sit-ins, SDS and community organizing. Largely conterminous with the 'New Left' label after 1965, it remained alongside the term counter-culture, as an overlapping category, and I have followed this usage throughout – even in relation to movements outside America. On the other hand, the term 'radical' (or 'new radicalism') was used less in the later 1960s whereas the term 'revolutionary' was only widely used after 1967.

At the outset, the NL was strongly implicated in reformism and I have dealt with this, the disillusion with Liberalism and the development of extra-parliamentarism in chapter 4. Like the British nuclear disarmament movement, the peace, civil rights, and student movements in America were all initially reformist and often liberal in tone, and the reactions to this experience were decisive in determining the radical character of the subsequent movement. It is obvious that the ensuing developments and changes in the NL reflect these reactions both in the black movement (chapter 6), the peace movement (chapter 9, on Vietnam), and in SDS (chapter 10). Moreover, black power and the Vietnam militancy precipitated the shift towards violence (chapter 12). The NL, despite its subsequent rapprochement with Marxism and even Stalinism, has to be understood initially as a reaction to the Old Left, and to bureaucratic Communism;[8] in chapter 1, I have emphasized this incomplete break with the past. The weakening of established orthodoxies, like that of working-class 'agency', meant a new appraisal of constituencies of change (chapter 5) and a search (albeit an unsuccessful one) for a systematic ideological position that would faithfully reflect the social character of the movement (chapter 7). In chapter 15, I specifically analyse the organizational relationship between the Old and New Lefts.

In order to re-examine assumptions about what was 'new' or 'left' or 'radical' about the NL, I have focused on certain critical dimensions, e.g. alignment and non-alignment, and the shift from one to the other; the dialectic of participatory democracy versus 'vanguard' types of organization; the Old Left/New Left/Old Left progression; the distinction between the movement and its developing public image (chapter 16); all revealing the major variations between the early and later movements. In my view, these represent the critical tensions, ambiguities and even contradictions in the movement.

I have emphasized the travails of the American Students for a Democratic Society (SDS) as a central experience of the NL, largely because SDS was the closest any organization came to capturing and expressing the movement, its style and its ideas. Moreover, the collapse of SDS was symptomatic of the various crises of the NL explored in later chapters. But the NL did not die with the SDS; as a movement it always transcended organizations.

The 'crisis' of the title is the movement's loss of its sense of self in the years around 1968 and after (see chapter 16). Later in the book, the dilemmas exemplified by events in 1968 like the Columbia crisis, the splits in SDS, the Vietnam Solidarity Campaign in England and the People's Park affair, are some of the crucial junctures examined. I have also examined the impact of such external events as those in France, Czechoslovakia and Vietnam in this same period.

In my view, much of what was new, and indeed radical, was lost or abandoned by the movement, in this crisis of the later 1960s. It can be argued that the ensuing identity-crisis had begun earlier; or that a firm identity had never been fixed, but I have argued that by 1966 a NL identity had indeed been formed, and have taken 1968 as a momentous watershed (chapter 11).

Murray Bookchin has argued that:

It is a remarkable testimony to the inner resources of the counter-culture that the debacle of SDS led not to a sizeable Marxist–Leninist party but the well-earned disintegration of the 'Movement' and a solemn retreat back to the more humanistic cultural premises of the sixties.[9]

But against Bookchin the thesis of this book is that the movement as a whole, and SDS up until 1967, *did* indeed embody such premises, and that it continued, outside SDS, to link up with the projects of the 1970s.

Of course the American NL was dealt a bitter blow by the crises in SDS – and indeed this was symptomatic of a general crisis of identity that affected the overall counter-culture just as deeply. But polarizing 'movement' and 'counter-culture' as Bookchin does, merely confuses the picture. The movement no more than the counter-culture 'died' in the late 1960s. Moreover, sections of the counter-culture 'ravaged' the values of humanism just as deeply as the political left – and indeed helped reinforce the influence of the latter.

The rediscovery of a movement's original identity depends partly, in my view, on understanding its roots and background, the beginnings of the movement's self-definition, and of comprehending what went wrong. This can be done only by first analysing the changes since 1966 in relation to this original self, and trying to explain why they occurred. Second, such rediscovery depends on avoiding the temptation to define the movement in terms of media images and the cult-left, or its more ephemeral leaders – Cohn-Bendit, Dohrn, Dutschke, Tariq Ali, Jerry Rubin, Mario Savio, Mark Rudd or Stokeley Carmichael – or its more marginal theoretical influences, on the one hand such as Reich, N. O. Brown, Laing or Sartre; and on the other, Debray, Guevara, Bakunin or Mao. I have also disputed the influence of Marcuse (see chapter 16). In attempting this task, I return very much to the definition and scope of some of the books written earlier in the NL's development (e.g.

Jack Newfield's *A Prophetic Minority* (1966); P. Jacobs and S. Landau, *New Radicals* (1966); M. Cohen and D. Hale, *New Student Left* 1966)).[10] These substantial accounts were, incidentally, by and large accepted *at the time* by 'Movement' participants as accurate summaries of what the NL was all about and also as summaries written by sympathizers active on the fringes of the movement. In that sense this book has an unconcealed continuity with them and the Movement as it was in this period of its first rapid and innovative growth up to 1965.

Initially it was intended that this study should focus equally on those two societies, Britain and America, where the NL first emerged. Not that the movement has not evolved outside the Anglo-American context – indeed the European experience especially contributed, by both ideas and example, to its overall development. But clearly it was in the early transatlantic interchange that the new 'mix' of radical elements appeared. Indeed it was to an English 'New Left' to which the American sociologist Mills wrote when he coined the label in 1958.[11] Even in 1960, the NL was still something mainly happening in England, and in view of its apparently more sophisticated analysis and its link to a more substantial movement, a continuing deferent reaction of American activists and theorists was perhaps understandable. However, many kindred spirits in the American movements at first failed to recognize any strong links between themselves and the groups to whom Mills wrote abroad. Perhaps this was because of the pre-association of the NL label with the English pilot project – and its much closer links with Labourism, Marxian revisionism, and single-issue reformism; as a result groups such as SDS and SNCC only slowly came to accept the term of themselves, or interest themselves in English approaches.

Of course it is true that any American Left in the years after 1957 would have been a 'New' one, such was the vacuum of organized socialism.

The McCarthyite persecutions, a *coup-de-grâce* to a Stalinist movement already in total disarray, confirmed the acute isolation of the wider scatter of critical intellects and independent literati: C. W. Mills, William Appleman Williams (the Marxist historian), Norman Mailer and Dwight MacDonald. Mills went so far as to assert that 'today in the US there is no left'.[12]

Yet the very fact of discontinuity enabled radicals to look back across a divide of forty years to the inspiration of pre-Communist Party socialisms, to populism and other indigenous radicalisms – feminism, anti-militarism and syndicalism – of an earlier period. At that distance it was possible to select afresh from earlier traditions, and produce a more innovative and original synthesis.[13] But it was also possible to lose sight of what had gone wrong in that tradition after 1917.[14]

In the process of writing this book, and particularly as the focus sharpened on the crisis and decline of the NL, events and ideas in the American context came to predominate in the analysis. In part this reflects, I believe, the actual historical importance of the latter, and the decreasing importance or originality of the British contribution over time; the American NL of the mid-1960s was both more sizeable and more creative than its transatlantic counterpart – and organizationally it survived longer.[15] Whilst the American crisis is subsequently reflected in British movements, the decline in the major manifestations began (in Britain) at a much earlier stage. The American movement took on a special significance because of its operations within a world hegemonic power and in the context of the Vietnam war, and the degree to which it exported (or re-exported) a new radicalism to Europe.

The relationship between the American and British movements, their cross-fertilization and differences, whilst only a subsidiary theme of this study, does underline these points. Even in the early English movement it is notable how much American-based theorists predominated; most of the theorists who shaped the NL, and who were read both sides of the Atlantic (discussed in chapters 2 and 3), were writing in the USA in the late 1950s. The predominance of the American situation of this NL theory can be seen in retrospect to have had a significance for the whole movement not apparent at the time – leaving English theory stranded between the former and continental Marxism, often parochial both in its reference and its scope.

The British movement languishes and fades as the American and continental NL flourishes; E. P. Thompson in 1963 had already resigned himself to the dispersal (organizational and to some extent intellectual) of the 'movement which once claimed to be the New Left' – in England at any rate;[16] from 1965, America becomes the fulcrum – and whilst I have dealt at some length with the 'false start' or early decline of the English NL, and the implications of the collapse of the Campaign for Nuclear Disarmament (CND) (chapter 8), the actual 'crisis' of the book's title, as far as Britain is concerned, is dealt with as much in relation to the fragmentary and imitative movements which still survived or partially revived in 1968. Indeed, increasingly the English movement becomes an echo, an ambiguous postscript, to American developments, rather than the leading section, as it had been both in ideas and actions, between 1958–61; as a result I have finally devoted less than a fifth of the book to British developments up to 1963, and the short-lived revival of 1967–9. Outside England the growth of a NL in Europe was a retarded one generally.

Largely an extension from the American experience, i.e. Berkeley and beyond, 'student revolt' did not reach Europe (even including Britain) until 1966; with less highly developed educational systems, relatively less affluence, no major foreign wars after Algeria, its youthful disaffiliation was at first less thorough-going than in America. Indeed, up to 1966, it was possible to describe the development of the NL largely in terms of the Anglo-American interplay, without doing too much violence to the record, though then this becomes more difficult as the movement is physically extended. The NL had begun its rapid trans-national growth in the late 1950s, and Mills had recognized this before anyone else: the movement increasingly looks beyond national politics, national issues and a purely domestic development. Even though the Anglo-American NL of 1957–65 was trans-nationalist or internationalist in action, orientation and posture (see chapters 1–3 esp.), and although the nuclear issue became important in over a dozen countries outside Europe, it was not in any genuine sense a broad international, trans-national and certainly not global movement, until the Vietnam war protests became coordinated.

In the mid-1960s, this political growth was centred in America; alongside the exportation of styles and ideas, came the influence of American social theories and models.

Conversely, the final stage in the growth of the counter-culture after 1966, owes a great deal more to non-American developments such as the French, German and Czech 'happenings' of 1968 and the injection of such European ingredients as situationism and provo. But again, in the present analysis, the need to compress and select has meant a conscious obliqueness with reference to these European movements, and an inevitable superficiality in the treatment of such phenomena.

A full, adequate history, or academic sociology, of the NL as a global movement remains unwritten, but meanwhile I hope that this particular focus and approach will contribute to that overall task. Moreover, by concentrating on 'the Movement' *as* a movement – and ideas and theorists as they relate to the NL in its actions; 'words-in-action', and 'on-action' (rather than on detached theoretical debates or polemical pamphleteering) – I hope that a sustained search for the essence of its radicalism can be deepened. Through this alternative perspective, it is hoped also to address continuing elements of that movement itself; to assist it to find itself again, to pick up the threads and reconnect them; to discover what was essential and what has been lost, and why it was lost, in order, hopefully, to recreate a more effective movement, a more sustained vision, and an identity that is secure.

1. Convergence and Breakthrough

The blocs begin to crumble

It is a central part of the argument of this book that the NL, which after 1956 emerged as an alternative to the Cold War and its Liberal and Marxist orthodoxies, eventually a decade or so after its birth returned whence it came; in other words the 'crisis and decline' of the NL represents an end of a cycle, a loss of an identity forged by its birth. Before examining this identity and the circular character of the NL's biography, it is necessary to look back at these origins, at first more European than American, to detect some of the clues and parallels with later developments. What subsequently turned out to be the weaknesses and ambiguities of the NL as a movement can indeed be detected in its first uncertain phases – not least in England.

The political movement of the NL emerged from a situation of global tension dominated by two vast military-industrial blocs. To a considerable degree these antagonistic blocs depended for their maintenance of internal pacification and legitimacy on ideological contrast.[1] As this contrast diminished, domestic cohesion declined; this was reflected in the declining unity of parties committed to support of each of the blocs.

The full understanding of the enormity of Stalinism, and the break-up of the Soviet camp, meant the decisive end of the hegemony of Russian-oriented communism on the left. Everywhere the Communist Party itself was in decline; in Britain membership fell by a third in 1956–7; in the USA the Communist Party youth group ceased to exist in 1957, and a third of what was left of the adult party were said to be FBI agents. The Cuban Revolution of 1959 was made, not by but almost in spite of, the Russian-oriented Cuban Communist Party, and at the outset was not supported by the USSR.

Any claims to revolutionary leadership were gone; hopes of survival could only lie in cultivating respectable domesticity – and that is what the Western communist parties did.

It is rather amongst the dissident communists of the West (and to a lesser degree those of Eastern Europe), that the intellectual origins of the

NL are usually first discerned. Politically isolated and alone, searching for a third way beyond the 'empty cant' of current liberalism, and the Marxist–Stalinist orthodoxies, some vacillated closer to Anarchism and Pacifism.[2] In Britain, where total apostasy was rarer, Marxian revisionism and humanism was the more typical response of those who left the Communist Party. There were those who reacted to the Old Left's domestic face – its style and tactics – its organizational élitism and dogma – whilst continuing to sustain a belief in the ultimately 'progressive' character of the Russian state. Others, rejecting and condemning the Russian model, were quite prepared to rebuild authoritarian Leninist cadres or parties of their own – on behalf of some new model or 'line'; such as the Cuban or the Chinese – or a not-yet emerged Trotskyist 'workers-state'.

Thus, within and alongside the NL, those who remain relatively uncritical of Russia, and those who remain largely uncritical of Old Left methods are not necessarily the same people. It is arguable, however, that only those who made a complete break with apologetics for either facet of Old Left orthodoxy, were the 'true' core of a NL, its real source of identity as an articulate force; but they were probably limited in numbers, and their dominance only partial; equivocation and ambivalence was much the more typical posture. The English NL from the outset involved a number of ex-fellow travellers, and party intellectuals who had moved away after Hungary. The various magazines they associated with[3] represented, in an important sense, responses not so much to the 'Imperialist' events at Suez, as to the Twentieth Congress of the CPSU, and the events in Budapest.

Thus, the first phase of the NL was, in the words of James Weinstein, 'in part a response to the collapse of the old left and in part a continuation of it'.[4] In America, and later in an Eastern European context, there were also the theories of ex-communists who argued that radical political ideas were exhausted. These views, in part generalizations from personal disillusionment, also reflected a declining relevance of 1930s' leftisms.

The reaction from those few who could remain more detached, was often one of either cynicism or despair. Even after 1956 there remained a predominant sense of loss of human control, a lack of faith in rationality or humanity.

Consensus and utopia

The period of the 1950s had been one of intense ideological consensus;[5] of anti-utopia; of existential resignation – an end of utopia certainly – if not an end to ideology. Ideology had become total and all pervasive; without opposition, it could, on both sides, disguise itself as value-neutral, scientific and objective, and thus pronounce its own demise.

Manipulative and corrupting media on all sides represented

indoctrination as 'objectivity'; the conspiracy of silence, or the cant-of-self-justification were, for example, methods by which liberalism concealed the deep contradictions reflected in various areas of Western life

Everywhere, education itself had become profoundly hostile towards utopian and optimistic ideals; pessimistic about human nature, it was dominated by conservative theories of politics and psychology.

Although development of a critical social analysis later proved fundamental in breaking out of this Cold War consensus, mainstream sociology and political science – in fact the whole range of social sciences – continued to play an enormously conservative role both in Europe and America in the 1950s and early 1960s.[6] Critics such as Mills and Marcuse detected the role of a crackpot 'technological' rationality, of scientism and pseudo-neutrality, a negative, positivistic outlook dominating both ideas and methods.

Whether officially Marxist or Functionalist, social analysis in the 1950s and 1960s consistently lacked vision, tending to reify a systemic 'present' and a focus on structure and function, rather than on 'contradictions', 'creativity', 'alternatives' or 'possibilities'; draining issues from politics, it sustained a theoretical apparatus that was no more than an abstraction of the dominant system in which actors (men) or citizens played appointed functional roles in a pre-ordained pattern (society) or polity. Western sociology, moreover, was predictably dominated by an idea of an ostensibly plural but cohesive society in which ideologically divisive issues had been eliminated.[7]

The tyranny of categories, the subordination of quality to quantity, tended to insulate sociology against innovative thought, sacrificing the future to the present, a characteristic soon reflected in the growth of a sociology in Russia.

The convergent orthodoxies

The years of the break-up of the simple contrasting polarities of the Cold War, which had been accompanied by notions of 'convergence' and 'end-of-ideology', also saw a discrediting of both Liberalism and Marxism. As the legitimacy of the Western states went into decline and the hollowness of liberal rhetoric and rules-of-the-game was challenged, opposition to authority became a universal ingredient of dissent in industrial society.

Liberalism stood ready to massacre millions at the press of a button, condemning unborn generations in the process, yet the slightest radical impropriety in opposition was met by a storm of abuse, and often prosecutions.

The long reign of Russian Marxism had not, however, led to any easier relationships with Liberalism's Eastern counterpart; indeed a convergent Marxism shared most of the liberal-technocratic assumptions; its positivism, its materialism, its belief in progress. By the 1950s it could not easily be seen as a polar radical alternative.[8] Even Mills claimed that both liberalism and socialism were bankrupt, even if the replacement of nineteenth-century ideology had not yet taken place.[9]

Some Marxian revisionists worked hard to re-open the ideological gap between a 'left' and 'right' – not so much on the basis of international re-alignments, but by showing that a theory of alienation, and a strategy of workers' control, could confront social systems in both East and West.

Many social critics remained unconvinced; one anarchist writer of the 1960s charged:

Marxism is the mirror image of bourgeois industrialism: an image reversed, and yet unmistakably identical. For both traditions the technocratic imperative with its attendant conception of life stands unchallenged. Ironically, it is the greatest single victory bourgeois society has won over its most irreconcilable opponents; that it has inculcated upon them its own shallow, reductionist image of man.[10]

In the ostensibly Communist countries, workers' control was perceived to be as elusive as under mixed-economy nationalization (Britain), federal intervention and corporate oligopoly (USA), or the more traditional enterprise–capitalism. As an anarcho-syndicalist group argued:

Industrial workers face increasing domination and alienation in their work. The work itself becomes more and more fragmented and more and more meaningless (*Solidarity*).[11]

The student movement too developed ideologically with a 'rejection of both capitalism and the bureaucratic communism of the Soviet Union; it shunned inherited liberal and socialist preachings as inadequate to the forms of the present'.[12] This reflected, according to Barrington Moore, the fact that

'The young' [had] 'become aware that Marxism and Liberalism have in good measure ceased to provide explanations of the world.'

'Neither one can any longer provide a convincing explanation of the causes of human misery in the twentieth century. The justifications for horrifying forms of cruelty and oppression that both Liberalism and Marxism have put forward, in the service of great powers, have more and more discredited both ideologies.'[13]

In particular, neither Marxism nor Liberalism had an adequate analysis or theory of the institution of modern war, and for a new peace movement appeared fundamentally inadequate; it was symptomatic of the ideological vacuum faced by a fledgling NL that, for the early movement, no ideology was available, which could accurately and easily locate the phenomena of nuclear weapons. Radical anarchist-pacifism had come closest, but even here effective comprehension was difficult and a preference for more immediate practical issues prevalent. Only a mediated memory of August 1945 and the glimpse of nuclear weapons' plants or bases could create some link in the imagination, some approach to comprehension.

The similarity of the two major war-machines, the comparability of both sides' nuclear threats and arsenals, were a far more significant factor than any ideological embellishments that might be given to them. 'We do not distinguish between Soviet and American H-bombs; all are planned mass-violence' (Muste). Each side had made the threat of mass-murder its major instrument of policy; political justification was an afterthought.

Marcuse, like Ellul and others, intimated that technology was developing its own independent momentum, regardless of the particular organization of society, of production, or of the relations between social groups – indeed that this dynamic was shaping social relations, rather than being an instrument wielded by powerful groups.[14]

In relation to this, convergence theory tended to deny the moral or organizational superiority of either bloc but rather focus on both as variations on a historical theme: the industrialization and centralization of society. Thus the USA and the USSR were following two amongst several 'routes to the modern world'; and for each route, 'mobilization', as a process, became synonymous with technological and organizational imperatives, drawing people and resources into a single common process of industrialization, state-building, and militarization.[15] Such a view did not appear a particularly radical idea; but many admitted its veracity in the NL. A decade later, Carl Oglesby, by then an elder NL statesman, was to affirm: 'Capitalism and Socialism are different means for pursuing the common and general aim of industrialization.'[16]

As against many orthodox Marxists, Marcuse too endorsed a radical version of convergence theory; the many common features of industrial societies; their tendency to military build-up and bureaucratic centralism, their technical modernism and urbanism, the reactionary similarities of their industrialism, might, in the long-term view, be as important as their differences. Much of this critique of repressive civilization, like the use of Marx's theory of alienation (see below), is thus applied to industrial society *per se* and not merely to the capitalist mode of organization.[17]

Orthodox Marxist dogma might still seriously identify technocracy with capitalism alone, but in occupied areas of the Eastern bloc, political alienation appeared complete, with the technocratic reaffirmation of state and military domination overwhelming. As *Liberation* in 1957 argued, 'The national, sovereign, militarized and bureaucratic state and a bureaucratic collectivist economy are themselves evils.'[18]

It was of course radical libertarians who most readily accepted the theory of convergence; this was exemplified in the plague-on-both-houses stance of the anarcho-marxist *Solidarity* group in Britain, as well as *Liberation* magazine in America. As *Solidarity* put it, 'The bureaucratic societies of East and West are coming to resemble one another more and more.'[19]

On the other hand, the common need for control from above, the *sine qua non* of modern industrial production *per se*,[20] forged at least potentially common links between workers' movements in Eastern and Western Europe. With the logic of domination, seen to be much the same in all industrial societies; with the 'robotization of existence' a common malaise prevalent in both Cold War camps, much of the radicals' faith in the progress and rationality hitherto identified by Marxists and Liberals with the two modes of industrialism, was undermined. The great consensus broke up, as critics perceived a technological totalitarianism developing both East and West.[21]

An offshoot of the 'convergence' and end-of-ideology theses was an undifferentiated liberal theory of totalitarianism; this held that there was basically no difference between right-wing and left-wing tyrannies. Both appeared to be highly centralized autocracies using terror and other means of repression. Both absorbed all social structure into that of the state, usually led by a monolithic single party; both shunned political choice mechanisms such as formally free elections.[22] Such comparisons became reinforced with the revelations of the real nature of Nazism after 1945 and of Stalinism after the Twentieth Congress and by various popularized and negative literary utopias.[23]

The fact that several NATO countries defending the 'free world' had an extensive apparatus of terror, secret police, torture, little freedom of speech and a number of political prisoners, whilst it showed that neither the left nor the right had any monopoly of these methods, hardly reinforced Cold War myths of a free world versus totalitarianism.[24]

Cold War and the critique of bureaucracy

Thus, despite the undoubted respectability of its origins, convergence theory and such counterparts began to take on new meanings. Deployed initially by conservatives to show the basic similarities of so-called movements or regimes of left and right, convergence had for early NL thought and action a different, radical implication. Although they were initially usually apologists for the Soviet Union or another self-styled 'socialist' country,[25] there remained those on the left who denied the similarities of Eastern and Western developments, or at least warned against stressing just those convergent elements they had in common, in case one was distracted from those elements where they differed. Nevertheless, in general the effect of such appraisals served to open up new alignments and possibilities and free the radical intellect for new formulae and critiques.

For example: Both Anarchism and Trotskyism fastened on the *convergent* notion of *bureaucracy*, East and West, State and party, as a central component in their critiques. Most Marxian critiques of the state, as an instrument of a dominant class, still begged the question of the enormously powerful 'socialist' state structures of both Russia and China. It was not clear, as critics had pointed out, that the Russian State bureaucracy was 'preparing the ground for any domination other than its own'.[26] Whilst critiques of *corporatism* had been gaining ground amongst revisionists, it was a vacuum which Marxism, oriented to class theories of the state, and without a developed theory of bureaucracy (Trotsky notwithstanding), was peculiarly unfitted to fill.[27]

Two alternatives presented themselves: a 'new class' theory along the lines suggested by Djilas and others, or an analysis of the state as independent from, autonomous, and in some cases, superior to, all 'social classes', even existing in a context of 'classlessness'. The latter point of view developed in a form closer to Max Weber's classical sociological view of the state on the one hand and to that of many anarchists on the other.[28]

In place of the Marxist notion of 'ruling class' which did not 'allow enough autonomy to the political order and its agents', and said 'nothing about the military as such', Mills suggested a concept of three major institutional structures of power: the military, the corporate-industrial and the politico-administrative. This was as close to a theory of the state as the early NL came.[29]

What had been perceived as a conservative theory of bureaucratism did not turn out to be the prophylaxis to radical ideas and action that was expected; indeed the loss of any need for the radical intellect to choose or defend either of the major bureaucratic systems allowed for the re-emergence of a vision that transcended both. For whilst such ideas might correctly seem to reflect changes in the Cold War towards a less ideological 'peaceful co-existence' between the systems, in fact they also reflected a declining internal ideological cohesion, and in turn assisted that decline in practice, as political disenchantment increased.

But the fact that convergence theory was seen to be an effective weapon by the conservative Right, and a threat by some in the NL, suggests the restricted vision of both. The idea that to demonstrate the convergence of two great powers would eliminate concepts or strategies of transformation in the West, reflected the blinkered pragmatism of American academic thought, and the equally obsessive fixation on Russia amongst many in the Left even after 'de-Stalinization'. The notion of convergence, often rejected by NL ideologues, partly for tactical reasons – it had a good deal of guilt by association with Cold War scholarship – was shunned as a concept which eliminated ideological discussion, or utopian possibility, by its scepticism of what had appeared to be the main model of socialist revolution and socialist organization. Yet, despite a rejection at the political level, such assumptions lay at the heart of much NL analysis, and became increasingly salient during the 1960s.

Although it has for long been a sociological truism that in the development of nation-states, external tension and internal pacification have almost always been correlated, this fact presented tactical problems for an emergent NL; on the one hand the fear of nuclear war and the desire for domestic transformation would have welcomed the possibilities implicit in relaxation of the Cold War, on the other hand the failure to make a complete break with the Russian-centred leftism which had dominated socialist movements for forty years, and the practical ambiguities of convergence theory, meant that considerable ambivalence was retained about developing a fully independent stance *vis-à-vis* the blocs.

Beyond the blocs

Clearly new formulae and critiques could not thrive on the slogans and doubletalk that dominated politics in either bloc. For example, both used the language of peace (and of freedom, justice and democracy). The Russian military machine was fronted by Picasso's dove, and the Stockholm peace appeal; the bastions of American deterrence carried over their portals the legend: 'Peace is our profession';[30] the USA described its foreign affairs in terms of peace-keeping or even peace-making. Such newspeak was one of the ingredients in promoting the great disenchantment with the political rhetoric of the military-industrial establishments.

A new trans-national sentiment also incorporated an increasing domestic unpopularity of foreign military adventures: Britain and France in Suez; France in Algeria; the USA in Cuba, Guatemala, the Dominican Republic, Vietnam and Cambodia; the USSR in Eastern Europe. Such ventures, creating doubts and disaffections even in the Western liberal middle classes, presaged a growing intellectual dissent, a crumbling of the Cold War consensus.[31]

A competition of national power blocs which threatened human survival also worked to undermine older patriotic beliefs. One symptom of this was the growth of a notion of 'positive neutralism', operating outside the military blocs, with the Third World non-aligned, and non-nuclear nations; working for an international *détente*, especially through the United Nations, and to strengthen international feeling against nuclear weapons. Third Camp internationalism represented a significant area of pacifist and socialist cooperation for those situated between the two blocs; between Stalinism and McCarthyism, between capitalism and socialist totalitarianism.

Such policies were linked to the initial orientation of various NL journals, towards a 'third way' beyond both Western Imperialism and Stalinism, but did not entirely transcend identification with nation-states.[32]

In contrast to the West, where relative international unity was maintained,[33] the break-up of the Communist bloc was along *national* lines, and for most of the time intra-national control was maintained, even if often in *totalitarian* fashion. *Polycentrism*, whilst rationalized in ideological terms, was rooted in questions of national power and interest within the bloc. Outside the blocs, however, within and outside the Communist parties, these nationalist developments were occasions for new ideological identifications and projections.

The 'new Marxists' were often tempted to join in the emergent international ideological conflict, moving from one national model or version to another, as positions shifted. Political choices seemed to be presented, especially for those uncommitted to the major blocs, in terms of the proliferation of autonomous national versions of Communism: Yugoslav, Chinese, Algerian, Cuban, Vietnamese, as well as Rumanian, Albanian, Polish, and fleetingly Czech and Hungarian.[34]

In particular, Third World movements did not seem to be slavishly following previous revolutionary models – least of all that of the Soviet Union.[35] This, and the positive, if superficial, identification with rural and peasant societies by a developing NL, partly represented a reaction to the compulsive consumerism and growing materialism of both Russian and Western societies. On the other hand, as hindsight later suggested, these identifications were perhaps the first indications of a preference for 'taking refuge from the distinctness of metropolitan conditions', 'in mirror models of the underdeveloped socialisms'[36] that was to have such disastrous consequences for the later NL. In any case, with the increasing momentum of mobilization in and by the highly industrialized war-machine states of the USA and the Soviet Union, the real prospect of many developing or socialist societies following suit, became increasingly clear, especially if they became militarized in inter-bloc conflicts.

Theory and language

Given the prevailing ideological cohesion within the blocs, it is hardly surprising that the initial NL appeals were made within the framework of assumptions of the respective systems and ideologies; this was manifestly true of the eruptions of dissent in Eastern Europe and the Soviet Union. The Budapest 'freedom fighters' of 1956, like the Berlin steel-workers of 1953, were dissident communists opposing Russian hegemony, rather than liberal or rightist anti-communists. Equally, the American NL grew in terms of unfulfilled liberal promise, 'incomplete' civil and economic rights, and unclaimed freedoms: they were at the outset, radical and dissident 'democrats'. Thus it was a 'Free Speech Movement' in Berkeley (the FSM) – even more than the movements against nuclear weapons – that was (somewhat arbitrarily) viewed as a first real sign of an erosion of domestic stability and the break-up of the great consensus.

Nevertheless, there is a certain irony in the fact that in the East, the radical intelligentsia wrapped the things they wanted to say in Marxist reference and language in order to show that they were neither radical nor subversive; whereas in the West many NL intellectuals, especially in Britain, to be 'radical', phrased things similarly, that could just as easily have been said in non-Marxist language and without reference to Marxism. Even at this stage the Left seemed unable to make 'the effort to find a language and to organize actions which are not part and parcel of the familiar political behaviour' (Marcuse).[37]

Perhaps inevitably, Marxism was chosen because it was the only major oppositional language still available intact, and thus might consciously insulate the development of independent perspectives that otherwise might get obscured in the meanings and assumptions of a dominant bourgeois language. In addition there was the urge to address former comrades in their own language rather than in the language of the establishment. Initially, this choice was also understood in England mainly as invoking a tradition of opposition, that affirmed the truly radical nature even of ideas and theories that were in marked tension with the old Marxisms; yet this manoeuvre foreshadows the 'more-radical-than-thou' fads of the NL in decline. Issues such as those of language explain much of the suspicion with which 'politics' was viewed by the isolated dissenters of the 1950s. There was hardly a word or concept that remained uncontaminated by cynical and manipulative misuse. Even after the 1950s, the problem of socialist language was still rooted in the Bolshevization of left experience; within debates about 'deformed workers' states', 'bureaucratic collectivism' or 'state-capitalism'.[38] It was an enormous setback for any 'new' Left that an alternative 'third' language took so long to develop.

Towards the end of the 1960s, the debate could indeed begin to operate with new concepts and language – those of 'post-industrial' or post-scarcity[39] – drawing from a decade of movement and experience, the burgeoning counter-culture, the growth of the radical communities, and the underground press. Such sources helped confirm the break with 'straight' society and make a new strategy of change inescapably available.[40]

A language evolved, rather than being created, haphazardly, eclectically, and to some extent marginally, for example, through the black community, or in a new sociology and psychiatry. A fundamental failing of the early English NL, this lack had its effect on an emerging American movement, especially as, floundering in the ideological morass of the later 1960s, it looked back to the English and European Left. This retarded development of a *new* radical language, was at the heart of the problem both of movement ideology, and the linked crisis of movement identity.

What was also true of the 'end-of-ideology' theme was the resulting largely non-ideological discontent of the protest movements; the lack of any desire for a nationally coordinated political party of the Left, and thus the inevitable heterogeneity and internal differentiation that characterizes the NL as a movement. The rejection of a 'power-accumulation model' of Leninist organizing or revolution, explains in part, the fact that no wholly coherent or unified 'New Left ideology' ever emerged amongst the radical utopians of the 'Movement'.

An end of politics?

In addition, what was more broadly if relatively apt about the end-of-ideology thesis *vis-à-vis* the NL was that political alternatives had, both East and West, largely disappeared in the early 1950s, or had been eliminated, either physically or intellectually; and the decline of Marxist or other Socialist alternatives to the instrumentalist orientations of a generally prosperous capitalist democracy gave a certain popular credibility to such claims.

A scepticism of purely political action, and an ambivalence about 'politics' attended the birth of the NL – a preference for the moral critique, the personal commitment.[41] Increasingly sceptical reactions to all ideology can of course be traced at the very roots of the re-emergence of radical activism.

When socialist politics was re-approached, it was – except for the very young without memories of the 1950s – with circumspection. For the rest, if there *was* to be a revival of alternative socialisms, it would have to lie in traditions that had escaped complicity in Stalinism, or were untarnished by the compromise, co-optation and sell-outs of left-liberalisms and social democracy.

The two obvious theoretical traditions to make this claim were Trotskyism and Anarchism, and there was a tendency to read elements of both approaches into developments of the national communisms outside Soviet control.[42] Trotskyism's revival was explicit and immediate after 1956; it could fairly claim that the revelations of Stalinist degenerations proved their attacks had been right all along; on the other hand its dissociation from the Russian experience was at most partial, e.g. its continuing talk of socialist deformations and 'degenerate "workers' states"'. Trotskyism did not transcend the pre- and post-1917 obsessions with the Bolshevik and Leninist/Stalinist experiences in Russia; its language and concepts were inescapably rooted in this debate and model, even when it turned to industrial Britain or America; this very fact encouraged its continuing sectarian introversions. The economism of the Old Left is reflected too in a continuing identification of the solution of the problems of recurrent economic depression and relative affluence, with the solution of all political issues.

Trotskyism's analytical sclerosis, its élitist top-down organizing methods, its love of discipline, dogma and official lines were firmly Old Left in character and thus remained marginal to the NL as a movement, though a constant if often minor element in its national coalitions.

Trotskyism's revival parallels, influences, and at times distorts, the development of a NL. Anarchism's rebirth took longer in coming, and was more implicit in the growth of new radical movements, than explicit in political organization. In so far as the NL involved the paradox of both a socialist critique of capitalism and a liberal critique of socialism, it was to that extent bound, sooner or later, to arouse a re-awakening of anarchist approaches in relationship both to centralism and statism in Marxism and continuing contradictions in bourgeois states. Moreover, the lack of an adequate historical theory or sociology of the modern state also created an intellectual vacuum into which anarchist ideas were likely to re-emerge.[43]

Alienation and control

The major theoretical attempt to transcend the convergence of capitalist and collectivist materialism and bureaucracy was the revival of Marxian alienation concepts.[44]

Both Fromm and Marcuse, eager to rescue the concept of alienation from the neglect of Marx's early writings, and deploy it as a major concept of a critical social theory,[45] introduced elements of socialist humanism and individualism, and idealist cultural orientations opposed to determinist materialisms, and stressed the importance of 'freedom'. Highly selective in their approach to Marx's work, together with others they sustained an entirely new emphasis on his writings; the sociological critique was made paramount subordinating both the economistic, historical and philosophical elements, as well as the political polemics.

However, mostly anti-capitalist and anti-bureaucratic elements of alienation theory were developed, rather than anti-industrial ones *per se*. This allowed some confidence in the possibility of a technology overcoming alienation, rather than deepening it, to be retained; a comfort to some in the Marxian tradition. But in the writings of Marcuse, that optimism becomes less marked, and an increasingly general critique of industrial societies seemed to be implied.

In the 1950s and 1960s few Marxian socialists were radical enough to carry through the anti-industrial implications of alienation theory to logical conclusions. That was left for a non-Marxian tradition and one whose confluence with the anti-capitalist and anti-bureaucratic critiques derived from alienation, was always tentative, and best expressed not in the theories, but the projects, of the 'counter-culture'.

The NL focused, in Bottomore's view,[46] on four main dimensions of alienation, each associated with one aspect of an industrialized society; 'capitalist society in which man is separated from his material products as a result of private ownership of industry'. (This, the Marxist problem, was tackled by Fromm as well as Marcuse.) 'Mass society in which man loses control over political decisions' (Mills's theory of alienated politics), 'technological society in which he finds his life regulated by the very machines whose creator he is' (a theme pursued by Fromm, as well as Goodman and Marcuse), and finally of 'collectivist society in which a similar separation proceeds from the centralized political and bureaucratic control of production'. It is significant, perhaps, that this fourth, the critique of collectivist alienation, left to others,[47] was the least developed of all.

Given the importance of war and peace as themes in the rise and development of the NL, it is significant that missing from Bottomore's list is a fifth dimension of alienation: that of 'militarized society' in which man is distanced from the weapons and institutions of war. In relation to this, Marcuse went so far as to suggest that technological society had not *relapsed* into the barbarism of Auschwitz or the Bomb and Hiroshima: mass violence was but the logical culmination of that same society's science and techniques, not least those of domination and war. Whilst Fromm and Mills both perceived that Marx's alienation theory could be extended to man's loss of control over his military products and techniques, and was closely linked to the other four types of alienation – and this was a theme touched on by Goodman, Marcuse and A. J. Muste[48] – the ambivalence of Marxism *vis-à-vis* organized violence, inhibited any thorough-going critique of this sort, a fact that became important in subsequent NL development.

The reaction to an authoritarian socialism, ostensibly guided by Marx, and to the loss of community implicit in capitalism and bureaucratic organization, precipitated a renewed attempt to revive pre-Marxian, utopian elements in socialism. Marcuse argued that such a NL utopianism would help to transcend existing blocks to consciousness, aiding people to 'imagine alternatives'.

Hitherto, few had been able to sustain utopian thought in the wake of mass war and totalitarianism – and under the nuclear threat. Those who did so were the inspiration of the new movement; alone, without a movement, their ideas were powerless; but as they became linked to minority action, they made change possible and conceivable, by clearing the space for it.[49]

In England, where the socialist tradition was stronger, and continental Marxism more influential, new sociological ideas generally played a less dominant role, but the English NL assisted the popularization and application of the sociology and social psychology of Goodman, Mills and Fromm, and echoed its American counterparts' analyses of power élites, mass-alienation, and critiques of the quality of life in industrial capitalism.

The NL in England after 1957 had as its fundamentally innovative concern that which linked alienation to questions of the 'quality of life' in mass society, and to a critique of the 'cultural apparatus' and its oppression; the role of the media, the position of the intellectuals, the nature of co-optation, and the new white-collar culture – not least the class and cultural base of political alienation.[50]

This reinforced a predominant concern with British social life, an appraisal of class culture; bourgeois – middle class and working class – as well as the popular arts. Burgeoning into a cultural critique of capitalist-industrial society, and the dominant values of the bourgeoisie, 'quality of life' also implied a positive search for what was vital, participant and expressive, and not yet co-opted or crushed.[51]

Back to utopia

The end-of-ideology thesis quickly became ridiculous, with its claim that 'the fundamental problems' of industrialism had been solved, its failure to see that the consensus society, the suppression of ideological opposition, was itself 'ideological' in the profoundest sense; and the 'end-of-ideology' was, in the words of one of the founders of SDS (Students for a Democratic Society), '*itself* an ideology'.[52]

In fact, such theories had had a boomerang effect: they helped precipitate the new search for ideology – and in some cases the revival of old ones – within and through a 'New' Left. In America such attempts were signally represented by *Liberation*'s explorations of the 1950s and early 1960s, a self-conscious effort to revive an independent radical option beyond either Liberalism or Marxism.[53] Comprehending humanism, tolerance, and concern with civil rights and individual liberty, all of which the Marxist tradition had hitherto neglected, it merged these with a socialist (if not necessarily Marxist) insistence on economic justice and equality; Liberalism was attacked for the shallowness and hypocrisy of its confrontations with major human problems, such as boredom and poverty. Marxism was accused of failing to confront the authoritarianism of oppressive and militarist states and the problematic relationships between political means and ends.

In their own quasi-anarchist version of convergence theory (more radical than the Triple Revolution statement of a few years later),[54] *Liberation* rejected the 'faith in technology, industrialization and centralization *per se*, characteristic of both the contemporary, capitalist and communist regimes'. Emphasis would be on

possibilities for decentralization, direct participation of workers and citizens in determining the conditions of life and work, and on the use of technology for human ends, rather than the subjection of man to the demands of technology.[55]

Sociology and the New Left

Revivals and renewals in socialist theory have often overlapped with new developments in the social sciences, and, for an American intelligentsia, it was within this location – in a critical sociology – that the major innovations occurred.[56]

Indeed, in the mid-1950s, non-Marxist social science had been one of the few arenas left with some semblance of freedom to manoeuvre. At first the dominant tendency amongst NL theorists is to re-vamp a Marxist sociology, through 'conflict' theory, or towards a mechanical synthesis of Marxism and Functionalism;[57] but economistic, holistic models did not allow for the flux and contradiction of emergent sub-cultures, or reflect the theory and action of the movement itself; or the emergent values and pluralist creativity arising even within the dominant frameworks of an existing society. Nor did it in any sense reflect the NL as a movement.

Partly as a result of the renewals in social theory, the NL, both in America and in Britain, derived its leadership primarily from universities and its support predominantly from students. An emergent student movement sought a radical social analysis and critique to match its radical actions; to deal with new forms of power and bureaucracy in mass society, and the relation between post-scarcity life and Third World problems, a new sociology breaking with the current systems of sociology, of roles and functions.[58] The role of sociology students and other social scientists in the early growth of the NL in America, and in the French student movement of 1968, is symptomatic of the growing influence of radical social theory and in turn reinforces it.

This early base was probably most significant in America where students first perceived liberties threatened by an authoritarianism implicit in wider corporativist and bureaucratic developments.[59]

The isolation of radical academics in the 1950s was totally transformed by the burgeoning of a radical intelligensia in America, sizeable and distinguished, alongside the growth of the NL itself.[60] The NL's search for ideology was characterized by a continuing rejection of what has been termed 'the ideological Manicheanism and political schematism' of the Old Left, especially the Stalinist subordination of means to ends. The discrediting of both orthodox Marxism and Liberalism, especially in the American context, at least allowed the NL there the advantage of starting as if from scratch. If one was able to predict the end of totalitarian revolutionary ideologies, and the resurgence of a libertarian pluralism, both of means and ends, it was because of a renewed ideal of 'permanent protest', an activist notion close to that of Camus's 'rebel'.[61]

The NL's version of pluralism sought the representation of all social groups regardless of their power or literacy or degree of organization. It did not interpret pluralism as 'pressure from multiple organized interests', as the democratic élitists put it. Nevertheless, the demand for a social order balancing the state by voluntary association, idealized by nineteenth-century liberals, and reified by the twentieth-century conservatives, became part of the utopian vision of radical critics.[62]

Mills's 'publics', Goodman's and Fromm's 'community', Lynd's and Hayden's 'participatory democracy', all point towards a recreation of a genuine and 'socialist' pluralism. Such concepts also provide a base for a more utopian and anarchistic sociology; populist, eclectic and experimental, 'from the bottom-upwards' – in tune with decentralized movement projects, and making possible, in contrast, a sociology of the structures of unfreedom, of war, the State, and revolutionary limitation and possibility.

Thus these libertarian radicals of the 1960s largely accepted an end to doctrinaire solutions and closed utopias, endorsing the sort of pluralism and flexibility that had been characteristic of much anarchist thought.[63] The projection of a single historical sequence, the single blueprint for a new society, the unified and reductionist theory of man or history, was replaced by an insistence on the need for different groups, a range of solutions.

This account of the initial conditions that made a NL movement possible, may suggest some of the constraints and ambiguities in this birth; the failure to make a complete break with the Soviet Union or the Communist parties on the one hand, and the acceptance of many convergent and shared characteristics of liberal technocracies on the other; the inhibitions of recreating a utopian thought and language out of a context of Cold War *realpolitik*; the resort to Russian centred Marxified concepts especially in Europe and amongst the Trotskyists; the failure to transcend nation states and domestic frameworks – whether in pursuing national models of revolution abroad or reformist-parliamentarist strategies at home. The uncritical idealization of Third World communisms (which in no sense represented a break with Stalinism – but rather with racism, and colonialism) may explain the ultimate failure to effect a full break with old methods and language.

A decade and a half later – still thinking in polar terms – one of the founders and visionaries of the English NL remained proud that the modes of discourse within a revised Marxist 'tradition' had maintained contact between CP and ex-CP.[64] Yet perhaps this pride reveals the very fact that the break was never decisive, the possibilities of a renewal of language and vision altogether too limited, to prevent the recurrent débâcles of 1963, and 1968, in the English NL – as well as those of 1967–70 in America.

The NL's libertarianism was genuine but weak, its language retarded, its vision tentative; yet despite this there is every indication – especially in the years of Movement growth in America (1963–5) – that the New Left was not 'doomed in its infancy' – and that the potentiality for transcendence clearly existed after 1958 – and remains even after the recurrent failures of its subsequent history.

2. The New Left: A Core Identity

Forces and movements for change

Much of the subsequent argument is based on the premise that a distinctive 'new' left orientation evolved in the years between 1956 and 1965 and that the movements and ideas oriented to it, distinguishable from both Old Left and Marxist formations, and liberal reform movements, went into a decisive crisis in 1967–9 and then declined. To sustain such a thesis, this idea of a NL identity needs, however summarily, to be justified, examined, and described – before any discussion of subsequent identity-crisis can be entertained, or detailed analysis of the evolution of specific characteristics of the NL begun.

It is in the middle 1960s that one can begin to define a core-identity for the NL, composed of certain common themes and theories. Some of them, like the emphasis on direct action, nonviolence and anti-militarism are links backwards to the initial bases of the movement, some of them, like trans-nationalism and counter-community, are more inchoate and emergent, innovative rather than traditional. This identity was a direct expression of a collective sense of fellowship on marches and demonstrations as well as in the ghettoes and rural communities in which radical projects emerged. As early as the Aldermaston marches, or the first Students for a Democratic Society (SDS) and Student Nonviolent Co-ordinating Committee (SNCC) projects, there was a notion of the movement itself as 'community', an alternative in embryo. Perhaps even more crucial was the existential emphasis on the necessity for action. Partly in response to the urgency of the nuclear threat, the use of various forms of nonviolent direct action were, as Mills noted, spreading in the West in the later 1950s; they are closely linked with the emergence of a NL.[1] The need to 'touch the popular imagination through projects which would point up the nature of the unimaginable' (Muste), whether it was the impossibly horrible effect of nuclear war (or the racist terror of America's small Southern towns), applied especially to the young. When Fromm announced, launching the organization SANE, 'We must bring the voice of sanity to the people', he seemed to endorse a growing quasi-existential awareness that it might be the world that was absurd rather than the individual, and that sanity lay in rebellion and change.[2]

With the drift unmistakably in the direction of nuclear holocaust, regardless of the possibility of alternative developments, there was no certainty, but 'revolt was honourable'; the development of existential action and collective response to nuclear weapons were equivalent to 'subversive experiences' breaking down people's 'entanglement in the thickets of false-consciousness and pseudo-events', enabling larger contours of domination to be perceived (R. D. Laing).

Nuclear-deterrent theory was depicted as the 'crackpot realism' of an insane system (Mills). Critics like Marcuse and Mills rejected the functional rationality that operationalized all problems within this framework; Fromm's concern as a psychiatrist was an attempt to stave off nuclear holocaust, 're-awakening the normal drive for human survival'. Resistance was imperative. Yet, as Marcuse feared, in lack of protest against preparations for genocidal nuclear war, might lie a loss of any real will to resist.

In 1960, a spontaneous piece of direct action initiated the heroic period of the civil rights struggle;[3] this landmark, the sit-in by four young black people from a local college at Greensborough, North Carolina, was as critical in shaping the American movement as Aldermaston 1958, proved to be for England. These, the noblest and most momentous demonstrations (and at Birmingham, Montgomery, Selma and Albany), represented dramatic eruptions by radical minorities into majority politics. SNCC's revolutionary spirit took it, within two years, beyond civil rights to make a series of connections between race, war, poverty, capitalism and personal identity: by creating its cooperative self-help community projects in the southern rural areas, it raised the issue of 'capitalism'. The word 'socialism' had not been much used by the civil rights movement, but SNCC's ideas had uncomfortably little to do with business-as-usual. Deeply influential on the student movement and the subsequent development of SDS, its similarity to nonviolent movements elsewhere was almost uncanny.

The year of the Greensborough sit-ins, the English Committee of 100 was also founded. Of all the organizations to arise in the international movement against nuclear weapons, it had the strongest affinity with the later NL: like SNCC it was part of a growing transnational movement and it parallels other direct action groups – radicals and socialists – Committee members were increasingly involved in local projects, community action or squatting assisting the growth of an anarchist movement in Britain. Within these the Committee provided a continuity of the moral protest, the expressive idealism, as well as some of the wilder, if nonviolent, fantasies of the first Aldermaston marches. Both organizations were 'ginger groups', injecting a new sense of urgency and vitality into the larger movement, especially into CND; this was exemplified in the first mass civil disobedience demonstrations held in London in the spring of 1961. Despite later setbacks, the NL as a movement was re-invigorated rather than destroyed by these departures, which symptomized a new mood of militancy and self-sacrifice, moving the politically virgin from personal symbolic witness to massive confrontation.

A sense of urgency led to attempts to transform nonviolent civil disobedience into a truly revolutionary weapon, and to burst through the boundaries of established organization; they represented the dynamic core of the early radicalism. Neither SNCC nor the Committee believed in compromise; both believed in merging aims and methods, including the use of participatory democracy in meetings. Both were infused with an anarchistic spirit of decentralism, direct action at centres of power, propaganda of the deed, non-cooperation with unjust laws, and symbolic revolution.

Challenges to prevailing perceptions of the world, implied by such breakthroughs into action, are also exemplified in campus rebellion; beyond the common use of nonviolent civil disobedience and direct action, each sustained social forces previously constrained by the initial organizational framework of existing movements; carried a new movement beyond its initial 'protest' frame-of-reference into a more revolutionary one: SNCC beyond integration and reform to a recognition of black culture, institutionalized racism, and the aspiration to community control; the Committee beyond the bomb as single-issue politics and tactical reformism towards revolutionary confrontation with a state structure. In turn both were inspired by an alternative of participatory democracy. Thus the Berkeley Free Speech Movement (FSM) represented a major further stage in movement radicalization creating, like the civil rights experience, a further core of full-time activists.[4] The outbreak of 1964 is also of significance because it was the first movement confrontation with a substantial corporate institution.

A haven of the 'non-student', Berkeley, in 1964, had long been headquarters and recruiting ground for strong civil rights groups in the Bay area. Immediately preceding the FSM, many from the university went to Mississippi for the 1964 Freedom Summer. In the subsequent autumn, the movement returned north, not least to California, bringing its civil disobedience, militant idealism, and sense of radical community to the campus; since student leaders who returned from the Mississippi Summer, Mario Savio, Jack Weinberg, and many others, were deeply influenced by their experience, it was inevitable that they should also re-import active politics to student life. Above all they brought with them the methods of nonviolent direct action and the FSM culminated in a massive sit-in of two thousand students.[5]

FSM acted as a sudden catalyst and opportunity for those anxious about stepping out of line for the first time on their own. As soon as that first action had been taken, those fearing for jobs and clearances, felt more free to act. It was a collective breakthrough, where individual breakthrough attempts had failed, and it by-passed existing organizational structures. From this, student movements quickly widened beyond the issues of free speech and reform strategy, to query the universities' basis and reflection of the larger society; in Europe as in the USA, they exemplified as well as demanded a right of free association, an ability to use the university as a political base for peace and civil rights activity. The Berkeley dispute of 1964 was only a symptom of a larger impending struggle for control of the university and with it, the consciousness of its students and teachers. Students, confronting an educational system geared more and more to training functional units of a social system, found themselves cogs in a machine which inhibited imagination, frowned on speculation about constructing alternative futures; and, above all, reified the present.[6] The FSM's call for bottom-up democracy in the university exemplified an overall challenge to authority, but with the early leadership of SDS clustered in a few big universities,[7] a strategic emphasis emerged in American NL thinking based on challenges to campus authority. The structure of the university was viewed, in its paternalism and hierarchy, as a microcosm of power in the larger society. Its authoritarianism might be less naked, its élites less irresponsible, but such organizations still appeared essentially undemocratic. From such specific issues a mass-based, non-reformist student movement could aspire to confront wider concerns. FSM points on towards developments in Columbia, as well as to Berlin, Nanterre, LSE and a thousand other campuses in the following years. Its principles of organization were to include the role of travelling student organizers, linking campus to campus; their method was to be non-cooperation and resistance, radical classroom organization, the activist transfer of work from academic theory to political practice. Mario Savio's invocations to students to put their bodies on 'the gears, wheels, levers and all the apparatus of the machine to make it stop', were only the first steps in such strategy.[8]

The bomb generation

In the early development of the NL, although external events such as the Algerian war, Pacific nuclear testing and the Hungarian – and later Cuban – revolutions were important influences, the initial growth of the NL can be better understood in terms of a shaping generational experience, of involvement in moving and impressive moments: the symbolic actions of the civil rights movement and the movements against nuclear weapons. Campus rebellion, such as the Berkeley 1964 police car demonstration (which initiated the FSM), released a stifled and hitherto unexpressed discontent with a university as a system; during days of sit-ins and arrests, mass meetings and strikes, students began to feel in their own solidarity and power, the possibility of new institutions.

Such an experience was the first march 'Against Nuclear Death' in England at Easter 1958. By embodying a sense of a new community on the move, it engendered a spirit of opposition to the manipulative pressure-group aspects of other political or campaigning activities; indeed in later marches, the younger marchers actively participated in challenges to the leftish bureaucrats, organizers and march dignitaries.[9] Partly because of the relatively greater freedom and tolerance of such styles in the *ad hoc* activism of specific-issue protest groups like CND, Anti-Apartheid, or the civil rights and free speech movements, these were notably more attractive options to the radical young than the Socialist or Communist sects or parties. By also inducing a response to the inadequacies and more negative aspects of these projects' experiences, they deeply shaped the political reactions of a second generation of political activists: a vision of young activists facing middle-aged quietist leaderships, permeated by compromise and opportunism; SNCC, an inspiration behind a new movement because it spoke directly to young, mainly black, people, made them responsible for their own programmes. The Committee, too, was to the British nuclear disarmament movement what SNCC was to the civil rights movement; it represented an upsurge of youthful militancy against tried reformist methods and an established middle-class leadership.[10]

For the young people[11] who joined these movements, this participation was everything; the feeling of solidarity did not end when each particular project came to an end; it moved on into other fields and other places. It represented a new synthesis, the beginnings of a visible social alternative – an immanent counter-culture, that merged personal expressiveness with political activism.[12] In a partial merger of youth and working-class styles, they expressed a common rejection of inherited middle-class and middle-aged life patterns and styles. The popular 'beatnik' image of 'Aldermaston' was fixed from the first days marching out of London, when it became clearly a march of the dissenting young. The notion of 'youth culture' is an elusive one, but helps summarize a dimension of consciousness and politicization, and an intensification of generational conflict. Just as the Women's Liberation movement was later to produce a feminist culture and consciousness, and the black movement asserted an Afro-American culture consciousness, both of which cut across existing movements, 'youth culture' implied a new age-related movement, and a consciousness which created conflict even within Left groups, civil rights and peace movements, but more especially between the middle-aged administrators who planned wars, and those teenagers drafted to fight them.[13] Not least, generation cut across 'bourgeois' families and helped create a 'classless' substratum in the NL often leaning towards working-class culture, in a revolt against the 'middle-aged', the 'straight', or the 'respectable'. The Port Huron Statement, a founding document of SDS, similarly expressed a deep agitation about nuclear war, testing and radiation disease. An underlying theme of nuclear holocaust is to be detected at the base of a number of movement developments in the early 1960s. Many talked of the 'politics of the bomb'. Such fusion of anti-nuclear political elements with youth culture and the avant-garde at the base of an English counter-culture, was aptly termed a 'bomb culture' (Nuttall).[14] In so far as these movements were overwhelmingly those of youth, connections between the terrible character of nuclear preparedness and the subterranean consciousness of the new, young culture were often made:

The orthodox culture they confront is fatally and contagiously diseased. The prime symptom of that disease is the shadow of thermo-nuclear annihilation beneath which we cower. The counter-culture takes its stand against the background of this absolute evil.[15]

This was perhaps the 'great refusal', to defy

an evil which is not defined by the sheer fact of the bomb, but by the total ethos of the bomb, in which our politics, our public morality, our economic life, our intellectual endeavour are now embedded with a wealth of ingenious rationalization.[16]

The 'Good Brave Causes', the issues early activists adopted, were morally based and simple, and an anti-political idealism was nowhere more marked than in reactions to the H-Bomb. Their refusal, certainly linked one way and another with the common threat of thermo nuclear terror, was a revolt of the politically virgin; for a generation whose politics began with the reality of nuclear weapons, the double-think of current Liberalism stood totally exposed in its cant and self-rationalization about mass-killing.

The Aldermaston generation in England seems closer in spirit to the civil rights movement in America, to Martin Luther King's marches and to the SNCC sit-ins, than to the mainstream American peace movement which developed at the same time and on the same issues. The generation of white and black students who moved south in the Mississippi Freedom Summers, like the CND marchers, helped shape a generation, bound together by the collective experiences of what Stokeley Carmichael later bitterly called the 'pepsi generation' – those who shared with 'Snick' in the beatings, jailings, killings, as well as the fellowship, elation and 'joy' of the southern movement of 1956–64.

Direct action spreads

Previous accounts have often neglected the fact that the major source for the revival and development of direct action on issues of war, peace and civil rights, a technique later to extend to community and student issues, lay in the revival of radical pacifism, in the later 1950s.[17] Moreover, many of the major breakthroughs which created the NL movements of the 1960s were made by small groups of pacifists, and even by individual actions.

Nuclear war was possibly something that only direct intervention, moral witness, and existential action could dramatize effectively. In the years 1957 and 1958, on both sides of the Atlantic, there was a series of actions, especially invasions and blockades of rocket bases, like those in East Anglia, by the DAC and linked to *Peace News*.

In the USA, a Committee for Nonviolent Action (CNVA) invaded the Atomic Energy Commission (AEC) sites in Nevada, at Omaha, and at rocket sites in Wyoming. On both sides of the Atlantic there was direct action against Polaris missiles. Mass confrontation first occurred in New York when 2,000 responded to A. J. Muste's call to resist civil defence exercises (1961).

Indeed it is in this event, and in the Committee of 100, that propaganda of the deed makes its most dramatic transition from individual to collective extra-parliamentary action.

In Britain, even after the mass sit-downs of 1961, the Direct Action-ists continued to be a thorn in the side of the establishment, with guerilla expeditions to rocket and bomber bases, and campaigns (e.g. Pat Arrowsmith's) to persuade workers not to work for military projects.[18]

The NL's direct action was not confined to these sorties against the war-machine, and one of the first signs of its widespread revival was the Montgomery bus boycott that began in 1955. The boycott, which lasted a year, and brought M. L. King to prominence, was effective in bringing the racial issue to world-wide attention. The nonviolent leadership of the early sit-ins, boycotts and freedom rides, closely interlinked with *Liberation* and the direct action wing of the American peace movement,[19] was not advocating passive resistance but active nonviolent communication: in confrontations with police, national guard, landlords, white racists, 'straights' or bigots, the attempt was usually made to throw the adversary morally off-balance.[20] In dealings with political authority and the state, the attempt was made both to transcend it and subvert it by good-humoured non-cooperation and dedicated affiliation to constructive alternatives.

As has been noted, most of the direct action of the 1950s began as propaganda of the deed, symbolic moral protest, emphasizing the non-coercive aspect of direct action and its compatibility with cooperation, persuasion and education; at the outset it was far from more violent direct action traditions. Nevertheless, the use of direct action, exploring the bounds of authority, also sprang from anarchist traditions. For over a century this aspect of anarchism had tended towards violence but had slowly come closer to nonviolent methods.[21]

'Much of it is direct nonviolent activism and seems to be working here and there', Mills observed, but given its utopian and experimental character no one could be sure. 'The commitment to action is made in the knowledge that the consequences of action can never be fully predicted in advance'.[22] At least such action, collective or individual propaganda-of-the-deed, could create new possibilities, 'light the first fuse, and make the first break-through' (Cohn-Bendit). Without it, it is doubtful if the NL could or would have developed its activist techniques: the civil rights actions, and, to a lesser degree, peace movements revived political engagement amongst both university students and black communities; the nonviolent stance of King, Evers, Meredith and others, caught the imaginations of young and black people in America and involved many in action for the first time.[23]

In these initial movements, the influence of Gandhi's activist projects remained strong,[24] alongside, as Lynd pointed out, the native American nonviolent traditions, which stretched back at least to Thoreau and early Quaker and abolitionist passive resisters, and forwards to Muste,[25] who, more than anyone else, had kept alive the idea of personal resistance as a special link binding Goodman, Lynd, Dellinger, and younger *Liberation* and NL activists to him.

Emphasizing nonviolent action against the bomb and racism, Muste advocated and planned interventions opposing both, during the deepest periods of Cold War passivity.[26] Few movement figures or theorists failed to acknowledge Muste's influence and inspiration. Subsequently, Lynd's own tactical ideas became influential; eclectically drawn from an American history of civil disobedience, strikes, non-cooperation and sabotage, these encompassed a range of direct-action experiences, from the Wobblies (the Industrial Workers of the World – IWW) of the first decade of the twentieth century, up to the Civil Rights Movement itself.

Lynd demonstrated the continuities of nonviolent civil disobedience, and a movement's right to resist injustice, even at the risk of undermining respect for the rule of law. As a result, in 1965, Lynd and the *Liberation* collective played a key role in generating the Vietnam war protests. As the Vietnam situation deteriorated, and following SDS's April demonstration, Lynd and others, including Muste, Dellinger and Bob Moses (then secretary of SNCC), had initiated the *ad hoc* Assembly of Unrepresented People at Washington; fusing participatory democracy, trans-national initiative, and radical anti-militarism. From this Lynd hoped to develop a full-scale civil disobedience campaign.[27] Three hundred and fifty were arrested in the August civil disobedience; despite SDS's earlier opposition to this method it continued to participate in such protests against the war. When the anti-war movement revived, on the issue of Vietnam, it was the symbolism of individual direct action, in some cases the most desperately dramatic and personal kind of self-sacrifice, which expressed the movement's trans-national concern;

embodied in the self-immolations of those like Norman Morrison, a Quaker, for whom other methods seemed insufficient;[28] these acts were paralleled by the sacrifices of individual draft resisters.

Such dramatic actions by individuals and small groups quickly evolved into mass illegal actions; the Vietnam Day Committee (VDC) in Berkeley, first came to national and international attention with the dramatic troop-train blocking demonstrations (September 1965), in Oakland and Berkeley. These actions, aimed at preventing the new shipment of fresh batches of draftees (conscripts) to Vietnam, came close to producing the movement's first martyrs; some protestors sat on the rails in Gandhian obstruction.

There had for some time been action on the Berkeley campus against compulsory military training, sparked off by Fred Moore's lone hunger strike in 1959, and continuing until 1961. With the intensification of the Vietnam war, such concerns again became a focus of resistance. In 1966, a non-student pacifist organization, the Berkeley Draft Information Committee, set up a table in the Union, alongside a Navy recruiting table, thereby triggering the massive student strike at the University of California, when it was ordered to leave.

With the development of resistance to the war and Selective Service, a wide range of actions and approaches, from those of the pacifist non-cooperators to those of the anti-imperialist induction-refusers, were introduced. Draft-resistance took many forms: refusal to attend for induction, seeking CO-status, going to jail, draft-card burning, emigration to Europe and Canada, closing down induction-centres, non-registration, and finally desertion. There were also more symbolic actions such as statements of dissociation or complicity, opposition to university cooperation with Draft Boards, refusal of exemption or deferment, 'We won't go!' statements, non-registration and the return of, or refusal to carry, draft cards. SNCC's draft-resistance programme which began in December 1965, expressed uncompromising opposition to a war it identified as racist. (SDS's first anti-draft programme (1966) was somewhat less militant.)

Draft resistance generally carried on the tradition of personal and collective non-cooperation, extended in spirit and method by figures such as David Miller, Daniel Berrigan, Benjamin Spock, Michael Ferber and David Harris.

By challenging the state's right to conscript, 'the resistance' was able to effectively dramatize popular opposition to the war. The only two points at which modern mass war closely touches the individual are typically at or after the moment of conscription, or when attacks on the civilian populations begin. But the draft-resistance movement managed to bring the war closer, in terms of organized non-cooperation, and solidarity with those drafted and resisting.[29]

Outside the national frame

The one movement to clearly spread across national boundaries was the nuclear disarmament movement; during the 1960s its symbol became the property of an international movement, and the spread of nuclear weapons was, together with the transformation of world communications, probably the greatest single factor in generating a more trans-national consciousness. Anti-nuclear radicalism, especially when crystallized in direct action and the unilateralist impulse, was an implicit (and sometimes explicit) challenge to existing national sovereignty. 'Fall-out knew no political boundaries', and neither did the new radicalism. With the gradual development of global ecological awareness, the notion of the sovereignty of the human community grew, and with it the belief that 'the age of nations is past' (Teilhard de Chardin).[30] The factor of trans-nationalism[31] may thus be seen to develop first in terms of these expressions: a 'unilateralism', linking international direct actions, and the solidarities of oppressed groups transcending national boundaries. The concept was defined by the actions and movements which developed regardless of national boundaries, subverting the nation states' framework.[32]

Trans-national journeys, the trips of NL radicals to Budapest in 1956, or Havana after 1959, voyages into the Pacific testing areas, or interventions in the Sahara – as well as support for the anti-conscription campaigns in France – expressed new solidarities which, ignoring political frontiers, pointed forward to developments in the later 1960s. The CNVA marches to Moscow and Cuba, and the voyages by the *Phoenix*, *Golden Rule* and *Everyman* into the Eniwetok US test zone; and the direct interventions by Western pacifists in Red Square expressed a similar spirit.[33] Like their American equivalents, these actions embodied an internationalism based firmly on non-alignment *vis-à-vis* the major blocs.

Extending this idea, the English NL, especially within CND, propounded the theory of positive neutralism, which became a major plank of peace movement policy. Close to the Third Camp ideas of America's veteran pacifist leader, A. J. Muste, the non-aligned Third Way position, already developed since 1953 by Muste and *Liberation* in opposing the militarism of the Cold War blocs, guided American radical pacifism in its exposition of a mildly anarchist socialism in its years of renewal. Together with its advocacy of pacifism and civil disobedience, this helped develop the theory of unilateralism.[34]

Involving a universal condemnation of nuclear weapons, Third Camp internationalism also had, for Muste, a parallel spiritual dimension; a faithful nonviolent 'Third Way' alternative, a moral power centre, opposing the power blocs, which was also intended to link Western radicals and peace movements with the Third World.

Such themes, unilateral disarmament, individual and collective resistance, a positive non-aligned autonomy, were to become the major ones in the development of the British and American peace movements in the early 1960s, not least those focused on the Testing issue, like the Student Peace Union (SPU).[35] A direct forerunner of American campus NL groups, SPU, with its Third Camp, anti-militarist position, broke through various Cold War apologetics with its advocacy of international initiatives independent of existing power blocs.

Radical pacifism

It is thus arguable that both intellectually and politically, the continuity of certain themes central to the growth of the NL, was linked to the theoretical and actual developments of radical pacifism after the Second World War. Beyond pure anti-militarism or a Third Camp peace position, its themes were communitarian utopianism, direct action, decentralist anarchism and nonviolent revolution. It is notable that SDS's founders shared a number of the anarchist-pacifist views of *Liberation* magazine, and even the 'Beats', or early hippies have been termed 'radical pacifists' at base.[36]

In bringing these elements together, the first mass protests against the war in Vietnam took on the broader overtones of a movement against war in general; the songs and speeches ('We are here to keep faith with those of all countries and all ages who have sought to beat swords into ploughshares and war no more', Lynd) gave a distinctively pacifist tone to the early climax of the anti-Vietnam war movement.[37] In SDS, the notion of building a peace movement to prevent the 'seventh war from now', the politics of the long-haul, fully aware of the power of US militarism, enabled strong cooperation with pacifist groups like WRI and CNVA which supported SDS's March on Washington. Despite a growing existential sense of the possibility that, as Norman O. Brown argued, in one sense, war might never be abolished,[38] pacifism as an opposition to brutalized, depersonalized or authoritarian killing represented a definite if inchoate strain of utopianism, that remains part of the NL throughout its growth.

The attempt at democratizing another sector of life – replacing national 'defence' by popular resistance – is symptomatic of this strain. Whether at the level of state or community, non-military action represents a more participatory, grassroots approach to the problem of war, making it attractive to liberals as well as libertarians. As the Czech events later showed, it could put the emphasis on those democratic and decentralized actions which minimize systematic brutality and destruction. A nonviolent or civilian resistance force would clearly represent less of an internally repressive threat than a normal military force; it had already been turned successfully against military coups, or attempts at totalitarian takeover.[39] But its main political advantage, from the NL point of view, was the wider popular base of decision-making inevitably involved in taking over and breaking down the monopoly of violence held by the State.

Goodman's pacifism was typical of the early NL; not a purist rejection of violence and aggression, it advocated expression rather than repression of violent impulses, but rejected rather *weapons* (the technological extension of personal aggression) and *armies*: the social organization of violence as a bureaucratic negation of personal aggression. War seemed an unnatural extension of aggression, combining bureaucracy and technology in the service of an authoritarian state, contradicting and repressing any natural community, thwarting creativity. Such activity was not spontaneous, but coercive and hierarchical.

The three main activist civil rights groups[40] were each from the outset committed to nonviolent action;[41] despite the part played by radical pacifists in developing the struggle, the influence of Muste and Gandhi on King, and the role of Christian ideas of love and brotherhood in the Southern movement, nonviolence was adopted by the desegregationists for practical as much as moral reasons. The civil disobedience strategy arose naturally and directly from Southern black experience; as well as a notable moral advantage, nonviolence faced the realistic consideration that 'the whites had the guns' (Abernathy).[42] But the working principle of King's nonviolence was an active and creative 'truth-force' not merely a disruptive or passive 'resistance of the weak'.[43] Such nonviolence was rooted in principles of interpersonal transaction: 'If men cannot refer to a common value, recognized by all as existing in each other, then man is incomprehensible to man.'[44] This sentiment, appearing in the founding statement of SDS, echoes Camus's plea that man reflect on species murder.

It was Camus's humanism and nonviolence, rather than Gandhi's, which were enormously influential on the first generation of movement activists (e.g. Mario Savio, Bob Moses or Tom Hayden); there is hardly a NL spokesman or leader in the early 1960s who does not quote him; at one climax of the FSM, a speech, quoting Camus's appeal against hate and murder, cooled a near riot. And in this phase the endorsement of such an appeal comprehended all organized violence: from war and revolutionary terror to state executions.[45] Indeed in the early 1960s, nonviolence went largely unchallenged in the movement and a humane optimism was predominant. For several years it was still possible to use the word 'love' in SDS without provoking catcalls: love is referred to in speeches and political pamphlets; Fromm's 'taboo on tenderness' had far from captured the NL in 1965.[46] Indeed when Fromm developed this critique he helped assist the import of such words as 'love' into the language of the early NL and the counterculture. For example, the phrase 'love of man', and the word 'love' appear in several places in the Port Huron Statement, the founding manifesto of the NL in America. Equally, SNCC's statement of principle reads:

We affirm the philosophy, or religious ideal of nonviolence as the fundamental of our purpose. The presupposition of our faith and the manner of our action . . . seeks a social order of justice permeated by love. . . . Through nonviolence, courage displaces fear. Love transcends hate.

The founders and rank and file of SDS were at first deeply influenced by such ethics: 'our best concern comes from SNCC' (Oglesby, 1965). That 'best concern' was 'to make love more possible. We work to remove from society what threatens and prevents it.' But though SNCC's opening statement was unequivocally committed to nonviolence, there was a wide range of attitudes within it; nevertheless SNCC added new dimensions of resourcefulness and courage to the nonviolent tradition; and its formal commitment to this nonviolence was to last for six years,[47] or two-thirds of its organizational life.

Morality and political rebellion

In their acts of nonviolent resistance, early New Leftists claimed they drew a line beyond which they refused to cooperate, affirming values, beyond that line, which they endorsed. Like Camus's man in revolt, by saying 'no', they were also saying 'yes'. As a counterpart to the affirmative aspect of Goodman's anarchism, there was a matter of what he called 'drawing the line';[48] resisting the encroachments of technocracy and the state on the individual, or of the production of one-dimensional men by a knowledge factory: in the words of one of the FSM leaders before the final sit-in; such an institution 'becomes so odious that we must put our bodies against the gears, against the wheels and machines, and make the machine stop until we're free'.[49]

This was the NL's rejection of a dehumanizing domination, a hyper-developed economy, an operationalist ideology, opposed by the 'as yet un-coopted feelings and actions of those who were conscious of servitude'. In the view of some, this renunciation of technocracy, a cultural phenomenon rather than merely a political movement, 'strikes beyond ideology to the level of consciousness'.[50]

An outraged, often a-political moralism was a fundamental characteristic of the early Movement; Camus's appeal to choice, Muste's demand that the political and the normative be reunited; King's insistence that love be brought to bear on the political institutions and struggles – all helped reinforce the Movement's belief that what Buber had called 'the ploughshare of the normative principle' must be 'driven into the hard soil of political reality'.

In Britain, like Muste, Ronald Sampson contributed much the same uncompromising moral attack on the structures of power.[51]

One of the movement's historians comes to the defence of this very element in the NL synthesis. 'To react in moral terms means to set a mechanism in motion in the area where the citizen is most strongly repressed: his morality itself.'[52]

That a political disillusionment with Liberalism could take place, demonstrated the immense idealism and moralism of the early NL: 'The best of the young take the proclaimed values of their elders with a seriousness which leads them to be appalled by their violation in practice.'[53] The establishment's moral indifference, even cynicism, stood as a significant counterpoint to the idealism of the early protests and their calls for a moral opposition. Within the established version of politics, 'ethics is subordinate to strategy' (Muste). It was therefore necessary to break out of the language and behaviour pattern of a 'corrupt political universe',[54] this 'moral politics' demanded a refusal to acquiesce in violent structures, a persistent non-conformity with the state, a 'holy disobedience' ranging from tax refusal to conscientious objection, or even to more assertive nonviolent acts.[55]

With the evolution of the peace and civil rights movements in America nationally, only the draft resistance movement developed the kind of character and integrity that typified localized, community-based responses to the war – like the years of action against weapons shipments at Port Chicago in California.[56] The Resistance attempted, with remarkable success, to combine local moral solidarity and example with practical non-cooperation and mutual aid.

In the first phase of the NL in Britain, with its fundamental reappraisal of the nature of war, triggered by the developments in thermonuclear weaponry and further catalysed by the Testing issue, the core of CND's message was that the reversal of a race towards almost universal and inevitable nuclear catastrophe, demanded a major act of military renunciation. CND built up its head of steam on the basis of a few simple truths and responses, and its most telling argument was always that the threat to use weapons, and to test weapons which involve the health and lives of future generations, and to contemplate the slaughter, indiscriminately, of civilian populations and the devastation, even of non-combatant countries, was 'just plain wrong'.[57] Such altruistic grounds for nuclear disarmament were predominant over the chauvinistic arguments for survival, though the early combination of an ethical socialism with moral opposition to the bomb, declined in relative importance as CND developed.[58]

Nevertheless, until 1963 the early NL in Britain appeared to be searching for new native and ethically based politics previously lacking both in the Labour Party and the Marxist groups. It is thus less surprising to find Camus figuring prominently in an early issue of the *Universities and New Left Review*; the native-born William Morris, with his strongly ethical and aesthetic socialism; or anarchists writing on nonviolent direct action.[59]

When Carl Oglesby remarked, a decade later, that the NL began with a mis-reading or misinterpretation of Camus,[60] as a philosopher of commitment and action, he may underestimate the novel synthesis (hinted at in Camus's most influential book, *L'Homme révolté*) of anarchist politics, direct action and existential revolt. Indeed the widespread 'existentialism' of the early NL was filtered almost exclusively through such literary and political writings. His was the emphasis on personal choice (victim or executioner?) and decision, in a world in which choice and decision seemed the property of impersonal structures and administrative or technical processes; it lay at the base of the renewed determination to re-possess such powers.

But the NL read in Camus's 'rebellion' a mystical stress on the act, rather than a presentation of personal and symbolic choice. Thus his lone literary and philosophical stance could be bent into service as justification for running battles with institutionalized power, continuous protest, and an individual confrontation with authority, that was the essence of the student revolt and the first movement projects.

It is true that the NL's interpretation of *L'Homme révolté* was an over-optimistic one – seeing the rebel as heroic rather than tragic.[61] But in an era of change and challenge, the critic, the creative radical, only comes into the fore and is given a sense of confidence in his or her own innovation and vision as an active movement arises. In the period of apparent stasis, before these forces and movements develop, such minority innovators are indeed isolated and marginal. With a movement to identify with, Camus too might have been able to stand more clearly for a third way, and thus identify publicly and positively his 'rebellion'. As it was, his stance had appeared at the time a lone and anguished gesture of despair; unlike Muste, Camus was unable to accept or overcome political isolation and enforced detachment.[62] Only when linked to actions, however small or symbolic, do such stances and ideas seem to have any connection with reality. Thus it is such actions that are the preface to a NL theory, and are central to its identity.

Theory and practice

Subsequent debates about 'praxis' led many to question whether the real breakthroughs that led to the birth of the NL were in the realm of theory or rather that of practice.

Most of the writers whose ideas first filtered through to the new activists, directly or indirectly, in leaflet, speech, quotation, slogan or conversation, stressed many common themes in relation to this synthesis; the need to reconnect the personal and the systemic, the moral and the political, is a concern running through the work of Mills the sociologist, and Camus the political moralist,[63] the social psychology of Fromm and the direct-action pacifism of Muste.[64]

The stress on individual moral responsibility for action, uppermost in the early direct action against the bomb, in the freedom rides and later the draft resistance movement, provided the deep foundations of moral resource upon which much of the early opposition to the Vietnam war was constructed.[65]

The NL's reaction to ideology was not merely existential rejection, it was located in a suspicion of theory divorced from fact; 'if the facts do not support our theories so much the worse for the theories' (Savio). Hayden argued that the movement should 'depend more on feel than theory', insisting that 'action produces its own evidence which theory alone can never do'.[66] 'We do not need theories so much as the experience that is the source of theory' (R. D. Laing).

This was a mood militating against academic pomposity or theoretical prolixity; regarding detached analysis with scepticism, preferring participation and experiential recollection; trusting the spontaneous and expressive as against the calculated and measured. The 1960s were a time, not for 'reflection', but for 'evocation'.[67]

Such scepticism was linked to a pragmatic emphasis in the NL, not on the liberal pragmatism (that was often counterposed to 'the psychopathology of dissent'), but an emphasis on 'praxis', on proof through action. The dictum 'ideology disunites . . . action unites' expressed this emphasis; as Lynd stressed the relationships between thought and action, theory and practice, were always closer in the American context.[68]

A few broke through the consensus with words and ideas alone;[69] others spoke almost exclusively by their deeds;[70] perhaps those who were most influential were leaders like Muste, King, Lynd, Dellinger or Hayden – also Russell in England – who merged words *with* deeds; for their own acts and ideas became fused with collective action.

Although this utopian activism of the American NL was often tentative and experimental in character, it was generally more successful than its English counterpart in closing the gap between professed ideals and everyday activity. The mystique of activism, calling for a closing of this gap, helped locate the intellectual in a larger context, arguing that by dividing the intellect from action, the hierarchical differentiation of social roles would be maintained. The litmus test of the quality of an ideology became whether its proponents acted in terms of it, i.e. did they act it out *personally?* For, it was urged, the 'truth we discover affects the lives we lead'.[71]

Both within and outside the Marxist tradition, concern over the movement's 'concept of man' was a central problem for the NL.[72] SDS expressed its utopian faith in human capacity early in its growth;

Men have unrealized potential for self-cultivation, self-direction, self-understanding and creativity. It is this potential that we regard as crucial and to which we appeal, not to the human potentiality for violence, unreason and submission to authority.[73]

Power in America is abdicated by individuals to top-down organizational units, and it is in the recovery of this power that the movement becomes distinctive from the rest of the country and a new kind of man emerges.

Later Marcuse was to envisage the 'new man' emerging in a counter-culture, in an unrepressed utopia, possible because most destructive aspects of human nature were products of unnecessarily repressive structures.[74] New personalities could emerge with the removal of all these repressive forces. Hayden, too, talked of the emergence of a new kind of man; a rhetoric that in 1959 had echoed the early hopes of the Cuban revolution, articulated by Castro and Guevara, continued in the NL. As Marcuse put it:

We must be able to show, even in a very small way, the models of what may one day be a human being [or] that what is here at work are human beings with different needs and different goals which are not yet and I hope never will be, co-opted.[75]

For the question of morality was bound up with life-style; and living in a new way.

Because our goals, our values, our old and new morality, our own morality, must be visible already in our actions. The new human beings whom we want to help to create – we must already strive to be these human beings right here and now.[76]

For the NL, living one's beliefs became essential, living like the poor, acting as 'anarchistically as possible', or embodying the 'new man' in one's actions.[77]

Thus moral authority in the Movement rested not only in the ability to translate theory into easily understood formulae and proposals for political action, but also as with Lynd, a personal unwillingness to allow oneself or others to separate this intellect work from practical activity. Lynd urged: 'Let the intellectual make insurgency a full-time rather than a part-time occupation.'[78] Weekend activism was no more allowable than weekend hippy-ism; and the activist was also participant-observer, and analyst. Lynd continually lived these theories whether in democratic participation, civil disobedience, or communitarianism. Such 'Do-it-Yourself-Politics' was, in Goodman's words, the 'painfully American answer'.

Paul Goodman was, in this tradition, a pragmatic utopian; the innovation of social hypotheses must become translated into social experiment – a form of theory-testing in a social context. Many of the projects of the alternative society could be seen as exactly this proliferation of semi-replicated experiments, following Goodman's own activist model, freed from the rigidities of either methods or theory.

As an example, Goodman threw himself into the draft-resistance movement in the last years of his life; the domineering state must be thwarted when it demanded its sacrifice of the young. At the centre of his draft-resistance work was the idea of complicity – his own and others' of his generation, with the acts of the draft-card burners and the non-cooperators.

It was such an idea that deeply appealed to the university radicals who had experienced the action-distanced academicism of their more liberal heroes; Goodman was on the streets, his body on the line, mixing with the demonstrators. Yet he also contributed an element of rigorous thought and analysis to balance the cynicism bred of their rejection of academic withdrawal. He understood this rejection, which often amounted to anti-intellectualism, but opposed its renunciation of the worth of ideas.

Goodman, sharing Mills's 'realistic utopianism', was an example of a theorist who transcended inherited categories; his opposition to bureaucratic centralization and mindless technology, refused to take much about the modern world for granted.

Though less of an activist, Mills also proved a significant influence among students; his tone was quite unlike other academic writing of his time, which at best was nervous and qualified. Like Camus, Mills actively identified with the alienated rebel, whether or not the historical situation could actually be changed. In a somewhat romantic remark, prophetic of a second generation of NL intellectuals, Mills said that, if necessary, he would be fighting alongside Fidel Castro.

Furthermore, there was the example of Fromm in linking his critique of personal alienation, and the dangers of nuclear war, to his own political activity, in the peace groups.

But how far did theory influence, shape, reinforce, as opposed to merely reflect the movement in its earliest growth? Clearly, such writers as these made available both original ideas and significant reinterpretations of 'classic' theory.[79] It was possible to apply the popular ideas of Mills, Fromm or, above all, Goodman, to everyday situations of life, if not those of a Marcuse.[80] In this sense they proved influential; in other ways, the writing and speeches of King, and later, Carmichael, and even Malcolm-X, had more formative influence on the American movement that did Fanon, Guevara or Debray; for the former spoke to their own (movement) situation.

Nevertheless, in any discussion of NL theory, such figures find a place. For example it can be argued that Marcuse's writing clearly reinforced ideas, themes and styles already current in the movement in the mid-1960s; yet he did not shape the early theory or character of that movement, since he was not widely read by activists; even as late as 1968, Cohn-Bendit discounted his influence, and few NL theorists seem to have been influenced by him (although Hayden and some others appear to have arrived, independently, at some similar conclusions about America and ways to change it).[81]

The major ideas in the NL, that Marcuse's writing amplifies, or reflects, are involved in his critique of American society, its consumerism and alienation and his advocacy of a non-repressive culture, all ideas that become widely influential *after* 1966. To some extent even this later coincidence of ideas, and the resemblance of Marcuse's major themes (e.g. anti-repression, alienation, etc.) to those of the movement is superficial. Yet abstract and often complicated, Marcuse's ideas obviously represent versions of some of the deep concerns of the NL – the threat of annihilation, technocracy and authoritarianism – that are articulated more directly by Fromm or Mills.[82]

Emanating from the movement itself, the Port Huron Statement, though its ideas were borrowed, proved more important and influential.[83] A founding declaration, it was a synthesis of ideas from Mills, Fromm, Goodman, Camus, *Liberation*'s critique of the 'Triple Revolution', and Michael Harrington's evidence about American poverty; it implied general support for revolution against injustice abroad. It revealed the approach of the disillusioned liberal who has not yet become an innovating theorist.

In it the 'civilized barbarism' of America, invisible to the majority, protected from attack, is seen as beset by issues – war, militarism, racism, alienation and above all poverty, that the young founders of SDS saw liberalism as powerless to deal with.

The early history of the NL represents in part the gathering of intellectuals around a number of radical journals,[84] concerned with publicizing new ideas, including Marxian revisionism, alongside news and views from movement campaigns and projects. Typical of this was the inauguration of the *Universities and Left Review* (*ULR*) in England a few months prior to the founding of CND. Many of the ideas of Marx seen as immediately relevant by such NL publications, had been filtered through other post- or neo-Marxian thinkers; Trotsky, Lukács, Luxemburg, Gramsci, as well as Sartre, Reich and Marcuse, or even non-Marxists – Fromm, Mills, Sorel or later Fanon. *ULR* (succeeded by *NLR* in 1960), was still strongly pointed in a libertarian direction; its continuing quality of life concern, its critique of alienation, initiated a critical appraisal of industrialism and industrial culture foreshadowing the ideas of the counter-culture. It emphasized humanism as the popular basis of socialist movements; the need for a cultural and social articulation of these ethical strengths.[85] This was the neglected aspect of the Socialist tradition, and it needed to be discovered again. In Britain, *ULR* encouraged it at a time when the traditional Marxian Left was still stronger than anything across the Atlantic; giving libertarian openings, and an awareness of writers and theorists previously marginal to the Marxian tradition, such magazines, including *Studies on the Left*, made available to a much wider audience a brand of socialist humanism which went beyond inherited categories and dogmas. By including those writers such as Camus or Reich, or reviving the ideas of Simone Weil, who had been largely neglected or isolated by the 1950s' Left, and even in its revival of Marxist revisionists such as the Italian Gramsci, it emphasized the idealist, humanist and democratic aspects of their work – cultural critiques, rather than Leninism. Moreover, it is significant that this first, English NL confronted, in a way that American Marxists never aspired to do, the issue of nuclear weapons and nuclear war.

Let the people decide

In assessing the role of theory in shaping a NL identity it is notable that a survey of SDS members found that most of them had in fact read Mills and Camus, many had read Goodman, some had read Fanon, Fromm and Marcuse.[86] But what the survey did not ask or reveal was the probably more important source of ideas, i.e. the NL journals, and the stream of duplicated discussion papers, statements and pamphlets put out by SDS itself in the early 1960s,[87] through which the ideas of these theorists were filtered. If SDS was anti-intellectual, it was as a form of nativism. At this stage it looked mainly not to Third World ideas, nor to the European (e.g. Marxist) traditions, but to American movements and home-grown ideas.

As this literature reveals, the movement produced, especially in America, its own 'organic' intellectuals and elder theorists, some active, like Muste, Lynd, Dellinger and (to a lesser degree) Goodman.[88] SDS itself was not without theoretical expression; a whole series of articulate and intelligent SDS leaders (Hayden, Flacks, Haber, Oglesby, Booth, Kissinger, Calvert, Davidson, Potter and Egleson) contributed to the growth of movement ideas. They ensured that such theory reflected and was moulded by movement experience in the fields and churches of Mississippi, in the poor communities of the North, and in the anti-war demonstrations and student confrontations.

Nevertheless, predominantly this was a movement of slogans rather than theories, gut-appraisal rather than analysis; in 1965, it was still the slogans of freedom on everyone's lips – shaped by the experiences in the South, from the Montgomery boycott to the Greensborough sit-ins and the Freedom Summers – the language of freedom was, as Newfield points out, dominant in both SNCC and SDS.[89]

As well as the Free Speech Movement and Freedom Summers, it passed on into the language of the counter-institutions: 'free' clinics, 'free' stores, the *Los Angeles Free Press* and the 'free' universities and 'free' schools. 'A free university in a free society' was an early SDS slogan; freedom schools in the South and the ghettoes and a 'Freedom Democratic Party' in Mississippi were established,[90] and, at the second national SDS convention, a resolution ambitiously proclaimed 'our hope is human freedom'.

It was these slogans of SDS, 'Let the people decide', 'there's a change gonna come' or just 'Join!', that critics saw as summarizing a 'mindless activism' placing the NL in a tradition of anti-intellectualism in American life;[91] certainly populist notions of going to, learning from, living amongst, and identifying with 'the people', were central.[92] 'Let the people decide' had a practical significance when organizing minority power, whether student, black or poor-white.

Libertarian perspectives generated a sophisticated practice which in turn produced a 'guerilla' or movement theory,[93] focused on the specific problematics of tactics and organization, stemming from experiences in the South, on the campuses and in northern ghettoes.[94] It is thus perhaps not surprising that the NL should respond at first by denying the necessity for ideology;[95] nor that the American movement could find such inspiration in the romantic defeatism of the IWW and its spontaneous from-the-bottom-up democracy, and repeat with new conviction a variety of Wobbly slogans and injunctions, 'We are all leaders – we have no leaders', 'An injury to one is an injury to all', or 'Build a new society within the shell of the old'.[96] Such ideas, condemned by Leninists and Fabians alike after 1900, found a clear resonance in the new movements of the 1960s. The NL shares with classical Syndicalism its anti-intellectualism, its cult of activism; its suspicion of theory and praise of spontaneity; the integration of theory and practice.[97]

The activists rejected the Old Left style, 'they wanted instead to go South and get their hands and their heads – their lives – into the dangerous, the moral and therefore the authentic. The instinct from the beginning was to discover the streets!'[98]

Lynd, as a historian, helped make conscious and explicit the stylistic and rhetorical links between SDS and earlier American radical movements: Populism, the Wobblies, agrarian radicals and communitarians, abolitionists and war resisters; all helped provide native models for an authentic response to problems.[99] Safer still, and most potent of all, was to draw on the most immediate movement experience as it was lived and unfolded. Such experience was seen as the most authoritative basis of ideas or theories. The rejection of liberal alliances and coalitions, of strategies of 'realignment' or extensions of welfare statism was temperamental rather than political; to accept such tactics would have been totally at odds with the developing style of the movement, just as much as to have endorsed the methodology of the old-style, politically aligned, Marxist grouplets.

Living the revolution

But there are a number of ingredients in this synthesis that need to be unravelled. The first, pragmatism, complements the belief in the elision of theory and practice, thought and deed. The second, moralism, supports the necessary connection between means and ends. The third is structural, the implicit organizational continuity between actions and goals. And the fourth, linking these, is personalism, the belief in living as a new person, and the stressed importance of both experience and expression.

Movement theory permeated by pragmatism, driven by populist impulses was, like American radicalism, often seen from outside (e.g. by English radicals) as peculiarly parochial and incapable of export – practically applicable ideas in a limited context – 'bottom-up' theorizing rooted in a specific movement base, and a uniquely American experience.

Strong populist elements run through most of the American writers: Mills (despite his later intellectual élitism), Goodman, Lynd, and Hayden in particular. These, and pragmatist elements, accompanied by a strain of moralism, are finally expressed as a radical pluralism, genuine, if implicit. Pluralism lay in the idea of flexible and proliferating ethnic and functional, power – black power, student power, workers' control, community control – each characterized by its own mode of direct, participant democracy. NL tactics were essentially multi-centred, aimed at creating pluralities of decentral power and choice, where none had existed previously.

Together with the elevation of ordinary life-style, folk culture and the values of the under class, whether in Mississippi, Harlem or Merseyside, such reactions could easily purvey an imagery of primitive rebellion; as a reaction to Catch Twenty-Two bigness and bureaucracy, it was conceived as an alliance of contemporary radicalism with definite tendencies in the economic and social structure (and even in the personality structure), towards a decentralized community.

Such a project, implying bottom-up reconstruction – alternative ways of filling a social vacuum left by a century of industrialism and urbanism – was a pluralism that expressed suspicion of the centralizing state, of overall uniformity, and the inflexibility of the monolithic structures of industrial society. Thus the NL came to occupy some of the ground held by agrarian populism; a growing suspicion that industrialism was not identifiable with 'progress'. As a result, participatory democracy and community-organization became part and parcel of this scepticism of urbanization and technocracy – these were no longer accepted as the inevitable 'facts-of-life'.

At the basis of such relatively non-ideological action lay a sense of community, 'the experience of participation, the feeling of freedom, and the expression of self'. It was inhibited by a 'healthy aversion' (in Zinn's words) to 'making instruments into absolutes or means into ends; against the deification of any party, any nation, any ideology, any method', insisting, at every level, on the spiritual and political connections between means and ends; for just as brotherhood was the way to the 'beloved community', 'there is no way to peace, peace is the way' (Muste).

Thus as well as voluntarism, the belief in the necessity of creating new institutions, the NL introduced personalism and an expressive political style

Changes in life-style and a personal creativity involved in counter-institutions, helped close the gap between ends and means, between structure change and individual change.[100]

NL organization had initially rejected the implicit idea of an apocalyptic leap from the present into the future, the millennial faith which believes that you could do now whatever you chose and that it would have no effect on the society which you constructed in the future. Repeatedly in Goodman, in Muste, in Camus and in Lynd and in a whole range of writers, the point is emphasized, 'Your politics is not your rhetoric or your positions on issues, it is the way you live your life' (Gitlin). 'To adopt a pattern of behaviour and a life-style which do not conform to those of the majority means demonstrating externally the re-conquest of one's individual autonomy.'[101] Alternative life-styles, the 'instinctual repudiation of old political forms, movements and practices', represented alternative roles, or even the abolition of roles, as was clearly shown later in the sexual liberation movements.[102] Such new patterns, eclectic and improvisational, encompassed the search for authentic experience, an existential humanism, a concern with quality of life, and could identify with the Beats or situationists, in their 'revolution in everyday life'. The experiential explorations of honest selfhood, characterized movement discourse, together with an emphasis on qualitative rather than quantitative needs; celebrating the joyful, even the momentary.[103]

Reminiscent of Malatesta, or Camus's rebel, expressed in the Provos' 'declaration-of-intent', NL activism thus replaces revolution by continuous revolt, involving complete identification – and personal commitment to social transformation. Rebellion, if it is to be permanent, can no longer risk its revolutionary ideals in the contamination of institutionalized power.

Participatory democracy

The dominant NL themes of the mid-1960s were those which linked decentralization and community decision-making in a 'participatory democracy' (PD). 'Power to the people' was a slogan reflected and translated in numerous projects and organizing experiences. Such sentiments, linked to a plurality of emerging power relationships; black people, young people, students, minority groups and including, finally, women, were rooted in assumptions that 'in a good society people participate fully in the decisions which govern their destinies and thus can create basic change in their day-to-day lives'.[104]

For SDS, like SNCC, the insistence that 'participation and control must be one'[105] derived from the belief that political impotence was associated with black people's loss of dignity, that only through parti-cipation would self-confidence and self-respect be regained.

Under Mills's influence, the early SDS organizers felt they were able to take up the connection that he had stressed, between the personal problem and the public issue,[106] in their idea of organizing around the poor in terms both of their individual sense of worth and identity, and their collective independence and dignity. The issues around which they organized were humble enough: housing repairs, urban blight, jobs, welfare payments or school lunch programmes, even street crossings.[107]

It is usual to date the beginning of the community organizing movement, in 1963, the year that the Economic Research and Action Project (ERAP) was formed out of SDS, to coordinate grass-roots community-action projects. After the first Mississippi Freedom Summer, young white organizers were beginning to be edged out of the black civil rights groups; SNCC's emphasis had decisively shifted from protest demonstrations and sit-ins, to bottom-up community organizing, mostly in the northern cities.[108] It was from here, and at the same time, that the idea of community control and community power emerged. The community projects expanded after 1963,[109] based not on an élitist Marxist idea of 'organizing', but in the belief, expressed in the Port Huron Statement, both in people's 'essential goodness', and the political effectiveness of a bottom-up strategy, even if this meant an ideology of simple activism, or no ideology at all. Participatory democracy in SDS and SNCC implied living with 'the people', a belief that only in this way could the real needs of the people be understood, and a community effectively organized. A little more abstractly the same sentiments were being expressed by sections of the English NL: 'good community, a living culture, will . . . not only make room for, but actively encourage all and any who can contribute to the advance in consciousness which is the common need.'[110]

It is in community-based action that the practical link between the NL and anarchism is first clearly indicated. In 'letting-people-decide' lay hopes that the tension between the individual and the community could be resolved in the immediacy and simplicity of direct, participant forms of organization. The stress on democratic decentralization and involvement, the suspicion of established leadership and inherited institutions, was closer to an Anarchist or Syndicalist, than a Marxist tradition. So too was the quasi-religious emphasis on community and action. Direct personal links connect the English community activism of the mid-1960s with libertarian developments in the peace movements, the widening of scope of concern, from the bomb to community issues.[111] Symptomatic of this connection was the squatting movement. The Committee of 100, always closer to Anarchism than Marxism, and progenitor of many local grassroots projects, engendered in its organizers both a 'classless' concern – organizing all the poor – and a stress on democratic structure and willingness to intervene physically that characterized SNCC and SDS in America. The community organizing that sprang from these groups was thus unequivocally libertarian in character; embodying a radical vision of a communal and cooperative utopia in its methods and organizations.

Lynd and Hayden, the foremost popularizers of such notions as 'community control', owed a lot to Mills. Mills's prior emphasis on decisions and decision-making, in *The Power Elite*, was reflected in the early NL concern with creating participatory publics. The ruling élite, seen to be irresponsible and out of control – was a sort of juggernaut, only made safe by direct control. Mills's philosophy of the revival of political 'publics', foreshadows the ideas of a community's control of decisions that affect it, representing an overcoming of political alienation.

The re-establishment or revival of local and voluntary organizations, through which people can repossess political power, reveals clear parallels between Mills's 'publics', and the strategy of counter-institutions. Through the decentralized character of the movements of the 1960s, participation was effectively extended to new groups and communities.

This view that 'people should control the decisions which affect their everyday lives', first clearly expressed in the Port Huron Statement, demanded that 'decision-making of basic social consequence should be carried on by public groupings'. Politics was defined as 'the art of collectively creating an acceptable pattern of social relations'. As SDS developed the concept, it drew from many sources besides Mills; from the Anarchists, a concern with decentralization; from the Quakers, ideas about how to run meetings without formal structure; from SNCC, a sense of spontaneity of expression. It also became influenced by such phenomena as the T-group, encounter session, and sensitivity training.[112]

Inevitably there was a tendency to turn the concept into an ideology and a programme, as well as a mere technique. There are few spheres of life that cannot be subjected to such claims; participatory democracy could be carried into the debates about workers' control, representative democracy, individual life-style – even alternative defence policies. Carl Davidson described the spread of participatory democracy as a

chronic and contagious disease; once caught it permeates one's whole life and the lives of those around us. Its effect is disruptive in a total sense, and within a manipulative bureaucratic system its articulation and expression amounts to sabotage.[113]

Initially, participatory democracy was interpreted in individual rather than collective terms, but in the twin themes of community control and workers' control, collective versions of the concept soon emerged. There was also some identification between the early English NL and the workers' control efforts of the Yugoslavs, however compromised by state structure and a one-party system these were.[114]

Decentralized, autonomous workers' movements were idealized, especially those in opposition to bureaucratic union structures. 'The means of production should be open to democratic participation and subject to democratic social regulation' (Port Huron). 'Repressive institutions' could be broken up and replaced by 'properly administered democratic workers' control organizations in all the different institutions of social life'.[115]

Even in the middle of marches and demonstrations, votes were taken, issues debated, decisions made, 'participatory democracy occupied'; such innovations appear in the FSM occupations at Berkeley, in the meetings of the Southern Freedom Summers and in almost every direct-democracy gathering including those of France in 1968, climaxing in the assemblies of the Sorbonne. They appear in England, in the Committee of 100, and in America in SNCC and SDS.

In 1961, on an Aldermaston march, an unofficial group emerged calling itself 'Let the March Decide', opposing the CND bureaucracy and unlike the early CND, or even the DAC, the Committee facilitated informal debates on tactics during demonstrations.[116]

In a black version of participatory democracy, SNCC's early sensitivity to the local grassroots needs of local people was translated into Carmichael's populist rhetoric. And on this, for most of the New Left, the black power slogan was welcomed as ushering in a new mood of militancy and activism, and a more positive political strategy, to fill a vacuum left by the decline of the integrationist Civil Rights Movement.[117] Amongst black theorists, even Fanon was quoted in support of anti-élitist democratism: his sentiments were interpreted as identical with those of NL organizers, who were scrapping Robert's rules of order in favour of *ad hoc* procedures and consensus.[118] A further attempt to fuse the idea of participatory democracy and counter-institutions with the Peace Movement, and the nonviolent tradition in America, appeared in the anti-Vietnam war resistance of 1965. The call for a people's peace, negotiated by the movement directly with the Vietnamese, at the Assembly of Unrepresented People, in Washington in August of that year, clearly exemplified the influence of ideas of direct democracy. The Assembly was without 'organizational structure or established discipline', no 'single policy was pre-determined and imposed; all policies could be established or modified by the participants'.[119]

Oppenheimer suggests two major reasons for the adoption of participatory democracy: first the desire to de-structure the type of group in which procedural manipulation through rules of order is possible; second, to avoid the factionalism inherent in voting systems, by adoption of a consensus system of decision-making.[120]

At times SDS practice came close to realizing the Wobbly claim, 'We have no leaders . . .',[121] and if there was one writer whose conclusions about means and ends in organization the NL thoroughly internalized, it was Roberto Michels. His pessimistic conclusions about the oligarchic tendencies of even the most high-minded organizations, were a significant justification for adopting safeguards: 'The democratic process of participation and control must be used in the movement for social change from the start; the means for change must be democratic.'[122] In this spirit very real attempts were made to find and develop new leaders and organizers,[123] and to spread participation more widely, including the patient encouragement of the less experienced, and eventually, and especially, women.[124]

As a central theme of movement theory PD was soon translated into the practical organization of SDS; rotating leadership; annual elections; decision by consensus; office-holding limited to one year; autonomy for local groups and chapters; no decision by national office to be binding.[125] This was a remarkable organizational experiment; in some ways more radical even than those of SNCC and the Committee of 100. As an experiment in decentralized organization, even the national offices of SDS were eventually divided and dispersed.

3. A New Radicalism

The movement crystallizes

The new radicalism that crystallized in these years was, in Newfield's words, 'pluralistic, amorphous and multi-layered'.[1] The movements of youth, peace and civil rights had certainly had no clear centre, and no 'stable message'. They represented a system of *ad hoc* leadership emerging as need arose, shifting centres and evolving messages, e.g. theories which arise spontaneously, change and have at best 'a kind of family resemblance to one another'.[2] 'The organization did not have a centre and a boundary', initiative rested 'in the hands of local groups . . . the national structures . . . existed simply to facilitate coordination, and exchange of ideas' between groups (Teodori). 'The centre's role is to announce themes of policy to the periphery, to initiate, facilitate and support learning efforts.'[3]

Groups also arose and dissolved as they were needed. 'Non-organizations' like the VDC, FSM and ERAP were remarkably quick and easy to dissolve; SDS and SNCC proved hardly more institutionalized; they conformed to a model of 'organized spontaneity',

the strength of the New Left may well reside in precisely these small contesting and competing groups active at many points at the same time, a kind of political guerilla force in peace or in so-called peace (Marcuse).[4]

As typical of the anti-war movement in America and Britain as the big national demonstrations and teach-ins and rallies, were local groups and committees, community-based protests and projects, often growing spontaneously, using innovative methods, sometimes civil disobedience.[5] Such decentralized, flexible, yet activist groups could even provide a framework for campaigning activity by women at home.[6]

Nuclear disarmament activity in England involved a number of major strands: the Direct Action Committee Against Nuclear War,[7] an amalgam of Anarchists and radical Pacifists; the formal CND leadership, a new coalition of Left liberals, Christians and prominent celebrities and academics previously active in opposing nuclear tests;

Old Leftist elements, such as the ex-Bevanites around *Tribune* and Victory for Socialism (VFS) and Labour Party activists close to the Communist Party; and finally the explicitly NL groups, mainly student based, such as *ULR*, or the ex-Communists (*New Reasoner*).

Just as CND had at first been an umbrella of many groups and tendencies, in the American movement each subsidiary group tended to be a coalition. The names of civil rights organizations are themselves a description of black coalition; a Southern, Student, Nonviolent, Christian-led, 'Coloured' and, even in the South, largely urban movement.

Equally FSM became a model for student alliances everywhere: its steering committee, composed of representatives drawn from all the participating organizations, like many campus organizations, existed as an *ad hoc* coalition of students, graduate students, teaching assistants, drop-outs, ex-students, organizational activists and occasionally junior staff.[8]

Free universities also reflected this alliance: linking a vast range of political views (liberal to Maoist), of projects, courses, events and publications.

In the years after 1965, it was SDS in America which came nearest to entrapping the New Left as a movement and canalizing its development organizationally. Until 1968, SDS was more 'movement' than 'organization'; reflecting in its 'three political strands, anarchism, pacifism and socialism, all mingled in different proportions' (Sale). As well as a wide range of tactical and theoretical positions, reformist to revolutionary, it was an amalgam of left-liberals, social-democrats, Marxists, radicals, and nonviolent anarchists.[9]

This type of organization, an amalgam of tendencies without centralized control, was far more resilient than the critics predicted. Not only did it survive, 'but it turns out to be darn near invulnerable, and its invulnerability in part depends on precisely those ways in which it is different from the centre–periphery model.'

The advantages to the NL of this loss of 'a stable state', i.e. of what was basically an 'anarchist' model of organization – decentralist, federalist and evolutionary – became obvious. It gave great flexibility and sense of participation.[10] A very powerful, informal, interpersonal network pulled the whole thing together. Travelling organizers sustained the movement's vitality and grassroots appeal, without bureaucratism setting in. It was difficult to co-opt such phenomena since 'the organizations did not develop permanent leaders, stable bureaucracies or hierarchical relationships between leaders and militants'.[11] Equally it was difficult to repress them by selective action, because there was no clear, stable centre to repress, and nothing specifically to strike at.

Travelling organizers, long familiar in libertarian tradition,[12] find counterparts in the SDS and SNCC field workers and project organizers of the 1960s. 'Outside agitators', like those who moved to Mississippi in summer 1964, and on to Berkeley in the fall; from peace to civil rights to student rights to community action, went back to 'peace' or on to 'black power'; as the issues and sometimes the venue changed, they kept travelling on.[13]

'The proliferation of centres' conforms to this model and the development of communities, projects, institutions, spreading through society (Schön). Indeed, in most Western countries, student organizers helped spread campus rebellion and anti-war action after 1966. The role of the organizer was that of the 'diffusionist individual', 'the moving centre, who carries his message with him, and creates new peripheries wherever he goes',[14] combining both communal and travelling experiences whilst locating himself in various projects.

For example, within a couple of years (by 1962) SNCC had two hundred full-time paid workers through the Southern States; this number grew to four hundred (by 1964). Some of them were white, some volunteers; many hundreds more flooded in to help with summer projects or take part in demonstrations in 1963 and 1964. In England, many Committee of 100 convenors moved on to coordinate community projects in various parts of Britain and a 'Campaign Caravan' travelled round Britain; some organized 'squats'.

Later, the Resistance, which reached its height in the years 1967–8, continued the tradition of travelling organizers within a loose federalist structure of communal based anti-draft groups in the USA.

Such organizational innovations, emphasizing the honesty of direct and unstructured dialogue, were only possible because of what was termed 'the degree of psychic community' (Kenniston) – a phrase that describes the highly relaxed interactions within the movement.

Such a milieu defined the NL and separated it from the repressed, impersonal style of the old-line leftists; for the NL style was more the style of an encounter group than a vanguard cadre. Retaining vigour and humour in the most critical situation,[15] emphasis on this kind of organization, on power from below or 'bicameralism'[16] reflected the NL's initial distrust of highly centralized or élite-controlled organization. It is remarkable the degree to which without explicit literature or decision this style influenced the decentralization of SDS, and much of the student and peace movement. Even before SDS, Women Strike for Peace had experimented with such forms, and even the concept of 'national organization' remained alien to many in the NL. The Vietnam war movement was fundamentally decentralist, and the civil rights movement was a self-consciously plural federation. Indeed, despite the creation of several new national groupings in the 1960s, the black movement may well have been becoming more and more localized during the period after 1964.[17]

This amorphous and decentralized character of the NL as a movement, was in marked contrast to the hierarchical organization of the Old

Left, its centralized decisions, and use of 'discipline' for dissenters. This difference was partly based on a political belief in 'structural-entailment' (i.e. of political means and ends); 'a radical movement always begins to create within itself the structures which will eventually form the basis of the new society.'[18]

As a response to a highly stable, centralized and homogeneous garrison-State, and to corporate organization, the radical movements for communal autonomy, black power, alternatives and communities, testify to the strength of the revolt against authoritarianism and homogeneity. It was as part of this drift from the urban-centralist norm, that the Freedom Summers in America established a pattern of 'going to the people'.[19]

Authenticity was also to be gained by making life in the alternative, a movement life-style, permanent rather than temporary. 'Participatory democracy at this point, speaks most clearly to the middle-class man, daring him to forsake powerlessness and act' (Lynd).[20] Going to the people also implied a rejection of middle-class styles, even an acceptance of a voluntary poverty ethic.[21]

The identification with the 'cultures of poverty' and blackness was partly rooted in a contra-cultural stress on selfless relationships, downgrading property and money in favour of free or cashless exchange, and gift. Challenging liberal concepts of growth, progress, material reward or incentive, movement scepticism of a consumerist affluence was endemic; itself, to some extent, the result of the expropriation of poor outsiders.

Community organizers, like urban hippies, directly shared or imitated the life and living areas of the poor: 'counterposing to the paternalistic social worker approach to the poor, a rugged willingness to live and work among them.'[22] Hippy ghettoes coexisted in areas where NL organizers set up their shopfront headquarters: each discovered not just a culture of poverty, but a living community.

The groups of middle-class drop-outs, beats and hippies also began to find themselves excluded; 'white-negroes' outside, and looking in. This sense of popular community was not confined to the States. In England, *ULR* stressed 'the need to meet people where they are, where they work, where they are touched, to give ordinary men and women direct control over their own lives' (Thompson). The NL prescription was 'look at your community, learn from it, respect the traditions and culture of the working class' (but without always suggesting forms that organizing might take). On both sides of the Atlantic, the positive side of this approach was that it encouraged appreciation of ordinary localities, showing greater sensitivity to popular culture and style.

Organizing a movement of the poor was Tom Hayden's key to revolutionary change; like Fanon's black, Third-World lumpen-proletarians,[23] the American poor on the bottom-rung, outside the pale, and with little to lose, appeared potentially the most radical: this view foreshadowed a widespread identification with the pain and dissatisfaction of powerless groups and outcasts everywhere: poor and ethnic minorities and peasants – inside and outside the American empire. Such identification also sought authenticity, for example, in projections of emotionalism and unrepressed sensuality in the black community or in the life experience of the poor, in the self-discipline of the Black Muslims or later on in the re-enactment of tribal interaction or guerilla styles from the Third World.

The appeal of the so-called backward or primitive societies lay also partly in the communitarian and egalitarian aspects of their social forms; communal democracy, the relative statelessness of village or tribally based society, the alien nature of bureaucratic apparatus and militarism in such societies, due to their decentralist, localized social organization.[24]

In Europe at least, the early NL has been seen as an intellectual response to the crises of Soviet and Western imperialism and to the débâcle of inherited, Russian-oriented versions of Marxism, leading in turn to eclectic identifications by sections of the NL with the Third World: this was especially true in England. The non-aligned developments of socialisms, Yugoslav worker self-management, Cuban 'moral incentives' (in terms of the whole community), Gandhian nonviolence, or communitarian village socialisms, were some of the disparate elements fused in the NL's eclectic vision of community.[25] But for the American movement before 1966 local versions of community and the culture of poverty are influential sources more linked to practical movement experience. As the decade wore on, however, there was a widening search for a non-bourgeois, non-bureaucratic and unrepressive version of socialism in the Third World.

This was an added inspiration for the 'Third Camp' ideal: neither a third military power, nor a collective neutralism of the Afro-Asian nations, but rather a positive trans-national movement to end colonialism, militarism, poverty, racism and the hegemony of American and Russian imperialists, and their threat of nuclear war. A growing, if implicit, trans-nationalism was expressed in links of movements and kinds and categories of peoples; the spread of a worldwide youth culture; the cross-fertilization of national peace movements, of the US Civil Rights Movement with CND in England, later the diaspora of draft resisters in Europe, and the trans-national identification with suffering in Vietnam or with Southern Africa; blacks, students and women began to move across political frontiers as self-conscious movements outside inherited frameworks.

The central themes of the movement

From all these aspects of a NL configuration or identity, by 1965 one can discern five majority strands. In some ways, each represents an autonomous movement in itself: first, the student movement for university change (of course, students were also to some extent at the base of each of the other four movements); second, the grassroots movement of radical blacks, developing earliest in the USA, through SNCC, towards black power; third, community action projects, the beginning of a universal movement of the poor; fourth, the nascent international movement against the war in Vietnam; finally, the cultural movement of the underground and the alternative society. All five overlap in ideas and personnel, although the youthful counter-culture develops to some extent separately at first and grows together with the Movement as a whole only after 1966.

The character of the NL may be seen as formed in the interpenetrations of these dimensions, and the common themes and strategies that link them. The immense influence of SNCC and the southern movement on SDS, the FSM and the community projects, thus establishing the character of the white American NL in this period, has been noted already. But it was the community organizing movement, smallest and least publicized of the five strands, that was in some ways the closest to an emerging central core of the Movement and its identity. It certainly established far more clearly than any other actions or tendency a coherent set of ideas for the NL as a movement, and an identity that could be translated into other types of projects, and linked to other movements arising against war, racism, and in the universities.

In many ways the central components of the community organizing movement are, by 1965, those of the NL itself. The stress on community; local focus and decentralized organization; the notion of participatory democracy and direct control of decisions; the emphasis on do-it-yourself direct-action politics; the extra-parliamentary character of the projects; the anti-paternalism and suspicion of 'do-goodism' (implying substantial self- and soul-searching); the belief in organizing 'all-the-poor' (inter-racially);[26] and finally the concept of building counter-institutions (under the influence of Hayden and Lynd), by 1965 came to characterize both the community projects and 'the movement' generally.[27]

From orientation towards existing values and institutions, what were initially labelled 'protest' movements (e.g. the Committee of 100 in England, SDS and SNCC in America) began the agonizing move towards strategies that aimed at replacing both values and institutions through the 'do-it-yourself' reconstruction.[28] The voluntarist idea began to emerge that the alternative society had to be created, and would not merely grow from the ruins of the authoritarian structure.

What we have got to do is build a movement which shows you in anticipation, the sort of institutions that will characterize the best revolutionary society . . . one avoids the system by creating alternative institutions which can replace it.[29]

The communalist vision

The 'myth' of community was a central one for the movement; Georges Sorel had once used the notion of myth to depict something that was not necessarily untrue or impossible, but an image of the future which guided effective action in the present; a truth *becoming* rather than existing.[30] Such was the idea of community in the growth of the NL and the counter-culture, reflecting the influence of anarchist and utopian socialist ideas, and filtered through writers like Fromm and Goodman; but it also reflected a general popular and sociological concern with a 'loss of community'; in the words of the Port Huron Statement itself, the task was 'bringing people out of isolation and into community'. That was a function of politics.

For Mills, 'mass society' described an atomized, amorphous social situation in which individuation had replaced true individualism: conformity replaced autonomy,[31] leaving only the alienation of 'pseudo-gemeinschaft', a phoney community of status-striving, the success ethic, and the rat-race. This society elevated individualism as an ideal, but undermined its social basis. Both the cult of organizational belonging-ness and the quite contradictory myth of competitive individualism are cultivated to disguise the real nature of the corporate conveyor belt.[32]

Fromm[33] perceived the atomized 'lonely crowd' not as a replacement of 'individualism', so much as a development from it. Only the illusion of 'individualism' had remained to justify privatized individuation in mass organizations; thus Fromm stressed the complementarity of individuation and organizational conformity; like Mills, he believed that the atomized competitiveness of capitalist society laid the divide-and-rule basis for the new forms of domination. The alienated conformity and isolation of politics was thus seen as the very basis of an increasingly irresponsible élite.

A solution could be to rebuild a community from these isolated, lonely 'crowds', to break conformism in direct personal action of a radical kind. Optimistically, Goodman saw basic evolutionary tendencies towards community counter-balancing such aggressive and competitive loneliness in mass society. But Fromm warns that in dialectic with a structural crisis, the decline of community, an alienated leisure, a manufactured education, may easily precipitate authoritarian solutions. Along with individual psychological disorders, his deep concern is with the weak sense of self in modern society; without community it can lead to an 'escape from freedom' into authoritarianism.[34]

Where other social critics saw a traditional polarism between individualism and group cooperation, these three writers urged that what was needed was a recovery of individual autonomy within manageable, identity-giving social groups; groups rather than organizations. For Mills this was the 'community of publics'; for Fromm, the 'democratic community', in which, drawing inspiration from the kibbutz, a form of workers' self-management would determine production of the basis of social need; Goodman,[35] proposing an alternative to organizational conformity for the isolated individual, made communitarian pragmatism his main contribution to movement thought and practice. Alongside this, and as part of it, the NL's anarchist dimension drew from the tradition of Kropotkin a vision of community scaled down to a level whereby it could be controlled by the democratic participation of its members; and institutions organically linked to their members and creators. Goodman proposed the building of cooperatives in which mutual-aid, and personal freedom and identity, are combined; not as polar opposites, but as complementary elements.[36] Goodman's advice was widely heeded: 'if there is no community for you young man . . . make it yourself.'[37]

As a critique and often constructive appraisal of city living and modern technology, these ideas proved enormously attractive.[38] As the counter-culture and the political NL grew together,[39] there was an increasing awareness of 'communes' as part of a strategy of change.[40] Together with anarchist decentralism and scepticism of technocracy, the commune seemed to represent a synthesis of a number of NL dimensions: participatory democracy, personalism, direct action, mutual-aid and an alternative life-style; implicitly linked to an alternative strategy of change[41] that was both nonviolent and extra-parliamentary, it represented a fusion of individual and collective concerns, the active and the expressive. Previous communal living situations experienced by theorists like Lynd, became extended to movement activity[42] through SNCC and ERAP projects, and then to the Resistance communes of the later 1960s: or the political communes of Berlin. They provided a key missing element in the NL revolt; a genuine subcultural context that could give continuity and reinforcement to a new life-style, and sustain and insulate political resistance.[43]

Contra-culture

The dialectic between the development of such a cultural base and the organizational growth of a NL politics will be seen to be a complex one; from the 'Beats' and the first Aldermaston marches,[44] through the community projects and the growth of communes and radical communities, the two co-exist. Of course extreme innovations in life-style, and the growth of hippy enclaves, can certainly be distinguished from the course of organizations like CND, SDS or SNCC.[45] But as the 'hippies' turned to action and structural creativity, there were moments when they had more in common with the NL, than the NL ever had with the Old Left.

Participatory democracy was just as much an expression of counter-value and structure, as 'doing your own thing' and cultural guerilla action; the idea of counter-institutions emerged in community organizing and other movement projects even before becoming embedded in the 'alternative communities'. The search for non-alienated work and leisure, for decentralized community, for an extra-parliamentary re-definition of political activity, for a humanized control of technology,[46] were common themes in both NL and counter-culture: such elements fused in the alternative society strategy of change.[47]

Yet the notion of cultural revolt grew largely independent or unconscious of a NL theory of counter-institutions; the development of alternative styles, and the growth of embryonic institutions, presented the vision of a different society and 'a consciousness of possibilities' (Marcuse), 'a conceptual formation of a different society that will enable that formation in fact'.[48] Linked to 'free universities', or free student unions, the 'Freedom Democratic parties', and community unions of the poor, a society-wide strategy of change along such lines seemed less and less utopian.

It is a nationwide network [Hayden claimed] of people with the same oppression, the same language, the same music, the same styles, the same needs and grievances: the very essence of a new society taking root and growing up in the framework of the old.[49]

It has been suggested that the success of this attempt is to be judged in terms of five criteria.[50] First the potentially revolutionary non-recognition and counter-definition of norms and reality; second the location of and rooting of these in the counter-society, third the confrontation of the predominant value system at central points of tension and contradiction; fourth the offer of an alternative life experience that is social and collective as well as individual; and lastly the concretization of these definitions and experiences in new institutions and projects expressing these counter-norms and meanings.[51]

By 1966, it had become obvious that the cultural underground had produced some of the most successful counter-institutions anywhere; together they represented a dramatic range of alternative possibilities within the communities in which they rose. For example *ad hoc* 'free' and exchange systems became an essential ingredient in the rise of the hippy communities,[52] and for a while, in small communities they could work, as the Diggers' exemplary actions pointed the way.[53] Even Marcuse felt able to announce that the 'new sensibility' had become 'a political force'.

These were alternative rather than parallel institutions and grew together with the counter-community, constituting a 'rehearsal in vivo' of 'a number of possible solutions to central life problems posed by the emerging society of the future', an 'island of deviant meanings' within the sea of a consensus society.[54]

The birth of radical community

The counter-community thus represented to many within the movement a scenario, and, to those outside it, a spectacle, or an alternative: in the four years which followed the FSM, an area such as Berkeley became one model for the development of radical communities in which the NL as a movement, and the counter-culture with which it overlapped, could thrive and flourish.

From 1965 Berkeley became a major focus of the American anti-war movement with the marches, teach-ins and troop-train stopping of the Vietnam Day Committee (VDC). It clearly exemplifies by then the developing alliance of hippies and activists, students and non-students, 'politicoes'[55] and drop-outs, that was rooted in common creation, of radical projects, *ad hoc* groups and actions, sustaining a set of community institutions.

Indeed, for most students, Berkeley was such a community *before* it was a university; but being one of imagination and action, the base that students wanted to build was not one which could easily defend itself in crisis either within the university or in the larger society; alternative alliances began to develop organization – only such a fusion could transcend the wedge that the campus administration had been so eager to drive between the university and its environment, between students and 'non-students'.

The fact that the 1966 sit-in and strike were mainly organized by students, did not make them willing to abandon the larger community which lent them essential support. In the words of a famous leaflet produced at the end of the strike:

A community which had seemed submerged has revealed itself again . . . what is needed now is the building of institutions fit for this community's expression and growth (Mike Rossman).[56]

Not all such attempts were centred on a campus with a major student movement,[57] but in the concentration of dissenting forces, radical in both cultural and political developments, these became major movement enclaves, and bases of growth, both in America and in parallels in Europe; in Amsterdam in the period of the Provos, the Kabouters and the Orange Free State; in Berlin between 1966 and 1969, during the period of the Communes and student activism (the APO); in Nanterre and parts of Paris in 1968; to a lesser extent in Notting Hill in London from 1965–7, during the period of the housing projects, free school and George Clark's community schemes.[58] Each hinted at the development of a radical and autonomous community, and in each case a sense of community is intimately linked to the growth of alternative life-styles and viable alternative institutions; the underground newspapers are a key mechanism of growth for the subculture and these communities.[59]

'There's a Change Gonna Come': the counter-institutions

New Leftists argued insistently throughout the 1960s for the creation of 'institutions outside the established order', for an 'anti-establishment network' of rival institutions which might make both reformist and revolutionary inroads on the existing system; in the long-run, helping to 'wither it away' and become the dominant institutions of an alternative society. Such strategic thinking, a form of latter-day anarcho-syndicalism, replaces the 'one big Union' (i.e. of the IWW) with the building of many counter-institutions,[60] and embodies a concept of revolution-without-violence, similar to that re-developed by radical pacifists.

Such a scenario, denying the tension between revolutionary change and building libertarian and radical institutions within existing society,[61] implied a rejection of a once-and-for-all cataclysmic struggle; substituting projects and engagements which might seem inconclusive, it represents a further development from the basic anarchist principle – an idea embedded in much socialist thought – that the natural society lies beneath state oppression and authoritarian structures, and can be 'liberated'. But the emphasis shifts: the alternative society now has to be constructed through will, work, and creativity.[62]

On all fronts, it appeared some form of alternative society project had emerged; ERAP's dream of a national poor people's movement, inter-racial and autonomous, was closely aligned to an ideal of communal institutions; local radio, tenants' and claimants' groups, police control groups, food co-ops, pre-school playgroups and free local papers, to be linked in with the Community Union. Spreading from Berkeley, student syndicalism was equally rooted in an idea of student power and autonomous students' unions and free universities.

Black Power, in its positive programme, stressed the growth of radical counter-institutions, black cooperatives or black businesses, black control of the police, schools, college courses and housing; it stressed the development of black media. An idea of developing black counter-institutions had long been part of SNCC's programme. 'We must form our own institutions', SNCC announced, 'credit unions, co-ops, political parties, write our own histories.'[63] CORE had had an even greater orientation to communal separatism and institution-building than SNCC, emphasizing black control of schools and ghetto business, throughout the developments of the later 1960s.

At the same time the more involuntary black and ghetto counter-culture had had an enormous impact on the growth of white and inter-racial youth culture in the 1960s.[64] The growth of such a culture exemplified the intensifying ambivalence of a white dominant group about its own cultural identity, and the thrust towards a cultural alternative to the success-ethic, consumerism, of America's way of life.

The appearance of Black Power cannot be understood except against the background of black contra-culture and its particular growth in the 1960s. This subculture insulated a sense of communal identity, and a number of significant components opposed to dominant capitalist ethics. It protected a black movement and culture from any simple capitulation to prescribed American norms, and it provided a further early suggestion of counter-institutions – in black media, stores and churches – and a model of alternative cultural development; in hipsterism, literature and music, distinctive styles, largely insulated from an American mainstream, and in the matriarchal family, an alternative to the nuclear patriarchy.

In England, as has been seen, similar ventures and movements were developing out of a fusion of the NL and the peace movement, especially from the Committee of 100 and the Anarchists.

Altogether more conformist, the peace movement nevertheless related to alternative institutional strategy itself; with the Assembly of Unrepresented People of 1965, draft-resistance and tax-refusal, Committee of 100 projects and local community-based peace groups and centres were moving towards re-possessing aspects of decision-making on key issues of war and peace.

In America and Europe, such institutional alternatives were also now growing in the university contexts; and SDS northern projects, modelled on the success of a variety of SNCC projects in the deep South, cooperative, participant and stressing self-help, were expanding.

In 1966, the phrase 'student syndicalism' emerged, after the events at Berkeley, as it became clearer that to succeed even the student movement had to institutionalize its own organization, and begin to create 'counter' (rather than merely parallel) institutions, maintaining them by its own communal élan, and the pursuit of a set of unfulfilled goals. It had to organize on issues specifically of counter-curricula, dorm regulations, classroom organization, free student government, a challenge to grading and marking systems, and a challenge to university involvements in the war-machine; such as cooperation with the Selective Service.

Goodman, understanding the anti-intellectualism of student activists, suggested an alternative project to their slide towards a book-burning, slogan-shouting nihilism. He urged the creation of intellectual alternatives – even counter-universities, within or outside existing institutions: free and experimental courses – experiments in cooperative learning, all linked to the radical movements. These were becoming aware of a need for new content in a university; student awareness, expressed in the subsidiary development of alternative courses, free universities within the movement, and operating during occupations, helped add missing dimensions to their struggle, and an alternative to the politics of pressure and confrontation.

One of the first of these projects, the Free University of Berkeley, an idea born in the sit-ins of 1964, was personally encouraged by Goodman.[65] An experimental set of alternative courses in the occupation led to more permanent structures; emphasizing bottom-up forms of learning, it was created to serve the needs of the whole community, not just, or mainly, students; like other counter-institutions, it crystallized a bridge between NL ideas and life-style radicalism, retaining an idea of nonviolent structural change, beyond free-speech reformism; the establishment of a truly experimental model of teaching and topics, not possible in the established university, helped break the isolation of the student movement from the larger community by resisting the élitist implications of the official version of 'University'.

Confronting the substance of the university at the level of curricula and educational methods, the Free University represented both a lever for change within, and exemplification of, an alternative without.[66] Abolishing grades, marks or diplomas, and teacher-roles in the inherited sense, it attracted students and others into a counter-organization of cooperative learning, and deepened commitments to change. Almost everywhere that strong student movements arose or radical communities formed, free universities were opened. By 1966, these experiments were establishing a function in relationship to the radical community much as had the underground press. The FU's moved from university, NL-oriented workshops and discussion groups, towards meeting the disparate needs of the whole movement.[67]

Emphasizing radical do-it-yourself attitudes to education, innovating topics and methods where needs were felt, and cutting across the inherited divisons between teachers and taught or established disciplines, of community and university or between theory and practice, such groups confronted the existing big universities, where they were most vulnerable.

The dynamics of radicalization

Despite these utopian aspirations and radical activism, the initial and formative and political contexts for many movement activists in the early 1960s, whether in civil rights struggles, peace agitation or student confrontations, were ultimately predominantly reformist ones in which 'petitions were made to power'. Dominant institutional structures were still conceived of as capable of concession and change; their evils were aberrations, not systematically connected. But this was a perspective quickly transformed by movement experience; frustration with attempts within the established, institutional channels (students with university administrations; CND with the Labour Party, and Parliament; SNCC with the Democratic Party; community organizing with City Councils), drove the NL towards extra-parliamentary action.

But although extra-parliamentarism was an essential and growing component of an NL identity, especially in America, its growth was in constant interaction with electoral ventures, individual candidacies, gestures towards the Labour or Democratic Parties and independent or third party attempts.[68] It was through direct experience of systematic brutality and harassment as well as censorship, slander or ostracism, but above all, through direct contact with the life of the poor, with institutionalized racism, and with military installations like Omaha or Aldermaston's death-factory, that ultimately undermined remnants of faith in 'Liberalism'.[69]

Such political traumas, whether outside the gates of a USAF air-base or rocket site, in a Mississippi jail, in a court or in a political gathering, quickly revealed society in a new light. No longer something basically sound with a few removable excrescences, the body politic was seen as fundamentally diseased. The pattern of racism, poverty and militarism was seen as part of its basic fabric and identity – ingrained, or as they put it: 'institutionalized'.

Disillusion was also possible for thousands of young American and British activists, because they had come often from sheltered middle-class backgrounds where the 'Other America' or the 'Other Britain' was essentially invisible. That disillusion and that loss of legitimacy set in only when the movement had participated in the life of those who were excluded; such as the second-class citizens of the American South and Northern Ghetto.

It was not until élite-educated white students directly experienced these things through direct action, community projects and freedom summers, that their radicalization was confirmed.[70]

To this extent the NL could become a 'revolutionary movement'; implicitly before 1966, increasingly explicit afterwards; it was always less in the business of reform within basic structures, than of the replacement of those structures: rejecting the partial change of existing 'core-institutions', in favour of their total transformation or abolition – and as rapidly as possible.

An important survey of the NL at this stage[71] selects a number of key characteristics of the American movement, seen to constitute in the mid-1960s distinctive components of a 'New' Left as a whole; the stress on moral revolt and non-conformity of life-style; the emphasis on direct action and grassroots organizing; the radical analysis of Western societies as 'systems'; slogans and strategies stemming from the term 'participatory democracy'; the stress on decentralized organization, 'community', and Movement autonomy.

The first characteristic exemplified by the moral revulsion against the bomb, political oppression, and racism, was also expressed in the personalist revolt of both radicals and hippies and the new life-styles of the counter-culture.

The second has been related to the development of a range of actions, projects and movements involving civil disobedience, nonviolent resistance such as the peace and civil rights struggles, as well as community and student organizing.

The third has been discussed in relation to the rejection of liberalism, the move away from reformism and the increasing stress, from the Port Huron Statement onwards, on a systematic rejection of society.

The fourth characteristic has been analysed here, in relation to the growth of counter-institutions; this is linked to the fifth dimension, community decentralization and community control, and the extra-parliamentary strategy of change.

It is the basis of the subsequent argument that all of these aspects define an identity that is unmistakably different either from the then current 'liberalism' or the 'Old Left'. Whilst it is the crisis, and partial loss of this core identity, that is the subject of the rest of this analysis, what was most remarkable in 1965 or 1967, as even hostile critics remarked, was the degree to which movements on the fringes of society were beginning to be able to have an impact on the whole of it, by highlighting a self-defined, social, value crisis, through subcultural non-conformity and response.

4. After Reformism: the Dilemmas of Extra-Parliamentarism

The liberal disenchantment and the origins of anti-politics

The attitude of unwillingness to compromise, the readiness to move outside institutionalized structures, which marks the early NL, partly reflects a growing impatience and disenchantment with liberalism. Everywhere nonviolent direct action politics was taking initiatives absent in parliamentarist reformism. Disillusion with the established system and with liberalism inevitably spread to its supposedly democratic rituals and procedures,[1] in part endorsing a deep suspicion of an orthodox and amoral politics as an instrumental pursuit of power:

Political scientists and politicians ... have conceived of the realm of politics or power as largely autonomous ... Every problem became one of strategy rather than ethics. ... In one realm this concept of power as autonomous leads to the nihilism of nuclear war and war preparations (Muste).[2]

There was also a growing scepticism about liberalism's own integrity; initially students were recruited into organizations (SANE, SPU, SDS, SNCC or CND) whose reference was to values proclaimed by the dominant system; 'peace', 'freedom', 'dignity', 'justice', 'equality', 'welfare' and 'democracy'. Thus Hayden, together with Al Haber and Bob Ross, the founders of SDS, were able to get money and support from liberals – including Walter Reuther – for their revival of a 'social-democratic student group',[3] but as they moved further from strategies of Democratic Party re-alignment ('part of the way with LBJ'), tension between them and their adult sponsors, the left-liberals, the coalitionists and the social democrats, grew deeper.[4] Some of their venom was reserved for their 'exclusionism';[5] the unwillingness to work with party-Marxists and Leninists (based on their elders' bitter experiences of the 1930s and 1940s), a crucial issue in early SDS, just like that of the liberal alliances for SNCC, or the Labour Party for CND.

Despite SDS's early renunciation of Civil Disobedience,[6] nevertheless, it became clear that in important senses, NL ideas could not be realized by or within the existing structures or institutions. Rejecting the Left-Liberal tactics of party manoeuvre, coalition and re-alignment, such a realization lay at the base of the deep division that opened up between the NL and the old Social Democrats.[7] With the changes within the student movement, and the loss of faith in representative democracy, Civil Disobedience came to be admitted as a major step in radicalizing confrontation.[8] Civil Disobedience in the early movements, justified only in the main in terms of specific unjust laws, or the implementation of existing, but unenforced law, was not seen as a mode of confrontation with an 'unjust' state. The Committee of 100 stretched the meaning of civil disobedience in so far as they were not disobeying 'unjust laws' (or implementing existing laws against local authorities – like the civil rights movement); they were, rather, involved in non-cooperation with and obstruction of the 'war-machine'.[9]

Slowly but surely, this came to mean a re-orientation away from established government or dependence on administrative and legislative changes. When, for example, the material concessions of the federal government came finally – under pressure from civil rights groups – they were understandably felt to be too little and too late to offset a widespread disillusion with the effectiveness of mere protest on bread-and butter issues.[10]

The dislike of party politics and the preference for extra-institutional action, which is at the heart of both British and American movements, were given a particular intensity by the nuclear issue.[11] As the peripheral censorship, boycott, and ridicule that met the peace and civil rights movements in the 1950s turned into systematic victimization, provocation and repression, it became clear what Liberalism meant when crucial areas of state policy were challenged.[12]

In England, CND faced a British Government that, in alliance with a stupid and acquiescent national press, effectively stopped up the information process about nuclear weapons. Subsequently, in order to sustain the supposed defence of democracy, it undermined free debate, even banning a factual film commissioned by the BBC in 1966.[13] To bolster up the credibility of deterrence, both sides of the Atlantic, the state depended on fall-out shelter programmes and an illusory 'Civil Defence'. Thus the peace movement was forced to devote much of its energy and finances to breaking through an information barrier, to disillusion those who thought that World War III would just be a tougher version of the preceding one.

Such censorship, and unhelpful or obstructive officialdom, together with the dismissal or harassment of supporters,[14] are typical obstacles to radical anti-establishment movements, and might seem a small price to pay for the advantages of a relatively liberal parliamentary system. But for those new to politics, like the political virgins of CND, such frustrations were intolerable.

Like its nearest counterpart, SANE in the USA, CND was first envisaged as an *ad hoc* traditional lobby or temporary pressure group on political, academic and scientific opinion. Its big names were deployed as speakers and signers, and it was a coalition of pragmatism and absolutism about the bomb. Both organizations were pitchforked by the enthusiasm of their rank and file, and the spontaneous formation of local groups, into creating a national structure. But in each case leaders had envisaged a short, sharp pressurizing campaign, organized on a top-down basis – in CND's case to change Labour policy.[15] The idea of a mock national structure to give weight to this pressure might be admissible, but the orientation to changing 'public opinion' was secondary, if not irrelevant, and any democratization of the organization was seen as decidedly dubious.[16]

The analogy can be taken further. SANE, like CND nationally, was increasingly tempted to substitute parliamentary lobbying and pressure-group tactics, for mass-campaigning and activism,[17] and yet, despite its substantial size and influential support, SANE achieved little more political influence than CND, by placing too great hopes in the liberal wing of the establishment. When Kennedy and Humphrey, like Wilson after Gaitskell's death, employed some of the language of the peace movement, many nuclear pacifists in both countries began to think they had allies in high places.

Even before the intensification of the war in Vietnam, the peace movement had partly run aground in this belief in sympathetic left or social democratic tendencies in government.[18] This was one of the main reasons why the anti-nuclear movement dwindled in both countries after 1963. Kennedy had been keen to co-opt movement rhetoric and harness its energies; the development of the Peace Corps was in part to channel these emerging forces. Yet the liberal idols quickly lost their appeal, endorsing obviously reactionary policies and often betraying even the mild and ambiguously radical platforms on which the young had supported them. This was especially true of a number of the Labour MPs pledged to support CND's aims.

Given the disillusion with the political process and professional politicians, it is not surprising that these should grow mainly as movements of political amateurs; individuals operating outside the traditional spheres of politics, against party bureaucracies, almost as much as against nuclear policies or racism. Their efforts highlighted a growing awareness of the snares of electoral politics, the relevance of an independent power base, and the importance of sustaining alternative institutions, and counter-definitions of democracy.

They are also symptomatic of a wider crisis than these crises of Liberalism: interrelated crises of the total political culture. Discrediting the fabric of politics itself, there was a period of deepening suspicion of public life generally.[19] The trend was towards a more manipulative political style, a declining role of the party conference, and a perceived decline in standards of representation.[20] Bi-partisan politics is met by apathy,[21] cynicism, satire and ridicule of politicians and the normality of the 'protest' vote. 'A plague on both their houses' attitude was spreading in domestic politics, as it was in international orientations.

But breaking out of bi-partisan frameworks was a slow and painful process. At the beginning of the decade:

The two-party structure as the principal vehicle for participation in the political process, seemed at the time not only a historical reality, but also a mental habit which set limits even for the new modes of thinking.[22]

Even some activists who from the start rejected work within the Labour or Democratic Parties, still argued that NL strategies were having their effects on the internal alignments of party in left or liberal directions.[23] This ambivalence remains embedded in the Port Huron Statement, despite an increasingly detailed attack on corporate liberalism, its control, through welfare, vested interest, and, if necessary, terror. The existing party structure, coalitionism, the electoral frame, itself only slowly came to be viewed as part of that apparatus of control.

Whilst many left-liberals were willing to accept that Liberalism 'in its current perversions' was 'institutional, corporate and debased', Lynd and Hayden and other New Leftists attacked them for their failure to come out in unequivocal opposition to American military adventures and the capitalist system. The apparent ineffectiveness of left-liberalism, its political double-talk, its failed strategies, meant that a push beyond it was bound to characterize the ensuing growth of the NL.

Symptomatic of this transition was the movement against the war in Vietnam; what began as a liberal and reformist protest at certain policies, quickly developed into a movement that challenged war as an institution, the legitimacy of the state, and the whole nature of American society and its relationships with other societies. In time it went further, both in 'naming the system' responsible for the war,[24] and moving towards anti-imperialism. After the Washington March of April 1965 and subsequent demonstrations, SDS became increasingly concerned to find a systematic analysis that connected local and international issues. The bombing of the North and the intensification of the war tended to confirm earlier emphases (e.g. by Hayden and Lynd) on the militarism, imperialism – if not creeping totalitarianism – of American society; through the teach-in movement, SDS helped spread and deepen a sense of the power, and contradiction, in the social system.[25]

The hollowness of the rhetoric of the erstwhile heroes, of Stevenson or Kennedy, or of Wilson and Castle, became acutely clear in this area of foreign affairs. Previously, where liberal camouflage had been successful, the contradictions in the value system, or between ideals and actuality, could be somewhat disguised. But in powerful assaults on notions of liberalism, SDS leaders endorsed a view, that was later to become dominant in the NL, that America was now drifting towards a form of Fascism, barely disguised by its ideology of corporate liberalism, and its welfare legislation.[26]

From pressure group to extra-parliamentary opposition: CND in Britain

For the Left in Britain and Europe, parliamentarism[27] was less closely associated with independent attempts and new parties than with major Left Parties (Social Democratic (Labour) and Communist). Once the break is made with either or both, the hold of electoralism is decisively weakened. The developing consciousness of the costs of sixty years of parliamentary socialism, in the English, Welsh and Scottish contexts, and the growing anti-parliamentarism of the movement – including the original NL groups – can be partly traced to the tactic employed by sections of CND itself, of flooding an alien organization (the Labour Party).

On the other hand it would be wrong, as some commentators on the development of the movement in Britain have suggested, to presume that the sequence is simply one of a conventional legal pressure group becoming frustrated with its attempts to change national policy within the established framework and responding to its failures by moving towards extra-parliamentary, and extra-legal, action.[28]

Indeed, as has been shown, nuclear pacifism began with unconventional and often illegal acts by minority groups – even before the DAC and Aldermaston. The CND pressure-group leadership was one highly influential element in a broader movement which, in alliance with other groups (Old and New Left), made the strategy of entry, for two crucial years, a dominant one. But acts of symbolic confrontation and obstruction continued alongside it.[29]

Extra-parliamentarism in the English NL developed alongside Labourist tactics; Civil Disobedience alongside party infighting; none was totally predominant, or seen as exclusive. Indeed, because of the structure of CND – an organization superimposed on a movement – it is possible to argue that the dominant tactic was in tension with the main tendencies in that movement (certainly cross-party, and to a large extent extra-parliamentary).

Ironically it was NL reformism that was partly responsible for the attempt to direct the British peace movement into the electoral framework in the first place. For several years after 1959, NL leaders helped to weld CND into the Labour Party matrix.[30] The dominant options advocated by *ULR/NLR* in the first phase were towards changing the Labour movement from within, which explains an orientation to persuasion, education and consciousness and a final unwillingness to rock-the-boat that even extended to pressurizing CND into compromising the unilateral principle that was fundamental to it.[31] The gradualist programme typical of this move towards 'multi-lateralism' has been seen as one of the biggest single internal disasters of the nuclear disarmament movement.

Throughout the first years of CND's growth, its leaders publicly endorsed a non-partisan policy of winning public opinion by education and protest. Privately they almost all pursued the aim of a majority within a future Labour Party Government. Other tactics, including civil disobedience, electoral abstention and independent candidacies, they consistently and vehemently opposed.

But those who advocated the Labour Party strategy overestimated both the commitment of CND members to the 'Old Left' or Labour voting and the strength and commitment of the left-wing unilateralists within the Party, both inside and outside parliament.

The formal structure of CND as an organization, which in some ways paralleled that of social-democratic parties, tended to release the executive from rank-and-file control, especially in crisis, when it proved more conservative: there was little consultation with those outside the CND leadership about positions adopted *vis-à-vis* the Labour Party: what the bulk of the movement failed to comprehend until too late was that unilateralism could not survive as a bargaining counter within the framework of Labourism.

The fact that the EC acted as a brake on the membership parallels the history of the Labour Party itself.[32] The ordinary CND members tended to have less investment in established politics and procedures, and be freer for spontaneous or extra-legal direction. But the nature of parliamentary projects demanded a pragmatic, deal-oriented attitude to defence questions: specific policy proposals were put forward and elements in them conceded in an attempt to achieve agreement. A major focus was Labour's foreign-affairs groups, regularly lobbied. A nuclear-pacifist stance was clearly at odds with such a milieu.

At the Scarborough Labour Party Conference of 1960, the Labour Party tactic was crowned with an apparently brilliant and unexpected success: a majority for a unilateralist resolution. But the Gaitskellite parliamentary leadership promised not only to reverse it but to resist, by non-implementation.[33] The bureaucratic and opportunist responses to all this by CND leaders were perhaps even more disheartening for the young rank-and-file. The so-called 'Crossman–Padley' compromise of 1960, thought up by a Labour-Left to maintain some sort of position in the Party, was in fact a foretaste of what would happen as the 'politicizing' of the Campaign silenced its arguing of the simple moral case; there would be sellouts to whatever seemed expedient and possible, and agreements (on nuclear bases or 'disengagement') which might never be honoured anyway.

To pressurize the parliamentary leaders, party and party machine, trades union as well as constituency support was needed; although initially (1959–60) there was a unilateralist groundswell in both, before long the dependence was on the union hierarchies. The issue in the party was fought, won and lost in the end on expediency and the votes of bureaucratic leaderships; the reversal of 1961 was a confirmation of the near impossibility of a populist revolt within such mass organizations maintaining any success.

Later calls to the movement to place its main hopes in Labourism, although nothing new, and seen by many as a belated but still urgent necessity after Scarborough, became sadly out of touch with many ordinary campaigners. The bomb as an issue was not easily handled by the political system: it had produced a radical response cutting across party lines, but CND leaders, influenced by a traditional Left, concerned only with Labour Party infighting and moving towards 'compromise', were unable to comprehend or cope with the fact that nuclear disarmament had won support across the whole spectrum of society,[34] and these attempts to harness or channel the energies they had helped unleash, were clumsy and inept.[35]

The early writings and speeches of CND, high in moral tone and idealism, had played down practical political considerations, and appealed to the young and a-political middle class, as well as the older politically alienated and disenchanted.[36] In common with the NL generally, early CND – even its 'political' leadership – made its main appeal a moral rather than a strategic one.[37] Nevertheless the appeal to move into the local Labour parties and work there was at first accepted by substantial numbers of campaigners, especially the young.

When, after the Pyrrhic party victory of 1960, renewed appeals from the centre to concentrate efforts on trying to infiltrate and secure the Labour position were made, it was conspicuously alien to the emerging style and sense of urgency at the grassroots. Thus much of the movement's subsequent extra-parliamentarism was a reaction to this experience of CND's entry into the manipulative context of Labour conflict, much of it still concerned with using 'Unilateralism' as a stick to beat Gaitskell and the 'Right' wing of the Party.[38]

In any case, as Nicholas Walter argued[39] in 1960, a unilateralist government was almost inconceivable, and a unilateralist Labour Party almost as far-fetched. With CND and the Labour Party as they existed in the late 1950s and early 1960s, unilateralism was never likely to be forced through the crust of the Labour Party bureaucracy or effectively operated by Transport House.[40] Certainly it seems likely that any Labour Government would have bungled a policy of non-nuclear neutralism.

Most people in CND immediately sensed the hollowness of the 1960 success and although, for a few months, the main field of campaigning did shift back, as in 1959, to the Labour Party, it was already far too late; in turn it was responsible for the melting away of a lot of the growing fringe support for CND once the matter seemed firmly back in the area of Labour politics.[41] Indeed the main strength of CND was never in the Labour Party; if it had been, the internal campaign would have been about foreign policy issues (especially non-alignment), or moral ones; but Scarborough merely emphasized the lack of contact between the minority of active Party 'unilateralists' and the rest of the nuclear disarmament movement.

Yet few campaigns in a democracy can have suffered the combination of subtle misrepresentation, crude slander, conspiracy of silence and political double-cross that attended the growth of CND from 1958–63. Nevertheless, the anti-nuclear movements were driven out, rather than opting out; the activity of parliamentarist allies and opponents in the Labour Party, the stopping-up of channels of ordinary democratic action, the loaded dice against independent electoral efforts, and the subsequent massive harassment of the Committee of 100, and the vicious sentences given to its leaders, did little to restore a wavering faith in the political system.

The betrayals and 'ministerialism' of various Left-Labour MPs, the response of Gaitskell and other Labour leaders, the picking up and subsequent dropping of unilateralism as a parliamentary tactic, were perhaps nothing new in the history of parliamentary socialism; many 'good brave causes' had suffered similar equivocation and abandonment by a labour-left. But the blatant reversal of positions by MPs once they achieved election or junior ministerial rank, explains some of the bitterness with which a generation of radicals abandoned the Labour Party. These were the idealists unused to the exigencies of 'real' politics; they did not take such betrayals lightly,[42] and a leading British Anarchist described his conversion to Anarchism as a response to this experience.[43]

The battalions who were marched into the Labour Party after 1959 were fairly substantial. But, despite the encouragement of NL journals, few stayed for long. Even those who had counselled the entry of nuclear disarmers into the Labour Party in 1960, often later left in disgust.[44] Indeed many thousands were alienated by this experience from the institutional procedures of both the Labour Party and of established politics. It was not a rejection of democracy in the larger sense, but a gesture of despair and resignation; the feeling of urgency which led to an impatience with letter-writing and lobbying MPs had now grown to encompass parliamentary procedures themselves.

Undoubtedly one of the reasons for the British movement's more thoroughgoing scepticism of traditional political methods and styles, was born of these experiences and frustrations. Their prior efforts lacked even the token achievements of Left-Liberal strategies in America such as the civil rights legislation, the Peace Corps and the War on Poverty. The Labour election victories of 1964 and 1966 merely confirmed the emptiness of promises to abolish Polaris or the independent British deterrent and the illusions fostered by the

Labourite Left about Wilsonism.[45] By then the movement had allowed the parties to remove foreign policy and defence from political debate, and few demurred at Wilson's claim (1965) that support for US policies was the price of defence of the pound. The acceptance of the Labour government's volte-face was symptomatic of the tiredness and resignation in the movement and the loss of clear direction once its political leadership had compromised unilateralism.

If CND could not alter from within and the Labour Party could not be changed, then the one other temptation was independent electoral effort. This took up less movement time in Britain than in America, where SANE as it began to decline had turned to peace candidates.[46] CND was probably (in 1960–1) in an even better position to create an effective electoral front that could make the issues of the bomb and neutralism priority national issues,[47] and many in the NL felt this to be, as E. P. Thompson put it, 'the right, the only response' in 1961 to the Berlin crisis, the Blackpool rejection of unilateralism in the Labour Party and the massive Trafalgar Square demonstrations.

But the Independent Nuclear Disarmament Committee (INDEC) was not set up until 1963, by a number of prominent New Leftists both active in CND and on its fringes.[48] INDEC was in part an expression of frustration with electoralism and parliamentary man-oeuvring, but also a gesture of last resort – giving the political system one more chance, with an implicit recognition of the irrelevance of the big parties to nuclear disarmament. Though the idea was to run independent candidates – prominent unilateralists, at parliamentary elections,[49] an ambivalence remained; how wide was the Labour Party door to be left open?[50]

The tactic was opposed by many in both wings of the movement; both the libertarians of the Committee of 100, and the Labour Left of the CND executive, anxious about proscription; the first wrote it off as an irrelevance, the second condemned it as a threat. Except for INDEC there is no widespread return to electoralism in Britain; even to set up an independent front for anti-nuclear non-alignment meant accepting a great deal that was disliked about politics if not party politics; even individual electoral campaigns in the protest tradition meant involving oneself in a framework that seemed loaded against the movement; a set of rules, vote-getting and a media-oriented campaign that many were not prepared to accept. In the 1964 election, the Committee of 100 supported a 'voters-veto' campaign, an idea taken up by anarchist groups in subsequent years.

The development of the NL in Britain subsequently cannot be understood without this piece of history – the pursuit of the parliamentary carrot through the Labour Party, the INDEC gesture of electoral autonomy, and the existence within CND of an extra-parliamentary mass movement. Whilst the English NL was not subsequently tempted seriously up the parliamentary cul-de-sac, or to work within the parliamentary parties, various Trotskyist groups adopted entrist or ambiguous stances *vis-à-vis* the Labour Party. The ensuing tactics of International Socialists towards Labour politics (or the Young Liberals in their adult party) as well as the growing Welsh and Scottish Nationalist parties, though they have some links and affiliations with NL ideas, do not really contradict the general tendency.[51]

In the 1967 May Day Manifesto, this extra-party reversal is partly confirmed in a call – 'to end tactics and allegiances which are *wholly* enclosed within traditional organizational forms' (my emphasis). But even though, in the manifesto's words, the strategy of the Labour-Left had involved the same kind of machine politics, the same manipulation of committee votes in the name of thousands, even though such a strategy 'wholly enclosed within the forms of labourism is directing energies into the very machines socialists should fight', even though these 'machines' had 'sought to expropriate political identity'; the manifesto's rejection of Labour Party strategies was reluctant and nervous, and hedged around with ambiguity.[52]

Civil disobedience was the most radical way out of the electoral frame; faced with the 'extremity of doom' many chose direct action only after a prior flirtation with party politics: from the first small actions of 1957, to the massive extra-legal rehearsals of revolution of 1961, the tendency to move outside the rules of the game confirms the existence of a substantial extra-parliamentary movement initially spawned by CND, and first clearly revealed in the orientation towards civil disobedience and mass marches. It was fully expressed in the groundswell of support for the Committee of 100. To the rank and file, CND's role had seemed to be dwindling from the heights of Trafalgar Square in 1960, to the pressure-group some Labour Party traditionalists had always wanted it to remain. On the Easter marches each year, frustration would grow as Westminster was skirted.

Underlying this was a myth and an apocalypse; the myth was a dream of an irresistible mass movement, independent of political organization, which would become large enough to swamp all opposition. At the end of the huge demonstrations of the early 1960s,[53] there was a feeling that the march should just go on and take over and abolish nuclear weapons – in the name of humanity even if not in the name of an electoral majority. This feeling, very similar to one expressed by Staughton Lynd after the Washington March of 1965, was the Committee of 100's portrayal of battle. The apocalypse which accompanied this myth was the ever increasing (and by no means unsubstantiated) fear of nuclear holocaust.

During the Berlin crisis and with the resumption of testing – in an atmosphere of U-2 flights and B-47 fail-safe missions, four-minute warnings, and major accidents involving nuclear weapons – people turned away from the 'politics of the long haul'.[54] This belief in imminent universal destruction, supported by the statements of world

DID

notables, was from 1958–63 counterposed by CND with advocacy of painstaking work in local ward Labour parties, union branches, trades councils and co-ops – or in churches, all of which might take years.[55]

With the growing élan and momentum of CND following three large Aldermaston marches, the tendency towards an independent mass movement that would not act just as a pressure group within existing organizations, became irreversible. The politicians found that CND was a threat because it would not be contained by the mechanism of party; the CND leaders saw the movement as a problem because it could not be harnessed by organization (there was no formal membership). A spontaneous national upsurge, channelled outside the framework of Labour politics, independent of party orientation, creating its own parallel structure locally, had never been envisioned by the leadership of CND; but it was this that made the 'victory' in the Labour Party Pyrrhic, and the Committee a logical necessity in the months that followed it.[56]

Those who broke away after Scarborough to support the initiative led by Russell, claimed that the technique of infiltrating existing political organizations along with leafletings, meetings and poster-parades, was out-dated, slow and of dubious efficacy: above all, it did not measure up to the urgency of a world-situation dominated by the possibility of accidental or escalated nuclear war.

The imminence of nuclear disaster, the malfunctioning of political democracy, the lack of public information about nuclear accidents or the nature of modern war, had produced a situation in which, it seemed, a normal politics no longer existed. To underline this, the Committee could point to a bi-partisan political system, which with informal press censorship excluded the nuclear issue,[57] or to government maintenance of a deterrence policy through refusal to argue the 'defence' question in realistic terms. The moral imperative of resistance to the bomb was rooted in this belief that only through extreme alienation and manipulation had the preparation for nuclear genocide become 'normal'. Thus the rights of a minority to conscientiously oppose policies seen to be evil was typically invoked (as later over Vietnam) in such terms as the Nuremberg principle.

This sense of urgency and impatience was not altogether an irrational one; the belief in nuclear threat, sincerely held by most CND rank and file, and indeed supported by expert opinions, made traditional political methods seem even more frustrating (even more than in trying to overcome racism and poverty). 'Politicking' and compromise in this situation seemed not only slow but immoral. Believing its own propaganda in a period of a most delicate balance of terror – including six major world crises (Berlin to Cuba) – the movement justified its extra-institutional methods in terms of such extremity. But once accepted, they were often preferred, and rationalized into a strategy of change.

Thus a key component of the NL, and one which took it in the direction of anarchism and syndicalism, adopted in terms of an unstable arms race, became a basis of day-to-day movement practice.

During CND's ascendancy, four major divisions in the movement emerged: the pressure-group tacticians versus the strategists of mass-politics; the parliamentarists versus the direct actionists; those who were aligned East or West, and those who espoused neutralism; and the multilateralist-disarmers versus the unilateralists or nuclear pacifists.

These divisions of policy and strategy were substantially super-imposed on one another; those involved in the Committee, advocating civil disobedience and principled nonviolence, insisted on universal application of the unilateralist principle, and typically wanted a mass movement free of parliamentary illusions or Labour Party ties; they opposed the Labourist realists' advocacy of practical pressure for multilateral initiatives.

But by no means all who held these views turned to militant illegal action with the formation of the Committee; many in CND openly opposed civil disobedience.[58] Some ridiculed it as a 'confession of impotence'; some, in despair, opted out of politics altogether; nevertheless, many, even though they did not accept theories of disobedient revolution or filling the jails, were willing to use such methods as a more radical form of pressure.

But a deep tension remained, even after the formation of the Committee of 100, between the tactics of a high-level pressure group, élitist in style, structure, and orientation, and the amorphous, participatory-radicalism of the grassroots; throughout this period, the English NL tended to straddle such positions, as it continued to do later when a group attempted to form a new national 'coalition of the Left'. It was a tension to be reproduced many times in the NL as a movement in the coming decades both in Britain and America.

With a lack of explicit overall anarchist perspective, this divide was inevitable: civil disobedience had mostly been accepted as a minority tactic, as propaganda of the deed which stressed communication rather than obstruction or even revolutionary change. Even those who accepted obstruction did not necessarily see this as a revolutionary confrontation with the state, but just with the nuclear weapons system itself. There were even revolutionaries who objected to the Committee's mass-confrontation strategy as minority dissent without majority support.

When the Committee declined in size, the English movement moved from direct confrontation towards an amophous extra-parliamentary opposition focused especially on localized community action.[59] The very impotence of the nuclear disarmament movement had both affirmed and reflected the need for dismantling the political structure within which the nuclear defence policy was embedded.[60] As the editor of *Anarchy* had written in 1958:

we are powerless to change the course of events over the nuclear arms race, imperialism and so on . . . precisely because we have surrendered our power over everything else.[61]

In three other countries, with amongst the strongest movements against nuclear weapons (Canada, Germany and Japan), there is similar evidence for a growing extra-parliamentary orientation – partly due to the trans-national spread of NL disaffection – partly as indigenous developments. Various accounts of the Japanese peace movement suggest that although its first and major constituency was a liberal one, even this group tended to view politics and politicians with suspicion, and that as the student opposition grew, so did extra-parliamentarism. In Canada too, there was a growing disbelief amongst peace activists, that peace programmes could or would be carried out by political parties.[62]

Organizing the excluded: SDS and power at the grassroots

Attempts by left-liberals in America to organize a national coalition of the poor in 1963 were rejected by SDS for fear that a new way 'had been found to contain and paralyze the disadvantaged and voiceless people'[63] through co-optation and concessions which would destroy the Movement. Such a viewpoint, expressed in particular by Lynd and Hayden, quickly became the majority one in SDS, and for a time of the Movement as a whole.

The objections to this coalition, and the strange ambivalent relationship of SDS and ERAP projects to the 'War on Poverty', was not a rejection of coalition in itself; indeed the dream of a national, even international, 'inter-racial movement of the poor' was at the basis of their strategy. Rather it expressed the tension between local, bottom-up concepts of socialism, in which the unit of organization was a natural community such as a neighbourhood, and the older left and liberal conception of statist national direction and planning and schemes such as nationalization and welfarism. What the left-liberals had not envisaged was the severely populist view of the role of the excluded; the emphasis on bottom-up purity of organization in the various grassroots ventures in the North. The culture of poverty, and the organizing projects, contrasted sharply with the bureaucratic depersonalization of federal programmes. Various state concepts of socialism had little to do with the NL's direct control and participation, and indeed idealized the advances in welfare and state control already made. SDS, ERAP and similar projects were, on the other hand, in constant tension with the public sector; urban welfare programmes, poverty programmes, 'Headstart' (a government training programme) – all appeared as devices for co-optation or suppression, or merely smokescreens. An emphasis on the capacity of the American system to deflect and co-opt, is at the basis of Lynd's rejection of a re-alignment politics which 'aimed at an extension of the welfare state':[64] this confrontation appeared far less sharply in England, where the tenacious hold of statist versions of socialism had not yet weakened, and the Old Left and part of the New, still clung to versions of nationalization and the welfare state. Participatory, anti-bureaucratic projects were as threatening to this brand of socialism (endorsed equally by Labourism and the Communist Party) as to capitalism.

However, some influential figures in the English NL, including E. P. Thompson, saw the continuing need for a Movement politics to get outside the institutionalized framework of parliamentarism and centralized decisions: at times closer to the participatory democracy of the American movement, he argued that socialism was something 'done by people, not for people, or to people'.

One of the great strengths of the American movements was that

they exist outside the democratic process ... their opposition hits the system from without and therefore is not deflected by the system ... the fact that they start refusing to play the game may well be the fact that marks the beginning of the end of a period (Marcuse).[65]

This identification with minorities still unintegrated into the larger national culture, unconcerned with the political 'charade', as the most clearly revolutionary in potential, is rooted in the belief that such agencies of change outside the electoral arena will be the least confused by its distractions.

For the same reasons reformism was rejected:

There is much evidence which suggests that the reforms gained (in the past thirty years) were illusory or token, serving chiefly to sharpen the capacity of the system for manipulation and oppression (Hayden).[66]

The claim to control decision-making by the poor, by students, by racial and ethnic minorities – often excluded from the system altogether – clearly challenged the legitimacy of established structures, and questioned their representativeness.[67] Liberal rhetoric did not comprehend any full or immediate extension of citizenship and democracy to to such groups, least of all at the workplace; yet there were few areas where such systems of 'rights' and participation could not be demanded, or created. Thus the movement to press these claims became in essence 'extra-parliamentary' by operating outside an established system of institutionalized 'rights and duties', and limited participation.

'Secondary' or dual citizenship systems of the oppressed often present a historical choice; at first their demand may be for the extension of dominant system-rights into their own constituency (for example, the black Mississippi challenge to the Democratic Party and their requests to the federal administration). But this may, after frustration, compromise, co-optation, and with growing revolutionary awareness, revert to a demand that the minority system of rights itself become predominant; e.g. that 'one-man-one-vote' be implemented directly by the constituency without further resort or petition to dominant structures of power.

Taking this view, the poor in the projects and the SDS organizers refused the invitation to ally with unions and civil rights groups and instead opted for this quasi-syndicalist strategy of constructing counter-institutional enclaves, calling for 'local reform movements and independent bases of power' such as democratically run Community Unions; of which the first model was NCUP.[68]

This idea of counter-organization, community government, and parallel institutions, developed out of organizing the poor, with the belief that in this way the gap between political means and ends could be closed, and could indeed be a good society in operation. But practically, its advantage was that it could empower the poor, not in terms of coalitions with liberals or mainstream politicians, but in creating alternative foci of power outside these institutionalized structures. Indeed Hayden believed that these could be the basis of a 'counter-government', which would 'compete with the existing structure of legitimacy'; such a process could 'culminate in the decision of hundreds of thousands of people to recognize the authority of alternative institutions of their own making'.[69] Such a language later passed on into the confrontations of draft resisters with the state.

Hayden's definition of radicalism in terms of disengagement and the creation of new social structures, external to the system, ensured that once confronted from outside, the State could no longer be sustained by the Movement's own legitimating actions.

The new phase of radicalism begins with this decision to disengage oneself entirely from the system being confronted, so that the structures sustained by our former attitudes can no longer endure.[70]

'We visualize and then build structures to counter those which we oppose.'

Critics argued that by using these tactics, a libertarian movement had 'focused attention on problems and contradictions in American society', but still 'lacked the political power to resolve them' on its own.[71] The years 1965 to 1968 thus see NL attempts to develop an alternative notion of coalition outside the established institutions,[72] not moving into the system, as Howe, Rustin, Kahn and Harrington had urged initially, joining various liberals of uncertain strength and credibility, but rather creating alliances of the excluded and the unrepresented outside the system, and wooing liberals into more radical positions, away from the establishment. The 'Poor People's Coalition' and the 'New Politics Conference', the 'Peace and Freedom' coalition and the various Vietnam war coalitions represent such attempts.

Do you really imagine that you can resist the inertial drift of all politics towards compromise without some of us . . . who stand outside politics and say things politicians can't say.[73]

Here the basic ambiguity reappears; extra-parliamentarism can become justified almost as a device to pressurize the political realm. Whether liberal or radical, such 'withdrawal' might be tactical in essence; it did not necessarily rest on any deep or long-term analysis or strategy.

The proliferation of organized groups and communities of people largely excluded from or marginal to the exercise of national power, was taking place in Britain and America largely independent of the NL and continued to take place after its subsequent crises and fragmentations. Their main aim was that enunciated by the NL itself in the mid-1960s, taking control of decisions which affected them in everyday life (or which often actually took their lives); the young, the immigrants, the poorly paid, old people, racial and ethnic minorities, tenants, women (especially working or unmarried mothers), were those whose needs and interests the ongoing system largely ignored. Substantially marginal to the parliamentary or electoral arena, they were no threat to it in a direct sense, although they organized new forms and levels of participation and representation.

The organization of the unrepresented, initially a matter of bringing these within a system from which they had hitherto been excluded, i.e. democratizing the existing system, evolved into an extra-parliamentary and counter-institutional strategy as disillusion with earlier tactics set in; it was thus an attempt to create the structure of a grassroots democracy.

It had been the claim of pluralists such as Riesman that countervailing power existed in America balancing the power of the élite; yet the NL could find none, and saw its most urgent task to be the construction of this 'counter-power', as a mode of undermining the power lodged in dominant institutions: only that common experience and language could prevent the top-down manipulation of masses, characteristic of representative democracies; only participation would increase the experience and skill of members, or stimulate the acquisition of greater information and competence to deal with human and social problems, and above all, combat apathy and alienation.

But with frustration at the slow growth of such alternatives, the NL switched to a third phase, an orientation to power at all costs, in which democracy itself became secondary. At its most fruitful, Black Power raised the possibility of sustaining control outside established institutions – a control that involved voluntary cooperation in existing communities – but the developments of the concept give a clear example of a drift from participatory democracy through community control, towards élitist concepts of power.

It was part of the NL's failure of nerve that it was not able to sustain and extend the second or 'Syndicalist' stage which would have developed parallel extra-parliamentary structures of innovation and involvement, but moved instead to an anti-parliamentarist, élitist, or purely negative and destructive stance.

The Democratic Party and the crisis of black reform

The leadership of the early civil rights movement, explicitly reformist and integrationist, was concerned with altering the existing structure of law and improving social justice. But in 1963, with John Lewis's denunciation of the Kennedy administration for dragging its feet on civil rights enforcement, SNCC broke the consensus of the massive Washington March.[74] After this march, and the passing of the Civil Rights Bill (1964), many moderate leaders hoped that a new phase of race relations would begin, and black scepticism of establishment concession be tempered. But it was quite the contrary; with Goldwater as a presidential candidate, an apparent white backlash under way, church burning in Mississippi and one of the worst riots in Harlem's history, the polarization intensified, and black nationalism moved from the margins of the movement towards its centre.

It was in John Lewis's words all too little and too late. The political polarization, further confirmed by the build-up of tensions on all sides during the months of filibuster and delay of civil rights legislation, seemed to indicate that gains could now only be made at the price of sustaining incessant threats of mass action. The final passing of the Bill did little to soften the struggle; the political costs of tokenism, assimilationism and deference had long been obvious, and for some, 'civil rights' had become synonymous with these. Institutionalized racism had come to mean not the highly obvious and visible forms of oppression, but the more subtle perpetuation of subordination embedded in the procedures of liberal institutional life: federal programmes, corporate activity, higher education, even the channels of 'legitimate' protest themselves.

Reformism was implicit in established orientations to federal government and legislation, to white, liberal politicans, and in protests against 'unjust laws' or petitioning for the implementation of just ones. It was clear that the major legislation fought for, through the courts by NAACP or by demonstrations by SCLC and CORE, not only did not itself precipitate change, but in effect withdrew responsibility from black people themselves. These attitudes, and the criticism of black 'Uncle-Tom' leaders, co-opted by the white power structure, affirmed a stress on black-controlled institutions, and a growing suspicion of the federal umbrella.

Federal intervention caused few misgivings in the early movement, indeed Martin Luther King's links with government were seen as a movement asset. But SNCC's radical rhetoric led to growing apprehension; what did 'nonviolent truth' mean when backed by federal bayonets? Lynd, in 1964, had described the resort to the Kennedy liberals by the civil rights leaders as a 'coalition with the marines'. How could one talk about building autonomous local-power, of decentralized community, and of non-electoral decision and participation, if one resorted to the ultimate power of federal government against racist and states-rights authority?

That, as Howard Zinn points out, was SNCC's painful dilemma: on the one hand advocating self-help and independent and autonomous black institutions – cultural, economic and political; on the other hand, as it moved deeper South and faced lynching, rape and torture, it was often faced by a choice between armed defence by local, black share-croppers, or invoking the armed federal umbrella, i.e. troops. Although SNCC heroes, like Bob Moses, tried to avoid such choices by refusing either's protection, by accepting these sharecroppers only as allies and friends,[75] they inevitably took more pragmatic positions.

At the same time re-alignment in the Democratic Party revolved essentially around a black and southern strategy to defeat the racist Dixiecrats in the party by a black-liberal-labour coalition. The threat of withdrawal of black votes was an increasingly substantial one to the Democrats by the 1960s. On the other hand, despite considerable black alienation[76] from the political system, the Negro community continued to give overwhelming support to the Democratic Party essential to its success in urban areas.

An acute ambiguity in the Democratic re-alignment strategy remained nevertheless. One of the central reasons for a lack of black political autonomy was monolithic attachment to the party of Dixiecrat racists in the South, and of cynical machine-politics in the northern cities. Despite distrust of white legislation, and scepticism of white dominated parties and politics, ultimately the black vote could be mobilized simply on the fear of white reaction – producing negative votes 'against' Goldwater or Wallace.[77] Exaggerated fears of white backlash were used for this purpose.

The belief that with greater consciousness and increased voter-registration, black majorities could shift the whole bi-partisan political spectrum, underestimated the power of that system itself. Except for voting, black involvement often remained marginal even when black mayors were elected in major cities.

This political 'backwardness'[78] began to confirm the NL's belief that a final rejection of the Democratic Party, graveyard of so many black hopes, was absolutely necessary. Convinced that integration into the Party inevitably meant its buying-off black leaders, the Movement now turned towards an autonomous politics. Such a mood was partly engendered by the experience of the relationship between the Democratic Party and the movement, both in the south where the Mississippi Freedom Democratic Party (MFDP) was rebuffed, [79] and in the North where, despite the massive solidarity of the school boycotts, Uncle Tom machine candidates were still winning elections. Yet whilst these changes of mood might make co-optation, oligarchic control, and 'sellout', less likely in local electoral activity, they did not preclude it.

In this context both SDS and SNCC leaders tended to become a little befuddled by their own rhetoric over the MFDP affair. The argument that the black delegation to the Atlanta Democratic convention represented 800,000 unregistered black voters in Mississippi was of course a myth, a symbolic claim, not even a partial truth. Yet it was as if the SNCC workers took it seriously. In fact, as Newfield points out, they had 'almost handpicked the MFDP delegation in Mississippi and controlled it whilst at the convention'. In formal terms it was not more 'representative' than the white racists; of course such formal considerations were instinctively rejected by the organizers, on the ground that any black delegation must be more representative in reality.[80] But the whole affair created some problematic precedents.

COFO (Council of Federated Organizations) was initiated by SNCC (1962) with the other groups involved in voter registration.[81] From this time on, SNCC's electoral emphasis was heavy, through voter registration drives[82] and Black Panther Parties. Yet these strategies, both before and after the Mississippi attempts of 1964–6, were still seen as intimately related to the reforms and concessions – such as civil rights bills and poverty programmes – with which many in the NL would now have no truck. Electoral programmes, even such as that of the MFDP, were recurringly linked to the need for white allies and establishment concessions; inevitably there was strong temptation to compromise over the MFDP; intense fears of co-optation gripped the movement. Politically, it was still unclear whether such electoralism meant grabbing some of 'whitey's power' in a zero-sum game (for example, black electoral power in white assemblies) or the continued creation of new types of representative power, outside the white definitions.

There was thus, so long as the Democratic Party remained monolithic and basically racist, a fundamental ambiguity in the voter registration and electoral strategy. The various attempts at entry or pressure such as MFDP, and the Julian Bond campaign, merely confirmed this situation, as both met refusal and rejection. Yet despite distrust amongst participatory-democrats of the 'distanced' politics of the vote, and the great dangers in all these campaigns that they would still focus mainly on vote-collection, the 'Free' Democratic Party of 1964–5 evolved into the independent Black Panther Party of 1966.

During this transition, there were times, in 1965 and 1966, when Black Power seemed close to being defined in narrowly electoral terms: 'vote-power', mobilized by groups like MFDP and the Lowndes County Freedom Organization, rather than social or economic power. Both organizations were outside the institutional structures of the South (by necessity rather than choice), and yet aimed at institutional office-holding or gaining footholds within national structures. In this lay the ambiguity of the clash at Atlantic City concerning MFDP's challenge to the Democratic Party, or the January 1965 challenge to the seating of the State Congressional delegation at Washington.[83] The Lowndes County Freedom Organization remained essentially a protest organization, registering votes and collecting evidence of voting discrimination; it was not clear how it related to counter-community and parallel organizations. When SNCC's Julian Bond was elected to the Georgia legislature in 1965, then rejected, then appealed, and was subsequently elected again, it created a great deal of uncertainty both about such tactics and its relative success. The costs of such a focus are exemplified in the virtual ending of the Southern movement by the electoral defeat of the Lowndes County Freedom Organization in November 1966.

After this, SNCC moved away from elections as well as alliances, if not from politics and organization altogether. An independent strategy, according to the SNCC militants, would now have to be concerned with taking what rightfully belonged to people, and tended towards an autonomist anti-coalitionism. Not only was the Democratic Party rejected but by now the strategy of building a political party itself was abandoned, at least until the later alliance with the Panthers developed.

This new militancy did not, like white militancy, reflect the impact of the Vietnam war; in fact many radical blacks expressed the view that to merge the issues of the war and Black Power would merely distract from the racial problem, or alienate essential community support. On the other hand the development in the NL as a whole of a decidedly 'Sorellan' streak[64] – the belief in direct action, the suspicion of intellectualizing, and the advocacy of purposeful polarization to prevent alliances, negotiations, deals and sellouts – becomes equally characteristic of this phase of the black movement, just as the intransigence of the black Nationalists and Malcolm-X's rejection of any truck with white liberals, or white power structures, had parallelled and reinforced 'separatist' tendencies in the movement in the previous phase, especially in the North; cultural and political 'separatism' began to merge strategically.

Electoral interludes: the temptations of re-alignment and coalition

Despite radical pronouncements, and a strong extra-parliamentarist spirit at the heart of many projects, the NL in America remained ambiguous about electoralism. Whilst in England, the CND experience had proved decisive, in America there is never the same clear tendency to reject parliamentarist efforts. The temptation throughout the 1960s and early 1970s, remains to try either to influence the alignments of the Democratic Party, or to create an independent electoral front, or to use independent candidacies to do both – or as merely educative ventures. Many of those who influenced the NL's early growth (Mills, Thomas, Fromm, etc.) supported Socialist Party candidatures, and Muste, whilst more sceptical, had like them, gone some way in endorsing Stuart Hughes and the rash of independent peace candidates of 1962.[85]

Moreover, as in the black movement before 1965, there was never at any time a conclusive NL break with the Democratic Party. A number of Democratic candidates, from Adlai Stevenson and J. F. Kennedy, through Johnson in 1964, Eugene McCarthy and Bobby Kennedy in 1968, and later Muskie and McGovern in 1972, were given a qualified 'benefit-of-the-doubt' by sections both of the Old and New Lefts, with the fundamental hope of bringing re-alignment. However extra-parliamentarism was given a powerful fillip by a meaningless alliance with Liberals at the 1964 Democratic Party convention, and frustration of the two major black challenges.[86]

Thus the account of the movement's relationship with electoralism and the parliamentary framework of parties and voters, is, in the USA, a complicated one; the withdrawal is a gradual and by no means unilinear development, influenced by shifts in movement theory, and re-inforced by movement experience. Various coalitions within, on the edge of, or even outside, established institutions and parties, were all deeply ambivalent about their relationship to the electoral system and their alliances. Few of these ventures, often seen as representing a 'failure' of NL strategy in America, were central to the NL experience; in fact many of them existed on its fringes.

Some (like MFDP) were more significant,[87] and in addition to the Southern strategies, there were after 1966, significant attempts made, particularly at congressional level, by white coalitions in the North.

Later Independent electoral campaigns, like Bob Scheer's in California, were subject to many of the same criticisms (particularly of operating initially within the Democratic Party); Scheer's campaign for congress exemplified many of the recurrent problems of electoralism and work within the Democratic Party.[88] As manager of *Ramparts* magazine, Scheer ran on an ostensibly NL ticket against a sitting liberal congressman for the Democratic nomination. His hope was to draw the support of anti-Vietnam war sentiment and the VDC. In fact, the campaign split the VDC, and SDS in northern California opposed the campaign on the grounds that it was vote-getting, not organizing and that short-term electoral success would be at the expense of basic educational work. The campaign was localized, the candidacy personal,[89] and after it was over the local movement went into decline.

One understandable response to the escalation of violence, to the sight of police clubs swinging in local communities, was to try to steer the movement back into the safety of electoral politics, and after 1967, a whole range of Old Left groups were attempting to draw NL support into 'Peace and Freedom' coalitions, especially the Du Bois clubs and Independent Socialists, and even the Black Panthers.

Long before the Chicago Convention of 1968, the Democratic Party had appeared to most in the NL a closed door. Yet the alternatives were not always more attractive; in 1966 and 1967, a strong case was made out by some groups, mainly Old Left/Liberals, for a new party based on liberal-radical coalition, such as a broadly based 'Peace and Freedom' party. Independent platforms such as the King–Spock ticket of 1967 were also proposed with substantial support: and the New Politics Conference was launched.

The beginnings of these moves can be traced, early in 1966, to the attempt at an alliance between liberals and radicals, engineered by Arthur Waskow and others, including Bond. Even this was rejected by many militants and organizers as a new co-optive and vote-getting venture – a bandwagon for careerists, organizing for organization's sake – usually opportunistically. The activists continued to argue that 'movement' was more important than 'party', and that if any electoral activity was undertaken, it should be a single, subordinate facet of a broad moving coalition, not the rationale of the Movement. They were opposed to the centralism and the bureaucratism associated with the notion of national party, and their suspicion was grounded in awareness of decades of electoral ventures on the Left in America and elsewhere; it was only with this kind of reluctance that some of the militant black groups entered an electoral alliance within the white coalition.

This political coalition of the 'New Politics' was, except in California, where it had already developed some strength, stillborn at the disastrous National Conference for a New Politics (1967) in Chicago. Never really a NL affair, it represented a weird amalgam of three major forces: the new militant Black Nationalist groups including Panthers and the remnants of SNCC; the Old Left groups, especially the Communist Party and Du Bois Clubs, but with some Trotskyists and Independents in attendance; and the scattering of left-liberals, radicalized by the war, especially such groups as Waskow's Institute for Policy Studies (IPS).[90]

In this mêlée, the main chance of unity around a relatively moderate King–Spock ticket, supported by the Independent Socialist group from Berkeley, was lost. As a result each element had to go it alone. The Communists produced their own presidential candidate, and the Peace and Freedom Party (PFP) in California put forward its Cleaver–Jacobs ticket, symbolizing the shaky alliance between black and white groups. In this, the period of Carmichael's ascendancy, dialogue between many black leaders and white liberals had already broken down, clearly exemplified by the final fiasco of the Convention, the debate over black control. The subsequent electoral alliance forged by the Panthers with the PFP, based on a formal recognition of mutual autonomy, was nevertheless a cause of great apprehension amongst the black nationalists, especially those in SNCC still arguing for a black front, excluding whites.

It is significant of its distance from the NL that over half the delegates at Chicago interpreted 'new politics' as an electoral platform – and equally symbolic that they should have got nowhere near an agreement on who the candidates, and what the platform, should be. Following this débâcle many drifted into the Eugene McCarthy and Bobby Kennedy campaigns.[91] The NL leadership largely condemned McCarthy's campaign, fearing the threat its growth posed to it, shown by the willingness of younger and potential NL supporters to join his bandwagon in the early months of 1968. But by the end of the spring this strategy too seemed largely to have failed, and the temptation for SDS in particular was now to 'go it alone'. Yet at the very moment when the problems of liberal coalition were being highlighted and reaffirmed by the McCarthy failure – and the impossibility of Left coalition underlined by the disasters of the New Politics – the practical need for alliances and coalitions was reaffirmed by the events in Chicago.

These events (August 1968), especially the indiscriminate violence of Mayor Daley's police, brought McCarthy supporters and left-liberals into a renewed and unexpected coalition – albeit a transitory one – with the militants of SDS and the Yippees. Of course the demonstration disclaimed any connection with the McCarthy or Kennedy opposition within the Democratic Party, but its interpretation by the American public was clearly as an anti-Daley/Humphrey protest, not as an expression of alienation from the Democratic Party and the American political system generally (as its organizers intended).

The USA election figures of that year gave absolutely no indication of the breadth and character of the NL movement which had now developed; of the hundreds of thousands of young people not eligible to vote, now drawn into the radical movements against the war and the draft; nor the high school and college students who had spearheaded protests against education and racism (and also who often could not vote). Beyond the minority voters and teenagers were the tens of thousands who rejected electoral politics altogether, as a path of change and abstained. For the first time the *Guardian*, a New York Old Left weekly that was moving towards the NL, had opposed any electoral involvement in 1968.[92] Hippies, anarchists, and NL militants, though old enough – even registered – to vote, refused to play yet again the game of 'lesser-of-two-evils' which had for decades been the liberal rallying-cry.

But the November 1968 elections came as a considerable shock and disappointment to all those involved in the political coalitions; the fact that left and liberal abstentions, minority votes, and youthful militancy did not show up in the 1968 figures, was compounded by the fact that Wallace and the populist right had mobilized effectively from non-voters and the previously disenfranchised.[93] Whilst there were certainly thousands who chose to buck the bi-partisan system by votes for the minority candidates,[94] the Peace and Freedom Party remained a largely submerged 'protest vote'. By the beginning of 1968 it had 66,000 names and within a few months 107,000, thus winning a place on the ballot in California: yet it still gained no more than 1 per cent in the actual elections (its best vote going to Paul Jacobs for Senate).

What had seemed to represent, only a few months earlier, a major alliance of white and black radicals, had suffered irreparable setbacks.

After the 1968 election, third party politics seemed to have proved yet again a time-wasting cul-de-sac, little less illusory than Democratic coalitionism. But this relation of the NL to the McCarthy and other Presidential campaigns in 1968 and later was neither analysed nor discussed. Certainly many more on the Left than had been expected had shown a final willingness to work with these electoral machines (and that still even included that of a Kennedy) as they would again with McGovern in 1972. Given all the radical alibis and rationalizations, there must still have been millions who, notwithstanding their belief in the 'choicelessness' of the election, grudgingly, perhaps without telling their Movement friends, pulled the 'Humphrey' lever in the automatic voting booths 'to try to keep Nixon out'.

Outside the system: Syndicalism revisited

1966 saw the growth of a new strategy, associated with the term 'Student Syndicalism',[95] wedded to direct-action and constructive alternatives, displacing the previous tactics and structures of student politics. Rejecting the weakness of student reform strategies, based on paper agreements, negotiations and winning the support of middle-opinion amongst faculty and students, it argued that the Free Speech 'victories' had brought mystification and a gradual erosion of gains made. No longer ones of free speech and civil liberties alone, the issues at Berkeley and elsewhere soon crystallized into demands for new institutions, new student participation in decision-making, a new powerful role in the life of the community. These were not petitions to be granted by a beneficent administration, or dependent on the intercession of a paternalist faculty, but demands to be backed by the organized power and dedication of thousands of students.

The term 'Syndicalism' was revived[96] to stress a parallel with workers' control movements, aspiring for full democracy at the work-place rather than merely seeking amelioration of wages and conditions. 'Student control' implied a new power of rule-making or rule-abolition, vested in the organized counter-power of student organization – ideally a Free Student Union (FSU).[97]

The growing importance of the universities as a key institutional sector, gave this shift great strategic significance. Control of one campus might be utopian, but a movement on every campus could generate real if uneven advance. On the other hand, a students' with-drawal and constant agitation might never be as potent a sanction as an industrial workers' withdrawal of labour. Moreover, administrations might combine liberal concessions on one issue (e.g. compliance with draft boards) with reaction or intransigence on another (e.g. autonomous student governance).

Such a strategy challenged at every point the legitimacy of the existing university, yet retained a certain ambivalence about whether the existing structures could be salvaged or not. Counter-curricula projects within the university were thus balanced by the Free Universities outside; many struggles – over mass-teaching methods, the use of grades for draft status, or complicity – implied that reform was indeed possible. Only when the functioning of the university was impaired, the classrooms emptied, was it difficult to avoid a more basic questioning of the validity of the institution as a whole.

Student Syndicalism is one of many symptoms of the deepening suspicion with which the whole movement was beginning to view Liberalism and supposedly 'liberal' institutions. Before FSM at Berkeley, both Kerr and Chancellor Strong, had had reputations as liberal administrators. Yet their behaviour during the months of the free-speech agitation was repressive – characterized by smear tactics, red-baiting and victimization of FSM leaders. In the student reaction to this, one discovers echoes of Sorel, the early twentieth-century Syndicalist writer, and of Syndicalist responses to betrayals and compromise, and its rejection of the established political realm. [98]

By 1966, student revolts and the burgeoning of a full extra-parliamentary opposition had spread to Europe, particularly to Germany (the APO). [99]

In Germany too, failures and frustrations within the system led to the development of an extra-parliamentary opposition, which was partly a pragmatic strategy (i.e. a more effective form of pressure than from within), partly expressive of disillusion with parliamentary politics, and partly political principle based on a growing radical critique of the 'capitalist state'.

The peace movement had gathered considerable momentum in the 1950s opposing German rearmament, nuclear weapons and compulsory military service – on all three issues the movement was defeated both nationally and within the SPD. Germany re-armed, introduced conscription and became part of the NATO nuclear strategy – all with the tacit approval of the Social Democrats. From these reverses, the German NL was born. Consequent opposition to bi-partisanship and parliamentarism by Niemoller and other peace leaders, led to a German anti-election campaign in 1965, including the return of blank ballot papers or the spoiling of ballots.

The extra-parliamentary opposition grew from this point, taking as part of its justification the new Emergency Laws which were perceived as turning the state in a decisively authoritarian direction; whilst the APO soon turned from the issue of nuclear weapons to the whole range of student and NL concerns, its origins lie with the reversal of the anti-nuclear position in the SPD (at the Bad Godesberg Conference, 1962), the series of mass extra-parliamentary demonstrations, and the disaffiliation of the German SDS (Socialist Student League)[100] in the period 1957–65 – closely paralleling the English experience, and leading into the Vietnam protests.

This extra-parliamentarism in Germany which by 1967 sprang mainly out of the confrontations of SDS was dedicated to the commune as a unit of its organization, adopted ideas of workers' control and decentralization as basic principles, and used the libertarian 'council' ideas of Rosa Luxemburg, and other models close to Anarchism and Syndicalism. This anti-authoritarian and extra-parliamentary opposition, like the American, stressed a bottom-up, democratic and decentralized movement,[101] especially SDS which was the leading group under the 'APO' umbrella. Many chapters, including Berlin SDS, leant towards a revolutionary syndicalism, based on a grassroots direct democracy – self-governing workers' and intellectuals' councils;[102] they rejected the notion of political party, maintaining that such a position was not incompatible with a brand of Marxism. But influenced by Marcuse, there was a strong anti-technologism and even anti-industrialism in their movement, and along with their identification with the Räte (the soldiers' and workers' councils of the 1918 German revolution) and the principles of Karl Liebknecht, they made a distinct theoretical contribution to NL ideas, through such figures as Rudi Dutschke.[103]

Sections of the NL discovered the tradition of Proudhon and the ideas of anarcho-syndicalism, of control by producers of factory and workshop, a policy advocated by the NL in terms both of democratization, and decentralization: control by working communities, independent of state authority, a direct democracy at the workplace, with units coordinated on a federal basis. 'Extension of citizenship into the industrial sphere' might turn out to be another way of describing participatory democracy and power at a 'point of production'. But in directly political terms, democracy in the workplace may be instituted at the factory level without reference to the parliamentary framework. Thus even though the model might derive from liberal formulae – of voting on issues, and popular control over decisions made – such an extension appeared to represent a push beyond and against liberalism – 'a non-reformist reform'.[104] The factory had hitherto been defined out of politics; the 'industrial citizenship' expressed by unions had at best been quasi-legitimate; the workplace, in so far as it is part of the 'democratic civil right' of property,[105] could not be subject to 'democratic' procedures. To demand this was to confront an inherited system of private and corporate property, and a whole superstructure of 'rights and duties' and frameworks of representation, constructed upon that basis.

Both on the campus, and in France, in 1968, in the factory, such confrontations brought crisis. In Britain as elsewhere, the Labour movement represented a latent source of extra-parliamentary activity of great power; despite its long involvement with parliament, it had its own tradition of democratic institutions, and principles of mandated and delegated democracy, offering substantially greater checks on leadership in its early development than had the dominant forms of representation (institutions reflecting a merger of middle-class power and aristocratic concession, geared to the protection of property).[106]

A Syndicalist potential – a latent autonomy – remained in the British Labour movement through the sheer size of its organized membership. Not all the Labour-Left and union leadership was entirely disingenuous about either the degree of representativeness of parliamentary institution or in whose interests it typically operated; as unofficial militancy revived in the late 1960s, it became clear that the unions were not yet quite the tame industrial arms of the Labour Party they had been taken to be.[107] Even unions, it could be argued, still embodied, along with some of the Co-operative Societies, some semblance of an original representativeness, which parliament still lacked.[108] When such historical awareness was fused with growing demands for 'workers' control' the Labour leaders began to attack a 'new Syndicalism'.[109]

Anti-parliamentarism and the rejection of the State

In its emphasis on decentralization, counter-institutions, community control and participatory democracy, it was inevitable that the movement would move towards a more fully developed 'Syndicalist' position outside existing representative institutions. Unlike revolutionary unionism, the NL had to hope to eventually create a separate power base which could allow it to ignore agreements and assume power – otherwise it too would succumb to repression, or co-optation, by a state it viewed as illegitimate, or be replaced by more authoritarian rivals (as had historically been the case).

Significant of these orientations, the May events in France reflected a tremendous ideological confidence in the constructive ability of people.[110] Both political parties and unions were viewed as structures which might inhibit this constructive and spontaneous creativity. Where possible, new forms of organization should come into being. This view was expressed by Geismar, one of the leaders of the revolt, when he identified it with a

rejection of existing structures, of all bureaucracy, centralized direction ... and granting power to producers at their point of production.[111]

Anarchist and Syndicalist scepticism of parliamentary tactics is certainly echoed in much NL rhetoric. But, in its relative ignorance of established political processes, and with a sense of the wider definition of political responsibility than that confined to voting, the movement drew closer to the counter-culture's rejection of traditional politics; 'the urge to replace politics by poetry', the view expressed by Norman

O. Brown, that 'the real fight is not the political fight, but to put an end to politics'. As the inevitable fusion of various 'deviant' life-styles, and subcultures, took place through their proximity in the urban ghettoes or drop-out communities, there was recognized a certain shared detachment from the society: typical of this same attitude, though less urban-centred, the commune movement developed with intense scepticism of politics. The hippy emphasis on confronting the manipulation of consciousness with counter-values, also engendered withdrawal: the creation of alternatives to the dominant media, a rejection of consumerism, the articulation of higher stages of 'post-scarcity awareness':

Drop-outs from political struggle they may be; they are some of the first enlisted troops in a new kind of politics of post-modern post-industrial society: the politics of cultural rebellion.[112]

Rejecting power struggle in favour of federalism and solidarity, Provo in Holland implied fusion of libertarian and counter-culture elements, re-synthesized (1970) by the Kabouters.

The underground society grows out of the ground now, and it begins – independent of the still ruling authorities – to live its life and to rule itself.[113]

They, and the Orange Free State, took such ideas one step further into politics; neither Provos nor Kabouters were a true extra-parliamentary opposition; anarchists in spirit, they were quite happy to exploit the arena of electoral representation, indulging in a number of electoral ventures which met with both numerical and propagandistic success – especially in the Kabouter victories in Amsterdam elections (1970). But generally the NL was constantly torn away from the electoral arena by its associations with cultural disaffiliation – the rejection of so many of the implications of established political rituals and procedure. Alliances with the middle-aged, the middle class, the liberals, seemed to be at the core of electoral alliances, and the official institutions bore that stamp; any coming-to-terms was deeply problematic except for those closest to the Old Left; in using such established tactics and techniques,

even principled rebellion, runs the risk of operating upon the body politic with instruments contaminated by the very disease from which the patient is dying.[114]

Such an instrument was the political party. Before 1968, the NL was as suspicious of the revolutionary, mass, or vanguard party as it was of a bourgeois democratic party. Either as mechanisms of representation or organs of control, both were viewed as top-down, élitist, and compromised institutions. 'The obsolescence of traditional forms of organization', such as the parliamentary party, was roundly rejected by Marcuse, no party whatever, I can envisage today which would not within a very short time fall victim to the general and totalitarian political corruption which characterizes the political universe.

The debate on organization was at first characterized by a consensus amongst the elder NL statesmen that

as a national network emerges from local resistance–politics, it may not take the form of a political party. It may resemble the old IWW rather than the old Socialist Party.[115]

Marcuse too, increasingly influential, warned of the obsolescence of 'traditional centralized forms of organization' and the need for spontaneous organization or an 'organized spontaneity' which 'corresponded better to the development of advanced capitalist society', foreshadowing

what may in all likelihood be the basic organization of libertarian socialism – namely councils of small manual and intellectual workers, 'soviets', if one can still use the term.[116]

But the organizational dilemma of the NL, springing from similar contradictions in relationship both to community organizing and electoral strategies, inevitably initiated discussion about the formation of 'a party'. It was stimulated by a debate in the pages of *Studies* between 'socialists' who wanted a new national party, and the 'activists' suspicious of any top-down organization. Until 1968, generally speaking, both inside and outside SDS, there was an agreement that a traditional Leninist model of centralized political organization was undesirable. It would, in the view of many besides Marcuse, militate against the likelihood that revolutionary means would remain consistent with its aims. In so far as the NL was involved in the anticipation of utopias here and now

its development calls for actual struggles for new social structures, new instruments of expression and political participation.[117]

Admittedly, at this stage, the Socialist viewpoint in support of party did not advocate a 'vanguard' élite structure, nor try to revive democratic centralism, but it did seek unity and national organization in a new party. Against this, the movement organizers advocated forms of action involving people without such centralized structured organization.

Anarchists, like others in the movement, were divided on their immediate attitude to the state. Most would have agreed with Gitlin when he wrote that 'bureaucracies stand between the people and their needs and should be disbanded'. But whilst some held it possible and desirable to work for the destruction of the state either now or in the foreseeable future, others considered it compatible with a libertarian position to seek concessions and modifications, partly in order to defend the radical communities standing outside.[118] There were still those who believed that to develop radical community detached from the structure of the state, was itself a sufficient response.

The assertion of the rights and moral responsibility of the person and the minority, both against the state and its requirements and the rule or will of the majority, constitutes a major link of Anarchism with civil disobedience: Zinn urged the movement to

show ordinary people that the state constitutes a special interest of its own, which deserves not unthinking loyalty, but criticism, resistance and watchfulness.[119]

Anarchist association with civil liberties campaigns in Britain and America was based on the rationale of an expansion of such freedoms and rights as existed, not so much as a liberal social-engineering project, but as a mode of making successively wider claims against the state on behalf of both group and individual.[120] Non-cooperation with the activities of the state had long been part of the armoury of Anarchism, alongside collective resistance, and is a connection fundamental to the growth of a NL attitude to legalized power, through campaigns for civil rights, peace, and nuclear disarmament.

Such an attitude, which characterizes the movement throughout, is most clearly brought to the surface in the Committee of 100's opposition to nuclear preparations, the revelations of the 'Spies for Peace', and the RSGs in the early 1960s.

Critics argued that CND and the Committee, like the civil rights actions, had established a precedent for others in violating the democratic-pluralist ground rules; the attempt to act directly at the centres of power was anti-majoritarian and often consciously by-passed elected majorities. Illegal action at rocket sites, flouting Official Secrets acts, was clearly 'unconstitutional' in the accepted sense. But when a war-making state begins to lose its legitimacy, when popular acquiescence ebbs, increasing numbers come forward to resist its demands or reveal their complicity in its enterprises.[121] The 'major assumption' behind military conscription in the USA was that 'the lives of young people in this country belong not to those young people'; their lives are 'instead possessions of the state, to be used by the state when and where the state chooses to use them'.[122]

Such an attitude opens up, as had some eighteenth-century enlightenment ideas, a deeply moral relativism, focused on the pathology of a political system – 'Moloch', as Ginsberg had called it, the false idol – not the real victims[123] with which it is fed. Hundreds of thousands of young Americans became involved in some form of personal resistance to the State over Vietnam, mostly on the draft issue. This intensified in 1966 when General Hershey started a new plan to draft college students, and within a short time a total of 40,000 a month were being called up. The 'Resistance' was not merely the propaganda-of-the-deed of committed activists, it was an effective mode of organizing ordinary young people, though for many of the movement's leaders, like David Harris, it was also a question of non-cooperation with an authoritarian state. Rejection of the war-machine thus came to rest on an explicitly nonviolent and libertarian foundation.

Organizing the counter-democracy

'Participatory democracy', an alternative to existing forms of representative democracy, based its call for alternatives to parliamentarism, on the principle of a direct, or at least delegated, democracy. The emphasis on the participation in all major decisions by the mandators could be interpreted either as 'parallel' or supplementary to existing structures, or as being in opposition to them; a 'dual power'. Some proponents, like Lynd, were prepared to argue that PD was essentially subversive of such a representative system rather than complementary to it.

Major dilemmas for PD emerged as it was translated from local and regional spheres to the arena of the nation state. What was the appropriate size and level at which such systems could operate? The usual answer had been given in terms of small groups and communities, rather than large geographical or territorial units. Certainly at the nation-state level, such entities were viewed as overlarge, over-centralized, often monolithic, and typically artificial as contexts for decision-making. It was, in one movement leader's words, a question of 'breaking up the big blocs of power' with their pyramid-like structures (Steve Weissman). The hypertrophy of the state, swollen and depersonalized, underlined the urgency of decentralization of control and decision-making – though in and of itself this would not have guaranteed different decisions.[124]

In this context, Mills's stress on the idea of 'political alienation' was a critical one; the idea that people had lost any comprehension of the whole political structure, sensing that an inhuman power seemed to rule over everything,[125] that people could not control it, or even begin to control it. Such a situation confirms the need for participatory publics to begin to re-possess the power from the power élite. Projects of this kind, representing the re-connection of the individual and the small group with day-to-day functions, could replace the state power that had both created, and filled, a vacuum in social organization; in a period of urban expansion and industrial growth, the Nation State had undermined social group alternatives, destroyed them, and occupied their space.

Mills and Marcuse seeing liberal democracy as a sham – 'slaves electing slavemasters' – viewed institutionalized tolerance of dissent as a prophylaxis against radical opposition. A. J. Muste too rejected the mystique surrounding formal state elections and voting as a 'patriotic duty'. Marcuse's condemnation of the 'rule-of-the-game', and electoral participation, or reformist or pressurizing tactics as reinforcing a myth of 'democratic freedom', echoed Mills's arguments against the rituals of electoral politics, 'images from a fairytale' of political participation and choice. 'Free elections of the master by the slaves doesn't eliminate the masters or the slaves.'[126] The Tweedledum and Tweedledee of Republican and Democrat, of Labour and Tory, engendered an increasing sense of bi-partisan, yet manipulative, consensus (especially on Vietnam, racism, and the bomb). Without opposition and managed by political technocrats, it manoeuvred issues in and out of the organized routines of electoralism.[127]

Theories of 'false consciousness' or 'manipulation' through the media enabled a majority to be seen as misled and thus the key underpinning of electoral politics removed; liberal choice became a 'mechanism of control'; the parties, narrowly defined and highly bureaucratic, were 'organizing devices'; this was not pluralism but an 'alienated politics', an 'irrational and uncontrolled system' hostile and external; and to the NL the language of 'system', and 'élite', depicted it even more accurately than that of 'class' or 'oppression'.[128]

Marcuse's anti-majoritarianism, unlike the tradition of civil disobedience (invoking Thoreau or the Nuremberg principle) was based on such perspectives: 'the majority of the people is the majority of their masters'[129] – a view that came to predominate in the NL by the late 1960s; the votes of the electorate, of MPs, of Congress, are simply dismissed; somehow the power structure has purloined or befuddled the masses and their political expression.[130]

Where Marcuse was seen to be most accurate, was in his stress on the inadequacy of 'majority' participation in political decision-making, and the dangers of accepting electoral or constitutionalist definitions of political reality. Yet established structures of politics and law were still of some consequence to many in the NL – and closer to 'orders of freedom' than had been achieved in most non-liberal states. Many NL theorists envisaged a multiplication of democratic institutions as the best antidote to parliamentarism rather than merely focusing on its abolition.

Others stressed the dangers of sweeping away existing representative bodies in the absence of viable alternatives at some level; other modes of representation were suggested (e.g. on the basis of function or occupation), a Syndicalist idea of producer-representation was revived along with Guild Socialist ideas of consumer-representation, in parallel structures.

But existing forms of representation were

profoundly inadequate and need to be extended by radical transformation of the context which condemns them to inadequacy or erosion rather than sweeping them away.[131]

Indeed Marcuse too seems to have recognized some of this in his stress on decentralized organization, and in the importance of political participation for those who were excluded. It was at least possible that this latter development could amplify and extend existing democracy.

Thus real dangers of nuclear war, and a fear of a drift into Fascism, were used to justify an abandoning of the pretences of liberalism by the Left, in order to effectively reject an illiberal system (Marcuse). But the theory of crisis, and emergency justification, coupled with the attacks on law and democracy as they existed, themselves carried other dangers. It was one thing to diagnose extremity, another thing entirely to justify and use terror; it was one thing to criticize unjust laws and even the courts and quite another to reject all institutional forms of justice. Equally there was a difference between criticizing a given system of democratic representation or participation (e.g. parliamentarism and electoralism) and abandoning the attempt to construct the various positive alternative forms of democracy that had characterized the NL up to 1968.

Marcuse (and many of his critics) stood accused of mistaking a rejection of the political mechanism of change of and within the system, for a rejection of politics itself. Unlike many Syndicalists of an earlier period, sections of the extra-parliamentary opposition of the 1960s, who identified with much of Marcuse's thought, failed to understand that politics outside the system could be both a potent force for change, and yet sustain a working alternative system of democracy.

5. The Problem of Agency

In quest of proletariat

One theoretical problem that classical revolutionary theory, whether Marxist or Syndicalist, had had no difficulty in facing was that of 'agency'; *who* would make the revolution. Both libertarian and authoritarian streams of socialist thought and action had agreed with Marx – it must be the army of producers, the working class. Yet in the American context, and in that of the 1950s and 1960s, such an answer was not only inadequate, it was unreal.

Rejecting the major Marxist tenets of the role of such a class, or of a 'ruling class' based on ownership of the means of production, Mills attacked Victorian Marxism and the 'Labour metaphysic' in a letter to the English NL:

> What I do not understand about some New Left writers is why they cling so mightily to the 'working class' in advanced capitalist societies as the historic agency, or even as the most important agency, in the face of the really impressive historical evidence that now stands against this expectation.[1]

Radical critics like Mills and Marcuse were agreed in abandoning hope of any revolutionary role for a 'working' class, and urged others, in Britain and elsewhere, to drop the orthodox belief in this class as the critical agent of change. Other critics stressed the increasing diversification of social classes, the fact that industrial workers in particular represented a declining proportion of the total workforce; they illustrated its class-collusion, conciliation, quiescence and 'embourgeoisement'. 'The working class is to a great extent integrated into the system; and on a rather solid material basis, and not only superficially' (Marcuse). But the changing *role* of the working class was accompanied by a more fundamental change – the break-up of familiar class formations.

Mills's comments laid the foundations of a general NL scepticism of the working class – or at least of the white, American working class – as an agency of change.[2] A class metaphysic of transformation had become outflanked by historical development; counter-values were no longer securely lodged in the working class; on the other hand the British working-class movement in particular (as the English NL stressed) had developed – like black Americans – a distinctive communal subculture representing a possible social alternative, suggesting a community-basis for reorganization or political autonomy; such highly-organized, conscious cultural groupings had for over a century engaged in an uneven political, economic and cultural collective 'self-advancement'; but no such classic formation existed in the American context even though the black community had shown some parallels.[3]

Thus the NL in America lacked the same sense of labour tradition, of a history of trades union movements or an understanding of the role of economistic types of demand; the NL's consequent disillusionment with labour was unremarkable; organized labour was viewed simply as another big 'institution', with a conservative, even reactionary, bureaucratic structure. Those Anarchists who continued to be wedded to a strategy of change involving the working class were able to explain its lack of attraction to twentieth-century Socialism by the restriction of its options largely to a simple choice between bureaucratic alternatives.[4]

Despite its early dealings with Reuther and others, SDS was under no illusions about the American working class as represented by the AFL-CIO, which had become by the 1960s an integral part of the system of domination, giving thoroughgoing support to American foreign policy, including counter-insurgency. It guarded with great jealousy the privileged position as workers in the decisive corporate sectors of its predominantly white members. Its bureaucratic hierarchies maintained an exclusiveness that was, as often as not, coincidental with racial divisions. Indeed the proletariat in general was, in Marcuse's view, now providing the key social base of a popular conservatism, defending the status quo; on questions of the war or race, it drifted to the right, sometimes to the far right, and the massive votes for Wallace, and working-class reactions to international issues, supported this latter view. The spontaneous racist militancy of industrial workers (e.g. the dockers) in Britain and America was unmistakable. The fervour of their support for tough lines on Vietnam or immigration went further than any other social group.

In Britain, where proletarian mythology died more slowly, most of these tendencies were denied or played down; there was, for example, strong emphasis on unofficial unionism as a counter-weight to socialist pessimism.[5] But besides voting in massive proportions for Conservative candidates[6] and supporting racist politicians of the right, the working-class rank and file in the early 1960s confirmed, in their rejection of the nuclear disarmament movement, that this was the very last section of the population to be interested in peace issues, let alone support an internationalist or unilateralist policy.

As has been seen, despite the votes of some union leaderships in 1960, CND had undeniably been a middle-class movement; and only later did working-class youth give some support and then only because of the overlap with an increasingly classless 'youth culture'. For all the rather pathetic harping on the need for working-class support, CND and the rest of the English NL had to settle for a basically middle-class identity, a small part of the leftward portion of Labour support, and a great deal of resistance in working-class areas.[7]

The fact that the early NL in England romanticized the English working class, parallels the American movement's romanticization of black and white poor in the ghettoes, slums and southern communities, or the migrant workers. The identification has a populist-democratic basis that shows as much resemblance to NL impulses on both sides of the Atlantic, as to inherited orthodoxies in Europe. Both leading theoreticians of the English NL (Thompson and Williams) found their grounds for admiration in working-class *culture*; they both stress the revolutionary implications for capitalism of the collectivist and communalist strains surviving in proletarian life and work. In Williams's view, the social collectivism of this class had been institutionally expressed by the creation of democratic unions and cooperatives. These represent latent negations of bourgeois individualism in its capitalist form, involving values of mutual aid, communality and solidarity. For Williams, though solidarity has hitherto been a defensive attitude, it is 'potentially the real basis of society'. Whilst this class counter-culture or set of alternative institutions has hitherto been predominantly retreatist, it could still aspire to revolutionary replacement of bourgeois dominance.

Moreover as yet, no other group clearly transcended the dominant culture, or seemed to have a similar transforming potential.

We have to admit that a large part, if not the majority of this population does not really feel, is not aware, is not politically conscious of this need for change. This presents, as I can see it, the first great problem of our strategy (Marcuse).

There was a certain paradox involved in the difficulty of detecting – in an increasingly unstable society – agents by which the opportunities for change could be exploited and sustained.

There was a shortage of allies even for change wrought by the movement itself. As Kahn remarks, the 'quest for allies outside the university intensified as the intellectual leadership of the SDS was graduated.'[8] Since the only cracks in the American consensus were provided by blacks in the civil rights movement, student revolt and the anti-war movement, allies and agents were first sought there.

As the secondary or industrial sector of production came to form a smaller and smaller proportion of Western economies, the actual size of the traditional working class was declining; more importantly, increasing social fluidity, including geographical transience, helped dissolve the 'reality' of social class in favour of a whole range of emergent and plural power relationships. Even Marx had seen that no society in the contemporary world exhibits classes in their pure form; stratification may include intermediate, transitional and vestigial groups, within and between classes,[9] and it was to these groups and strata that the NL generally now turned in its search for alternative agents of change.

The NL's development in this respect can be characterized in terms of the proliferation of confrontations across authority lines, the increasing ideological salience of these social divisions for conflict, and the growing consciousness of these power-related characteristics, as against 'class' characteristics in their traditional form.

Table 1   *Emergent power relations*[10]

(State/Community)	Rich/Poor	Employer/Employee	Old/Young
	White/Non-White (esp. White/Black)	Teacher/Student	Male/Female
	Urban/Rural (e.g. tribal, peasant)	Parent/Child	
	Ethnic Majority/ Ethnic Minority		

This was but one further aspect of the decline of Schön's 'stable state': a dichotomous class formation was relatively stable in comparison with the multiplicity of divisions now revealed.[11] As examples of the range of subordinate groups, he lists blacks, poor, rural families, women, aged, sick, children, prisoners, mentally ill. Of course, the lines of subordination and oppression are not simply coincident; in America not all blacks are poor, not all poor are blacks; women may find themselves subordinated in movements of blacks or students; the urban/rural division may cut across the constituencies of the poor and coloured. Though there is often a superimposition of these divisions, the problem of agency now becomes in part a problem of coalition – what kinds of *alliances* can be built between those who are unified only by their common subordination or powerlessness.

The variations of these relationships are well illustrated by the two constituencies that organized themselves more distinctively in America than in Britain (where they simply co-existed beneath the same 'left' umbrella): *students* and *women*. The emergent power relationships they imply also appear as trans-national categories of solidarity. In the same way there is a growing temptation to try to create a universal stratification system of the poor/coloured/rural communities of the world – an alliance of the 'outcasts', the fringe elements, or an attempt to see the 'lumpen' elements in all societies, including the metropolitan west, as having common interest and links.

The NL in its populist adulation of the life-styles and culture of the under-class in America, ultimately fantasizes about alliances with the under-classes and lumpen-proletariat of the Third World 'who have nothing to lose and everything to gain' (Fanon). The greater the disillusion with agencies of change in the heartland, the more pressing the need to find such external agents, or allies, as the peasantry of Vietnam, or of other Third World countries. Marcuse, too, shares this hope that despite their lack of revolutionary consciousness, these elements 'outside the system' will constitute a new proletariat whose opposition may prove decisive. 'The substratum of outcasts and outsiders, the exploited and persecuted of other races and other colours, the unemployed and unemployable.'[12]

Drawing Millsian conclusions about power in American society, SDS and SNCC acted far more closely with these constituencies (even though Mills had in fact disparaged them) than their English counterparts could approach with an already organized and somewhat stereotyped 'working class'. But while the 'poor' were quickly identified as major allies, like much else in NL thought, the view of the poor as agency, was based on the 'moral correctness' of such a strategy rather than its realism. Hayden's search for such a constituency, for *the* revolutionary group, led him to these agencies written off by Mills simply because they were *not* involved in the ideology and values of liberalism; because they *had* been excluded. Lynd agreed: 'the poor will produce a truer, sounder radicalism than any which alienated intellectuals might prescribe'.[13] Transient minorities, young and single people, the flotsam and jetsam of a mass society, did not easily weld into the inherited Marxist left concept of a 'class.' The enterprise was far closer to the Anarchist tradition of belief in organizing all the poor, Bakunin's 'great mass of the oppressed'.

This imagery of 'the outsiders' had an undeniably dramatic appeal, but under-emphasized the depth of divisions cutting across such multi-faceted constituencies; it romanticized the natural relationships and alternative values of the under-class, underestimating the degree to which these could be manipulated. Nevertheless the idea of an alliance between 'the most advanced consciousness of humanity and its most exploited force' remained a powerful one. However, none of the SDS rhetoric of organizing 'all the poor' really spoke to these problems or disunities, and any detailed NL analysis of the concrete possibilities of these various alliances was lacking.

The belief in the poor as allies in change, if not its sole agents, came from participation in SNCC's joint southern projects and Harrington's book *The Other America*,[14] but was soon taken up by the SDS leadership.

The suggestion that the NL organize the poor communities of the

North, also came from blacks as far apart as Bayard Rustin and Stokeley Carmichael: Rustin had encouraged the shift of focus from protest demonstrations to coalitions of the poor and the organization of the poor white communities; and Carmichael was actually instrumental in moving white organizers out of the southern movement. From the outset it was not the working class but disaffected middle-class youth who became the only possible ally of this inter-racial constituency, but in such a relationship with the poor (as with that between whites and blacks) the question was soon raised: could 'the oppressor', or at least renegades from the oppressor group, be a source of liberation for the oppressed?

Thus the concentration of the various organizing projects in America, and even Britain, was on groups often marginal to the working-class community; the poor, the welfare recipients, the elderly, claimants, the unemployed, the young and ethnic minorities, even tenants – rarely specifically industrial workers. The Dutch movement explicitly appealed *not* to the working class, but to the 'provotariat', the lumpen riff-raff and revolutionary youth; they repeated Bakunin's call to 'all the oppressed' to resist wherever possible.

Marcuse, too, contrasted the mass base of the traditional working class[15] with the 'local and regional political action against specific grievances – riots, ghetto rebellions and so on; certainly mass movements'. The sum total of such projects was closer to activation of the lumpen-proletariat and the unemployed, than any kind of stimulation of an organized working-class constituency. Even in England where the preoccupation with Marxian analysis and remedies was typically stronger, and where some community organizers employed a class-rhetoric (some were also later members of socialist sect-groups), the focus was predominantly the same, although nothing could have been further from orthodox Marxism.

A black proletariat?

The growing identification with black people in America as a major internal agency of change was partly engendered by those in the Old, white Left who were prepared, in their growing disillusion with the white working class, to turn to black people as a surrogate proletariat.

Black people, less than half of the thirty to fifty million 'invisible poor',[16] were nevertheless seen as the group most likely to engage in concerted class action. Marx, after all, had perceived that one element in a class may focalize itself in consciousness and struggle – possibly on the basis of occupation (in trade union organization) or on the basis of race. Certainly he had predicted that ethnic-racial conflicts might prevent, as in the USA, the crystallization of ordinary class struggle. Despite organizing attempts, a class opposition which united the proletariat across racial lines had never really existed – Negroes always, and often other minorities also, were isolated: excluded from most unions, they were a discriminated minority in others.[17] Economically, Negro trade unions and cooperatives, black-strikes, boycotts and trade competition had never operated as an autonomous, independent sanction of any great strength. The idea that Negro business enterprise or syndicalist initiative could develop power in the ghettoes maintained some element of credibility in peaceful economic competition with the white majority. But the white exclusiveness of trade unions began to provoke the entirely predictable recrudescence of black labour unionism, including the militant Dodge Revolutionary Union Movement (DRUM) in Detroit.

As has been seen black struggles had already indicated that they too could be co-opted; twenty million black Americans might be the single most powerful potential agency of change, yet their acute needs, their ghettoization, and the history of their exploitation, made them also peculiarly vulnerable. Black culture – the black community – was not essentially geared to political action; in some ways both the civil rights upsurge, as well as ghetto riots, were misleading as political indicators.

One NL hope was that in black culture there could emerge a structural alternative to American capitalism; but in so far as this culture was shaped by exclusion and oppression, it was unlikely that these hopes could be met, beyond an aspiration to local control and the injection of a quality of simple spontaneity into living.[18] Plantation legacies of ritualism and deference, the hyper-conformism of the black bourgeoisie, the escapism of drugs and black youth culture,[19] even the retreatism of the Muslims, did not encourage positive attitudes to radical political action. Ghetto culture was, if not a-political, pseudo-political.

Carmichael's lack of confidence in the ability of black people to survive alliance with whites without being 'absorbed and betrayed', is grounded in a fundamental suspicion that they may lack the dynamism to lead an attempt to transform America, and should settle for something less. Hayden also admitted that the ghetto was a slough of conservatism and stagnation even after the start of the Newark project. It confirmed that most negroes desired the comfort and security which white people possessed, that there was little revolutionary consciousness – even less readiness for violence.

If rising colour consciousness produced greater group solidarity and strength, was this merely a tactic strengthening an ultimately *integrationist* bargaining position (the pluralist view of integrative and functional conflict)?[20] Was it a mode of transforming society, culturally as well as politically, through alliances; or was it an attempt at some essentially separatist solution? At first it looked as if Carmichael accepted the pluralist view of ethnic groups, 'buying into' the system on its own terms through its group strength, but *what* terms these could be economically, or culturally, was not clear.[21]

It would be incorrect to simply contrast the 'dropping out' of middle-class youth with the 'opting-in' of blacks and workers; but by social definition and institutionalized prejudice and by discrimination in the economic sphere, the Negro clearly exists as an 'interest group'. The direction of this 'interest' is less clear 'objectively' than 'subjectively', and the directives of Negro strategy, the problem of 'assimilation' *versus* 'organization' as a conflict group, relate directly to economic advances within the framework of capitalism; why and 'when is it that mobility is desired more strongly within a given prestige order than alteration of the prestige order itself?'[22]

The demands of the civil rights movement were essentially classless; they emphasized the needs of a *black* community, though without necessarily stressing race-pride and identity. Advancement as a group – human rights, dignity, equal economic, social and political opportunity, and integrated institutions – these were the mass concerns of the movement. Some, like Rustin, believed that these demands could not be satisfied within the framework of existing political and economic relations, and were therefore radical (e.g. in expanding the public sector dramatically). From an NL standpoint, however, that in itself was not as revolutionary as Rustin might maintain. The tendency towards a statist organization of capitalism made such change more and more compatible with only marginal modifications in social and political power.

With a median income only somewhat over 50 per cent of that of white workers, blacks were faced by a situation which still admits of enough upward mobility to encourage a feeling of deprivation, whilst not enough to raise the condition of the mass of Negroes for decades. In any case, the primary concerns of Negroes appeared to be neither middle-class values nor individual mobility and acquisition, but with community, class and racial consciousness, new dimensions of an emerging 'group' feeling; 'class' as a dimension of blackness was first re-introduced in response to the hypocrisy of integrationist liberalism which proclaimed 'class doesn't matter – we're all brothers now' in the face of gross inequality. But this was still 'class' without a socialist vision; a pure 'interest' formation without a 'collectivist' end.

Black power offered instead the hope of group solidarity as an essential precondition of power. Whether the ultimate vision was separatist or integrationist, only communal organization could offer the position of strength to achieve it. It was not only the 'lack of a matured social vision' (which Lasch and other critics deplored), but the lack of any real renewal of social organization, that was ultimately to give the Black Power slogan its hollow ring.

Thus, although racial divisions were increasingly salient in the 1950s and 1960s, reflecting the growing ambiguity of other social divisions of a pure class kind, they were not easily the basis for organizing change. The defining factors dividing white from black become reasons, or occasions, for continued exploitation. As social mobility creates a declining clarity of social division at the middle levels of society, 'race' or 'colour' becomes a defining characteristic of a massive lower class. This social definition, historically derived, was both the basis for economic subordination and in turn reinforced by it.[23] It laid the basis for something which the NL, not altogether inaccurately, described as 'internal-colonialism'; the economic oppression of minorities within America itself.

Perhaps an essential characteristic of modern economies is the manipulation of depressed and distinctive ethnic and racial sub-groups, who have inevitably filled the lowest paid and regarded jobs in the prestige order, and been regularly unemployed and easily transported to new industries; they have been described as the modern, mobile 'lumpen-proletariat'. Most industrial countries in the past decades have shown a vast mobility of labour, and racial distinctions have a bureaucratic usefulness in isolating the mobile segment. Few of these workers are unionized or politically or communally organized, their atomized family life enables easy transfer, the influx of cheap labour keeps wages and prices down; governments have subsidized this influx, cutting off the supply when the labour market was satiated. Moreover, the regular infusions of migrant unskilled labour provide elasticity in the labour market and relative full employment and upward mobility for the dominant racial group. The waves of immigrants starting at the bottom of the prestige order in the USA have often performed this function. Unlike black people, most of these groups had achieved integration and a more elevated status. The hope, shared by both liberals and SDS, of an inter-racial movement of the poor, was thus faced by a range of groups not only disorganized and depressed in themselves, but split by racial enmity (as were Puerto Ricans and Negroes in New York). The common long-run economic interests of Puerto Ricans, Chicanos, blacks and even poor whites, might be the same 'objectively', but until the 'Poor People's Coalition' of 1967–8, there was little sign of a breakthrough into joint action.

The most problematic alliance of all was between the poor blacks and the poor whites. The position of the poor white was a conundrum for the NL analyst. With increased Negro urban migration, the competitiveness of an increasingly bourgeoisified and united white working class against any influx of black workers, was intensified. Amongst the unemployed and 'lumpen' whites (many of them urban immigrants themselves), resentments ran even deeper. Most white working people saw themselves as having more in common with white poor and white middle class than with black workers, awkwardly situated between the 'lumpen' whites and skilled white workers.[24] For poor whites, though united with many Negroes by economic depression and a 'culture of poverty', the social distance from blacks remained immense; their racial self-definition seemed to be decisive.

EID

A new class: 'Students as niggers'

A quite different perspective on the agency of radical change emerged in the second half of the 1960s that was in deep tension with the strategy of organizing either the poor, or black people, or the 'working class'.[25] Students had constantly organized other social groups, but rarely themselves. Often university struggles had little directly to do with students as students. Yet suddenly the proposition was put forward that 'no individual, no groups, no class is genuinely engaged in a revolutionary struggle unless their struggle is for their *own* liberation.'[26] The message of student syndicalism was a novel one: 'organize yourselves'. Hitherto radical students had mostly been involved in ventures that had gone out to organize other constituencies. Now they were told that liberation began at home. Everywhere the students, Rudd, the Columbia leader wrote, wanted to 'fight back against the oppression of the blacks, Vietnamese and *themselves*' – students had to 'move for their own liberation as well as others'.[27]

A number of NL spokesmen elaborated this same theme: black power was clearly intended to say to white civil rights workers 'get out!', 'go and organize your own racist, violent and exploitative caucasian community'. As one white radical, an SDS worker, remarked, 'That's much more difficult, and Marxists among you don't want to organise the middle classes.' In fact the very term 'middle class' had become almost redundant in the new perspectives on post-capitalist stratification and as the traditional productive class dwindled.

Counter-posing it to Progressive Labor's revival of traditional labour metaphysics, Greg Calvert, Carl Davidson, Dave Gilbert, Carol Nieman and others, developed a theory of a 'New Working Class'.[28] College-trained workers, such as professionals and those who had sustained the growth of the NL, were perceived as crucial to the system. There was no need to fight other people's battles, 'your own are more important personally and politically'. The failure to do this, Carl Oglesby blamed on the NL's late discovery of its own oppression. Moreover, both he and Weinstein argued that the further the NL moved away from its own constituency, the greater the danger of engaging in the 'politics of guilt and self-repudiation' (Weinstein) in which concern with other people's welfare would predominate: the further away the group, the more problematic for the future of the NL, and the greater likelihood of the projection of desires and anxieties on to them. Davidson and Calvert were both concerned in developing the organization of students and the 'class' which emerged from universities, and thus stressed the need for an experiential consciousness of oppression by the revolutionaries themselves, rather than projecting this oppression on to others, or organizing revolutionary action only in terms of others.

But slogans which implied that the NL was getting others to act on its own behalf in the Third World or the ghettoes, or that its own action was on others' behalf, was usually a self-conscious half-truth, at times sheer impasto or pretence.[29] It gave credibility and drama to what was essentially a personalist and generational revolt, though it could easily rationalize such revolt in familiar categories of agency and change. The Free Speech Movement, and a number of other student revolts, were clearly substantially self-orientated; and an unmasking of the self-delusion which portrayed them as something else explains some of the introversion which followed this growing awareness after 1969.

These emphases led to one of the major splits in orientation in SDS between those who (even before 1966) argued that organizing should focus on the immediate student constituency and those who emphasized community or anti-war work, off-campus. Davidson and Calvert's 'student syndicalism' – building a radical movement with mass-support in the universities – had developed in contradistinction to the idea of mobilizing minorities in the South, in the ghettoes and in the communities. The 'new working class' is a term which sometimes comprehends, and sometimes overlaps with, these two other concepts of agency: 'youth as a class' and 'students as a class'. It is certainly from the latter that the more general concept first stems.[30] The quest for levers of change included the universities: these represented contexts in which many in SDS saw new possibilities for organizing by radical intellectuals, in addition to anti-war movements or civil rights. But even if the whole of the potential constituencies of blacks, students and disaffected radicals from other groups, were mobilized, it would constitute less than 15 per cent of the total population in America – and would represent a group which lacked the ability to paralyse the economy at the point of production. This power lay now in the hands not of blacks, the poor, students, women, radical pacifists, or the intelligentsia, but rather in the ranks of the middle aged and middle class.

Fear of economic collapse, exhaustion from the experiences of the 1930s and 1940s, the need for escape and leisure, the seductions of consumption, and the unthinkable nature of nuclear war, made this constituency the very last likely to engage in radical action. It was upon its conservatism and quiescence that the successful control of managerialism was dependent. Adjusting to this 'fact of social life', others opted back into the structure, to work with groups like 'Movement for a Democratic Society', or 'Radicals in the Professions'.

Mills himself had been under no illusion about the possibilities of challenging such a system. Even the universities, where his best hope, the intelligentsia, was mainly situated, were deeply incorporated into the military-industrial structure. Mills saw new sociological work as a major task for the radical intellect, because it might prove a possible means to influence and understand such power, if not to possess it.[31]

Mills's intellectual élitism was a response to his pessimism and his isolation from any political movement. Yet ironically, Mills helped to create the movement he had despaired of; having written off the disorganized poor, the co-opted blacks and working-class leadership, the accommodated unions and the middle class dominated by consumerism and bureaucratism, his continued search for the 'insurgent impulse' wherever it could be found, led usually back to the radical young and the activist students. By the early 1960s, they had already taken a leading part in European peace movements; students also played a continuing role in internal change (such as the overthrow of Menderes in Turkey, and Synghman Rhee in Korea) and after 1960, their role in Japan and Latin America became a constant echo of actions taken in North America and Europe. US college students also made up the bulk of the early civil rights demonstrations, some from white northern, but mostly from black southern, universities.[32]

The new working-class concept developed in America out of the notion of students *as a class*, partly because they had become significant potentially, in terms of numbers, by the 1960s in America. The seven million full-time college students (in 1968 3 per cent of the population)[33] included an estimated quarter of a million who were active politically. They were gaining a sense of being part of a larger transnational collectivity. Students now viewed themselves as a sort of unwilling proletariat, lacking control of meaningful everyday decisions or situations which affected them. The FSM was like a first peasant jacquerie against feudalism signalling decades of conflict. The university was changing everywhere; it was also growing. The enormous expansion of the student populations of the world was most marked in America, but there were now a million full-time students in Japan, half a million in France and 400,000 in Germany. As in America, the student revolts everywhere reflected the standardization and formalism of this mass higher-education, geared to late industrial society's hunger for specialized personnel.

The series of actions at Berkeley, especially the 1966 strike, had proved the strength of the student base. These actions were the most radical, the most serious, and the most dedicated to the realization of student power, that had yet taken place on any American campus.

About 50 per cent of all American eighteen- to twenty-one-year-olds were in college or university by 1970,[34] and it was from this constituency that many argued a 'new class' could emerge. Yet clearly students themselves were not a 'class' in any traditional sense. Although they might feel common interests and a subcultural identity and, indeed, a common *objective* status and role, these were all essentially transient.[35] Their relationship as students to the means of material production was tenuous, and by this criteria they were a parasitic 'class'. Yet, it was argued, in post-scarcity economics, such a Marxian criterion is unsatisfactory; they are really apprentices in a scheme of ideas-and-services production. Materially better off than the 'free poor' (like the eunuch or the house-slave), the student is pampered yet dependent and impotent; this paradox generates many of the tensions of the student position, and in turn stimulates attempts to humanize the situation.

How could seven million students, mostly white, mostly middle class, ever be a class in themselves? Student culture, despite the enormous impact of the NL as a movement, was by no means solidary. External ties, training differentiation, seniority, size of student community, living situations, and finally sex and race, were all factors that could cut across the solidarity of students. As in the development of all classes, occupational and interest differentiation will be the most stubborn obstacle to the development of communal identity. Engineers versus humanities students, those whose first priority is exam-taking against those whose objective is the humanization of the university environment, is paralleled by the opposition between craft and industrial unionism, between different racial groups, between the individual striver and the collective solidarist, which has characterized the history of classes in modern societies.

On behalf of the concept of a student class, it could be argued that this student interlude was at least a time of maximum volatility when the purchase of society was less strong. But for all this, the likelihood that students could organize effectively on a national scale as a political force, was small.

Perhaps the most telling opposition to the use of the class label for the student community came from those who stressed the evanescent quality of the status. Even if a majority of twenty million high-school leavers in the USA went through university, it remained an interim time for most of them; rarely lasting more than four years, the stakes in it are not that high.[36] It is significant that graduate students played a leading role both in spearheading student revolts and in developing the NL. Like the medieval apprentice, only free within the confines of a unilinear process of elevation according to strict rules, graduates are often moving from apprentices to the 'system' (the state), to apprenticeship of a 'guild' of the higher socializing instruments of that system (the university faculty). They have to reproduce the pattern already imposed on them; they are the intellectual journeymen who lead revolts of the apprentices against the entrenched power of the guildmasters, except that in this case the guildmasters themselves are intermediary agents of power and authority – their own being more apparent than real when system needs and assumptions are opposed or thwarted.[37] At this point, even some of the guildmasters begin to side with rebellious apprentices and journeymen against external regulation.

The other elaboration of the theory was in terms of 'youth as a class'. Somewhat distinct from the 'new working class' and 'student syndicalist' positions, and indeed from the 'counter-culture' strategy, this was at base a generationalist theory, and emphasized the polarization of youth from the larger society; 'no-one over thirty was to be trusted'.[38]

Vietnam was depicted as a war advocated and planned by one generation, and fought largely by another; America over thirty was held to be unreformable;[39] and the idea of youth as a class was often made compatible with an import of change into America through the revolutions sustained by Third World guerilla armies.

In summary, the new working-class theory focused on those who had graduated, and those who had yet to graduate, from universities. As the NL leaders themselves moved outside the university orbit, they stressed new needs, new objectives and new possibilities transcending industrial society; and it was arguable still that theirs was a class which had no more *actual* control over its work, its means of production, what was to be produced and how, than the traditional working class, even if its potential *sanctions* were growing.

Neither Mills nor Marcuse were initially impressed by such theories, whether focused on white-collar workers, the college educated or the technocratically trained.[40] But by the later 1960s, with an increasing movement stress on 'radicals in the professions', even Marcuse had modified his view:

new working class simply comprehends and anticipates tendencies that are going on before our own eyes in the material process of production in capitalism, namely that more and more highly qualified salaried employees, technicians, specialists, and so on, occupy a decisive position in the material process of production.[41]

The fact was that the university was not only becoming a central institution, but its personnel were increasingly dominated by graduates and researchers. Their sanctions, too, had moved from petty threats to a genuine challenge to societal functions (e.g. defence) as the 'ownership' of ideas-production itself became an issue.

Again the question of alliances arose; some identity with working-class youth or youth in general was intimated. A student-worker alliance was mooted (and in Europe was taken seriously). Oglesby suggested that a 'new class' would *seek* such an alliance, just as the proletariat in early industrialism sought alliances with the liberal bourgeoisie. Others suggested that just as the historic bourgeoisie had used the proletariat as its shock troops, drawing it into conflict despite itself, it was possible that the students might be similarly exploited by industrial workers (and May 1968 in France suggested something of this). The student/worker alliance appeared likely to be highly one-sided, the former supporting union demands and strike actions as well as working-class socialism, with little to show in return.[42]

In SDS itself, the new working-class theory always had other contenders for theoretical primacy; some Marxists, especially PL, still emphasized the traditional working class. On occasions, Rudd referred to a 'working class' also. For others, the idea of a 'youth class', coming to be more closely identified with the counter-culture, was seen as an alternative to any idea of a 'new' working class. Fairly typical of NL approaches was Rudd's eclectic view of agency:

any revolutionary programme must fight in the interests of the most oppressed – the blacks and the Vietnamese – as well as in the interests of the working class.[43]

The fact that no consistent view of class came to dominate the NL was not least due to the increasing influence of Marcuse[44] as his revised version of class, itself a highly selective interpretation of movement ideas and forces, gained attention.

6. Black Movements in Crisis

Blackness and integration

The Civil Rights Movement, even its most militant offspring, had been southern based, whilst its northern allies had been largely middle-class and white. But by the 1960s, the Negro no longer lived predominantly in the rural South. Seventy-five per cent of all black people lived in towns and cities; and the deepest resentment and hostility existed in the ghettoes of the urban North. The appalling living environments of many American black people existed in strong contrast to the lilywhite suburbs. These latter, although they had never been attacked physically by black groups, remained a constant goad to black militants who threatened to turn them into 'shooting galleries' (Cleaver).

It was here in the cities that the diffuse frustration and social disorganization reached its zenith in the riots of Los Angeles (Watts) in 1965 and the following years. Only the most militant rhetoric could match this anger in its own terms: the speeches of Malcolm-X or Bill Epton, Baldwin's *Blues for Mr Charlie* and LeRoi Jones's *Dutchman* echoed rather than created the frenzy. But the reinforcement of race pride was the essential ingredient added by the political slogan of 'black power'.

Of all the groups involved in the NL, the most self-conscious in their trans-nationalism were those who saw themselves as part of a new and separate black subculture; only with the growth of negritude, a pride in being black, did such cultural forms become assertive.[1] Increasingly aware of their own Afro-American heritage of slavery and beyond, and identifying with the upsurge of African independence, the black movement in the USA was psychologically dependent on this sense of trans-national belongingness. There was a growing understanding that to some extent the clash in America – the subordination of black and coloured groups – reproduced in microcosm a world-wide hegemony of white over coloured peoples.

The later 1950s and 1960s are punctuated by trips of black leaders to Africa; Muslims, including Malcolm-X, civil rights leaders, and later

Stokeley Carmichael who turned this into a world tour, intended to stimulate black power movements elsewhere. Other Black Power leaders went to Cuba, to Algeria and other black states; some went as political émigrés. Links were forged with ex-slave cultures and black movements in the Caribbean and Latin America.[2] As many African leaders in turn came to the UN, the impact of the new states through UN delegations in New York reinforced this black trans-national link, which became one of the strongest and most concrete links between the Movement and the Third World, especially Africa and the West Indies. Though the diaspora of blackness had few states which could encapsulate with clarity its dreams and strivings,[3] the models of Africa's autonomous states created a new conceptual world for black Americans as for black Africans.

Black intellectuals, Fanon in France, writers and playwrights in New York, sharpened a racial ideology; the speeches of Malcolm-X, the novels of Baldwin, the theatre of LeRoi Jones, emphasized a bitter, aggressive blackness. Previously, Black Nationalism had been merely the most primitive political expression of this mood,[4] but the separatist instinct was never far from black rhetoric and programmes in the 1960s, or from the projections of 'black power'. In its extreme form, arguing for separate armed defence, and communal separatism, it urged non-cooperation with tax-paying and the draft. As early as 1964, a survey found one in five black Americans saying they might not 'fight for white America'. Operating mainly at the level of 'myth' this black trans-nationalism was highly plural and eclectic; the 'nation of Islam', 'Afro-Americanism', 'Pan-Africanism', the cultural nationalism of 'black power' and black-separatism, were all included under the same umbrella. Yet it is perhaps significant that this global consciousness was expressed against white power wherever it was, rather than just Western capitalistic forms of racism: since there were rumblings of discrimination on the basis of colour in 'socialist' Cuba, black power advocates were generally happier in identifying with *non*-white Marxisms, such as Asian or African versions, than those which might have a white, and racist, complexion (e.g. Russian).

But what of the rest of the Negro community? Whilst most black people tacitly supported the NAACP and King,[5] frustration and disillusion divided them. Early splits were mostly about ultimate ends and degree of cooperation with the white community, rather than about methods. Various attempts to create an umbrella organization resulted in low common-denominator programmes, and tended to increase frustration and tension, especially with the systematic subversion of the Civil Rights Act in the South after 1964. SNCC quickly perceived the problems of the existing movement, its deference both to whites and its own middle-class leadership, its ambivalence about blackness, expressed in the desire for integration, and its dependency on federal intervention, official protection, and state legislation.

Although this was to be seen as the movement's heroic period, nevertheless deep latent tensions existed in the early 1960s, producing divisions in the leadership, basically over strategies; not least it was an inter-generational dissension, between the youthful, rebellious and innovative CORE and SNCC, and the often ritualist, conformist Urban League and NAACP.[6] The militants tended to move the moderates several degrees towards more radical and more militant interventions – as the Birmingham, Alabama, campaign suggested in 1963. But this was also due to the fear of some of the mainstream leaders that otherwise they would be outflanked by the young activists. The continued orientation of NAACP and the Southern Christian Leadership Conference (SCLC) towards traditional forms of authority in the black community set it against the youthful egalitarianism and participatory democracy of SNCC; the more reformist groups like Urban League and NAACP never came fully to terms with civil disobedience – the former never abandoning legalism – and the NAACP only slowly accepted a role for direct action. SNCC on the other hand, like CORE, was formed around the idea of civil disobedience.

Even the role of religion as a uniting factor soon began to decline; SNCC, which had initially shared the religious basis of the southern movement, began to reject the respectability and reformism that they associated with the leadership of King, SCLC, and the southern ministry, whose authority in the black community rested on its links with the churches. This leadership, in turn, forming alliances with Uncle Tom elements and white liberal politicians, seemed basically prepared to accept a continuing white leadership role. On the other hand, Negro churches continued to play an important part as a focus for community and political organization (remaining a starting point for many civil rights marches and meetings).

In the north, however, where both church and community organization were weak, none of the civil rights groups – Urban League, NAACP or CORE – all active in the urban ghettoes, were able to gain any sort of stable loyal following. Where groups *were* formed, they tended to be both maverick and militant. Far stronger were the ritualist-retreatist groups such as the militantly nationalistic Black Muslims.[7] CORE and SNCC leaders later shared platforms with Malcolm-X, but also could gain no northern base, even after 1965.

By 1963, SNCC and CORE had already started pushing a radical or revolutionary position without yet abandoning nonviolence; socialism versus capitalism; direct action versus legalism and reformism; black consciousness against assimilationism and white leadership; local organizing against federal pressure; a new youthful leadership against the traditional, religious-oriented authority structure of the black communities – the transition to militancy was underway.

For a variety of reasons, the civil rights movement in its first phase had tended to take a liberal view of race – that it had 'no reality' – that it was distinction born of prejudice alone – thus to deny its existence. In so doing, any race pride was denied, cultural nationalism was muted, and pluralist integration was easily confused with black self-effacement; 'integration into a burning house', as Baldwin put it, was on white terms; an ethnocentric adaptation to dominant white Anglo-Saxon Protestant (WASP) norms, language and culture, its work ethic and its nuclear, father-centred family.

None of the various Negro organizations, from the Black Muslims at one end of the spectrum to the NAACP and Urban League at the other, were fundamentally assimilationist. But they varied considerably in their attitudes to 'blackness'. In the mid-1960s the positions of both integrationists and segregationists hardened, and as black awareness increased, it was met by a white conservative reaction. The cultural gap between the communities was widening too, and with it the lines of political division crystallized; such attitude changes first became noticeable and pronounced in the black movement between 1964 and 1966, and were the prelude to a major alteration of course.

Black Power and the grassroots

Whatever meaning was given to it, 'integration' by 1965 was coming to be seen as a cultural and political distraction; despite the dangers posed by polarization, the possible isolation of the black community and the dangers of exacerbating the white racist reaction, many outside SNCC had come to the conclusion that it was time for communal self-assertion and political and economic control in the ghettoes, aligned to a sense of black pride.

As the issues polarized in the 1960s, the northern urban movements began increasingly to lean towards the Muslim nationalists and Malcolm-X, as well as hear the voices of the northern black literati – at first especially Baldwin, and then LeRoi Jones. In the South, the long postponed crisis came to a head on the Selma–Montgomery march, and the power struggle became an open one. It was one in which the traditional community-based leadership and its cautious liberal versions of integration and reform, were confronted by a growing identification by a minority of the movement with a NL version of cultural nationalism bordering on separatism, expressed in the cry: 'Black Power!'

During the Meredith march, the new slogan was shouted against the traditional chant of 'freedom', a significant counterpoint in terms of the increasing stress on both power and liberation throughout the NL. Despite the dangers that a phrase like 'Black Power' would be misinterpreted and distorted (as it was), it captured exactly the changing mood and deepening frustration of the militants. The slogan, first widely used in June 1966, when Carmichael defined it as the 'acquisition of economic and political power at the local level' by black people, became the name of a movement when CORE came out openly for a 'Black Power' platform.[8]

But such positive aspects of black power were complicated by the nature of the transition in SNCC and the character and ideas of the man largely responsible for the birth and career of the slogan.[9] Stokeley Carmichael's defeat of John Lewis as chairman of SNCC in spring 1966, meant several things.[10] It implied a success for the Lowndes County Freedom Organization – the first 'Black Panther' party[11] – and Carmichael's successful work with it. It also meant the beginning of the end for nonviolence in SNCC; John Lewis stood firmly for nonviolence, whereas Carmichael was equivocal over 'self-defence' of the black community. It also meant the stress on an 'all black' organization (like the Alabama ticket) and the move towards exclusion of whites.[12]

The election of Stokeley Carmichael as chairman of SNCC, and the launching of the slogan of 'Black Power', was greeted in the liberal and establishment press with a universal hostility. Misrepresentation came even before definition, when it was labelled as 'racism in reverse', 'extremism' and a 'new tyranny'.

Yet despite such reactions, with a shift of the focus of the black movement from rural South to the urban North,[13] both psychologically and tactically, the notion of Negro control of the Negro *movement* as well as the Negro *community*, had become probably inevitable. It was the consensus amongst young radicals that for too long, white liberals, Uncle-Tom politicians, token-integrationists and welfare-colonialists had frustrated black aspirations and needs. These, it was felt, had acted as a buffer and a diversion, and had incorporated Negro leadership.

However, as race lines had hardened, white civil rights workers, in ghettoes and rural communities, began also to be identified with the enemy – and 'civil rights' advocates with compromise and paternalism. King, Rustin and Farmer consistently argued for maintenance of contact with the white community, not least to prevent repressive violence, whilst retaining black authority in their own communities. But Carmichael made some telling strategic points in emphasizing that whites should now leave the black movement in order to organize racist white communities. Neither poor whites, nor middle-class whites, had yet been successfully organized as potential allies for a black movement. It was understandable that an emerging Negro identity should demand an all-black leadership and authentic black institutions where it could define its own needs, free of white influence. As Paul Goodman remarked, people have the right of self-definition, they 'have to humanize themselves in their own way'.

But what was inessential was what Goodman terms the growth of 'racial spite'.[14] Carmichael's gratuitous remarks about the 'Pepsi Generation', his assertion that oppressors may not tell the oppressed how to rid themselves of the oppressor, strike a new and sinister note. Carmichael crudely blamed the white freedom volunteers for the fact that a dead white freedom worker was priced higher by the press than a black one. It was clearly not the whites' fault that the press betrayed this undoubtedly racist bias, but Carmichael captured the widespread and understandable, but essentially irrational, resentment against them.

The 800 or more volunteers (mostly white) and the white SNCC staff workers were a generation who had responded to SNCC's call in the first place; experienced its murderous suffering and humiliation and 'come alive' in the compassion and nonviolence of the black community and its culture. These jibes, however, now forced them to prove themselves yet again and in a new context; it played upon their guilt as whites, a factor which was to have profound consequences for the larger movement, and the subsequent relation between 'Black Power' and the NL and the ultimate crisis of both.

The launching of the 'Black Power' slogan, amidst all the bravura of media presentation and charismatic appeal, confirmed the *élitist* tone of an ostensibly 'participatory' strategy. This was illustrated by the manipulative methods of some SNCC members on the Meredith March through Mississippi, or the cult of personality that had characterized the Berkeley black power jamboree.[15]

Ironically, SNCC's move to 'Black Power' had begun with an attack at Atlantic City on mainstream American liberalism, especially the top-down style of manipulation by leaders; yet in the ensuing months Carmichael's prima-donna performances and his refusal to define, or even engage in dialogue with black critics, all augured ill for popular control, let alone Movement control of Black Power. Indeed those who had initially identified Black Power with popular control and participatory democracy in the ghettoes, were soon given cause for second thoughts.

Evasive about strategy, only the rejection of nonviolence came across clearly in Carmichael's rhetoric. Refusing to define the label for white audiences 'because they were white', to black audiences he talked about 'identity'. The reticence to clarify was perhaps a necessary part of the mystique of the slogan, and the ambiguities, the contradictions, the lack of concreteness, were perhaps neither all 'hustle', nor all accident. The attempt to maintain a suitably vague aura around the term, served a double purpose; it allowed various trial balloons to be sent up in terms of alliances, and it could be seen also as a political 'myth' or bluff, to test white (and black) reactions. Carmichael refused to show his hand, partly because he was a politician (and believed politicians had to be opportunists) and thus kept open both a Black Nationalist and an 'integrationist' strategy. Without any organizing, such bluffs might bring concessions. Moreover, it could genuinely give people in the ghettoes the chance to define 'Black Power' for themselves. Above all it could give time for the myth to prove itself as an organizing device (the argument made by SNCC staff at the time).

But no evidence accrued that it was resulting in any new surge of organizing in the ghetto. In fact, after the inception of Black Power, SNCC declined just as fast as Carmichael's personal prestige rose. The exhaustion of initial organizing tactics, the attempt to make SNCC a more bureaucratized, centralized organization, as well as the exaggerated fear of co-optation which had driven Lewis out of the leadership – all contributed to the growing internal crisis. Predictably, most of SNCC's sources of funds, both black and white, began to dry up, and it was forced to turn elsewhere, including abroad, for support; Carmichael's substantial speaking fees became a significant part of SNCC's budget.

The tension between blacks and whites, between black nationalists and others, between Southern veterans and students from the North, was accompanied by a new influx of angry young black people, many of the unemployed, who attached themselves in the South, as in the North, to projects and demonstrations. These were to be the shock-troops of the future, but they drove SNCC in directions that it had neither contemplated nor discussed, and whilst both Moses and Carmichael sympathized with the 'young bloods', the newcomers created the paradox of chaos in an organization that was trying to organize more efficiently.

'Black Power' never proved itself a successful organizing device; from a 1964 high-point, when issues of race, poverty and war were being broadly discussed and linked, SNCC, under Carmichael and the 'Black Power' label, went into a precipitate decline.

Most of the old leadership of SNCC stepped down in 1966; not only Charlie Cobb, Ivanhoe Donaldson and John Lewis, but the more militant James Foreman also: internal decline is reflected also in the drop in the number of full-time (paid) organizers, from 200 in 1964 to 120 in the winter of 1966, and to about half that number the following year.[16] When one remembers that, with unpaid organizers, Moses and Lewis and Foreman had had about 1,200 field-workers in 1964, the degree of collapse becomes manifest. Indeed, the Lowndes County Freedom Organization's election of November 1966 in effect marks the virtual end of the *mass* movement in the South.

By 1967, the Black Power movement was no longer a continuation of the Civil Rights Movement, nor even a successor to it. It was a *new* movement with a largely new leadership and social base, developing in different locations from the old movement, mainly in those cities where the Civil Rights Movement had been weakest, and chiefly in the North. It had already touched raw nerves in the northern communities: even those liberals hitherto sympathetic to southern protest were caught out, and embarrassed, when the campaigns came nearer home.

'A slice of Whitey's pie'

It has been argued that the development of a strategy of Black Power was an almost necessary outcome of the tendencies and strains within the civil rights movement.[17] Yet the version of black power which became predominant was *not* inevitable: it owes a great deal to one figure – Carmichael – and is the version which started the development of the black movement away from both the civil rights tradition *and* the NL as it had formed up to 1966.

Stokeley Carmichael's profoundly conservative view of power and violence made it difficult to develop any alternative *vision* for the black movement to underpin a slogan of 'Black Power'. Whilst maintaining the rejection of any 'seizure of power' strategy, Carmichael introduced a more primitive notion of power into movement debate, and one that could easily capitulate to narrowly chauvinist or nationalist or simply reactionary interpretation. As he was later to admit (in 1969), 'Changing powers is not a revolution'; that power must emanate from and express 'a community'. But Carmichael was less explicit on how to build that community. In Cruse's view, the fundamental weakness of black power was its apolitical nature and its inability to create viable political organizations based in the community.[18]

Despite Carmichael's recognition that black power would reinforce black pride and identity in a political fashion (as Negro literature did not do), he still failed to answer Baldwin's ultimate question about 'integrating into a burning house'. The new 'political project' of the young black militants was, in Roszak's view, so narrowly defined in ethnic terms that despite its urgency it had become as culturally old fashioned as the nationalist mythopeosis,[19] which led to some deeply contradictory attitudes to existing black institutions in America. Like Fanon, Carmichael called for a sweeping away of white Western institutions and culture:

When you talk of black power you talk of bringing the country to its knees, of building a movement that will smash everything Western civilization has created (1966).

Yet an element of manipulation or confidence-trick has been detected in such claims; it has been argued that hustling is the inversion of US status-striving and acquisitiveness. Carmichael's version of 'Black Power', with its inbuilt lack of clarity, has something of the bluff or hustle about it, yet in it, too, there seems to be a reflection of that jostling for position and power seeking that is central to American culture. As one critic remarks, 'point by point, his is an upside down version of the most genteel, middle class, liberal position'. Everything is explained in terms of the authority of white people, in terms of white skin rather than in terms of the control of violence and wealth.[20]

'For racism to die', Carmichael wrote, 'a totally different American must be born.' Yet Carmichael gave few clues as to what that difference might be. Throughout the contradictions and ambiguities of the slogan's career, it was hard for critics to tie the concept to a particular political ideal or perspective. Indeed, despite the occasional lulling reference amidst Carmichael's rhetoric to the 'spirit of community', the 'co-operative concept' and 'humanistic love', the dominant tone sounded to many critics like an echo of white power. His speeches gave the impression of an attempt at public 'tough-mindedness', or an expression of black virility. 'We had to work for power because this country does not function by morality, love and nonviolence, but by power.' Yet how, critics asked, can one 'bargain from strength' about concepts like 'humanistic love' or 'cooperation'? Were immorality, hate and violence (i.e. power in practice as societally defined), indeed the better method either to transform America,[21] or even to join it?

'Black Power', the leaders answered, was the power not to have to define itself. If indeed such power came to be little more than a mirror-image of white power – racist, élitist, jingoist and violent – that was a harsh judgment on it. But 'no-one ever *talked* about white power', Carmichael replied, 'because power in America is white'; yet, he also argued, that same power was exploitative, authoritarian, cruel and corrupt – as well as almost totally male. If Carmichael knew all this, his critics asked, what went wrong?

Perhaps the answer lies in relation to two major variables; on the one hand, to the question of economistic interests – getting a bigger slice of 'Whitey's pie' – on the other to black culture and institutions as they had developed since emancipation.

Even before Black Power, Negro movements had made such demands as local control of local businesses – either under black capitalist or cooperative control. These now included those jobs involved in non-economic black demands – such as control of police, or schools – where jobs in these sectors might still mainly be occupied by whites. Muslim strategy suggested an alternative perspective; construction of a black separatist economy based on institutions created to serve its own community.

Already there had been substantially increased attempts to move towards cooperative Negro enterprises. Wresting of control over Negro magazines and radio stations from white or 'Uncle Tom' hands had taken place, together with the use of boycott, sabotage, phone-ins and sit-ins to extend black control. Demands of 'Black Power' leaders in 1966–7 included black-controlled PTAs in the urban areas, dispossession of ghetto-exploiting tradesmen, and pressure against slumlords through tenant action.

There was also a growing attempt to take over government-aid programmes in the ghettoes, precipitated by attacks on welfare paternalism and internal colonialism. These culminated in ambitious attempts to incorporate separatist black communities (such as Watts) detached from white cities, with autonomous black institutions. All these developments were occurring without 'Black Power' and it is not at all clear whether either Carmichael, or the slogan's career, particularly assisted or strengthened that vision.

The other component, implied at least in SNCC's early usage, was the idea of popular participation and control at the local level, 'the coming together of black people to elect representatives and to force those representatives to speak to their needs' (Carmichael). PD had always seemed an intrinsic part of such an alternative vision. But this would need more, not fewer organizers; Oglesby of SDS proposed that SNCC concentrate not on a few charismatic personalities addressing mass meetings or going on whistle-stop tours, but a return to basic organizing at grassroots, with mobile black community organizers of the kind that had defined SNCC in the past: Carmichael repeated that it was not for a member of the oppressor group to give advice, and a role for the renegade white revolutionary did not seem to be one any longer available to NL radicals, even though, it was argued, white guilt might actually aid an understanding of the relationship of power.[22]

Yet despite this antagonism to whites in the movement, his increasing opposition to alliances with whites, his Fanon-like attacks on white civilization, and his adoption of the term 'cultural nationalist', Carmichael's attitudes to both white and black culture were deeply ambiguous. On the one hand he claimed, 'We must stop imitating white society and begin to create for ourselves and our own, and begin to employ our own cultural patterns.' On the other hand, there was no clear grasp of the role of culture in social or political transformation, and the willingness to overplay the role of the white media is significant of this.[23] Even more significant is Carmichael's continual underestimation of the positive value of existing black institutions, such as the negro family.

Influenced by Fanon and the Muslims, he tended instead to look to Africa as a source of models. Missing from all this was any concrete programme that would help ensure that a black mayor of Newark or Detroit would act differently from a white counterpart – become something other than a 'black-faced bureaucrat' or authoritarian, who would call out black police squads to maintain white 'law and order'. The closest Carmichael came to enunciating an alternative was a naive faith in the purity of African political experience: 'The reality of black men ruling their own natives', he wrote, 'gives blacks elsewhere a sense of possibility of power.' But where and how, critics asked? Should black power mean black autocracy and black coercion? And who should be the model of leadership? Tshombe? Mobutu? Nkrumah? (All of whom Carmichael quoted approvingly, yet each was deeply influenced by white rule.)

Like power in proletarian dictatorships, one of the tragedies of power in black Africa had been exactly the failure of post-colonial leaderships to abandon inherited white, bourgeois and colonialist styles and concepts of state authority, including bureaucratic institutions and violent social control.[24] Fanon had recognized that white-trained black police and army officers, party politicians and bureaucrats have, with their neo-colonialist and authoritarian regimes, mimicked white power;

yet this does not seem to matter to Carmichael, because they reveal a willingness to be as tough-minded and as 'virile'[25] as the white 'racists' and 'imperialists' themselves.

At the same time, this approach created some paradoxical attitudes to black-American institutions: despite Carmichael's protestations about integrationism, his position looked at times like a subtle acquiescence in – if not incorporation into – the core assumptions of white American 'civilization' – as an example, he seemed to accept tacitly the notion of a 'cultural lack' in the black community.

For years, assimilationists, liberal social-scientists, like Myrdal, Moynihan and Glazer, had been arguing that the Negro had little or no 'culture', was psychologically and socially deprived and thus inferior; they argued that blacks needed 'achievement motivation', and that to be 'aggressively competitive', the negro needed a strong father-figure, a stable family, and a sense of masculinity.[26] Not once did Carmichael attack such assumptions behind the Negro 'manhood crisis' thesis, or argue the positive values of the existing black community or of the matriarchal family, and of the heroic role of the Negro woman, Negro communalism or black nonviolence which had accompanied it. This contradiction clearly surfaced at the Newark Black Power conference of 1967 where there were both attacks on the traditional matriarchal black family (as a legacy of slavery) and defences of it against 'white sociology', and male chauvinism.

Carmichael's position seemed to deny that already black institutions, black culture, black consciousness in America had itself begun to evolve societal alternatives (even offering these to the outsiders – the 'white Negroes'). Certainly after the Newark conference, black culture and counter-culture began to drift apart;[27] with the increasing stress on machismo and armed violence, and the growth of materialist aspirations in sharp contrast to 'flowerpower', the dissolution of sex-roles, and the rejection of bourgeois consumerism; black militants attacked hippies for occupying urban districts that had previously been black dominated and accused them (without much evidence) of 'driving blacks out' of areas like Haight-Ashbury. These were occasions when key individuals (especially Cleaver, and Leary in his sojourn in Algeria) within the two cultures linked and overlapped. But it was also a period of deepening estrangement: only the Yippees attempted to maintain any bridgehead between them.

Integral to Carmichael's 'realistic' approach to black power at the societal level was an ambivalence about 'Whitey's pie'. In the first place (revealing a superficial internationalism), not too many questions were asked about how the pie was acquired and maintained. Yet this was clearly crucial, if the Afro-American was to build the kind of international alliances that Carmichael planned.

Not least of the factors that divided the black and youth counter-cultures at this point was the excessive commodity fetishism of the black community, already legendary. In the mad scramble for consumer 'durables' (reaching a zenith during the ghetto riots) and in the worship of the automobile, the black man becomes indeed in Myrdal's phrase, 'an exaggerated American'. It seemed that white imperial control was dropping not inconsiderable crumbs from its table – crumbs that most black Americans would be loath to endanger by too serious an alliance with the world's economically oppressed, in Vietnam or anywhere else.

Carmichael did seem also aware that part of the tragedy of integration was the implied assumption that 'white is better' – leading to aspirations to enter the white school and the white neighbourhood, draining skills and talents from the ghetto; he appeared to understand the denial of culture and of identity which this implied,[28] i.e. that negroes both want the same material pie, and to be in the white man's place, 'because that is where a *decent* life can be had'. Yet like other black leaders he rarely chose to ask whether the hopeless cul-de-sac of American middle-class life was really 'decent' – as long as it was free of cockroaches, rats and racial oppression, that, it seemed, was enough.

But white radicals perceived its other indecencies and critics accused them of bemoaning

this desire because they don't want the negro poor integrated into a rotten middle class society, and thereby end up with two cars, barbecue pits and ulcers . . . even more than wrong, those intellectuals seem to me snobbish. For negroes should have just as much right to suburban pleasures as anyone else; but he should be in a position just as much as whites to change the middle class style of life.[29]

A Black Power Movement was caught in an impossible bind, one that could be best termed 'ressentiment'; at the same time it both desired and resented middle-class consumption and affluence; it aspired both to destroy it and to possess it, to smash the technocracy and become its most devoted slave. Assimilation and mobility are thus pitted against negritude, class solidarity and loyalty to Negro culture. Yet internal mobility within the black community is still more permissible – since caste defines class solidarity here – than mobility outside. This fact, which had previously allowed middle class Negroes to assume leadership roles in Negro mass-protest organizations, affirmed that the main unifying factor was race rather than class.

Indeed, any black power of this sort could be bought off by a 'bourgeois' strategy of concession, 'the solution of minimising discontent by increasing the size of the pie';[30] this was only working to a limited extent,[31] but already the guaranteed national annual wage had been a demand of a number of black groups. As Rustin argued: 'though the militant black might be motivated by a thoroughly bourgeois ambition . . . he will end up having to favour great expansion of the public sector'; the logic was towards a reformist, welfare-state solution.

All this partly betokens a failure on the part of Carmichael, and those

who uncritically supported him, to polarize the issues societally as well
as racially. Initially 'colour blindness', equality of opportunity, the
stance of the civil-rights liberals, had been seen not to work for the
negro; it was alienating and ineffective, and it was inevitable that the
movement would shift to colour consciousness. But now the strategically
important question was raised: what about ultimate integration? And
it was at this level that Carmichael's tactical ambivalences appeared
most inadequate to the crisis of the black movement and the black
community, and by extension to the NL as a whole.

The Black Panthers

Despite King's attempt to revitalize the Civil Rights Movement
through an inter-racial coalition of the poor, the dominant factor in
black politics after 1967 was the final eclipse of SNCC and its replacement by the Black Panthers (BPP) as the vanguard group of the Black
Power Movement. Formed in Oakland in October 1966, the Panthers
from the outset called themselves 'revolutionary nationalists' and
actually merged formally with SNCC in 1968. Unlike SNCC, however,
they had been able to build a small base in several northern ghettoes.

The founding of the Oakland chapter by Seale and Newton – both
soon in jail – was followed by a chapter in New York the same year and
more chapters elsewhere in 1967. The Oakland chapter was always the
predominant one, with a membership of 700 by 1968. Probably no
other chapter approached this size, and the peak national membership
was in the region of 2,500. After the large Newark Black Power Conference of 1967, a broad alliance had been seen as possible involving
most of the 1,100 delegates, with SNCC and the Panthers operating as
equals.

Indeed, the official merger of the two organizations seemed to confirm
this, but in 1968 was complicated when Carmichael himself split with
SNCC (or was expelled). Their differences were centred on the
questions of Pan Africanism and the creation of a Black United Front;
issues that subsequently also split the BPP.

The Panthers, and Newton in particular, had been strong advocates
of 'utilization of the media' by use of militant direct action. Typical of
this was the Panthers' first major public action in 1967 – their entry,
fully armed, into the California state capital Sacramento, to oppose
firearm restrictions. Such exhibitions, and increasingly wild rhetoric,
tended to move the Panthers swiftly from defensive to offensive
postures, with media-oriented gimmicks substituting for organizational
tactics in the ghettoes.

This orientation towards a strategy of urban violence reflected the
cumulative symbolic impact of Watts and other ghetto outbursts – and
did not seem to reflect a particular ideological stance. At first, the
ideological leanings of the Panthers were towards a synthesis of black

separatism and a brand of anarchism, but they quickly moved towards a bizarre form of Marxist-Leninism. The complexity of their ideological make-up and the reasons for later splits, can be detected from this early background; in fact the Panthers drew their name and symbol from SNCC's political arm in Alabama (active in 1965) – the first 'Black Panther Party'.

The BPP drew together elements from many disparate black developments – from SNCC or CORE to African nationalism, the Deacons, the Muslims, and Malcolm-X; a black political organization with all whites excluded, standing for black social cultural autonomy; no coalitions with whites; a stress on power rather than moral persuasion; self-defence including violent retaliation; and advice to white sympathizers to operate against racism in their own communities. Integration, even on the basis of communal organization and a position of strength, was explicitly rejected. The Panthers capitalized on the widespread belief in the potential power and autonomy of the black community as a self-sufficient strategy, which was perhaps rooted partly in a basic demographic misperception.[32] The major political demands for the 'power to determine the destiny of our black community', and the main programmatic aim, initially black 'community control of the police', clearly had separatist overtones.

Whilst Newton and Seale were in jail, the leadership was taken over temporarily by another 'ex-con' and Malcolm-X follower, Eldridge Cleaver, an author and poet, as well as self-confessed ex-rapist and felon. Whilst he too was returned to jail again, it was possible to create a campaign for the BPP against 'political repression', successfully portraying all three as victims of unjust legal actions. During 1967–8 widespread sympathy and support were gained by this move, which previous actions, though obtaining great publicity, had not achieved.

But from 1968 onwards, the BPP began to seek white allies in lieu of expanding its black base in the community, which it was finding increasingly difficult to do. The subsequent splits with Carmichael were mainly on this issue. Despite his flirtations with white radicals after 1966, Carmichael most strongly articulated the widespread fears of a return to such alliances:

any premature alliance with white radicals has led to the complete subversion of the blacks by the whites, through direct or indirect control of the black organisation.[33]

To this fear – that whites would directly or indirectly subvert black organizations and replace them with white control, Cleaver and his Panther lieutenant Hilliard in New York, responded that this revealed a lack of faith in the intelligence and organizing power of black people.[34] Over this issue the split developed, with Cleaver increasingly condemning cultural nationalism, although it was a position he had once held himself.

Carmichael, who, along with two other SNCC leaders, Rap Brown and James Foreman, had become an honorary officer of the BPP in 1967, had at first drawn closer to the Panthers. But during 1968, the tension between himself and Cleaver occurred. At the end of the year, Carmichael returned to Africa, opposing the Panthers' version of 'revolutionary nationalism' with his own more clearly nationalist position. By 1969, both Cleaver and Carmichael were in exile in Africa, and Carmichael had now resigned from the Panthers and SNCC. Although the formal merger with the Panthers had been maintained after Carmichael's switch, many SNCC members had also left the alliance and to all intents and purposes this was the end of SNCC.

At the time of the Panther coalition with the largely white PFP[35] in early 1968, the party claimed substantial roots in the Oakland-Alameda black communities, and appeared to be growing. But there seems little evidence of any real attempt to organize the black community generally, and the Black Panther breakfast programmes, started a year later, were a belated and face-saving innovation in which anti-racist education could be coupled with a social service for ghetto children.

Yet even here there were rumours of coercion and protection rackets; in the tradition of Malcolm-X and the Muslims, many Panther recruits were young black criminals and gang members – some joining whilst still in prison.[36] Even these apparently innocuous breakfast programmes were accused of being financed by a form of protection 'hustle' against local traders – most of them black. Moreover the programme served only the purpose of 'political education' and had little other function in the community.

The use of violence within the movement, including threats to Carmichael's and Brown's lives, intensified these schisms. Such physical clashes, first with SNCC, then involving Carmichael, Newton, Seale and Cleaver, occurred partly over the two major and overtly divisive issues, alliances with whites, and the role of Marxist-Leninism. But in fact the issues of armed offensive action and internal 'disciplinary' violence were also a major, if covert, factor in the growing crisis, particularly as the costs of the self-defence strategy became clearer with police attacks on the party.

The demand for Black Panther police to replace white police in the ghetto had increasingly problematic implications for white allies and black people alike, given the provocation and internecine violence that had already occurred in the ghettoes. In this period, actual murders, as well as continual threats of shootings, marked internal exchanges and feuds. Members of black groups were 'executed' as spies, often without evidence. Even the white left began to cool in its admiration. After 1969, the Maoist PL, hitherto thought to be close to the Panthers, denounced them as all black nationalists, and thus reactionary; other leftists called both the Panthers and Carmichael 'racists in reverse', and 'black Stalinists'. It was at this point too that the moderate groups like

NAACP openly condemned the 'racism, anti-semitism, intimidation and violence' of the Panthers. After these developments, with the shootings and increasing harassment by police, terror in the ghetto, problematic alliances with white radicals, and the ideological turn towards Marxism-Leninism rather than black nationalism, the final and deepest cleavages appeared in the Party membership.

Although it was the Panther version of 'Black Power' that had become widely publicized, and SNCC's that began to fall into the background, the Party was finally torn asunder by this internal dissension. In 1970, Seale summarily purged those who were not 'true' Marxist-Leninists, leading indirectly to Cleaver's first split with Seale and then in 1971, with Newton, who was by now also moving away from the BPP's armed tactics.

The final collapse of the Panthers was centred on the issue of the priority to be given to this Seale-Newton version of Marxism-Leninism as against racial self-definition. Even Newton claimed by 1970 to be going 'beyond' Marxism-Leninism into the enunciation of an 'inter-communalist' ideology. But by now the Panthers had tragically failed to give organizational meaning to black power and far from making the black movement more assertive and outgoing, it proved to be just as retreatist and introverted as its many black predecessors had been. As Newton in 1971 admitted:

we thought of ourselves as a vanguard . . . when we looked around we found we were not the vanguard for anything, we lost the favour of the black community and left it behind.[37]

7. In Search of Ideology

Marxism and the ideological vacuum

Throughout the 1960s the ideological core of the NL remained ambiguous; 'Marxist or non-Marxist, socialist or non-socialist, violent or nonviolent, centralist or anarchist'? In 1966 and 1967, as Sidney Lens argued,[1] no one was very clear. The Port Huron document had stated that 'Not even the socialist and liberal preachments of the past seem adequate to the forms of the present',[2] and the angry young man's complaint of 1958 that there was an end to 'good brave causes' was not entirely confined to the 'end-of-ideology' school.[3]

The emergence of massive and militant factions of blacks and youth to some extent gave the lie to the proposition of an 'end of ideology'. On the other hand these movements were at the outset acutely circumspect about ideology. Given the experiences of the 1950s that shaped the NL (see chapter 1), there was an understandable lack of final commitment to a comprehensive ideological position[4] – a reluctance, despite the vacuum of organized belief, to endorse a genuine Marxist framework. As Bottomore put it:

The great 19th century ideologies which divided societies, have developed cracks and appear to be crumbling... (they) no longer exercise anything like their former sway over the minds of social critics.[5]

Barrington Moore echoed this: 'We are at a point (1968) where both reigning orthodoxies, official Liberalism and official Marxism, are subject to vigorous challenge.' On the other hand, as both agreed, so far 'no intellectual current has emerged as a clear alternative'.[6]

An alternative to replacing the old ideologies, the belief in pure activism, offered to fill the theoretical vacuum. But inevitably this was also accompanied by a strong scepticism about ideology, even about theory, that some in SDS deplored. Theory, it was argued, should emerge from the activist core, not the intellectual periphery: for this reason, there must be fundamentally tentative approaches to questions of ideology. 'The New Left is not only hostile to adults, it is hostile to ideology.'[7]

Reich talks of this as the NL's 'radical subjectivity' that brought together 'conscienceism' and a 'deep scepticism about both linear and analytic thinking';[8] but experiential radicalism was at best local or subcultural in its understanding of reality, and temporally restricted. Egleson complained: 'We have slogans which take the place of thought; "there's a change gonna come" is our substitute for social theory.' There was a general agreement that such lack of ideology might eventually lead to crisis and that the anti-intellectual currents might be a subsequent cause of weakness: 'People (in SDS) do not want to oppress others with their views.'[9]

From summer 1966 until fall 1967 was a period of uncertainty in which the ideological character of the NL in America was molten and indeterminate. Very much the same was true of its European counterparts. As a result, as one SDSer put it, by summer 1966 there was a tendency to 'over-worry ideology',[10] so much so that at one point, SDS was compared with a hapless maiden wide open to ideological assault. Other groups on the NL spectrum were criticized for a similar lack of any accompanying holistic analysis of society. They lacked a comprehensive scenario of transformation or a clear specification of an agency of change, and revealed a fundamental failure to produce a theory of structure and process to distinguish the major social forces.

Traditional Marxism, on the other hand, had been characterized by all of these. When forms of Marxism were eventually re-adopted, it was not because they were necessarily appropriate, but because they contained these properties and met these needs. The tragedy for the NL was that 'once we took up the only available revolutionary ideology we lost the impulse to develop another.'[11]

To some extent this 'crisis' of ideology was an artificial one; the confrontation with Marxism created a sense of inadequacy that was more apparent than real.[12] The NL had ingredients of an original ideological system, which was evolving steadily with Movement experience, whereas the Marxists had arrived with a ready-made and comprehensive orthodoxy – albeit a dated one. For example, by the 1960s C. Wright Mills's notion of political and social alienation, 'the war machine' and the power élite, had already been popularized in Europe; he helped provide a language and framework for a non-Marxist analysis of both American and European societies. The components of Mills's social analysis most central and most relevant to the development of NL ideas were the concern with the transformation of class and the material basis of the new élites. Criticizing the Marxists, Mills rejected the notion of 'ruling class', counterposing an élite-mass model to the class model; second, his critique of bourgeois pluralism was not a critique of pluralism per se; third the idea of a new sociology rooted in a theory of alienated politics was linked to the decline of communities and publics; fourth, his critique of mass society and the role of the media; and finally, the analyses of military-industrial hegemony. Mills's emphasis on the political order and the military establishment, as distinct from the purely economic emphasis of traditional socialism, had already become a distinguing element in NL theory by the mid-1960s.

Influenced by these approaches, 'Port Huron' and 'America and the New Era', together with the 'new working class' ideas and 'student syndicalism', indicated one direction that ideological formation in SDS was already taking. Participatory democracy, community action and counter-institutions was another, not entirely irreconcilable, direction.[13]

SDS in particular seemed to represent this continuation of an indigenous tradition of radical populism that combined such activism and democratic ideals. To succeed, in Kopkind's view, the NL only had to reaffirm such traditions of 'native American radicalism' of which it was 'the guardian'.[14] PD offered itself not merely as a practical principle, but as ideology or political philosophy. At its heart lay an idea of mutual aid, as against individual competitiveness; cooperation rather than opposition; it could simply be extended to a socialist critique of the individual status-striving of capitalist society. Lasch argued that by its espousal of 'decentralization, local control and a generally anti-bureaucratic outlook', and by insisting that these values are the heart of radicalism, the movement showed 'American socialism the road it ought to follow'.[15]

The failure to develop these components into a fully developed NL ideology has been well summarized and explained by the main biographer of SDS, Kirkpatrick Sale:

Those theories, and their defences, because they had to be created anew seemed too hard to formulate and polish in the instant, especially in the face of attacks from people like the PL dogmatists and especially at a time when action brought its own rewards and resistance seemed enough to create visions of the revolution. SDS'ers involved in theory tended to give up the hard work of fashioning their own, of finding formulations that were new, particular to their time and place, valid for a post-industrial system, consistent with the Movement they had seen develop, true to their own experience, coherent with their own reality. They turned more often instead to something ready-made.[16]

The NL has often been interpreted as a further revision of Marxist ideas and this relationship has been widely discussed in various contexts, e.g. the Marxian revisionists in England in the late 1950s, the ongoing debate with Mills about organization and agency (class), and the search for ideology by the American movement. Of course, any search for a new revolutionary strategy had inevitably involved dialogue with Marx, as well as Lenin's and various other European revisionisms.[17] But it would be quite erroneous to suppose that the NL was ever a 'Marxist' movement – even after 1968. Undoubtedly a substantial concern both with the historic Marx and with twentieth-century revisions dominated the intellectual NL in the late 1960s. Certainly in its identification with the historic institutions of the producer, in its recognition of the role of peasant communes, its concern with Petrograd, Kronstadt and the experience of the 'Soviets' – even with a Marxist like Rosa Luxemburg – the NL entered into intimate dialogue with aspects of the Marxist tradition, especially in its more libertarian or quasi-syndicalist moments.

But the principal impression remaining is of wide-ranging ideological eclecticism: the early movement drew at least as much from other traditions – the Anarchist, the Gandhian, the native American theorists and from classic sociology, Weber and Michels – as from Marx.[18] In an extreme form this heterodoxy passes on into the later NL splinters. It is expressed in the kind of statement put out by Cleaver in the Black Panther Party paper, 'Our thinking is inspired by Che Guevara, Malcolm-X, Lumumba, Ho Chi Minh and Mao Tse Tung.'[19] As PL influence increased, many of the earlier fears in the NL about the impact of ideology were confirmed in the heterogeneous mélange of Old Left rhetoric, half-understood clichés from contemporary Marxist-Leninism, and a naive but extensive iconography of Third World leaderships. 'Backwards as it is', wrote Gitlin, 'our practice is more advanced than our theory and our theory therefore becomes an obstacle to our practice.'[20] As it stumbled in its attempts to fit its praxis into alien theoretical moulds, the NL helped create its own crisis of self-recognition, thus undermining the source of its activism.

Nevertheless, the movement shifted far enough towards Marxism to confuse the other two options open to it, i.e. a firmer development of its own native insights, or a more definite commitment to the Anarchist tradition. In the end, all three options were kept open, and each failed to provide the ideological recipe for survival. Application of American-based ideas remained tentative until reinforced by the post-scarcity ideas and theories of Marcuse and Bookchin and the re-discovered Reich. But the coherent development of post-scarcity ideas, whilst these found ready acceptance amongst surviving elements of the earlier NL, occurred only in the 1970s, when the NL was past rescue by any updated libertarian analysis.

The New Left as Anarchist revival

Throughout the 1960s and early 1970s, critics and commentators used the term Anarchist to describe part or all of the NL.[21] In Zinn's view, what characterized the NL's fundamentally anti-authoritarian character as a movement was that it 'would burn draft cards in any society':

it is anarchistic . . . not just in wanting the ultimate abolition of the state, but in its immediate requirement that authority and coercion be banished in every sphere of existence, that the end must be represented immediately in the means.[22]

Ideologically, the only political tradition which, over the previous century, had clearly expressed such an integration of personal revolt against oppression with the political strategy of dismantling coercive structures, was the tradition of Anarchism and libertarian or utopian Socialism.

At the outset, Camus's emphases on rebellion in thought and action had been close to, if not synonymous with, the Anarchist position, and was widely influential, as was Paul Goodman's Anarchism, on the early NL. Subsequently, the ideas and events of May 1968 were frequently described in such terms; Cohn-Bendit refers to libertarian Marxism and himself as a Marxist, 'in the way Bakunin was';[23] it is also significant how Bakunin is quoted again with favour in the later 1960s. With the spread of Marcusian ideas after 1968, the terms libertarian-Marxist or even Anarcho-Marxist were also used of many NL ideas and movement actions. Despite some distinctly authoritarian strains in Marcuse's thought, he too was often identified with Anarchism or 'anarcho-Marxism',[24] not least because the Marcusian Utopia coincided with the belief of classic anarchism, that a non-repressive civilization can emerge as a natural expression of 'man's unfettered nature'.

Mitchell Goodman surveying the movement in 1970 still called it 'Anarchist in its deepest impulses'.[25] A number of activists and theorists invoked the tradition, or described their own ideas or practice as Anarchist. For example, David Harris, one of the main organizers of the Resistance, re-echoed an Anarchist position, averring that 'the state' was a relationship between oppressors and the oppressed, that could only be broken by rejecting that pattern of behaviour.

A range of NL movements and projects such as the Squatters, Tupamaros, RYM I, Weathermen and the Resistance were all in their different ways linked to Anarchism.

Earlier, FSM, SDS, SNCC and the German SDS had each in some sense and at some stages, also embodied this ambiguous tradition. So too, in Britain, did the Committee of 100, and of course later, and much more explicitly, the March Twenty-Second Movement in Paris. Moreover such projects might often appear to observers libertarian in both their essence and tactical logic, even when participants saw themselves as outside or hostile to the Anarchist heritage. For example, the Black Panthers started by publishing Nechaev and Bakunin.[26]

Anti-bureaucratic and anti-authoritarian elements became integral ingredients of the 'a-political' avant-garde in many spheres. For example, the Beats, Situationists, Provos, Kabouters, Diggers, Yippees – in fact, all the most active groups in the counter-culture – were continually labelled 'anarchist'. Indeed, Roszak lists amongst its major sources and ingredients 'remnants of Left wing ideology and Anarchist social theory' (alongside Dada and Eastern religion!); Oglesby too termed the counter-culture 'the new anarchism',[27] and a close integration of the youth culture with anarchism was noted by commentators on both sides of the Atlantic.

It was British developments in particular, out of CND, that gave impetus to the inital spread of the new anarchism; one main development of libertarian ideas came with the founding of *Anarchy* in 1961. Although Anarchists at this time still wrote for *Peace News* and *Freedom* as well as *NLR*, this new magazine ranged more widely than these others into alternative projects and topics such as alternatives to prison, intermediate technology and current sexuality. Anarchism had re-emerged as an actual movement in Britain in the early 1960s, by building on the direct-action wing of the peace movement, which itself had developed its own theory and analysis, as distinct from the *ULR/NLR* group.[28] Libertarian tendencies were able to recruit more déclassé elements than the largely middle-class Marxist-groups, and the 'worker-intellectual' tended to gravitate more to small libertarian and activist groups, like the Solidarity group, outside the orbit of the *NLR* or official Anarchism; many were often active also in the Committee of 100, and its industrial wing.

By 1964, the Committee had moved to an overtly anarchist position; though it had from the outset been anarchistic in essence – in its ad-hoc spontaneity of organization, its chaotic democracy, and its fundamental belief in direct action for change – the Committee's opposition to the bomb, always both extra-parliamentary and anti-authoritarian, only slowly developed a view of the problem of nuclear war as embedded in a wider struggle against authoritarian and militarist structures generally.[29]

But the emergence of libertarian characteristics in earlier movement projects – not only in the Committee of 100 and its offshoots in England, but in the New Left activity in America (1960–5) – remained an augury of Anarchist revival rather than a revival itself.

Indeed such a revival when it comes is not necessarily an organizational one;[30] except for the brief resurgence of English Anarchism in the 1960s, Anarchist organization seems constantly on the retreat, and in the later 1960s, organizationally, even in England, it was the Marxist-Left that appeared to be taking command. Indeed it has been widely debated[31] whether an organized Anarchist tradition or movement still existed in the 1960s. Heroic and brilliant as many of those were who carried on the traditions of classical Anarchism and Syndicalism after the experiences in Russia and Spain, organizationally Anarchism had been reduced to tiny unrevivified fragments in Europe and America, often maintained by ageing émigrés. This explicit inheritance had all but died away before the resurgence of the more implicit anarchism of the NL and the radical movements of the early 1960s.[32]

This discontinuity and amorphous quality of the Anarchist tradition was revealed yet again in the new libertarian effusions of the 'young rebels' of 1968. The association of this later, post-1968 resurgence with Anarchism is partly an accident; the NL often backed into Anarchism loudly proclaiming its adherence to other traditions, or playing down its libertarian origins whilst engaging in direct-action politics or syndicalist strategy. NL leaders, like many previous major spokesmen of anarchist ideas, from Tolstoi to Camus, mostly denied they were Anarchists, or masqueraded under other titles; there is continual evidence of the sensed need for activists and theorists alike to play down, camouflage, disguise, or even abandon and forget Anarchist associations, in order to organize more effectively; the historical liabilities of the Anarchist tag were not lost on those whose *prime* concern was to build a movement.

Given the ambiguity of this relationship, yet the widespread description of the NL as anarchist, it is necessary to attempt to specify the connections between the movement and Anarchism, to ask just *what* ideological elements they had in common. Of the classic libertarian ideas the following components have been identified as prevalent also in the mainstream NL.[33]

An insistence on workers' control.

The organization of the poor and the déclassés, the marginal elements.

Anti-intellectualism, irrationalism and anti-theory.

The romanticization of spontaneous violence (*but* also a tradition of anti-militarism).

Direct Action; Propaganda of the Deed; Extra-institutional, extra-parliamentary and extra-legal activity.

A stress on 'community' and the decentralization of society.

Loose decentralized organization; the rejection of permanent leaders.

The belief that the revolutionary movement itself foreshadows the character of the new society; a stress on the means/ends continuum.

Certainly these dimensions occur in most of the movements described here and represent significant ingredients in the NL's ideological make-up (for example, all make their appearance in the Paris events of 1968), yet *none* of them is part of the orthodox Marxist canon. The new breed of Anarchist theorist argued that 'the task was to try to build' the new society 'through anarchistic action', a view close to anarcho-syndicalism, and clearly compatible with the NL's view of 'counter-institutions'. This belief that a state could be eroded, slowly

but surely, rather than through an apocalyptic revolutionary transformation, was reassuring to the progressive middle-class elements. It
also left open a continuing role for the individual in 'propaganda of the
deed' – rationalized not so much in terms of personal salvation as of
publicizing visible alternatives.

Some NL projects shared a romantic defeatism with the tradition of
Anarchism; an attitude expressed also in the fatalism of many
community rebellions.[34] Despite this, the creation of counter-
institutions, which for the mainstream NL was situated in the revolutionary as much as in the reform tradition, made the term 'protest'
movement a misnomer. When on the offensive, such opposition was
aimed directly against centres of power (or at least helped provide a base
for such confrontation).

If there is a moment of genuine re-birth for Western Anarchism, it
is clearly in the France of May 1968; whether conscious or not, the
libertarian character of the movement cannot be doubted. But it also
illustrates just how fluid and ambiguous the anarchism of the later
twentieth century in the West is, and how far it is predominantly the
anarchism of the middle class. It is also of course the anarchism of the
young; historically it is the first time that the doctrine, outside its
appeal to a few renegade gentry and students in Russia, had made any
kind of purchase on this young middle-class constituency, and many of
its projects and issues represent the concerns of a leisured 'post-
repression' strata of late capitalist society; the focus on environment,
on culture, on life-style and on 'free' speech, 'free' schools, 'free' radio
and other alternative media, represent the extension of areas of freedom
within the existing society, and a running battle on many fronts to
construct alternatives in such key areas as education.

the task of the Anarchist is not to dream about the future society; but
rather to act as anarchistically as he can within present society.[35]

That, in effect, was what much of the NL continued to do.

Thus the urge towards local control and the repossession of decision
making through direct action and cooperative alternatives, can be
viewed as a continuing aspect of historic Anarchism's opposition to the
centralized state.[36] In its anti-bureaucratic, 'anti-bigness' guise this
was an essential component of the NL. Opposition to the paternalism
of welfare, or a university, and the impersonalism of state schemes, was
thus merely a new facet of an historic belief in 'the community' against
the state (as well as of the individual against the state). Thus resistance
to the draft in an anarchist and libertarian context, also took place at
two levels; at the communal and the individual.[37]

Movement-slogans of people 'controlling their lives' and participatory
democracy have therefore to be seen as springing from similar anti-
authoritarian and utopian traditions.

Marxism, Revisionism and Anarchism

Given the openness and eclecticisms of the NL, the especial appeal of the Anarchists, less encumbered by a grand theoretical apparatus, was that they were ideologically more flexible than the Marxists in appraising changes in advanced industrial society. This flexibility was expressed in two ways: first in abandonment of a single-minded focus on the working class; second in the development of a body of post-scarcity theory on which to base an anarchist critique of modern society.[38]

Certainly if one compares the theoretical and practical development of the NL in America with its counterpart in Britain, the lack of a 'working-class-based' Marxist heritage operated as a distinct advantage.[39] Its freedom to manoeuvre outside the frameworks and suppositions of class analysis, its lack of preconceptions about organization and its avoidance of an outmoded language, gave the Movement of the mid-1960s flexibility and strength, and a belief in humanity as an end in itself.

Whilst the rhetoric of the early movement is almost as often drawn from Marxist humanism as from Camus, the relation of the Marxian 'intellectual' NL of the late 1950s to activist movements remained problematic (see above). When for example, *Studies on the Left*, stressing the US NL's theoretical weakness, attempted to engender its own 'Marxist' ideological orientation, there was less than enthusiastic support (1965).

Certainly segments, especially of the intellectual leadership grouped around one or two journals, had firm attachments to Marxian revisionism throughout the 1960s and it is equally true that other leadership sections saw themselves as converts to Marxism in the later 1960s. But the rank and file of these movements, especially of the black and student movements, was at best only superficially touched by Marxism.

Even alienation, a concept which had promised to revive a universal Marxian critique of both sides in the Cold War, was soon reduced to a cover-all term with little analytical rigour and an accretion of meaning which made it less and less useful.[40]

In America, *Studies on the Left* was the closest NL journal to Marxism, emerging in 1959 at Wisconsin, partly under Marxist influence.[41] Other magazines, less Marxist in orientation, echoed the Port Huron Statement: 'Marx the humanist has much to tell us, but his conceptual tools are outmoded, and his final vision implausible.'[42]

There were many radicals who, in this vein, suggested that Marx himself might have been the first to satirize the deification of a social philosopher almost a century dead: as for Sartre's claim that Marxism was the 'philosophy of our time', and close to infallibility, many endorsed Camus's implied response: that we had indeed passed beyond the circumstances that had created Marxism and that if this philosophy was in its 'infancy', as Sartre claimed, then it was a *second* childhood, beyond senility.

Acting as a filter both for Marxist and movement values, Marcuse, like Sartre (and like Sorel), seemed to endorse Marxism less because he 'believed in it' than because he saw it as an effective instrument for advancing reason and progressive social change.

Whilst the founders of the original English NL, the young editors of *ULR*, or those intellectuals who had founded the *New Reasoner*, were after Hungary prepared to reject the Communist Party and Soviet Marxism, Marxism itself remained somewhat sacred. Whilst they might have a great deal of admiration for Mills's work in America, they were uncertain about his warning to avoid the 'proletarian metaphysic'. Their two leading writers, Williams and Thompson, gave intellectual endorsement to an assumption of the continuing transforming potential of the working class, even though this was articulated almost as a critique of inherited Marxisms, and included a developing anti-determinist and populistic historiography.[43]

Despite criticisms and revisions, and largely through the Marxisms of PL and the Du Bois Clubs, as well as the Independent Socialists in America and the IS and IMG in England, the 'concept that the working class could be an agency of effective change' gained some ground again after 1968. It became reinforced as a frame of reference, not only for these Marxist groups and theorists, but for sections of the NL as well. But despite this revival, and the impact of some Old Left concepts, and Trotskyist figures like Ernest Mandel and Deutscher, none of them succeeded in widely popularizing a traditional class analysis.

The changing make-up of the working class, the movement of American blacks into heavy industry, and women into the tertiary sector, made such analysis complex, as Nicolaus had pointed out. American Old Left groups and theorists, confronted with this dwindling and far from militant working class, tended, as has been seen, after the New Deal to move towards a class analysis of the Negro community – even of the lumpen and mobile blacks.[44]

The relationship of the black movements to Marxism had in any case always been ambivalent,[45] and one critic remarked that 'American Marxism has disastrously misled negro intellectuals over a period of fifty years.' Its relationship with white Marxists, however radical, in the period after 1968 is marked by increasing scepticism and aloofness. Nationalist critics in particular warned of any relationship with Marxism; Lester declared 'because Marxism doesn't concern itself with the race question its relevance to the black struggle is extremely limited.'[46] The Black Panthers' explicit adoption of Marxist-Leninism was based more on the 'hand-me-down' variety of Marxian revisionisms than on the ideas of Marx or Lenin directly; as with the RYM and Weatherpeople, the principal filter of such ideas was Maoism – but one cannot underestimate Fanon's influence.[47] Whilst the Panthers turned towards their own novel version of 'Marxist-Leninism', they also turned away from the white SDS and PL versions of it.[48]

The older orthodox Marxism had made most impact when translated into simple and relevant descriptive propositions. Older American Marxists like Baran and Sweezy were able to point up the irrationality of a capitalist system, governed by profit rather than need.[49] They were able to make links with ecological concerns in stressing the use of surplus as waste. They linked militarism, over-consumption, advertising, squalor and unused capacity in a way that avoided the sterile terminology of Marxian economics, yet provided a more telling indictment than that of liberal critics such as Galbraith.

In the view of many libertarian critics, however, Old Left options were by now largely 'reformist' ones in the West – whether they worked towards 'state capitalism' or retained private monopoly capitalism, whether totalitarian in implication or not, and whether revolution was envisaged as the path to 'state capitalism' or not. It was to this type of critique that the post-1967, Marxist-leaning segment of NL leadership was most vulnerable, rather than to the head-on confrontation of some post-scarcity Anarchists.[50] The NL, whilst it might find class-analysis unwieldy, was by now in any case basically sceptical of capitalism; reformist social democrats, whether left-of-centre Labour MPs in England, or figures like Howe, Rustin or Harrington in America, might be hostile to the NL's amorphous (or 'non-existent') ideology, but they lacked any thoroughgoing critique of capitalism themselves – either humanist or collectivist.

In the late 1950s, the example of the Yugoslavs with their experiments in workers' participation seemed of especial relevance[51] to an emerging NL, and was the most widely popularized version of 'industrial self-management'. It was from this model that the English NL had developed its view of worker control as part of its repertoire. But its American counterpart was far more nervous of a concept which had such accretions of Old Left meaning, even though its own ideal of participatory democracy, logically extended to the workplace, implied a similar democracy of ownership.

In so far as the possession of industrial property is seen as a critical mode of control, such an extension should have constituted an approach to a socialist critique of property. But the slogan 'workers' control' had been given very many meanings, including the social democratic, the Syndicalist, and even the Stalinist, and had in fact been treated with scepticism by Marx, and even more by Engels. If discipline and hierarchy were accepted as an inevitable counterpart of modern mass-production, to abolish this type of authority, as the Anarchists proposed, would challenge the very basis of industry.

Anarcho-Syndicalism had developed historically in terms of a synthesis of elements of Marxism and Anarchism, focused on production, and although it is not the only form which such synthesis may take it finds recurrent echoes in the NL.[52] This was not least because its appeal transcended many of the sectarian divisions in socialism through its main strategic and practical focus of thought and action to further the spread of authority at the workplace along egalitarian and participatory lines.[53] (Though Anarchism generally was moving away from the traditional Syndicalist focus on industrial workers at the point of production towards a more eclectic view.) Such ideas came to be associated with the anti-bureaucratic tendencies in Left-revisionism after the 1930s and both Titoism and Trotskyism moved cautiously in this direction. Mandel, a popular Trotskyite mentor after 1968, argued along similar lines, even including the old Syndicalist scenario of the General Strike. The YSA in the USA too, stressed a libertarian and Syndicalist line, especially with regard to France, perhaps in order to attract the younger 'politicoes'.[54] Certainly, there is a growing influence of Anarchism on Trotskyism and Marxism generally in this period (as well as, at the other end of the spectrum, on liberalism), though this largely went unremarked by its practitioners.[55]

If there was a common attitude in the NL to Marx's ideas it was to respect them as those of a major theorist, amongst many. But the view amongst some was that, despite the predominance of such ideas in Movement discussion, the most 'Marxist' thing would be to forgo the Marxist label; after all Marx had insisted on the primacy of social development which changes theory and practice, and classical Marxism could hardly escape such analysis itself. But it was not merely that conditions had changed, and that with it Marxism had been revised out of all recognition; it was also that within the Marxian canon lay the two parallel strands of socialism – the libertarian and the authoritarian – which were, in part, a matter of two revisionisms, alternative schools of interpretation, and partly two contrary perspectives within Marx the thinker. These 'two souls' of Marxism were in tension, not only within the Marxian system, but reproduced contrasting aspects of the actual traditions of the organized Left;[56] and it was a tension that NL theorists searching for reformulation seemed, at first, aware of.

The division may be summarily represented in terms of two lists of attributes; they are 'ideal types', that is they exaggerate the polarity and clarity of distinction in practice; neither thinkers nor socialist organizations fall clearly to one side or the other. But the following figure may help identify the poles between which debate runs:

Table 2   *Attributes of the two types of Marxism*

Libertarian Marxism	Authoritarian Marxism
Stress on Free Will	Tendency towards Determinism
Radical consciousness as wellspring of change	Economic contradictions as source of historical development
Idealism	Materialism
Revolution as Freedom	Revolution as necessity
Emphasis on community-based organization (Soviets, Councils, Communes, Unions, Locals, Strike Committees)	Emphasis on class, party and state
Socialist trans-nationalism	National 'self-determination' and the unity of proletarian nations
Abolition of state	Retention of state in foreseeable future
Critique of Industrialism (broad alienation concept)	Optimism about industrialism/technology
Alienation as total concept (i.e. in all industrial societies)	Alienation focused on capitalistic system
Opposition to bureaucracy	Pragmatic necessity of bureaucracy
Opposition to armies/militarism, conscription, etc.	Necessity of 'progressive armed struggle' and national defence (e.g. conscription)
Reconceptualization of revolution (situationism, alternative society, 'revolution of everyday life')	Revolution on the Bolshevik model (with later Chinese, or 'guerilla' modifications)
Development of new society 'within the womb of the old' from the grassroots upwards	Development of new society only after seizure of state power, nationalization of production, etc., abolition of classes etc.

The dialectic between such conceptual alternatives represented by these two columns, reflecting the dialogue and revision of Marx's own work is, in turn, reproduced in the history of Socialism generally, and in the development of the NL especially after 1967.

The alternative libertarian Marxism is obviously often closer to Anarchism than to the official Marxist movements, and closer to 'revisionist' theories developed later, than to much in 'orthodox' Marxist thought. Yet Marx himself denied being a Marxist in part as a renunciation of the authoritarian dogma that, with Engels's help, was gaining ground.[57] The need in the later 1960s to call the alternative libertarian strain 'Marxism', or 'Anarcho-Marxism', betrays in part a recognition of the prestige, size and continuity of an alternate 'subordinate' brand of Marxism. But it also reveals the astute realization amongst libertarian radicals that the main recruiting ground for such anarchistic tendencies would be amongst those disillusioned with the Marxist groups, and amongst the *soi-disant* 'Marxist' young of the later NL.

On the other hand, Anarchism represented quite a different transcendence of bourgeois liberalism from Marxist forms; rejecting the anti-individualism of state collectivism, the Anarchist attempted to extend the logic of liberalism whilst embracing a critique of oppressive structures that were both economically and politically exploitative. It is this counterpoint between liberalism and Marxism, and the re-emergence of Anarchism, which is perhaps the key to understanding the ideological meaning of the NL in terms of a libertarian revival. Barrington Moore was not alone amongst progressive or socialist critics in believing that 'unless future radical movements can somehow synthesize the achievements of liberalism with those of revolutionary radicalism, the results for humanity will be tragic'. This was a lesson that had appeared to be learnt by the early NL in the period of de-Stalinization, and the later phases of the Cold War. But it still had to be re-learned by a new generation of radicals.

8. The New Left in Britain: 1956–70

A false start

Any discussion of a NL in Britain is bedevilled by terminological problems – especially in any attempt to compare its nature and developments with the movements in other countries. The problem lies with the initial label, used by Mills in his letter to the then largely English NL. From the start, the term NL was largely identified not with the oppositional movement as a whole, but with the relatively narrow groupings around the *Universities and Left Review* (*ULR*) and *New Reasoner* published from 1957 to 1960; and for some years subsequently, not with CND, but with their successor, the *New Left Review* (*NLR*).[1]

Many of the tendencies, most comparable with the American movement (and indeed with developments in Europe) that have been elsewhere identified with a NL, did not so identify themselves in Britain. Indeed libertarian radicals in England, especially those in the Committee of 100, consistently rejected the NL tag because of its association with Marxism, or the Labourist strategy (e.g. in CND), or the compromising of Unilateralism. This refusal to see the NL as a broader phenomenon was one reason why so few elements in English radicalism identified with the simultaneous Movement evolution in the USA.

This negative attitude to the term 'New' Left was compounded when after an internal coup, *NLR* passed out of the hands of the relatively anti-authoritarian and humanist editors of its earlier years into the control of a more doctrinaire and traditional Marxist-Revisionist group after 1962; these had much stronger orientations to European and Third World Communist parties.[2] Thus, by the mid-1960s, the NL label in England, predominantly associated by radicals or the broad Left with this small and increasingly sectarian grouplet in Britain, was no longer used of the larger trans-national movements. Indeed, adoption of the label NL by SDS and the broader movements in America, worked to create an artificial barrier between them and fellow-spirits in the British movement (e.g. the community organizers). This confusion is further compounded by the fact that when developments in *NLR* after 1962 took it outside the orbit of the NL proper (i.e. as here defined) many subsequent Anarchist and Pacifist attacks on the 'New Left' in England, are in fact critiques of 'Old Left' orthodoxies and organizational styles henceforth advocated by *NLR*.[3]

The differences between the developments of the transatlantic NLs also have to be explained in terms of the very different contexts, especially the tenacity with which older social formations survived in Britain and its less vigorous anti-Communist atmosphere in the 1950s. Whereas some sort of Marxist tradition had survived in Britain, by 1958 there was no American Left to speak of, with the breakdown or incorporation of working-class institutions, the co-optation of 'the new men of power', and the collapse of organized socialisms.[4] But the labour movement in Britain was still too powerful and too implicated in left-wing thought to be bypassed, and in particular, 'the possibility of the Labour Party becoming the vehicle of radical and socialist movements' proved 'sufficiently great to divide the British Left permanently on the issue of whether to work within or outside the Party' (Carter).[5] This existence of a massive and institutionalized working class with a still distinctive culture, made the emergence of a genuinely 'New' Left much more problematic, and the continued purchase of more traditional groups like the International Socialists[6] or the Communist Party, much firmer than in a society like that of the USA.

Thus, any 'new' Left in Britain was more or less forced to accept the whole movement and radical tradition at the point it had reached in 1957 or 1958, and as a central component of it, the hoary mystique of the working class, although the NL's focus on working-class life included a cultural celebration of folk life and popular arts (concerns that had also been located in a Communist Party milieu previously). In fact, many of the first English New Leftists were either ex-Communists or Left-wing Labourites still willing to work closely with the CP.[7] This explains the centrality from the outset of the British NL's 'tactical alliance with the Bevanite rump'.[8] The novel element was the re-alignment with radical pacifism which gave the English NL a conscience during its short early life.

At first, in 1958, in Notting Hill and elsewhere, *ULR* associated itself with community organizing and also supported direct action,[9] attracting a vigorous infusion of young and new ideas into the movement. Those who associated with the partisan coffee house and NL clubs in their first days, generated a genuine *élan* and identity with a youth revolt that *ULR*'s 8000 readers and its packed London meetings attested. Thompson believed that these 'clubs and discussion centres will be places beyond the reach of the interferences of the bureaucracy, where the initiative remains in the hands of the rank and file,' that the influence of the NL derived from the power of its ideas.[10] After 1959, when *ULR* and the *New Reasoner* were merged into the *NLR*,[11] this provided both the 'theoretical analysis which gives the movement perspective' and the 'clarion call to moral principle . . . which gives the movement guts'.[12]

But like *ULR*'s cultural analysis, *NLR*'s limited critiques were not linked to any positive strategy or theory of change. At best it implied a creative do-it-yourself response to the cultural crisis – grassroots community action or projects like 'free cinema'. At worst it could be taken as an endorsement of an uncritical labourism, or traditional leftism. Indeed, Birnbaum suggests that even at this early stage, the 1959 NL merger implied 'an implicit abandonment of *ULR*'s programme' and hints at the ex-CPers' responsibility for this.[13]

One could, however, in any case easily exaggerate both the impact and the importance of the English NL theorists in helping to create a new movement. The relatively sophisticated intellectual level of the magazines meant a widening gap between them and both activism and practical ideas. More practical, immediately applicable ideas were available.[14] Unlike their US counterparts, the Oxbridge intellectuals of the *ULR*, or those of the *New Reasoner*, became increasingly remote from the movement. The younger ones might turn out for a couple of Easter Marches, or act as 'consultants' to CND or community projects, but they were not the 'organic intellectuals' that the English movement needed, and lacked.[15] In England even more than in America, university-oriented theoretical magazines, with their sociological and philosophical concerns, even though they started with links to direct action, became divorced from the anti-intellectualist activism and style revolt of the Movement.[16] The academic approach of the editors, and a failure to escape the left-sectarianism deriving from the positional differentiations of the 1930s, soon struck activists as a ponderous irrelevance.

Such various weaknesses of the NL were reflected in and reinforced by the theoretical lack, and absence of strategic vision, in CND as an organization. Though it did not owe its birth to the NL theorists, there were too few others in CND ready 'with the will and the capacity to transform the movement into a different and more political entity'.[17] In influencing CND to abandon unilateralism for a 'realistic' political package, the luminaries of *NLR* showed the same fundamental misunderstanding of the nuclear disarmament movement that had first led them to advocate a Labour Party tactic. Admittedly, the appeal to scrap moral arguments was addressed to CND first by other sympathetic political sophisticates, the left-liberal defence strategists, the Crossman–Padley 'convenient' unilateralists in the Labour Party, rather than the 'realists' of the intellectual NL.[18] But it can be shown, whenever NL theorists did intervene, it was either as blunder ('Steps towards Peace') or with only tentative awareness of the latent possibilities of the larger movement (May Day Manifesto). Certainly, throughout the early years of the British nuclear disarmament movement, the opportunity was offered of something more than speculative, limited or ex post facto analyses, and consultant relationships.[19]

It is this lack of genuine NL options which enabled Marxist sects or organizations to successfully take over or supersede some of the offshoots of nuclear pacifism in the later 1960s, moving into a vacuum of ideas and tactics. The closeness of *ULR* to activism in the years 1957–9 is quickly replaced by *NLR*'s alignment with the traditional left, at times supporting the Communist Party against the Trotskyites; in the main pursuing a traditional and fellow-travelling tactic within or alongside the Labour Party. Over the coming years, the Old Left background (never shaken off), the influence of the Bevanite Labourleft and the Communist Party, tended to grow stronger again. So much so that when, by 1963, it was becoming clear that the Labour Party strategy had failed, and with the recurrent disappointments of nonaligned internationalism, there was a notable tendency within parts of this English NL to return to semi-Stalinist solutions.[20]

This failure of NL strategy and lack of any forward-looking theory, created an ideological gap which the Sartrian–Marxism of a new batch of NL editors began to fill. After the loss of Ralph Samuel, then a split in which Stuart Hall, E. P. Thompson, Raymond Williams and others left, the magazine was transformed in character into a narrower, more doctrinaire and mandarin journal of Marxist criticism – apeing at times *Temps Modernes* in France, idolizing the French Communist traditions. Its popular appeal disappeared, and its circulation fell; its alignments and associations from then on were strictly 'Old Left'. As a result many, both Marxian revisionists and CND activists, prised themselves right out of this 'New Left' orbit.[21]

After the split, *NLR* became abstruse and didactic, remote from any active movement, oriented more and more to élitist and Leninist groups, both in Europe and the Third World.[22] The somewhat weird Francophile obsession, apparently rooted in an admiration for Sartre and other figures in French Marxism, also expressed itself theoretically in regret for the lack of a comparably strong CP intellectual tradition in Britain. Perhaps also, it was with the fading memory of Stalin, and of Hungary, that the style and the rhetoric changed, and the best spirits left.

These changes and the decline in the NL faction associated with the *NLR* journal continued through the 1960s.[23] Still deeply influenced by the intellectual currents of French Communism it moved from its Sartrian stance to embrace other luminaries as mentors. Althusserian counter-revisionism; and the associated structuralist school linked with the name and work of Lévi-Strauss, became popular, camouflaging Stalinism in new and more abstruse ways. In addition, there was the revived interest in the Frankfurt school of critical-social psychology and social philosophy. But except for some of its domestic analysis, *NLR* had little influence outside academic left and fashionable intellectual circles, and came to be principally known as a rather sectarian and abstract backwater of both traditional and revisionist Marxist thought.

At its worst, the later *NLR* degenerated into a convoluted and jargon-ridden never-never land of Marxian scholasticism, or even a revamped Stalinism, 'tarted-up' – as one of the ex-editors put it wryly – with a few 'Sartrian neologisms'.[24] By the 1970s, this performance made it something of an intellectual curio.[25]

More in touch with the larger movement in Britain were those who had broken with *NLR* in the early 1960s to form the loose grouping that brought out the 'May Day Manifesto' in 1967. The early NL which had been linked to these individuals had expressed its belief in the 'humanist strengths of socialism' as a basis of a popular movement, strengths to be developed in cultural and social terms as well as economic and political. But this belief too was dissipated and diluted during the later 1960s. In one recent critique the English forerunner is seen as having a critical impact 'antedating the formation of an independent left in other countries by some years and setting intellectual and organizational precedents which have been highly influential.'[26] On the other hand, the 'Old' NL as it had been termed, was certainly a 'false start' as far as Britain was concerned because it led nowhere; whether it had any real influence on the NL elsewhere is doubtful – though sections of the American NL of the mid-1960s did turn to its writings with interest, as their own search for ideology intensified.[27]

CND: decline and fall

Peggy Duff argues that CND was so large that it had already been responsible for swamping the English NL by 1963: 'In one way, CND did them no good. It swallowed them up as a political force', despite the latter's numbers and potential.[28] Certainly the understanding of the break-up of the nuclear disarmament movement is essential to an understanding of the fate of the NL in Britain in the later 1960s.

The dissolution of major organizations like the Committee of 100 and CND is far more significant in the British context than the rather earlier decline of their lesser American counterparts like SANE, WSP and SPU.[29] As has been seen, the nuclear issue had been defused sooner in America and had in any case never developed a movement on the same scale, since peace protest had been effectively rechannelled, first of all into civil rights and students activism in the early 1960s, and then into the Vietnam issue after 1965. Unlike these developments, the British movement found no major issue like Vietnam or civil rights or even student revolt until much later on.

No factors objectively justified the decline from the intense opposition to nuclear weapons that had accompanied the birth of the NL. The danger of war had only slightly receded. CND's demise has to be explained principally in terms of the movement's own history.[30]

The crisis in morale of the nuclear disarmament movement can be traced not least to internal factors such as the exhaustion and failure of a number of tactics, especially parliamentarist ones (discussed earlier). Most movements have a definite life cycle, during which a certain range of possibilities is explored; the weariness of any movement, after five years' campaigning in the context of anxieties about an ever-present nuclear threat, is understandable enough. Both symbolic civil disobedience and parliamentarism had proved severely limited approaches: there was a dearth of concrete victories, and the movement found itself searching for organizing issues to sustain itself.

As significant as these factors, was CND's continued failure to have any real impact on the British working class. Despite the unilateralist votes in the unions, despite all the rhetoric of the Labour-left in the early years – especially of those Marxists (like the 'Newsletter' group) in the campaign at the outset – the failure to organize the working class around the nuclear war-issue was well illustrated by the vain efforts of direct actionists to get union 'blacking' of work on bases or rocket sites, or even token strikes of an official kind. Few workers left their jobs, and even unofficial action was minimal. Attempts to prevent supplies reaching Aldermaston and other plants were equally unsuccessful. Bomber and missile production continued smoothly despite union positions on the bomb, and under the noses of Communist shop stewards.

Moreover, throughout this period, the leadership of CND proved itself, in the words of Peggy Duff, then CND's general secretary, 'paternalist, vicarious, and plebiscitary and basically lacking the imagination and courage to accept and lead the movement as it was'.[31]

The thrusts from the grassroots had been powerful in the early years, and with its self-democratization, the campaign had outgrown its initial old figureheads.[32] But though it had developed (organizationally, ideologically and constitutionally) beyond the pressure-group stage,[33] the influence of Labour Party strategists in the executive of CND (who saw it still as a lobbying organization, feeding and depending on the strength of the left of the Labour Party) remained very powerful. Under this influence, and after four frustrating years fighting in the Labour Party, CND looked as if it was about to stagnate as a sort of Fabian Society of the anti-nuclear movement: the experience was deeply destructive of a NL.

The official CND leadership, together with the *NLR* grouping, and the more orthodox Tribunite Left, must take substantial responsibility for the collapse of CND after 1963. Its failure to do creative work in the area of trans-national policies, non-military resistance, theories of direct action, and radical peace research, its inability to explore alternative strategies to flooding the Labour Party, its distance from grassroots projects, its unwillingness to recognize and harness the moral outrage at the heart of unilateralism, led both the NL and CND into the cul-de-sac of reformism.

That CND's fortunes should begin to wane soon after the winning of massive union support and the immense 1961 Aldermaston rally, can thus be traced to the cumulative frustrations of various kinds; partly to the inevitable split on civil disobedience; partly to an over-estimation of actual strengths; but above all to a psychological over-dependence on Labour politics.

This was never shown more clearly than in 1964. The new government contained many erstwhile CND supporters; but although Wilson made none of the promised concessions to the movement, the Labour-left still found the nuclear issue an embarrassment and were never prepared to bring the leadership to account.

Whether as demagogy, or sheer political realism, it had to be recognized that a mass-movement such as CND could only thrive on simple formulae; once it had dropped its first principles, its 'political case' collapsed as well. By moving away from the unique and guiding principle of unilateral action, 'Steps Towards Peace'[34] took away the central moral impact of the campaign, its main source of recruitment and motivation, and was met with fury and resignations from grassroots activists, producing the moment when many chose to leave CND.

The fact that CND was not able to find a popular formula for British non-alignment or proclaim it with the vigour of its later anti-NATO stance, was due to the failure of both the traditional Left and the NL to spell out trans-national alternatives to a national nuclear defence policy. Indeed it was easier to foster a distinct nativist element that opposed American presence as an alien, cultural and military dominance, exemplifying in part, hurt national pride.

This anti-American dimension which figures mainly in the campaigns against the bases, and was exploited by the CP, was later to be developed as a major feature by sections of the Left, and provides a forward link to the Vietnam war movement. As other tactics, issues and styles fell away, there was a tendency for the Old Left – especially the CP – to gain ground after 1965, principally on the Vietnam issue. CND became deeply compromised on the issue of alignment: the refusal or failure to work out and publicize a systematic and positive neutralist foreign policy to replace continued participation in the Atlantic alliance,[35] helped to give credibility to Gaitskell's accusations that 'Communists and fellow-travellers' dominated CND with their crude anti-Western slogans.

The 'issue' and 'event' orientation of the English movement made it very much a creature of context, reacting to crises and developments as they occurred. The intensified call for nuclear disarmament first arose as a direct response to the change of Britain's world status revealed by Suez; it reflected a 'loss of Empire', as well as escalations in nuclear weapons technology, the Cold War and an ambivalence towards Europe.[36] But as well as issues of national role and defence, CND reflected a broad cultural crisis, the impact of immigration and Americana, and changes in class structure; the eventual decline of anti-nuclear protest partly reflected a growing impatience with the manic preoccupation with international crises and single-issue orientations, at the expense of basic domestic social change. The Committee of 100 had begun to reflect this in its diversification towards wider ranging projects in the early 1960s.

At first these were local and spontaneous projects linking the bomb to topical issues and community action. The CND leadership tended to ignore or dissociate itself from such ventures, and the fragmentation increased; milk for Algeria, independent candidacies, demonstrations against the Greek regime, campaign caravans, factories for peace, spies for peace, RSG (Regional Seats of Government) demonstrations, fasts, squatting, tenants and eviction fights, were typical of the spread of activities the movement engaged in under the nuclear disarmament umbrella – whether officially endorsed by CND nationally or not. The CND leadership particularly condemned those actions which had a disruptive or anarchist flavour, such as voters, veto campaigns, and the invasions of the government RSGs.[37]

As the initial heat aroused by the Collins–Russell split cooled, CND concentrated on its organizing and educational work, and the complementarity of the two wings of the nuclear disarmament movement was recognized. But by this time the period of mass civil disobedience was over: the Committee was not so much smashed by mass arrests as by its inadequate sense of tactics; it made unrealistic estimates of what people would do, when and where,[38] especially when it began to talk seriously of flooding the jails, again. The Committee's newly won support was dissipated in a number of ill-planned and poorly publicized actions, and the government was not to repeat its inept handling of the arrest of Committee leaders (September 1961). The public bewilderment of the autumn was replaced by a return to 'normality' – the Committee of 100 became again part of the 'lunatic fringe', and though public attitudes had shifted in the movement's favour, the decline of the Committee after the December demonstrations of 1961 was precipitate. Although liaison with CND now increased, the Committee was never to repeat its early successes. Despite severe sentences, publicity for the Committee declined. The conspiracy charges, the twelve to eighteen month sentences, had a deterrent effect. Symbolic confrontations with the state had either to develop into something more concrete, or different tactics were needed. Decentralization and diversification was sound in principle, but only partially successful in practice. Decimated by prison sentences, demoralized by reluctant resignations and actual defections, the Committee was tempted into its misconceived strategies for demonstrations outside London.

The juxtaposition of nuclear disarmament with the growth of youth and counter-cultures, was also often cited as a source of CND's demise. But when the Aldermaston marches finally declined, it was not because marchers had danced in the streets, or brought a notion of community into their political style, or that this had allowed the growth of an idea of a 'whole person' being expressed on such occasions; it was because that sense of community was waning and had moved on elsewhere.

Between about 1963 and 1965, the counter-culture develops apart from the bomb issue, and adopts an increasingly critical attitude to CND's tired and now rather staid image and its respectable rituals.[39]

In America, as in England, the press was always eager to bury the peace movement alive, but it took a lot of burying. The Test Ban Treaty, and failure of the Cuban missile crisis to produce war, were seen as finally undermining the position of such groups as CND and SANE, and it is certainly true that the year 1963 marked a substantial recession in CND activity. Yet it is often forgotten that regardless of the premature obituaries after 1963, and despite the Test Ban Treaty, the Cuban brink and Wilson's Labour victory, CND remained for five years more, not only the largest peace organization in Britain, but the largest single radical organization (outside the CP), until it was finally eclipsed at the end of 1967 by the Vietnam Solidarity groups.[40] During this period both the limited Test Ban Treaty and apparent shifts in Labour policy after Gaitskell's death, were quoted as CND successes, but it was hard to demonstrate any concrete connections between the movement actions and such achievements. It is probably true that CND, like its American contemporaries, SANE and SPU, had over-emphasized the reformist issue of testing, and the signing of a limited Test Ban Treaty lost it one of its major platforms. Yet the Treaty, although welcomed by the movement, was seen as only a small step towards nuclear disarmament or even nuclear detente.

The 1962 Cuban missile crisis was a far more ambiguous event as far as CND was concerned. The reaction by the movement in London was conspicuously weak and confused[41] and political differences of attitude prevented a single response. The crisis certainly revealed the relative impotence of the peace movement in preventing any actual escalation towards the use of nuclear weapons. Indeed the paralysis of the Left and CND in Cuba Week was caused by a sense of just how close catastrophe was. But this belief that the crisis had *vindicated* CND's warning and appeals, was not shared by the larger population in any straightforward sense. The main NL sentiment was both of the reality of the dangers of nuclear war, and the pervasive sense of impotence in the face of such threat.

Just as in the early years it had never been clear whether CND demonstrations were a cause or effect of mounting public support, it was now doubtful whether they were sufficient as responses to inter-national crises. The first marches and sit-ins had seemed to be effective organizing devices, communicating to a movement if not to the public. But after Cuba, both CND and Committee of 100 demonstrations became increasingly ritualistic, serving a mainly expressive function for supporters, as became the case with Vietnam demonstrations in the USA.[42]

In the early 1960s, American students polled on the major issues facing man, acknowledged the likelihood of nuclear war, yet did not consider it to be a 'great and important issue'.[43] This illustrates one of the great problems of the peace movement, its inability to close the gap between popular consciousness and the reality of such war. Mediated experience has little impact in comparison with directly experienced reality, and distant or nuclear war had not touched most people's lives. Whilst the media, and growing resistance, brought Vietnam closer to home and one could experience and analyse racism, the consumer society, poverty, or even conventional war through conscription, the experience of nuclear war was beyond fact or theory. Only briefly, in the early 1960s, has such awareness made any widespread appearance.

Despite the decreasing public awareness after 1962, in reality the dangers of nuclear war had probably only been marginally diminished by the Test Ban Treaty, the Cold War thaw, the Cuban experience, the hot-line and the arms control talks and treaties (e.g. later the SALT negotiations). Against these developments had to be placed nuclear proliferation, hot-war in Indo-China, and a technological intensification of the arms race, including new weapons systems. By the 1970s, the overkill capacity of the great powers was far greater than a decade earlier, deterrent systems were even more sophisticated and still developing in relation to advances in space technology.

With renewed atmospheric nuclear testing in the 1970s, a new trans-national movement – 'Greenpeace' – arose especially emphasizing ecological aspects, and focused on the French Pacific and US Alaskan tests. But 'Greenpeace' did not represent a revival of the nuclear disarmament movement so much as a symbolic project that re-awakened awareness of the universal significance of the bomb – spurred by France's ostentatious nuclear programme, and others like it – both in terms of the ongoing arms race and the contamination of the atmosphere, and genetic damage to future generations.

The Communist Party's role

The dilemma of Communists' influence and anti-Communism was not dealt with any more effectively in the English NL than in the American situation, though the developments are different. In the American case, the movement associated with opposition to nuclear weapons disastrously weakened itself by a purge in the early 1960s. Against a background of McCarthyism, SANE's response was understandable, but it led to an over-reaction against exclusion in the NL.

In England, with little background of anti-Communist harassment, and a Labour-left that had long indulged in popular front tactics and fellow-travelling with the Communist Party, the situation was different. In Britain, as in America, the CP-initiated World Council of Peace and Stockholm Peace Appeal of the early 1950s had not only dominated the peace movement in the period, but created a widespread antipathy to the concept of 'peace' in the Cold War context; nevertheless Communists had played little part in sustaining the first anti-nuclear protests.[44]

Had the CP been in CND from the start, the story might have been more similar in England, but as it was, the initial embrace of the Party came not until 1960, after nearly three years of non-aligned campaigning when CND's size and success were already assured. In these years, the old Marxist left had a weak foothold in CND; they muddied its public image but they could not hope to control it.[45]

The years 1958–60 had been the years of CND's consensus, and the first three Aldermaston marches had been marked by a strong sense of community and purpose. After 1960, the entry of the Communist Party, whilst the more active attention of some other Marxist groups was declining, was certainly one factor causing the attrition in cohesion and morale; but in these early years, first the Trotskyists (e.g. the SLL) and later the CP, were an organizational nuisance rather than a threat; CND's sturdy political independence tended to take both the CP and fellow-travelling organizations by surprise; and the anti-Stalinist groups, continually obsessed with sectarian trench-warfare and archaic political debate, both in the USA and Britain, continued to isolate themselves and their political standpoints in terms of a self-defining analysis of the Soviet Union – not only of Stalinism, but also Leninism, Bolshevism, and the post-Stalin regimes.

These fixations, perhaps an inevitable hangover of the thirty-year Comintern hegemony on the Left, were accompanied and sustained in Britain by recurrent myths of capitalist crisis and impending working-class insurgency. After an initial alignment with CND, the *Newsletter* group and Socialist Labour League (SLL) mainly kept aloof.[46] But other Trotskyites who had engaged in CND much earlier than the pro-Soviet left, partly (and correctly) viewing it as a good recruiting ground, constituted factious and often disruptive minorities at meetings and demonstrations: along with Anarchist grouplets, they spent most of their time attacking the tactics, leadership platforms and character of the movement. For example, during the Cuba crisis, the debates about the dangers of nuclear war, US brinkmanship, Russian and Cuban 'adventurism' and Russian 'capitulation', had tended to split along sectarian lines. It had been this hard, grating, political edge, the old style of the Left in CND, which drove many to try to recreate the style and spirit of CND's first two 'years of grace', within the Committee of 100.

After 1963, CND itself became year by year more steadily compromised by the CP; by now, most of the Trotskyists and many of the Anarchists had moved out, but the CP at about this time seemed to decide to make CND its major peace front; over the ensuing years this political embrace tightened, finally becoming fatal. Having survived initial overtures, CND was slowly strangled as the CP was allowed not only to retain its influence, but to take over key positions in the national organization. No other group had this kind of staying power; the libertarians had moved on into the Committee, into community action, or out of active politics; those Pacifists who had entered and remained, wanted peaceful co-existence with other groups (as well as the Eastern bloc); CND's Labourites typically entered into tactical alliances with the CP. Dedicated, manoeuvring and repetitious, the Party 'bored from within' in every sense; a resolute CPer could usually outwork and outwit a dozen politically inexperienced, if not naive, CNDers. In the mid-1960s, virtual control over the CND national office, its newspaper and its major committees passed into the hands of the CP, or its closest sympathizers (some of them officially 'non-card-carrying' or ex-party members). By this time, CND was already in decline, but its destruction can be detected in the years of this stranglehold.[47]

None of this should obscure the skill, experience and perseverance of CP workers; but far from reversing the decline of CND, it must on balance be judged to have been a major contributory cause, not least because it foisted on the movement the CP's rather tired political style in place of the youthful energetic and fairly novel style of the late 1950s. Tactically the CP encouraged a return to pre-Aldermaston reformism, a generalized 'peace' appeal, and endorsed the entrist Labour Party tactic (though it certainly could not be blamed for setting the Campaign on this path).[48] By giving CND nearly three years' grace, the CP had missed these early experiences, and despite the integrity of some CPers in terms of faith in their own dogmas, this lack led them astray in relation to the moral idealism of nuclear pacifism which they only further subverted, thereby helping to destroy the very substantial movement that still remained in 1963.

The most telling part of the early CND style and appeal related to a moral call to the non-conformist conscience; it was that part of its programme which had helped develop a mass base. Yet this was something which the CP, just like the Trotskyite and Bevanite Left before it, was totally unequipped to deal with. Instead it attempted to substitute the economistic arguments about military costs which dominate CND propaganda in the later 1960s (together with predictable attacks on NATO). CND was thus compromised partly because of its own exhaustion, because of the lack of a solid ideological counterbalance, and because, for a variety of reasons, the theoretical NL, as in America, was chary of developing (or sustaining) any thoroughgoing critique of CP activity and policy within the peace movement.[49]

Clearly those in CND who advocated withdrawal from NATO were not necessarily aligned with the Soviet Union, and Gaitskell's original charge of 'neutralists and fellow-travellers' was at best only half truth. Given the transparency of most Cold War 'peacekeeping' claims, it could be argued, as some traditional left-wingers did, that Western defence was geared solely to meet an illusory threat – that of Russia – or to defend the spoils of Empire – and as such should be dismantled rather than replaced. Indeed the idea of the Red Army occupying Britain, did appear more fantasy than reality.

What divided the neutralists from the CP was the refusal of the latter to insist on the dissolution of the Warsaw Pact, but even the former lacked vehemence; the crude anti-NATO, anti-American slogans of 1961 and 1962 were for CND the thin end of a wedge which led towards increasingly Moscow-leaning formulae. The lack of predominant alternative policies outside the Cold War framework tended to pitch CND into debates about 'peoples'' bombs and 'workers'' bombs, or 'progressive' nuclear testing, which sapped the initial integrity of its protest.

This disastrous hiatus began soon after the CP's entry, when the British Peace Committee was developing its own anti-American nuclear line, and survived through the discussions about European security a decade later; the Warsaw Pact's nuclear weapons policy was never unambiguously challenged by CND, though later the British CP, unlike its American counterpart, was willing to make mild criticism of the Soviet invasion of Czechoslovakia.[50] There was little follow-up however, and the CP found itself embarrassed by more open opposition to the occupation in the ranks of CND and sought to dampen it.

The English and American CP's, despite their differences over issues like Czechoslovakia, continued a reformed Moscow line. On issues such as Vietnam, there was little evidence of flexibility or detachment from the exigencies of Soviet foreign policy, and during the 1970s, their obsession with 'European security' reflected the Russian view of continuing nuclear dangers, and strategy of both nuclear deterrence and peaceful co-existence, with some controlled and limited disarmament. Echoing this standpoint, these kinds of focus remained an unmistakable trademark of CP activity in the peace movement, in both the 1960s and 1970s.

It is difficult to make any final judgments on the motives for the CP's attentions to CND.[51] It is obviously crude to suggest that its only concern was to weaken the defence system of the West, aid Soviet hegemony, or weaken threats to the 'socialist camp.'

Nevertheless, this clearly was the motivation of some CPers in CND some of the time – for a few, perhaps their main objective. But there also is abundant evidence that some of the moral idealism of CND rubbed off on others. Nuclear pacifism sapped many tried loyalties over the years, and after the major Russian test series in 1961, CND membership was a dubious asset. In fact some YCL members, won over to genuinely CND positions in 1961, participated in a sit-down at the Russian Embassy in London against the fifty-megaton bomb. Most Moscow-oriented CPers truly believed CND's warnings of the imminence of holocaust, and yet on the other hand were now prepared to accept the formulation that 'war was no longer inevitable'. In the past many Marxists had held that global war was unavoidable, but only the Maoists continued to argue this in the 1960s. On the other hand, the CP did not share the Chinese view of nuclear war as a 'paper tiger'; the genuine Russian fear of German revanchism, and the real danger of nuclear disaster, were faithfully reflected in CP attitudes. In fact, many members were prepared to maintain restrained criticism of both Chinese and Russian nuclear policies, though again, how much this was necessary for credibility in CND and how much genuinely motivated is debatable.

After CND

Tired, split, tactically and ethically bankrupt, trying to be all things to everyone, straining to recapture lost crowds, early successes and forgotten idealisms, CND and movements like it, perhaps deserved to decline.[52] The growing disenchantment both with the strategic bankruptcy of CND's leadership and with the growing influence of the Old Left, accelerated a tendency, already noticeable in the movement, towards fragmentation. It would be as foolish to ascribe the decline and fall of the Campaign to the activities of the CP alone, as it would be to ignore the very real importance of the Party's influence. But it was the fact that the anti-nuclear movement itself ebbed and divided, leaving a political vacuum, that was crucial to the renewed growth of *all* the Old Left groupings in the later 1960s – including the CP.

Indeed, such is the disintegration after CND that it is hard after 1963 to talk of the NL in England as a 'movement'. To describe the continuing struggle between authoritarian Old Left groups and libertarian tendencies over the dispersing legacy of CND is to depict something less than a movement. Certainly nothing like SDS or SNCC or even the Resistance emerged as a major organizational expression of a NL movement as in America, and this is a further principal reason why this first English NL fades just as the American movement expands.

The Anarchists, in particular, lacked the coherent, nationally organized formations of an earlier period in Europe. If a comparable movement exists, it was the amorphous set of alternative projects and institutions which most closely resembled the American pattern; lacking any coordination or unitary character, it is the one development which survives into the 1970s.

In the USA after 1965, populism and pragmatism could be merged in action and located in a student base. But the British movement lacked such traditions;[53] its populist and pragmatic gestures were left to anarchist and community action projects: it failed to establish a major student movement.[54] In fact it is significant of the contrasts between the movements' development in the two countries, that outside CND, which was always debatably NL in its political orientation, and the Committee of 100, the early NL developed no real independent mass-base, and thus could be overgrown by CND. Moreover, partly because of the relatively small élite nature of the British university system, nothing comparable with the American or even the European student movement developed, and it is perhaps a significant factor in under-standing the different character of the British NL.

The far greater fragmentation in the British situation, whilst in part reflecting the same centrifugalist and decentralist tendencies that defined the American movement, was caused by these special factors which created a confusion of issues, and competing small organizations, which the Old Left groups could more readily take advantage of, or destroy.

To define a British or an English NL, to understand its nature and subsequent history, it is necessary to summarize these various segments into which the anti-nuclear movement broke, for it was from such fractions that a NL struggled to survive in Britain, or indeed to re-emerge, in so far as it had been absorbed, or had dissipated itself, within CND.

As the Committee of 100 and tendencies within CND turned to-wards long-term social change, and movements and projects flourished at the grassroots during the early 1960s, libertarian groups fastened on issues like housing and rents to develop direct action campaigns. The later squatting movement, rent and eviction fights, especially in the London area, stemmed directly from this and were an important ingredient in the Anarchist revival. This was a period of genuinely intense local activism: community projects in provincial cities, stemmed partly from the Campaign Caravans of George Clark[55] and the Mobile Voluntary work teams of Barnaby Martin; and the activities of Ron Bailey, Jim Radford and Des Wilson move out from the same milieu to develop radical organizing experiments.

There are also a variety of single-issue movements and one-shot campaigns throughout the 1960s, many of them associated with the Old Left, or sponsored by the socialist sects, or the Anarchists; squatting, community issues, immigration, workers' control, Vietnam, Biafra, anti-apartheid – including the militant 'Stop the Seventies Tour' (STST) campaign (1969–70) – and various student campaigns. But this proliferation of groups and issues from tenants' and claimants' unions and other community-based projects, to national organizations related to the Third World events, workers' control or 'student power', was not a linked development, even in the inchoate way in which the segments of the American NL were linked. Though their organizers talked of 'links', most of the groups, local and national, were evanescent, protest campaigns, often media-oriented – mini-movements that rarely survived a year. This was even true of the big Vietnam coalition of 1968.

Far more significant than CND's activity (1965-8) on Vietnam, was the emergence of this massive VSC coalition in 1968. It brought to the surface the impact of developments already apparent in the American NL, especially the influence of events abroad, in Bolivia, in Vietnam, in France and at Columbia. The ethos and symbolism of violence fused with Third World cults and finally arrived in London. The publication of new papers like *Black Dwarf* and *Red Mole* reflected these changes, as did the new fashions of revolutionary activism and moves towards confrontation expressed in student occupations and street battles. The spontaneity and anger of Grosvenor Square were not clearly ideologically based, but were emotions shared by most of the activist groups, whatever their view of the NLF or Ho Chi Minh. Despite the willingness by sections of the Old Left to continue quies-cence in face of the Wilson government's equivocations, these groups, particularly when they cooperated, could represent themselves as recreating a broad left extra-parliamentary coalition, reuniting various splinters and fragments again under one umbrella on the Vietnam issue, as formerly CND had done on the bomb.

Thus it is only briefly, in 1968, that a NL in Britain regains the mass base that had been attracted through the nuclear weapons issue;[56] in that sense, it is a good deal less significant than its American, and perhaps its European, counterparts in this period. Even amongst the smaller university populations of Britain, the movement of the later 1960s mobilized proportionately fewer students than SDS had done.

Briefly it seemed that the London based Radical Student Alliance (RSA) might play the same sort of role after 1966 that SDS had played in the American context. But it was soon eclipsed by the more ideo-logical, and even more transient RSSF (Revolutionary Socialist Student Federation).[57] Though never as widespread as in America, student militancy did develop after the 1967 activities at the London School of Economics (LSE), partly modelled on the Berkeley actions.[58] The period produced a number of occupations and other militant actions during 1968 – particularly at Essex, LSE, Hornsey and Birming-ham.[59] Certainly this student activity was the most important single factor in providing a mass-base for the Vietnam war protests of 1968, drawn disproportionately from the campus constituency. But the student movement was unable to forge the firm links between itself and issues such as war, racism or community issues or workers' control that student movements abroad, particularly in France, Germany and the USA, had achieved: it is perhaps not inaccurate to see this pheno-menon in Britain as a 'temporary excitement' within British liberalism.[60]

The attempts, such as that of the 1969 National Convention of the Left (NCL), to bring together both Old Left organizations (like International Socialists, the Communist Party and smaller groups like IMG) with the range of projects that was closest to a NL or with the alternative society experiments (communes, underground papers, free universities, etc.) were a hopeless failure. Inevitably, the organized Old Left dominated such a conference that aspired to ignore any difference between Old and New. It was subject to an effective takeover by the CP in competition with the IS. Even more clearly doomed than its American counterpart (the Conference for New Politics held two years before), the NCL, like the CNP, shunned or ignored any attempts at sustaining a distinct NL identity, refusing for example to take a clear stance outside electoralism or the party machines.

The same criticism could be levelled at the Janus-facing 'May Day Manifesto' with its zealous anti-imperialism, and economistic analyses, straddling a no-man's land between established and alternative institutions and strategies. Its swansong was this disaster that befell the National Convention, which it helped organize, and which marked the end of the post-*ULR* developments.[61]

The Anarchists had initially put in a strong claim to inherit the legacy of the nuclear protests, but in so far as each political tendency remained close to the traditional sect model of Old Left politics, unselfconsciously adopted by the British Trotskyite groups and the Maoists, libertarians never constituted any sort of loose national movement or organization – such as the Committee of 100 had been. Perhaps because of their sectarianism, the Anarchists lost considerable ground in 1968 to the Trotskyist groups, to IS, and the newly-formed IMG, as well as to Maoists and the CP itself, which was still making some headway on the Vietnam issue.

The IS, and to a lesser extent the IMG, represented the two British groups most capable of capitalizing on the Trotskyite revival of the later 1960s. For all the eclecticism of the IMG rhetoric and identifications, it was ultimately another form of revision of the Bolshevik experience applied to the British situation. Where it differed from the IS was in its diminished obsession with the proletariat, and its NL orientation to the Third World and students. Several of its leaders, such as Tariq Ali and Robin Blackburn, associated with the leadership of student movements, linked themselves with 'anti-imperialist' actions on Vietnam and Cuba – Ali being a leading spokesman of the VSC. The IS, whilst lacking the flair of the IMG, or the same glamorous leadership, was more systematic and theoretically sober; building from a solid base established over a decade, it was able to replace IMG as the main recruiter of student revolutionaries, though its orientation to the coming British working-class revolution, was a good deal more guarded than IMG rhetoric.[62]

Its paper, the *Socialist Worker*, which unlike the IMG's *Red Mole*[63] (which split from the *Black Dwarf* after 1968) did not attempt to make bridges with the counter-culture or underground press, built up by far the most substantial circulation of the Left periodicals by the 1970s, but was not NL in tone.

The IMG and IS indulged in continuing polemics with each other, and with other groups such as the CP and WRP, and their humourlessness and lack of vision seemed merely to reproduce Trotskyite sectarianism of earlier decades on a larger scale. Moreover, despite the unexamined Old Left assumption of impending class polarization and industrial volatility, the main recruiting grounds for the Trotskyites, like the Maoists, were colleges and universities rather than factories; they fought actively within student groups and organizations, both radical like the RSA and the RSSF, and later the established National Union of Students (NUS) and individual student unions.[64]

Workers' control was another major issue that both libertarians and the Old Left shared and contested in the later 1960s. Sedgewick of the IS talks of a 'militant-gradualism' drawn from Owen and G. D. H. Cole, centred on workers' control.[65] From *ULR* onwards, the NL had preferred such an approach to 'industrial democracy' rather than 'nationalization' – a formula which appeared unable to confront the central problem of bureaucracy, the distance between workers and decisions, or the alienated politics of over-centralized states. 'Workers' control' was viewed by the CP on the other hand as tactic rather than principle. But as the Yugoslav model was widely studied, and with the growing industrial militancy in the late 1960s, a coalition around the Institute of Workers' Control (IWC) was formed, with a strongly libertarian dimension.

This showed remarkable growth after 1968, reaching its zenith after the fillip given by the strikes of ten million workers in France and the challenge of the government's incomes policies. Its large Sheffield conference of 1968 was remarkably free of sectarian presence and control. Within a year, however, the scene had changed, and both the major Trotskyite groups had poured members (many of them students) into the 1969 conference, with the result that IS seemed to wrest control from the existing Institute leadership and the Labour Party unionists.[66] Nevertheless, the years 1971–2 were marked by many factory occupations influenced by the principle of workers' control.[67] And the International Socialists emphasized the 'rank and file' movements of workers in the private and public sectors as against the official trades union bureaucracies; this they did in both industry and services.

The most clear example of various Left tendencies moving in to contest the organizational legacy of CND were, in addition to the Vietnam issue, the area of community politics. As has been seen, the campaigns in Ilford, Notting Hill, Southwark and in Kent against homelessness had their roots in earlier Anarchist activity. But as such community action spread, given the changed atmosphere of the later

1960s, a Marxist rhetoric was increasingly used, and some organizers were, or became, members of IS or IMG. There was considerable tension between these two groups, and with the Anarchists, especially in so far as the latter felt that the Trotskyists were not only destructive in their criticism of the squatting campaign, but infiltrating, 'politicizing', and in some cases taking it over, on an élitist basis.

This growing antagonism between Anarchists and the IS and the IMG over the squatting campaign, was symptomatic of the differences between them. The latter's Leninist style of organization and stress on class-vanguard and the IMG's lack of domestic ideology or strategy made most Trotskyites appear alien to local organizers; yet their greater cohesion enabled them to take over squats, and later many Claimants' Union groups also, in the name of 'radicalization'.

The IS criticized the Anarchists in turn for a lack of any coherent long-term strategy of change, and an a-political emotionalism which focused on the homeless rather than relating to leading sections of the working class. The IS were, however, quite willing to organize around the issue, to move in on the squatting campaign, and use it for political advantage as a radicalizing influence; and generally those who believed in a centralized revolution made by a Leninist vanguard, especially the IMG, brought this style and language even into community action.

But in the 1970s the scene alters yet again when the major Leninist groups tactically abandon the field to libertarians and an assortment of leftists and liberals, some of whom make a more definite bridge with alternative society approaches and projects. It is in this area that the continuity and growth of the early NL impulses can most readily be detected, but the legacy of fragmentation and localism rooted in the collapse of CND showed few signs of being overcome.

9. Vietnam and Alignment

Non-alignment and internationalism: the third way

The failure of Third Camp positions as a version of Left internationalism in the early 1960s, was itself bound up with the old problem of nation states. As long as the nation state survived, it was clear that major conflicts would continue to revolve around them and their conflicting interests. What was also clear was that external hostility was used as a means of internal stabilization and integration. Any particular enemy might be largely an ideological invention, a justification for defence spending, or a purely transitory threat.

Smaller societies or revolutionary movements would inevitably get caught in these conflicts, particularly exchanges between the superpowers or supra-national blocs. In addition, such territorial units were seen to inadequately represent the needs of minorities and subcultures, especially ethnic and racial ones. Thus the widening transnationalist challenge to the territorial basis of political units, including the nation state, was in part an expression of the movement's pluralism, as well as its politically libertarian character. There was a growing doubt whether territoriality should define decision-making units at all, and this was expressed in theories as diverse as 'participatory democracy' and 'civilian resistance'.

The Third Camp idea which had first become translated into various novel forms of internationalism, non-alignment or 'positive neutralism' in the late 1950s, had a fatal weakness.[1] Since at least 1917, Left internationalism had been rooted in a faith in groups of countries or states, or the Comintern, rather than in a trans-national alternative. Influenced by this tradition, the 'non-alignment' of the NL thus was conceived in terms of a non-aligned bloc of neutralist nations, mostly Third World countries.[2] It was not a trans-national conception, and in so far as the middle-ground occupied by some Third World governments was eaten away during the 1960s, there was a decisive movement towards alignment.

Moreover, although positive neutralism in Britain in part had to do with support for the existing non-aligned bloc, it also implied a role for Britain in the world, as arbiter or honest-broker, resolving world conflicts. Such a notion clearly contained delusions of post-imperial grandeur and of independent national action that was a hangover from former attitudes to the Commonwealth. As such it implied an often superior and patronizing stance to the Third World that had little relation to the actual development of these *tactically* neutral states.[3]

It was particularly when these countries failed to remain either non-aligned or neutral or even united, that the position weakened and collapsed. In addition, since the regimes of many of these countries turned out to be far from exemplary in their domestic activities, it was hard for many radicals to identify with their foreign policies. At this juncture, sections of the peace movement veered on the one side towards explicit alignment – usually with parts of the Communist world – and on the other towards greater trans-nationalism.

Despite the early NL's non-alignment, there was a distinct suspicion that when the cards were down, some of the *ULR* editors would have plumped for alignment with the Russian bloc, even though an 'unambiguous choice was virtually unbearable' and 'no fully supportable political choice existed'.[4] From the outset, some groups and publications like *Studies on the Left* in the USA and *New Reasoner* in England, clearly leaned slightly towards Russia.[5]

For many in the NL, the hope of a revived working-class internationalism died hard; but with working-class support for the Tory invasion of Suez and for Enoch Powell's racism in Britain; for 'Algérie Française' by French workers; for the Cold War anti-Communism and the Vietnam war by American workers – it was clear that this was the last constituency in which now to look for anything but the narrowest of trans-national links.[6]

The vain but classic hope of Socialist Internationalism, at least up to the 1914 débâcle, had been that massive non-cooperation, a general strike, refusal of military service, or the desertion of, or fraternization between, troops could prevent any imperialist war. In so far as these beliefs did not involve arrangements between nations or states, but only solidarity between members of a single homogeneous class across political boundaries, the term 'trans-nationalism' was perhaps more appropriate than 'internationalism' to describe them.[7] This contra-distinction of notions of trans-nationalism and internationalism proved critical to the basic problem for the NL facing nationalistic developments in the Third World, and economic nationalism at home.

It is significant that a major NL anti-imperialist, Oglesby, failed to even understand points made by Isaac Deutscher in the old Internationalist tradition of Socialism. In a speech at Berkeley,[8] Deutscher called for a class-conflict that was not linked to nationalism: 'The divisions may once again run within nations rather than between nations' and thus give back 'dignity and meaning' to class struggle and 'great ideas'. Deutscher's remarks reflect the insight that when 'class war' is fought within nations, it competes with nationalism for the loyalty of working people. When it is fought by nations, i.e. between rather than within the national frameworks (if Deutscher's Trotskyism can embrace such a concept), it may be claimed that one nation has managed to embody 'proletarian interests' over against other states which are seen to embody 'bourgeois' ones.[9] When a national war effort uses proletarian rhetoric or symbols to reinforce its appeal, the evidence of history is still that the nation, rather than the class, will become the dominant symbol of affiliation and frame of organization, and national chauvinism, rather than international socialism, may prove to be the primary source of motivation.

That this tension is not perceived by Oglesby, reflects the extremely limited consciousness of the problems of nationalism of the NL leadership generally. On the other hand, Oglesby's dismay at Deutscher's remarks is understandable: why should conflict be limited to a national framework? Why should political conflict be limited only to class conflict within given states? For example, the Maoist model of the world countryside surrounding and defeating the world's towns was a prestigious analogy: as in China such strategy had brought revolution. It coincided with an awareness that the confrontation of white and non-white, or rich and poor, was also involved in a confrontation of the rural and the industrial sectors of the world.[10]

Oglesby probably had in mind these struggles between global classes. Yet conflict between the coloured poor societies and the white rich, and between rural peoples and urban ones, between the peasantry of the world and its oppressors, had never been represented or crystallized except in the most partial ways by nationalist wars, or nation states. Indeed nationalism was usually imposed artificially on such conflicts, or merely sought to represent itself as embodying one of these multiple dimensions (e.g. a 'peasant' nation).

Yet it is significant that whatever theorists like Oglesby or Deutscher were deciding, and despite the pseudo-nationalist identification with the NLF (i.e. as the 'true representative' of 'all the Vietnamese people'), the movement was still manifesting practical trans-nationalism in its growth both at home and abroad. The trans-national alternative to both Deutscher's and Oglesby's positions was expressed simply by the view that struggle should be contained neither by conflict between nations nor within nations, but transcend national borders, subverting both the national state and such boundaries.[11] Liberating national cultural communities (without organizing armies or bureaucracies in their name) might be one of these struggles – but one amongst many. For nationalism as such, whenever used as a military and political mobilizer, has been typically bureaucratic, élitist and centralizing, and this could be shown to be true no less of Vietnamese nationalism than of the Russian, American or German varieties.

Peasant peoples having never been fully integrated into a national frame, embody a trans-nationalism of a different sort. Living on the land, tied to it for subsistence, they have little sense of the national political unit, its boundaries or its relevance.[12] Their communal focus is the village and their solidarities are with other peasants. This regional, ethnic, or communal consciousness stands in an alien relationship with the modern state, and with the national market, whose boundaries often cut artificially across immemorial bonds. This latter characteristic is most marked in ex-colonial territories such as Africa where artificial boundaries (lines on a map) were inherited from metropolitan diktat.[13]

As the state grows, it demolishes these links to tribes, families, localities, or the larger peasant society, in favour of unification within the nation state. Revolutionary war is one way in which this nationalism is imposed, and the sovereignty of locale or region broken in favour of new centralized state-structures. Far from expressing peasant trans-nationalism or community, wars of liberation typically destroy both. It is ironic that the growing identification with the peasantry of the Third World by the Western Left, should be an inevitable accompaniment of its own growing trans-nationalism; it also reflected movement frustrations at home, as well as increasing consciousness of revolutionary activity in the 'tiers monde' itself.

The acceleration of liberation wars in Indo-China, Algeria and other parts of Africa, in Cuba and other parts of Latin America, was accompanied by the precipitation of further peasant-based nations, joining China and India on the world stage. But this process too was as much *trans*-national as national. Factually and ideologically the division between the urban advanced sector and peasant society was a world-wide division that cut across national boundaries. An imagery was needed to express this opposition, and the images of Fanon and Mao were combined with dreams of a Third World peasant revolution strangling and dispossessing the exploitative metropolitan areas. In the West, this was an imagery compounded of romanticism, guilt, compassion and pure misunderstanding about the relationship between the peasants and their 'liberators'.

It is true that, with the popularization of peasant-focused writing like that of Fanon or Mao, and Lin Piao, there was an increasing rejection by the NL of the old Marxist view of the peasantry as 'backward' and 'reactionary'. But this was not accompanied by genuine insights into the transformation of peasant society, although Mao's model of rural base areas, or Debray's talk of 'focos'[14] and 'mobility', could be made to seem analogous to movement tactics, or the building of an alternative society, in the industrial West. The character of these superficial identifications can, it is also argued, be explained in their association with a more generalized attack on Western values, mounted both by the counter-culture and black American writers, in common with both African and Asian theorists, and Western metropolitan intellectuals like Sartre.

Undoubtedly Fanon's appeals to the developing world to avoid the mistake made by the West: 'not to pay tribute to Europe by creating states, institutions and societies which draw inspiration from her', was advice ignored not merely by the Algerian revolutionary élite, but by most of Fanon's Western admirers.[15] In forming these global re-orientations, which radically challenged some Old Left orthodoxies, the NL on the whole drew its information and imagery of the Third World movements either from the established Western media or from official revolutionary Third World propaganda.

Many nationalist Communist leaders in Asia and Africa publicly announced their avoidance of centralized Western or Russian models of development, endorsing, it seemed, alternative paths chosen to avoid the over-emphasis on industrialism. On the other hand, it was quite clear that both the infrastructure and superstructure, the technological and institutional aspects of industrial societies, could be developed rapidly, when harnessed to national-liberation wars and political unification.

Alongside the rise of the nation state, modernization and indus-trialism evolve in relation to such changes in the rural sector. In the long run, the model of progressive change which fetishizes industrial production, modern political structures, and often armed violence as well, is substantially (if tacitly) accepted by Third World leaders (especially by Western- and Russian-trained élites). A synthesis of old and new, East and West, is the main innovation. Despite such evidence, some in the NL were still reluctant to recognize these processes, arguing that the Third World movements were avoiding forced development to industrialism, and citing favoured aspects of Tanzanian or Chinese experience.[16]

If the Western movement clutched at anti-industrial straws, equally, the belief in the heroic guerilla was a myth that died hard; there was a tendency to exaggerate the role and importance of military struggle in political change. Commentators from Debray to *Newsweek* concen-trated on it, and such sources tended to exaggerate the role of charis-matic leadership. The *NLR* writers lauded a 'fraternity between people and leaders formed in the revolutionary party',[17] but were either ill-informed or unhelpful about the actual relationship of these struggles and leaders to Third World peoples. There was an easy identification of peasant peoples with the leading armed resistance organizations.

Through the role of guerilla armies in the Chinese, Cuban, Algerian and Vietnamese contexts, a myth was purveyed that here was a less directed and authoritarian mode of violent change than conventional military force, and one which stemmed from 'the people' themselves. Such an endorsement would thus disguise the fundamental opposition between peasant society – decentralized, communal, stateless; and the alien hierarchical structures – military, political, and economic – imposed by the nationalist-Marxist formations on these societies, both as a means of the 'liberation' and destruction of the peasantry in the name of progress.

Guerilla war was interpreted, in terms of its apparent spontaneity and decentralized character, as arising naturally from peasant society rather than being imposed on it, as even a cursory reading of Mao or Giap or Debray would have confirmed. Such approaches should be contrasted with Fanon's theory, much closer to a peasant decentralized and spontaneous theory of revolution 'from the bottom up'. Although in practice the Algerian FLN did not conform to the theory, Fanon insisted that: 'when people have taken part in violent liberation war, part in national liberation, they will allow no-one to set themselves up as "liberators".' Tragically the lesson of Algeria, as with other liberation wars, was just the contrary. The decimation of the internal forces ushered in the domination by first bureaucratic cadres, and latterly military élites, who had kept at a safe distance from the war zones. Whilst in his well-known paean to violence, Fanon had not clearly given any endorsement to conventional armies of liberation, his writing could easily be used for such an endorsement. He did not live to assess the final cost of the war he supported: the misery of Algeria both in the huge human and social destruction and the dire political results of such a strategy.[18]

Although strikingly different from orthodox Marxist or Leninist strategy, still lacking an adequate critical appraisal of the Algerian struggle, the Fanonist failure to understand the implications of military and political organization created external to a peasant society, helped sustain the fatal myths and ambiguities, that soon led the NL (or much of it) into a similar myopia about Vietnam. At the intellectual level, the NL, still lacking any thoroughgoing sociological analysis of war and militarism, could not compare the war-machines of the post-industrial context with those of the developing world, the 'liberation' armies. As well as capitulating to the exigencies of modern bureaucratic organization, ultimately each national armed struggle came to terms with its context of world power and became, to a greater or lesser extent, aligned to, or sponsored by, a major power. It was a process which inevitably controverted and dissipated the non-aligned and trans-national impulse at the heart of the NL, as well as anaesthetizing its pacifist conscience.

Pacifism and national liberation

It is doubtful whether this cult of armed violence and iconography of the heroic guerilla would have come to dominate the NL as it did, or have been sustained as long as it was, had not the radical pacifists' position on wars of liberation crumbled during the 1960s. One can trace this capitulation back to the early years of the decade; the disarray of European pacifists over the war in Algeria, the loneliness of figures like Camus in his refusal to endorse the FLN; this isolation and detachment in the constrained context of 'the Algerian crisis, little different from that of Muste faced by the Cold War balance-of-terror, has many parallels with the situation of those later faced by similar choices in relation to Vietnam in the mid-1960s. When it came to both the Vietnam and Algerian wars, the attempts to avoid the roles of victim or executioner became an anguished one. Camus could not choose the military revolution that he had condemned in his work, even against an oppression that he fully acknowledged. Opposing the torture of the 'paras' and the terror of the FLN, he drew hostility and slander from both sides. His call for a civilian truce, as a gradualist and nonviolent solution to the Algerian bloodbath, won him few allies, just as the call for ceasefire and reconciliation in Vietnam later isolated non-aligned pacifists.

Nevertheless, the intellectual foundations of the NL's position lie more in the analysis of Cuba in its first years of revolution (1959–61) e.g. by Mills's *Listen Yankee*, and in the pages of *Liberation*.[19] Exemplifying the ambiguous tightrope walked by American pacifists on Cuba, it was perhaps understandable that Muste and a majority of the *Liberation* editors should give qualified support to the Cuban revolution. It had after all been achieved with minimal bloodshed, and despite the later military images of the revolution, it was its very lack of protracted warfare that could explain the relatively libertarian elements of its first years. Before the Bay of Pigs, the revolution was still mildly nationalist and socialist; though indications of its authoritarian character existed, thoroughgoing Marxian dictatorship developed only later, and largely in response to American encirclement. However, this pragmatic stance, whilst it kept *Liberation* close to the mainstream of American radicalism, was a thin end of a wedge. If a violent military coup and political executions were acceptable in Cuba, why not elsewhere? Moreover, *Liberation*'s tendency to give Cuba's degenerations the benefit of the doubt (it published far less criticism than some more explicitly socialist journals) contributed to popularizing a blanket endorsement of Castroism.

Ironically, support for the Cuban regime increased at the same time as the revolution reverted into a more unrelenting authoritarian pattern; this support partly represented a reaction against US military pressure, partly the growing radical identification by the young NL. From 1959, Cuba was an essential part of the American NL experience; no 'liberation war' came as close in the British experience – the proximity of Cuba and the initial independence of Castroism made it model, magnet, and inspiration for young mainland revolutionaries.[20] As they were to do subsequently on Vietnam, movement spokesmen like Dellinger, Hayden, Lynd, Muste, and McReynolds gave prestige to a position on Cuba that came close enough to endorsement of armed struggle; only if they had held the line at this point, might there have been fewer openings in the movement to crude anti-imperialist, pro-militarist positions.

That this occurred, it has been suggested, had a great deal to do with the changing leadership role of *Liberation*, its entanglement with SDS and influence on NL attitudes to the Vietnam war. Of those associated with the magazine, Muste, Lynd, and Dellinger and later even McReynolds, drifted away from absolute pacifism in the critical years after Cuba; of the four, only Lynd, the least absolute to begin with, maintained some elements of a genuine pacifist critique. *Liberation* itself flirted with the cult of violence surrounding both the Cuban revolution and the NLF; and those caught up in this process, like Dellinger and McReynolds – who had initially been closer to absolute pacifism – moved away from it; Dellinger in 1965 significantly refers to both the 'heroic forces' of the Fidelistas and the Viet Cong.

Reactionary or oppressive roles by other groups than the USA were increasingly and flagrantly ignored, as the growing anti-imperialism of SDS in turn reinforced these double-standard tendencies. Tom Hayden, bridging SDS and *Liberation*, although not a pacifist, had also at the outset been ostensibly opposed to 'militarism and nationalism',[21] but he quickly and easily came to terms with both the militarism and nationalism of the NLF; the visits of most of the *Liberation* group and Hayden to Cuba and North Vietnam appeared to affirm and take this identification one stage further.

It is ironic that it was this very weakening of their pacifism that was a factor in enabling such erstwhile pacifists around *Liberation* (Muste, Dellinger, Lynd and McReynolds) to take decisive leadership roles in the American peace movement during the following years.[22] Muste's concern with 'neutralization' of potential world flash points led him naturally to urge a unilateral US ceasefire in Vietnam, negotiations and re-unification, independent of his general 'Third Camp' politics. Lynd's appearance in the leadership of an alliance of SDS and *Liberation*, forming in 1965 the first major anti-Vietnam war coalition, was a significant early indication of this new development. Whilst most older Pacifist groupings and traditional peace groups tended to keep aloof from this SDS-initiated coalition, some Old Left groups, such as the Socialist Workers' Party (SWP) with their slogan 'Bring the Boys Home Now', as well as Muste and some of the radical pacifists round *Liberation*, joined.

Having been involved with this initial Vietnam coalition during 1965, by 1966 and right up to his death at eighty-two in 1967, Muste played a leading role in both the National Co-ordinating Committee against the War, and the Spring Mobilization Committees – a mantle that was to pass on to the shoulders of Dellinger, Muste's chief lieutenant. But no one walked the knife-edge closer than Lynd; calling himself a 'personal' pacifist, he made distinctions enabling him to adopt positions on the Vietnam war in which his political pacifism became highly selective, since it was not derived from any overall analysis of war and militarism, but from personal religious preference.

Lynd's equivocation on the Vietnam war primarily stemmed from the common belief that the USA were altogether more culpable than the NLF, the DRVN and their allies. Thus the outcome of the 'struggle' was 'not a matter of indifference'. As a result he took a stretcher-bearer attitude to one of the armies, maintaining that his personal pacifism was compatible with non-combatant participation in a 'just war'.

This standpoint, adopted by several *Liberation* editors, endorsing both the 'just war' thesis, and a non-combatant role in that war, re-occupied positions previously rejected by radical pacifists. In so doing it left any anti-militarist analysis in tatters, and a truly pacifist movement virtually leaderless. This subsequently had enormous implications both for the Vietnam war movement itself and the NL generally.

However, unlike some of his colleagues, Lynd did not thereby abandon all his critical senses in relation to the armed solutions of the NLF/DRVN, and he showed this in dissociating himself from the bias and selectivity of the 'War Crimes Tribunal' when it refused to entertain substantial evidence of terror and atrocities by the NLF and the North Vietnamese Army. Lynd also insisted on sending medical aid to *all* civilians and combatants (unlike the Medical Aid Committees) and condemned terror on both sides although he wrote that one should not '*absolutely* condemn revolutionary terror' (no reasoning given). At the same time, he expressed the hope that we would react to torture by the NLF 'exactly as to torture by the other side';[10] here again the fatal ambiguity, if not contradiction, that characterized Muste's position, was also evident in Lynd.

Muste, like the others, expressed a surprisingly simplistic view of the relationship between a nonviolent revolution and the attempted military revolution by some sections of the Vietnamese people. He almost implied that they might only differ over means. Yet Muste had, over the years, consistently criticized various revolutionaries and political sectarians for separating means and ends, or believing that after a military victory or after 'the revolution' 'things' would be different.

The *démarche*, that began with the *Liberation* pacifists, and later briefly included Daniel Berrigan, accelerated, each new convert finding some reason for identification with the NLF, and fewer taking note of the non-NLF, non-Communist resistance groups in Vietnam, such as the Buddhists. By 1966, Muste had clearly qualified his previously non-aligned and fairly consistent pacifist position, elaborating on the Vietnam issue, an apparently contradictory stance; on the one hand he claimed that he still 'rejected all war and organised violence regardless of who or what nation or movement resorts to it', and that he did 'not accept and condone violence on the part of any people, any group'. On the other hand, he believed that a 'distinction between the violence of liberation movements' (i.e. the NLF) and 'imperialist' violence has to be made and allowed the pacifist to 'support some who are engaged in violent action' because their violence was morally superior. This elusive distinction, between refusal to condone violence and yet willingness to support those who used it, laid the fatal, if ambiguous, foundations for a shift from an anti-militarist analysis into an anti-imperialist one. It was a drift that moved not only *Liberation*, but substantial sections of the movement, across Camus's 'tragic dividing line', from pacifism to militarism.

This change of position was reflected in the evolution of two distinct policy positions on how the war could be brought to an end (as distinct from a third calling for an unambiguous NLF military victory – which few in the NL, at this stage, were yet prepared to do).[24]

The first more general position was to call for a ceasefire with the slogan 'Stop the Killing Now' and implied an agreed or unilateral cessation of military activity by the USA, pending withdrawal. The second position, taken by Lynd, Dellinger and McReynolds (and by some Anarchists in Britain) was that since the USA had no right to be in Vietnam it should just unilaterally withdraw, even if this led to an eventual end to the war by Communist victory. This latter position either did not call for a ceasefire *at all*, or called for it only after unconditional troop withdrawal or an agreement to so withdraw. Though these subtleties were largely lost on the larger peace movement, it became clear that those who held out for unilateral and unconditional withdrawal by the USA without ceasefire, gave overwhelming political and military advantage to a specific armed formation in taking over the South Vietnamese, with heavy support continuing from its big-power allies. The arguments amongst pacifists centred on whether any self-styled pacifists could take positions either way which actually meant the continuation of killing, and thus implicit support for a military solution.[25]

The parallel argument over 'realism' was as to whether, on the one hand, the USA would in any case accept a withdrawal *without* a prior ceasefire, and whether, on the other, the NLF and the North Vietnamese (DRVN) would ever accept a ceasefire without agreement on withdrawal; this was of course eventually the nub of the Paris peace negotiations, but even before that, it provided a sort of watershed for the peace movement both in the West and in Vietnam itself.

Though many in the movement did not firmly commit themselves or make their position plain (this was largely true, for example, of the generalized Trotskyist call for troop withdrawal, without calling for NLF victory), it opened the way for an eventual and substantial identification with what in 1965 was still the slogan of only a handful of Maoists: 'Victory to the NLF'.

The Resistance alone among the anti-war groups and tendencies, retained its morale, unity and integrity in this period of movement crisis. This was largely because it was rooted in undramatic, morally based, personal action and a non-violent ethic. It combined mutual aid with individual responsibility and local organizing. It is significant that, from the start, it had least need of identification with a foreign military force, such as that of the NLF or North Vietnamese, and did not in fact concern itself with supporting their violence.

It may well be, as one commentator (Zinn) suggested, that some Resistance members would have equally resisted the oppressive conscription systems of both the Vietnamese combatants, in the North and South, even though the penalty for such resistance was often – as from both sides during Tet – summary execution; they may well have identified with the actions of their Buddhist counterparts, resisting even to the death the forcible conscriptions of Thieu and the NLF, and deserting from both armies.

Yet it is a tragic irony that despite this potentially common identity, the Resistance failed to make stronger trans-national links with those resisters in Vietnam closest to them in spirit and action, e.g. the young, militant and neutralist Buddhists, often monks, using nonviolent techniques against successive Saigon regimes. Calling for immediate ceasefire, the 'Third Way' monks, nuns and social workers encouraged draft-resistance against both armies, refusing to fight themselves and sheltering thousands of deserters. Their fearless opposition to the militarism of both Saigon and Hanoi led to often fatal results; the destruction of pagodas, assassination and execution or mass imprisonment of Buddhist workers, or else wounding or involuntary exile.

Yet even Resistance leaders like Lynd, with his Quaker background and his long record of civil disobedience, failed to publicly identify with this thoroughgoing and massive anti-militarism by ordinary Vietnamese, and instead juggled with inaccurate formulae that endorsed the 'just struggle' of 'the Vietnamese'.

That the Western anti-war movements failed to identify with these forces until it was far too late[26] can only partly be explained away by their ignorance of these groups' existence and activities, and the fact that the National establishments and the Left establishment both presented the war as a simple dichotomy between polar military formations. It was a symptom of the tragedy of nonviolence in the late 1960s[27] that those Vietnamese of similar style and politics should actually be consistently excluded or eliminated from peace movement platforms in the West, or even accused of CIA links.

As has been seen, in the origins of the NL, both in Britain and America, radical pacifists had occupied influential positions and played key roles, but during the 1960s they were faced with the choice of either retaining influence at the expense of their pacifism (the case in America) or retaining their pacifism with a consequent loss of influence (the case in Britain). Had a nonviolent critique of the spread of national liberation movements been developed early enough, things might have gone differently, not only in the peace movement, but in the NL as a whole, including the black movement and political groups like SDS. But such was not the case: the result of this theoretical vacuum, the deep compassion for those suffering the rigours of colonial rule, or American bombardment, and the lack of effective nonviolent strategies to alleviate these situations, was the typical defensive pacifist double-standard position of the later 1960s; nonviolence at home, but tacitly endorsed 'just' violence abroad.[28]

The New Left and the Vietnam war

In 1966, both SNCC and SDS issued statements entirely uncritical of the 'other side' (also referred to as 'forces for liberation').[29] From then on, an increasingly one-sided view of the war developed, which concealed the deep contradiction between, for example, support for participatory democracy at home, and support of indisputably authoritarian regimes and movements abroad – formations that were quite clearly not dedicated to the principle of 'let the people decide'. In the long run, this identification helped not only to undermine the belief in participatory democracy, but also to tempt many to jump out of the frying pan of US imperialism into the fire of a new oppositional Stalinism.

Thus almost from the start, criticism of the Vietnam war by the NL excluded critiques of authoritarian leftism.[30] One of the left social democrats critical of SDS – Bayard Rustin – prophetically characterized the Lynd–SDS coalition of 1965 as being one between those giving covert, and those giving explicit, support to the NLF.

In 1965, SDS went so far as to vote to remove any anti-totalitarian statements or criticism of the NLF from its constitution, and restrict its criticism to the policy of the USA. From this moment, SDS's attack on 'anti-Communism', as Kahn pointed out, failed to differentiate between criticism of, for example, the NLF, by democratic libertarian socialists, and criticism by people in the establishment or on the far Right.[31]

The NL failed in this context to create criteria by which to judge either the ideas or the methods of such movements and regimes. The very word or concept 'totalitarianism' was rejected because of its previous deployment as a convergent Cold War term.[32] NL leaders also argued, with some substance, that since Communism was no organized force in American politics, then domestically the question of pro- or anti-Communism was irrelevant.

But whilst in domestic terms this was possibly true, in international terms, particularly in relationship to Hanoi and the NLF, and to a lesser degree China and Cuba and Russia, it created deep ideological ambiguity. Popular front politics was no longer an organized phenomenon associated with a strong Communist Party, but rather an atmosphere or milieu in which adulation of Communist leaders and movements could grow unchallenged. Double standards in the Vietnam war, an uncritical attitude to the concept of 'liberation', and a failure to condemn excesses by America's opponents inevitably ensued. All this indicates the growth of an extensive, emotive and predominant anti-Americanism that was a principal basis for the growing unwillingness to criticize any authoritarian regimes and movements on the Left, including the NLF. After all, even if 'national liberation' turned out to be the same type of double-talk phrase as 'free world', at least it represented an effective stick to beat America with.

But equally, this shift represents the revival, encouraged by Guevara and mentors such as Marcuse and Sartre (and to a lesser degree Fanon), of a revolutionary morality that is selective in its criticism and uses relative standards for judging 'liberation'. Sartre had defended revolutionary regimes at the War Crimes Tribunal, arguing that opposition to them is a form of treason, just as criticism of bourgeois states is morally necessary. The standards of individuals (e.g. freedom) are irrelevant; in such a debate, it was argued that these formations could not be judged by the same moral criteria as bourgeois states; whereas the errors of the former can be rectified, the crimes of the latter spring from their inherent evil. Indeed such was the horror at the American presence, and the much greater destructive capacity of Western militarism, that undoubted evidence of Communist excesses was neither sought out, nor countenanced.

The stunning success of North Vietnamese propaganda amongst young radicals[33] is not entirely to be explained in terms of public relations. Some within the NL not only wished to believe certain things – they were as willing to distort, select, omit and exaggerate the facts of the war, as part of their dedication to the cause it represented. Such a conscious development was nothing new in the history of the Left, but it did represent a departure for the NL, and re-enacted the deception and self-deception of the Comintern years.

Probably when the NL identified with the NLF and the 'whole Vietnamese people', and argued that their resort to arms had *only* occurred after all other channels had been blocked, this was sometimes sincere. On the other hand, many were undoubtedly encouraged by both the Maoist and post-Marcusian views that propaganda must be met with counter-propaganda, lies by lies, distortions by distortions; it was certainly a view that the Cuban and Vietnamese regimes seemed to share in practice; 'truth' was whatever served the cause of the revolution.

The NL's precipitate descent into propaganda, largely born out of compassion and frustration, was partly based on the felt need to counter-balance biased information with slanted material on the other side. If any radicals still wondered whether more than two parties were involved in the Vietnam conflict, their doubts had to be removed and the 'David and Goliath' image reinforced. When in December 1966 SDS first used the formulation 'Vietnamese people in their struggle for self-determination', it may well have been an unselfconscious, well-intentioned phrasing. But such resolutions helped to eliminate the greys from the Indo-China situation,[34] and actively discouraged alternative modes of resistance.

The newspeak of 'people's war' would probably have been challenged by the early NL; however, by the later 1960s, such formulae were not. The consideration of third or fourth choices in Vietnam (i.e. involving the millions of progressive Buddhists and others) was thus discounted. The majority disappeared, as in other wars, between two forces, two propaganda machines. Much of the NL consequently became aligned with one of them as a lesser evil,[35] purveying images, symbols and slogans direct from Vietnamese materials, and making any balanced or accurate view of the war increasingly elusive.

It became typical for radicals to hold up Vietnam as an exception to any generalized criticisms of 'revolutionary degeneration'; traditional 'class analyses' of the peasant role proved inadequate, however, since they ignored the conscious nationalist manipulation of the rural masses by party cadres. As one radical critic put it:

the NLF is controlled by an incipient bureaucratic ruling class. The fact that the mass base of the NLF lies among the peasantry does not mean that the NLF is controlled by the peasantry, nor that an NLF victory will establish peasant control of the state.[36]

The charge of 'Stalinism' regularly levelled against both the North Vietnamese and the NLF, had to do with the reproduction of the Stalinist organizational imperatives and an apparatus based on deception, relentless regimentation and precisely managed terrorism that recalled similar excesses in China and Russia.[37]

Yet the imagery of a popular, spontaneous and decentralized 'struggle' in which the NLF and the 'people of Vietnam' were synonymous, persisted long after Tet. The anti-war movement had accepted an imagery of the war drawn from the early 1960s, and preserved it long after the reality had become transformed. Indeed there was plenty of evidence around in the early 1960s to suggest that Ho Chi Minh's regime (like the NLF) probably had one of the more brutalized and repressive, as well as highly bureaucratized, leaderships in the history of Communism.[38] Its strong links to Stalin and Stalinism in the past, and its reproduction of Stalinist ideals and models in the present were beyond doubt.

The 'Titoist' interpretation of the DRVN was harder to sustain after Tet; by 1968 there was substantially less autonomy; the war became firmly situated in an international power struggle (where it was 'solved') and its continuation depended critically on Russian and Chinese arms.[39] Even while the image of NLF independence from the North was being accepted in the NL, it was becoming less true (i.e. from 1960 onward). Equally, the independence of both NLF and DRVN from Russian and China was being accepted on the Left, at a time when this too was in rapid decline.

But whilst the NL was initially partly accurate in stressing a relative national autonomy of the NLF – e.g. independence of direct control by Hanoi before the early 1960s (let alone by Peking or Moscow) – its analysis of the internal structure of the war, and of its relationship to those external models, was always wholly inflexible and inadequate.

To say that at one stage the NLF and DRVN were not 'puppets' of the great powers, and had interests of their own, independent of one another, was one thing. It was quite another to deny influences and similarities, or to deny that the war steadily drew the North, and subsequently Russia and China, into deep involvement; increasingly the context altered the nature of the internal struggle until finally it could only be sustained or halted at their will.

Indeed, the increasing conventional fire-power of the NLF/DRVN forces and the degree to which the North, armed by its great power allies, took over the main operations of the war, made almost any kind of 'guerilla' analysis factually irrelevant. On the other hand, this development merely confirmed processes – bureaucratic and militarist tendencies for example – that had already clearly existed in the first Indo-China war, and lay at the foundation of the Hanoi regime.

Rather than allow the original illusion to be shattered, the 'David and Goliath' imagery of the Vietnamese war was maintained, enabling Western radicals to identify with an Asian pygmy struggling against the imperialist giant. This version of the war, e.g. an ill-equipped peasantry brutally oppressed and spontaneously struggling against monstrous odds, documented by pictures of black pyjamas and old rifles pitted against long-range artillery and napalm – projected an 'underdog' image which went down well with the NL and liberals alike. At one point, significant of this, Lynd used the extraordinary phrase 'the oppression of Vietnamese guerillas'.

The myth springing from all this, that the struggle was a spontaneous, mass-based upsurge against Saigon and the USA, that half-a-million troops of the most advanced military-industrial power were stalemated by popular heroism, obscured the tragic reality of a North Vietnamese numerical superiority on the ground enabling an appallingly profligate use of life in combat (almost as careless as the Communists in Korea); that it was essentially *the pattern of control* – over masses of men and resources – that had emerged North and South, that was able to meet and check American power on its own terms. Although at hideous costs, the growing political infrastructure and expanding industrial and armed strength of the North, together with substantial Eastern-bloc aid, reinforced the immense organizational effort in the South, and marked the increasingly 'conventional' nature of the struggle. The guerilla armies, far from the romantic image of decentralized spontaneity, turned out to be small versions of the military machines of the great empires, East and West; carefully wrought bureaucratic, military apparatuses.[40]

Thus the image (never the whole truth) was overtaken by the reality of the increasing conventionalization of the war. Such imagery had depended on a notion of voluntary, majority support and sympathy for military struggle; after 1968, and probably a good deal earlier, evidence to sustain this was also lacking.

Between 1960–3, in the last three years of Diem's regime, military resistance, although Communist-led, had been clearly widespread and often spontaneous. But it was mass Buddhist opposition that had actually led to Diem's overthrow. However, in the first years of the military rising (1957–60) and again after 1963, this kind of unified resistance did not appear; thereafter the NLF increasingly depended on force and terror rather than consent in mobilizing opposition (as Tet confirmed, much later).

The evanescent nature of the NLF's mass popularity also created major dilemmas and problems for that informed section of the NL which now openly supported the NLF. On the one hand, it could accept the necessity for terror and accept the subordination of means to ends, justified by the same 'revolutionary morality'. Or, on the other hand, it could deny that this terror existed and maintain an imagery of the war as a 'spontaneous' people's struggle. The first 'realistic' position was taken by a militant minority (e.g. PL) and eventually was used to justify terror in America itself: the second that adopted by sections of the more liberal, mainstream Vietnam war movement was reinforced by Eastern bloc propaganda.[41]

Many in the NL seemed unwilling to relinquish an idealized image of the NLF, a force 'respecting and respected' by the 'people'. This impression even survived the events of Tet, and the use of civilians as hostages; Oglesby could still call the protracted militarized insurrection in Vietnam 'as honest a revolution as you can find anywhere'. Since the movement leaders had become unwilling to adapt their theory to the facts (i.e. that the NLF *was* top-down, élitist, centralizing, bureaucratic and often brutalized, and the DRVN very deeply influenced and imbued by Stalinism), the facts were adapted to the theory, an anti-bureaucratic movement from the bottom up. Thus it was continually claimed that the 'struggle' had developed not as a planned strategy of armed takeover, but only as a heroic and instinctive resistance to US aggression.[42]

As has been argued earlier, much of this would not have happened if pacifists and libertarians in the movement had not capitulated to propagandized versions of the war. The pronouncements by Dellinger, McReynolds, Hayden and Chomsky in particular, made this possible (even Muste's early visit to North Vietnam was easy to misinterpret). The key importance of these identifications with élitist or bureaucratic military leaderships of the Third World guerilla armies is revealed by their reflexive impact on the domestic movement of the NL. Openly organized support for wars of liberation did not fully emerge till 1967; in that year, the small 'revolutionary contingent' with miniature Viet Cong flags, appeared on the April marches in New York; during the next three years, however, they became a sizeable and assertive minority on demonstrations.

Had NLF styles in organization and leadership entered the Movement in 1965, they would have faced immediate rejection; but the transition in two or three years is dramatic. The NLF flags and portraits of Ho or other rather superficial symbolic identifications with revolutionary war remained a fringe element in 1966 and 1967. But tolerated by a 'non-exclusionary' movement in these years, and in the context of a growing shame and anger focused on Vietnam, by 1968 and 1969 such styles and identifications became the predominant tone of many demonstrations, along with all the paraphernalia of pseudo-militarism or the attempts to create a revolutionary 'discipline'.

Indo-China solidarity in Britain

Naturally the Vietnam issue was slower to take hold of the peace and Left-wing movements in Britain than in the USA. The reverberations of the first teach-ins and Vietnam Day demonstrations – especially the troop-train blockage attempts in Oakland were felt in Britain in late 1965. Wilson's uncritical relationship with Johnson's policies was widely deplored on the Left, and Cabot Lodge was given a tough time in a teach-in on the war at Oxford. But CND was the first major group to take up the Vietnam issue in a big way, even though it was later outflanked, especially during 1968. In addition, significant activity was stimulated by American anti-war émigré groups and draft resisters such as the 'Stop-It Committee', and groups sheltering deserters and draft evaders.[43]

By 1966 and 1967, CND, with the British Campaign for Peace in Vietnam (BCPV – the Communist Party's front organization), ran a number of demonstrations, but with little impact. In these years, CND's attempt to switch to campaigning on the Vietnam issue subordinated its concern with nuclear weapons to a secondary role. Such a shift was predictable after 1964, particularly given the shifting balance of forces in the peace movement, and the closeness or overlap of key CND personnel with the BCPV and Communist Party on the Vietnam issue, and it confirmed the growing hold of the CP on CND's national office. But the degree to which a CP line could be easily outflanked by more militant groups on the Left, led by Maoists and Trotskyites, was soon in evidence.

Support for national liberation movements, especially the leaders of various colonial freedom efforts, had long had warm if generalized endorsement from the Labour Party left, as well as from the CP and other Marxist groups. The massive and militant anti-Suez demonstrations of 1965 foreshadowed both CND and anti-imperialist confrontations in the later 1960s. But in the period after Ho Chi Minh's war against the French, and with the advent of the Algerian and Cuban revolutionary wars, such struggles became much more overtly situated in a global power struggle. In the process, they became increasingly and openly aligned with the Eastern bloc and identified with overtly Communist leaderships and Communist takeovers. The rather uncritical approach taken by the Labour left[44] to such changes was merely the prelude to the large-scale shift in the NL towards advocacy of 'progressive' war *à l'outrance*, as the increasing number of Western external adventures made imperialism once again a dominant concern on the Left. But as one critic put it: 'Their Imperialist theories are too narrowly class-based and too America-centred – thus lacking adequate critiques of bureaucratic Communist states.'[45]

After 1967, the CP line in CND lost ground in two directions. Whilst some Liberals, libertarians and pacifists more vocally rejected the tacit support for the NLF's military efforts (and a number left CND) others on the other hand – mostly militant and committed revolutionary socialists – increasingly rejected the CP's moderate line and cautious tactics in the movement, opting for an overt 'solidarity' line instead.

A whole new generation of student militants thus came to see CND as an embodiment of cautious conservatism on the one hand, and pro-Communist alignment on the other; a classic example of having the worst of both worlds. Though at times such a stance allowed the CP to depict itself as a unifying and 'moderating' force, it too eventually decided to compete with the Vietnam Solidarity Committee (VSC) in the mobilization of militant youth, and the degeneration of CND into a pro-Hanoi stance reached its peak at the end of the 1969 Easter march.

This occurred in Trafalgar Square, when the tough NLF/PRG bureaucrat Mme T. Binh greeted a mildly surprised CND crowd with a lecture on Stalinist ethics and the justification of 'revolutionary morality' (which she identified with progressive killing). The connection with nuclear disarmament, however, was not at all clear[46] and from this date, CND's numbers dropped dramatically – in terms both of demonstrations and members. On this march and in the following year, the organization declined to insignificant proportions; for many who had hung on in the hope of a CND revival, this was finally the end of the road.

As has been seen, this final eclipse of CND created a vacuum in the British context into which both the CP and the Vietnam Solidarity coalition moved. Neither Anarchists nor Trotskyites had been effectively able to block CP activity before 1968, so many Trotskyists chose instead to take over the Solidarity Committee themselves. The IMG predominated in the coalition, which held its first demonstration in the autumn of 1967. Its two main operations were publicizing the War Crimes Tribunal and organizing confrontations under the slogan 'Victory for the NLF'. These affrays culminated in October 1968 with its third and largest demonstration which proved a supreme anticlimax, no more 'revolutionary' than the end of an Aldermaston march.

In fact the VSC was far more like its peace movement predecessor than it liked to believe. 'This then was no peace march' commented one reporter on the 1968 demonstration. But oddly enough, although the VSC was constantly keen to distinguish itself from the 'empty moralism' and nonviolence of CND, the majority of its rank-and-file supporters had in fact been active in CND (*New Society* survey of 1968), and even shared its orientations. The leadership nevertheless harped on the weakness and ineffectiveness of nuclear disarmament right up until the moment of its own precipitate collapse.

In so far as CND remained the largest single peace organization up until 1968, the only real factor that could have prevented a Communist Party takeover on the Vietnam issue in the peace movement, was a strong radical pacifist wing either of the Vietnam movement or within CND. But in contrast with the American situation, rather than capitulate on the issues of the war, British pacifism remained largely isolated and silent, or at most gave tacit assent to Old Left positions. Instead of either a firm non-aligned, anti-militarist stance, or the double-standard sympathy for the NLF that many US pacifists adopted, there was mere acquiescence. The leftover pacifism of the 1930s, never particularly acute in its strategic or analytical thinking, and hopelessly inadequate as a basis for understanding and evaluating these developments, withdrew from the debate.

Nevertheless, in Britain, unlike America, there was at least one section of the NL which was ideologically consistently and openly opposed to any direct identification with the NLF or North Vietnam, especially after the Tet offensive. The Anarchists helped maintain the integrity of their position, through their critique of Stalinism and in slogans of 'neither Washington nor Hanoi'; but the slogan which must have most embarrassed the Trotskyists in their support for the NLF, or their acquiescence in pro-NLF formulae, was the quite accurate Anarchist cry 'Ho, Ho, Ho Chi Minh, how many Trots did you do in?'[47] Sometimes Anarchists created parallel demonstrations, sometimes they abstained, sometimes they joined the major demonstrations with these 'plague on both your houses' slogans; but undoubtedly they also lost out in what was a period of guerilla euphoria and which so much favoured identification with national liberation struggles.

Support amongst activists for Palestinian Arab organizations, for the IRA in Ulster, as well as the NLF, was opposed by most Anarchists because of the authoritarianism, Marxist-Leninist orientations, backward-looking nationalism, or élitist manipulation of civilian populations characterizing each of these groups. But these Vietnam war demonstrations and the VSC signalled a decisive weakening of the libertarian left. Anarchists were caught in a no-win bind. If they avoided the mass demonstrations of March and 27 October they would be accused of irrelevance and sectarianism; if they joined the VSC coalition they would seem to be giving a blessing to and legitimizing its slogans and leadership. In the end, they chose a sort of compromise, the best available to them in the circumstances, which was to organize parallel demonstrations at the same time, but using different slogans and different routes.

Anti-imperialism and anti-America

The tendencies towards alignment in the NL cannot be understood outside the development of a variety of positions styling themselves anti-imperialist. Alignment with military revolutions and post-colonial regimes, as well as a growing anti-Americanism, was usually explained and justified in terms of such a theory. Certainly the generalized guilt about the heritage of Western colonialism and imperialism – the long-term legacies of slavery and racism for example – was deeply felt by the white Western intelligentsia. Identification with anti-imperial symbolisms and strategies was a small price to pay for exonerating this inheritance. Radical nationalism and aggressive Third World communisms were effective counter-weights to US domination, and even when the authoritarianism of such movements and regimes was noted, this could still be blamed on American pressure and encirclement. Indeed, the belief grew in the NL that only through an efficient dictatorship such as Ho's or Castro's, could any effective defence against imperialism be organized; the 'luxury' of democracy was something the Third World could not afford.

Such a view, as well as the cult of anti-Americanism, was particularly purveyed by Old Left and liberal renegades like Mary McCarthy, but it was eagerly endorsed by many younger militants.[48] David McReynolds wrote in *Liberation*: 'The New Left is profoundly alienated from this country. It is anti-American with a bitterness that is new.' Certainly, the NL's so-called 'anti-imperialism' is actually a misnomer. It was an attitude that reflected a much more complex response both to American hegemony and the expansiveness of advanced capitalism than anything associated with Leninism and the Old Left. But it involved an awareness of the domination of the technological society over the traditional society, the urban sector over the rural, the industrial over the agrarian, the bourgeois-proletarian over the peasant and tribal, the white over the coloured.

It perceived the crisis of European white civilization's hegemony in the world, exemplified by developments in China and Japan, and the de-colonization of Africa; a crisis accentuated by the existence of coloured minorities within the Western countries. Black militants perceived the racism that characterized the Negro-white relationship in the West as symptomatic of a global white dominance over three centuries. 'Internal colonialism' and 'external imperialism' were phrases which attempted to depict inter-connected relationships.

Carmichael audaciously attacked the growing numbers of negro youths enlisting for the Vietnam war, as 'black mercenaries' fighting for a 'freedom' they neither knew nor shared. To those fighting in Asia, such phrases reinforced a bitterness in those who already saw the irony in 'poor blacks being shipped to kill poor Asians on behalf of wealthy whites'. But despite this growing sense of solidarity with the Third World, the disproportionate use of black combat troops,[49] and the ridicule of America's free-world role, Carmichael chose not to identify these black troops as protectors of the artificially big pie they wished to share. In so far as the ghettoes shared the consumerist fruits of American hegemony – its elevated standard of living – it was impolitic, and inopportune, to point this out. And to be fair, it took some time to unravel all the implications of claiming a slice of affluence created in part by the exploitation of black and yellow men, and now defended against them by an armed force, that was itself increasingly black.

The anti-imperialism of the NL in part attempted to unravel this by stressing the inter-relationships between these various dimensions of control. The domination of the USA or the West, or of capitalism, was only one such dimension inter-related with the others. Racist domination, technological domination, as well as political, economic and military domination, were subtly intertwined.

Indeed many in the NL viewed the imperialist West and non-white Third World as constituting a more basic polarization than that between universal capitalism and a universal working class. With the rise of liberation wars, Lin Piao and Fanon had also provided the vision of trans-national revolution, based on encirclement of the cities by an insurgent world countryside – with peasant violence midwifing historical change, even exporting revolt to the industrial-metropolitan areas.

On the other hand, whilst it may be true that the NL became more anti-imperialist than anti-capitalist, it remained opposed primarily to state aggression, internal or external, and state capitalism, like corporate capitalism, was seen to oppress both at home and abroad.[50] The NL's model thus did not exclude the possibility of other imperialisms –

including non-Western, non-capitalist and even non-white empires – though these were not stressed. By the 1970s, however, there is a growing awareness of the possibility that there were in fact 'one, two, three, many imperialisms'. Castro found it necessary to attack the heresy that there were at least two imperialisms (Russia and the USA), a view put forward by both Guevara and the Chinese.[51] Whilst Sartre saw US imperialism as the main enemy, he too increasingly used the term 'imperialist' to describe Russia after 1956, not as a matter of value, but of fact. Other possible candidates were: Japan; the old colonial powers of Europe forging a new alliance; possibly also China herself; and even North Vietnam appeared increasingly expansionist.[52] This type of development aided an anti-imperialist stance independent of the socialist power blocs, just as the NL had aided the growth of an anti-capitalism independent of class-analysis.

These libertarian tendencies, in both cases moving towards an anti-economistic analysis of systems of global power, encouraged greater openness and experimentation in ideology. In this sense the 'anti-imperialism' of the 1960s was more deeply trans-national in emphasis than previous anti-imperialism had ever been. It was flexible enough to allow new permutations to emerge, even though these became frozen into more rigid formulae later. Even from a classic Leninist standpoint, there were clearly ambiguities in an imperialism of the American variety, which had most of its investment in the advanced countries, and which actually had a loss-making relationship with a number of its supposed dependencies.

The new capitalism was both flexible and powerful, dominated by multi-national corporations, but it did not, even its critics admitted, depend on the 'looting of the rest of the world' for its existence.[53] Alongside American military involvements, the corporatization of the Third World had proceeded by way of overseas sales and investments, but it was not clear that this was essential to any post-scarcity development. More critical was its internal incorporation of a dwindling working class into its expanding structures, and the trans-national bases of its operations.[54]

Guevara's attacks on the Western working class for its complicity in imperialism and decreasing militancy were widely echoed in the NL. But these 'racisms and national chauvinisms', complained the critics, were not inalienable characteristics of the white working class. Moreover, the attacks on white 'skin-privilege', which accompanied the increasing glorification of race war,[55] focused on privilege relative to black and coloured peoples abroad, and excluded more privileged whites in the metropolitan countries.

It has already been argued that the anti-imperialist stance had its most significant impact on the NL through the changing nature of the Vietnam war movement. Initially the NL attitude to 'liberation wars' in Asia was the liberal one, of minimizing the military potential of such communist regimes and movements. Typical was the SDS critique of 1966, which reassured the establishment that the domino theory was a myth and that US withdrawal was safe because there would be no expansion of China or North Vietnam in South East Asia if South Vietnam was abandoned.[56]

By 1969, this position was almost entirely reversed; not only was such extension of the war admitted as likely, it was welcomed as the impending victory of the Indo-China 'People's War'. The proliferation of liberation wars throughout Laos, Thailand, and Cambodia was endorsed as a form of radical domino theory. The slogan 'one, two, three, many Vietnams' taken up by many militants, expressed this volte-face into an 'anti-imperialist' militarism: the imperialist powers must be met on their own terms, on their own ground.

This tended inevitably to the situation where a political blank cheque was written for any 'anti-imperialist' movement that happened along, and large sections of the peace movement had shuffled off the complicated and often unrewarding burdens of non-aligned internationalism in favour of this open-ended call for 'national self-determination'. Oglesby, a key figure in this transition to an anti-imperialist stance, traces the route from a 'peace movement' in the traditional sense, towards an 'anti-peace' movement favouring continued armed struggle, rather than a ceasefire agreement (SDS in 1969).[57]

By this time the very word 'peace' had become suspect. From sympathy for the NLF, the NL evolved through anti-imperialism to support for sundry Third World armies; it was a transition aided and abetted of course by a scatter of Marxist–Leninisms, official and un-official: the first and principal agents in America were the Maoists – the Progressive Labor Party (PLP) and especially M2M, its front organization on the campus (1964–5), which proved the earliest and most effective anti-imperialist, 'pro-liberation war' group within the 'anti-war' movement.

But even before open identification, it had been easy enough to interpret anti-militarist activity as 'anti-imperialist'; indeed leaders were often glad to sophisticate simple anti-war activity with that title; after all, was not anything which hurt the war-machine, hurting American imperialism? Many Left papers were glad to write up events as anti-imperialist, even if the main impulse of those who took part was anti-militarist, outraged opposition to sophisticated methods of killing, or hatred of war as an institution; but Marxists claimed to know its 'real' meaning. Even if the motivation of the demonstrators was closer to pacifist instincts than Old Left ones, the 'historical significance' of their action lay in its contribution to the success of the military oppo-nent in Asia. Such interpretations raised many questions: was napalm 'neutral'? If 'anti-imperialists' started using the same 'oppressive means', then would these protests against them then cease (as they tended to after 1969)? Or would anti-war groups reject usage of such weapons by either side (as a principled radical pacifism might be expected to do)?[58]

In such moral and ideological confusion, it was those NL groups least obsessed with anti-imperialist analysis, which retained their identity longest; draft-resistance had a myriad of motivations, but endorsement of 'anti-imperialist struggle' was the last and least of them. This is not to say that among the groups like the Resistance there was any lack of awareness of the oppressive role of American world power, but there was a sense that *all* imperialisms – and not just imperialism, but militarism and authoritarianism as well – were being opposed. The concept of 'imperialism' was viewed by them as yet another slogan – an inevitable oversimplification; it was enough to oppose the war-machine where it stood; if that made an impact abroad, it was a welcome, but subordinate, dimension to their activity.

Certainly for a considerable time there had been an awareness throughout the NL of the inevitability of further wars after Vietnam, and a belief, expressed in the then current phrase 'the seventh war from now', that a US peace movement would only actually prevent the US involvement in such conflicts, in the very long term. The point is that initially this had *not* implied any one-dimensioned imperialist analysis, nor had it called for 'one, two, three . . . (let alone seven) . . . Vietnams' – the slogan that emerged, however briefly, in 1968 and 1969.

The Third World trap: 'thinking with the blood'

The Movement crises of the later 1960s can be analysed substantially in terms of the inter-relation between internal weaknesses and external factors – the events of 1968, the Third World movements, the identification with groups either promising revolutionary change outside America (like the NLF) or those like the Panthers, detached from the movement, but apparently offering a revolutionary lead at home. In particular the one-sided view of the revolutionary movements of the underdeveloped countries, the unwillingness, or inability to see them as they really were, was perhaps, as an erstwhile SDS leader charged, a reflection of the NL's own restless search for a 'revolutionary tradition which would give it memories and spirit'.[59]

As Lasch argues, under the influence of these imported ideologies, models and myths of imminent revolution, the NL eventually 'loses sight of its own peculiar traditions of local autonomy and democratic decision-making'.[60] Libertarian instincts fail to be translated from the campuses, communities and ghettoes of America or Europe to a systematic appraisal of Third World movements, free of guilt, self-repudiation and self-delusion. Thus the gut anti-élitism of the NL organizers becomes aligned with the self-conscious élitism of organizers of the Third World's poor and peasantry. The democratic praxis of the movement becomes fatally intertwined with the bureaucratic and even

Stalinist mobilizers of 'Peoples' War'. As the New American Movement's (NAM) manifesto put it:

The focus on solidarity with the third world grew out of a correct reaction to United States' national chauvinism – but it has gone so far in the opposite direction that it has lost all possibility of communicating with the American people and has lost touch with reality. [61]

Whether on the basis of guilt, misinformation, physical distance, wishful thinking or double standards, this kind of external identification became widespread by the end of the decade. It was based on what Weinstein called self-repudiation and had 'the implicit idea of redemption through identification with one of the true, or key revolutionary agents', whether 'ghetto-blacks, freaks, youth-as-a-class (students), industrial-workers or colonial-revolutionaries'. It was a result of the unresolved dilemma of agency (previously analysed) [62] and the apparent failure to communicate to the more immediate constituencies and communities. For SDS, 'students and déclassé intellectuals became strictly appendages or tutors to the "real" social forces'. [63] For some it was an excuse not to organize at all.

There were, however, many in the Movement who resisted these tendencies; an underground paper editorialized:

The sooner SDS gets back to white America and changes that [the better] . . . forget about Mao, China, Ho, the NLF: forget about Che, Debray and even forget about Fanon, Malcolm, Huey. . . .

Weinstein maintained that the effect of such identifications had jettisoned some major tenets of the NL as a movement; for example that 'radicalism is based on awareness of one's own oppression' and that 'popular participation in the process of decision-making is central to radical politics'. This abandonment meant their replacement by the Leninist élite-vanguard model of revolutionary politics (at least in theory), older versions of class, or the prime emphasis on military action. [64] Accompanying this, as can be argued in the case of the Weatherman faction, for some in the NL the only political role available to Western white radicals was as *francs tireurs* for the Third World struggles or commandos behind enemy lines.

Strong parallels exist between such positions and those adopted by Fanon, Marcuse and Sartre, not least in their abandonment of the Western proletariat in favour of other agencies, [65] and their faith in the outcasts and lumpen proletarians of the Third World. These analogies, imitations and transplants were all rooted in a belief – or a hope – that the post-industrial and pre-industrial struggles could somehow link hands, merge, or become a unified cause. But such a scenario created thoroughgoing ambivalence as to the role of the metropolitan movement. Was it a revolutionary movement in its own right or merely a support group for the Third World? 'The rootless detached shock troops of other peoples' revolutionary movements' following programmes designed for fundamentally different societies?[66] Either way, did it merely imitate Third World movements, or did it actually pursue the same tactics?

Some of the worst failures of the Movement can be traced to this kind of mimicry, or implementation of the programme of another movement outside the realities of its own time and place. As Julius Lester pointed out, 'Ho and Mao and Fidel, each used Marxist-Leninism to suit his own particular problems'.[67] But exaggerated versions of military action, over-emphasizing the role of militarism in politics, whilst it reproduced the press version of Che Guevara's ideas, bore little or no relationship to those of ordinary Americans, and their needs.

The switch in Movement language from the term 'freedom' to the more negative 'liberation'[68] represents in part the growing identification with liberation struggles abroad. But more than this, it is symptomatic of the growing crises relating to internal attitudes to freedom; glorification of the Third World is associated with increasing self-censorship within the Movement as far as national liberation wars or 'progressive' regimes are concerned. In the unwillingness to criticize Chinese or Vietnamese policies, in the apparent indifference to the degeneration of the Cuban revolution, its émigrés and 40,000 political prisoners, or its cultural and sexual persecutions, this one-dimensional attitude to freedom in 'revolutionary' contexts betrays a further reversion to standard Old Left procedure.

This, a failure of intellect and imagination by the NL in relation to the people of the Third World, presages its increasing internal crisis. Just as it settles for an Old Left solution in the Third World, it begins to turn to Old Left solutions at home. Slowly but steadily, the Movement itself begins to aspire organizationally, and even resemble or imitate, 'the autocratic bureaucracies of the Stalinist period against which SDS and other groups had originally rebelled'. The Movement becomes more centralist, more militarist, and in those organizations which leant towards a more disciplined para-Leninist organization, or for those joining existing Leninist organizations, more bureaucratic.

These authoritarian tendencies in the Movement, were in part an attempt to 'catch up with' an authoritarian reality in the Third World movements; since the initial identification had been made on the basis of a libertarian ideal – and compassion for the mass-base from which these armies were recruited – profound adjustments were necessary. In this way, the prevailing guilt about imperialism, and the militarism of America, together with compassion for Third World peasant peoples, opens a trap. Guilt and shame, as Gitlin argued, although an antidote to privilege, become poisonous in large doses. Compassion on its own proved a snare that had led much of the Old Left into inhumanity, and Algeria, Cuba and Vietnam in cumulative intensity now threatened to do the same for the New.[69]

10. SDS in Flux

Several perceptive leaders of the NL were concerned about the dangers involved in the Movement's rapid growth through the years 1966–8, and discerned the roots of the subsequent crises in the developments in SDS in these years. By 1968, student support in America may have stood at around a million sympathizers, of whom probably 150,000 were actively linked to the movement or its organizations (e.g. by membership), over half of these were linked to SDS, locally or nationally. Certainly, by 1968 and 1969, SDS itself was undeniably numerically larger than ever, and with 60,000–100,000 members of local chapters, by far the largest organization on the Left.[1]

A movement which had begun with a few thousands on a few major campuses (the large and prestigious, usually state, universities) had, after the Columbia rebellion, spread to literally every campus in America down to the smallest junior college; and even in black colleges in the South, where a new wave of militancy was apparent in 1968, comparable movements existed.[2]

But SDS's rapid expansion is a basic factor in its own crisis of identity and organization. The Movement had neither time nor capacity to organize the influx of new people (several hundred thousands of them within three years in America alone), let alone absorb them into its ideals and style; it was 'instant participation'. Students entered SDS and became 'militant' radicals within months of existing in an a-political uncommitment. They were often recruited second-hand, not directly by the groups, but through the selective images and publicity of the media. They entered the organization often with a distorted media version of radicalism, attracted by SDS's young and student image. They did not share any of the movement experiences of existing NL activists, and thus did not necessarily understand or identify with the ideals or principles of the Movement as it had developed up to 1966.

Certainly they can have had no previous experience of the Old Left. Yet this was also a period of entry for Old Left groups, particularly

Maoists into SDS, and Trotskyists within the anti-war movement. One of the penalties of non-exclusionism was that new recruits would not necessarily distinguish the 'new' from the 'old', and often were undoubtedly an important source of support for Old Left challenges to the existing Movement structure and ethos.

'The Movement' was not easy to 'take over' because of its amorphous decentralized nature – but the balance of forces was undeniably altered by the flood of new supporters. Not only was the already unstable character of SDS changed, but an illusion of sudden strength was given to bolster an already unstable mix of fantasy and rhetoric; local SDS chapters were thrown into chaos by the influx; ideological confusion crystallized into caucuses and in-fighting; an increasing air of unreality filled Movement gatherings. The totally inadequate development of the idea of PD³ was reflected in student formulae of direct democracy – simply organized, and easily abused. In the mass meetings of the FSM, the freshness of the approach saved it, but as university confrontations developed in the 1960s, the need for quick decisions in crisis showed up weaknesses in these exercises in participation.[4]

As has been seen, the eclecticism and openness of the NL was one of its early strengths, and at first it was able to maintain a balance between new ideas on the one hand, and its basic humanity, its concern with human relationships expressed in terms of peace or freedom, on the other. But in this latter period, participatory democracy is severely tested if not actually abandoned. To some extent participatory democracy required a basic consensus to operate successfully; it created a strange setting for factional dispute, and as a result, many key organizers decided to move into more specific projects.

These events partly reflected a general crisis in Movement democracy (to be discussed later) and partly the indecision and incoherence at the heart of SDS. The ambiguity and openness of SDS, its refusal to define itself or to exclude, was both its main attraction and its principal weakness. The populist slogans and coalition character of this group helped make it the largest organizational expression of the NL – appearing fresher and more radical (as well as being more youthful) than any of its competitors. But these characteristics were also major liabilities.

To understand these developments it is worth tracing the balance of tendencies in SDS back to its earliest years. With the decline in the SPU in 1962, and the relative weakness of the various leftist student parties, like SLATE at Berkeley, a vacuum in radical student politics resulted. The FSM whilst it signified a profound change was still, in 1964, a localized outburst. But SDS, filling the gap left by the SPU, became almost by accident first the foremost student peace organization (although foreign policy issues had not been a predominant theme in SDS hitherto) and then, during the course of 1965, the vanguard of a revived national student movement.[5] Certainly before 1965, community themes had come prior to campus organizing in SDS and its involvement in generating the Vietnam war movement was almost an afterthought; but it was in part its involvement with the initial 'Teach-In' movement which focused these protests on the universities and the student constituency.

However, the fact that it was primarily the issue of the Vietnam war that made SDS a major national movement, an issue that SDS was not well equipped to deal with, was not without its political costs. The interrelation between campus, community and peace issues was often obscure and uneasy, reflecting the fragility of the early SDS coalition.

An organization that ranged from the Texas anarchists and Jeff Shero to the New York 'coalitionists' (Steve Max) had little that was stable or coherent at its centre. Indeed, the National Office regularly changed hands, as well as policies and strategies. If there was a core of SDS it was a moving one, associated with figures like Hayden, and its changes roughly paralleled his development from moderate to militant, from non-aligned student radical to aligned professional revolutionary. Nevertheless, the fact that no single faction became predominant before late in 1968, kept the SDS coalition, albeit a changing one, in business.

An early crisis developed as the movement against the war grew during 1965, and preoccupied SDS. A split occurred between many of the organizers on the question of relationship to the Vietnam issue, and the dangers it posed to long-term grassroots work. Those who argued for continuing emphasis at the local level, maintained that distraction of energy to immediate international issues would weaken the growth of a movement against racism and for America's internal victims, the poor and blacks. Against this, others argued for a shifting focus to the role of the poor as white and black mercenaries in Asia, and the Asian victims of these American executioners. They also stressed the diversion of funds, 'from welfare to warfare',[6] and federal budgets suggested that they were undoubtedly right.

Just as the development of the anti-war movement and SDS involvement, was a major factor in the recession in the community projects after 1965, and the collapse of several of them, it also meant that Student-Syndicalism failed to gather the momentum that it otherwise might have done. After the Clear Lake, Iowa, conference of August 1966, SDS returned to the campuses with the main aim of organizing students as the major agents. But in terms of power-political confrontation, the student movement was totally defeated; the Berkeley strike of 1966 gained none of its five main demands, the administration did not even recognize the legitimacy of the Strike Committee or of its affiliated groupings by negotiating with it.[7] Moreover, despite the immense support the strike received, it was weakening at the end. The need for a new content of a university, although recognized by the movement, had not been given enough emphasis in the campus protest struggles, and this was only partly counterbalanced by SDS support for the Free Universities.

Although there was still tension between those who focused mainly on anti-war action, using the campus as a base, and those who focused on student power, student issues and organizing that constituency *per se*, these two tendencies were fused in many of the anti-draft actions and opposition to army and navy recruiters. The SDS anti-draft exams of 1966, not the failure that they were sometimes made out to be by opponents, did not herald a forthright SDS leadership of the draft-resistance movement, but they did emphasize the needs and interests of students.

SDS became less clearly 'interest oriented' in the demonstrations against Dow Chemicals (then the main napalm manufacturer), the CIA, and government representatives. In addition, encouraged by PL, SDS was involved in increasing opposition to the ROTC, taking up where radical pacifists had left off in the early 1960s; substantial confrontations with the military occurred at Berkeley and Chicago in 1966 and 1967. Following these, SDS chapters and other campus groups launched a call for the severing of university ties with the military.

SDS participation in the growth of draft-resistance opened up major debates within the whole of the NL, and specifically between the resistance and anti-resistance wings of SDS. A draft-resistance movement represented both a political and moral revulsion to the war, and against war in general, with specific objections to Vietnam policy and the Selective Service (SS). In it, individual conscientious resistance was combined and contrasted with collective solidarity and organized civil disobedience.

But despite its apparent militancy, SDS was still nervous of direct action; the leadership initially was chary even of civil disobedience; in 1965 its National Council had turned down Lynd's Washington civil disobedience proposals.[8] There was a tendency to conform with the law; it was significant that although the SS test was voluntary, and although SDS offered a counter-exam, a number of SDS militants and others were willing to take the exemption exam, despite denunciations of it (and them). They argued that this too was largely a question of personal choice.

In such a context the resistance debate inevitably polarized into a number of false dichotomies; political versus moral; symbolic acts versus realistic action; collective versus individual resistance. But as Lynd and Greg Calvert later argued, it was the Resistance which stayed true to many of SDS's early ideals and methods during 1967 and 1968, even when SDS itself had begun to abandon them and was attacking the Resistance, which became a distinct and separate entity as a result.

The development of black militancy also had a decisive impact on SDS: as has been seen, the white NL movement outside the South, now mainly represented by SDS, despite its earlier ousting from the southern movement, remained the closest and most vocal ally of the black community.[9] Although Black Power moved away from the NL as it is usually defined, SDS activists were able to relate to its slogans (as they did to anti-imperialism) as theories or models that were in some senses developments of their own positions on the war, on organizing, and on blackness. Yet at the same time, such ideas were recognized to be to some degree alien importations from parallel movements, and from a distinct sub-culture.

As a result, from the outset, many in SDS entered the defence of Black Power against its opponents. In the months that followed the Selma march, in which Carmichael emerged as the dominant prophet and interpreter of the slogan, intense discussion over it took place within the Movement. Instead of dialogue about black power, however, it became clear that NL radicals (whites), on the one hand, and Carmichael and his immediate entourage, on the other, were not interested in resolving the variety of dilemmas and ambiguities it represented, nor in eliciting a firmer definition. Rather, everyone was reading into the slogan their own largely uncritical interpretations, from the libertarian to the authoritarian, from the reformist to the revolutionary.[10]

The strong and lasting influence of SNCC on SDS has already been remarked, and is still a key factor in assessing the 1967-8 developments, even though by now organizationally, SNCC was fast becoming a shadow, and the Panthers had taken over their 'vanguard' position. Although SNCC had avoided ideological associations and doctrinaire positions at the outset, the theoretical and rhetorical overkill of a later NL should be understood in relation to the experiences of white SNCC workers in the early 1960s, and SDS's white 'brothers and sisters' who joined them on projects, e.g. the Freedom Summers.

In the uneasy period of transition, and in order to prove their worth, there developed a competition of black and white militancies, a more-militant-than-thou escalation, to try to ensure that 'white' and 'liberal', at least within SNCC, could not be seen as conterminous. As black militancy increased, so too did the rhetoric of white organizers; even after they were ousted from SNCC, this contest continued; explained by the desire of white Movement people to be respected by the black groups, and accepted in alliance with them, it also underlines, how, until the end of the decade, 'the New Left was particularly willing to accept black organisations and leaders as vanguards of change.'[11]

With the development of the war, the rise of student power and the radical shift in the black movement, the predominance of community organizing in SDS dwindled, especially after the dissolution of ERAP in 1965.[12] Though the proliferation of local projects continued, SDS had passed beyond its 'going to the people' phase. Early hopes were not yet realized; deep problems of coalition, alliance and reformism, as well as the relative smallness of their organizational structures, showed that these projects needed years, perhaps decades, of patient and often unrewarding work. The young organizers rarely had that time or were willing to take those risks.

On the whole, however, whilst students were not ejected from the northern projects,[13] as the white SNCC workers had been excluded in the South, they left either when the local projects had no longer need of them, or when they chose to move on and work elsewhere, or, as in some cases, when the projects collapsed. As for the prevalent rhetoric of 'base-building', it could now mean anything; radicalization through repression; continued organizing work either in the communities or in the universities; even new forms of creative communication through cultural confrontation, such as Agitprop or street theatre. But the main tendency in SDS was towards recruitment by militancy, gaining publicity through street or campus confrontations.

At this stage, also, other divergent tactics were developed in the Movement outside SDS such as new forms of draft-resistance, or community projects, middle-class and professional organizing, new unions, women's groups and university reform. But these tendencies became largely separated from SDS itself, leaving the confrontationists very much in charge, and in 1967 the Movement for a Democratic Society (MDS)[14] was formed by old SDSers to focus on organizing professionals and technocrats within existing institutions, or occasionally to set up alternatives for these groups.

But SDS itself was now beginning to move in quite a different direction; like SNCC, it was organizing less and less, it was losing touch with any community base, and even subsequently its campus base. The national factions were now each tempted towards an élitist centralism, one actually becoming a closed cadre organization (and later going underground), another becoming an adjunct of the Maoist PLP. The elder statesmen, often more moderate and by now outside the mainstream of SDS politics, either threw themselves into draft resistance or anti-war organizing (such as the National Mobilization Committees) or began creating adult groups such as Radicals in the Professions, the New University Conference, MDS (which grew out of the former) and latterly the New American Movement (NAM). Also many of the women in SDS at this point became involved in Women's Liberation groups outside SDS.

Both the SDS conventions of 1968 and 1969 were remarkable for the lack of concrete reference to such realistic base-building possibilities; abstract and sterile debate, strongly interlaced with slogans, made little direct reference to programme. Very little discussion took place on the issue of the renewed and massive campus militancy of 1968.[15] The national office and national conference of SDS had never been particularly representative of the student movement or even of the local chapters, and this divergence became acutely obvious after 1968. Many local SDS activists ceased to find any point of identification between themselves and what the media was relaying to them about the various 'national' factions of SDS. By 1969 this gap proved unbridgeable.

Three overlapping splits in SDS developed during 1968. The first which to some extent represented the 'base-building' versus 'confrontation' debate of previous years was now formulated in terms of consolidation versus revolution ('action faction'). The second which at first seemed more a matter of style than ideology was PL versus 'the National Office' (NO). The NO cadre or caucus which was later to emerge and be termed RYM I was only one of the three or four major segments to emerge from the total fragmentation of SDS one year later, and only at certain points did this conflict clarify itself as PL versus non-PL. The third, which worked to PL's advantage, was the growing division between the National Office and the rank and file of SDS, particularly those who had joined in the middle 1960s, the period of solid growth.

In no simple way did these splits coincide, but there is substantial evidence to suggest that the grassroots members, whilst opposed to Maoism, were increasingly sceptical of the new leadership, and prepared to support PL on specific issues as the only organized opposition to the increasingly élitist NO group. Certainly the local chapters were far less prone to endorse the pro-NLF, pro-Panther, pro-Cuba, pro-Marxist, pro-confrontation package, than the NO seemed to assume.

PL's blatant but successful opportunism was never better displayed than in its arguments for an open, destructured SDS (in which it could most successfully operate). Thus despite its own democratic centralism and rigid discipline, it could pose, both in 1968 and 1969, as the champion of traditional SDS libertarianism, openness and decentralization. Even those who saw through this tactic by an alien cadre, were still forced to vote with PL against the National caucus's authoritarianism – or else abstain. The SDS leadership might demand that PL operate in a principled fashion, but without effect as long as SDS was 'open' and non-exclusionary; PL could recruit at will.[16]

It should be noted that whilst SDS conferences had always been unrepresentative of rank-and-file opinion in the chapters, by 1967 the gap between the ideologues at the Convention and the grassroots members was great indeed. The 1968 and 1969 conventions were almost wholly unrepresentative of the organization as a whole, as were the NO and *New Left Notes*. Many activists made conscious decisions to boycott the conventions and thus deny them legitimacy – a tactic that failed to take account of the enormous national attention that these gatherings would receive. The libertarian elements in particular stayed away from what promised to be Marx-oriented and jargon-ridden talk-shops – others were in fact not invited, but the results were disastrous, both for SDS and the local groups.

Although PL became a major force (and nuisance) in SDS during 1967, the so-called 'action-faction'/'praxis-axis' split that developed during that year and carried on till the 1968 national conference of SDS, can by no means be simplified into a PL/SDS split. PLers were in fact to be found on both sides in different circumstances; it would be much more accurate to depict it as the SDS mainstream of 1964–6 versus the newcomers, the organizers versus the confrontationists, the base-builders versus the 'militants' of the action-faction. Although PL increasingly emphasized base-building during 1968, this had long been the emphasis of the SDS veterans as well as those moderates who wanted to 'consolidate'; PL was usually opportunist in such matters, thus at Columbia active PLers lined up with Rudd in the action-faction. But the support for the 'praxis-axis' orientation from SDS chapters was obvious from the amount of support given by the mainstream to PL throughout 1968.

In that year, the major tactical debates in SDS were over these questions of confrontationism.[17] The hyperactivism that had long marked the NL as a movement, reached frenzy pitch in the years 1967–9, and became translated into a conscious *tactic* of street confrontation embedded in a *strategy* of provocation, repression – and, it was hoped, revolution. 'Confrontationism', as a major movement orientation, had begun to seize hold of SDS during the latter half of 1967 and developed almost into an ideological alternative to offset the political inroads being made by PL. The Ten Days of Resistance of Spring 1968 were typical of a number of ambitious, but ill-construed, projects initiated by the NO which, both before and after 1968, revealed an unrealistic understanding of its own relationship with SDS chapters, and the need for conscious publicity and preparation.

This became even clearer after the débâcle of the SDS election-day demonstrations in November, which though coming at the apparent height of SDS expansion, drew only minimal support. Moreover, oddly enough, despite the influence of the action-faction in SDS, the national organization tended to follow rather than lead in the six months after Columbia, and did not openly identify either with the radical bombings or the Chicago mobilization.

Confrontationist tendencies had first been clearly apparent in the build-up to 'Stop-the-Draft-Week', and in the 1967 Pentagon demonstrations, where every section of the movement revealed a far greater willingness to use aggressive direct action – from the pacifist wing's escalation of tactics into militant, obstructive, mass civil-disobedience, to the 'crazies', the groups who tried to force entry into the Pentagon, or Gerassi's 'revolutionary contingent' with their pseudo-violence.

In the strategy of confrontation and provocation, the role of manipulation of demonstrators was first marked in Berkeley in the 1966 and 1968 Telegraph Avenue confrontations, in the Oakland 'Stop-the-Draft-Week', at the New York draft board demonstrations, at Columbia, and then later at the Chicago Convention. Though such developments evidenced a growing gap between leader and led, the process cannot be just explained in terms of manipulation of unsuspecting political innocents by a cynical élite, though this was one real ingredient. More significant was a growing willingness on the part of the street people and SDS activists to be directed in this way, to accept 'revolutionary discipline'.

By 1968, SDS had itself become self-consciously revolutionary; the French events in particular, reinforced by Tet, Columbia and the ghetto risings, were taken as the proof of the viability of such an extreme project. The events of the NL's 'year of wonders', both inside and outside America, undoubtedly had a profound, though confused and contradictory, impact on SDS – not least in encouraging young white activists to look for identification outside their own traditions and constituencies. The red and black flags at its June Convention symbolized the inspiration of both the Columbia rebellion and the French events. Both the new Anarchism and Marxist-Leninism were ingredients in this development. The appearance of the 'Up Against the Wall Motherfucker' group at the meetings and the later emergence of 'Weathermen', suggested that the red flag of Socialism (i.e. of Marxist-Leninism) had not yet completely obscured the black flag of Anarchy. As if to underline the influence of these events, Mark Rudd, later to become SDS President, and SDS's NO group, claimed that the Columbia revolt exemplified the success of their new 'strategy'; whilst at the same time PL claimed that the workers' role in France confirmed *their* (Maoist) analysis.

But in fact the 1968 convention at Michigan more clearly revealed the effect of internal developments in SDS, already apparent during the previous year; the growth of factionalism, following the entry of PL and other groups; the increasingly dogmatic violence-prone, ideological orientation; the shrillness of movement rhetoric; all these had been foreshadowed during 1967 and cannot be explained solely in terms of sudden reactions to external events. The changes were, however, certainly sweeping enough, and rapid enough, to catch many old-hands in the Movement off-guard; those who had been out of touch with SDS organizationally were amazed at the extent to which its character was transformed at the centre; many, including some of the founders, were already abandoning it as a lost cause, despite its expanding membership.

These deepening splits were, in O'Brien's view, partly due to the reaching of certain 'natural limits' in campus organizing; but since many campuses had still only been touched superficially by anti-war organizing, draft-resistance or student power issues, this is unlikely. Moreover, other constituencies remained virtually unorganized; rather it is the loss of a populist and democratic orientation, and the drift towards terrorism and authoritarianism in SDS, that can principally be blamed for this loss of organizing potential.

There was undoubtedly a much quicker turnover in SDS membership from the end of 1967 onwards, and this tendency accelerated as the changes of 1968 were realized at chapter level. Although the absolute numbers of SDS members continued to grow throughout 1968, its substantial loss of members was only counterbalanced by a remarkable flood of new members, often freshmen out of high school. But by the early months of 1969, this balance changed, and for the first time in its history SDS was losing members at a faster rate than gaining them, reflecting the impact of the splits, and discrepancy between local groups and the NO. The fact that SDS did not actually decline numerically until relatively late, may be misleading: recruitment took place on the basis of media-image and past reputation, and a definite 'culture-lag' at local chapter level existed. Knowledge of the new ideologies espoused at national level since the June convention took time to filter through.

The strident and superficial pronouncements of the NO group after the June 1968 convention, indicate the declining calibre of SDS leadership in this period – often naïve both in analysis and prescription. The period of militant control by the NO from June onwards was also a period of declining efficiency at the centre; mismanagement was rife in every field of SDS activity. The new leaders were poor administrators and planners; financial and organizational chaos followed during the next twelve months, even though new members were pouring in. Thus the new SDS élite made little effective use of its new-found hegemony over an apparently growing structure.

In the summer of 1968, SDS officially sidestepped the planned use of violent provocation tactics at Chicago – yet although it actually discouraged some members from attending, many SDS rank and file finally took part in the confrontations, forcing the leadership to 'keep up' with the militancy of the membership in this post-hoc reversal. At this stage both the PL and their new front, the Worker Student Alliance (WSA), opposed such tactics, and SDS, largely opportunistic in its relations to the Chicago demonstrations, did not expect the groundswell of local youth support – especially from ethnic and working-class backgrounds – that eventually became involved in the mobilization's actions.

At first SDS opposed the Mobilization Committee on tactical grounds,[18] which varied from opposition to the un-revolutionary nature of the leadership, to the irrelevance of demonstrations in general, or of the Convention in particular. During the Convention week, SDS involved itself first in communicating with young McCarthy supporters; but as days wore on, it became involved with 'radicalizing' the confrontations by street-guerilla actions, revolutionary rhetoric, 'affinity groups', and proclaiming a black-white-and-youth alliance.[19]

The Revolutionary Youth Movement (RYM), born in the fall of 1968, gave ideological finality to a trend which had begun with the anti-imperialism of 1966, and acclaimed the cult of the working class by 1968. Ad hoc tactical involvement in the Chicago events quickly led those sections of SDS who were there (many RYM and NO people were already physically located in Chicago as opposed to PL and other groups) to envisage a working-class youth-movement, as distinct from a 'student/youth' alliance.

These sudden and opportunistic turns moved SDS towards the fully fledged RYM position of December 1968, evolved to counter PL's 'student-worker alliance' position. In it a 'youth-culture' – 'class-consciousness' synthesis emerged, advocating a 'reaching out . . .' to the young workers who after Chicago might join the movement. But, whether this implied an alliance, or an SDS sponsored organization of these groups, was still left ambiguous. Only the rejection of campus-strategies was clearly beyond doubt: RYM showed by now as much contempt for its student base, as had PL.

The SDS and PL leaderships' contempt for students was at least one ingredient in the changed atmosphere which greeted SDS on campus in 1969. The growing hostility to SDS in the universities marked a new watershed in the student movement; it was a hostility that other radical groups did not experience to the same degree, and was a symptom of SDS's rapid loss of its campus base. From the Columbia strike onwards, it had typically developed a reputation as factious and disruptive for its own sake, as well as unpredictable and high-handed in relation to campus issues and attitudes. This was plainly revealed at the major campuses – Columbia, Berkeley, Ann Arbor and Harvard – after fall 1968, where its manipulative and élitist image led to its early downfall.

Some reaction to the various tendencies in SDS during 1968, both to the rise of PL and of the 'confrontationists', was revealed in an attempt at retrenchment and consolidation by those more moderate elements who remained, together with some veterans still in SDS, but by the end of the year this move too had petered out.

The organization's strategic bankruptcy can be illustrated by the fact that no detailed analysis or even position was taken on SDS's relationship with black nationalism, or the new, armed domestic-militancy; nor were the role or implications of Women's Liberation theoretically confronted. The Yippee and other manifestations of cultural revolt were hardly mentioned. At the SDS conferences, there was no longer any concern with community organizing, although the possibilities of organizing around the high schools, the draft, urban renewal and ethnic group issues, remained as strong as ever. Despite theories of the working class, even labour organizing – especially of poor and migrant workers and many skilled and professional groups, still disadvantaged, or often non-unionized – was avoided.[20]

All this is a remarkable commentary on the vacuum in SDS, its lack of contextual relevance in its later years, as well as the lack of any basic agreement on major issues. By 1968, SDS was fast losing touch with all the basic processes of change, in a welter of rhetoric and jargon and a collage of Old Left ideological fragments.

In the view of SDS's chief biographer,[21] during the period from later 1967, until early 1969, SDS opted for Old Left's ideological solutions by 'happenstance/and osmosis'. 'It is as a result that SDS becomes a melange of sects repeating the "sectarian spiral" of the organized left of the past' (Gitlin). Its failure to develop other options was because of a shortage of time and a failure of nerve and imagination. Although ideology was not the root problem for SDS, any more than for the NL as a whole, a number of major ideological divisions were to develop over class-analysis and action in America (including the Marcusian, 'student-worker' and 'new working-class' perspectives), over the relationship with Black Nationalism and the Panthers, and the attitude to the NLF/DRVN.

But both the ideological and organizational crises in SDS were brought to a head by its bizarre and paradoxical relationship with the Maoists.[22]

The final polarization was caused by the NO's decision to use PL's Old Left methods of manipulation and caucus to prevent a Maoist coup. Thus one of the ironies of the demise of SDS is that the leadership, in its attempt to fight PL, finished up so extraordinarily close in tactics and even ideas to Maoism. Indeed, RYM takes on most of PL's least attractive characteristics, and its own *version* of Maoism.

This is confirmed in the consistent NO censorship of PL views from mid-1968 onwards, and the suppression of Maoist articles which were flooding into *New Left Notes*; the exclusion of certain PL factions in some local chapters also took place. Not only PL, but other groups like the semi-Trotskyist Labour Committee, were then expelled. Anarchists were refused credentials for the 1969 convention by the NO (in 1969) because of 'deviations'. And eventually PL itself was declared no longer 'a member' of SDS by about a third of the 1969 convention delegates.

Thus SDS, originally the most anti-exclusionist of organizations, was driven to expel these other 'Communists' and revive the most blatant of Old Left methods – a move that proved utterly destructive, not least to SDS, but to the American NL as a whole.

As Jacobs points out, most of the anti-PL factions to develop in this period were made up, not of old SDS activists, but of newcomers to SDS, some attracted by instant revolution, and a mass base. In addition, at the 1969 conference, there were other small anti-PL groups such as 'Action Faction', as well as the Detroit Organising Committee and the 'Revolutionary Union' (which again ironically tended to adopt PL's narrow view of the working class). There were also other assorted smaller factions including Anarchists, YSA, and Independent Socialists who attacked PL.

But the national membership at large was deeply alienated by these sectarian squabbles; during 1969 the internecine strife between the factions, which had openly surfaced at the 1968 conference, turned from venomous words to physical assault; particularly as by now PL had developed a strongly critical stance towards the three sacred cows of the new militants: Cuba, the Panthers and the NLF. It was thus a further irony that many NO spokesmen were left defending positions in 1969, on the Panthers, on Vietnam, etc., which PL had earlier introduced but had already themselves abandoned (though not for NL reasons!).

The pitched battles at the 1968 convention had taken place mainly between PL and the mainline SDS. In 1969, the split was by no means so clean. Many delegates, including many non-PL supporters of the worker-student alliance, were largely bemused by the split. Many WSAers seem to have been genuinely unaware of PL's dominance, and even actively denied it. Moreover, many SDSers, whilst they might accept criticisms of PL's methods and dogmas, were equally ready to oppose SDS National Office on some issues. For example, it was easy for radical libertarians to sympathize with PL's attacks on all forms of 'nationalism' as reactionary; equally, though for quite different reasons from PL, they might wish to withhold support from the NLF. Moreover, they might sympathize with PL's attack on 'racism in reverse' which PL now argued characterized some Panther pronouncements. Of course, those who temporarily supported PL on such issues, did not necessarily remain with them after the split. A substantial number of delegates seem to have 'shopped-around' the various factions.[23]

The other splinters which formally emerged in 1969, in addition to PL and the WSA, were the three main fragments of the 1968 SDS National Office group – the 'RYM I' – part of it becoming 'Weatherman', and part RYM II. A sizeable number of SDS chapters clearly supported and identified with neither of the main national factions (PL or RYM I/Weatherman) nor with the relatively unorganized RYM II – many of these chapters declared their autonomy from SDS; one chapter declared that neither of the 'bureaucratic Stalinist' National Offices represented them. Not a single SDS chapter affiliated with Weatherman or what was left of the National Office; though PL/WSA already firmly controlled a number of chapters, it gained few more from the split; and RYM II did not in reality exist as a national organization, and soon faded away. The few dozen Anarchists who had still remained after the 1968 débâcle, now left SDS with final denunciations of 'the new Stalinists'.[24] The YSA and the IS who had been waiting in the wings of the final SDS convention, were the only groups to gain members. The fight with PL had turned out to be a 'death rattle' for SDS rather than a 'life struggle'.[25]

It can be argued that in the last analysis, the leadership of SDS had pulled out of its own organization rather than having actually successfully expelled PL. It is generally conceded that no clear majority for the expulsion declaration ever existed at the 1969 convention; perhaps logically the expulsion of PL *should* have meant a stronger SDS rather than the instant atomization that occurred. But the way in which the purge was performed meant that a supposedly common enemy had sustained only a partial, temporary and artificial unity, amongst the opposition; in the end large sections of the movement were not prepared to fight fire with fire.

This is perhaps why SDS had become a silent majority in its own organization; opposition to PL was an insufficient common denominator to sustain coalition; and in answering the challenge of PL, the NO had produced a mirror image of PL's ideology and tactics – even though never able to match it in its relentless discipline. It was never altogether clear what Mike Klonsky had in mind when he announced, when still SDS national secretary, that 'our primary task is to build a Marxist-Leninist revolutionary movement'; PL of course already claimed to be exactly that. But in Klonsky's view, and in the name of 'revolutionary vanguard organization', a tightly organized and self-conscious élite (the SDS 'caucus') was created mainly to engineer PL's defeat and expulsion from SDS, as early as summer 1968.[26]

The finality of Lynd's consequent attack at this point on the NO may be seen as a highly significant disavowal: in SDS, he argued,

both PLP and the national collective are working to recruit a cadre, a revolutionary cadre, out of SDS no matter what the cost to SDS as an organically evolving revolutionary movement.[27]

It is also important to note how both of the major organizations left within SDS were also related to the development of 'Weatherman'.[28] In the 1968 split between the PL/WSA factions on the one hand, and the NO caucus and future RYM I faction, on the other, it was future 'Weatherpeople' who organized the main opposition to the PL/WSA line, and it was Mark Rudd, a founder of RYM I who, together with Bernadine Dohrn, Bill Ayers and Mike Klonsky, took the leading role in SDS until mid-1969.

A separate stage of NL history marks this subsequent period of Weatherman predominance, the period in which the mass membership of SDS, in the months before and after the 1969 Convention, finally – and rapidly – evaporated.

It was the attempt to impose the straitjacket of authoritarian organization on SDS which represented the most marked change from the pre-1967 movement; by doing this (ostensibly in self-protection), SDS created an authority structure worth taking over – a power centre to be competed for, either by groups or individuals – and thus probably encouraged rather than discouraged PL's attempted coups. But in addition to PL, the organizational careerists, usually vying in the militancy of their rhetoric, made an appearance at this stage. These 'leaders' who tended to have a fairly opportunistic or eclectic attitude to ideology, promised, in utter contrast to the existential defeatism and sacrifice stressed by early SDS and SNCC, a string of easy victories without apparent cost.

Perhaps the greatest failure of SDS in its last two years was its inability to relate to the hundreds of thousands of young people who, aware of the organization's name and tradition, were searching for a humane and libertarian radicalism. In his history of SDS, Sale concludes: 'it failed to provide a radical politics for a sub-generation of militant students who were then forced to look elsewhere or more often chose not to look at all.' Oblivious to this mainstream appeal, contemptuous of such grassroots impulses, the NO group transformed SDS beyond recognition, and beyond the sympathy and comprehension of its base. In organizational terms, the SDS leadership 'simply failed to reach great segments of the membership or potential membership',[29] in the colleges and universities of America. Sale aptly summarizes this gap:

At a time when many young people wanted some explanations for the failure of electoral politics SDS was led by people who had long since given up caring about elections. . . . To students just beginning to be aware of their own radicalisation and potential role as the intelligentsia in an American Left, SDS offered the wisdom that the only important agents for social change were the industrial workers, ghetto blacks, or the third world revolutionaries. For . . . students . . . ready to take on their administrations for any number of grievances, SDS provided an analysis . . . emphasising de-studentizing, dropping out and destroying universities . . . for youths in search of an integrative ideology . . . SDS had only the imperfectly fashioned tenets of a borrowed Marxism and . . . the theories of other revolutionaries; not even the serviceable explanations of an earlier day were available.

Intolerance had now spread to its own constituency. The effect on SDS was particularly disastrous, the ethos of one-dimensional tolerance and counter-violence was taken further than Marcuse himself had indicated, and created a strange mirror-image reaction to the sickness of American society. The growth of factions advocating hyper-militancy was a further aspect of the growing sectarian division within SDS, culminating in the Weatherman 'Days of Rage', a conspicuously para-military exercise organized by the Weather-group in Chicago in October 1969.

America was violent; SDS apparently had to become increasingly violent to defeat it. America was racist, so this section of SDS prepared to support racism in reverse (and the call of 'Off pigs', 'slaughter white people', or 'Burn, Baby, Burn' was not unfairly characterized as that by some SDS moderates). America was Imperialist, and this fact could consistently be used to justify, apologize for or ignore other imperialisms, including Chinese, Russian or Vietnamese expansionism, or the invasion of Czechoslovakia. America's legendary militarism became mirrored and echoed in SDS's own armed mythology, rhetoric and posture; in its final year, *New Left Notes* literally portrayed guns on every page (and many other Movement and even alternative papers were by now following suit), even whilst railing against police-armouries and the militarism of the right.

H𝟙D

Even the personality-cultism of the dominant media was reflected in SDS behaviour and Movement icons – such as posters of Che, Huey Newton and Ho Chi Minh, which dominated SDS offices and demonstrations.

When earlier theorists had urged the domestic NL to become a specifically American movement, they had hardly intended this; an inversion of mainstream Americana masked by the trappings of an alien and exaggerated leftism. As many of the founders of SDS quietly dropped out of it during the years 1967–9, they remarked that it had become increasingly a neurotic symptom of the societal malaise, rather than a potential cure for America's ills.[30]

11. Annus Mirabilis: 1968

Point of no return

The year 1968 may be taken as marking the major watershed in the development of the NL. By the later 1960s, the movement had become a spectre haunting Europe as well as America and Britain. In Germany, Holland and Italy, and also in Scandinavia, Czechoslovakia and France – even in Latin America – similar tendencies were beginning to come to a head. Most of these were emerging with the greatest clarity in the universities, and through student action,[1] accompanying the massive international developments of the anti-war movement.

In these years, student interchange and communication was advancing more rapidly than any other section of the movement; transnational links of study abroad were paralleled in the exchange of student political leadership. It is no accident that American graduate students were active at LSE and a German at Nanterre. The student subculture was becoming its own form of global village.

During that year the NL became recognized in official circles as undeniably a serious movement; as it reached the zenith of its mass support, it moved to near-revolutionary militancy in the spring and summer. This was true not only in America but in Europe – quite clearly in France, increasingly in Germany, and with some signs of such growth in Britain.[2] A growing awareness of the development of the American movement marked the European militancy of 1967 and 1968, not least the student revolts, just as the American movements absorbed the influences from Berlin, Paris, Prague, and Amsterdam.

At the time, the momentum of events of the early months seemed quite irresistible; the apparently irreversible American setback of Tet, the Johnson withdrawal speech, the April nationwide ghetto risings, the May events in France, and escalating radical confrontations at the Pentagon, induction centres and at Columbia, were gathering impetus on all sides. It seemed that the whole Western establishment was on the run. Even in England the scenario of revolution was translated from movement rhetoric into alarmist press predictions of upheaval.

Everywhere the NL seemed to be moving from the wings to the centre of the stage. Yet only two years later, it was possible to say 'The New Left as a social movement has been decisively defeated.'[3]

To understand this great divide in the movement, it is necessary at this point to consider several occurrences outside America and Britain, which had a fundamental impact and implication for the Western NL as a whole; the first in January, in Vietnam, the second in May, in France, the third in August, in Czechoslovakia. In addition, three major movement events inside the USA – the murder of Martin Luther King at Memphis, the crisis at Columbia university and the happenings at the Chicago Democratic Convention (together with the failure of the McCarthy campaign), are each intertwined in their effects with the crises outside America, just as events in England, especially the two militant Vietnam Solidarity demonstrations and the student occupations, reached their climax.

The year began with an event of universal significance in Vietnam, which had little or no direct connection with the NL. It is true that some commentators believe that North Vietnamese and NLF leaders were disproportionately influenced in their strategic thinking by the apparent strength of the American anti-war movement during 1967. But the influence, in terms of symbolism and reinforcement, of the Tet offensive on the NL and on the whole of Western consciousness was probably of far greater moment.

To the mass of ordinary Americans, Tet revealed a stalemate in Vietnam, confirming that neither side could win. None of the Movement developments of 1968 can be seen, particularly in America, without reference to the groundswell of support for – almost at any price – a cessation of fighting in Vietnam. There was a growing awareness of the costs of the conflict. This presaged a sudden shift of public feeling towards the Movement, reflected nationally in America with the McCarthy victories in the Democratic Primaries, and Lyndon Johnson's announcement that he would not seek re-election, and confirmed by public opinion polls. It is in this context, and in interpreting Tet as a 'victory', that the NL itself escalates its rhetoric and tactics; it acted almost as if it sensed a new mandate for extreme action.

The year 1968 was certainly a watershed in terms of the Movement's willingness to employ violence; the major shift of attitude towards violence which had come at least a year earlier with the rise of the Panthers and Stop-the-Draft-Week, was now openly expressed at Columbia, in Chicago and at San Francisco State College.

The happenings of 1968 themselves lent reinforcement to this growing ambivalence about means; whilst the Czech popular resistance, like the May events in Paris, was based predominantly on unarmed confrontations, both experiences marked a new moment in European thinking about the use of military violence in political conflict.

Yet nonviolence itself was by no means dead; the actions of the

Buddhists in Vietnam which both preceded and followed the Tet offensive, signified the most unlikely and remarkable revival of all; nonviolent draft-resistance and the California Grape Strike, together with King's Poor People's Campaign, continued such traditions in America. But then the assassination of King at Memphis, and NL reactions to King's death and its context, reveal and illustrate the growing confusions surrounding the movement's ostensible changeover to violence.

It is difficult to remember that despite all the movement rhetoric, the self-confessedly violent events like the Tet offensive and the Chicago confrontations were by no means clearly 'successful' even in their own terms, and the former created dissension both in the NL and the pacifist movement over the ethics and character of terroristic revolutionary war. Whilst Paris (like Columbia) was a confrontation which involved un-armed physical violence, many of its tactical successes could still be claimed in terms of the *nonviolent* armoury. The Czech resistance, predominantly without violence, whilst it did not succeed in reversing the Soviet invasion, slowed and tempered it; though it ironically, and graphically, also helped reinforce images of street confrontation, already so prevalent in movement imaginations in the West.

The events in New York, at Columbia, culminating in the early spring of 1968, also represented a new stage in the development of on-campus student protest in the Western countries. Militant and physical confrontation had already taken place at the LSE in London the previous year, but this was a sustained action that marked a new stage beyond the Berkeley events of 1964 or 1966.

The so-called French May events that erupted mainly in Paris in the May of 1968, created the first major national crisis provoked by a NL anywhere. Here the novel element that was stressed was the van-guard role of the students, and the initiating of mass industrial unrest: this was at once interpreted as both cultural revolution and a 'student–worker alliance'. In Marcuse's words 'the students showed the workers what could be done' and the European revolutionary tradition was 'revived', to a great extent spontaneously.[4]

But the predominant imagery of the events which most influenced the movements outside France was of the 'great festival of youthful solidarity' (Edgar Morin), the notion that this was 'the great game that is the revolution', or as Raoul Vaneigem described the happenings in Paris, a 'break-through into freedom'.[5]

The impact on the Western NL of the Czech developments in August, can be compared significantly with the previous decisive impact of Tet and Paris. Tet had not been fully understood by the NL, and at first had been misinterpreted; nevertheless, it was absorbed into the move-ment experience; Paris was far simpler both to understand and to absorb, given a certain idealization of 'worker-student alliances'. But the events in Prague were so out of line with recent NL experience, expectations and orientation, they jarred against so many assumptions and predictions that for many they had either to be grossly slandered, or ignored and rejected. Whilst the NL had now become unable to cope with such events ideologically, it was on the very ideological plane that the Czechs won overall a moral victory, reinforcing the political superiority of their position for world opinion, and making Russia's wholesale use of terror and reprisals, as in Budapest, much less likely.

Then there was the Democratic Convention, or 'Czechago' as it was later termed, after the assaults by Mayor Daley's police on predominantly unarmed, though militant, NL demonstrators; these actions represented a self-conscious synthesis of slogans and tactics and icons drawn from the year's previous events and confrontations. The images and influences of Paris were reflected in the Situationist aspects of cultural confrontation and the Yippees. The impact of Tet was reflected in the Viet Cong flags and the almost universal call for NLF victory; Mark Rudd's presence marked the link with Columbia; there were also token appearances by Black Panthers. A number of posters referred to the repression in Prague; and varying attitudes to Eugene McCarthy's candidacy were expressed. As a result, overall the demonstrations presented one of the oddest spectacles in the whole history of the NL; 'Pigasus'[6] juxtaposed with McCarthy supporters, street theatre broken up by police batons, anti-Imperialist rhetoric interspersed with rock bands, violent confrontation with lip-service to nonviolence by some pacifist leaders. The seven who were later arrested for conspiracy only indicate a partial impression of the range of elements represented in the streets outside the Convention.

Two other contradictory elements surfaced during the days of the Chicago confrontation – the extra-parliamentarists in SDS and the coalitionists attracted to McCarthy's campaign, or those who had supported Bobby Kennedy, within the Democratic Party. On the whole, NL reactions to both the Convention and the subsequent election was to try to ignore both events; up until the elections of 1968, the American radical movement appeared to itself and to its opponents, including the President, a good deal stronger than it actually was. After Nixon's 1968 election, the reverse seemed true. For all the scoffing at electoral results amongst the militants of the NL, there was little doubt that the November figures left a pervasive feeling of impotence; nor could the toll taken by internal dissent, tiredness and deep divisions over strategy and ideology be any longer ignored.

Finally, emphasis must be given to the impact of the events of 1968 on SDS in precipitating the extraordinarily rapid and sweeping changes that, as has been seen, completely transformed the organization between March and October of that year. Whilst the changes in the SDS leadership were only in part a reflection of such events, by the end of the year, SDS was not only altered beyond recognition, but had a substantially new membership, and was irreversibly split. During these ten months, the movement as a whole, unable to give perspective or rational form to a series of external and internal eruptions, entered its deepest and most enduring crisis.

At the time, and indeed in retrospect, 1968 appeared to be the NL's 'year of wonders' – it was also a year from which the Movement, everywhere, has never recovered.

Tet

In January 1968, in the middle of the Tet holiday truce, whilst most Vietnamese were with their families, celebrating the annual festival with the equivalent of a Western Christmas dinner, the assembled NLF and DRVN forces launched a massive surprise attack of unprecedented speed and ferocity on every urban centre in South Vietnam. Parts of Saigon and the whole of the ancient Buddhist city of Hue were occupied and days and weeks of vicious terror ensued, including at least one full scale massacre (Hue). The event showed that at the very height of US involvement (550,000 men committed by 1968), the greatest military-industrial power in the world could become stalemated in a small Asian country, when only indirectly in conflict with the other great powers involved.

America could clearly *not* guarantee security to Vietnamese people by its presence, and much of the Western NL typically celebrated an event which symbolized the apparent discomfiture of an 'aggressive' imperialism. At a time of accelerating identification with armed liberation struggles, and the iconography of the heroic guerilla following Guevara's death, Tet seemed to suggest American vulnerability, and, for the movement, the chance of a much-needed victory. The year 1968, thus sees the elevation of slogans such as 'create two, three many Vietnams' (Che), 'Ho, Ho, Ho Chi Minh' (neatly linked to Mao's admonition 'Dare to Struggle, Dare to Win'). There can be little doubt that the immediate effect of Tet was to intensify militancy and determination in most of the Western movement. Coming at a time of deepening frustration and anti-Americanism, it became a symbol of resistance and rejection of the status quo.

This was its symbolic meaning and significance; but it had quite other political and military ones. In the first place, it was certainly not a 'victory' for the NLF except in a certain immediate propaganda sense. Militarily it was a crushing defeat involving appalling, almost suicidal losses, which partly meant that the NLF after Tet played an increasingly minor and subordinate role to the Northern troops. Politically, it was a defeat within Vietnam, in the sense that there was absolutely no general or urban or rural rising to support the NLF cadres; indeed these groups became during Tet, totally isolated. In turn, sympathetic peasants blamed the NLF for not achieving promised victory. In addition, enormous civilian losses, partly due to drawing firepower on to

NLF positions in towns and cities, partly due to direct executions, mortaring and terror by the NLF, further alienated a large section of the population. Although it was not an aspect of the offensive emphasized by the Western press, and certainly and predictably largely ignored by the NL, it also revealed the terroristic nature of the NLF, and appeared to confirm some of the accounts of earlier terrorism in the post-1945 and post-1957 periods, which had also been previously played down or rejected by most of the left.[7]

The terror of Tet, like that of the early years of the second Vietnam war (1957–60), was selective, organized, bureaucratically directed, and not merely a spontaneous 'settling of scores'. As a result of the terrifying ordeal at the hands of both sides, the third force opposition in Vietnam at first seemed utterly demoralized by the violence of Tet; after years of oppression and harassment the cessation of nonviolent struggle could have been predictable. But despite growing victimization by both sides, and overt repression by Thieu on a 1963 scale, mass demonstrations for peace, neutralist political work for a ceasefire, against forcible conscription, and for land reform in the villages, continued and actually spread in the subsequent period.[8]

Memphis

The idea that the assassination of a single leader could extinguish a tradition which had developed in scores of cultures and countries over at least a century, was, as one commentator pointed out, somewhat equivalent to suggesting that Che Guevara's death marked the end of guerilla violence.[9] But whilst it was not true that the year 1968 in general, or Martin Luther King's death in particular, marked the 'death' of nonviolence, the violent episodes which preceded and perhaps precipitated King's assassination, clearly illustrated many of the tensions and problems which attended King's life and the movement generally.

It was not so much nonviolence that failed, as that the particular movement and ideas which King represented had become demoralized and outpaced by events. It was the tragedy of both King and nonviolence that throughout the 1960s they had become increasingly identified with one another. King's was advertised as the only genuine brand (it was clearly often the most explicit brand). Thus the assassination of King could purport to represent the 'end of nonviolence'.

King had been forced after 1965 into a somewhat isolated stance by the emergence of the black power leadership. Nevertheless, it was also true that he had regained substantial prestige by the year of the King–Spock nomination (1967). Moreover his Poor People's Coalition, the Memphis sanitation workers' strike, the Resurrection City campaign in Washington, as well as his increasing militancy on the war, had brought him back well within the Movement orbit during the year before his death. Indeed, these last campaigns were seen by many as a further test-case for nonviolent militance in the changed atmosphere of 1968.

King was still a predominant figure in the black community in his last year, as he had been in 1964. Few men's deaths could have triggered nationwide rioting on the scale of April 1968. It was an ironic but natural epitaph to King that the ghettoes should erupt in this violent grief and anger, with spontaneous waves of burning and looting. It was an event foreshadowed both in Watts and Detroit in 1964 and 1966, and in the streets of Memphis, a few days before his death. The climate in which King was killed was created not only by racist sentiment, the escalation of violence in the ghettoes, the Vietnam war, and the obduracy of the politicians (and directly or indirectly their possible complicity in his death), the atmosphere was in part created by black militancy itself. Grief and anger were emotions which King had never succeeded in tapping or harnessing through civil disobedience or nonviolent action; he had spoken too little and too late to these Northern cities. An atmosphere of intense violence attended the Memphis march, and King clearly was involved in a continuing struggle to contain the tension seething within the black community and movement, as well as deeply threatened by the fury of the white backlash it promised to provoke.[10] He returned to Memphis to prevent this violence escalating.

King's own life was often at risk; but as Andrew Young, King's aide in Memphis suggested, this particular attempt might not have been made if the militants had not provoked the Memphis actions into greater violence. King felt, despite the immense danger, that he must return to vindicate the power and truth of nonviolence on the street, and his last speeches had all the intensity of a premonition of death.

It is nevertheless ironic that the increasing militancy of white and black radicals was partly reinforced by MLK's death: at the memorial rally to King, at Berkeley, black militants tried to break up the speeches with a call for armed Negroes to take to the streets; only violence, they announced, could be revolutionary. This was Carmichael's own reaction to the news. Many whites reacted similarly. At Columbia, the 'racist' plans for uprooting blacks in Harlem through the Gymnasium scheme, were highlighted by Rudd's intervention at the university's memorial service for King (9 April).

Such outbursts, like the ghetto violence, were strange tributes to a man whose philosophy of transformation had shunned violence, and whose final political agony had been worked out in the attempt to contain the violence of his own followers.

But far *more* alien to his work and life were the pious epitaphs of the Establishment, which praised nonviolence in terms he would have rejected (i.e. as a form of social control, thus reinforcing the jibes of all his radical critics). Even whilst calling out the troops, those who had opposed him in life and supported repressive violence elsewhere, now attempted to co-opt King's memory on behalf of an opportune quietism and passivity.[11]

King's death was also catalytic and revealing in terms of the nature of American society; it bore out the NL's appraisal of its sententious rhetoric; the shocked grief of the whole black community, even of those black leaders who rejected nonviolence, was seen as acutely real; the unctuous hypocritical grief of the white politicians who at the same time were ordering out the National Guard, was displayed as ludicrous, unbelievable and false. The commercializing of emotion and the thoroughgoing racism embedded in the fabric of American culture seemed to stand revealed in the media's glib and prurient handling of King's death. The dubious quality of its justice was affirmed in the inadequacy of its investigation of the killer and his motives. LBJ could only call for an end to 'lawlessness and divisiveness', whilst a parade of apologetic white politicians was still apparently wheeling and dealing in the game of political manœuvre for self, class and race. The assassination and the response mark an important symbolic turning point in the massive alienation from American society; but it did not, as some claimed, teach a simple lesson about the tactics or methods by which that alienation could best be channelled, expressed, or overcome.

Columbia

By the spring of 1968, the Columbia chapter of SDS was under attack, and with its leaders threatened had already made plans even before the April eruption to go on to the offensive, rather than wait for the expulsion of Mark Rudd and others. The university's involvement with the Institute of Defense Analysis (IDA) had come under heavy attack, along with the continued presence of military recruiters and the CIA. An SDS Resistance group had been active and was being harassed. Its specific opposition was aimed at the submission of class-grades to draft boards: students voted overwhelmingly to support it. In addition, Columbia SDS had been involved, together with other groups, on both racial and student issues, and coordinated a number of actions on these and other themes.

As in a number of universities, SDS, since 1966, had been organizing coalitions around black and student interests using a variety of methods; campus CORE had also raised problems of the university's relationship with the ghetto; the university was a Harlem landlord planning a construction project on hitherto public parkland. SDS took this up, condemning the Gym that was being built in place of much needed housing, and in 1967, six student members of SDS and the Resistance were arrested and threatened with expulsion. The three major themes were now clarified; 'amnesty' for the arrested students, an 'end to links' with the IDA, and suspension of the construction of the Gym. It was on this last issue that black students became involved.

Nowhere did SDS develop a range of activity as effectively as at Columbia; only there was confrontation backed by as much research and many of the subsequent actions were thoroughly planned in advance, though the timing and scenario were not. The previous leadership had succeeded in preparing much of the ground for the April outburst, and had organized effectively, if not actually creating a 'mass base'; in March Rudd was elected President of Columbia SDS. He represented the activist wing, and whilst he rejected any split between theory and organizing, he criticized the 'wait and see' moderation of the previous 'praxis' leadership and stressed the need for vanguards.

Although the main events started on 21 April and lasted one month (until 22 May), several militant demonstrations had occurred in March and early April, one against the IDA on 27 March and the disruption of the MLK memorial service (unsupported by the black students) in April. In the latter, Rudd denounced the hypocrisy and racism of the university.

The notorious 'up against the wall' statement from Rudd appeared on 19 April. In it Rudd rejected both a student-power position and a worker-student alliance position, as well as a more traditional working-class analysis. His views seemed closest to an advocacy of a student activism that linked itself to the universal oppressed. Consciously rejecting student-reform strategies, Rudd denied that his struggle had anything to do with a lack of democracy and communication in an archaic university; there was no question of Columbia being 'reformed'.

Although initially led by Rudd into Hamilton Hall on the 21, the the vanguard role seems to have been played by the Afro-American student group, who first occupied it, accompanied by some whites, on that day. This uneasy black-white alliance seemed broken after an expression of considerable anti-white feeling, and a split on the question of barricading the occupied building; this led to the walk-out (or ejection) of white SDSers and others.

But soon other buildings were occupied, starting with the Low Library; communes were established in all five of these buildings. This occupation, initiated by a minority in SDS under Rudd, after a split in relation to the black occupation, was at first isolated from the mass of students. But Rudd, by now the principal spokesman, initiated the escalation of the occupation from temporary to permanent when the white students barricaded themselves into these buildings.

But it was only the administration's threat, and then use, of police intervention that swung massive support towards SDS; Daniel Bell, by no means a sympathetic observer, wrote 'for most of the students it was their first encounter with blood and brutality and they responded in fear and anger'. The next day almost the entire campus responded to a call for a student strike. In a few hours, 'thanks to the New York City Police Department, a large part of the Columbia campus had become radicalised'.[12]

Part of Columbia's significance, within the larger movement, was that this event apparently confirmed what many had said before the Oakland Stop the Draft Week the previous October: a police attack on a demonstration was an instrument of radicalization. This moved some SDS strategists to begin, tacitly, even overtly, to advocate deliberate provocation of such response. It was partly for this reason that Paul Goodman attacked the Columbia events as exemplifying a growing authoritarianism and manipulation which used people as tactical and strategic pawns, and which presumed to radicalize people for their own good. This, said Goodman, was a piece of élitist intellectual arrogance.

Yet, as against these factors, and the growing impatience with dissent within SDS-organized meetings, as well as the uneasy relationship with blacks, there seems to have been genuine attempts to extend the idea of participatory democracy within the occupation, and in the strike committee. The occupation emphasized the communal aspect of the enterprise, and PD was stressed in all the meetings.

The language of Columbia is full of this rhetoric of community – the idea of the movement as 'a Commune', and it was this element that another observer, Stephen Spender, saw as the most characteristic. But a student participant and observer, Dotson Rader,[13] saw even its PD as spurious; he noted that an SDS line always triumphed in meetings, through both the acquiescence with an organized leadership minority, and the lack of organized opposition (or quick suppression of any alternatives). In addition, other participants reported strict censorship and control within each of the occupations.

Although Rudd admitted that the growing élitism of the leadership of SDS was one of the reasons that it failed to sustain itself after the mass arrests, he denies that the leadership foisted its anti-imperialist demands and quasi-Marxist programme on the rest of the radical students, or that the demand for amnesty was an inflexible one. The major reasons he gave for the strike's relative failure (though both the demands on the Gym and the IDA were largely met) include the growing sectarianism of the meetings (mainly blamed on faction fights with PL and other groups), and the escalation of SDS rhetoric and action (including that of the 'Up Against the Wall Mother-Fuckers' group) as well as on the police repression and expulsions.

Other critics, including some within SDS, criticized the movement at Columbia, and Rudd in particular, for shunning aspirations in terms of the university itself (other than that of a 'Liberation' school set up later). The grudging willingness of SDS to even accept a further demand, for democratizing the university, was too little and too late: 'Leaving the issue of student power to the Liberals was a bad mistake' according to an SDS activist, Eric Mann; yet Rudd freely admitted that building a student power base had never been the intention. It was rather to create a model, and highlight issues nationally – which he claimed Columbia did.

On the other hand, Columbia also undoubtedly lacked the initial kind of groundswell of solid mass student support that had characterized Berkeley in 1964 and 1966, and thus SDS was tempted into radical minority actions that inevitably turned towards élitism and manipulation. Whilst over a thousand took part in the occupations, there was not the same large intervening support group as at Berkeley.

Moreover, in insisting on the six demands initially, SDS had effectively isolated itself from the mass of students; in particular there was little general support for the amnesty appeal, for which SDS, understandably, held out even after concessions on other major points. Indeed, SDS was only saved by the police intervention which at last brought support from the left-liberal middle ground of students and faculty. But this was again alienated in the following months, and the militant 'five per cent' effectively isolated once more. In large part, this failure to mobilize behind the actions (except in the period of classroom boycotts immediately following police intervention) probably had as much to do with the style, tone and methods of SDS's actions as with the demands themselves, which (even including amnesty) were not unreasonable ones.

A number of features which exemplify the developments in the Movement generally, characterized these events at Columbia; in the first place, black and white students organized separately; there was often tension between the two groups; different demands (the blacks included black studies demands), and separate negotiations with the university, police, etc. In the second place, as an additional symbol of the changing nature of the NL was a dominant iconography in the revolt; portraits of Che Guevara, Malcolm-X, Stokeley Carmichael, and Marx; slogans from Che, Mao, Rap Brown and LeRoi Jones abounded.

Third, the style and tone of the confrontations was more militant, involving more verbal violence than before; Rudd warned the President (Kirk), that if the students won, they would take 'control of his world'. Thus Columbia (even though partly because of police over-reaction) exemplified a further stage in the growing provocation-repression strategy of the NL – especially SDS; henceforth, the violence of the police was almost desired and elicited to prove a point; it pointed forward to Chicago in August.

May 1968: France

The Parisian explosion came unpredicted, with a magnitude unmatched by anything in America, Germany, or Britain. The nationwide seizure of universities and high-schools, followed by street battles and a massive quasi-general strike and factory occupations, was more militant than even many ardent anarcho-syndicalists had dreamed of over half a century earlier; and it came close to its fruition in a revolutionary general strike. The decentralized actions of first students, and then students and workers, were deployed against a state structure that at first seemed paralysed in a centralized impotence. It also seemed to represent a culmination of the strategic implications of the NL's projects and ideas that had been evolving in America, married with a more traditional Socialist scenario of worker-rising. In addition, it embodied the new rhetoric of post-scarcity radicalism: 'The consumer society must perish a violent death. The society of alienation must disappear from history. We are inventing a new and original world.'

From such slogans and manifestoes, the posters and pamphlets of May 1968, one gains a single predominant impression of the events, of their ideologically eclectic character, and the undoubted predominance of anti-authoritarian ideas.[14] Prominent amongst these were the principles of direct democracy (applied in France in the various assemblies), Rosa Luxemburg's ideas of worker control (and also her critique of Bolshevik methods), tirades against Leninism as well as Stalinism (and even Sartreism).

By including the critique of bureaucratic methods in revolution drawn partly from Luxemburg, Trotsky, and from the tradition of the 1871 Paris Commune, they established their NL identity; the radical Spontaneists called the Russian Revolution a 'counter revolution'; and the critique of bureaucracy was extended even to Cuba and China; the ideas of workers' councils were developed particularly from the interwar German libertarian socialists who had already influenced the German SDS, and the most prominent figure, Cohn-Bendit, identified himself closely with the Anarchist tradition.

But just as typical were also manifestly non-political elements, or at least elements which saw themselves outside the purely political traditions of ideology, such as Dada and Surrealism. These together with Situationism (which they influenced) also represented rejections of any bureaucratic apparatus – whether of the Establishment or the revolution. Expressing the ideas of Raoul Vaneigem, Situationists called for a revolt against alienation, a breakthrough into freedom, a revolution in everyday life; from these groups emerged the slogan 'All power to the imagination', emphasizing the cultural dimensions of revolt including poetry and theatre.[15]

Thus from the Sorbonne came the manifesto: 'Imagination is seizing power'. 'The Revolution which is beginning will call into question not only capitalist society, but industrial society.'[16] These were the symptoms of what Oglesby saw as the first *mass* revolt against the forces of modern production.

The group that came nearest to the core of the movement was the Movement of the 22 March; accepting that politics in the traditional sense was only one aspect or dimension of the revolt (unlike the Trotskyite or Maoist dominated sects), the 22 March coalition managed to combine the activist and expressive character of the events.[17] It may be contrasted with the Situationists who focused on structure and manoeuvre as well as content and atmosphere. M22 managed to capture the spirit and style of the overall movement and generate it by exemplary actions unlike any other group or organization; it was actively anti-authoritarian, helping to put a libertarian stamp on all the events, and, together with Situationists and the smaller 'Enragé' groups, it initiated the direct democratic control of the Sorbonne.

There was considerable tension between their sporadic agitation and provocation and the bureaucratic methods of the more authoritarian groups. Both in ideology and practice, they expressed a suspicion of the use of others as objects – even in the name of revolution. They were critical of the call for sacrifice on the behalf of revolution in the name of some unfulfilled future. In the same spirit, they advocated and implemented a multi-centred organization and leadership, which was reminiscent of the pre-1968 American NL.

This movement proved most dynamic when least closely linked to traditional orthodoxies. Whilst most of the groups indulged themselves in the rhetoric of urban guerilla warfare, in practice this meant different things to different wings of the movement.

The second phase of the events in France, the period of the workers' revolt, a massive and non-institutionalized wave of activism outside the control (at first) of the Confédération Générale du Travail (CGT) and the CP, has been called a workers' *jacquerie*, a spontaneous outburst against the factory system, without clear purpose. Certainly it is hard to estimate the political as opposed to the economistic demands of the workers. Within the movement, however, there remained a tension between a traditional Syndicalist respect for unionism, and an Anarchist suspicion of the reformist tendencies of all organization.

Worker actions were clearly triggered by the student protests and police reaction, but in the end, the Communist Party (which in the view of many students, was anxious to defend capitalist institutions) manoeuvred control of the workers' movement, on the basis of economic concessions. But rather than the proclaimed ends of the strikes and occupations, it is also important to look at their methods; some argued that aims and means came together in the widespread factory occupations; in some of the large factories, their running, and the organization of local communities, was organized by workers' councils, strike committees, factory councils, action committees – even Soviets or Communes. These, operating with remarkable autonomy, took control of almost every aspect of day-to-day existence. Thus the character of such events had great ideological significance for Western student revolutionaries, even raising in an immediate and practical way the problems of how communal or collectivized production might be organized without resorting to state capitalism.[18] As a result they engendered a far more serious and realistic debate about the nature of revolution, or post-scarcity rebellion, in advanced industrial society, though at the same time encouraging an even greater penchant for revolutionary symbolism and posture in the NL.

Prague summer

Despite placards on a few demonstrations, the general failure of SDS to respond to the Czech events in August revealed not only the growing lack of political balance and awareness in the NL, but a decisive loss of that moral imagination and intellectual courage which had marked the early movement. As it loses identity, the NL also seems to lose character and integrity. The bankruptcy of the NL leadership, so fulsome in its support of Ho Chi Minh, and so grudging in its support for the young Czech resisters, was clearly revealed even before Chicago; as someone rather plaintively asked an SDS theoretician – 'Can't you see that SDS has more in common with these people on the streets in Prague than with Uncle Ho?'

The thaw in Eastern Europe and the new wave of intellectual dissent during the 1960s, were taken by many to be a simple mirror-image of the growth of the NL in the West. But of course, despite many similarities, this was in no simple sense true. Like the Western developments, these changes represented a response to the general détente, and polycentrism of the Communist world, as well as a concern with a humanist socialism and opposition to bureaucracy. But in a very real sense, the reforms and movements in Czechoslovakia represented liberalization, an aspiration for many of the very things Western radicals took for granted or dismissed as irrelevant or without real basis. The rights and freedoms of bourgeois democracy and civil justice, as well as a more flexible attitude to distribution and exchange, were very basic to the programmes of these reformers, and can explain the ability of hard-liners in the West to write them off as 'capitalist reformers', 'petit-bourgeois-revisionists' and 'liberals'.

It is necessary, nevertheless, to distinguish between the top-down liberalization sponsored by post-Stalinist regimes in the other satellites, and the movement towards democratization – a wholesale institutional change with popular support from below – which was beginning to take hold by 1968 in Prague. Dubček's 'socialism with a human face' was probably intended more as the former, but it became an aspect of a social movement with its own momentum in the direction of participatory democracy, a genuine worker-control and isolation of the party hard-liners: a repetition of the pattern of 1956 in Hungary.

Like the NL elsewhere, the reform movement invoked theories of alienation and the revolt of the youth, and stressed decentralization of power away from the hands of the party hierarchy and the state. The resistance which took place against the Russian military invasion, illustrated clearly this character of the Czech movement; spontaneous, decentralized, democratic, socialist. It produced a genuine civilian non-military defence (the army played almost no part) against overwhelming armed force and it stressed its socialist character.[19]

The Russian invasion on the night of 20 August 1968 was a crude combination of military incursion and coup d'état. It reflected a fear of a loss of balance of power in Europe, of economic control in the satellites, and the infection of expanding liberties – even affecting Russia itself. This was perhaps no more than the Western alliance might have done if a Western power went neutralist or opted out of NATO (certainly CND's neutralist ideas for such reasons had been totally rejected at official levels). Like the events in Budapest a decade earlier and partly as a result of internal Soviet division, such a shift was seen as strategically unacceptable. But whereas the military aspect was overwhelming and by and large efficient, the political side was inept, faltering and with an almost complete lack of Czech collaboration. Without this internal support to legitimate it, it was embarrassingly impotent in face of popular resistance. Political communication and a general strike thus became the Czechs' primary weapons.[20]

If no resistance had occurred (as in 1938), demoralization and renewed collaboration would have been complete. Instead, the Czechs chose non-military struggle, not only because of the terrible long-term costs in lives and resources of armed resistance (as Hungary had indicated), but because of the political costs of such a response. The distinct advantage of nonviolence was that it also tended to shift the conflict from the military to the political sphere – from violence to ideas, thus keeping communications open.[21] As it was, Czechs were able to capitalize on the Russian political weakness, by a brilliant use of political literature and an underground network – even using official media of communication to give structure and content to the resistance. Through them they argued that they were not heading for a Western-style party system nor a capitalist system, and Marxism was deployed to refute Russian actions and claims.

The resistance, strikes and mass meetings of workers and political representatives were possible only because of the widespread development of an incipient democratic political culture; the nonviolent character of the resistance, which included all the classic methods of non-military conflict – fraternization with invading troops and the attempt to undermine their morale; underground communications and parallel government; a wide range of non-cooperation including boycotts, sabotage and strikes (as in Hungary 1956); and massive street demonstrations – developed from the bottom upwards and made this democratic organization possible, and reinforced it.

But the strength and breadth of the resistance came as a surprise to both the Czechs and the Russians; there was no prior Czech tradition of non-military action, nor any widespread knowledge of, or training in, nonviolence. Gandhi's thought was relatively unknown; only Jan Hus and the 'Good Soldier Schweik' provided any sort of cultural model for what occurred, and only slowly did the official leadership, always a follower rather than initiator of the humanization and democratization movement, begin to crumble. From the start it was acutely vulnerable, and it was inevitable that it should eventually compromise.

But the Czechs themselves, close to the agony of invasion, would have found it hard to fathom the sense of Western NL positions; indeed, they were positions taken quite external to the events themselves. There was a great deal of relevance and poignance in the Czech developments for those who had experienced the Old Left's traumas. But for a new generation of radicals, to whom the experience of Hungary in 1956 was unknown or irrelevant, this re-enactment in the streets of Prague of one of the formative occurrences of the 'old' NL, meant little in the climate of 1968.

Figures such as Gunther Grass condemned the European NL for its hair-splitting and mealy-mouthed attitude to the Czech reform movement operating under the most difficult conditions; in comparing police state attitudes in Berlin and Paris (he was writing before Chicago) with those in the re-occupation of Czechoslovakia, he deplored the failure of the NL to support its Czech counterpart, or even take notice of it, even though the brutality of international power politics was so similar in different contexts. 'Undoubtedly', he wrote,

The New Left in Czechoslovakia is being suppressed by the superior strength of reaction.... [The West European revolutionary left had] every opportunity to try to understand the brave efforts of the Czechs and Slovaks and take them up as their own cause. That they did not do so betrayed a lack of understanding, an intellectual failure which made them partly culpable for the events in Prague, and condemned them to ultimate failure.[22]

Indeed far from learning any lessons from the Czech spring, the German SDS sent delegations to preach a 'correct' line to the Prague movement. The fact that the Czech movement did not identify with either the Cuban or Chinese road (indeed the two cult figures, Ho Chi Minh and Castro, both supported the Russian invasion, and China proved highly equivocal) was taken as evidence of its liberalism and tolerance of reformist tendencies.

NL slander, such as the accusations of 'petit-bourgeois revanchism', echoed both Russian propaganda and pronouncements by the non-pro-Russian, but hard left sects. The fact that several current heroes endorsed the Russian invasion might explain why almost nobody still in the SDS leadership by August 1968 was willing to openly condemn it. The usually small rallies and marches, sponsored in Berkeley, New York and London were arranged by alliances of independent Socialists, Pacifists and Anarchists to denounce the Russian tanks; the slogan 'Prague equals Chicago' and 'Czechago' were used by some SDS demonstrators outside the Democratic Convention, but beyond these and some critical political and verbal opposition within some Western Communist parties, there was generally little mass reaction.

'Czechago': the National Democratic Convention demonstrations

Few events in the development of the NL were infused with greater ambiguity than those which took place inside and outside the Hilton Hotel in Chicago in August 1968. On the one hand, the convention symbolized the end of any hopes of a liberal democratic candidacy, such as McCarthy's, achieving success. On the other, it marked the ability of militant NL demonstrations to provoke a police riot. It also revealed and affirmed the genuine dangers of provoking repressive reactions on the right, at a time when Wallace was gathering support. But furthermore, it well illustrated the least anticipated achievement of the NL (and Lasch has argued that this was in fact its 'chief contribution to American politics'), its ability to move 'many liberals several degrees leftwards'.

A confrontation that was intended to reveal the unreformable nature of corporate liberalism, revealed instead the deep polarity between liberal opinion and a right-wing police force used for political repression.[23]

What is certain is that a wide variety of groups became virtually indistinguishable during the televised demonstrations, and it was ironically widespread liberal shock resulting in sympathy for the demonstrators that was the most marked and perhaps the most positive response to the events – even within the Convention itself.

Moreover, once having been artificially created, this bizarre coalition – the young McCarthy supporters, the anti-liberal SDS militants, the Yippee cultural revolutionaries, and the peaceniks of the National Mobilization, as well as the assaulted newsmen and by-standers – were driven further together by the repeated climactic violence of Convention week, into a recognition at least of a common enemy.

In Chicago, the loss of restraint began when the police chased madly after frightened demonstrators.[24] Hayden retrospectively talked about what he termed, the 'pitiful attempts at peaceful confrontation' at Chicago as a 'final justification' for the turn to violence – a baptism of blood for future Weatherpeople. But the offensive guerilla tactics of the militant minority at Chicago were consciously chosen; whilst outflanking Hayden's leadership, the eventual SDS decision to 'bring the war home' was made largely independently of Daley's police. From that standpoint the Chicago confrontation was certainly never intended to be one more peaceful march, and marks a further escalation in confrontationism, from the Pentagon and Stop-the-Draft-Week. Certainly and predictably to some extent, the clashes were provoked, and many demonstrators carried weapons; of course none of this could disguise or justify the over-reaction of the Chicago police, and their wanton brutality appalled even the supporters of 'law and order'.

As for the professed legality of many of the Mobilization's actions, this too was in part rhetorical. From the start, it was essentially a direct-action demonstration regardless of legality, that was transformed by a militant minority, with the acquiescence if not support, of the main organizers. In part the actions of the demonstrators represented an insistence on the right to demonstrate near the Convention; an injunction had been required to hold the demonstration at all, but confrontation was then necessary to assert these 'constitutional' rights to protest.

The Yippees and their mascot 'Pigasus' had clearly aimed to introduce a lighter tone to the proceedings, whilst being equally dedicated to contestation – even if it was mingled with street theatre. Jerry Rubin, who first issued the call to gather at the Convention, interspersed these collective happenings with more individual exhibitions and appearances, his approach combining theatrical confrontation with a saving ingredient of humour.[25] It was symptomatic that such a maverick figure should place himself at the heart of events which in some ways crystallized, in some ways further confused, the American movement's situation in the late summer of 1968.

12. Turn Towards Violence

Nonviolence in crisis

Nonviolence in its civil rights phase, had reached the peak of its influence and effectiveness in America in the early 1960s.[1] Nonviolence itself was not at issue in the Movement, at least until after the March on Washington, when the civil rights movement began to wane. Even then dissent was not between proponents of violence and nonviolence. Nevertheless, by 1964, after the massive Washington March, non-violence in practice was beginning to ebb. As an explicit phenomenon, it went into decline during 1963. Despite its dramatic later usage in the peace and student movement; despite the implicit nonviolence of community organizing and counter-institutions or the proclaimed non-violence of the early hippy movement, increasingly, nonviolent means were not identified as such. The openings to violence – in the rhetoric of movement leadership – first in SNCC and in many cases elsewhere, including the pages of the underground press, became more and more apparent. Thus nonviolence as a philosophy was driven on to the defensive, and whilst King remained a paramount figure in the black community, his ideas became more marginal to the NL as an activist movement in the years after 1965.

Nonviolence in the civil rights movement, despite its link to the universalistic ideas of love and brotherhood – of Gandhianism, Christianity or socialist internationalism – had a curiously restricted and piecemeal character. Its limitations of aims, and commitment to given issues, was the Movement's immediate strength; masses of local people could be mobilized around segregated transport or lunch counters, public accommodation or segregationist barriers to voting. But it was a long-term weakness, because these incremental, sequential demands were seen to be implied in the narrow scope of the method itself. Thus total comprehensive demands would, it suggested, need a new method.

Gandhi's distinctions are relevant; that between 'Satyagraha', which seeks to change the opponent through 'love without coercion', by 'speaking truth' and through self-sacrifice, and 'Duragraha' which is coercive nonviolence, with the possible ultimate or covert threat of violence. Clearly both were used by the movements and there were certainly cases where both had profound and lasting effects; but it was the latter version – the economic pressure and political threat – that was seen to be working, and most widely endorsed.[2]

Nonviolence has been advocated as a tactic for organised demonstrations in a society where negroes are a minority and the majority controls the police.

But in Gandhi's terminology, this was a nonviolence 'of the weak' – a pragmatic choice, rather than the nonviolence 'of the strong' – chosen on principle. As one organizer of the SCLC put it: 'one reason why we urge thousands in the street to kneel and pray is because it is very hard to run on your knees'. (The police also proved less brutal confronted by stationary rather than running targets.)

In a situation where the white majority had guns, such nonviolent actions by the black minority made such pragmatic sense; nonviolence, controversial at the outset, became increasingly legitimate because public sympathy in the North was extended to its methods of protest by 1964. At first NAACP opposed all direct action, but such groups were pressurized towards more militant actions by the radical methods of younger leaders. Partly because of its legitimacy, its lack of real principle and the context in which nonviolence operated, many weaknesses appeared. The two main nonviolent constituencies in this period were the black and white volunteers from the North, and local black community support, mostly from the churches and rural areas – the latter a highly stable and controlled base.

King was easy to personify as associated with the latter's pattern of deference and paternalism, to some extent inherited from slavery and its aftermath. Nonviolence as a result could be portrayed as a confidence trick, foisted on 'dumb Southern niggers' by King's white Northern backers or his 'Uncle Tom' allies, manipulating a traditional subservience and willingness to defer through use of religious appeals.

It is clearly not true, as even Julius Lester has argued, that nonviolence was adopted in the early black movement *only* out of respect for King.[3] The very assertive spontaneity of the earlier direct actions of black people such as Rosa Parks, James Meredith, Medger Evers, of the black students at Greensborough and of SNCC itself, substantially controverts this image. It confirms that King had given leadership to a movement (or part of it) which already existed anyway, and was nonviolent in essence.

Before King, nonviolent direct action had already been used in the freedom struggles of the 1940s and early 1950s. Bayard Rustin had helped organize marches and sit-ins in these years, and freedom rides were initiated in the early 1950s; the Montgomery boycott had begun independent of King, just as had the Greensborough sit-in movement of 1960 and the birth of SNCC. SNCC and CORE developed their forms of nonviolence quite separately from King; indeed there were many in these movements at the outset who accepted nonviolence as a principle, whilst only a minority were willing to announce merely a tactical acceptance. Nevertheless, a wide range of attitudes – from the dedicated principled acceptance of men like John Lewis, Bob Parris, Julian Bond and Ivanhoe Donaldson, to more opportune endorsement – existed; there were those too who adopted a purely temporary, and even cynical, willingness to go along with nonviolence.[4] It is also true that those radicals who did reject principled nonviolence waited until Robert Williams and Malcolm-X had spelt out the armed alternative before beginning the full-scale challenge to King's leadership.

Nevertheless, as the movement grew, the pragmatic 'Duragraha' basis of its nonviolence created problems of discipline and control. As early as 1963 at Birmingham (Alabama), King warned of ominous expressions of violence, and his letter from jail was interpreted as a covert threat of violence if the movement could not contain its pent-up emotions.[5] Before and after 1963, with the increasing militance, many groups found problems in maintaining a dividing line between assertive nonviolence and violence, both in practice and for the public.[6]

The numbers who were dedicated to a principled nonviolence, became proportionately fewer; the numbers of those untrained and willing to be provoked, grew larger. Clashes broke out on the fringes of demonstrations – a few physically retaliated to police action, and as the movement moved North, these problems grew worse.

In the South the problem could partly be faced by the civil rights groups in their established schools of nonviolence, and in special training camps for workers in the 'Freedom Summer' project in Mississippi; this training was rigorous, and produced many new young leaders, but the fact remained that even here the commitment to non-violence by many of the rank and file was increasingly tenuous.

There was of course never any guarantee that the movement or the black community would remain nonviolent; the civil rights movement was only one active section of that community, and only a sub-section of it was dedicated to nonviolent principles. Like all such leaderships in all such movements, it tired; its charisma became routinized; it failed to adapt to change. Political movements, cyclical in nature, are mostly very limited in duration; often they evolve through marked phases of development. Frustrations were inevitable in this case, and limitations of tactics and ideas were always apparent.

It is perhaps remarkable that a movement composed of at least five major organizational segments, held together for all the years it did.[7] By becoming a mass movement in the early 1960s, like the student NL later in the decade, the civil rights movement had faced its own acute problems of identity, organization and leadership. In such circumstances self-discipline and nonviolence became increasingly uncertain and training for large numbers in nonviolent techniques almost impossible.

There are strong transatlantic parallels in the decline of nonviolence in the English peace movement. In Grosvenor Square, as in Birmingham, Alabama, a new fringe violence erupts in the later 1960s, that expresses an impatience – even contempt, for the self-discipline and self-sacrifice of the earlier direct actionists. The tendency is towards the spontaneous and the expressive, the angry gesture, and the physical clash. A sudden escalation of violence in England is symbolized in events at the LSE, where in 1967, under the influence of American ideas and events, mob-tactics took over, gates were smashed, staff assaulted and speakers shouted down and ejected.[8]

This tendency appearing on demonstrations in England, had partly been influenced by Anarchist contingents on CND marches, keen on precipitating confrontation. The dignity and self-discipline of nuclear disarmament demonstrations rapidly declined after 1962 – a product of the same kinds of crises of leadership and strategy and the frustrations that they brought to civil rights. In CND, as in the black groups, a leadership which advocated nonviolence, whether as principle or tactic, became identified with quietism and reform, and began to lose control of the demonstrations.

The movements were faced with common problems in their non-violence; the Committee of 100 confronted a similar lack of training, a lack of nonviolent leadership and a loss of control in expanding demonstrations which proved to be far less organized or disciplined in their nonviolence than previously; CND, like the Committee, faced such issues *after* the event; SNCC dealt with them just in time, and even in the face of murders and beatings, solved them. On the other hand, in the process, SNCC entered a debate about self-defence, which finally led to a weakening of its nonviolent faith, that in the end transformed the organization.

From about 1962, one of King's major preoccupations became that of maintaining nonviolent self-discipline on demonstrations: commentators remarked on the appearance at these of gangs of black, working-class youths who were often provoked to violence after police maltreatment of the regular demonstrators. Sometimes their outrage could be channelled into nonviolent expression; often it could not, and riots resulted.

Many considered the Movement was fortunate in having a powerful middle group, between the young militants and the old and more discredited compromisers, who were still able to control large numbers of frustrated, and often frightened, people.[9] But, as Carmichael put it, all the black community knew was that 'Dr King was being slapped by whitey', and they could see it all, at least on TV and in the press photos, or hear of it on the radio. Meredith was being shot at, little Negro girls murdered, churches burned, and 'whitey' was getting away with it. The nonviolent leadership came to look to many like a buffer, compromising with whitey, and insulating the misery and anger of the ghettoes; thus King's attempt to mediate between rioters and police in 1965 in Watts was easily depicted by the black militants as the action of an Uncle Tom.

Carmichael claimed that by 1966, no Negro leader would any longer be listened to by black people in riot situations, for such figures had helped to create the crises. He believed that the nonviolent strategy had helped develop a 'revolution in expectations' which the Movement could not now meet and that this had merely increased the frustrations of the Northern ghettoes. Nor had civil rights been able to fulfil the aspirations of a new generation of black young militants. The situation swung first towards the elimination of whites, and then to an escalation of rhetoric – including that of 'armed self-defence'.

Carmichael may well have been correct in much of this; there was no logical basis, however, for the consequent absolute rejection of nonviolence. Black Power stemmed indeed from the failure of the 'civil rights movement to produce a viable non-reformist strategy' (i.e. a nonviolent 'revolutionary' alternative).[10] Frustration for a movement mainly using nonviolence in a tactical, pressure-group fashion to attain integration and other concessions, was inevitable. Equally unavoidable were the brutalities and humiliation suffered by the movement and its leaders (like the Gandhian movement before it) – and possibly, the co-optation of some of them. Yet it is crystal clear that Carmichael never grasped the central meaning and potential of nonviolence, in so far as he identified it with a position of 'weakness' and the white liberal 'rules-of-the-game' (a view that Marcuse also endorsed). For Carmichael, strength came to mean only 'violence'; to build a position of 'strength' meant the rejection of nonviolence, now seen as an integral part of the position of weakness. Even those who still saw the use of a communal nonviolent action as appropriate at the local level, began to seek other methods for 'the revolution'.

Although it was the nonviolence of the civil rights movement that gave impetus, a new dignity, and self-respect to the black community, this was not enough. For it was the tragedy of nonviolence that it had become tarred with the brush of integration, reformism, and the tactics of an inherited middle-class leadership style. Through no fault of its own, it was easily depicted by the militant 'tactical' nonviolentists, as part of such a package. The possibility of nonviolence as an instrument of communal autonomy, of increasing black dignity and consciousness, of economic cooperation and even of defence of the black community, largely went by the board.

King and the others had clearly failed to persuade the movement[11] that a social revolution through nonviolence was a possibility. Indeed, this stems in part from their own ambivalence. Very often, black nonviolence, reflecting the culture from which it sprang, was indeed an expression of weakness or deference, a prayer, a supplication, a gesture of despair or suffering. But this was also close to one of its strengths, as some of its most moving and successful actions showed. It 'spoke truth to power', as the Quakers put it – it had an impact on the conscience of America, and it actually created extensive social, cultural and structural change; it made the later black movements possible.

This raised a long-term question, and one to which there was no simple answer; certainly the civil rights movement cannot be isolated from the subsequent movement it had spawned, or the vast changes in public consciousness it helped trigger off. Again, its successes and failures cannot be simply judged as a success *or* failure for 'nonviolence' itself; since so much of the activity was 'Duragraha', or economic and political pressure, sometimes with covert violence in the background; it was thus no test of pure nonviolence or 'Satyagraha,' which even King himself rarely employed.

Nor did the civil rights struggle have the elements of constructive programme which Gandhi had deemed essential; most of CORE's nonviolence was the passive-resistance of the weak rather than the positive *communicative* nonviolence which SNCC came closest to. Where creative and positive forms were used (as at Birmingham), its most substantial victories were to be judged in terms of its ability to communicate with immediate opponents, and, by proxy, both with white racists and black self-negation throughout US society.

A further argument (or legend) encouraged by the far left, was that the civil rights movement had, even in its own terms, completely failed; that the nonviolent sit-ins had gained nothing, that voting rights and public desegregation were worthless or insignificant advances, or had not in fact materialized. Yet as most accounts reveal, there was some quite remarkable personal changes of position through these encounters; and change in southern society was dramatically accelerated by these events. Moreover, without the 1963 militancy it is unlikely that Kennedy's hand on civil rights would have been forced; the South was substantially de-segregated, the rule of the Ku Klux Klan (KKK) broken in most areas and incommensurate changes were disguised only by their slow pace; uncelebrated, they continued throughout the decade; in the four years of voter registration alone (1961–5) SNCC, COFO, and other groups had completely transformed the electoral situation.[12] Despite appalling brutality and humiliation, the Movement thus did not fail within its own terms of reference: momentous changes were made at the cost of relatively few lives; whereas violence would have initiated a racial bloodbath.

Despite his increasingly clear opposition to the Vietnam war, and the militancy of some of his urban campaigns, King did not speak, nor perhaps understand, the language of the NL; partly as a result he was driven into isolation. The inherited image of King, reformist and integrationist, the small-town minister, manipulative of submissive negro attitudes, was effectively purveyed within the white Left by those who accused him of reinforcing the prevailing order (e.g. this was Marcuse's view).

Nonviolence was always vulnerable to this type of interpretation, even though King's strategy of active and massive nonviolent confrontation, had clearly as often created *disorder* as sustained 'order'. Indeed, King had been willing to take the risk of provoking violence and counter-violence, or the loss of control on the fringes of the movement. If King failed it was in communicating, both to the Establishment and the NL, as well as to his own community, the larger possibilities of the methods and tactics he adopted.

For a number of years, King had been a consistent target of those on the Left, especially the Maoists, who wished to shift the movement towards an armed strategy. The latter in the form of PL repeatedly called King an 'Uncle Tom', and since 1964 had identified itself with Robert Williams's 'rifle squads' and the 'Deacons' for self-defence. It always proved easier to attack a *man* who negotiated with Kennedy about concessions – respectable, middle-class, middle-aged and Christian, advocating at least some form of integration – than it was to attack the *philosophy* of nonviolence itself.

King was caught between the white backlash, which never really materialized (except partly in electoral terms), and the very real escalation of both ghetto violence and Movement rhetoric in the black community. This spiral of violence, fear, and increasing race-consciousness (and the insulation of the two groups) had its own momentum: the prophecies of race-war a self-fulfilling quality.

But King also played a role in containing such Movement and community violence before Watts, and in preventing the major split in the movement until after 1965-6. Through his courage and example in building and sustaining SCLC, and the movement generally after Montgomery, and in his own self-transformations after 1965 – coming to terms with the new militancy, black power and anti-war platforms (though they were the actions of someone now *following* rather than *shaping* events) – he revealed, nevertheless, a remarkable ability to adapt to new conditions.

Between 1966 and 1968, the armed rhetoric and tactics of the black militants[13] contributed to the polarization in which nonviolence became anathema to many: King now faced an impossible task; the escalation of violence by both police and the state, on the one hand, and the militants, on the other, created a gulf in which many of King's actions (such as the open-housing marches in Chicago) became near-suicidal; it exemplified one of the key weaknesses of nonviolent strategy: that it can be simply submerged in violent polarizations.

Yet despite significant eruptions of ghetto violence, there is a great deal of evidence (even from those who wished it otherwise) that the black community was not basically violent.[14] It was despair of nonviolent methods, and fear of backlash and existing white sanctions, that pushed some militant groups and leaders in these directions.

As a result, the demagogues also gained new audiences; in the Harlem riots, it was the PL firebrands, Jesse Gray and Bill Epton and others, who were listened to – though there is little evidence they 'caused' the events. Moreover, for those in SNCC and CORE to whom nonviolence was only a tactic, Watts was a symbolic moment when they could join those like Malcolm-X who had openly rejected it. Their move towards more violent direct action and 'self-defence' began to parallel Malcolm's talk of rifle-clubs, which after 1963 became the explicit alternative to nonviolence. Yet though O'Brien believes that 'for many militants, Watts must have seemed like the death knell of the nonviolent civil rights movement',[15] this unexpected explosion quickly claimed by black militants as their own, was an external event, not linked directly to the Movement or its preceding developments.

In fact largely unpublicized, nonviolent civil rights activity continued after 1966, especially in the border states, in the mid-West and in Texas; elsewhere, even before Watts, it had been declining anyway. Later the 1968 Memphis strike, an ambiguous mixture of tactics and styles was, although at unacceptable cost, a success in its own terms. Equally the Poor People's Campaign, though overshadowed by King's death, constructed a significant coalition. The degree to which its 'Resurrection City' was regarded either as a 'possible swan-song' or a 'revival', for nonviolence, was typical of further over-simplification: but it was not the failure of nonviolence that both the pro-violence militants and established media made it out to be. The leadership of the coalition was tired and cumbersome, and substantial criticisms could be made of its strategy, but it was the Old and NL's that made Resurrection City into a scapegoat, endorsing much Establishment ridicule with such enthusiasm.[16]

The great divide

In the years 1967–9, the mainstream of the NL passed over Camus's tragic dividing line between violence and nonviolence: the line that divides:

Those who accept the consequences of being murderers themselves or the accomplices of murderers, and those who refuse to do so with all their force and being.

At the outset, Camus and Fromm, both willing to give free rein to tenderness and concern with the human 'soul', were of considerable influence; but Camus was already concerned with the way in which left intellectuals were constantly engaged in rationalizing violence and murder, or re-erecting the 'taboo on tenderness'.

The intensification and reinforcement of this tendency must be analysed as a final and critical factor in the general crisis of the NL, together with its two major sources – the drift towards violence in the black movement and the romantic identification with military 'liberation'.

Under the influence of the shifts in the black movement – especially SNCC after 1966 – and with the growing identification of sections of the Movement with Third World guerilla war, a major change of course was involved. The swing towards violence in the Negro leadership can in particular be seen as part of the growing violence of a society involved in the brutalities of the SE Asian conflict. The intensification of the Vietnam war in part explains also the turn in the movement generally: several groups adopted sabotage against property as a 'next step'.

The period is also marked by a notable vacuum of articulate defences of nonviolent attitudes to change; within a few years, three major voices for alternatives, Muste in 1967, King in 1968, and Goodman in 1972 were silenced. The predominant domestic impact was now that of black power leaders, Marcuse and, to a lesser degree, the example of the Yippees. As a result, by 1968, those who wished to denigrate the NL were more than ever able to focus on the protagonists of violence, whether or not they were part of the movement; Sartre emerged again as a relevant figure, the streak of fanaticism in his writing, the willingness openly to advocate terror and assassination, coincided with these new more desperate attitudes. Thus in the later 1960s, as nonviolence went out of fashion and authoritarian and Marxist solutions were more in vogue, it was Sartre – with his syntheses of anti-imperialist alignments and shrill advocacy of counter-violence, of getting 'bloodied hands' – who, although outside both the NL and any familiar Marxist-Leninist mould, clearly replaced Camus in Movement esteem or public attention.[17]

Yet the founding statements of SDS had expressed its abhorrence of violence; the Port Huron document had stated, in a vein that is pure Camus:

The brutalities of the twentieth century teach that means and ends are intimately related, that vague appeals to posterity cannot justify the mutilations of the present.

It is a long way from this humanistic rhetoric, with its talk of man as 'infinitely precious and possessed of unfulfilled capacities for reason, freedom and love', to Carmichael's call (referring to Camus) to black people to become 'executioners of their executioners'. It is equally far from the Port Huron statement of opposition to 'the depersonalisation that reduces human beings to the status of things'[18] to the rhetoric of 'offing' (killing) the 'pigs', the fetish of the gun as a revolutionary object, and the belief in the tactic of radicalization through calculated violence.

The NL of the later 1960s succeeded in reawakening that taboo on tenderness which had been so characteristic of the Old Left; the new cult of 'machismo', a new vindictiveness and brutality (coupled with an inevitable paranoia), came to dominate most active, militant groups. A loss of sensitivity in human relationships was part and parcel of the brutalization involved in the street-fighting and confrontation tactics on the one hand, and the manoeuvring and politicking on the other; these were especially associated with the growing rifts in SDS. Predictably the process ended with sections of the Movement becoming what Camus had termed 'accomplices of murderers', in a very real way.

The earlier NL, partly due to this alternate influence, had emphasized a humanistic respect for life and with it for the individual person. But for black leaders like Carmichael, it became a 'cop-out to talk about the individual'. Guevara too was widely quoted in his remarks about people being components of an historical process in which it was necessary that there would be both victims and executioners.[19] His view that historical causes transcended the lives and deaths of individuals accorded well with the coincidence of a new revolutionary romanticism and a revival of Old Left ideology.

At the theoretical level, Marcuse, like Sartre detached from mainstream Marxism, had also made important justifications for this change in sensibility. Just as Debray had offered (quite erroneous) justifications of violence in strategic terms, and Fanon in terms of personal identity, Marcuse's focus on the distinction made between the violence of the system and the violence of the rebel, constituted, in terms of the NL's own endorsement of violence, a critical re-orientation, with an important bearing on softening attitudes to the systemic violence of other political orders (including 'socialist' ones).

Like Hayden, Marcuse, more explicitly than most, interprets the USA as drifting towards Fascism as a logical development of corporate liberalism. This leads him eventually, in an influential essay of 1966, to abandon a libertarian stance on the means-ends connection, and to move *against* the then current spirit of the NL, by preaching both anti-tolerance and the rejection of nonviolence.

Marcuse's starting point was the cultural context; wherever the media is dominated by a ruling group and ruling ideas, counter-violence will be condemned and state violence ignored or camouflaged: the same may be true of a dominant race's violence, as opposed to that of its subordinate. As one civil rights leader (Bayard Rustin) had remarked of violence between the races, 'if it's white it's delinquency, if it's negro, it's race war'. In the same manner, academic critiques of 'violence' will mainly treat the overt violence of the rebel, not the covert violence of established order. This leads Marcuse to make a further key differentiation, and reversal; the 'actual' violence of the legally constituted powers exists, even if not always used; the 'non-actual' violence of subversive movements is largely potential and non-institutionalized. To criticize this counter-violence, in Marcuse's view, weakens the protest against the violence of the system, and serves its cause.

Significantly, Marcuse's concrete example is drawn from the civil rights struggle: he attacks the hypocrisy of calls for 'nonviolence' by black people, parallelling Carmichael's exhortation: 'Let them preach nonviolence in the white community.' He condemns the renunciation of counter-violence in protest demonstrations; criticizing the nonviolent idea of Gandhi, King and others: it harbours the illusion, he argues, that 'history is made in accordance with ethical standards'. The nonviolence of the weak may be tactically necessary, but remains a matter of necessity not ethics, and he notes the double standards involved in accepting the violence of the state (mystified as the 'rule of law') as 'noncomparable' with the violence of the revolutionary rebel. They are comparable in so far as both are violence, but the first is 'reactionary' and the second 'progressive' violence. To criticize the latter is to aid the former.

In essence these are fundamentally simplistic arguments, though elaborated in philosophical terminology; they lead on, in effect, to Marcuse's acceptance of the normative differentiation of Establishment violence and Oppositional violence; but he decisively *reverses* the accepted appraisal of each; and it is established violence alone that is condemned.

Despite his critique of Stalinism and totalitarianism in general, Marcuse's searching attack on the double standard by which the violence of the state is judged to be ethically defensible, whilst the violence of the rebel is condemned, creates an opening for a later advocacy of meeting violence with violence; Establishment terror with Oppositional terror; Establishment indoctrination by counter-indoctrination; Establishment versions of tolerance with committed intolerance; and finally, even replacing existing institutionalized power with alternative forms of institutionalized power (though on this Marcuse is ambiguous and contradictory).

Camus had argued of the radical that through what he called a 'casuistry of the blood', 'to justify himself . . . each relies on the other's crimes' Marcuse comes close to doing this when he argues that the critique of violence by the Establishment should be stood on its head. So does Sartre, endorsing the need to 'fight violence with violence' (1969). The latter shares the view that the violence of the dominant groups must be condemned unequivocally, and the secondary 'justified violence' of the opposition given uncritical support or ignored. Thus in Vietnam, such a position expressed itself in the view that the main armed resistance organization (the NLF) was historically incapable of 'illegitimate' or 'unnecessary' violence (thus of 'atrocities' or 'war crimes'). The critical focus must therefore be entirely on the 'imperialist' violence and war crimes of the USA and Saigon, never on those of the PRG or DRVN forces, even though evidence of terror or overkill by the latter could easily be produced.[20]

It was of course possible to accept some or all of Marcuse's premises about Establishment violence without arriving at his conclusions:

nevertheless, a generation of NL activists did convince themselves of the necessity of 'progressive violence'. In general, as long as the violence was limited and unorganized, it was perceived as legitimate if used for a libertarian end; this contrasted with the double standards of the Establishment which denied much of its violence.

The alternative view was that whilst it was dangerous to differentiate qualitatively two faces of violence in this way, the violence of entrenched power was so much more extensive and oppressive than the violence of opposition, that they were not *quantitatively* comparable. In other words, one might still use the same human standards to judge violence on both sides without needing to resort to a metaphysic of 'progressive violence'; this in effect could criticize both, whilst searching for alternative modes of subverting the established order, and hopefully breaking the cycle of violence and oppression. Such an alternative might still accept that the spontaneous, angry eruptions of the ghetto or peasant society could not be condemned to the same extent as the calculated violence used to uphold a repressive system – though the actual development of the Vietnam war made even this distinction problematic in practice.

This general ambiguity was reflected in the title and proceedings of an internationalist symposium in London in 1967, with the Marcusian title 'The Dialectics of Liberation – Towards a Demystification of Violence'. In addition to the protagonists of violence, like Carmichael and Gerassi, Goodman, a leading nonviolent spokesman, was invited, as well as Marcuse himself, and a number of anti-psychiatrists. The aim of the conference, held at the Round House, was never clear; on the one hand it was taken to be an exercise in the 'demystification' of 'bourgeois violence', the violence of the state, war, racism, and even of psychiatry and education. An alternative interpretation was that this was an attempt to remove the taboo against violence operating amongst the opponents of bourgeois violence. The overall result, however, was primarily of reinforcing the mystification of violence amongst revolutionaries themselves, though the organizers of the conference (Laing, Cooper and Joseph Berke) steered clear of military rhetoric.[21] Goodman's contribution, outstanding but critical, was of course not given the reception accorded to the newer 'wild men' like Gerassi or Carmichael – he was, in the words of McReynolds, 'too reasonable, too practical, too old' to be one of the heroes.[22] But he still won a surprised respect as he punctured the inflated rhetoric of the conference with simple incisive queries.

The youth culture was by now full of the rhetoric of guerilla war and liberation struggle in America; and the underground press now tended to canonize some homegrown military heroes, as well as Che Guevara and Ho Chi Minh. This rhetorical indulgence in violence was often vicarious – and in that sense irresponsible; it rarely if ever extended (as the Panther rhetoric *did*) into military organization. Like the NL generally, the counter-culture retained an ambivalence about the Third World's revolutionary wars, and emotional identification almost never extended to the fantasy of white revolutionary armies in America.

By the late 1960s, the numbers of those in the radical movements willing to make articulate pleas for an alternative approach or against blanket justifications for counter-violence, were dwindling. The few with the courage and vision willing to spell out an alternative to matching violence with violence, were reduced to a handful;[23] by 1968, theirs was an isolated and exposed position.

This growing equivocation over violence generally explains the changing public image of the hippy, from a 'flower-child' stereotype of 1966–7, via Yippee (of 1967–8), to the 'street-fighting' one of 1968–9. The question of self-protection and retaliatory violence plagued both the counter-culture and the student communities in facing the threat of repression.

In Holland, for example, the Kabouters in 1970 raised the question: 'If the movement is successful, if it spreads, will not the authoritarian structures fight back and use violence?' An optimistic view was that these movements would not in fact be attacked because they were considered not as threats but rather as safety valves. This argument held that whether or not the counter-culture was actually an escapist opiate, the established structure would probably tolerate it or attempt to co-opt and commercialize it, rather than act repressively.

But another viewpoint was that any viable set of counter-institutions would eventually be seen as a threat and be attacked, even though this did not necessarily invalidate the strategy. Hayden believed radical communities could defend themselves, and by talking about the 'free territories defending themselves physically, including self-defence training and the use of weapons', he encouraged a myth of communal self-defence. Against this, it was argued that to centre a counter-institutional strategy on physical rather than cultural confrontation was a pseudo-revolutionary venture that might well provoke full-scale right-wing repression.

As has been seen, the 1968 Russian invasion and Czech resistance spoke directly to one of the major lacunae in NL thought – its attitude to organized armed violence in general and the question of military and national defence in particular, especially in an industrial society. Czechoslovakia had demonstrated the possibilities of non-military resistance to authoritarian regimes elsewhere, Fascist or Communist, and also suggested again the advantages in the nuclear context of keeping the struggle limited.

The 'silent fight', as the resistance of August and September 1968 came to be called, was one of the most extraordinary examples of unplanned nonviolent response to enormous military strength; indeed natural weapons of strike and sabotage were combined with the kinds of textbook techniques advocated by the theorists of civilian defence,

IID

illustrating both the weaknesses and strengths of such a theory.[24] These nonviolent methods had the great distinction of granting an opportunity for political communication. But the attainment of a minimization of violence remains a key problem, if such political communication is to be maintained; it was the Czech contribution to demonstrate this possibility.

The disciplined nonviolent character of the Czech events and the lack of violent provocation were particularly remarkable,[25] in that the problem of containing violence on demonstrations was largely overcome; exhibitionists and 'agents provocateurs' were isolated. Had armed violence taken place, it would have provided the occasion for a far more oppressive occupation regime and the Soviets could have politically isolated the resistance and driven many more Czechs into collaborating at an early stage. Nevertheless, especially at the outset, the contradictions between the violent and nonviolent elements in such a movement remained – between the use of 'stick' and 'carrot'; such mixed actions could cancel each other out and prove self-defeating.[26]

Generally the events were greeted with considerable confusion by Western radicals; both those who identified with the young people on the streets of Brno, Bratislava and Prague, and those who opposed them, tended to believe that violence must be both correct, and necessary. Those who had adopted 'militant' or violent postures on Vietnam, Black Power or US imperialism, seemed bound to find a similarly aggressive stance on the Czech events.

Some identified with the Czech resistance and said that the Czechs should get guns and fight. Others condemned them as a bunch of liberals and revisionists, justifying the Russian use of military force (some self-styled NL leaders in England took this view). In the NL almost nobody clearly identified with the nonviolent resistance or found much meaning in it – it was as if it had moved outside the Movement's framework of understanding.

One of the lessons of these events was particularly relevant to the Western radicals; namely that the Establishment (in this case the USSR) always prefers to fight on the traditional grounds it knows best – for the Russians this was military confrontation, rather than a nonviolent political 'hit-and-run'.

The other lesson, for those who cared to examine it, was the complicated nature of alternative forms of resistance in a modern urban setting, not easily dealt with in terms of the stilted categories of 'violence' and 'nonviolence' as they had developed in NL debates. Such a non-military defence typically represents the influence of various groups involved in a coalition; their tactics and methods display a widely varying commitment to non-military methods. The result, as Czechoslovakia showed, is neither systematic, organized violence, nor, inevitably perhaps, pure nonviolence.

The continuum between violent and nonviolent disruption tended to highlight the ambiguous Anarchist position on violence, and pointed to the distinction between two separate traditions of Anarchism, one of them very close to, or indeed overlapping with, Pacifism. The dividing line between non-alienated spontaneous or personal violence and the alienated, distant, technological violence was a growing dimension that also created problems for libertarians. Like the distinction between authoritarian and non-authoritarian violence, such lines were difficult or impossible to draw in practice. The implications of this distinction for the types of impersonal organization related to alienated violence – such as the modern state – whilst dimly perceived, were not widely debated.

The break with nonviolence was, of course, never as clear in practice as it was in theory and rhetoric; the proliferation of militant demonstrations on most American campuses did not at first, except in a minority of cases, yet involve real major outbreaks of physical violence; as can be shown, the Resistance, and parts of the counter-culture, as well as the Poor People's Coalition, retained strong links with the nonviolent tradition, and although neither Memphis nor the Washington campaign signalled a genuine revival of nonviolent activism, the deep ambivalence which had surrounded King was only partly resolved by his death; after it the problems of nonviolence and violence were even more sharply and explicitly articulated. The easy attacks on nonviolence or on King were replaced by a growing wariness of alternative formulae and eventually, by the 1970s, an openness to thinking again about both armed and unarmed possibilities of change.

Thus even the 'violent' period, from 1968 to 1972, showed that nonviolent methods were still alive in parts of the student and radical movements. The Resistance was close to the older, nonviolent tradition of conscientious objectors to war; civil disobedience was by 1970 more generally being used again in the anti-war movement; the hippy movement, having turned away from its early 'love, flowers, and freedom' ethic, still retained important links with the methods and ideas of nonviolence, and the People's Park episode showed that a radical-hippy community could still employ largely nonviolent methods of struggle. In the central valley of California, Cesar Chavez was still leading the migrant fruit-workers in a successful phase of a long-term, but nonviolent struggle, invoking the Gandhian idea, just as the Memphis strike had itself confirmed the essentially nonviolent possibilities of an industrial conflict.

It is worth noting that the violence practically endorsed by the NL and exemplified by its actions was largely the proximate, personal violence or the violence of local confrontation, rather than the organized violence of disciplined militarism and the state (despite the rhetorical endorsement of North Vietnam and the NLF).

For example, the street-people and those involved in the counter-culture who engaged in trashing, fighting and bombings, often remained opposed to armies and all war; in this sense, they retained links with pacifism. The German SDS too, despite its aggressive militancy, announced its rejection of violence against individuals, though the position clearly weakened in relation to their so-called self-defence. The president of German SDS announced that their strategy was to 'abolish violence', through nonviolent anti-institutional action.[27]

The problem of self-defence

As has been seen, to a large extent the turn towards the actual use of violence was initially justified by the NL in connection with the problem of communal defence. Subsequently the theoretical problem, first raised in the black movement, of how a radical community could defend itself when attacked, became relevant to the counter-institutions and the Movement generally, both in America and Britain and wherever else they emerged. In Berkeley, student strike leaders announced: 'Direct action against the administration can only create us the space we need for freedom . . . we can't defend that space. . . .' As this type of debate about collective defence became widespread, it was particularly linked to the tragedy of the black movement which in its role as model for large sections of the NL failed after 1966 to develop an alternative vision of black power or defence rooted in its counter-institutions. That it did not do so was in part related back to its obsession with the specific problems of *armed* defence.

Boycotts and sit-ins against unjust laws, non-cooperation with taxes and conscription, hinted at the possibility of defence of radical counter-institutions through militant though nonviolent means; already a range of such institutions existed in the black community, some vitalized by the community organizing projects (such as those SDS and SNCC had launched); such an innovative fusion of energies might have developed more creative approaches to defence. CORE's initial attempts to use imaginative sabotage and obstruction tactics against symbols of white oppression and discriminatory institutions, did not necessarily jeopardize the possibility of serious attempts at fraternization with police or other agencies of social control – especially with black police or National Guardsmen.

Already some such methods had met with successes even in the un-favourable milieu of the northern ghettoes. But the appalling experiences in the South in 1963 and 1964, following hard on the groundwork laid by left-wing and black advocates of armed response, had turned the movement away from such alternatives. The exceptional violence of 1963 had brought the debate about violent self-defence to a head. The bombings and shootings and Klan activity in the South, the fear of a white backlash in the North, had for some years stimulated a growth of armed defence squads such as the Deacons; the Muslims had become widely admired both for their self-discipline and apparent willingness to use weapons.[28]

From 1957, Robert Williams, a NAACP member in Monroe, N.C. (also an ex-marine) who visited Cuba after the revolution and subsequently became openly linked to the first pro-Chinese splinter from the Communist Party, had begun to advocate reorganizing the local chapter, forming 'rifle-clubs for self-defence'. This move in a North Carolina town, although developed alongside nonviolent activity, proved to be the thin end of a wedge as far as the later civil rights movement was concerned: a racial arms race was under way; the arming of sharecroppers and movement personnel was used as further justification for an escalation of official armour.[29] Mayor Thompson of Jackson, Mississippi, had a tank and squads of police with sub-machine guns.

Such highly organized potential violence was linked to the growth of white citizens' councils, active after 1954, and the revival of the KKK, which emerged in the context of massive Southern support for Goldwater and Wallace.[30] Actual violence on both sides was increasing.

With the awareness of this threat and lack of a Gandhian perspective in the nonviolent actions of this period, it was not such a leap from an increasingly aggressive 'Duragraha' (nonviolence based on coercive sanction) towards accommodation with ideas of military self-defence. Economic and political pressure had in any case often appeared to depend on an ultimate threat or sanction of violence, rather than on any purely nonviolent 'truth-force'. Thus despite their physical courage, the militant wing of SNCC around Carmichael had developed little understanding of principled 'Satyagraha'; indeed they attacked it, arguing that only violence could be ultimately revolutionary; other black figures like LeRoi Jones began openly to ridicule it (as the pro-Peking Communists had from the outset): Jones equated it with being 'bashed over the head' to 'prove Mr Gandhi was right'. Others attacked nonviolence as being 'unAmerican'; the 'ethos of this nation is not non-resistance' argued James Farmer, and Franklin Frazier, a black sociologist, condemned nonviolence as the 'method of slaves'.

Thus all the pressure from the Left was increasingly against both King and nonviolence; and Malcolm-X implied that the choice of 'bullets rather than ballots' was close at hand.

As this suggests, the debate about self-defence in the early 1960s had become a debate between prominent personalities rather than confrontations of ideas and strategies. King's dialogue with Williams about arming black people, or his later confrontation with Carmichael, turned the debate around fundamentals into one about King's own personality and ideas, something which those who attacked nonviolence welcomed. Such an irrational polarization took place that, as all nonviolence was written off as conservative, almost every act of violence by implication tended to be endorsed as 'progressive'.[31]

A final turning point for SNCC can be detected during Mississippi Freedom Summer in 1964; after sustaining 1,000 arrests, thirty-five shootings (including six deaths) and eight beatings in the one state alone (Mississippi), SNCC wearily announced that it reaffirmed 'the right of black men everywhere to defend themselves when threatened or attacked'. Whilst the statement did not explicitly mention guns, the meaning was clear enough: the link of 'black power' to 'armed self-defence' was forged from this moment.

Carmichael said that he hoped initiating violence would not be necessary, but it was 'not for SNCC to tell black communities what particular form of action to take'. Since SNCC and Carmichael were exhorting and instructing the Negro community on almost every other aspect of its political actions, there was a certain irony in this disclaimer.

The polemic of violent self-defence quickly became significantly military in language and tone; the term 'deterrence' became familiar and the notion of using the opponent's 'escalation' of threat as justification for one's own.[32] As in every arms race, deterrence, escalation, and ultimately the temptation to strike first, characterized the continuum from defensive to offensive violence.

The criticism made on the left of armed self-defence was, in part, that it was ineffective and often suicidal, and identified targets for right-wing attack; partly, that it was always impossible to draw the line between defensive and offensive violence. Those who still maintained a nonviolent position argued that it had a deleterious effect on the black community and undermined the sense of community and communication of participants with their opponents (thus preventing true nonviolent action).

The polemic of self-defence was, however, a persuasive counterpart to the rhetoric of black power; it met the frustrations of many movement activists, it appeared to give blacks a sense of 'manhood' and 'potency', which the civil rights movement, like the society at large, it was argued, had failed to provide.[33]

Yet even at the level of the isolated rural sharecropper, where the debate began, the rifle was at best only a temporary means of insurance – only able to scare away the KKK for a while; it was not a long-term preventative. To extend the analogy to the ghetto, as did a number of militant blacks and Left protagonists – preparing the way for the Panthers – was fraught with political non-sequiturs.

Thus the general confusion of black power with armed self-defence is not hard to explain; although initially, supporters of black power insisted that the 'violence' implicit in it was a fabrication of the Establishment media, given the difficulty in identifying the relationship between slogan and practice, it soon became obvious that for those who took up the slogan 'black power' with most enthusiasm, the two were in fact linked. 'Don't pray for power, don't beg for power,' Carmichael admonished, 'take it with a gunbarrel.'

In 1966, even before his election in SNCC, Carmichael promised he would recruit the toughest Negroes he could find in Watts, Harlem, Chicago and Washington to defend the Black Panther Party candidates in the Alabama elections of that year. James Foreman and Rap Brown also supported this tendency towards a more militant and violent interpretation of black power. 'Black people must have guns', 'we will have the means and ways to obtain those guns' (Brown, 1967). The same year, SNCC as a body, also adopted this stance despite its retention of 'nonviolence' in its title. CORE, too, had moved in the same direction: Floyd McKissick announced, 'we have no alternative but to use aggressive violence'. Again, immediately the riots (1968) following King's assassination flared, Carmichael said 'the only way to survive is to get some guns'.[34]

As on Vietnam, black militancy, and a range of issues, it was the middle ground that collapsed. Moderate commentators like Christopher Lasch and Todd Gitlin, who in other contexts remained often critical of Movement excesses, were both driven to accept 'the right' and the 'necessity' of 'armed-self-defence',[35] and to imply that criticism of black self-defence squads was outside the arena of acceptable discourse. In July 1966, a Professor Freedman, writing in the *New York Times* on the alien nature of nonviolence, wrote:

The doctrine of nonviolence in the face of physical attack is foreign to American law and morality. Its rejection by negroes is long overdue. The vast majority of Americans have long consistently recognized the moral imperatives of self-defence both in international relations and private action.

Just as criticism of the NLF was now being shouted down in the movement, any critics of self-defence were told: if you have no alternative means to offer – your criticism is invalid.[36]

Many of the middle-of-the-road critics capitulated to these arguments for arming black people, with an apparent sense of historical inevitability; unable to provide alternative proposals for protecting black people, they therefore felt forced to accept as 'realistic' or pragmatic a political option that they were equally aware could easily lead to a genocidal racial polarization. Thus by acquiescing in the talk of 'threatened genocide' and 'armed polarization', these critics encouraged American radicals to engage in a 'self-fulfilling prophecy'.

The idea of the defensive arming of the whole Negro people, initiated by the Deacons and later taken up by Carmichael and others, was always fraught with deep ambiguity. Whilst, for some, the 'defensive' posture adopted at first may have been genuine, it inevitably moved along the continuum from self-defence and deterrence towards preparation for terrorism and guerilla war. As Oppenheimer concludes:[37]

Civil rights workers of the South, who lacked nonviolent means of protection against rightist terrorists, began armed defence which became the prelude to much current talk of urban guerilla warfare.

In the North, the language of self-defence was in fact used partly as a cover for what was seen by many as a 'next step' towards guerilla war.

When Carmichael used the phrase 'by any means necessary' (BAMN) and called for a 'fight for liberation', the offensive nature of these preparations became more clear. There was never any guarantee that men once armed would know where aggression began and defence ended, even less would a white police force, highly trained, armed and paranoid, make subtle distinctions; indeed, armed black 'defence' squads helped create the fears and self-justifications for the massacres of the years after Watts.

The fetishization of armed self-defence as a 'right',[38] can only be understood in the American context (it has not developed elsewhere) in relation to an American individualist tradition of gun-owning politics; from the Minutemen of the War of Independence, through the right to own guns in the Constitution, through the Western mythology of armed frontiersmen and cowboys, the tradition continued right up to the contemporary proliferation of (often right-wing) rifle clubs. In the cases of the new Minutemen, of Lee Harvey Oswald and the Panthers, an aggressive-defensive individualism, and insistence on democratic rights, are fused in the instrument of violence – the gun.

The fact that this piece of Americana, like so much else, should find its place in black radicalism in a collectivized form, should not disguise its origins; to some extent, the object of the gun represents the familiar aspiration to 'opt in', just as much as did other consumer objects and status-giving commodities (the colour TV or the Lincoln Continental). There was very little willingness to approach the more basic problems such as disarming the police – either by the black groups or, even less, by their white allies. Indeed, every murder, whether in the name of self-defence or law-and-order, made that possibility steadily diminish.

To many, this escalation was perceived as merely a further expansion of the American civilian arsenal, already larger than in any other society. With an overkill capacity in some cities consisting of more guns than people, it was a truism to talk of America as dominated by the syndrome of violence. Carmichael asserted that 'responsibility for the use of violence by black men . . . lies with the white community', and in an ultimate historical sense this was a valid claim. The white community was indeed responsible for the Negroes' situation, though this did not in itself constitute evidence of likely genocide: nor did it follow that the wisest course was for blacks to arm or that black people in America should immerse themselves in a dominant culture of violence, which in some ways, their traditions and community – even their religion and music – had previously insulated them from.

Whilst suicide and murder had been typical of ghetto life, organized terror and militarism had not, which helped confirm the view that in part the advocacy of 'killing whitey', was a tongue-in-cheek effort to get the white community to reappraise its own attitudes to the black experience. Thus the amoral determinism of Carmichael's rhetoric, like Fanon's, was in part a desperate appeal against existing forms of social oppression and control. But tragically, as so often, rhetoric became fact, words led to organization.[39]

The emergence of the Black Panthers represents the first organizational synthesis of black power and armed self-defence. Formed as a uniformed and armed police-watching group in Oakland late in 1966, the first chapters were directly inspired by the death of Malcolm-X, killed by former Muslim colleagues in February 1965. Malcolm's exhortations to armed defence, and the previous experience of the Deacons (still active in the same year), as well as the Watts riots, made the Panthers in essence a para-military formation, actively opposed to anti-gun legislation.

Such tendencies confirmed that by the later 1960s, black power and armed self-defence had come to be seen as inseparable: 'Black people should arm themselves', was the Party's advice; and Mao's dictum 'political power grows out of the barrel of a gun' was constantly reiterated by Panther spokesmen. Soon much of this 'defence' advocated was of a distinctively pre-emptive kind: 'if you don't get [the pig] today, he's gonna get you tomorrow'.[40]

In 1968, to signify this movement on to the offensive, the actual words 'self-defence' were dropped from the Panthers' title (at the same time as the word 'nonviolent' disappeared from SNCC). As I. F. Stone remarked, the black ghettoes had long regarded the white police as an illegitimate army of occupation and the murder of 'the pigs' was now openly advocated by the Black Panther newspaper (and depicted in its cartoons) as was Cleaver's declaration of 'urban guerilla war'. But as leftist liberals had long predicted, such language and tactics proved suicidal, leading into a 'cul-de-sac of isolation, exhaustion and heroic blood'.[41] Even in Stone's view:

The effect of the ambushes which have begun to occur in various cities is to deepen police hatred . . . and therefore to stimulate those very excesses and brutalities which have made the police a hated enemy.

Panthers only slowly learnt the first guerilla lesson; to avoid the confrontations in which they would lose; by 1969, this meant almost that every direct contact or clash with police was evaded, awaiting a more favourable balance of forces. But during 1968–9, after twenty Panthers and four police had died in armed clashes, the terror began to turn in on the Party itself as well as on the black community. This development involving internecine murders, physical violence and intimidation, confirmed that the Panthers' dual orientations to the media on the one hand and their expressed concern with community defence on the other, were almost always in tension; armed organization, berets and guns attracted the white press more than their own black community; and the Panthers' status there became decidedly ambiguous. As both black and white critics argued: if the BPP had had a 'sound base in the ghetto, then the police would never have dared to come in and shoot them in cold blood'.[42] And this became clearer; Newton after 1971 shifted ground, announcing that 'we have rejected the rhetoric of the gun', and many Panthers moving away from the urban guerilla stance and calling for a united front on the Left (in defence of the Panthers!) urged the white NL to work for community control of the police; they were beginning to genuinely fear a drift towards fascism, and thus they were assuming defensive positions, which Weatherman now threatened to undermine.

From confrontation to terror

It is important at this juncture to distinguish between those tendencies towards violence in the black movement and those in the white NL, though they are of course in many ways linked; from the pressure on white ex-SNCC workers to prove themselves, from the admiration for Malcolm-X, from the exuberance over the symbolism of the Watts outburst, to identification with the Panthers, white radical attitudes to armed action were constantly intertwined with the phases of the black movement.

Nevertheless, the escalation of actual violence in the white NL has a distinct course of its own, independent of the black move towards 'self-defence', and later, urban guerilla tactics and individual terrorism. It begins with confrontation tactics and rehearsals of street-fighting, passes through a phase of training for the actual street violence, and then reaches from the extension of strategic sabotage to the radical bombings that are later associated with the Weatherpeople.

Whilst black groups, beginning as early as 1957, through the Deacons and the ghetto marksmen, to the Panthers, repeatedly turned to guns, the white NL, particularly SDS and sections of the anti-war movement, turned finally to violence only considerably later – and then very rarely in terms of armed self-defence. White violence, which began as physical provocation in unarmed but violent street-fighting, then escalated to the sabotage and bombings. It emphasizes the differences between black and white 'riots' that white radicals could embark on such open contests with the police; the almost total absence of black people in such ventures was always significant.

As has been argued earlier, none of these transitions can be detached from the development of changed attitudes towards revolutionary violence and guerilla war in the context of Vietnam, that Hayden and Lynd helped hasten. From the mid-1960s on, the substantial identification amongst student radicals with guerilla violence in the Third World, and black self-defence and ghetto revolt at home, was plain enough. But the move to the actual use of weapons on their own behalf was a much more agonizing step, and one in the end taken only by the very few in the NL. In each case one has to distinguish between the theory and practice; there was excessive talk of urban guerilla war but virtually no actual armed organization in the white and even to a large extent the black movements.

The major way-station to this point of no return, a point at which the NL virtually disintegrated, was the development of 'confrontationism', a phase which the black movement had barely passed through, except perhaps on the fringes of the later civil rights demonstrations. The term 'riot' had been used so loosely in relation to such demonstrations and confrontations of various sorts during the 1960s, that it was difficult for those dependent on the media to discern the real change taking place in the nature of these clashes in America.

Certainly, student occupations such as the FSM at Berkeley (written up as a 'riot') were relatively disciplined, involving few real physical confrontations that were outside the nonviolent tradition. The scuffles by demonstrators in Sproul Hall (Berkeley) during arrests were minor in comparison with later struggles. Moreover, most of the subsequent street clashes and confrontations designated as riots at Berkeley, were only a little more violent than the mêlées which took place at the end of the later (post-1962) English Aldermaston marches,[43] or on some of the less disciplined civil rights actions.

After 1967, with both the use of CS gas and an increasing loss of discipline by demonstrators, and with more noise, chaos and hysteria generally, the whole character of the confrontations altered. Though many of these later clashes should still be more fairly characterized as 'police riots', Oppenheimer argues that the peace movement simply did not re-learn from the 1967 Pentagon confrontation the plain fact that any violence by demonstrators, even defensive responses, could serve only as an excuse for violent retaliation, or provoke extreme repression, as happened in Berlin that year.

The evolution is well illustrated by the Berkeley case, contrasting the street demonstrations of 1965, 1966, 1967 and 1968. The 1965 VDC marches to Oakland, which despite the city's refusal of a permit the Berkeley police actively protected from attack, were relatively 'orderly'; the police were not seen as the main target. The 1966 and 1968 Berkeley street demonstrations, like the 1967 Oakland Stop the Draft Week, were much more clearly confrontationist. The two street demonstrations of 12 April 1966 and 1 July 1968, were similar in many ways: YSA-created fronts precipitated the two clashes; the issues were those of student solidarity (with Saigon students in 1966 and Parisian students in 1968); both demonstrations were held without permits and were provocative in tone.[44]

But in the 1968 clash, it was obvious that police were at times clearly frightened, and they responded in fear as much as anger; the assorted YSA, PL and ISC militants were more or less in control of a larger and more hostile crowd,[45] and a new pattern of 'riot' emerged, in which the 'street people' became the new shock troops of confrontation and 'trashing'.

What had happened in the intervening period[46] was not unlike changes in the NL and society as a whole, but strongly focused in a small urban area; the key development in these two years had been the emergence of a 'radical-hippy alliance' or rather the dissolution of the two groups in a common identity. Many of the hippies who had abandoned love, psychedelics, and the pacifist poets, now opted for radical postures, aggressive rhetoric and confrontation politics. In Berkeley, for example, the fusing of the two as 'street people' is crucial to any understanding of the growing crisis; the 'street people' were now using fairly crude but political tactics; boycotts, strikes, commune-building, bail-funds, etc.[47] In addition, with the growing influence of black power, the official abandoning of nonviolence by SNCC and SDS, and the growing strength of the Marxist-Leninist sects both in themselves and within the NL – an inevitable reduction in communicability marked the character of ensuing demonstrations; there were few 'petitions to power', or even formal demands.

The 1967 Oakland clash, reflecting the influence on Stop the Draft Week of the previous Pentagon confrontation, was again utterly different from preceding 'peace' demonstrations in the Bay Area. Like VDC, STDW asked for no permits, but it was different not merely because it had renounced civil disobedience and nonviolence, but because it was openly provocative and saw the police as a number-one target. These were attitudes also reflected in the 1968 Berkeley street clashes and the Vietnam Solidarity clashes in London and Berlin. Fringe elements, dedicated to violence and 'to fight America' (to 'the last Vietnamese' their critics asserted) began to appear on every mass demonstration: 'Kami-kazi' tactics seemed to express the growing frustration, sense of impotence and even despair, bearing witness to the inability of the movement to alter American policy in Vietnam, and foreshadowing Weatherman.

The reality in which organizers manoeuvred political newcomers into physical danger to 'radicalize them' by cracked skulls was always more ugly than poetic; at the Oakland Induction Centre, the nonviolent sitting crowd at the entrance to the Centre was 'protected' by several noisy lines of helmeted and crudely armed demonstrators. When the police charged, part of the line was able to retreat, but the rest was driven back onto the immobile sitting crowd who then became the main target of the charge. Their vulnerability – and the likelihood of the charge being triggered – would have been minimal without the prior provocation. Whilst the role of police agents in these confrontations is unclear, this instance was later used to document the uselessness of nonviolent tactics! The élitism of organizers who wanted a few martyrs (not themselves!) or who consciously put demonstrators unknowingly into vulnerable situations, indicates the shift from the early 1960s when demonstration leaders had taken the most vulnerable positions and when the dangers were stressed to all at the outset, in frank discussion. Significantly, Carmichael had taken even at that time a similar line on radicalization: 'people won't fight; they won't fight unless you push, so you push'.

This decline in the ethical climate of demonstrations is intimately associated with political decline – a growing contempt by the leaders for the led, strangely parallel with the ethics of political leadership adopted by some of the movements abroad now being taken as models. From the STDW demonstrations of 1967, there is marked growth in both verbal and physical violence in SDS revealed at the level of symbolism.

Shortly before this, a smallish faction in SDS, close to the Maoists, put out a 'clenched-fist' symbol which was quickly taken up by broad sections of the Movement;[48] whilst such adoption of aggressive postures and symbolisms did not yet signify an actual embarkation on the path of planned physical violence, these were clues symptomatic of a growing escalation of physical confrontation, and an identification of the Movement with on the one hand the Old Left's toughness and on the other a romantic 'solidarity' with 'militant', 'armed struggle'; it represented a distinct breach with the SDS of an earlier period.

Sale, the principal biographer of SDS, dates this turn towards violence in the Movement considerably later, i.e. late during 1968, but this is because he confines himself to *armed* violence; certainly as late as the spring of 1968 the official view in SDS was still against a full-scale commitment to violence. Davidson and Calvert, deeply divided on strategy, nevertheless agreed that the 'crazies' and 'left adventurists' who advocated violent revolution, were a liability to the NL. But though the membership might agree with them, the powerful faction close to the National Office were increasingly inclined to the turn towards physical force.[49]

STDW and the Pentagon confrontations (1967), it was announced, would 'deepen and extend the anti-war movement by escalating the militancy of movement tactics'. As long as this remained at the level of pseudo-violence, confrontation in the streets and on the campuses had not yet reached riot proportions. In the long run, however, these postures would have to be acted out more fully; the pseudo-militancy of the gesture would in the next two years become caught up in bloody adventures on the streets of Berkeley, Chicago, Berlin, Paris, London and on the lawns of Kent State.

Each escalation of the war brought an escalation of urgency and militancy and a series of increasingly physical and hysterical confrontations. The hope was expressed that 'rioting would bring peace', based on an analogy with Watts and other ghetto outbursts which had seemed to engender poverty programmes. Hayden declared that the era of 'organised, peaceful and orderly demonstrations is coming to an end, other methods will be needed'. On and off campus, clashes with Dow Chemical recruiters, attacks on draft boards and the first political acts of sabotage such as the bombing of power lines in the Bay Area and the destruction of SS offices, expressed these sentiments clearly.

Although student-based, demonstrations began to take on a more threatening appearance as the Movement escalated its tactics; wearing helmets, using picket signs as weapons, looking to the street-techniques of Japanese or Parisian students as models to adopt,[50] and beginning to deploy a rhetoric of physical struggle and military analogy, fronted by the beatific icon of the dead Guevara; each in turn encouraged sacrificial venture.

In many cases the actual language of guerilla war was used, including Debray's advocacy of 'mobility'. The tactics used at the Stop the Draft Week demonstrations were not of course 'actual tactics of urban guerilla warfare', as one commentator called them, but a sort of theatrical imitation of such tactics; hit-and-run offensives where police numbers were smallest.

These actions also became the model for the next planned confrontation at Chicago the following year (1968). The helmets and protective clothing indicated that the organizers of the Chicago confrontation certainly planned for violence, even if not all of them sought it. Dellinger and Hayden had said that 'the responsibility for any violence which develops lies with the authorities, not the demonstrators' but this was somewhat pious, since street-fighting had been all along expected and prepared for. Indeed Hayden openly announced beforehand that they needed people who could 'fight the police'; in the event, fringe elements, at first Chicago ethnic and youth gangs and later militant elements from SDS, obliged. Turning the confrontations to violence, much as had similar elements in the later civil rights demonstrations, almost certainly these groups also included agents provocateurs planted by the Chicago police to stir up trouble, and to justify their response.

On such occasions of course, the line between defence and offense was always hard to draw; in any case the extreme over-reaction of the police was probably not quite expected, and it was this loss of self-control which may have had something to do with the demonstrators' own lack of discipline. As George Lakey remarked, running away can touch off a police riot far quicker than anything else. Whatever the actual chain of events was, certainly some of the bloodied militants of Chicago took this as the signal for new and bloodier confrontations: even a move to armed resistance; and at this point, Mike Klonsky (later to become SDS president) urged SDS members to arm themselves and fight; here too the Weatherman faction was foreshadowed – and possibly precipitated.

The Paris barricades and the various European street battles of 1968 had been taken as further endorsements of a change of course. In the past, New Leftists had, as Lens points out, proved by their willingness to accept personal suffering, jail and beatings, that they stood for the higher order of morality, while the state adopted the violent repressive stand. As Sid Lens put it:[51]

Whether the New Leftist believes in nonviolence or not [therefore], most of his actions will be nonviolent if only because in most instances violence will alienate the potential constituency.

But in the new strategy, this tactical and political advantage was now lost. Even amongst those radical groups still shunning violence there was a refusal to condemn the trashing and physical assaults of the 'crazies' continuing to alienate mainstream America – otherwise increasingly sympathetic to some Movement aims. Thus although the evolution from nonviolent defence to violent offence had initially taken the ostensible form of 'violent self-defence', it was often sustained in such a way as to provoke, or indeed to threaten, the adversary. Certainly there can be little doubt that many of the initial clashes between white radicals and the police were engineered consciously by steering committees or Old Left segments dedicated to a confrontation/provocation strategy.

As a result, predictably, the police were also by now spoiling for blood: even if sections of crowds had been still oriented towards nonviolent obstruction, police charges often preceded any kind of warning that could have enabled on orderly sit-down (though in fact such a warning was given to the Oakland STDW blockade). As for nonviolent groups which tried to act as human barriers between the combatants, these often suffered, beaten in the mêlée, even though one such experiment, organized by Dick York's 'Free Church of Berkeley', was partially successful in 'cooling' a police riot.

Meanwhile the spread of campus violence, often spearheaded by black and Third World students, continued: between autumn 1967 and spring 1969, there were over 500 confrontations on over 250 campuses.[52] Dozens of university bombings occurred in early 1969 – only a few directly linked to SDS. The most significant escalation, that at San Francisco State College, which had begun in the autumn of 1967, was characterized by what even Movement critics called 'mindless violence' including the destruction of classrooms; the following autumn a protracted and bitter strike and occupation was marked during its four-and-a-half months' duration by intensive violence, shifting political coalitions, intolerant factionalism, establishment repression, and inconclusive but militant engagements. Black students also escalated their actions especially in the southern and border states; the influence of the Panthers was exemplified in the Cornell University incident of 1969, where students hovered between symbolism and armed threat when they took rifles in with them to occupy a campus building; that they seemed to be finally ambivalent about the guns' actual purpose was symptomatic of such ventures.

More than any other group, the Panthers encouraged this worship of the gun amongst radicals; parallel with the pro-NLF cult of small-arms, and echoing the gun-fetish in American culture generally, the Panthers elevated it to a major movement symbol within a matter of months. The language of 'pigs' was introduced partly in an attempt to reduce people to something that could be slaughtered, and partly to emphasize the venom of anti-police tirades. Though this piece of rhetoric largely misfired, certainly hatred of the 'pigs' reached frenzy-pitch in 1968-9, during which time some major clashes with police occurred.

For the youth culture this is a period of songs such as 'Revolution' and 'Street Fighting Man', and for many the new violence of street-fighting appears more as expressive experience than political strategy. Many seemed to feel in this desperate discontent a need to emulate the dramatic violence of Tet and Paris; as revolutionary gestures, like the sporadic bombings and burnings, the street-fighting episodes were seen as part of a 'theatre of resistance', which extended into the verbal and symbolic violence of much rock music,[53] reaching a climax in the actual murderous violence of the Altamont music festival (California). This suggested that the degeneration of certain elements in the counter-culture into sickness and violence was no longer merely a satire, or an attempt at 'anatomy of the system', but rather an excrescence, symptomatic of the larger society's sickness; it threw up some increasingly extreme symptoms.

As the overt violence and hate in the movement grew, sado-masochistic and nihilistic elements in the counter-culture that were reflected in the music and the underground press became pronounced.[54] Although the Manson Family, bastard offspring of the counter-culture, was disowned by some sections of the Movement, there were others, including Yippees and Weatherpeople, who proclaimed some kind of identification with their murders (the 'heavier the better'): bestial as these were, they were seen, like the terror of the Black September or Red Army guerillas or Sirhan Sirhan's killing of Kennedy, to belong to a general escalation of savagery by a counter-culture against an Imperial Establishment which was always itself prepared to use its million times more savage, nuclear weapon, and which itself could now only be purged by a 'holy war'.

There remained in these global outbreaks of terrorism, a detectable and recurrent sense of sacred mission. The ritualization of political murder was indeed taking place on the fringes of the political counter-culture; acts of terror or hi-jacking could be politicized, often almost as an afterthought or rationalization. To some extent this represented a continuity with the Marcusian argument that, in comparison, the incredible violence of advanced industrial societies is often disguised or represented in terms of surrogates.[55]

Thus the new types of violence of the 1970s are partly a legacy of the NL evolution of the late 1960s: too many radicals, Lester argues, came to see violence as a principle to be adhered to regardless of circumstances:

As long as the radical movement continues to view violence as the sine qua non of revolution, then it will continue to be out-manoeuvred and manipulated.

Cleansing, cathartic, the trigger of historical change, violence became an independent variable, valid in itself, prior to and detached from political programme: the language of violence and threat, from burning down cities to blowing up draft boards, from 'death to Yankee imperialism' to 'killing the pigs', reproduced this equation of the true revolutionary with the adoption of violence.

Even by 1967, as SDS leaders admitted, there was 'increasing talk along these lines'.[56] It was part of the growing militarism of a movement which, taking its graphic imagery of the Third World from partisan propaganda or from media (and public) which could only understand *military* action and which underplayed *political* ideas and revolts, condemned the 'reactionary nature of pacifism' and its 'failure to analyse violence in class terms' (RYM). This 'revolutionary youth movement' proclaimed that the 'armed struggle was the only road to revolution', and *New Left Notes* reiterated (December 1968) 'we must use any means necessary, including people's violence'.

From the romanticization of peasant war, guerilla values could reinforce the growing worship of violence of all kinds; so much so that by the 1970s some of the adulation for revolutionary guerilla figures shifted to the Arab terrorists (such as Al Fatah), to the IRA, and to such extraordinary culs-de-sac as the SLA (Symbionese Liberation Army).

Indeed, SNCC, by expressing support for Arab terrorist organizations, cut its last tenuous links with the Liberals; SDS leaders gave their first support to Al Fatah, and then to other Palestinian guerilla groups, in 1969.

This type of relationship with the Third World was most cogently reinforced by Debray: partly under his influence, political and military aspects of change were merged (for example in the organization of the Panthers), with the military arm predominant. These analogies were extended from guerilla organization abroad, to justify the imposition of similar structures, even by terror and violence – in the ghetto organization of the Panthers; they were stretched to include Weatherman and other NL cadres trying (unsuccessfully) to bring more oppressive military discipline to bear on the Movement.

A great deal of black and white rhetoric of the late 1960s, warning of impending genocidal moves against the black community, was used to press the need both to arm and to prepare for pre-emptive violence.[57] Those on the Left, who talked of genocide, of an Algerian parallel, of cathartic 'polarizing' violence, of analogies between black people and 'Jews' or slaughtered peasants, were, as some critics warned, entering an area that could so easily turn the American situation into a futile bloodbath of enormous dimensions.

The arguments of Marcuse and the proponents of self-defence had been that counter-violence would weaken or deter the actual violence of the state and ruling groups. But even from a radical standpoint, this had not been borne out by the events of these years; the violence of Newark and Detroit, even of Watts, was overwhelmingly the violence of reaction, not of the initial riots themselves. It was mostly black people who died, and white police armouries which expanded. The self-destructive violence which promised identity, also made people targets and scapegoats.[58] However, in Oppenheimer's view:

Para-military affairs in the black ghetto may be largely a creation of the press which has resulted in a self-fulfilling prophecy.

Certainly, the minority violence *was* manipulated and sensationalized by the white media – like many previous facets of Movement growth. But this time there was evidence of an even greater danger looming; violence was used to isolate the radicals from the mainstream; going underground merely assisted this process further.

During 1969, the second major split between RYM II (led by Klonsky) and Weatherman developed, mainly over this issue of para-militarism. RYM II called this a 'petit-bourgeois inclination to violence' that would 'alienate working people' (which was almost indistinguishable from PL's criticism). The violence of 1969–70, widespread and uncoordinated, reflected the influence of the NL's lurch towards violence, but lacked any direction by what was left of it organizationally. Independent of SDS, or any other group, the scattered violence ranged from killing police and taking hostages to arson; during a phenomenal fifteen months of bombings, there was a rapidly escalating violence on campus (especially against ROTC buildings) and trashing (attacks on shops) in the community; there were sharply violent responses to the Conspiracy Trial convictions. These violent direct actions and street-fighting, which were now[59] being met by enormous counter-force, were at last provoking a conservative law-and-order response. There was a danger of creating a situation the NL could not control. Such left minorities could soon lose the initiative (and the streets) to armed groups, official and unofficial, and the right; for in addition to such NL ventures, a three-cornered arms race was on. 'Blacks are arming, the police are arming and the ultra-Right is arming' (Oppenheimer). The escalation of armouries both official and unofficial, and the growing strength of the forces of control during the 1960s,[60] suggested that any attempt at armed tactics by the left – black or white – would be met by an overwhelming overkill response.

The lessons of this period had been learnt on the left many times before; libertarian radicals, in particular, are ineffective at sustaining organized brutality of the kind necessary to destroy the violence of an entrenched power. Moreover, terrorism involves the use of ordinary people as hostages for change, therefore it becomes difficult to reconcile it with democratic strategies or theories of revolution; it is essentially élitist, breaking off communication with opponents and supporters alike.

Marcuse, amongst others, significantly turned sharply away from it in the 1970s;

Terror groups trying to gain power have never been able to use terror effectively. Terror has been effective historically only if the terrorising groups are already in power.

A number of radicals were now regretting that they had employed the facile rhetoric of violence and thus helped create the 'unnatural climate of violence'.[61] It began to dawn on the Movement that the protagonists of violence had helped justify the enlarged counter-insurgency budgets; that the agencies of control were only too glad to meet expected challenges on the familiar ground of violence, rather than in the arena of ethics and culture, or moral or intellectual argument. The police always preferred to act 'as if' the Movement were armed or violent (whether it was or not), since by reacting to their (ostensibly) counter-violence, the Movement would prove that the NL was the aggressor and itself wedded to the use of weapons.

In such contexts still the methods of nonviolence were probably always the more appropriate; traditionally they had allowed greater communication and continuation of politics – even *during* confrontation. Indeed the recognition of this possibility of militancy *plus* dialogue, presaged a surprising renewed interest in nonviolence amongst some of those who had previously rejected it.[62] It was on this front that the political wing of the hippy movement, the Diggers – now Yippees – still seemed to have something to contribute, but even here, frustration and impatience after 1968, led to self-identification as 'street-fighting men'.

Nevertheless, the declining numbers in militant street confrontation demonstrations during 1969 and 1970 suggest, as Weinstein has argued, that many people were now turning away from the constant violence of America, official or unofficial, established or oppositional. Aggressive militance could after all only serve as a substitute for strategy 'when the power of the state was primarily held by *force* rather than by ideological means',[63] and that was something that the cycle of provocation and repression, conspiracy and trial, failed conclusively to demonstrate.

13. Revolution and the New Left

Theories of insurgence

Many of the misfortunes of the NL, from its inception, and through the crises of the later 1960s, may be attributed to its lack of any comprehensive theory of revolution that would fit the circumstances of an advanced industrial society. In Gitlin's view, the premature definition of the NL as 'revolutionary', especially by the Establishment, was a setback in any case, since it reinforced exaggerated self-images. After the self-conscious change in the movement from 'protest to resistance', the word 'revolution' was increasingly used, and the movement conceived of itself as involved in an effort 'to liberate through an overall transformation of society' (Calvert). The NL in itself, moreover, may be seen as representing some essential components of any revolutionary process, not least the disenchantment and desertion of the intelligentsia.

But although the word 'revolution' had been on the lips of activists since the early days of SNCC,[1] there was predictably little consensus on what the term implied. From its inception, SNCC talked in terms of revolution; yet it was the only civil rights organization to do so, even though, after 1964, commentators widely argued that the negro movement as a whole was 'implicitly' revolutionary in that its demands could never be met.[2]

One cannot avoid the judgment that the lack of a NL theory of revolution was largely caused by the belief that such theory would emerge naturally from movement practice; the closest to this was the counter-institutional strategy, but it was not widely recognized as such. The crude conceptualizations that later emerged, the piecemeal strategies, were an inevitable counterpart to the anti-intellectualism, pragmatism and moralism of the movement; as a result they left a vacuum that would be filled by concepts and strategies drawn from dated or external models.

The attitude of the NL to revolution cannot be understood without at least some reference to the classic Marxist revolutionary model, as well as its development through various theoretical revisions such as Leninism and Maoism to the ideas of Guevara, Castro and Debray and even further from Marx, to those of Fanon. Outside the Marxian mainstream, Sorel's earlier stress on the need for a scenario of transformation linked to revolutionary myth and symbol, laid him open to a charge of élitism, but he too undoubtedly influenced the NL.[3]

To some, Anarchist strategy offered itself as something of a synthesis, a third way (like some brands of Trotskyism) outside or beyond the political developments of the major blocs, East and West, as well as bringing together the critiques of capitalism and Marxism, of private greed and state bureaucracy. Anarchists had, however, remained perpetual rebels, unable to produce a viable model of revolution or social organization that could replace the existing state.

When, in the years after 1967, serious discussions of revolution began, it was mainly the inherited definitions and conceptions of it – for example, those purveyed by the Old Left, including and especially in the new guise of Maoism – that were easily available. These were an important influence, and their impact should be examined in greater detail.[4] Not that Maoism was entirely novel – the Chinese communists,

looked back to the Russians, and further back, to Marx, though they went ahead and did something that had very little to do with either of them (Moore).[5]

Increasingly sceptical of left-wing revolution in the West, and calling for revolution in the East instead, figures like Sweezy and Sartre thus turned to the Maoism of the cultural revolution as a solution. Yet this claim that it could offer a more realistic, but also more utopian alternative, like that of other NL solutions, merely confused the picture.

In any case, by the 1960s, any attempt to impose a unitary character on Marxian revolutions, whether in theory or practice, was clearly doomed to failure.[6] Yet despite the multiplication of such revolutionary ideas and models during the twentieth century, most of them still paid lip-service to Marx. The resultant and additional problem was that revolution meant different things to different people, even amongst those who accepted a broadly Marxian version of change.

Guerilla struggles in Latin America, including Castro, further exacerbated the polycentric fragmentation of Communist theory and organization. Whether such tendencies were Marxist is more problematic: Oppenheimer argues that contemporary revolutionists who style themselves Marxists, are not Marxists at all, because they represent rule by an élite and merely 'use Marxist language and peasant revolution to justify their present or future role'.[7] As both cause and result of these changes, it was arguable that there was 'no Marxist theory of what twentieth century revolutions in fact look like and what they mean.'[8]

The link between these experiences if there is one, lies more in Leninism than Marxism. The climactic élite-led violence focused on state power, associated with the Bolshevik coup, is the component in

Lenin's thought which links the variety of *soi-disant* Marxist revolutions, even though in other ways they may be unique.[9]

Peasant rebellions had provided a model of change that was different from the Bolshevist image, but were increasingly suppressed by the Leninist methods, and centralizing goals of Third World leadership.[10]

It has been remarked how revolutionaries tend to look backwards even as they 'resolutely march forwards', and the NL was no exception;[11] just as in the Old Left there was an inevitable tendency to look back to Russia in 1917, the NL was to turn back primarily not to European or American revolutionary traditions, but to those of China, Cuba and the Third World.[12] Yet as Gitlin argued, 'any design that tries to repeat history will come to naught'. Many socialist groups had hitherto defined themselves mainly in terms of their stance on the Bolshevik revolution and when (or whether) it had begun to decline. Amongst Anarchists, independent Marxists, Leninists, Stalinists and Trotskyists innumerable models, versions and interpretations of Russia existed, but to the mainstream NL, witnessing the proliferation of new revolutionary experiences, independent of existing Russo-centred CPs, such an obsession with revolution in one country had become almost incomprehensible.

Despite all these alternative options one has to explain the lack of a clearly articulated NL model of revolution evolved from domestic Western experience; the burgeoning of imported revolutionary rhetoric and the alien theoretical traditions of Third World Marxisms and liberation wars only came after the tentative efforts to build a programme around the NL's own unique ideological insights. Why were these abandoned?

Increasingly one of the problems of the NL was that of direct transplantation of theories (such as peasant-based revolution) to an industrial setting. As practical revolutionaries, Tito, Mao, Ho and Castro adjusted their revolutions to local conditions, later adapting their theory to this experience – just as Lenin later justified Bolshevism.[13] But the NL made little attempt after 1967 to adapt theory or practice to American or Western conditions;[14] Oglesby's constant use of Cuban and Vietnamese analogies proved as problematic as the images of Russia and China he rejected. In the same way, Weinstein calls the subsequent Weatherman theory of revolution

a strange conglomeration of insights . . . the result of years of haphazard action and thought . . . (inappropriately) . . . framed in a model of revolution borrowed from revolutionary nationalist struggles abroad.[15]

Whether the sources were Cuba, China or Vietnam, such borrowings exemplified the problems of adopting what Gitlin called 'prepackaged versions' of revolution.[16]

As the preamble to the New American Movement put it several years later,

In lieu of building a serious struggle in this country, the Movement has lived off the glory of third world struggles. The Movement has attempted to portray third world revolutions as the embodiment of all virtue and wisdom.[17]

This idolatry, the search for guidance from external authority, was one of the clearest symptoms of the NL's loss of self. Moreover, as, by way of the Third World, this pointed back to the Old Left and even to Stalinism, 'SDS leaders persuaded themselves that they were the sole repository of a revealed revolutionary truth'. When New Leftists came to opt for guerilla struggle, it was often in the hope or belief that it represented a decentralized, community-based and relatively spontaneous violence: yet as Goodman's critique had pointed out, already there was the technology and bureaucracy that must doom such hopes that this was a qualitatively different, or 'more natural' form of revolutionary war.

The fact that the NL's cult of activism and confrontation should find identification with mystiques of peasant revolt, or the emphasis on will and spontaneity in action expressed by Fanon, is understandable enough. What is more difficult to explain is the extent to which the NL failed to comprehend the lack of relationship between this *imagery* and the *realities* of Vietnam; or the fact that there as elsewhere, peasants had become mere instruments of urban bureaucratic-élites guided by rationalism and programme.

Whether in Algeria, or Indo-China, terror too played an important role; but, this clearly was not 'spontaneous popular violence'; peasant violence, typically a mindless, often a-political destructiveness, involving frenzied attacks on local targets, was never systematic terror. In this sense, like all the NLF/DRVN structures, Vietnamese terrorist organization was imposed from outside peasant society; the systematic assassination of officials, like the careful strategic occupation of urban areas, or the calculated shelling of civilians, were not 'spontaneous acts'. The planned strategy of FLN or NLF political terror was directed as much against 'the people' as by them. Once full-scale fighting began, such activity continued; appeals to nationalism, unity, patriotic duty were enforced with ruthless discipline: the killing of local representatives was a selective sanction. Once implicated in the struggle, villagers, exposed to counter-violence, were faced by a 'lesser of two evils' dilemma: into this situation, the NLF introduced both forced labour and forced conscription.

The writings of Giap and Ho remain close to the Chinese model, but in the Cuban model, or in Fanon's ideas, the role of violence takes on other distinctive forms. In both, commentators have detected a tendency to 'separate the use of armed force from any analysis of social and political conditions' and an emphasis on the 'primacy of violent action over social analysis' and of 'military over ideological or political leadership'.[18] (Debray argues that only such men can be 'truly revolutionary' and therefore 'proletarian'.) The views of the counter-insurgency advocates in the Pentagon, and a 'guerilla theorist' like Regis Debray, thus become almost indistinguishable. Oppenheimer points out that this is unremarkable since both now conceive of revolutionary war in terms which 'minimize the role of masses and see change as the work of tiny vanguards'.[19]

The Cuban legend loomed large in all this because its mythology most deeply met the apparent needs of Movement youth. Some SDS leaders helped initiate the 'Venceremos brigade' – a PR project for the Cuban Establishment, not unlike the 'Fair-Play' trips of several years earlier, and with links to fringe groups like Gerassi's 'revolutionary contingent'.

Oppenheimer stresses the degree to which the prominence of Debray, Castro and Guevara, as well as Fanon, in Movement mythology, is also linked to its activism and anti-rationalism, i.e. the impatient praxis of individualistic leaders, 'practical revolutionaries, initiating our own struggle', rather than waiting for conditions to ripen. This lack of comprehension extended from Vietnam to Cuba, and to China and elsewhere, where the same mystique was identified with the revolutionary regimes of Ho, Mao and Castro. The NL clutched at straws: lip-service to anti-industrialism and decentralism by Asian and African revolutionaries, Guevara's paradoxical emphasis on 'humanism' – 'love' and 'voluntarism' – man as the 'architect of his own destiny'; Mao's stress on 'moral incentives' and idealism. But the effort to apply in an urban context, tactics and strategies derived from rural movements, was as Moore concludes, an important but misleading current in American radicalism; the analogies of 'liberated' base areas which could undermine the existing system, were based on false parallels.[20] In China these areas were self-sufficient, territorially independent, and attractive to much of the population in a way that the counter-communities were unlikely to be.[21] The long period of prior disruption out of which such areas developed, would be unlikely to be reproduced in an urban setting, indeed no industrial society would tolerate it.[22] For such a process to have any chance of success in the West, a great mass of the irreconcilable elements that Fanon describes would have to exist; only the ghettoes in the USA contained anything approaching this kind of hostile 'surplus' population, and most of the ghetto violence was self-destructive, turning inwards on itself, and with almost no links with the NL.

Not all Third World identifications were at this level of seriousness, and early on in the process, Nick Egleson, a former SDS national officer, challenged the tendency towards symbolic moralism and posturing in much talk of revolution:[23] 'instead of good and bad, we talk of revolutionary and unrevolutionary'. Another critic argued that the cult of 'borrowed revolution' was the attitudinizing of 'revolutionaries without a revolution' –

Not your revolution nor mine, nor even that of the proletariat, but just revolution in the abstract which is available in various parts of the world in different brands and packages.[24]

SDS itself, deeply implicated in the eulogizing of cult figures, especially Guevara and Debray, adopted such revolutionary affectation, along with the pollution of language and exaggerated images derived from the under-developed world, crystallizing graphically the romanticization, especially of armed violence, guerilla fighters and the community of the 'struggling' oppressed. It was a public style, expressed in the 'personality' posters of Mao, Ho, Che and other leaders, that decorated walls almost as a pathetic substitute for developing a 'native revolutionary tradition, or an independent basis of revolutionary power' in the West.[25]

This reluctance to adopt fresh scenarios can be partly explained in terms of the forces arrayed against any urban revolutionary movement. No decisive splits among the groups controlling key institutions had appeared such as those preceding previous revolutions; nor did the system appear overly oppressive to the mass of the population: the system had

considerable flexibility and room for manoeuvre including strategic retreat. There was no probability of easy success.[26]

No urban rebellion had been successful for more than a few months in an industrial society; inter-urban rebellion in modern conditions seemed even less likely to succeed.[27] Neither in any case had come near creating a full-scale long-term revolutionary breakthrough, not least because working-class organizations had been largely incorporated, and because the increasing power and efficiency of the state were reflected not only in its sophisticated technology of repression, but in its elaborate ideological manipulation. The complex differentiation of such societies, the rising standard of living which accompanied this atomizing process, the individualizing tendencies of bourgeois domination, all worked against the creation of 'revolutionary classes'.

The urban guerillas

The accentuation of armed violence as a national or civic right and the growing violence in the streets were neither entirely a natural or even accidental growth of Movement developments, rather they were in part the fruits of fairly determined efforts by sectarian groups to discredit nonviolence and move the ghettoes towards violent strategies. Encouraged by the Watts revolt of 1965, and the three years of urban violence that followed, many such groups (most of them white) began to proclaim urban guerilla tactics, and it was increasingly claimed that returning GIs, especially black ones, would provide the trained and motivated recruits for urban guerilla outfits.[28]

This retrospective romanticization of the urban revolts, has already been analysed as largely the result of the importation of scenarios of guerilla war from abroad, e.g. the impact of PL's image of China, Vietnam and Cuba, the ideas of Debray and Fanon, the lessons of Algiers, etc., coinciding with the later growth of the IRA, the Tupamaros and Black September's activities. These aided the portrayal of black self-defence groups like the Panthers, as potential vanguards in America's guerilla struggle. A neo-colonial analogy[29] was widely used to draw the parallel with anti-colonial war:

If white America is the mother country and black America the colony, the white police are occupation troops.[30]

This kind of thesis naturally coincided with various theories of revolutionary militarism associated with the anti-colonial wars,[31] but the fascination of armed adventures tended to relegate political and ideological aspects to a minor position. There were others, who, whilst they did not believe the time had come for talk of guerilla war, nevertheless believed that the self-destruction of the ghettoes might serve a useful political purpose by 'making the unengaged blacks worse off and so swell the cadres of revolt'. A further ingredient was the sense of fatalism in the ghettoes; in a survey in 1964, over a quarter of all black people thought that major violence was inevitable. But most commentators agree that, far from the romantic imagery, the ghetto revolts were in the main expressions of despair, a plea against going unnoticed.

The group from outside the black movement which probably played the most significant role in this development in the early 1960s was PL. On the whole, such elements were unsuccessful in permeating the Movement organizationally before 1967, but PL's ideas and example did have an effect. The causal nexus is always hard to establish; much of the evidence is circumstantial inference, added on to the proclaimed ideas, aims and achievements of such groups.

Their ideological role will be discussed separately, but their stunning strategic victories in swinging much black radicalism towards their methods and ideas of armed guerilla rebellion, deserve consideration here: the pro-Peking splinter was never more than a sectarian fraction in the early 1960s, yet its influence always far exceeded its size. More than any other group, it was able to sustain the myth of the failure of nonviolent tactics, and move American radicals, white and black, towards armed self-defence and the glorificaion of ghetto violence.

Nonviolence was a significant road-block as far as such groups were concerned; its stress on communication, patience, suffering, respect for the opponent, were anathema to them; they succeeded in persuading many black militants that such a policy meant compromise, betrayal and incorporation.

The beginning of what Christopher Lasch describes as this 'cult of armed self-defence as revolutionary action' can be traced back to Williams's actions in North Carolina in 1957–9.[32] As someone already closely linked with Maoism, Williams's task was to provoke and to polarize; the ideas of 'self-defence' were accepted first; then later 'armed self-defence'. From assertion of the right to carry guns (which many in the civil rights movement accepted), Williams went on to a polemic against nonviolence. Violence, he argued, was to be the catalyst whereby two clear sides could be created, subjects and objects; ideological polarization, provocation and the escalation of violence would then inevitably follow.

This was, or became, PL's tactic; to use the widely accepted civic right to bear arms, as the thin end of the wedge of an armed insurrectionary strategy. In the early 1960s, this strategy developed a dual emphasis in North and South; in the South, the main task was to move blacks away from nonviolence with attacks on King, and towards armed violence through the example of figures like Williams. In the North, the main aim was to organize armed Afro-Americans, and give leadership to ghetto riots and rebellions.

With the lack of any other comprehensive *black* vision of social change, North or South, some aspects of PL's systematic, if rigid, Marxist–Leninism began to influence black militants; the weaknesses of the Northern movements were exploited, and the new goals and new methods introduced.

That PL did in fact harbour dreams of provoking guerilla resistance in this period, is borne out by their actions in importing arms, including dynamite to blow up bridges, into Hazard, Kentucky, in the white miners' strike of 1963.[33] A year later, they were active in the Harlem riots; in these outbursts of largely spontaneous anger and looting, they were the only political camp to announce that they were both Communists and revolutionaries and aiming to lead both these events and the revolution itself.[34]

Epton in Harlem called for the 'smashing of the state',

kill a lot of these cops, these judges and we'll have to go up against their army. We'll organise our own militias and our own army.

Both Jessie Gray and Epton were arrested for incitement during these riots, but later PL emphasized their 'defensive' role, and both the ensuing 'Plot against white America' statement and PL magazine, were filled with pictures of 'defensively armed negroes'.[35] But PL had consistently advised the masses to arm themselves and had argued that in the USA, revolution could only be brought about by armed struggle.[36]

After the Sino-Soviet split in 1962, their rhetoric significantly escalated; the riots in Harlem were seen as proof of native revolutionary potential. PL sensed that the black leadership was no longer either capable or willing to prevent mass violence once it started: 'When massive violence comes, the USA will become a bedlam of confusion and chaos', Williams announced.[37] The police in Chicago and New York were hinting that they could not contain it either. By operating against both the old community leadership and the police at the same time, all restraints could be swept away; any attempt to stay the hand of city police departments was condemned as reformist. The police were 'an occupying army'. It was PL too who popularized the idea of fighting back when police attempted to clear a crowd; they also instigated the circulation of diagrams for making molotov cocktails, later to be widely distributed and used in the underground press of the later 1960s. Although they later opposed what they termed 'individual terrorism', and although they denied the 'plot to kill whitey' myth, PL in this period was clearly an important model and influence on the later growth of both Panthers and Weathermen.

With the projection of Third World liberation ideas, PL was no longer alone in the shift towards urban guerilla tactics: the swing towards violence in the Negro leadership during the later 1960s gathers a momentum of its own, and a direction which even PL eventually rejected. Initially, Carmichael had proclaimed black power as an alternative to prolonged destructive guerilla warfare. But over the years, his emphasis changed.

More and more people are now beginning to plan seriously a major urban guerilla war . . . where we can move seriously within this country to bring it to its knees.[38]

During the long hot summer of 1967, his successor Rap Brown appeared provocatively at crisis points, including Newark, one of the worst of urban eruptions, where Tom Hayden had been actively organizing and LeRoi Jones had been involved. Each had predicted the ghetto violence or race war, though no direct links existed between them and the 'riots'.

Hayden tended to encourage the myth that ghetto riots could become the springboard for genuine guerilla warfare,[39] and LeRoi Jones's move from a posturing guerilla theatre – a sort of cathartic shock therapy – towards the advocacy of urban guerilla war, suggested that the distinction was not always clear between theatrical rebel violence, and the reality of race war; and Jones did identify himself with armed organizations.

By 1971, Cleaver too was very seriously calling for immediate urban guerilla war, since 'war can only be abolished by war'. Whilst there was little demonstrable link between such figures, or the NL movement generally, or for that matter to the initiation of these ghetto uprisings of the mid-1960s, they helped create a climate and attitude whereby the idea of guerilla war could move from fantasy towards actuality.

Moderate critics of the black leadership during this period argued that they had not only given up the effort 'to control violence or even understand it, but are themselves making a cult of violence'.[40] Certainly the role of King, Rustin or Farmer as a mediating or nego- tiating force was long since undermined or abandoned; many were now prepared to let the revolts take their course as the only way to convince whites that the 'Negro would not wait'. Others argued that the fear of a racial bloodbath was a significant sanction, or again that it would act as a kind of blackmail.

Those who saw violence as cathartic for the black community, believed that it might be therapeutic for the white community also; but ghetto violence – despite the claims about 'urban guerilla war' and 'political insurrection' – was essentially disorganized and uncontrolled. This largely expressive and spontaneous violence, which Goodman termed partly 'racial spite', had some positive aspects – an assertion of freedom against irrational authority, the looting of a rich society by the desperately poor, the 'vitality of the powerless' – 'Burn Baby Burn' was a way of 'not being resigned, of keeping a lost fight alive, by preventing the dominator enjoying his dominance'.[41]

The last major occasion when Negroes had armed and collectively defended the ghetto was in 1919; the result had been a rapid escalation of violence with widespread black bloodshed, and the political gains were nil. In the 1960s, nothing comparable occurred; spasmodic looting, burning and rifle fire did however lead to massive repression and substantial loss of life.[42] These events reached their climax with nation- wide rioting after King's assassination: like previous outbreaks it was purely self-destructive – most of the property burned was black, most of the amenities and services disrupted or destroyed served black people, and most of those killed were black. Though on a smaller scale much the same was true of some subsequent Panther ventures.[43]

For the American establishment, as Oppenheimer observed, such violence might be functional: 'A violent movement, or one which for any reason can be perceived as violent, permits the society to evade ghetto problems': urban riots were used as much as justifications for cutting off urban-aid programmes as creating them. White radicals, concerned with protecting the black community, preventing race war, and creating change in the larger society, were thus caught in a paradox as long as they indulged a tempting fantasy of change being launched from the black community – e.g. as a base for guerilla activity – or of armed 'self-defence' groups turning to the offensive when the next ghetto 'blew'.

One theory of urban guerilla action was focused on sabotage of the fragile systems which supplied the functional necessities of urban living; the garbage strike and the New York blackout were used to illustrate the vulnerability of electric supplies and mechanized functions. It was believed that, through sabotage, the city could be brought to a halt. Gerassi, at the Round House Conference, went so far as to talk about poisoning water supplies.

Yet in territorial isolation, such strategies could only bring disaster, not least to the blacks themselves (this may explain the cool reception given to the Panthers by most black communities, and the actual hostility shown by middle-aged and middle-class blacks).

The vulnerability of the ghetto population is becoming evident to black leaders, arguably the most expendable, backward and bankrupt area in society.[44]

Moreover, there was now a school of thought that was convinced that 'armed struggle' in any advanced urban-industrial setting was doomed. Black urban guerillas in particular would be territorially and logistically isolated and would be dealt with almost solely in military terms.

While the city is vulnerable to dislocations caused by insurgency warfare, it also jeopardizes the very population which it is trying to help by revolutionary methods.[45]

In addition, the Panthers' evolution created fears that a new black oligarchy based on military terror – black against black – might emerge in a context of race war. Guerilla warfare, urban or rural, has normally been seen in terms of massive majority support or acquiescence by the population; where this support is lacking or declines, urban guerilla war, as with the Tet offensive or the IRA campaigns, is likely to degenerate into terror. It was never clear that black guerilla groups would have this majority support from America's ghetto population, let alone support from outside it.

A racial bloodbath might indeed act as a suicidal catalyst for the next stage of social transformation, but this could only be justified to black people if the myth of genocidal preparations by whites could be made persuasively real. Certainly by exacerbating the backlash, armed tactics could help bring this nearer. A minority in the NL were concerned to shift the nationalist polarization in the black community back to the political and cultural fronts, and were disturbed by the blanket romanticism of black violence – whether the spontaneous chaos of Watts, Chicago or Detroit, or the organized armed projects culminating in the Panthers.

In opposing the proponents of terrorism and guerilla violence, this section of the NL argued with a guerilla metaphor. Given that a large counter-revolutionary movement is growing, the radical movement has to choose the ground it knows best, to struggle on. It does not provoke the enemy where he is strongest, but rather where he is weakest and least expecting attack. They claimed, and even some of the Old Left Marxists agreed with them,[46] that there was a war still to be won on the cultural and educational front – to outwit, not outgun, the opponent.

For many in the radical-hippy youth culture, the brutalization and disciplining involved in the whole 'bag' of terrorism and 'armed self-defence' units, were still basically repulsive:

It turns too many 'cool' people into our cops, our 'green-berets' or our 'Minutemen' to seem a meaningful kind of personal transformation.

Even if the radical movement had the manpower and firepower, even if the radical communities were not logistically vulnerable, the military experience would prove essentially an alienating one. Ultimately that is why the urban guerilla and terrorist fantasies began to lose their attraction: they were not seen to be clearly linked to any vision of social or individual change.

It is questionable whether the violent propaganda-of-the-deed of the underground bombing-groups in Germany, USA, Britain and elsewhere can be usefully termed 'urban guerilla' activity, although the German groups received training from Palestine guerillas in terrorist techniques. Nor were armed defence groups, however aggressive and provocative – like the Panthers – truly guerillas either, principally because they were above-ground. Most of these groups espoused revolutionary ideologies and para-military structures – but lacked a community base or a scenario of hit-and-run warfare.[47]

One concrete and contemporary test case of urban guerilla and terrorist theories presented itself after 1969. There were some very real parallels between the Catholic ghettoes of Northern Ireland and the situation of the American black minority – both were faced with problems of neo-colonialism of an internal kind, and the identifications of a minority with forces outside the country. Moreover, the events in Belfast gave some clearer examples of what real urban guerilla war might mean than the ghetto revolts had done. The development of the Irish movement from moderate nonviolent civil rights to a vicious nationalist and sectarian terror, going through stages of self-defence, army intervention and limited guerilla war, presented an oddly compressed parallel with the American movement in the 1960s and indeed was directly influenced by it.

The progression of the Irish movement towards near civil war, encapsulates almost every stage of the NL, by which, in some ways, it was shaped. The major difference is the enormously foreshortened time-scale (1968–71) of the Irish developments. The Civil Rights Association (CRA), formed in 1967, was a successor to the Campaign for Social Justice, and both were inspired by such movements as CND in England and the American civil rights struggle. Its nonviolence, direct action and militant reformism were modelled on theirs.

From 1968 to 1969, the CRA was engaged in a series of demonstrations, supported by trades unions, left-wingers – including the CP – and involving both Catholics and Protestants, not confined to intellectuals and the liberal middle-class young. But despite this nonsectarian character, and its demand merely for an extension of British rights to Ulster, the CRA was met with repressive actions by both government and Protestant extremists and forced into civil disobedience. By December 1968, the escalation of confrontations had already persuaded the moderates in the CRA that they should scale down their activity; but this was 1968, the year of Paris, Chicago and the mass Vietnam demonstrations. Students and young socialists fought back against the police, the CRA strengthened its mass base, and a new ginger group – the People's Democracy, also non-sectarian but Marxist in inclination – was formed around the activist students at Queen's University in Belfast. The demonstrators began to see themselves in a revolutionary light, playing down both the movement's nonviolence, and its limited aims.

In these conditions, the situation quickly went out of the control of either the CRA, trying to de-escalate and backtrack, and the People's Democracy aspiring to create the working-class revolution. Riots in Londonderry and Belfast, a near pogrom, and attacks on the Catholic community by uniformed Protestants, were the occasions for the intervention of British troops (initially and ostensibly to protect Catholics), a massive revival of the nationalist IRA, the ascendancy of the militant Provisional wing, and the beginning of a terror offensive. This escalation was foreseen by many commentators who argued that direct action would 'thaw out' frozen violence and liberate it.[48]

Unlike most other Western terrorist groups, the IRA fought against a long background of nationalist and colonialist violence, a substantial para-military tradition and with a community base clearly defined by religion as well as economic and political deprivation; however, by no means all in the community endorsed either its means or its goals, and much of its 'support' was maintained by terror or other sanctions. By 1969, violence and sectarianism had destroyed the civil rights movement, and within a year anti-British and even anti-imperialist slogans began to predominate. The younger militants and student radicals in the People's Democracy had totally lost the initiative to the 'hard men' in the old Republican movement and had to choose which of the Republican factions to side with (or drop out); whilst the liberals and moderate left (like the Communist Party) tended to reject the revolutionary but sectarian path the Republicans, especially the Provisionals, were pursuing. As Catholic IRA[49] support increased, the possibilities for a non-sectarian alliance collapsed, and the campaigns of urban terror after 1971, with extensive civilian killing, but few significant political gains, dominated the scene.

Modern revolution: violent and nonviolent

Though events in industrial societies had suggested that revolutionary masses could still emerge and that they did, as in 1968, paralyse urban centres and beyond for brief periods, it was not clear where they could proceed from there. Under modern conditions, the fact that the lack of concentration of the multiple sources of power represented not a political decentralization as much as an impersonal division of labour, strictly controlled, made the task of the mid-twentieth-century revolutionary an entirely novel one. 'The old model won't do any more', Marcuse argued,

the notion . . . that under the leadership of a centralised and authoritarian party, large masses concentrate on Washington, occupy the Pentagon and set up a new government

is totally unrealistic.[50]

'What is certain is that we are moving towards power', Hayden proclaimed, but no scenario could adequately answer the question of where in fact such an élite would go to 'seize' the power – with, or without, mass support. The centres of power are multiple in a society like the USA: Omaha, Nebraska; the Pentagon and other (some secret) military centres and bases; the CIA, the FBI; the media: CBS, NBC and other networks; the telephone companies; the Post Office and key plants, as well as all the formal political centres. And even if the takeover of such centres by dedicated cadres was feasible, how could they get them working again? As Paul Goodman observed: to seize and maintain the existing system as a going concern would require

centralised coercion on a Stalinist scale simply because it would have to force the technicians and the experts, the bureaucrats and the managers, to operate them and to serve new masters.[51]

This imagery of taking state power, one which had almost become the defining imagery of twentieth-century revolutionaries since the Bolshevik coup, had not hitherto been an explicit part of NL theory, and even when élitist fantasies proliferated, the notion of armed seizure of power remained largely in the realms of rhetoric. Nevertheless, by the later 1960s, the dream of a small 'dedicated' vanguard directing revolutionary masses (from its underground equivalent of a Smolny Institute) had gained some appeal, though given the atomization and complexity of the American apparatus of power, it quickly turned to parody.

The May events in France had convincingly demonstrated that industrial societies can still be threatened by mass disruptive action, even when of a largely unplanned kind. But there was a widespread assumption that revolution in advanced industrial society would be characterized by urban guerilla strategies, and similar tactics of disruption. As Robert Williams had put it,

The new concept of revolution defies military science and tactics. The new concept is lightning campaigns conducted in highly sensitive urban communities.[52]

Despite its flamboyance, this kind of urban guerilla rhetoric and the

KID

inspirational legends of urban revolt, had at least one factual component: the real vulnerability of the city, and by extension, of the larger
society; as Oppenheimer points out, obviously this urban

vulnerability to disruption and para-military attack jeopardizes such
societal decision-making centres as may remain in it (such as Wall
Street).[53]

In so far as the legitimacy of the industrial system is partly based on
consumerism, the breakdown of goods and services may well undermine it. Concerted dislocation of food and other essential supplies,
communications, power, sanitation, and other necessities of urban life,
together with obstruction of police and fire and other crucial services,
or dislocation of schools and hospitals, indicate the urban dependency
on such activities at critical points. In addition, strikes in key areas,
blackouts, power failures, sabotage and bomb scares, even in non-
revolutionary situations – have indicated in Western societies the
existence of these potential crisis points and the fragility of their
urban systems.

Undoubtedly, part of the fear of revolution, the nervousness of
radical experiments in living and working, that is embedded in the
whole cultural milieu of the West, and that had so hampered the growth
of the political alternatives, was rooted in the belief that, without
expertise and control the whole 'great mechanism would surely bog
down, leaving us in the midst of chaos and poverty'.[54] The very
complexity of the division of labour was the key to the vulnerabilities
of modern society, but also revealed the redundance of earlier models
of revolution.

One result was an intensifying debate between those advocating a
revolutionary movement and those a revolutionary party: 'the
Leninist vanguard, as against collectives, affinity groups or communes'.[55] Significantly, Marcuse took his stand very firmly with the
latter:

No political party, but also no revolutionary centralism and no underground – because both are all too easy victims to the intensified and
streamlined apparatus of repression. The same circumstances that
militate against democratic persuasion, also militate against the development of a revolutionary centralised mass party, according to the traditional model. You cannot have such a party today, not only because the
apparatus of suppression is indefinitely more effective and powerful than
it ever was before, but even more and perhaps most so, because centra-
lisation today does not seem to be the adequate way of working for change
and obtaining change.

The closest the NL ever came to spawning its own vanguards were
Weatherman and the Panthers, though neither articulated any vision
of how such vanguards would act. Weatherman was content to spell
out the destructive side, the strategic meaning of radical disruption: 'we

have to force the disintegration of society creating strategic armed chaos where there is now pig-order', though the implication was clearly that such ruthlessness should extend to the re-imposition of order, with or without popular mobilization. Indeed, in the midst of chaos, the restoration of effective, 'efficient' state power might even emerge as the revolutionaries' trump card.

As a number of commentators have pointed out, a collapse of a system of power, without a basis in popular support, is an obvious recipe for an élitist and coercive solution. In turn, the lack of either an alternative political apparatus or majoritarian sympathy is bound to reinforce the resort to the 'seizure of state power' model. But by no means all the NL leaders ever accepted such a dogmatic, Old Left eschatology of change. Oglesby, in many ways one of those closest to Marxism, left open the question of whether revolution would or would not take place. Cohn-Bendit envisaged the possibility of a 'non-catastrophic revolution', 'I don't say a nonviolent one'.[56]

From a neo-Marxian standpoint, Barrington Moore suggested the possibility of 'recreating' the democratic framework peacefully, through 'a limited amount of disorder that falls short of real revolutionary upheaval'.[57] Julius Lester, spokesman for many black revolutionaries, argued that revolution was first and foremost a 'question of morality, a question of values and the inner life as opposed to guns, ideologies or organisations'.

This had long been the pacifist view – stressing individual transformation and the means-end connection – and the *Liberation* group had maintained this ethical concern with the 'humanizing of revolution'.[58] This was seen as particularly critical in so far as the technology of violence had transformed the nature of fighting, depersonalizing the process of revolution. As the gun rather than the person of the revolutionary became the symbol of political change, the dangers of authoritarian organization and brutalization became more acute.

There clearly did not exist, even among anarchists or pacifists, any thoroughgoing NL analysis of the inter-relationship of the problem of revolution and violence; there were few structural critiques of the costs of violent means.[59] The negative organizational implications of violence were usually shrugged off as either inevitable or forced on the revolution by 'confining conditions' and external circumstances. The continuities between authoritarian and terrorist hierarchies of revolutionary war, and the coercive structures and brutalized leaderships which emerged after the accession to power, were the inevitable costs of change.

The vicious oppression that such structures typically entail, the subordination of societal goals, the breakdown of human communication into murder – above all, the replacement of politics by force – were guessed at but not detailed. The power that violence gave to the brutalized, the new states it created, were obvious enough – but this could be blamed by anarchists or pacifists on ideology and organization, rather than violence *per se*. This 'inevitability' in revolution was accepted in part because the Bolshevik coup, élite mobilization of masses, and dictatorship of the proletariat, had passed into the Marxist tradition as the essential model. But it was also related to the fact that revolutions had always been processes linked to that of moderni-zation; involving the creation of centralized nation states, usually militarist and expansionist, and spawning vast bureaucracies, as a 'by-product'.

In this apparently inexorable development, as one theorist observed:

The revolutionary response takes its structure from what it reacts against, with nothing to put in its place where it takes direction from established institutions themselves. [60]

Such were the limitations of the historical dialectic. It is true that this inherited experience of revolutions had created certain misgivings amongst movement spokesmen. Echoing Camus, Norman O. Brown warned of the 'recurrence in revolution' which some movement people refused to see: 'Revolution is not a slate wiped clean, but a revolving cycle ... the idea of progress is in question'. [61] Warning against any repetition of the mistakes of socialist regimes, now even Sartre was arguing (by the 1970s) that revolution was not justified if it produced totalitarianism (thus repeating precisely Camus's position of a dozen years earlier). [62]

The prime example of a radical movement creating and sustaining revolution was still that of the Bolsheviks – yet they had turned towards draconic oppression: and subsequent events had never entirely reversed that relationship. Barrington Moore maintained that rather than accept bureaucratic components as defining revolutionary success, it was necessary to 'redefine such success as making some lasting contribution to human freedom'. [63]

In the past, the ebbing away of the central authority of the old order had constituted an anarchic core to revolution, paradoxically enabling the success of even the most authoritarian groups. Such a collapse of power had often more to do with the withdrawal of obedience, than with the prior activities of such revolutionary élites: it confirmed that the state can only exist on the basis of obedience. This was something long understood by revolutionaries of all sorts; without the decom-position of the armed forces, revolutions are usually stillborn; but when the police and army refuse to obey, then a revolutionary situation may usually be said to exist. [64] Revolutions have been able to occur solely because the refusal of obedience, of taxes or conscripts, of food or of work, had weakened the structure's capacity to resist. Such actions, usually precipitated by external factors which help weaken or destroy the legitimacy and institutions of the state, assist in creating a power vacuum in which alternative revolutionary institutions might survive.

The question which posed itself to the NL, was whether through their strategies such a power vacuum could be created. Together with internal domestic action, such as radical disruption, there was at least a hint that such a loss of control by some Western states was beginning to occur especially with the intensified anti-war opposition of the late 1960s.

The Ellsberg case,[65] the Pentagon papers and the various forms of resistance to the state by figures like Spock, the Berrigans and others, especially such as Harris, provided clear examples of renewed non-cooperation with authority; dropping out of the war-machine was a continuation of the kind of defection from the bureaucratic systems that had characterized the student revolt and the counter-culture from the early 1960s.

This was, implicitly, what the counter-culture was about as far as Anarchists were concerned. The upheaval in the army was the most grave threat of all to the government, and the counter-culture and the NL were at its source. The very survival of the nation might be threatened, in the view of a presidential commission, which admitted that the USA had 'lost the allegiance of part of its youth'.

To evolve from these elements a strategy for revolution was dependent on the view that such a process of resistance could be transformed into the revolution itself; in other words, that the refusal to obey, coupled with the creation of a new order 'within the womb' of the old society, could produce the very transfer of legitimacy that revolution implies.

Yet when some in SDS proclaimed the *transition* from 'resistance' to 'revolution', they usually meant quite the reverse: i.e. that revolution was a distinctive orientation – unrelated to mere resistance. It was the libertarians who believed that disobedience, including the political strike, could foreshadow a particular type of societal collapse:

we will see that what we have to envisage is some kind of diffuse and dispersed disintegration of the system, in which interest, emphasis and activity are shifted to local and regional areas (Marcuse).

In this scenario the permeation of a society by decentralized alternatives would also provide bases sustaining ongoing resistance and confrontation: free cities with free schools, clinics, universities, stores, churches, press, radio, would not just be *parallels*. 'Enclaves of freedom' 'would to some extent avoid this problem' (Hayden); both in creating this change and sustaining it, such new forms would help weaken and dismantle the old structures by accelerating a transfer of allegiance. Thus a refusal to render unto the old order, coupled with a switch of loyalties to the new, could create a transfer of legitimacy without producing the fatal power vacuum into which élitist revolutionaries have typically transported their organizational structures, laws and agencies of control (or revived old ones). The orders of freedom would thereby be given the enhanced strength they had lacked in previous revolutionary crises.[66] Thus the legends of the Commune and the Paris sections, the Soviets and the workers' councils, could again be resurrected to compete with the Bolshevik image, or the Leninist vanguard. Like Lynd, Marcuse echoed this strategy of counterinstitutions, possibly aided by a general strike and radicalization through disruption, as offering itself as a more natural concomitant of such breakdown.[67] Some had called such institutional creations 'artificial'; but in most previous revolutionary experiences, despite the conceptual inheritance which had emphasized the top-down power seizure, such democratic institutions had emerged from the bottom up, challenging and competing with the vanguard parties and leaders. Lynd believed this largely spontaneous creation of a new order, springing from organizing efforts 'within existing society', could become the dominant characteristic of the American revolution: 'As the revolutionary situation deepens, the broadening of the decision-making process becomes institutionalised'.[68]

Only this type of strategy avoided the classic NL dilemmas about working 'within' and 'outside' the system, about gradual versus climactic change, or the relationship between community organization and social transformation. The alternative institution approach, stressing revolutionary continuity against the apocalyptic vision, placing the humble organizing projects into a larger setting, made the choice between coalition and independence, reformism and revolution, immediate demands and long-term aims, largely irrelevant – representing both, or neither, according to the will and nature of each local movement. For the mainstream NL, the seizure of power as an implicit model was thus rejected in favour of one which was explicitly utopian in trying to close the fatal disjuncture between means and ends in the form of the revolutionary movement itself: that is, that the movement should foreshadow the type of society which would emerge during and from the revolution. Only in this way, it was argued, could an authoritarian revolutionary movement be offset.

Such a perspective endorses a view of the continuity of revolutionary experience

within which the revolution is only the accomplishment, the setting free and extension of a reality that has already grown to its true possibilities.[69]

The belief that new structures, institutions and relationships could themselves represent a revolutionary process – and that if this process was accelerated during social crisis, it would at least offer alternatives for those radicalized during a societal collapse – was the NL's crystallization of its own experience around an inherited theory of revolution.

The idea of a revolutionary nonviolence had also been kept alive over the years, not least by *Liberation*, as well as its young rival and successor

Win, in America.[70] Its founders had, from the outset, predicted that nonviolence would be the instrument of mass revolution to occupy the factories and to defend the revolution. As active pacifism became more radical again in the later 1960s (and more explicitly linked to Anarchism) this option was looked at from a new standpoint and as a possible source of alternatives to the cult of violent revolution then sweeping the NL. In the West, the explicit concept of nonviolent revolution was first developed by the Dutch Socialist, De Ligt (influenced by Gandhi) and developed again in debates over civil disobedience and the state, in England though the Committee of 100's revolutionary and anarchist aspects tended to develop in tension with its Gandhian principles.

During the Czech actions of 1968, the East German leader, Walter Ulbricht, condemned the civilian resistance as an insidious new form of counter-revolution: 'a nonviolent uprising'. Ironically, the evidence assembled by the civilian resistance theorists, which made an extremely limited impact on the NL, led on (largely unintentionally) to strategic elaboration of nonviolent revolution, as the next major development in pacifist ideas. Whilst the idea of an alternative national defence was greeted with substantial scepticism, even amongst pacifists, the work of its proponents did turn up some very substantial research on non-violent techniques of resistance.

Gene Sharp was foremost in creating an awareness of the extent of this nonviolent armoury;[71] in addition to the nonviolent creation of the orders of political freedom, previous revolutions had also been characterized by many other, sometimes neglected or ignored, components. Many of these were 'unviolent', or certainly non-military, some of them straight out of the Gandhian armoury; for example, massive unarmed demonstrations, fraternization with troops and police, strikes and go-slows, non-cooperation and tax refusal, war resistance and desertion, occupations and sit-ins, boycotts, underground communications, or alternative services. Trades unions had become radicalized by such situations producing new permutations of social forces. And even sabotage represented a further element short of armed struggle or terrorism. Such elements had, however, rarely been related to non-violence as an explicit philosophy.

With the writing of George Lakey, the idea became more explicit and more practical; evolving a strategy of nonviolent revolution came to be seen as the major theoretical task for pacifists in the 1970s: pacifist manifestos and manifestos for nonviolent revolution began to proliferate, and identification with these by pacifist organizations and anti-militarist sections of the NL, became more open.

The 'nonviolent revolutionaries', in evidence even after Chicago or Grosvenor Square, could still reject both armed struggle and electoral tactics, but did not necessarily oppose confrontationism, even if they urged a move towards more educative and creative, and less provocative forms. Alternative forms of society – alternative democracies – represented another way of confronting a repressive system. Meanwhile, work within communities and universities offered a complement to direct-action pressure to develop the mass base of a movement which could become revolutionary; even trades unions could be radicalized, they argued. For these largely a-theoretical and optimistic revolutionaries, the recipe was 'more of the same' – more draft-resistance, more community projects, more work to transform universities and other institutions, more work to create new ones, including new unions, new schools, and a proliferation of alternatives.

Whilst they might not openly adopt such notions as 'nonviolent revolution', something that many NL spokesmen accepted as one of the major tasks of revolutionary theory in the 1970s was to evolve concepts of *libertarian* revolution in which the seizure and exercise of state power could be avoided or bypassed; a 'new model', more evolutionary and less apocalyptic, was sought on the basis of activist experience. Thus for most radical theorists, the principle dilemma of strategy for the Movement was not between reform and revolution – the counter-institutional strategy, for example, avoided this choice. The main problem was the redefinition of revolutionary 'success', and thus of scenarios of change and models of organization which fitted it. For many of them seizing central power and staying in control was seen not only as an inadequate criteria for the success of revolution, but also an outdated model of change for any industrial society. It was generally accepted that the world had changed structurally; and Oglesby and others maintained that it needed to be looked at through new eyes.[72]

Imperialist America, with more mental workers than manual workers, and more students than farmers, requires its own revolution . . .

Since the fixing of the basic radical definitions, [structural] shifts meant that the world needed to be understood again, conceptualized and acted upon from a standpoint uncommon to classical Marxism, and through political modes suggested no more by the experience of the Bolsheviks than by that of the parliamentary socialists or the Stalinists.[73]

Given this altered reality it became necessary to reconceptualize the process by which social transformation could and might take place. Though many critics, such as Marcuse, believed new strategies could emerge, carrying with them the redefinition of revolution, the element of backwardness in radical theory, the urge to recall the last period of ideological stability, seemed opposed to pressing ahead with any revolt which 'totally rejected the past'.[74]

Thus, at the very moment when the alternative conception of revolution was becoming available to large numbers in the NL, the drift towards violence had reawakened an identification of revolution with the forcible seizure of power; when this happened to the NL, as

O'Brien remarks, 'the term "New" had lost all meaning; revolution had become an impossibility.'

Weatherman

The Weatherman experience represents the culmination of certain revolutionary tendencies in the white NL, just as the parallel developments culminating in the Yippees in the counter-culture and the Black Panthers in the black movement represent a logical outgrowth of similar tendencies. These processes are both linked and analogous; each represents the actions of activist minorities, extending the logic of violence to certain extremities. At the outset the three lines of advance are conceived as mutually re-inforcing and supportive. In some senses Weatherman moved into the vacuum left by the BPP as it moved away from urban guerilla ideas after 1969,[75] though this was one factor in the growing tension between them.

But despite the generally growing factionalism amongst most radical political groups in this period, there is initially a surprising amount of mutual solidarity between these three groups. The Yippees openly identified both with Panthers and Weatherman. Of the three, the Panthers were a little more reticent. But even here black militants, especially Cleaver, made sympathetic remarks about each of the other groups, and Panthers supported Weatherman in the SDS split. Vehemently endorsing the vanguards of 'youth' and 'blackness', Weatherman consistently identified with both the Panthers and the Yippees. Weatherman was soon announcing that 'Freaks are revolutionaries and revolutionaries are freaks'.

Such formulae indicated that the times had indeed been changing and were by now changed; that an urban terrorist group could be born, taking its name from one of Bob Dylan's songs,[76] is symptomatic of the changing political face of the counter-culture. Undoubtedly a key component in the move towards the Weatherman bombings, terrorism and urban guerilla tactics, however suicidal, was this form of cultural romanticism: there is a distinct element of what Howe called 'pop art guerillaism' in both Yippees and Weatherpeople and perhaps in some of the Panther actions also[77] which proved something of a liability.

Yet whilst all three are undeniably heirs and offspring of the NL, all have pushed beyond and outside its limits, and perhaps for this reason prove to be political cul-de-sacs. All three have the limitations born of an obsession with style and method as against content and agency; they have an element of fad, and are predictably evanescent and short-lived.

The roots of Weatherman have been seen at various points; during the attacks both provoked and suffered by SDS militants at 'Czechago' in August (Hayden), or amongst those who chose to be arrested in the final sit-in at Columbia in May 1968 (Sale), but they can probably be sought earlier in the growing confrontationism, especially street-fighting and revolutionary rhetoric, of Fall 1967. One spokesman of the Resistance dates the emergence of the Weatherman ethos in the Oakland Stop the Draft Week clashes of October when the rhetoric of physical confrontation first emerged at its shrillest and with an accompanying intellectualization of the impulse towards violence.

In a strange way, Weatherman offered yet another means of obeying C. Wright Mills's injunction to translate personally-felt problems into public political issues. The felt issue for Weatherman was fundamentally the Vietnam war and the attendant alienation from American capitalist society. The outrage against American overkill, the identification with the NLF, sought a mode of expression. Such profound horror and frustration could not be contained by traditional peace demonstrations; as each year of the war progressed, the necessity for channels for these emotions, especially physical and verbal violence, grew stronger. At last, after the 'Days of Rage', the Weatherman solution was offered. Bernardine Dohrn announced

revolutionary violence is the only way. Now we are adopting the classic guerilla strategy of the Tupamaros . . . in the technically most advanced country in the world.[78]

This self-image was essentially an élitist one, a minority consciously provoking masses into action ('you have to push people into action' – Carmichael) by catalytic and exemplary acts of violence.

But even the 'Days of Rage' themselves were ill-conceived and disorganized. Terms like 'masochistic', 'suicidal', 'fascist' and 'adventurist' were used even by erstwhile sympathizers. 'Custer's last stand' cost the movement over 200 arrests, 200 injured (many seriously) and over 200 million dollars in bail money. In fact nearly everyone who took part was either arrested or hurt, and many suffered both. A significant number of participants also dropped out of Weatherman during the four days, and there were no signs of working-class youth involvement or sympathy as there had been in 1968.

PL condemned the days as the work of police agents, provocateurs and 'hate-the-people lunatics'. The more sober PL approach was at this period still able to win sympathy for its worker-student alliance ideas; PL consistently condemned the individualistic terrorism of Weatherman,[79] and Calvert too condemned the 'left adventurists' who think that 'sabotage and terrorism' will bring the revolution tomorrow.

Whilst the direction of the movement as a whole was not towards underground violence – such as the Weatherman phenomenon – the rest of the movement did also turn away from 'above-ground organizing'. As David Horowitz remarks, this was a period when the move was towards new life-styles rather than new constituencies; towards political communes and collectives rather than parties and coalitions.[80]

This shift was very much reflected in Weatherman itself. The Weatherman underground was organized into communes, collectives and affinity groups or gangs, rather than traditional types of political or military unit. But far from realizing the new rationality and the sensibility of the new revolutionary personality, these units created an irrational caricature of the relationships in the larger society; insensitive to the needs of individuals, riven by aggressive rivalry; dominated by hierarchies that used threats and coercion to maintain themselves. A deep dependency on leadership, amounting to a leadership cult, emerged in the crises of this development. Members of the Weatherman collectives commented on the psychological violence, hierarchy, élitism and aggressive competition (including male chauvinism), within them.

Initially, Weatherman saw the whole white youth constituency as its major base. Violence would catalyse its response; but gradually when this response did not materialize, the identification was with the more narrow youth culture. Yet even here, Woodstock (the immense and relatively placid three-day music festival) was far closer to where this latter constituency 'was at', than Weatherman. The attempt to forge an alliance with the white cultural radicals (Yippees, White Panthers, and other youth revolutionary groups) failed dismally at the infamous 1969 Weatherman 'war council' at Flint, Michigan. Far from being a celebration of youth culture, this gathering – or a 'gathering of tribes' as advertised – was a 'heavy' and introverted gathering, full of ritual paeans to violence. A Weatherman apologist describes it as that group's 'political Altamont' and characterized by 'a glorification of violence'.[81]

The major debates that took place following these splits were over the Weatherman approach to building a mass base; how does bombing, any more than burning down ghettoes or destroying draft boards, win popular support, or the support of the blacks or those to be drafted? Would the sabotage of an urban renewal project win the support of the poor? Such questions had been asked before in the movement.[82]

Whilst the media focused a great deal of inflated attention on Weatherman violence, even for Weatherpeople themselves, results were hard to discern. As Jacobs remarks: 'The provocativeness of their flamboyant rhetoric provided them with an illusion of strength'. The media helped make Weatherman a national force after a series of street-demonstrations, including the 'Days of Rage'. It also helped create what Jacobs calls the 'Weather-myth' of a 'white fighting force willing to sacrifice all in a headlong assault on the state'.[83]

Weatherman, like other sections of the NL, developed a self-conception of being a support group for Third World revolution. Basing itself on a quasi-Maoist analysis of worldwide change, it emphasized white racism and Western imperialism. The NLF and the Panthers were the major insurgent models and their domestic constituency was to be revolutionary white youth.[84] When the underground

'Red Army' was officially initiated in January 1970, with about 200 members, it compared itself with the small armed cadres with which General Giap had precipitated the first Indo-China war. Weatherman called its affinity groups 'Focos' after Debray's account of Cuba, and the analogy with fifth columnists or saboteurs 'behind enemy lines' consistently characterized the subsequent Weatherman communiqués which signified its final alienation from 'white America'.

The over-identification with Third World insurgency, and the failure of early hopes in the revolutionary potential of white working-class youth, left the Weatherpeople isolated. Jacobs comments that 'having lost confidence in their own revolution, Weatherpeople could not but doubt their own authenticity as revolutionaries'. The new self-image of Weatherman was as a guerilla operating within alien territory; yet the American people had become 'the enemy' in a way that the Cuban people under Batista, or the Vietnamese people under Diem had never become 'enemies' to the NL guerilla heroes; such attitudes were rationalized as stemming from America's world hegemonic role.

Closer home, the influence on Weatherman of the black militants had proved critical; in Julius Lester's words,

Weatherman, in its willingness and readiness to engage in physical confrontation, is a very logical outgrowth of the rhetoric and actions of the black movement and the Black Panther Party.

Weatherpeople consistently used Carmichael's phrase 'By any means necessary', endorsing his view that 'people who see themselves as part of the system are going to get smashed with it'. Mark Rudd, before he became a leader of RYM I (and subsequently of Weatherman), quoted LeRoi Jones in his prophetic speech at Columbia:

We will have to destroy at times, even violently, in order to end your power and your system but this is a far cry from nihilism ... this is the opening shot in a war of liberation ... up against the wall, Mother-fucker, this is a stickup.

As Lester had argued, for several years blacks had been telling white radicals

for us to respect you, you must be willing to kick ass. You have to prove that you are willing to suffer and die for the sake of the revolution.

When LeRoi Jones enjoined the slaughter of whites, and Cleaver promised to turn white residential areas 'into shooting galleries', it looked as if nothing short of terror against white society would win such respect, and such rhetoric matched the Weatherman need to outrage white 'middle-America'.

It also alienated the bulk of the rest of NL: there remained a 'public' fraction of RYM I which associated with the remnants of SDS National Office after the Weatherman split-off and went underground; it, like several of the anti-PL splinters, continued to associate itself with 'youth as a class', the guerilla cult, and the glorification of the Vietnamese and Cubans. But at about the same time, Weatherman began to lose its other allies; the alliance with the Panthers grew shaky, then fell apart. (The BPP subsequently identified more with Klonsky and RYM II.)

A further attempt to forge some sort of coalition with the Chicago conspiracy defendants was also never clinched, and the more isolated Weatherman became, the more hysterical its rhetoric. At this point the slogans 'Bring the war home' and 'Fight the people' were introduced – ushering in Weatherman's terrorist period; as one sympathizer put it,

fighting some of the people makes sense (if by this you mean keeping pro-war vigilantes from breaking up peace demonstrations), but never all of the people all of the time.[85]

There were undeniably terroristic elements in the Weatherman approach – with a definite tendency to endorse violence against others. This willingness to envisage such threats, not entirely outside movement experience in the 1960s, was a final admission of the breakdown of communication with other Americans. It represented what O'Brien called the 'final scary abandonment of the NL's attempt to think through the meaning of a more humane society in the US'. Though in fact all the Weatherman targets were, broadly speaking, 'property', they were far less scrupulous even than groups like the First of May in Europe. Moreover, like the Angry Brigade in Britain, they were very lucky not to kill more than they did (three of their own, and one other), and there was a certain amount of carelessness both in planning and operation that perhaps betrayed an ambivalence about killing.[86]

Precedents for the movement's support of terror existed, particularly outside the American context. There was support for the acts of Latin American urban guerillas, Arab terrorists and even for the IRA and NLF's use of terror. In addition, the exploits of the Spanish Anarchist cells in Europe were already being publicized during the period of Weatherman's growth. Moreover the film *Battle of Algiers*, which depicted the FLN terror in the Algiers casbah of 1960, had been well received by these groups and interpreted (probably erroneously) as endorsing such tactics.

At the outset, during 1967 and 1968, SDS's relationship with the first (non-SDS) bombings was an ambiguous one; PL openly condemned such acts as alienating the workers. But through films publicizing violence and urban bombing tactics, as well as the revelations of Tet about the Vietnamese NLF, the notion of such acts had a definite impact on the thinking of some white militants.[87] The revival of interest in Sartre, a man who wrote polemically on behalf of several such organizations, gave further intellectual reinforcement: a decade earlier, opposing Camus on Algeria, Sartre had advocated getting 'bloody hands' in righteous causes. Like Sartre, Weatherman now indulged in the fantasies of unrestrained physical violence. They shared with him the orientation to the militant conspiratorial fighting groups; Weatherman euphoria is reminiscent of Sartre's existential identification of freedom with such collectivities wilfully defining history – bound by oath, brotherhood and terror – disciplined hierarchies avoiding the dangers of individualist anarchism.

On the whole such identification remained at the level of fantasy, but in 1971, Weatherman, mostly weaned on Marcusian pronouncements, found itself finally disowned by its erstwhile mentor, when he firmly denounced their terror. With an obvious reference to Weatherman tactics, Marcuse condemned acts of violence by 'pseudo-political radicals' that 'are stupid, criminal and play into the hands of the establishment'.[88]

In retrospect this violent episode can be fairly claimed to represent the final dénouement of the mainstream tradition of the NL. It was not directly provoked or inspired by the Old Left; indeed in some senses it was developed in direct opposition to groups like PL and the Trotskyist seots and the Communist Party, despite their own involvement in the promotion and, in some cases (e.g. PL), implementation of violence. The Old Left condemned these developments as 'anarchist adventurism'. The street confrontations, the blockades of induction centres, the trashing and street-fighting (together with that of the Yippees), and finally the bombing campaigns, undoubtedly sprang genuinely from the Movement, and indeed major confrontations occurred independently of Weatherman including a wave of radical bombings unconnected with them, and the September 1969 clashes at the start of the Chicago conspiracy trials and the following year when the conspirators were sentenced (although Weatherpeople took part in each) were not organized by them.

Whilst ideologically eclectic, Weatherman, like the Angry Brigade and Baader-Meinhof gangs, its nearest European equivalents, was probably closest in spirit to the Anarchist and terrorist violence of the late nineteenth and early twentieth century, though most anarchist groups condemned this 'liberal irrationalism'.[89] It was a form of romantic rebellion that aimed more to shock and dramatize, to 'épater le bourgeois', than to terrorize. Like the ghetto revolt, it complained of invisibility; it was expressive, desperate, existential and in a basic sense, spontaneous. It lacked the selfless, systematic approach of professional terror; it had none of the cold, calculating approach to killing or traditional military organization of Third World terrorist groups or the IRA, though certainly from the 'Days of Rage' onwards, the model was a military one based on discipline.

But, like their counterparts in Germany and England, the Weatherpeople were extraordinarily personal in their relationship with violence.

Strategic sabotage and radical bombing rather than individual terrorism such as 'offing pigs' characterized Weatherman actions, almost as if recognizing the transformation of violence by technological change. There was an attempt to make the bombings personal acts, since by the alienation and depersonalization of violence through modern weapons, technology had to some extent drained the expressive and thus the satisfying element from the experience of aggression.

Whilst there was still hope that they would spark a mass uprising, Weatherman actions were also seen as an end in themselves. Indeed, Howe condemned this form of political expressivism as 'desiring a social conflagration to satisfy apocalyptic yearnings'.[90]

In the past, when the NL's idealism had been condemned as apocalyptic, this had been unjustified – the earlier movement had been incremental and pragmatic in the extreme. But now, with a new emphasis on will and spontaneity, a major sector of the NL *had* moved towards millennial confrontation, mainly at the level of ideas and symbols, with the implied aim of a sudden and lasting transformation. But Lasch argues that this aim, together with the revolutionary rhetoric which accompanied it, merely disguised a profound sense of impotence and despair, as well as deep distrust of others.

The Weatherpeople have been inevitably analysed in social psychological terms, as betraying in their attitudes the 'fanaticism of radicalized intellectuals bespeaking their impotence and malintegration into either class or community'.[91] Revolution, one critic argued, had 'almost ceased to be a strategy of social change and has become instead a yoga of perfection'. Even a Weatherman sympathizer wrote of their 'religious mode of revolutionary action'. But there was also the danger that, as another commentator put it, such militancy and attitudes could reinforce the Left's own 'worst image of itself as a band of isolated desperadoes'.[92]

This tendency towards increasingly 'catastrophic and glorious acts of martyrdom' through the 1960s, cannot be separated from other particular way-stations; the dramatic political suicides of Buddhists in Vietnam or Quakers on the steps of the Pentagon, and of Palach and other young rebels in Prague, represent the continuity in these acts of outraged despair and defiance.[93] This interpretation becomes less tendentious when viewed on the basis of Weatherman memoirs and documents which express this strong streak of chiliastic resignation. As the main Weatherman historian puts it, there was a sense that 'they would be unlikely to reap the fruits of the revolution for which they were prepared to risk their lives'. This seemed confirmed when three Weatherpeople exploded themselves in an armoury of dynamite in the New York Townhouse explosion of 1970.[94]

Some months after this event, Bernardine Dohrn announced from underground that 'Townhouse forever destroyed our belief that armed struggle is the only revolutionary struggle'. The Townhouse explosion 'ended the military conception of what we were doing', a Weatherman communiqué announced.

This tendency to consider only bombings or picking up the gun as revolutionary, with the glorification of the heavier the better, we've called the military error.[95]

Without the vacuum of revolutionary theory that characterized the NL, perhaps the Weatherpeople, any more than the Panthers, would not have found themselves in this cul-de-sac in the first place. The purity of Weatherman demands made even their terroristic actions almost symbolic moral acts, in the tradition of previous propaganda of the deed. The apparent inclination towards sacrificial, even suicidal self-assertion, may be seen to exist on a continuum from the nonviolent self-sacrifice of the civil rights struggle, through the self-inflicted martyrdoms of the Weatherpeople, and on to the calculated self-destruction of Black September or the Japanese Red Army guerillas.

However irrelevant these methods were to the task of changing America, undoubtedly the terrorist orientations of the later NL had a spin-off effect on other movements, developed in other contexts. The growing global popularity of hi-jacking, political assassinations and kidnappings, as well as shooting of police, sabotage, and bombings of the 1970s, owes at least some of its appeal to the precedents set by earlier Movement ventures and rhetoric. New styles of para-militarism were ironically and tragically one of the NL's most enduring legacies to the world.

14. Provocation: Response and Repression

Confrontation and reaction

The concept of 'confrontationism'[1] was based on a theory of change (reinforced by Marcuse) stressing the need to delineate, through praxis, the contours of repression. It began as a strategy of provoking corporate liberalism to show the limits of even the most flexible 'totalitarian' consensus; this society, it was argued, could not ultimately give real equality or participation to blacks, students or other dispossessed groups and liberal values had become cover-all clichés, disguising unresponsive authority. The difference between universalized values and rationalization of private interests had dissolved. Thus confrontation could have a revelatory character:

You create disturbances, you keep pushing the system. You keep drawing up contradictions, until they have to hit back; once your enemy hits back, then your revolution starts. If your enemy does not hit back, then you do not have a revolution (Carmichael).[2]

However, there were also those in the Movement who argued that such a strategy begged the question of repression and might in fact be a 'self-fulfilling prophecy', *creating* the rightist reaction by its adventures. Others, like Carl Oglesby, argued for confrontationism on the grounds that, through the repression and reaction it created, it would prove to New Leftists beyond their self-doubt, that they were a real threat to the state.[3] He maintained that such a consciousness was only possible for the NL when it had actually provoked its own repression (e.g. by police, state troopers and national guard). Only when repression intensified, could the idea that NL activists were making changes for themselves (rather than through or on behalf of some other group) predominate.[4] Moreover, it would reveal to the Establishment who their enemies were; once they knew whom to attack, realistic struggle would be joined.

A further justification of provocation tactics resulting in repression was in terms of its 'radicalization' of movement recruits through such an experience. Oglesby waxes lyrical over the educative powers of the swinging night-stick and truncheon:

the policemen's riot club functions like a magic wand under whose hard caress the banal soul grows vivid and the nameless recover their authenticity – a bestower, this wand of the lost charisma of the modern self – I bleed, therefore I am.[5]

Such an attitude lent itself to an extremely manipulative interpretation in relation to the tactics of demonstrations.

This orientation gradually shifted towards one that held the system to be basically 'fascist' already with only a veneer of corporate 'liberalism'; protest was allowed, Hayden argued, until it constituted a real challenge to the power structure, at that point it was repressed. Protest could act as a safety valve, but never a threat; the NL could not expect any real concessions. Thus Marcuse's formula of 'repressive tolerance' was put to good use in justifying street battles, or campus violence.[6]

As early as 1965, Oglesby was predicting that 'heresy may soon no longer be permitted'. Yet ironically, probably no nation state in wartime had ever allowed the freedom and dissent that the USA allowed during the Vietnam war – including even certain rights of free organization and free press within the armed forces.[7] But Lasch urged the need to defend remnants of liberalism (free speech, safeguards against arbitrary arrest, separation of powers, etc.), 'without which further democratic experiments will come to an end'.[8] Nevertheless, many asked, was this not the very repressive tolerance which made Marcuse argue that only provocation could unmask the coercive basis of its social order? The moment it was pushed or threatened it would reveal its true nature. Sartre talked of 'pre-fascism', a fascism into which America was now moving; and those in SDS heard constant predictions of an impending police state.

The corporate liberals were, from the NL's viewpoint, well and truly exposed by Chicago, but what came next? If the NL analysis was correct, a growing radicalization of the movement, and a winning of new support should have been a reaction to the police repression. Yet although millions saw, on TV, Mayor Daley's police run amok, beating young middle-class participants and doctors, priests and newsmen on the periphery, there was some sympathy, but little widespread popular response nationally.

Only a few years earlier, when Southern racist police chiefs like Bull Connor were doing this sort of thing to Selma's 'uppity niggers', there had been national outrage. But this authoritarian brutality which had moved north with a new-found assertiveness even against what at the outset was a 'whites only' demonstration, gained self-confidence from a still generally anti-NL climate of opinion (especially in the mid-West) which, despite considerable public opposition to the war, was a paradoxical but noticeable counterpart of events after Columbia. Moreover, with Humphrey self-consciously ignoring these beatings outside the Convention hall, such repressive reaction could still be made to seem at least partly 'legitimate'.

But confrontations, like the Chicago affair, drew a number of criticisms even from those within SDS; in the first place, such tactics involved manipulation; in the second, the belief in radicalization via repression was superficial and simplistic; in the third, such tactics were divorced from the everyday politics of ordinary Americans, and last, and most importantly, such actions threatened to create a major right-wing reaction. The first critique has already been mentioned; the tactic could only be defended as helping to sort out the radicals from the liberals. But in terms of the second criticism, though repression initially heightened activity and drew the involvement of many thousands, its long-term efficacy was dubious. Critics argued that except at the most primitive level, a night-stick blow across the scalp – or a lungful of CS gas – was no kind of substitute for radical education.

As long as the Left merely reacts to events, exposing and disrupting the 'system' without offering anything to take its place, it suffers endless defeats and frustrations out of which grows, not a consciousness of alternatives, but a rising demand for more and more militant tactics.[9]

Certainly such actions expose one aspect of the system, the readiness to use uniformed violence at the slightest provocation. But without analysis, this might be taken as the cause rather than the symptom. Indeed the phrase 'police state' which came into vogue, betrayed an implication that this was part of the system's central dynamic, whereas even for the Marcusians it was its last resort.

The organizers in the Movement tended to stress the third line of criticism. Lester perceptively remarks[10] that whereas a black man has good reason to 'go up against the cops', whites do not. If they had been attacked unreasonably in a legitimate project it would have made their confrontation appear justified. As it was, it was not immediately clear to people why exactly they were fighting.[11] Confrontation tactics, particularly on international issues, were divorced from ordinary life and felt issues and needs in the community. They operated in millennial terms at the level of ideas and symbols, and could not easily be translated in terms of contestations within everyday routines and institutions. Yet the organizers maintained that it was in the latter that lasting transformation would occur, and that SDS was polarizing itself from mainstream America.[12]

The fourth line of criticism had to do with SDS's claim that the strategy of polarization, repression, confrontation and reaction could reveal the contours of corporate liberalism in its harshest light. The nonviolent confrontation of repression in the earlier NL had indeed revealed the violence of the system because the system hit first – but when the *demonstrators* hit first it was much less clear. As one contemporary has remarked:[13]

Confrontation designed to expose repressive tolerance cannot in itself expose the mechanisms of manipulation, only the forces of repression.

Moreover, such attacks may isolate the radicals; the use of violence rather than unmask the system, may in fact draw attention away from political issues to the drama of the actions themselves.

Even normally permissive systems may react in a repressive manner to such acts, and America still has areas of unrepressed dissent. Critics like Lasch argued that the main need was not to talk 'glibly about the tactical advantages of repression' (as Mary McCarthy did) which only people in a 'country where political freedom was taken for granted' could afford.[14] Rather, the task was to defend what was left of liberalism – free speech, safeguards against arbitrary arrest and the separation of powers – 'without which further democratic experiments will come to an end'.

'Is corporate liberalism really fascist?' such critics asked. 'Was America yet a police state?' 'Could not such actions create these facts rather than reveal them as persistent (if latent) conditions?' 'In particular, might not confrontationism, by concentrating on the police as a target, reinforce the alliance of the police and the ideological right?' Certainly as has been noted, every militant act of street-resistance was being used as an occasion for further escalating police armouries and tactics, as well as becoming a rationale for increasing police budgets.[15]

NL actions could, in addition, confirm all the traditional paranoias of the Right: during the election, heckling and disruption tended to help rather than hinder Nixon. The likelihood of draconic repression, even genocidal moves against the black community, came a little closer to reality as radicals began to act as if such a situation had already arrived.

Provoking counter-revolution

The parallel with the pre-Hitler anti-Fascist Left in Germany and Italy was often quoted against the provocation strategy.[16] It was difficult to estimate the validity of the analogy, but there were some at least in the Movement who, after Chicago, saw it as an instructive one, and who began to turn back towards ideas of coalition, and away from imitation of experiences outside America.

The strategic dilemma, and problems of analysis that faced the NL after Chicago, might have at least partly been resolved by accepting that a number of quite contradictory social tendencies were coinciding with one another; for example, the growth of authoritarianism and repression, alongside the growth of an anti-authoritarian, non-repressive culture; and that the working-class, black and white, new and old, was at once both bought-off or incorporated into the structure of empire, and also still deeply oppressed and exploited by it.

As right-wing reaction and the government counter-insurgency preparations increased, the idea that things might have to get worse to get better, was a view by no means confined to the lunatic fringe. Groups uninvolved with the 1968 election, were even ready to welcome the massive accession of support to George Wallace which showed up in the results. There were radicals who claimed they would vote for Nixon or Wallace – either because the Democratic Party had to be taught that it could not 'flout the popular will and get re-elected', or because a right-wing candidate would, through repression and reaction, provoke such a response that the radical movement would grow, or a liberal president be swept into office in 1972. It is remarkable that such positions, despite the oft-repeated qualms of those in the peace movement at having a Nixon or Wallace finger on the Omaha controls of nuclear deterrence, could be taken seriously at all.

Wallace's movement had, by the summer of 1968, temporarily mobilized a far larger segment of society than any the NL could contact. Wallace's constituency involved much that was idealized by the NL – it was anti-establishment, it was deprived, and it involved a populist protest against bureaucracy at the centre; moreover, this 'Right' had more influence amongst the white working class, and Wallace's movement was a genuinely grassroots one, tapping radical sentiments far more successfully than did the 'Left'. But its populist-racist admixture (not unlike aspects of Powellism in Britain) also spoke to lower-class and middle-class anxiety and prejudice, exploiting their ignorance and confusion. Quite correctly the large Wallace vote from the working class was taken by some in the NL as showing a continuing working-class potential and the need to organize there.

The far Right in America had remained a major latent force in politics throughout the civil rights period; the long-prophesied and in part media-created 'white backlash' took long in coming and never fully emerged. The Southern backlash of the early 1960s, extremely powerfully armed and organized, nevertheless appeared in retrospect as something of a last-ditch stand, and more virulent extremisms had existed there before. Despite the revival of the Ku Klux Klan or Goldwater's twenty-five million presidential votes in 1964, and the other ominous rumblings, a relatively inarticulate and only semi-organized Right, did not re-capture the initiative as it had in the era of Joe McCarthy and the anti-Communist crusade of the 1950s.

But far Right sects still abounded; the Ku Klux Klan had success-fully infiltrated the Chicago police; the Minutemen and White Citizens, as well as Birchers and para-military veterans, and other organizations, remained active, and such groups were mostly involved in the Wallace movement; this gave them a constituency the SDS militants could not hope to tap, putting them in direct alliance with many local police forces.

Racial polarization in the 1960s became much more significant in the North, perhaps as a result of the urban revolts, and it was here that Wallace picked up big votes from 1964 onwards. It was here too that police behaviour became indistinguishable in its brutality from that which had symbolized the South's reaction to civil rights.

To translate a minority politics of racist extremism towards a real threat of genocidal mass-politics, a widespread paranoia had to be revived. Several NL segments pursued a strategy which recognized the possibility of a major polarization and right-wing reaction: Weatherman viewed race war not as a tragic possibility, but as 'progress'.[17] In the words of the slogan, people were 'either part of the solution or part of the problem, there is no middle ground'.[18] It was a polarization that could only favour Fascist fantasies on the Right – already underpinned by armed organization and ideology; but not all, in either the black or white movements, were ready to indulge in such death-wish strategies classically repeating the errors of premature polarization made by the German Left in the 1930s.

The great danger in these tactics employed by Weatherpeople, the Panthers and to a lesser extent, by Yippees and various anti-war militants, was that they would provoke a revolution not of the Left, but of the Right. 'To dramatise the threat of violence, where the power to consolidate a revolutionary movement does not exist, is to maximise the opportunities of authoritarian or fascist groups' (April Carter). Moreover, the use of means identical with those of right-wingers tended to cloud the distinction between NL ends and those of Fascists. The prediction of gas chambers and the problem of survival was even extended to white radicals, in the constant talk of 'repression', a type of thinking which led to further calls for armed polarization and defence, feeding paranoia both on the Left and the Right; 'Mobilise against the racists' might be a slogan or strategy for a large and organized section of a society; for the disorganized minorities of the NL, increasingly detached from or shunning liberal allies, it was clearly calculated to bring disaster.

Just as in 1964, the preparations in Mississippi against Freedom Summer had given the impression of totalitarian efficiency,[19] there was now increasing support for a violent official response such as that which greeted the ghetto rebellions. In 1968, Ronald Reagan talked of a bloodbath in California, and Wallace announced to a cheering audience 'we ought to turn this country over to the police for two or three years and everything will be all right' – such was the reflex of a nation, traditionally violent, brutalized and divided by a savage war.

What made the Rightist movement most threatening to the NL however, was its relation with the forces of social control – the police and the National Guard; the politicization of even the most 'professional' police forces in America was a relatively new phenomenon. The Right-wingers who carried bumper-stickers on their cars, 'support your local police' were celebrating a political marriage of potentially outstanding significance, between 'law-and-order' and right-wing ideas.

In Oppenheimer's view, the time was approaching when many police forces would no longer enforce the law against the right-wing or counter-revolutionary groups:

Many law enforcement agencies are infiltrated by the Right and work hand-in-glove with it, by no means exclusively in the South.

Lasch argued that the police could no longer be viewed just as the 'agents of corporate liberalism', but that they had 'developed what can be called a Fascist mentality', emerging as 'a political force in their own right, a force that has to be appeased'.[20]

The strategy of manichean polarization succeeded in cutting off the NL from its constituencies; and whilst a large liberal public opinion on the war had been sustained, it operated decreasingly in touch with the Movement, and widespread opposition to student demonstrations was revealed in opinion polls; fear of the NL represented a further scapegoat to take the place of the domestic Communist conspiracy.[21]

It has been argued that radical violence in these years was in the best interests of the state – since the activists' attacks could be portrayed as offensive, initiated by the Movement without just cause. The NL, far from pre-empting the Establishment's violence, found it already prepared, and increasingly, police were equipping themselves to specifically handle urban disturbances.[22] Even in England, where almost no armed challenge existed, the government's counter-insurgency plans were well developed under the guidance of Brigadier Kitson.[23] The attempt to meet the state and the agencies of control on their own ground, appeared only to strengthen its armouries and its resolve.[24] Many radicals were convinced that any attempt by the NL to reach parity with police departments or the National Guard was a road to inevitable disaster.

In the second half of the 1960s, new ingredients appear: a more highly armed but less disciplined police, acting with greater zeal than necessary; the increasingly indiscriminate use of tear-gas or CS; the gross over-reactions, indiscriminate clubbings (often beating media people and bystanders), the loss of any recognizable discipline, constituting veritable 'police riots'.[25]

This escalation of police violence can be documented from the Berkeley situation; the use of flying wedges of police with batons was first used in front of troop trains to 'protect' them against nonviolent VDC actions in 1965. The following year they were used at the Berkeley campus to charge lines of demonstrators trying to block exits of buses of arrestees. In each case, obstructors were beaten to the ground to clear a path – in the latter case into the path of the vehicles. This use of clubs against unarmed demonstrators, initially terrifying to spectators, became normal practice in following years, and it was accompanied by increasingly selective, violent, and often arbitrary arrests. VDC leaders were beaten and handcuffed during the 1966 actions. In the street confrontations of 1968, massive violence was used to clear the streets; tear-gas was widely used (even from helicopters), there were numerous charges of brutality and an undoubted police riot developed; all restraint disappeared, police hurled rocks from buildings, threw people through windows, and threatened to shoot.[26] Finally in the 1969 People's Park episode, weapons were used and one demonstrator was killed.

The reaction of the authorities throughout this period became more violent and the flouting of normal procedure more contemptuous; as the battles became more bloody, the numbers of arrests increased to massive proportions, and curfews were imposed. It was these developments that gave substance to fears of a developing police state, reinforcing an imagery of repression.

Faced by such a possibility, confrontationism and provocation tactics looked imitative, a revolutionary pose, and irresponsible and dangerous to many critics on the Left (even the Maoists now condemned such adventures). The nonviolent actionists caught in the middle, between two tactics, advocated continued action in the streets, but of a less provocative, more communicative kind, which could expose the system without any loss of political understanding, and yet be less threatening to the potentially repressive forces.

Other critics stressed the growing isolation of the NL (even though it might be actually expanding numerically). They argued that the movement had never been in any position to make violent revolution, and was in any case still a minority even within its 'own' constituencies of youth, students, blacks and the poor communities. They drew the conclusion that the main need of the NL was for allies.

Repression and the New Left

In the later stages of its development, the crisis and decline of the NL was often rationalized as the results of government repression. This was particularly so in America and Germany where the Old Left saw its own history in terms of the oppression and persecution of itself and its predecessors and projected it on to its successors. In America, the Haymarket affair, Sacco and Vanzetti, the Rosenbergs and the victims of McCarthyism were part of a legend of 'why the Left had failed'. Such a martyrology is hard to judge objectively[27] – but by the 1960s, it was no longer a predominant factor.

Whilst various forms of overt repression slowed the movement's growth and at certain points – for example the selective and often violent arrests of Committee of 100 members in England and the brutality and official harassment of Mississippi Freedom Summer – actually created temporary reverses, on the whole such explicit action tended to strengthen rather than weaken the response. It was police actions, in the Southern towns, that stimulated the civil rights movement, and later, in the ghettoes provoked urban conflagrations.

The student movements in particular were stimulated by the presence of police on campus and as has been seen, the escalation of police actions at Berkeley and Columbia were the prelude to further radicalization and increased student militancy.[28] What the Establishment had not realized was that police actions and arrests in a university would lead in a few hours to strike demands for student power. There was a traditional antipathy (not only in America) to police on campus – where a notion of 'sanctuary' prevailed: and whether it was at Berkeley or Nanterre, Columbia or the LSE, the breach of this privilege was a sure recipe for outrage.

Police excess had a similar effect elsewhere. The Provos grew directly from reaction to police repression in Amsterdam in 1965, and the police killing of Benno Ohnesorg in Berlin sparked off the German extra-parliamentary opposition. Dutschke's near-assassination in 1968 further radicalized and broadened the German SDS.

But whether civil liberties in America had been deeply threatened by McCarthyism or not, the NL emerged in the shadow of its aftermath. The fear of repression remained, especially in the universities where Loyalty Oath dismissals were recent memories, and massive demonstrations against the HUAC and the execution of Chessman were part of the earliest political memories of movement leaders. This nervousness was borne out by the fact that, despite the relaxed tensions after the McCarthyism and Loyalty Oath controversies of the 1950s, the expression of latent dissent was slow to emerge.[29]

But as the 1960s progressed and the movement grew and gained confidence, federal investigation by HUAC or other committees in America became a form of accolade or diploma of merit for movement organizations. Such investigative bodies were no longer taken so seriously. Indeed it can be argued that by the middle 1960s, both overt and covert repression was declining, and SDS felt deeply flattered when Attorney General Katzenbach ordered an official investigation of SDS in 1965 for its anti-war activities. When Reagan, with extreme Right-wing support and on an anti-students' rights platform, became Governor, he immediately called for an official investigation of the campus (with the support of the administration), which merely confirmed Berkeley's status as a radical centre.

So valuable were such official moves towards repression that the Movement increasingly sought such confrontations and investigations in the later 1960s, whether through civil disobedience in the civil rights demonstrations and draft-resistance or through provocation, street-confrontations, and armed self-defence ventures. Each time that the state or the local Sheriff's department acted, it seemed to act clumsily and too late, often bringing more publicity and more recruits to the Movement as a result.

One of the great virtues of such quasi-repression was that it brought press and public attention often previously denied the Movement. For the main and worst forms of repression faced by the Movement was covert and implicit rather than overt physical force; censorship and selective reportage had been the peculiar form which 'one-dimensional tolerance' had taken *vis-à-vis* the early peace and civil rights movement. It continued to suggest that despite the increasing readiness of the state in Western societies to physically repress, it was predominantly through ideological means that it maintained its monopoly of power.[30]

Establishment control of the media had been a major factor in hampering and distorting the development of the NL since the 1950s. For these reasons, the NL grew with a deep distrust of the over-thirties press, radio and TV.[31] From the start, even sympathetic younger journalists were treated with circumspection. In the early days of the student movement, the press took a near hysterical anti-student position; it tended to accept the press releases of university administrations without question.[32] At Berkeley an information office was set up to smear the movement by inaccurate information about its political character and actions; and to prove the strike 'had failed' Kerr put out several demonstrably false charges.[33] Equally, as has been seen, the peace movement had had a bad press in the 1958–63 period, with the blackout or vicious reportage of movement activity and of issues that the NL and peace movement had felt important. In Germany this resulted in campaigns against the Springer press.[34]

Such treatment had substantial impact on CND in England; unprinted letters and articles, editorial bias, and censorship, created the 'conspiracy of silence', that was remarkably blatant and coincided with a government and official press campaign to suppress CND arguments.[35] This blackout, which had attended CND from its inaugural and unreported mass meeting of February, 1958, was reinforced by the closing down of channels hitherto open to minority views and by the inherent disadvantages of the radical media; as movement militancy increased, this worsened. Intimidation, the use of the Official Secrets Act, phone-tapping, agents provocateurs, planted evidence, planted weapons, physical assault and harsh sentences increased as the Committee of 100 grew, and the flimsiness of the whole 'democratic' façade which needed to give its deterrent this sort of protection, became apparent with it. It was a measure of the increasing seriousness with which a liberal establishment viewed any threats to the American alliance, as 'treasonable activity'.

But the Committee of 100 experience also revealed what became obvious later with the student Left: a relatively small amount of repression was sufficient to deter the young, the professional or the middle class who had indeed much to lose. 'They had', comments one Committee activist,[36]

examinations to pass, jobs to keep, mortgage payments to make and marriage partners and children's wishes and interests to be taken into consideration.

The NL in Germany suffered repression rather earlier and rather more harshly than elswhere: the combination of police brutality, press distortion (the Springer monopoly had much to do with the repressive atmosphere) and new and harsh 'Emergency Laws' suggested continuities with German authoritarianism of an earlier era, and confirmed that the Cold War hangover was still strongest here. The self-consciously 'extra-parliamentary' nature of the opposition was in part a result of this situation.

Whilst one cannot accept repression as a primary explanation for the demise of the NL, certain sections of it did suffer fatal experiences: the jailing of anti-war leaders in Britain in the early 1960s, and in America at the end of the decade, *were* major setbacks. The Panthers were finally victims of their own provocation strategy and were run to ground in an excessively ruthless strategy of police raids, in which their active membership was decimated. The hippies were particularly acutely harassed in the counter-cultural ghettoes.

But worst threatened of all were active groups in isolated or remote communities such as those of the deep South, Texas or the midwest. Out of the public eye, local terror could reach frightening dimensions: the legendary violence of the Mississippi police, of Bull Connor and Ross Barnett, the use of electric cattle prods on CNVA marchers in Georgia (which became widespread), of dogs, clubs, hoses *et alia*, showed that sanctions were not left to extremist groups and individuals, and typified the organized brutality that defended segregationism, and which had caused some to turn to guns.

A clear example of this is given by the experiences of the day and night anti-war vigil at Port Chicago, California (1965–8); although only thirty miles from the Bay Area, the naval weapons station was isolated enough to make Vietnam demonstrators acutely vulnerable. At night the nonviolent vigilers were often attacked, beaten senseless and even maimed, by a local vigilante group who harassed the vigil. By day arrests and beatings of demonstrators continued. Over sixty arrests occurred in a single mass-blockade. The vigil's rest house was once burnt, and twice wrecked, by incensed hostile locals and marines who viciously assaulted the pickets. By 1968, the vigil itself was tiring, and this treatment was taking its toll, and the demonstration was no longer continuous; the commune from which it was run had been forced to move several miles away for safety. Nevertheless, this was a pioneer effort in directly confronting the points of delivery for Vietnam, and withstood immense repression.

To draft-resistance the state responded as it had so often done before, with selective action, scapegoating, harassment, selective arrests such as those of Spock, Coffin, Goodman in 1967, conspiracy charges, and yet refusal to prosecute most of those who claimed complicity. There was of course always a considerable tension between this principled core of the draft-resistance movement that was willing to face jail – in fact to turn itself in – and those who wanted to avoid arrest and punishment whenever and wherever possible. Such a dilemma clearly linked the Resistance to Anarchist experiences, resulting for many in the enforced or voluntary emigration of perhaps hundreds of thousands of young Americans.[37] The Spock indictments in January 1968 represented a further escalation in the attack on draft-resistance, and it became clear that the call-up was to be used politically, as a sanction.

Particularly amongst the more politically inclined draft-resisters, there was an attempt to develop, like anarchistic movements before them, including the Committee of 100, techniques of reducing the sacrifice of the individual act; these included sanctuary, complicity, collective action, collective leadership and refusal to accept arrest.

These examples of 'repressive' measures against the peace movement illustrate the way in which state action against those who disobey its laws (many argued that the draft laws were themselves repressive and punitive) can be complemented by the individual actions of 'outraged' citizens like those on the Port Chicago Vigil, who take the law into their own hands.

Much repression was of course of this kind, carried on by private citizens outside the law – actual or attempted assassinations, beatings, bombings and sackings of left-wing and peace headquarters, assaults on demonstrators and threats of violence: these became part of the day-to-day expectations of the NL. The wire-tapping and mail interception seems mostly to have been official however, though examples of private sabotage also occur from time to time (e.g. the destruction of mail). Drug and other charges (often spurious) against Movement personnel were often results of citizen informers.

Few of these actions against the Movement were commonly accepted as repression, first because it was 'official' – often merely the enforcement by state or federal agencies of enacted laws, e.g. the punishment of civil disobedience in the case of principled draft-resistance – or second because it was not 'official'! Yet both forms of coercion were part of a chain of repression in the view of the NL, not least because of a police force and legal system that operated with local bias, not only in enforcing the law and in turning a blind eye to vigilante action, but by actually acting in an openly oppressive and partisan fashion, as it did in the North as well as in Mississippi. It made little difference whether it had tacit approval from the state (as over Vietnam) or not (as over race).

Biased law enforcement, a marked characteristic of the South in the civil rights movement, was also a hallmark of the later crackdowns on the white and student Left. The FBI was no ally in such situations. During the systematic subversion of the Civil Rights Bill, state devices were used to prevent registration of black voters in the South. The FBI dragged its feet, and Bobby Kennedy was hamstrung in attempts to enforce the legislation. A further constant form of curtailment of ordinary rights of convocation and protest were the bans and ordinances which greeted almost every march during the peace and civil rights period (including even CND marches in England) and was still markedly evident at the time of the Chicago mobilization in 1968.[38]

A further form of subtle harassment that the NL consistently suffered was job insecurity – threats of firing or actual dismissal, as in the case of a number of academics.[39] Students too put their livelihood at risk when they were expelled or suspended. Activists in universities were treated much the same as employees in a corporation – sometimes worse – because they had no union, and their legal status, in loco parentis, was vulnerable.

It is interesting to note that when the student movement first emerged, Kerr and the other chief administrators used tactics highly reminiscent of the worst that old-style factory employers have adopted to break strikes and union activity. For example, actions against students were usually selectively repressive.[40] This, and breaches of faith, stimulated protest at the personal stupidity and impersonality of both the administration and its machinery – both human and computer. It would not willingly allow students more power, even if repression had to become more severe, because that would create the possibility of some real autonomy for the university.

The repression which preceded and followed People's Park symbolized the outrage with which the Establishment had seen the growth of a radical community in and around the university. For long the press had assisted the propagation of a conspiracy myth of revolutionary implications in such off-campus developments. In judging this, one has to comprehend the isolation of the Berkeley radical community in the general rightwards drift of the California politics, and the key nature of the campus in relation to the personnel-training and research of the military-industrial establishment.[41]

The ruling class views this pattern with growing alarm. They analyse places like Berkeley as 'red zones', like the ones they attempt to destroy in Vietnam. Universities and urban renewal agencies everywhere are busy moving into and destroying our communities, breaking them up physically. Tens of thousands of kids are harassed, busted, moved on (Hayden).

In Berkeley these attacks represented a new stage in a long-term struggle by various landlords, including the university, to clear out the radical community from the Berkeley area.[42] Authorities had attempted, and often successfully, to clear this housing, replacing it with parking lots, office blocks or blocks of remunerative flats for people or property speculators from outside Berkeley. The university administrators had been slowly winning the wars of attrition.

The years 1968–72 were marked, both in Britain and America, by more consistent harassment and surveillance of radical groups, and in the USA this was reflected in new legislation as it was in Germany; the federal anti-riot law was actively used after 1968 and, foreshadowing Watergate, FBI infiltration began in earnest after Nixon's election.[43] Surveillance, infiltration, phone taps on SDS sharply increased after 'Czechago'.[44]

In the more repressive atmosphere of 1968, engendered by the 'law and order' electoral programmes of the major parties, there were over 1,200 campus student arrests in the late fall; and off-campus many more were picked up. Many administrations, as Berkeley had until 1964, continued to curtail political activity on campus, with specific clauses aimed at civil disobedience (i.e. civil rights) and outside student political involvements.

But the decline of SDS had begun long before harassment and repressive surveillance began to take its toll. Even this was no worse than that suffered by other radical organizations in Western democracies. It paled into insignificance beside the treatment of such groups in truly authoritarian regimes of the Left or Right; indeed the main response of the National Office Collective was to encourage such attentions as proving the 'revolutionary character' of SDS's threat to the Establishment; the attentions of a House-investigating committee were positively welcomed. Nevertheless the main effects on the organization as a whole was to strengthen the grip of paranoia, suspicion and scapegoating already predominant in the mood of 1969.[45] One further effect was to make more financial inroads, though internal factors were mainly debilitating in this respect.

As a result of Weatherman activity, there *was* an intensifying political repression, and Americans experienced a more authoritarian atmosphere than for well over a decade and civil liberties in the Nixon era were threatened probably at least as severely as during the McCarthy period of the 1950s. There was an increased manufacture of charges in the post-1968 period, especially those involving drugs, which were seen to help undermine the credibility of political radicals. Even internment, along the lines of the British action in Ireland, was advocated and contemplated.

The sinister nature of the Nixon apparatus had become clearer by 1970 with its support for both official and unofficial harassment and repression; it was significantly slow in disassociating itself from the

National Guard killings at Kent State which brought the total of New Leftists (excluding Panthers and others)[46] who died at official (federal or state) hands during a decade in America to at least eighteen.

Whether real or illusory, such actions affirmed the image of draconic repression in the minds of most radicals, and indeed it symbolized the degree of reaction which followed the NL's decline in America.

15. The New Left and the Old

Waiting in the wings

As has been seen, the initial development of the NL was to a significant extent precipitated by the organizational and theoretical bankruptcy of the Old: 'its destructive factionalism and sectarian infighting'.[1] In the period of the NL's birth, the organized Old Left – especially the Communist parties and the anti-Communist Left, the social democrats – had been in disarray. Anarchism as an organized tradition in North West Europe and the USA was more or less dead. And though the Trotskyites made marginal and temporary advances in the period after 1956, it was probably true that, they repeated 'orthodoxy with an air of fresh discovery'[2] (Gitlin). In America 'denied a native tradition, Marxism or Anarchism considers itself lucky to exist at all'.

With the non-exclusion policy and organizational openness of both the nuclear disarmament movement in Britain, and the NL in America, both Trotskyites and a gradually reviving Communist Party, became more active in the early 1960s. In America it was the post-McCarthyite thaw and the gradual lifting of bans on Communist speakers that made this possible.[3] Indeed the popular front opposition to the HUAC was the opening of a new period for the still tiny CPUSA which later in the 1960s welcomed the rapprochement between the USA and the USSR as helping to legitimate its co-existence line, quite independent of the NL.

But the Communist Party's problems in the USA were not entirely over; a major split had been caused in the peace movement in 1960 when Senator Thomas Dodd accused it of infiltrating SANE.[4] The importance of the civil liberties theme, coupled with democratization of the peace movement, caused a crisis over the question of Communist participation. As in Britain, the fundamental ideological problem of the CP stance hinged on the degree of its independence from Moscow foreign policy relating to Western defence. In the same year that its counterpart in Britain was unobtrusively joining CND, the CPUSA was being purged from the main anti-nuclear organization; this had major repercussions and made exclusionism a key issue, with the CP itself condemning McCarthyism and witchhunts. In Britain this was never an issue, partly because of the late entry of the Communist Party (1960) and its relative unimportance in CND until after 1963. As a portent of things to come (and in response to the purge) the anti-exclusionist youth section of SANE disaffiliated and disbanded in 1962.[5]

SDS, the major organizational expression of the NL, emerged out of exactly these kinds of boundary defining skirmishes between the Old Left and the New. The growing division between them (the Left Social Democrats and the new younger radicals) had partly to do with the insistence of the former on explicit anti-Communist, anti-totalitarian statements; the birth of SDS occurred amidst tense running battles about 'exclusionism' and 'non-exclusionism'. SDS can well be contrasted with YPSL (Young People's Socialist League) to which it was in some senses a successor.

For many in the SPU, YPSL had been too theoretical, too intellectual, too hung-up on the Communist issue, pro and con. The rejection of YPSL's factionalism, the endorsement of participatory democracy and non-exclusionism led SDS into a new politics. As a reaction to Cold War attitudes and sectarianism, SDS had moved against exclusionism, dropping its anti-Communist clause officially in 1965. In the following years, such terms as 'a-Communist' or 'anti-anti-Communist' were typically used to describe SDS's stance.

It is ironic that the NL's prior contact with the bureaucratic rigidities of the anti-Communist Old Left, made it far less critical of the similar rigidities of the bureaucratic fellow-travelling or pro-Moscow Old Left. Undoubtedly the early SDS cult of complete tolerance, unwillingness to suppress dissent, was born of a genuine libertarian spirit, but in its actual expression it did represent both an over-reaction to the legend of McCarthyism and a tendency to favour, rather uncritically, those who had genuinely suffered its persecution.[6]

The advocacy of civil liberties for Communists and peaceful co-existence were still important issues for the early SDS, and some members joined the thousands who demonstrated against the HUAC in San Francisco and elsewhere, but the somewhat naive reactions to Cold War attitudes, exemplified in opposition to the HUAC, in anti-exclusionism, and in the refusal to be drawn into the debate between Communists and anti-Stalinist socialists in the Old Left, inevitably tended to favour the aligned Marxist groups. As a result, such rejection of Cold War anti-Communism, sooner or later meant a fresh willingness to cooperate with supporters of Cuban or Asian Communisms in anti-war demonstrations, which helped create the first major ideological problems in the American NL.

In the ensuing over-compensation for anti-Communist excesses, SDS often developed a sympathetic, uncritical attitude to CP positions, in marked contrast to their obvious antipathy to the Left liberals and the Social Democrats. Even more ironically, the exclusionism actually worked almost in reverse, in relation to both the Moscow and Peking oriented groups, as well as to Trotskyites; Dellinger, Hayden, Lynd and others were quick to welcome PL (Maoist), May Second Movement (M2M, aligned to PL), the DuBois clubs (Moscow Communist), the CP itself, and the Young Socialist Alliance (YSA, Trotskyite) into the SDS anti-war coalition of 1965. Liberal, Social Democratic and mainstream peace groups on the other hand, like SANE, TTP, League for Industrial Democracy (LID) and the NAACP were made to feel unwelcome from the start.

Basically the clash over exclusionism was a clash of two coalitions, involving the competing concepts of coalitionism to the right and to the left of the Movement; a coalition between young radicals, radical pacifists, NL, and Pro-NLF Old Left, on the one hand; and on the other, between a group of left liberals, social democrats, some peace and civil rights leaders and a few other anti-Communist Old Leftists.

The latter's aloofness in part was justified: Stalinist political practice, as well as that of some of those sects on the Left most bitterly opposed to other aspects of Stalinism, was typically to combine a broad external strategy of front groups, coalitions, alliances and popular fronts, with their own internal repressive discipline and control. Tolerance of deviation inside 'the party' was minimal, but outside tactical cooperation with groups to the right was smiled on. A dual personality functioned – split between external tolerance and compromise and internal dogmatism and witchhunts.

In December, 1965, seeing its new openings, the CPUSA etched out a firm cautious policy of approach to the NL:[7]

for too long we have avoided contact with the New Left and held them in contempt, our new policy should be to join struggle with them, whenever it is possible and prudent for us to do so. This does not mean that we can give a blanket guarantee to the NL; in our disagreements with the NL we are confident that we are right. In order to be able to criticize the NL effectively, we must also play the role of trying to bring the NL closer to the other Left groups.

The fears that the American movement would quickly be taken over by the Communists, was unfounded. The process by which the influence, not so much of the CP but of other Marxist splinters and Old Left methods, increased, was a great deal more subtle and probably could not have been prevented by mere exclusionism. And indeed the authoritarianism implicit in the wish to exclude Communists, had tended to rebound.

The history of Marxist sectarianism is the chronicle of small, but resolute, Leninist minorities lingering in the wings of history, waiting for their cue. Such was the case of most of the Marxist groups which were, both sides of the Atlantic, survivals, like the CP, from the 1930s.

Despite the recession of the 1950s, they had not actually died; most importantly they were able to reform their youth groups which were not only more effective levers and modes of entry into the NL, but also in several cases became larger and more influential than their adult counterparts: the Trotskyist Socialist Workers Party (SWP) for example, spawned the Young Socialist Alliance which became fairly sizeable by the 1970s; the Maoist PL formed a youth front organization (M2M) which was initially widely successful; the adult Socialist Party for some years had an active youth counterpart (YPSL) at first quite effective in the peace movement.

The Communist Party itself formed the Du Bois clubs in the early 1960s, which though never outstandingly successful, and eventually wound up, were able in part to develop the bridgeheads with the NL implied in its 1965 policy statement.[8] Like their CP parents (literally in some cases), the Du Bois club members collaborated with those left-liberals believing in re-alignment within the Democratic Party and similar established institutions, including the Labour movement. It was issue-oriented like the rest of the NL, but willing to support liberal candidacies; it also succeeded in making common cause with some elements in SDS in the mid-1960s.

Nevertheless, one should not exaggerate the significance or size of these Old Left youth fragments. The combined membership of all these groups in 1965 – including M2M, PL, YSA, YPSL, Du Bois and the Spartcist splinter from YSA – has been estimated as less than that of SDS (i.e. under 3,000), and certainly with far less influence than SNCC with its hundreds of organizers. On the whole, the Marxist groups throughout the 1960s were less successful than NL groupings in mobilizing mass support. It has been argued that Progressive Labor's decision to abandon M2M and move its members and sympathizers into SDS in 1966 was a confession of this failure to organize an independent mass-base of its own. They were essentially bandwagon jumpers – waiting for a relatively open-ended or non-ideological issue like nuclear weapons, workers' control, civil rights or Women's Liberation to gather momentum before joining in.

Jacobs and Landau in 1966 suggested that for 'the new radicals these political sects of the Old Left of the thirties and forties' were mostly irrelevant 'left-overs', and so indeed they seemed in the context of the early and mid-1960s.[9] But redundant as these 'groupings' may have appeared they played a decisive part in changing the direction of the Movement and precipitating its break-up as well as, in the case of PL and the YSA, surviving long enough to pick up some of the pieces.

In the late 1960s, as the movement floundered, the Old Left itself, particularly the Trotskyite and Maoist versions of it, prospered. Events were working with them; the NL, lacking analysis and theory, lacking vision and identity, turned to them, not always readily but in the belief that this was where serious militancy must lead. Trotskyism, originally an apparent swan-song of the Marxist movements, was able to make renewed contact with the NL as the events of 1968 developed. Its opportunism caught up with the overall drift of the Movement and was able to present itself in its various guises as a logical next step.

The Old Left counter-attacks

The rather complicated dialectic relationship between Old and New Lefts has to be understood in terms of the range of Old Left positions and the changes in attitude to the NL as it grew and as the Old Left itself evolved through various stages. In the early years of the movement, in so far as the NL could be differentiated from the peace and civil rights movements it tended to be ridiculed or ignored, or occasionally patronized by Marxists. There seemed to be some hope that it might just go away, or at least be tolerated as ephemeral. But as SDS gained strength and the peace and black movements grew under NL leadership, the attitudes changed; fiercer attacks on the one hand – attempts at alliance or common fronts on the other. When one failed the other was repeated. The early hope that the NL could be absorbed into Old Left groups or alliances faded, even the belief (as with the NCL and 'New politics' affairs) that some Old/New coalition could be achieved, met with failure. It is at this stage that *infiltration* becomes the dominant tactic.

As each new issue or movement developed, the typical attitude of the Old Left, or sections of it, had been to write it off, or try to strangle it at birth, as 'limited', 'naive', 'reformist', 'single-issue', 'spontaneous', 'irrelevant', 'easily co-opted'. Marxists, including the CP, condemned the ecology issue of the 1970s, just as they had condemned the nuclear weapons issue of the 1960s in these terms. But as soon as it was clear that there was a growing movement, the criticisms would be muted, the bandwagon would be mounted, and a 'correct line' in conformity with a Marxist analysis (on nuclear weapons, ecology, Women's Liberation, participatory democracy, etc.) laid down.

But throughout the 1960s at least one section of the Old Left is always engaged in fierce polemic against the New; whilst it is important to differentiate between the bases of their objections (Social Democrats, Moscow Communists, Maoists and various Trotskyites) many of their criticisms are remarkably similar, both in tone and content. In the early movement the common criticism by all these segments of the NL is of the movement's idealism, moralism, individualism and hopeful optimism. Its personalistic, existential political morality and respect for Camus were chided by Old Left critics as 'self-righteous'. Carmichael's later attacks on these traits in the 'Pepsi generation' echoed such Old Left attacks. However, this moralism revived again in the guise of spiritual renewal in the 1970s, despite the sneers of the Old Left, whose continuing and scathing ridicule had little effect on the main period of growth (1960–5) since it was largely external to the Movement; more-over although many – like Irving Howe – saw moralism and indivi-dualism as the great weakness of the NL, others saw it as its source of strength, even its raison d'être.

The Old Left attitude to NL violence was also selective and oppor-tunist – on the whole, except by PL, in the early 1960s, domestic violence was not openly advocated or encouraged. But on the other hand, none of the Old Left groups would have any truck with pacifism, except in a tactical sense, e.g. such as the support, especially from the CP and Social Democrats, for King and civil rights actions: nearly all of them were ready to endorse military violence abroad.[10] However, during the later 1960s the relative positions of New and Old Left on domestic violence underwent changes: PL tended to turn away from confrontationism and condemn the 'petty bourgeois' violence of SDS after 1969, and generally the Old Left disassociated itself from the 'anarchist' ventures into violence after 1968. But there were exceptions: The New York *Guardian,* hitherto a moderate Old Left journal, leaning towards the Communist Party, began to adopt a more-militant-than-thou attitude, apparently to attract a newer, more radical readership.[11]

Predictably PL and all the other Marxist groups pilloried the NL as ideologically confused, and suggested adoption of their own line as the path to enlightenment. The social democrats were equally scathing about the amorphous ideas of SDS and SNCC. Both to the Left and to the Right the Movement was attacked for its deviation from, or unawareness of, Marxian orthodoxies; for from the CPUSA to the Socialist Party, there were shared framework assumptions about 'class' and domestic strategy that were the basis of such denunciations.

The Old Left reaction to 'Student Syndicalism' was predictable: here was a movement of the privileged, seeking more privilege for themselves instead of turning to those who needed help most. Whilst its proponents argued: 'You can't communicate to other communities until you have successfully communicated to your own', the Old Left could not recognize that the university was no longer the old élite enclave of bourgeois privilege of its orthodox imagination, but a way-station for over half the population under twenty.

At different points, the black movement too, especially Black Nationalism, came under fire from Marxist and Social Democratic groups. Cultural Nationalism did not ride easily with universalistic Socialist doctrines[12] of brotherhood and solidarity, and most of the Old Left groups were fairly opportunistic in their relations with Malcolm-X and Carmichael; but in the later 1960s there was intensi-fying criticism of SNCC and the Panthers for their 'racist adventurism', 'isolationism' and 'narrow nationalism' – criticisms that had been reserved for the Muslims previously, but which even PL endorsed by 1968.

Though the Left liberals were constantly in dialogue and debate with the movement, they were never quite sure if they were taking it too seriously. There was a liberal ambivalence about the NL:[13]

The problem is not in determining how much weight to assign the good as against the bad elements embraced by the Movement, but in deciding whether to take it seriously at all ... [perhaps] ... the New Left will not in fact make history, but rather will turn out to be a symptom of history, a fleeting moment in which radical 'energies' [will be] released into the larger society.

One important distinction between the approaches of the various groups – is that whereas the aligned Old Left Marxist groups were if anything the more biting in their critiques they were still willing to work with and if possible within, NL organizations, whereas the social democrats and left liberals mainly kept aloof after 1964–5. Progressive Labor constantly attacked the early NL for its moralism and idealism, condemning nonviolence, civil rights, reformism, student protest and traditional 'peace' orientations; yet it was deeply implicated in the Movement, constantly inserting its critiques into the programmes of SDS and the VDC. Such activity had the effect of driving a further wedge between the NL and the traditional peace and civil rights movements, thus precluding coalitions with liberals and social democrats.

The social democrats, many of them in America still nominally Marxist, were most concerned with the movement's anti-liberalism; its willingness to throw out Dewey and J. S. Mill and the tradition of 'humane tolerance'; its willingness to work in harness with the 'totalitarian' Left and its failure to criticize political tyrannies in the Eastern bloc. This rapprochement, especially *vis-à-vis* Cuba and Vietnam, created a deep fissure in the mid-1960s, between SDS and its former allies and sponsors. On the other hand, Marxists and Western liberals continued to find much common technocratic ground in endorsing the advance of the centralizing nation state, in place of the 'backwardness' of the decentralized, peasant-based or tribal society.

The new sympathy of the Movement for rural people and pre-industrial forms of life – expressing a solidarity and identification with non-Western culture – when it developed its more explicitly anti-industrial orientation, naturally alienated the more traditional Left, with its overwhelming faith in technology and progress.

As with the subsequent concern with conservation issues and environmental crises, most Old Left ideologues wrote them off as a distraction from the main issues. During People's Park, when despite criticism by the hardline Left, the ecological aspect became paramount, the Marxists typically stood aside, labelling such emphasis as 'co-optation'.

But above all, the Marxists condemned the counter-culture's idealization of the rural pace and integration of life, the existential symmetry and ecological balance of pre-capitalist and pre-industrial culture. Many Old Leftists dismissed this as an entirely romantic projection by discontented bourgeois; the fact that most peasants did in fact exist in a relative isolation and detachment from, indeed estrangement from, modern business, industry and state was a sign of backwardness.

For other critics NL romanticism lay more in identification of this society and this life-style with the new revolutionary leaderships and with the leading military resistance organizations which mobilized peasant societies as if these were anti-industrial. As Irving Howe remarked, the belief that the Third World military leaderships were dedicated to preserving peasant society was illusory, the NL was deluded in seeing any anti-industrial impulse in these movements:[14]

They fail to see that such leaders of these underdeveloped countries, who in their eyes represent spontaneity and anarchic freedom, are themselves, perhaps unavoidably, infused with the same mania for industrial production.

The social democrats and traditional aligned Leftists also shared a deep scepticism about the NL's extra-parliamentarism, its tendency to flirt with anarchism, and worst of all its 'romantic defeatism'. The Old Left's insistent need for, and claims of, 'victory' set it off clearly from the element of resignation or the mindless activism of many movement projects which, like the Provo experiment: 'Realizes that it will lose in the end, but cannot pass up the chance to make at least one more heartfelt attempt to provoke society'.[15]

The Newark project (NCUP) in particular was presented in such a light.[16] This style was condemned by Old Left critics like Howe as 'the dismissal of society'. Deploring what he conceived of as the defeatism of such 'withdrawal' in extra-parliamentary action, Howe argued:[17]

Movements that are powerful, groups that are self-confident do not opt out of society; they live and work within society to transform it.

It was this, and the elevation of popular life-style which also drew sharp criticism from 'hard Left' groups, like PL, who saw it as a fundamental weakness of the community organizing work of SDS.

In part, the decentralism, communalism, and, despite the Left's dislike of the term, 'pluralism' of the new movement, set it clearly apart from 'democratic centralism' and orthodoxy of the Old. The tension between the need for collective action towards institutional change and the imperatives of moral militancy was an illusion cultivated by the Old Left, to hinder any alliance with the counter-culture, and prevent any final rejection of its own styles and tactics in favour of the counter-institutional scenario.

Seen by the Old Left as backward-looking and romantic, refused even the status of relevant experiment, communes and other alternatives were dismissed as a strategy of change that had predated Marxist–Leninism, and were thus historically irrelevant. As for the developing youth culture, and the counter-communities, for the most part the Old Left groups were equally contemptuous. The radical-hippy alliance represented a conception of the young and middle class as both oppressed and anti-bourgeois: a perspective that was unacceptable to the Old Left.

For all its equivocations over exclusionism, there was thus a fundamental difference in style between SDS and the Old Left groupings. Up to 1967, SDS embodied all the elements rejected by these groups; it was experimental, activist, spontaneous, expressive and personalistic. It was a balance of pragmatism and idealism, well within the American radical tradition, that led it to its 'anti-anti-Communist' stance. This was typified by its attempt to avoid the tyrannies of theory and categories in sectarian Left debate. There was a noticeable tension between Old and New Left members within coalitions, not just over goals but over methods and style. One can detect a clear difference between Old and New members over the use of Marxist language and doctrine, the constant references to seemingly irrelevant and distant debates, or the insistent reiteration of 'correct' slogans.

Lipset comments that many Old Leftists and Social Democrats found the general flouting of conventional norms with regard to dress and behaviour by many in the NL, difficult to accept, and suggests an urge amongst the latter to be 'as outrageous as possible' and mentions Lenin's condemnation of such behaviour.[18] With the partial exception of PL in its earlier period (i.e. the M2M, 1965–6) and to a lesser extent Du Bois, the Old Left groups consistently attacked the counter-culture, especially its drug use and permissive sexuality, even long hair and unconventional clothes, as 'escapism'. The developing NL alliance with hippies and drop-outs was thus condemned as making common cause with 'bourgeois degeneracy'. Straightest of the groups was the YSA which, despite its organization of street confrontations in communities like Berkeley, was unable to make any inroads on the cultural milieu of the street people, finding them difficult to organize, and impossible to discipline on demonstrations.

The NL activists who saw common ground between themselves and the hippy rejection of middle-class values, were alienated both from the Old Left life-style and the puritanism of its internal codes.

For the Old Left it had been largely irrelevant whether you lived the revolution or not – any ethical content in socialist action largely faded after 1917 along with the more conscious rejection of bourgeois values.[19] Certainly the Old Left had often stressed the priority of structural change, and even expressed an anti-voluntarist belief in the irrelevance of personal change of life-style. Irving Howe criticized white intellectuals who 'bemoan the desire of black people to enjoy the fruits of American society as it now is',[20] and none of the older Marxist groups could give support to alternative modes of 'non-bourgeois living'.

Indeed the Old Left groups denied its necessity; yet, with one foot within established institutions such as universities, this had been a basic problem for the NL and student groups; however comprehensive the embrace of left sects and parties, they could not provide a personal or domestic environment that was a genuine alternative. In fact, groups like the Communist Party, on the contrary, endorsed a life-style in which domestic and political affairs were separate, with the former being even more bourgeois, conformist and puritanical – if not actually suburban – than the latter.

Within the movement, in the later 1960s, the communal house could act as a refuge and a cushion against shocks of political and cultural withdrawal and became a crucial component in the NL. Since such urban communes rarely saw themselves as directly conflicting with the state, to that extent, they were often condemned by the orthodox. But whilst they were rarely seen, even when activists from NL groups began to join them (especially in the period *after* 1969), as actual 'foci' of revolutionary change, it was conceded that it was sometimes 'necessary to retreat, to de-totalize first, in order to advance'[21] and then 're-structure' society.

But the strongest attacks from the Old Left predictably came against the fusion of NL politics with the apparent 'anti-politics' of the counter-culture. Such a synthesis merely reinforced the withdrawal, the idealism, and the defeatism inherent in the earlier movement. The fatalism and resignation indicated by Norman O. Brown's view of revolution as 'not a slate wiped clean, but a revolving cycle'[22] implied the rejection of an idea of progress; the mystical idea of recurrence that seemed embedded in hippy ethics was an anathema to all forms of Marxism. The mystique of the imagination proclaimed by Situationists and the Paris rebels, the Yippee phrase 'revolution for the hell of it', or the widespread endorsement of rebellion as 'theatre' were an affront to political orthodoxy of any kind.[23]

Such an attitude – often implying almost the dissolution of politics – quickly drew sharp attacks from the Old Left who accused the hippies of substituting happenings for programme. Indeed such attacks had been initiated in the early 1960s in relation to the expressive psychologies of Fromm, Goodman and Marcuse. One critic accused Goodman, in his search for a natural, spontaneous culture, of laying the 'theoretical foundation of the great dropout' from a society which cannot tolerate such free play of imagination, direct awareness, impulsiveness and self-assertiveness within its regimented routines.

However, not all Marxists attacked the alternative society or the innovations in life-styles: and some fairly hard-nosed politicoes rallied to their defence; as has been seen Stuart Hall, one of the founders of the English NL (first editor of *NLR*) was one; Julius Lester, the black political critic, was another; he commented:

Smug self-righteous NL ideologues limply put down the yippees for being politically immature and irresponsible . . . [but] . . . this is America not Russia, China and Cuba, and in America maybe, just maybe, the baths to revolution will be clothed not only in guerilla's uniform, but peads and incense.

Thus the basic style of the Movement at every stage tended to derive from within a frame that was essentially alien to Old Left approaches – at Berkeley an ostensibly political strike for student power ended, in the words of its own leadership, in a 'mood of stoned euphoria' and the singing of the 'Yellow Submarine'; the Old Left leaders left the final meeting bewildered. The following day, its resolution was printed with remarks, a very yellow submarine and a cut-out lone-ranger mask to wear to classes, with the legend:

And so we made a resolution which broke into song; and we adopt for today this unexpected symbol of our trust in the future, and our longing for a place fit for us all to live in. Please post, especially where prohibited. We love you.

It was decided, in the words of Mario Savio, 'if we can't beat them down', to 'blow their minds': this might be 'cultural revolution', but certainly not along Chinese lines.

The Old Left takes over

In the main, the Old Left of the 1960s does represent a continuity with the groups of the 1930s, whereas the NL, at least before 1969, does not. It was said of the latter that in comparison with this earlier Left, the NL was both less dogmatic and less exclusively political in commitment,[24] 'focused from the outset on issues of self-determination and autonomy rather than material security . . . New Leftists were rebelling against both the ideology of historical inevitability and the routinised bureaucratic activity' of the Old Marxists.[25]

Certainly this is true of the early movement; of the NL of the Port Huron Statement and after, expressing its faith in 'no sure formulae, no closed theories'. And to some extent even in the complexities of the crisis of the late 1960s, this heterogeneity together with an anti-systemic, de-totalizing response to closed systems of thought, is retained. But overall the tone has changed; the 'avoidance of dogmatism, and in an extreme form the outright rejection of any ideology', is replaced by a collage of dogmas, or a transition from one sure formula to the next. The anti-authoritarianism is less confident; the 'basic opposition to the Communist system' of Port Huron has long since been abandoned, and in its place there are even those, conspicuous in

SDS by 1968 and 1969 who, in Oglesby's phrase, believed that Stalin-ism was 'Right on'. The search for 'truly democratic alternatives' seems to be largely forgotten. The humanism and scepticism of infallibility which had made Camus a movement mentor earlier in the decade has largely disappeared. The stress on choice or conscience has become identified with certain wings of the draft-resistance movement, rather than with the Movement as a whole. As a participant reminisced, 'our arguments became more and more stale, parched and withered trans-plants of the divisions amongst the Old Bolsheviks ... our self-importance was grafted onto its opposite – insecurity'.[26]

These changes have been largely located in terms of the movement's failure to develop its own central themes and insights. But such changes also have to be related to the activities of Old Left groupings who both helped to create this crisis of identity, and then actively altered the core identity of the movement as they entered the growing vacuum of ideas and organization.

In any attempt to understand this Old Left takeover, emphasis should not be placed on the counterpoint of the NL with the Old Left's ideas and theories. Rather, the subtle intertwining of each has to be unravelled in the relationships between NL projects – organizations, demonstrations and movements – and the organized Old Left (or in some cases Old liberal) sects and formations. In some cases these fuse and become hard to disentangle, but as has been argued, the main operations of most of them *can* be distinguished from the history of a NL as such, and an estimate made of their impact on it.

There is of course a direct connection between the nature of Old Left ideology and analyses and their organizational tactics and style in relating to the NL. A number of attempts have been made to differ-entiate between a libertarian and authoritarian tendency in the Marxist tradition;[27] and connections consistently made between the NL and Anarchism.[28] In order to clarify these relationships in terms of methods, a set of ideal types can help contrast the organizational style and political emphases of the Old and NL as they confronted each other initially and before they became confused. (See Table 3 overleaf.)

Such a tabulation helps to suggest the initially clear disparities in procedure and orientation of the New and Old Lefts. But it was a difference which steadily disappeared with the transition after 1967 towards an older Left style. Some New Leftists blamed the transition on external pressure:

The IS clubs, Du Bois, PL and the YSA have pressured us into adopting their style and language; movements abroad have conned us into identi-fying with an idealised version of their struggles.

Other analyses stressed internal factors as precipitating the shift, including the limitations of participatory democracy: whatever the source, such changes brought the movement closer to the Old Left's

Table 3   *The Old and New Lefts: a typology*

Old Left*	New Left
Authoritarian outlook, organization, etc.:	Libertarian outlook, organization, etc.:
'The old parties were highly centralized, disciplined, organizations with clear lines of decision making.[29]	'The New Left was above all a highly decentralized movement that put its emphasis especially in its early years, on participatory democracy.'[30]
Intellectual orientation to theory and analysis: reflected in importance of sectarian debate, 'correct positions', etc. Political training and education stressed.	Anti-intellectualism, suspicion of theory. Spontaneism, cult of activism, anti-sectarianism: theory to arise from practice. Tolerance of deviant positions.
Importance of class analysis; ancestral faith in organized 'working class', its culture and its institutions – parties and trades unions (plus immigrant organization in USA).	Search for new agencies of change: women, poor, blacks, students and college educated (white and black), young people, Third World peasantry, etc.
Economistic; stress on materialistic progress and technology. Cultural emphasis weak.	Stress on cultural factors, idealism, anti-materialism, scepticism of progress via technology.
Tendency to be culturally 'square' or philistine.[31] Critical of counter-culture; 'straight' life-style accepted.	Openness to cultural innovation[32] and experiment; alternative society, communes, *et al.*
Repressive attitude to self and others. Opposition to sexual expression, drugs. Puritanism within Left organizations.	Permissive and experimental attitude to sexuality and drugs, etc.

proclivity for vindictiveness and personal brutality, as well as the 'institutionalized hatred' in many class perspectives.

Initially, both in SNCC and SDS, NL style was opposed to manipulation, élitism, and Stalinism's 'use of slander as a political ploy'.[33] Nevertheless, through sheer persistence, Old Left factions tended to gain ascendancy in many *ad hoc* committees and coalitions. The Old Left, however small its representation, could gain the initiative in such situations; and if not the Old Left itself, then its organizational techniques or crude plebiscitarianism could replace NL methods.

* The left-hand column is a summary of the dominant characteristics of most of the Old Left groups active in this period – all of them Marxist of one kind or another. The right-hand column summarizes some typical characteristics of the movement of the NL, comprehending both libertarian Marxists, Anarchists and many others. Of course such diagrams exaggerate the separateness of the Old and the New, and the coherent identity of each; the picture is in fact more complicated.

As a number of SDS activists and peace people discovered, non-exclusionism was fine in principle and as long as the group sustained a core identity and some ideological precepts – but in an amorphous and quickly expanding movement it could be fatal. Those not experienced or trained were at the mercy of Old Left formulae – often reinforced by media attention. By the late 1960s, suffering this lack of clear selection criteria and unaware of the contradictions implied, white radicals drifted back towards the political style of the Old Left, ostensibly to defend the ideals of the New.

As participatory democracy, like nonviolence, came to seem the product of naive early stage of protest before the magnitude of the movement's task was fully recognised, more authoritarian and centralised styles took over.[34]

In this context of crisis, the dedicated, ideologically based activity of a Marxist–Leninist caucus eventually brought some rewards. The Old Left groups were predominantly focused on power; the control of the meeting, the rally or the demonstration; the right or chance to determine the content of leaflets and posters; the power to decide slogans to be used, or the agenda to be followed, or the line to be taken. It was an orientation towards in-fighting; and they wished to define all Movement activity in terms of locating power and confronting it.

But Old Left groups which tried Leninist infiltration tactics often ran into considerable problems; in the first place, NL groupings were often too amorphous to take over; the juxtaposition of centralized Old Left groups and a more decentralized NL, created an organizational tension that often worked to the latter's advantage. PD did not favour the long-term control of the faction, which were often left holding a disappearing baby.[35] It has also been remarked that from 1965–7, often many of those who were supposed to be infiltrating, influencing, even taking over NL groupings on behalf of an Old Left sect, were in fact converted the other way. As a further example, a number of active militants left PL in this period to give their first loyalties to SDS or the Resistance, or the Free Universities.

But in the years 1968–70, the tendency turns the other way; PL and YSA in particular, begin to gain recruits from the NL, just as did the IS and to a lesser degree the IMG, in England.[36] Although in Paris in 1968, despite the claims of every Marxist–Leninist group and tendency, none of the Stalinists, Maoists or Trotskyists actually initiated the events or controlled them, the Trotskyist 'Jeunesse Communiste Revolutionaire' (JCR) *was* highly influential. For example the JCR, able to insert its critique of Soviet Communism into the ideological ambience of the revolt, had limited organizational success, though in the long run it was the Anarchist tendencies which gained most from the May events, just as the Communist Party, heading off the revolution, probably gained least in terms of recruits from the NL.

But the CP was influential in the short-term negative sense, even if it lost ground to all its rivals. For the Movement Old Left takeovers, especially by the CP, had earlier come to signify domestication, staleness and reform, even repression, and such incorporation of the CP represented, very clearly in the view of Parisian student leaders, an 'objective anti-Communism'.

But despite the ambiguity of its role in Paris, the years 1968–9 marked a new peak for Trotskyism both in Britain and America; it became the most popular of the Marxist options, as represented by groups like the YSA/SWP and the Independent Socialists in America and IS and IMG in Britain. In their claims to the authorship of the French events, in their co-optation of the memory of figures like Malcolm-X and support for Robert Williams, in their timing of sympathy demonstrations and solidarity with movements abroad (Cuba, Vietnam, Paris, etc.), the YSA/SWP showed a brilliant opportunism which paid dividends in the atmosphere of 1968.

Despite its criticism of Russia and China as bastardized Marxist states, YSA was able to identify with at least the 'permanent revolution' aspect of Maoism; moreover the Trotskyite idea of permanent revolution, however varied its interpretation, had a definite appeal for the NL itself. In December 1968, the YSA convention was attended by over 800 delegates, reflecting a growth expanding into the 1970s.[37] YSA's success in recruitment partly reflected its active work in the anti-war movement, playing an important role in the mobilization committees, but mainly reflected the growing problems of the NL.

For also, of all the Old Left groupings, the YSA was most wedded to the 1930s' tactics of takeover and infiltration. Not only were such tactics not alway successful; they could be the 'kiss of death'. For example, despite their criticism of the Castro regime, YSA showed consistent sympathy for the Cuban revolution: in 1961 the parent body (SWP) took over the 'Fair Play for Cuba Committee' – previously under PL influence; and within two years they had unintentionally destroyed it. YSA's techniques are worth comparing with two other examples of Old Left infiltration and attempted takeover in the NL: PL in SDS[38] and, during the decline of the English peace movement, the Communist Party in CND (analysed previously). It is significant that in all three cases the Old Left entered where the NL either feared to lead, or was incapable of doing so.

Undoubtedly the Old Left's most successful arena of operations in both Britain and America was that of the peace and anti-Vietnam war movements. As early as 1965 the Trotskyites attempted to take over the National Co-ordinating Committee (NCC) 'to end the war in Vietnam', in Washington. But as has been seen, it was the NL, especially SDS with its large demonstrations of 25,000 in 1965, which had made much of the initial running in the Vietnam issue. After June 1965, however, seeing itself as a multi-issue organization, SDS refused to retain the leadership of the anti-war movement. Though it continued to take a lot of initiatives in campus peace politics, promoting the issues of the draft, imperialism and university complicity in the war amongst students, it was the YSA which tended to take over the initiative nationally from SDS after 1966. PL and the CP also played significant though less prominent roles in the Vietnam protest movement.

The Old Left – including the Du Bois clubs, YSA and the CP had dominated at the outset an organization called the Student Strike for Peace Committee, which helped to organize the Vietnam week of 1967. Whereas the pacifists and traditional peace movement were associated with the more successful Spring Mobilization Committee set up separately after the SDS demonstrations of 1965. The Vietnam Week rallies of April 1967 showed the success of the popular front tactics, with over 20,000 participants and addresses by King and other celebrities.

YSA combined united front tactics with infiltration techniques; in Berkeley by 1966, together with the parent body (SWP), it had gradually taken control of the Vietnam Day Committee, when VDC was already past its peak, and a Trotskyite majority of one on the steering committee was enough to wreck the organization. Although the role of Trotskyites in the Student Mobilization Committee was by 1968 equally destructive, the decentralized nature of such national coalitions helped to offset the worst effects of these attempted takeovers.[39]

Nevertheless, the YSA remained at the centre of peace movement faction fights for over five years. In late 1967, after bitter caucusing and sectarian in-fighting, it gained hold of the student 'Mobe' which sponsored the student strikes, international demonstrations and the Cleveland demonstration of fall 1969.[40] It was able to do this in liaison with fellow groups in Britain (the Vietnam Solidarity Committee) and other countries. Together with the National Vietnam Mobilization Committee these formed the National Peace Action Coalition (NPAC) of 1970, sponsoring large demonstrations in October 1970 and even larger ones in April 1971. These were the biggest in the whole development of the anti-war movement, though probably hardly any of the million participants in America had any affinity with, or even idea of, the Trotskyite ideals of the organizers. It merely proved that slogans like 'Bring the boys home' could be the basis of an effective and wide-based coalition.

But in opposition to the NPAC, in summer 1970 the New Mobilization was formed, eventually changing its name to the People's Coalition.[41] Although the two organizations sponsored joint demonstrations in 1971, with dwindling turnouts, they maintained at best an uneasy relationship. These bewildering changes of names and coalitions reflect the constant manoeuvring of Old Left groups and their changing NL and peace movement alliances. On the whole YSA managed to keep itself aloof from the factionalism of the 'new politics' and the Peace and Freedom Party, but like the CP, it was condemned for its opportunism – particularly in relation to the Student Mobilisation Committtee – in which both YSA and CP, fearing to get too far ahead of any of their constituencies, retreated to 'minimal' programmes.

By the early 1970s the YSA was the most active, and possibly most sizeable single left-wing body in America, Old or New. It was the best organized and had maintained the most consistent line (an advantage not shared by groups tied to the foreign and domestic policy shifts of other powers). O'Brien maintains, for example, that YSA was 'much quicker' and more systematic than SDS in organizing GIs, and indeed it was also YSA, rather than PL, that was the greatest immediate beneficiary of the decline of SDS.

Through the 'Student Mobe', it gained many NL recruits in its period of domination of the anti-war movement (1968–71). Yet YSA-led opposition to the Kent State killings and the Cambodia conflagration of 1971 remained a massive, but relatively traditional, protest with no sense of strategic growth. The initially successful Moratorium Committee equally lacked militancy or ideological perspective, and was subject to changeable tactics and policy; and in 1972, like PL, YSA devoted itself to liberal-baiting, attacking even leftist and anti-war candidacies.

By this time, not only had the peace movement declined, but any NL presence had, outside draft organizing, largely evaporated. The Vietnam war issue had been abandoned to the liberals on the one hand, and to the Old Left, mainly the YSA/SWP on the other. It is ironic that as the anti-war movement had become a truly mass movement in the later 1960s, the NL militants had found it increasingly difficult to relate to. The massive Moratorium Day protests had in fact such a wide base, and such a respectable image, that not even the trashing and provocation of Weatherpeople, 'Revolutionary Contingents' and other tiny groups e.g. the 'Crazies' on the fringes, could undermine its image or exploit it in the cause of confrontationism.

Progressive Labor: killing the goose

The classic example of Old Left influence on the NL must be that of PL in America; it deserves extended attention in any analysis of the NL in crisis, not only because of its tactics of infiltration and takeover, but because it came closer to the heart of the NL organizationally than any other Old Left group. This was perhaps partly due to the fact that at some stages in its career PL shared some common ground with it. For all its links with Stalinism, and the nadir of the Old Left tradition, Maoism did also represent a 'new wave', just as Stalinism had in the 1930s. With its ascetic self-assurance it vehemently challenged existing orthodoxies and subverted prevailing assumptions, as did the NL.

It had particular novelty – for example, in its view of the peasantry, the Third World, and guerilla war, a perspective which most of the Old Left sects in the Trotskyite or Moscow mould lacked.[42] From Maoism much more than from Trotsky, came the populist images of worldwide peasant revolution,[43] and M2M drew its imagery from such sources.

But the special status of Maoism was that it represented the only fully developed political arm of a non-white, Third World revolution. The Vietnamese, the Cubans, the Algerians and others had to make do with sympathetic front organizations, or groups like PL as representatives, which were primarily Chinese-oriented.

Whilst probably no single political system was given the same kind of broad commitment as an ideal, that old-style Communists had given to the USSR, if socialist regimes and revolutions were to be discussed, then the prestige of China after the cultural revolution rode as high as Guevara's Cuba, or the NLF and Ho's North Vietnam. Even Fanon's Algeria warranted more attention than the Soviet Union once the practical abandonment by the international Left of the Russo-centred identification and activity which had characterized it for forty years had taken place. It took rather longer, however, for the Left to cease stressing the centrality of the Russian experience in its theoretical debates.

The most important sequence of events as far as the NL's relations with PL are concerned, are those which follow PL's growing influence in SDS between 1965 and 1967. But first it is worth remarking on the background of Maoism in America; as well as precipitating the crisis in SDS, PL has already been noted for its role in the growth of an anti-imperialist position in the Vietnam war movement, and in fostering the cult of armed defence and offence, especially in influencing the black movement.

It was on this point that the relationship between PL and the black movement first became of significant importance; as early as 1962, the CP had condemned PL's influence on the black community, calling them 'parasites on the body of the negro freedom movement'. Their influence in shifting black people towards armed organization in the South has often been noted; they scoffed at nonviolence, scorned the role of the black clergy and King within the civil rights movement, and showed their fearless militancy in the Harlem riots of 1964.

PL aligned itself with the Black Nationalists against the civil rights leaders in the cities in order to divert the movement from integration and nonviolence. It even attempted to force the Negro into the role of 'working-class vanguard' – the true and un-coopted proletariat. But at the same time there was a growing tension between their language of Marxist–Leninism, their 'correct lines', their notion of historical mission (of 'alighting on other people's struggles to radicalize them or raise their consciousness'), on the one hand, and the self-consciously autonomous spirit of Black Power or the Panthers and nationalists of the later 1960s on the other; ultimately a break had to come, and it did.

PL also played a very influential role in the campus community in the 1960s, initially largely through its front group, the M2M, and through its organization of the trips to Cuba, principally as highly dramatic publicity and recruitment exercises. Operating with a semblance of autonomy, the May Second Movement, in its work on the campuses produced an effective paper, *Free Student*, but this soon ran into censorship problems from the old guard. On early M2M demonstrations it was PL leaders who sought confrontations with police.

After 1965, with the dissolution of the M2M, PL began a conscious infiltration of Maoists both into the anti-war movement and into SDS. But by this time, PL, through its front organization, could already claim to have initiated both refusal of military service and the first thorough-going anti-imperialist denunciation of the Vietnam war. On the whole, however, PL itself advised people to 'infiltrate' the army and organize there,[44] though there is little evidence to link PL's advice with the subsequent outbreaks of non-cooperation and disobedience in the armed forces, such as at Fort Hood in 1966, or the court-martials of that year.

Both M2M and PL were also active in the Free Universities, helping to establish the Berkeley and New York models, and later taking over the Palo Alto (peninsular) Free University. Although they lost control of these initial experiments, the move was partly successful in lobbying for explicit Marxist criteria for courses and teachers, though these were substantially less doctrinaire in the mid-1960s. In fact part of PL's initial appeal was its comparative openness about its Communist affiliations in comparison with the CP. Nevertheless, like other Old Left groups, PL did have a secret membership, especially of prominent figures who could be used to provide the semblance of support by independent celebrities, and of some of the leaders who remained largely anonymous, incognito or sometimes underground.[45]

Although created out of the Sino-Soviet split, and the consequent rupture in the CPUSA, PL maintained some independence from China in its initial years of growth.[46] After the cultural revolution, however, it adhered rigidly to the Chinese line for several years. This meant a number of potentially embarrassing shifts of line, similar to those of the Communist parties of the 1930s and 1940s. The initial Sino–Soviet split, regretted by the CPUSA, was welcomed by PL as a sign of militancy. But China's later rapprochement with USA was an embarrassing reversal; there were also some significant and damaging changes of line over Vietnam. The support of Arab terrorists, support for Boumedienne's takeover in Algeria, support for Pakistan against Bangladesh, and of the repression of the indigenous revolt in Ceylon, especially the swing towards sharp criticism of the Panthers, were all positions difficult to explain and maintain on the Left.

But PL captured Movement attention partly because it always had the capacity to shock by its often outrageous positions, including its support for nuclear weapons and its opposition to the Test Ban Treaty. It was fundamentally opposed to 'bourgeois idealism', and intended to show it; Robert Williams announced after the Chinese test: 'the bomb is not just a Chinese bomb, it is a freedom bomb'.[47] Whilst the Marxist defence of Chinese nuclear weapons, and the view that any socialist state could legitimately use such weapons represented nothing new on the Left, it did mark a break from the 'peace' attitudes of the early 1960s. Accepting the Chinese version of the Western paper tiger Paul Sweezy, like a number of Old and New Leftists, openly defended Chinese nuclear weapons: 'The Chinese possession of nuclear weapons does not increase the danger of a nuclear war – quite the contrary.' This was a position that Maoist sympathizers shared with Sartre: the view that the dangers of nuclear war could be ignored or minimized. Moreover, in adopting this 'paper-tiger' theory, Sartre launched a hysterical appeal to the Russians to risk a Third World war on the Vietnam issue; urging them to launch nuclear missiles against US bases in Asia, he was widely quoted in the NL press. Denouncing what they called the Russian 'sell out' over Vietnam, PL condemned Russia's reluctance to supply ground-to-air missiles to North Vietnam, echoing Sartre's call for a full-scale invasion of South Vietnam.[48]

This cavalier attitude to the use of nuclear weapons, coupled with the critique of Russia's lack of revolutionary zeal, is symptomatic of PL's more-militant-than-thou posture: indeed, this eventually led it to criticize both Cuba and North Vietnam as well as China for a similar backsliding. It is an attitude bound up with what can only be termed a Stalinist revival.

'Stalinism' is a label that has been often and loosely used[49] – typically a mode of abuse, it can be legitimately employed to refer specifically to the actual reinstatement of Stalin himself, the resurgence of the Stalinist cult in China, the use of his portraits alongside those of Mao and Lenin, the widespread use of quotations from Stalin's works and the defence or imitation of his policies whilst in power in Russia. It can also be fairly stretched to cover the associated resurgence of methods and attitudes that are linked with the 'Stalinism' of the 1930s.

This revival can mainly be dated from the Sino–Soviet split of 1959 onwards. During the following years, criticism of the Moscow-line, especially by factions still within Western Communist parties, often tended to focus on the changes since Stalin. The loss of militancy was blamed on Khrushchev, his successors and other 'revisionist' leaders. From the mid-1960s, Russia and the CP were roundly condemned for their detente with the USA, and their coexistence line. Support for and identification with Stalin thus became an excellent new way of censuring the current Soviet leaderships, and supporting China.

The true nature of Stalinism was probably unknown to most younger New Leftists except in the most superficial terms, whereas there were many older Leftists still willing to condemn it. Indeed, in Mills's view, Stalinism had almost extinguished the Old Left:

Many leftward circles were so closely identified with Communism that when Communism was reduced to Stalinism those leftward circles declined or collapsed.

They had become too dependent on this orientation to survive intact, much less to flourish.[50]

But as the memories of organized Stalinism faded, polycentrism developed, and the Western CPs became domesticated, a number of NL critics, as well as survivors from the earlier Stalinism, came forward, who were prepared to minimize or play down its excesses. That Stalinism became a definite factor in SDS (although denied by Klonsky), is revealed in the defence of Stalin by certain groups and the widespread quotation from his works after 1968.[51]

Fairly typical amongst the older generation of Leftists was Paul Sweezy whose classic understatement about Stalinism: 'Forty years is too long for a dictatorship to remain temporary', confirms that the 'dreams of the older Left were perverted by Stalinism and never recreated', but to some, like Sweezy, Maoism offered the hope of such recreation.[52] Sweezy was a significant convert from the Moscow position to Maoism, on the grounds of the moral ascendancy of Peking in the Third World. And Sartre, too, despite his reservations about its 'numeralized order', endorsed China for its purity and the integrity of its opposition to the bourgeois world (rather than for its Stalinism). The ultra-Bolshevism of the Maoist sects in the West, also seems to have appealed to Sartre's existentialist outlook. But against this, he still insisted that Stalinism could not lead to socialism.[53]

With the development of a number of quasi-Maoist or Stalinist sects in addition to PL (such as Venceremos, the Revolutionary Union, the Revolutionary Youth Movement, and several others, including for a time the Panthers), there was an attempt to fit the American experience into the Chinese mould, and link it up with the Stalinist tradition. Since the anti-war movement had never developed into the surrogate revolutionary party that some claimed it to be, PL offered such a party. As they themselves claimed, PL and the Chinese were the true 'children of Lenin', or as Bill Epton, a PL leader, put it: 'You need discipline, you have to be ready to give your life. This is a revolutionary organisation.' Discipline, secrecy, dedication, underground operations – PL had all the appearance of a truly Leninist party.[54] It was a 'democratic centralist' organization, in which criticism of established policy would lead to expulsion. Thus those who refused to recant the teachings of Liu Shao-Chi were purged after 1966.

In so far as Old Left dogmas did re-enter the movement, it was typically first through Maoism; PL influence was first noticeable in the fall of 1966, and in each successive year its involvement became more intensive, until SDS became its main field of operations.[55] On the East coast it made open moves to control regions and chapters in 1968. But the initial reaction to these advances was overwhelmingly negative. Bob Ross, SDS vice-president, wrote at this time: 'The PL people I know are crazy and very undemocratic and all hung-up on violence.'

Yet despite their irresponsibility and disruptive factionalism, many critics were willing to admit that PL was having a significant influence on SDS, by turning its attention to 'anti-imperialism' and towards class analysis and a more sophisticated view of the working class; it was this in part which generated the debate about agency in 1966–7.

Marxism also influenced the language of the NL; as Oglesby wearily commented, largely through PL's presence 'Lenin's phrases (or what is worse the Chairman's truistic maxims) are gnawed upon by every tooth'.[56] In the midst of crisis, Marxist–Leninism was adopted by various SDS splinters in 1969, in response not to experience, but to the relentless pressure of the Stalinist tradition, and Oglesby repeated E. P. Thompson's reference to tarted-up Stalinist formulations finding their way back into movement discourse.

Nevertheless despite its work in the student and anti-war movement, its undoubted influence on the black movement, and its organizing projects in the Lower East side of New York, Harlem and the Mission district of San Francisco, PL had still failed to attract a mass-base anywhere. It had gained notoriety in the early NL because of its sponsorship of illegal trips to Cuba, but was unable to secure any permanent foothold. It thus eventually decided to take control of the one organization which had a substantial base of its own: SDS. If it failed in this it could at least hope to gain through destroying the organization by sabotage or obstructiveness.

At first PL created Worker–Student Alliance groups within SDS, as a front group, along the lines of M2M, expressing PL's belief in the revolutionary potential of the industrial workers alone. But by late 1967, it had clearly decided to make a bid for total power, in order to impose its own version of Marxist–Leninism. PL had come to identify SDS with the NL as a movement, and thus the capture of the SDS structure with the capture of that movement.

For some time within the Movement, PL had been criticized; by earlier SDS leadership for its authoritarianism and manipulation – for its uncritical acceptance of Chinese Communism or its romanticization of the working class (even though PL was in reality not a working-class party). As Hal Jacobs remarks, the new (1967–8) SDS national leadership found itself in an odd position. During the crucial months they:

found themselves adopting PL's Marxist–Leninist Maoist rhetoric in order to regain the initiative, while, simultaneously rejecting PL's political line.

Despite its own democratic-centralism, PL was able to attack SDS leaders for their top-down organizing and manipulation, especially in fall 1967 and early 1968, when there was supportive evidence.

Aware of the growing threat, the leadership of SDS had decided that it needed more hierarchy, more discipline, more vanguardism, a 'mass-line' and its own ideology to compete successfully with and fend off the Maoist threat. They discovered, however, that PL had greater advantages in this exercise, greater fluency in Marxist language, greater self-discipline, better organization as well as a tried manipulative and secretive style.

PL was accused by the SDS leadership of spending as much time attacking its rivals in SDS as 'the state or the ruling class'.[57] But it had managed, as it had hoped, to become the main focus of attention during the debate in SDS. It had won certain strategic victories also; it managed to destroy its major rival in the South – the non-Marxist 'Southern Student Organizing Committee' – after this had been abandoned by the National Office (although previously SDS's southern affiliate) because it 'wasn't revolutionary enough'. Although the Maoists failed to capture SDS as a whole in 1968, the organization was transformed by the impact of PL. An ostensibly Marxist–Leninist-led structure resulted, and within a further year, this too had split into three or four pieces, with PL the largest single remnant.

From the outset PL dissociated itself from most of the NO's activist orientations – it denounced the Chicago mobilization and various groups involved, such as Yippees. It condemned 'trashing' for tactical reasons, as well as the 'radical bombings' of 1968; and it grew increasingly critical of the black militants. As a result there was increasing pressure from the Panthers on SDS leaders to expel PL. In the faction fights within the Peace and Freedom coalition during 1968, PL had developed deep antagonisms towards the Panthers, and the Panthers despite their apparent Maoism, not only broke from PL, but excluded it from their subsequent common-front conference. In turn PL denounced SDS's dependency on the black movement.

By 1969, PL had become deeply critical both of North Vietnam for its peace moves, and of the Panthers for 'adventurism' and nationalism. Although PL came up with a blanket attack on 'nationalism' as reactionary because it was based on national rather than class identity, this was only made specific in the case of Black Nationalism and the Panthers. PL did not attack the nationalism of the Chinese, Vietnamese, Cubans or Russians – although it had other criticisms of these latter. Nevertheless, such positions won some sympathy from quite moderate SDSers, as did PL's condemnation of Castro's regime as 'a personalistic and paternalistic' one-man rule. Even its wide-ranging attacks on hippies and Yippees, Herbert Marcuse, drugs, Guevara and the NLF (as revisionist) won odd pockets of support for all sorts of reasons – not only those which were motivating PL.

In 1970 came PL's formal break with Cuba, and then, most shocking of all, for some, the break with China herself on the issue of Cambodia. Only when the final break with China had been made, with PL support for repression in Bengal and Ceylon, with SDS broken, and the left in disarray, did PL itself begin to fragment and decline. The split in SDS had not brought PL the advantages it had hoped,[58] and by 1972, it was again devoting itself to liberal-baiting and other isolating activities: moreover though it had made pro-Chinese positions paradoxically more respectable, the Chinese–US rapprochement was now deeply embarrassing to PL. PL's defence of Stalinism was nevertheless continued, not only by the new Maoist splinters, but by small groups like Venceremos, RYM II, and the Revolutionary Union, each of which had once been part of SDS.

Paradoxically, some of the groups, especially the Detroit group and RYM II, sharing PL's identification with industrial workers, supported the tactic of sending SDS members to work in factories. Moreover, as the cult of Stalin spread from the Maoist factions to groups which had earlier opposed them, including RYM II, this scattering of SDS splinters and fragments such as RYM II, Bay Area Revolutionary Union, RUM, and the American International Socialists (no connection either with the English group or the Independent Socialists) mostly turned back towards a more orthodox Maoism; unlike PL, none of them showed any signs of staying power after 1969.

From the start of PL's serious attentions to SDS in 1966–7, they had had the effect of alienating many who had joined SDS to avoid sectarian argument and Marxist theology in the first place. At Berkeley and in other chapters where they gained ascendancy (especially in the East), they actually lost members – or caused the creation of oppositional 'SDSs'. There was probably never a time when they could realistically capture the organizational Goose and the Golden Egg of mass support. Like the Trotskyites, they could dominate organizations but not win the sympathies of people.

Whenever PL took over SDS it would become an unrecognizable rump – that they did this by default, with the defection of the most powerful rival faction in June 1969, did not alter that fact: PL sustained the masquerade of a PL/SDS during the year 1969–70 – but it was increasingly a shadow without substance – especially as the material accoutrements of the organization had been seized by the previous NO group.

Given a choice between two authoritarian and unrepresentative factions, the mass membership of SDS predictably (and sensibly) chose neither. PL/SDS looked no different from a series of PL front organizations sustained and controlled during the 1960s – and in fact was probably rather less attractive than M2M had been: even the WSA's support for the new PL rump was by no means assured. With its own intensifying internal and external problems to deal with, PL's support for its own version of SDS became increasingly half-hearted after 1970 – and no further national gatherings of it were held.

A verdict on PL's version of SDS in America might be equally apt of the CP's version of CND in England. It would go on 'as long as PL felt it was getting its money's worth out of it'. But it would have little relation with the organization that had borne those initials in the 1960s.[59]

Back to square one

With the dénouement of SDS, there were certainly many in the NL by 1969 resigned to the inevitability of Marxist–Leninism filling the vacuum of New Left theory. As one critic lamented,[60]

The more complex the problems appeared, the more the political movement turned to solutions others had used with success, namely Marxist–Leninism.

Such was the Movement's failure of nerve that it had intensified its crisis of identity; the NL found itself, in Lasch's view 'trapped in the rhetoric and postures of its predecessors'; Weinstein observed that the 'militants had nothing to fall back upon except the Marxism of the Old Left sects, which they had earlier rejected'; and Oglesby's critique was the most trenchant of all:

On every quarter of the white New Left, high and low, the attempt to reduce the New Left's inchoate vision to the Old Left's perfected remembrance has produced a layer of bewilderment and demoralisation which no cop with his club or senator with his committee could ever have induced.

It is an inescapable fact that the Movement floundered as soon as the Old Left's ideologies, language, and styles began to catch up with it; the small groups, and fetishist concepts which Marcuse deplored, succeeded both by infiltration and influence. Indeed more than influence was involved; the chronicler of the Weatherman development wrote that theory had re-entered the movement 'as an instrument of coercion and control, which one faction of the movement uses against another'.[61] Threat and browbeating took over from dialogue. This was Oglesby's stance; he attacked both the scholasticism and the 'intellectual tyranny of Marxist–Leninism'.

But to some extent the Old Left triumph was illusory; the movements and forces which the Old Left and the newer Marxist wings of the NL were able to control, often dissolved or fragmented; what remained now, outside organizations altogether, was a loose re-grouping of original elements very much in the libertarian spirit of the earlier Movement.

None of the much-vaunted Marxist–Leninist 'vanguards' survived,[62] and despite the rhetoric, neither Weatherman nor Klonsky's faction lasted long enough for anyone to be able to judge how far the NL was capable of successful regression to an Old Left pattern of organization.

But the 'anarchization' of the NL turns out to be the longer term and broader process; the movement's apparently overwhelming 'Marxization' between 1967-9 turns out to be, in the end possibly, the more minor and more transitory process, although this was not what some NL commentators expected; it could be observed by some that the Old Left 'trip' was more akin to a painful learning experience.

In retrospect it seems to be a phenomenon encapsulated by a larger process. This is not to say that all the new Marxist groups which picked up substantial support in those years collapsed; but it is clear that they began to lose touch again with the larger historical movement which they had, momentarily, seemed to control. Amongst radical activists, those who had not become attached to the ephemeral Marxist–Leninist sects in 1968 or 1969 often moved away towards philosophical and political anarchism, or into various extensions of the counterculture.

But for many thousands, this was an end, not a beginning, a period of profound disillusion. It reflects as well as a personality defect in the NL, a decline of utopia in the Movement that was a symptom of the loss of illusions in the larger society; a loss of vision – and a loss of hope. Both Oglesby and Gitlin, like the 'end-of-ideology' theorists, maintained that such despair had become a defining feature of contemporary life, one which the Movement now more accurately mirrored.

Camus's sense of isolation, 'the solitude' that had begun for every man, was rooted in 'the disappearance of a political hope from the world'. 'The greatest event of the twentieth century' for Camus, had been the forsaking of the idea of freedom by the revolutionary movement; the capitulation of the socialisms of freedom when confronted by Caesarisms and 'military socialisms'. It is the tragedy of the NL, that starting from Camus's insight, it had within the space of a decade re-enacted this capitulation, a reproduction, in miniature, of the tragic history of socialism.

16. A Crisis of Identity

A movement loses itself

In searching for the source of the NL's loss of identity, it is important to recognize its relative incoherence and amorphous quality from the outset. Its ephemeral organizational expressions, its evanescent issues, eclectic theory and transient movement formations were hardly calculated to stabilize a recognizable core-identity for generations of activists: 'SDS is intentionally ambiguous', Oglesby claimed, and when another commentator (Birnbaum) called the NL more of a 'mood than a movement', he expressed a common scepticism about the organizational coherence of the NL[1] especially in Britain.

Nothing is radiating out from the centre to its periphery. It's a kind of amoeba, with very unclear boundaries, with no clear centre, with no clear structure.[2]

It was argued that a core NL identity was established in the early 1960s during the rapid evolution of several major social movements. The dissolution of the important civil rights and peace coalitions of the early 1960s were symptoms of the Movement's dynamism; but the price was heavy in terms of the inability to pass on a central stabilized NL tradition, or socialize incoming activists and recruits with certain basic movement principles.

It has been suggested that the loose nature of the NL organizationally merely reflected the general break-up of what Schön termed the 'stable state' in all industrial societies, and that in this lay great advantages of flexibility, libertarian-authority patterns and expressiveness. But there were disadvantages as well as advantages in these new forms of organization; the lack of a stable core, of an accepted pattern of meaning, made for an unstable identity – and indeed was to some extent open-ended as far as new values were concerned. The Movement after 1966 could be all things to all persons – press and other media versions could stand unchallenged.

Schön links the break-up of this stable state with personal identity crisis, and in this the Movement was a microcosm of the larger society:

We are experiencing the actual or threatened dissolution of stable organizations and institutions, anchors for personal identity and systems of values.[3]

Social mobility creates inconsistent statuses and this fragmentation and the status anxiety and social isolation caused by it has been distinguished as a major source of motivation and recruitment for young radicals entering the NL.[4] In the context of fragmentation, the NL was in part a symptom of this process. As it lost touch with the proliferation of groups at the grassroots, partly under the influence of external events and models, it lost its own sense of meaning, identity and direction.[5]

Moreover, this was a problem that was getting worse rather than better. An increasingly rapid movement from project to project, from theory to theory, from fad to fad, suggested partly the impact of a novelty-seeking press, but also a certain instability in the character of the Movement which could no longer give the assurance or community that individual recruits clearly needed.[6] Open-endedness might represent libertarian instincts – or it might reflect nervousness and uncertainty. And many felt that participatory democracy symbolized just that: '"Let the people decide" has been an escape from our own indecision.'[7]

Just as the NL as a whole suffered a lack of coherence in its welter of ill-defined groups, SDS as an organization was beset with problems not only of a mass of new members, but a myriad of new chapters (as many as 200 in 1967–8, mostly at colleges and universities). The vast majority of them were led by people with little or no previous experience of SDS or any other political organization. This influx of recruits thus entered a movement that was itself multi-centred and without a single coherent body of theory or analysis. This made it particularly vulnerable to facile interpretation or distortion by the media. Newcomers might well find a militant guerilla rhetoric closer to the received image (from *Newsweek* or *Time* or *Harpers*) than the inherited styles of participatory democracy.[8] Any new theorist or idea, however marginal to the NL's development, could be foisted on the Movement without any single coherent position that could be counterposed to it.

Thus the roots of the NL's identity crisis can be sought in the development of the Movement as it has been described prior to 1968: in reinforcing these changes, two particular 'villains' have typically been selected for attention because they stand out in the degree of their influence in the crisis year of 1967: Herbert Marcuse and Stokeley Carmichael.

Given his pedigree, it was not surprising that Carmichael's ideas should have an impact. Marcuse, partly through media selection, partly because of his originality, became equally influential. Both men helped to undermine the strategic orientation to counter-institutions, grass-roots organizing and the utopian orientation to a democracy of participants, though both had to some extent paid lip-service to such ideals.

Initially Black Power had raised hopes that it could serve the black community in some more direct and constructively radical way than did either the civil rights movement or ghetto revolt. Yet Carmichael's adventurist rhetoric had ultimately lacked any theory which could transform 'social myth' into social reality. Whilst other figures were influential on the movement, they did not direct their remarks specifically and regularly in these years to SDS or to the NL as a movement. External heroes like Fanon, Che Guevara and Malcolm-X were all influential, but mainly posthumously; Debray was in jail, Sartre more distant and detached. The fact that Marcuse and Carmichael, on such issues as violence, tolerance, race and power, spoke self-consciously and specifically to white radicals had undoubted effect.

When the movement later adopted the more exotic or abstruse intellectual or political figures, including Marcuse, it was often as a response to externally derived self-definition,[9] or else as a form of politicial theatre – to shock and to awaken – just as it also produced scenarios of guerilla war, or a home-grown guerilla theatre. But there are also suggestions in this period that for many militants the political sphere becomes infused with spirituality – religious utopian needs are projected through movement action, gaining an intensity, a non-national even millennial emotionalism. This tendency can perhaps explain movement eiconics – the deification of ideological leaders, the increased role of political saints, sacred texts, relics and symbols, martyrs and prophets.[10]

Such tendencies inevitably helped to foment a virulent right-wing intellectual response to the movement. As well as those who did have some obvious links to the movement (Carmichael, Cleaver, Rap Brown, Gerassi, Rubin, Hoffman or members of the Weatherman faction of SDS), it was possible to quote figures recently elevated as mentors by sections of the movement (Malcolm-X, Guevara, Debray, Fanon, Sartre and Mao). By such selective treatment, it was possible for critics to piece together and attack an apocalyptic 'New Left' that bore little or no resemblance to the NL of the mid-1960s[11] (though even then Howe for example, had talked of the NL as 'Black Maoism' and white 'Malcolmism'). The label Maoist-Castroite, earlier used of the Berkeley FSM, could now be used, and with greater credibility, of the new SDS leadership; the old charge of Stalinism now too had substance. Whilst such versions were not pure inventions, they led to a distorted public image of what the Movement was and had been.[12]

It has been argued in this book that up until the later 1960s, the central NL strategy was located in the building of independent power bases, counter-institutions and the mobilization of new constituencies: a form of 'nonviolent revolution'. Broadly speaking, two other strategies which marginally overlap this one, become more prominent after 1967; the one of electoral politics,[13] the other of violent confrontation escalating towards terror, urban guerilla tactics, and even advocacy of full-scale revolutionary violence. It was often argued that the creation of forms of counter-power was inescapably linked to the possibilities of both increased voting strength on the one hand, or potential armed strength (offensive or defensive) on the other; occasionally (as the Panthers maintained) all these sources of potential power could be combined. But both strategies proved distractions from the prior and originally established meaning of the NL enterprise, and tended to become ends in themselves, in either a cult of violence, or a fetish of the ballot.

The fear of reactionary and repressive moves from the right had always accompanied strategic thinking on the Left, and intensified in the late 1960s; given the frustrations and proven disadvantages of electoralism, the mainstream NL in 1967 was moving into a deep dilemma. It was caught by its failure of nerve between what Zinn called 'the bloody futility of civil war', on the one hand, and 'the ineptitude of parliamentary procedure, on the other'. But these were not the only two choices: proponents of the third option, the 'nonviolent revolutionaries', caught somewhere between the two, tended also to lose their nerve, hedging their bets by urging both more work *within* the system through educative pressure *and* more militant direct action.

As has been seen, moreover, the NL now entered a period of crisis in relation to its own constituencies. On the one hand it was using the language of 'majority' revolution; but on the other it was alienating that majority with an escalating rhetoric of militancy, and the growing violence of confrontation and street-battle, which made the spectre of civil war as real as had the ghetto revolts. As a popular writer of that time put it: 'They failed to offer a positive vision, an example of an affirmative vision.' 'They frighten and make enemies of potential allies.'[14]

Moreover, the pessimistic realism of Marcuse was at the same time generally accepted.

Radical change seems to be unimaginable. But the obtaining of a mass base – at least in this country and in the foreseeable future – seems to be equally unimaginable.

Such a paradox was of course a recipe for élitist solutions; provocation, terror and urban guerillaism, which raised deep problems of leadership and organization implied in the relationship between the NL and its potential agencies. Despite its proclamations to the contrary, throughout the 1960s, the greatest failure of the earlier NL seems to be the divorce of its theoretical work from action. This emerges first in its failure to develop an appropriate debate about strategy, either for the nuclear disarmament movement in Britain, or the civil rights movement. At first the American radical critics of the later 1950s had at least the excuse that there was, until 1960, little movement to relate to. But this was no longer the case in 1967. Moreover, after 1965, as the NL became more and more deeply implicated in these strategic dilemmas, it moved further away from concern with organizing around interests, whether in terms of labour, of student unions, community organizing or even electoral demands, towards 'posture', and confrontation.

It is true that the Vietnam war movement had never derived from a 'natural' constituency as had the civil rights movement; peace activity was not clearly linked to any obvious agency of change; 'interest' politics could only be directly focused in terms of the draft. On the other hand the civil rights movement had managed to serve the black community, just as the draft-resistance movement could claim to serve conscripted youth. It was much less clear how ghetto rebellion served the black community, or how street confrontations or bombings could serve any other constituency.

To compound and accelerate this process, the NL – or its mainstream – abandoned publicly and openly its asset of nonviolence, although there is solid evidence that violent tactics antagonized key potential constituencies; nonviolence had for over a decade enabled the movement to appeal on the basis of conscience first and self-interest second, and to continually identify in the public mind the agencies of control with physical violence, rather than itself.

In retrospect this crisis and its causes have two discernible dimensions; the first being self-generated – implicit in these internal limitations of ideology, strategy, analysis, movement leadership and organization. In O'Brien's view,[15] it is in the period 1965–9 that

the New Left's internal weaknesses became accentuated to the point where, at the peak of its apparent size and strength, it fell apart.

But the second cause lies in the NL's consequent search for a solution outside itself; the identification with the armed solutions of Third World guerilla armies, or the militarist posture of nationalist black militancy in the ghettoes of America, or the imitation of the Marxist-Leninism of the Old Left sects. These solutions – as well as being usually illusory and irrelevant – proved profoundly destructive. Whilst such an overview of the causes of the NL's degeneration is not novel, the roots of this crisis and decline, and various precipitating factors in the NL's development at earlier stages, have not been hitherto given much attention in an overall analysis.

In the American case, the growing tensions of the movement have been partly explained in terms of the differing orientations of the various civil rights organizations, their offshoots and successors. Together with the impact of external events and the new anti-imperialism of the Vietnam war movement, the shift away from participatory democracy and counter-institutions was the single most important factor in the loss of the movement's coherence and identity.

But initially it was the changes in the black movement that were of the most critical influence in causing the shift away from nonviolence and tolerance. In so far as the white NL from the early days of SNCC tended to take cues from the black movement, their change of tactics and style was bound to have effects.

The loss of a social basis has equally been seen to be rooted in the reaction to the Vietnam war. Within a year or so of the failure of some of the major community organizing projects, the growing scepticism about the possibility of creating a mass movement of the poor, and the switch to the anti-war front, the NL began to go through 'a number of contortions resulting in the rise of authoritarian and vanguardist fads'.[16] After 1966, there are signs of an increasing willingness to move from a leadership based on openness, feedback and participation, rooted in popular disaffection, towards a more manipulative style, 'manufacturing synthetic disturbances and manoeuvering them'.[17] Thus there develops a crisis in the notion of participatory democracy, as 'decision-making by consensus gave way to caucusing, factional polemics and voting'.

Amongst movement theorists, it was Lynd (even more than Oglesby) who was most aware of these shifts in the movement in the later 1960s, and showed considerable concern that

the tendency in the second half of the sixties was away from the distinctive atmosphere of humour, emotional expressiveness, experimentation and . . . chaos, which had characterized the early years of the white NL.[18]

But rarely are these insights linked to an analysis of shifts in the external context. Although both Calvert and Lynd detect the fateful shift in SDS strategy in the fall of 1967 when SDS was 'reverting to the . . . politics of middle class self-flagellation', and making people 'auxiliaries to other people's radicalism',[19] it can be more accurately located in the crisis of the black movement of 1964–5, and of the peace movement in 1965–6, reflected in SDS at its 1966 conference.

Whilst in understanding the changes of course in the subsequent development of the NL, it is difficult to assign primacy to the influence of either of these developments, in the later civil rights movement or the development of the Vietnam war opposition, what is certain is that the subsequent modifications in both these major influences, and the ideological shifts within them, come, to some extent, from outside the Movement.

But in understanding this, a reverse process is just as critical; Black Power grows from *within* SNCC and the NL, and yet gradually moves outside and away from it; to a lesser extent, sections of the peace movement, too, begin at the heart of the movement and move in divergent but tangential directions towards its margins.[20] It also is significant that by 1968 there were even elements in the National SDS caucus (RYM I) who no longer identified themselves as 'New Left': in fact the term was used pejoratively of elements in the National Mobilization!

In retrospect, the year 1967 can be seen as the year when various dilemmas, unresolved problems of organization and leadership, of ideology and agency, begin to assume the proportions of crisis. Bardacke was probably right when he announced 'Stop the Draft Week changed the movement' – though not perhaps only in the ways he thought: Weissman was probably equally correct in believing that, had a strong counter-move against the National Office faction of SDS been made in fall 1967, things might have gone differently.

But as these problems become linked to a further dilemma, that of the use of violence, one can begin to talk of an *overall* crisis of strategy and a deep ambiguity about the character and identity of the NL *as a whole*. Together with the impact of the Old Left and the climactic events of 1968, the turn towards violence intensifies this, until finally identification of a NL no longer becomes possible.

As has been seen, the phases of this crisis overlap – the degeneration is not total; it does, however, overwhelm some of the major organizational expressions of the movement such as SNCC, CORE, SDS in the USA; *NLR* and CND in Britain, and most of the Vietnam war organizations on both sides of the Atlantic.[21]

Most significant, this was a period when key figures made dramatic volte-faces; Calvert swung against participatory democracy – surprising in view of his continuing libertarianism – and Carl Davidson moved from Student Syndicalism to Marxist-Leninism within a matter of months. Oglesby, who had drawn so many into anti-war activity, suddenly urged SDS to become an auxiliary of the black struggle instead. Hayden, always changing, turned towards violent militancy after Newark, and like other leading figures, made his identification with the NLF and Hanoi clearer than ever. (He later stood for Congress.)

Calvert and Lynd were, however, concerned with defending the Resistance against the attacks of both white SDS and the black militants; after spring 1968 both these NL veterans switched all their energies and attentions from SDS to draft-resistance; Lynd attacked as the 'politics of guilt', Oglesby's exhortation to students to turn away from their own problems such as the draft etc. towards the problems of blacks and racism.

In the 1968 vacuum of strategy and ideas, LBJ's climb-down and the Paris peace negotiations tended to take substantial impetus out of the anti-war movement for over a year; liberal electoral candidacies took attention away from resistance. After the election, as the Paris talks and the SE Asian fighting continued, both the anti-war movement and draft-resistance gained a new lease of life during 1969. But many of the tens of thousands of young people who had flocked into the McCarthy campaign in 1968, and later joined the McGovern campaign in 1972, had been barely touched by the NL; even though, perhaps indirectly, their political shift was a result of the Movement's actions, it no longer offered them a home.

At the same time there developed in these years an amorphous growth of high-school leftism, ethnic youth gangs, and scattered militancy in various contexts almost unrelated to the previous NL. The obvious effect of SDS's demise was that although student and anti-war protest continued on an often massive scale (and in some senses it spread in this period), it was now highly localized and un-coordinated; there was no longer the sense of being a national movement, and the various Mobilization and Moratorium committees and coalitions failed to give it that sense. The return to electoralism was one result, encouraged by 'votes at 18', a concession granted on both sides of the Atlantic at about the same time, as a final ironic official tribute to the NL's impact on youthful electors.

In summary, this final collapse of most of the major NL projects and organizations may be gauged in terms of a wide range of tendencies and factors; violence and terror, intolerance, the renewed impact of Old Left ideas and organizations, identification with terrorism, guerilla warfare and authoritarian regimes, abandonment of emerging movement language, styles, and strategies, and the cessation of effective organizing in various communities. But they all led to one fundamental conclusion – that the NL no longer recognized itself, and in effect denied or negated its own existence. 'The party of hope and change was not defeated in combat', Schaar argues, 'it just evaporated.'[22] O'Brien's view that the NL's final disintegration was for the most part a natural result of its own internal weaknesses is substantially accurate,[23] yet one must maintain that it was external events and identifications that helped cause and exacerbate these weaknesses, and that, together with actual infiltration or influence of Old Left groups, proved fatal.

Crisis of the counter-institutions

The crisis of the project of the alternative society, the faltering belief in the possibility of the creation of counter-institutions as a viable radical strategy, emphasized the ill-effects of the Marcusian apocalypse, and the limitations of Black Power as it was interpreted by Carmichael and the Panthers.

Community control as advocated in the first versions of BP included black parent boards, black tenants' associations, and black businesses or cooperatives, and economic sanctions against other traders; but in the heady atmosphere of 1967, such concepts seemed small-beer. Whilst Marcuse paid lip-service to counter-institutions, like Carmichael he failed to spell out fully enough, or early enough, the development of an alternative concept of revolution. Without explicitly rejecting the counter-institutional idea, both had by default or vague rhetoric helped steer the movement away from its implementation.

Marcuse seemed to clutch at the 'alternative society' notion as an unexpected institutionalization of the utopian motive. In reaction to Leninism, such a network seemed to offer an alternative at the theoretical level to a centralized, disciplined national vanguard party. Moreover, it answered Marcuse's utopian demand of the movement that it respond to the public question: 'What can you offer us that is better than what we have?' ('We cannot simply brush that question aside', he argued.) In rejecting traditional Left strategy he criticized its postponement of utopia, and its self-destructive ideologizing in which everything was sacrificed on the altar of 'realism' (defence, GNP, industrialization, defeat of internal and external foes, etc.).

The apocalyptic gap between means and goals that has characterized the Marxist tradition, and creates the hiatus that can be filled only by a Leninist vanguard, a disciplined party, or a seizure-of-state-power, conceives only of the forcing of such change from the top. Yet this belief can demonstrably lead to a surge of millennial activism – the authenticity of the blind, often destructive praxis, that has typically been portrayed as belonging to Anarchism but may be just as firmly related to many other political traditions, as the crisis of the NL reveals.

Marcuse's speculations were never rooted in the pragmatic, actual experience of movement projects; his ultimate failure[24] to take up a strategy which could avoid the millennial leap of Marxism, both reflected and reinforced the NL's own failure to opt decisively for the road of counter-institutions. The temptations of Weatherman-style praxis on the one hand, or Leninist organizational plans on the other, proved in the context of 1968, and in the absence of strongly argued alternatives, too strong for most militants.

The strategy of counter-institutions, as has been seen, embodied the 'Wobbly' principle of creating new social forms, unencumbered by dogma. But the NL, like Syndicalism before it, failed to develop an adequate strategy in relation to power in America – the 'shell of the old society' within which these new structures were supposed to emerge.

By 1967, it was becoming clear that the embryo of an alternative social order never easily forms within the womb of the old one especially under modern conditions. The decline of the 'free' institutions, the cessation of organizing projects, as well as the crisis of the alternative press, were accompanied by the weakening or disappearance of many other experiments and communities, under the strains of external pressure and internal decay.

The free universities, relatively undemanding amongst counter-institutions in terms of commitment and resources, fell on harder times, reflecting both the changes in the counter-culture and the ideological dissension in the political NL. Any attempt to impose either the straitjacket of dogma and organization on the one hand, or total anarchy on the other, was a source of immense tension.[25]

In many alternative projects, just as in SDS, the search for a 'non-bureaucratic' centre to coordinate activities was fraught with problems. Some groups, like Women's Liberation, preferred to operate outside any umbrella.[26] Without a centre, publicity and interchange was retarded; with it, there was a danger of overstructuring, or a takeover by an ideological vanguard. The problems of openness versus restriction, structure versus total informality, created deep crises of leadership, and were the common problems of every do-it-yourself project.

In any discussion of a strategy of parallel institutions or counter-institutions, a major source of dispute was whether such a strategy should attempt to build institutions *parallel* to the present ones or as 'negations' of present institutions. Hayden, in Millsian language, had expressed his belief in the possibility of keeping both those options open; in listing a number of examples of viable counter-institutions – community unions, freedom schools, experimental universities, community-formed police review boards, people's anti-poverty organizations (lobbying for federal money), and independent union locals, Hayden argued these could be at one and the same time separate bases 'pointing towards a new system', and 'practical pressure points' from which reform in establishment institutions could be launched.[27]

The ambiguity of MFDP, as has been seen, was that it had been both 'within and against' traditional political systems.[28] As Lynd confessed, 'the intent of these structures is still unclear to those involved in organizing them.' He too suggested that both options must be kept open, parallel institutions on the one hand coexisting with and transforming their establishment counterparts, and on the other, genuine alternatives slowly expanding into a counter-society.[29]

Lynd and Hayden both saw the dangers of the co-optation of parallel institutions by what they termed 'corporate liberalism', or their diversion by merely token success; Lynd admitted that parallel *economic* institutions were the *least* likely and the *last* likely to emerge. But there was also a great fear in hippy communities and amongst some NL groups, about becoming parasitic, of becoming part of the consumer society. The limited efforts to create alternative forms of production and creative work, and to re-distribute the goods and services within the community, as well as making use of the waste and surplus from the larger economy, were genuine attempts to break free of these dependencies.[30]

Thus the central dilemma of the strategy of counter-institutions had to do with the degree to which such institutions could be inside or outside existing systems, societies, or institutions – and whether they should merely provide 'alternatives' (functional substitutes for existing institutions) and thus be either 'counter' in the sense of being 'opposed to', negating, or replacing, *existing* structures. For this was related to a further profounder problem; the need to assess the salience of current institutions and existing social needs for the counter-culture or any alternative society.[31]

If some 'needs' are in fact artificially sustained, and not necessary at all, then many institutions of the dominant society require not so much replacement by alternate versions (functional substitutes) as *abolition*. Equally, many basic needs may not be met by existing institutions, and so structural creativity can evolve into entirely new ones. Thus the conceptualization of 'negating', or 'countering', or 'paralleling' or even providing 'alternatives to', *existing* institutions was extremely limiting in so far as each started from a base line of existing structures.[32]

Donald Schön remarked on the weakness of negations, of traditional reactive modes of confronting existing power. For this reason, the radical position opted for total alternatives (e.g. providing functional substitutes for present institutions where necessary, but also demanding *new* institutions as part of the re-definition of needs implicit in a counter-culture). As this idea of self-controlled, self-directed communities, insulated from the dominant culture, grew, 'parallel institutions' or organizations, the term first used by the NL, was dropped.

But as Barrington Moore argued, 'To sustain itself, any oppositional political movement needs to be able to obtain for its members day-to-day benefits and protect them against reprisals.' Taking unions as a classic example of the major counter-institutional innovation of an industrial order, Moore pointed out that in modern societies:

this necessity has so far always led to compromise with the existing order, to working within it to achieve piecemeal benefits. It is also precisely this need for protection and continuing benefits that New Left semi-revolutionary movements cannot provide through such symbolic gestures as offering sanctuary to draft resisters or 'liberating' a university. Neither of these is a step toward setting up a real working community, a base from which influences can be expected to spread outward and transform the existing social order.[33]

Moreover, as Keniston also pointed out, the NL would also have to find ways for those who perforce became involved in the predominant institutions of conventional society 'to retain their active commitment to the movement'.[34]

Schön, too, despite his emphasis on decentralization, saw the counter-institutional response as an inadequate one if it became separatist:

The same technological changes that produced the loss of the stable state, connect every piece of society to every other and no separate enclaves can survive. If decentralization is a response, it must be a connected decentralization.[35]

For these reasons, Barrington Moore argued, the counter-community was likely to remain parasitic upon the larger society.

The creation of a liberated area that is really independent culturally, economically and politically would be extraordinarily difficult if not impossible.[36]

A number of the more sympathetic critics also argued against the realism of any all-out counter-institutional strategy, and against the viability of separate economic and political units, in industrial society.

Oppenheimer, discussing the possibilities for the black community, observed 'separate economies are no longer viable even if they were not prevented by the dominant social order for racist reasons'. CORE's successful experiments with cooperative communities in the South could not be translated into organizational or institutional tactics for the ghetto. To be successful, even at the cultural level, to create and sustain a revolutionary subculture or counter-organization on a significant scale, innovative institutions would have to embody processes of social learning. They would have to insulate people from the larger 'hegemonic' culture, creating the room, the time and the space for people to adopt and practise new forms of behaviour, thus cutting them off from old forms.[37]

Hayden increasingly stresses the role of 'turf' or 'territory':

Instead of dropping out individually 'in their heads' or into tiny enclaves, people drop out into free territories.

Hayden defined these as utopian centres of new cultural experiment, breaking down a decadent culture, internationalist in character, enabling confrontation *and* defence, acting as centres of retreat and survival. Only where the whole range of alternative radical institutions coexisted, could such projects effectively and credibly operate. A free university could not operate in isolation; only where a strong student movement and a counter-community coexisted, could it survive in some form or another. These alternatives by degrees found a level at which they could directly meet the needs of a community – rather than the spare-time needs of students alone, and as a result, it was on the whole a less focused radicalism and a more 'hippy' style which flourished.

Nevertheless, by the end of the decade, these and similar projects like free schools, arts labs, free stores, and purposive urban communes were finding times far more difficult than in the heady days up to 1968. There were many sceptics; many who were impatient; the failure of many projects reinforced both attitudes. Co-optation and incorporation on the one hand, and repression and intransigence on the other, seemed to raise the crucial question of whether either complementary or negating roles were open to these institutions. Paul Potter, one of the few SDS leaders openly sceptical of counter-institutions, believed that the counter-community had not developed the organizational strength or cohesiveness to withdraw respect and support from existing government agencies.

The only chance for the growth of 'liberated areas or communes or something similar' in Moore's view would be 'if the process proceeded slowly and quietly' without provoking repression. But it would still be difficult to achieve any real autonomy for such communities or for them to become or remain, distinct, except in trivial ways which would not threaten the system.[38] Even if it grows at the expense of its host, it is unlikely to be able to strike at the instruments of domination or to undermine them in the ways that liberated areas succeed in doing in peasant revolution.

Other commentators were convinced that America's Establishment might prove inherently and inevitably hostile to such strategy, unwilling to tolerate the expansion of viable and popularly based rival institutions. The probably inevitable intermediate (and perhaps ultimate) confrontations with these institutional innovations, did not necessarily invalidate the strategy, although it did raise the critical question of defending them. Demonstrably there was little more likelihood of the transformation of existing institutions towards participatory democracy than the survival of alternatives.

Participatory democracy and after

Participatory democracy, more than any other concept, represented a fusion of the main elements in a NL identity. Yet it was at this juncture of its crisis and flux that leading sections of the Movement abandoned this very principle, and moved towards a permanent, militant élite of leaders based on an authoritarian control 'from the top down' (or so it was hoped). Such perspectives, whilst keenly concerned with winning new recruits, were not interested in their participation or control in the movement; 'Grassroots democracy' became a remembrance of the past.

PD, which has been identified as a central theme in SDS actions, began as a genuine and radical alternative to Old Left bureaucracy. Its lack of permanent leaders gave – at least in theory – a number of advantages. For example, it was arguable that it avoided the risk of selective repression, though in practice it rarely made the identification of key personnel so very much more difficult. It was also held to offset the dangers of takeover by élitist groups, yet in the event it proved vulnerable to both the influence and disruption of such groups. Moreover PD had inevitably allowed the most experienced and sophisticated SDS leaders to get their own way most of the time. But as the decade ended, a new self-conscious willingness to 'rig' meetings and manipulate agenda, becomes apparent. Even as early as 1965, the call to an SDS conference had already expressed alarm: 'We scream "no leaders, no structures", and seem to come up with implicit structures which are far less democratic.'[39]

Although PD was introduced to re-invigorate the decentralized community, by reviving a spirit of solidarity and practical cooperation, critics argued that amorphous spontaneity and lack of structure could actually frustrate democratic control.[40] Small-scale tyranny through informal manipulation was as likely a result and demagogy could replace bureaucracy. Certainly as a style, participatory democracy was to many a refreshing alternative to the overstructured formalism of traditional Left sectarianism; however, it only partially solved the problem of leadership and equality of participation, and it was not always successful in dealing with infiltration and takeover. As Lipset comments: 'Political factions often stemming from the Old Left have frequently been able to use the organizational looseness for their own purposes.'[41]

The FSM was unplanned; much of its leadership was politically inexperienced, it was decentralized and amorphous in organization; meeting in large, chaotic sessions at Berkeley, it set a pattern which produced as many organizational dilemmas as solutions; no one was quite clear about the mechanisms by which large numbers of people could participate in decision-making at such movement gatherings. Far from the 'small group' imagery, meetings were often far too large, and still the activists, the articulate spokesmen, the strategists who had decided beforehand their approach to issues within the meetings (plus the inevitable exhibitionists), tended to dominate the meetings and to coordinate their resolutions, sometimes outside the gathering.

Often the equally large VDC meetings of 1965–6 in Berkeley, with several hundred participants, turned into chaotic mêlées that became typical of PD in action.[42] At best PD of this kind was 'a very time-consuming method', as Lipset comments.[43] At worst, the inarticulate, the incompetent and the less active, or those, like many women in the Movement (before Women's Liberation) who were given mainly menial tasks, remained as silent or subordinate as in any other organization, even though the style and intention were different.[44]

The proclaimed ideal (that each 'individual share in those social decisions determining the quality and direction of his life' and that 'society be organized to encourage independence in men') did not indicate a precise method of decision-making. Thus as an ambiguous response to twentieth-century political crisis, despite the importance of populist solutions and the slogans of popular control, the development of a theory of PD, ideal or in practice, was with few exceptions, lacking.[45]

Martin Oppenheimer, attempting a sociological appraisal of PD, highlighted the problems of consensus-style meetings – the difficulty of opposing the 'sense of the meeting', the emotional isolation of dissent, the lack of formalized opposition, the tendency to acquiesce in demagogy as a result.

Participatory democracy may turn into plebiscitary democracy in which the reputation and skill of leaders may become paramount, rather than direct participation.[46]

Indeed it was easy for the movement's most vehement critics to place a sinister interpretation on what was going on, even in the more genuine attempts to diffuse initiative.

The 'participatory democrat' had no use for elections, votes and parliamentary procedures – since the masses are non-participant, the élite activists must act on their behalf.[47]

Whether opportunistically or not, organizers qualified the idea of participatory power for the masses: 'to make or participate in making the decisions which affect them'. Sartre accurately stressed the widening gap between historically minded intellectual-cadres and the stultified, patronized, satiated masses who have been co-opted and corrupted, and have become immobile; this was a position towards which Marcuse had also seemed to gravitate.

But Hayden had earlier warned of the dangers of

maintaining a dependency on fixed leaders, who inevitably develop interests in maintaining the organization (or themselves) and lose touch with the immediate aspirations of the rank and file.

Such populist sentiments are echoed in Fanon's criticism of manipulation of the people by self-appointed élites, through techniques of language and management from above; although his critique is aimed at Third World leaderships, both revolutionary and neo-colonialist, it found strong echoes in the American black movement. Urging the masses to participate directly, Fanon expressed a populist faith in their ability, as long as they are not blinded by expertise and tricked by procedure. The radical who uses complex language and other such methods in the name of their education, is in Fanon's view, guilty of their betrayal.

But many had perceived a profound discrepancy between actual organization and idealized participation which invalidated the communitarian and libertarian aspirations of the Movement.[48] The populist rhetoric, the belief in the people, which represented one side of PD was easily compromised, not least in the black groups.

Particularly in relationship to a revived Marxism, there emerged a deep tension between the anti-élitist idea of organizing or representing the poor on the basis of their desires for material advancement, and the strategic attitude that saw the poor as agents of systemic change, regardless of the short-term needs or desires of this constituency. The former idea tended to be associated with the belief that the poor could best identify their own problems and how to solve them, lacking only competence, expertise and skill, which the community organizer could help the inexperienced gain. The other view, which was that the poor cannot understand their real historical interests, and that to some extent these have to be defined by the organizer himself, created the classic dilemma: grassroots leadership in neighbourhood organizations might or might not understand this 'real need'.

Nevertheless, initially, reformist demands were included, usually as organizing devices, but also because they were demanded by the constituency. The inclusion of such claims points up some of the paradoxes and contradictions of the SDS (or indeed any syndicalist) concept of organizing. The SDS organizers were not expected to make decisions on behalf of those they organized; his or her task was to assist people to make their own decisions; the organizers were to try to make themselves redundant in the long run. Yet the people whom the organizers were to help, were those with little to lose: helpless and often without hope, their spirits depressed. As Kahn observed: 'between these people and the student or ex-student organizer', there exists 'no essential identity of interest such as one can assume to exist between the union organizer and the factory worker'.

The student organizer can escape from the ghettoes into security, the poor cannot; the poor are often materialistic and may yearn for the very life-style which the students have rejected.

The costs of libertarian organization and democratic leadership were clearly exemplified in the NL's attempt to do without centralized parties or a national structure of power. The classic Syndicalist dilemma had been recreated by revolutionary ideals superimposed on a populist style: operating partly within the framework of the status quo, giving implicit recognition to an existing power relationship, this exacerbated the crisis of PD.[49] Just as early twentieth-century revolutionaries, then leading trades unions, had been forced by their members into bargaining agreements, the NL was faced by parallel dilemmas in its dealings with local administrations, campus authorities, or the legal structure.

As domestic stability appeared to be eroding in the later 1960s, the temptation to create a single new oppositional power centre, almost by definition centralized and authoritarian, grew stronger. In the events of 1968, despite clear indications of a widespread if inchoate libertarian revolutionary vision, and a series of utopian actions, an ambivalence remained about the organizational dilemma and the temptations of the Marxist-Leninist solution.

In this respect, Marcuse deepened the ambiguity; his practical rejection of liberal values in the contemporary context, whilst this had to be placed alongside his critique of Leninist forms of organization, and his critique of the Soviet Union, revealed that he both recognized the trend towards 'decentralized forms' and felt that such could be the basis of a new style of 'national organization'.

Like Marcuse, many movement critics with traditional socialist orientation, such as O'Brien, acknowledged this need for a 'broad radical organization', and Oglesby called for a 'post-Leninist theory and post-Leninist practice'. Gitlin, like Teodori, argued largely on pragmatic grounds: 'A highly central structure is not appropriate.'[50] Marcuse argued against the Leninist model, on both realistic and principled grounds,[51] maintaining that the 'mass base' had become large but diffuse and dispersed, and the only organization which will channel its force is one which is entirely overt, diffused and concentrated in small groups which are highly flexible and autonomous.[52] He contrasted the diffusionist model of such NL organization with the classical system of clearly defined leadership and a fixed centre. 'A large, centralized and co-ordinated movement'.[53]

Marcuse's endorsement of the new model of 'small contesting and competing groups . . . active at many points at the same time, a kind of political guerilla force in peace', suggests sharp divergence from the neo-Leninist and manipulative vanguard ideas of some in both the Marxist groups and the ascendant SDS leadership. Clearly arguing for a 'libertarian' model of 'revolution', and an apparent rejection of Leninist forms of organization, at the same time, just to confuse matters, he stressed that these were:

mass movements which in large part are lacking political consciousness and will depend more than before on political guidance and direction by militant leading minorities.

Thus Marcuse merely reproduced the dilemma of PD in SDS or SNCC with statements remaining open to vanguardist interpretations.

Symptomatic of this organizational turmoil, the language of freedom could not survive; as the crisis of the movement grew, the language of 'liberation' – 'national liberation', 'women's liberation', 'liberated' areas – took over; it betokened a lowering of sights; once more the construction of the new political order was to be postponed on the altar of necessity. Hayden, earlier one of those most insistent in warning against leadership abuse, begins to talk ominously of 'liberation' in terms of 'new guards' established by 'the people'. The long-term effect of the NL's split over organization is to resolve nothing: with a leadership increasingly élitist in rhetoric and aspiration, the larger movement remains amorphous and chaotic in practice.

SDS and SNCC at their peak had been movements of organizers; in Britain, to some degree this was true of the Committee of 100 and its offshoots. In other cases, as with the Resistance, a whole new generation of organizers arose in the same mould as their predecessors. But with the shifts of the NL into black power, Left sectarianism, and terror, these organizers largely disappeared or became inactive. Some of them moved on to new things. With the transition of the revolutionary youth wings of SDS into 'ideologically disciplined organizations of cadres', the shift of a major segment of the NL towards a top-down model of change is completed.

The turn away from bottom-up organizing also loosened the restraints against élitism and dogmatism; humourlessness and intolerance are the prerogative of a movement or organization that is losing touch with ordinary people. In addition, this drift from a populist democracy meant that the fundamental insight that movement actions in the present determine the kind of institutions that are built, and in turn the kind of society that will be reproduced in the future, was by 1968 fast being lost or abandoned.

Keniston, having noted the NL's 'hostility to formally structured roles and traditionally bureaucratic patterns' – enabling the movement to develop 'an open personalistic, unmanipulative, and trusting style of leadership' – points out a tension between this and a more apparent need for tight organization as a national Vietnam programme developed.[54] The first serious move by an SDS leader to oppose PD came surprisingly from the libertarian Calvert, in a December 1967 pronouncement, perhaps misinterpreted, and later regretted (judging by his later verdicts on SDS decline). He cited PD's 'inadequacy as a style of work for a serious radical organization'. This turnabout confirmed tendencies in the National Office. By 1967 it was clear enough, Weissman wrote, 'that a new Marxist group was taking over, and a new style – without a vote' had come to dominate SDS. It was a significant portent that Dohrn should also reject PD.

The abandonment of PD was not immediate or universal. Even at Columbia and Chicago, control of the events retained some semblance of participation; at least, in Dellinger's view,

the role of centralized formal leadership was minimal in these events. A crude but creative kind of participatory democracy was at work.

Somewhat unsuccessfully, similar attempts to spread participation occurred at the Sorbonne, and in Britain PD characterized the Notting Hill organizing projects in the late 1960s; George Clark stressed how the Golborne council involved local residents in direct democracy, bypassing the local council and holding neighbourhood elections. But by and large the NL was passing into the hands of those contemptuous of such self and group indulgence. Much closer to the ideal of many new leaders, was the RYM blueprint, later implemented by Weatherman, which advocated 'city-wide' 'cadre organizations' with 'effective secrecy' and 'self-reliant' 'collectives'.

One-dimensional tolerance

During the year 1967 and after, it was clear that in terms of the changing internal milieu of the Movement, the NL was already entering an entirely new phase. During its early growth, SDS had shown a great deal of patience with irrelevant, repetitious, even down-right 'reactionary' speakers. There had been little or no exclusion of unpopular viewpoints from movement meetings. In CND there had been no attempt to suppress the right of free speech for opponents. But during 1967, the next stage of movement away from 'liberal values' became clearly exemplified in both the Vietnam protest and student movements in both Britain and America.

A section of the NL noticeably shifted in its attitude to opposition and dissent in Movement actions and forums; in movement meetings at Berkeley, in the planning for Stop the Draft Week, in the meetings at the LSE (and subsequently in the SDS conferences of 1968 and 1969), opposition speakers were persistently shouted down or drowned out: no longer was 'anything goes' the prevailing norm; platform censorship, restriction of debate, ejection of opposition, howling down even left-wing dissent, became increasingly common. The use of planning, agendas and credentials to eliminate 'undesirable elements', for long part of the organizational style of the Old Left, became increasingly typical.[55] The use of platform privilege, or white or Western guilt, or even male supremacy, to suppress debate and brow-beat questioners, was characteristic of these years. 'Internal democracy degenerates into the rippling of self-righteous slogans hurled across a convention floor' (Sale).

Calvert and Nieman note this decline of tolerance in SDS, the growing 'intellectualization and parliamentary manipulation of meetings' which represented the stepping stones towards the full-fledged faction-fights of 1968. Rigid and intolerant debates had by this time, in the view of these two erstwhile SDS leaders and theorists, replaced the 'anarchist style of earlier years' by the 'pseudo-scientific language of Marxist-Leninism'. This battle of humourless orthodoxies represented in their view by 1968 'a deep malaise in the body politic of the NL'.[56] It reproduced the 'class guilt and messianic pretensions' associated hitherto with the middle-class intellectuals of the Old Left.[57]

Those from within the NL who opposed these tendencies did so not so much on behalf of liberalism *per se*, as of basic principles which had made limited advance within its framework; not a defence of 'bourgeois' democracy, but of democracy itself; not of 'repressive' or selective tolerance, but in the cause of *tolerance* itself. When Raymond Williams, a founder-theorist of the English NL and the May Day Manifesto group, entered his plea for tolerance it was both to promote the movement's own growth and a larger humanism.[58]

Those who entered a defence of the limited advances for human rights and liberties made within the framework of capitalism, did so in the knowledge that such rights and liberties, however restricted, had not made their appearance in non-capitalist societies.[59] By tolerance it was argued, one might imply not trimming, compromise and co-optation, but a respect for people where and as they are. This was arguable from socialist premises – that human beings are educable, rational and mutable by argument in preference to force.

Wherever we have started from, we need to listen to others who have started from different positions. We need to consider every attachment, every value with our whole attention for we do not know the future, we can never be certain what may enrich it, we can only listen now and consider whatever may be offered and take up what we can.[60]

Gitlin also argues that authoritarian trends in the NL become barriers to mass involvement: workers in revolt

will not surrender their beings to a movement which promises dictatorship of the proletariat yet offers merely dictatorship. The same is true of the GI's turned off by military discipline per se.

The rejection of corporate liberalism by radicals in the years after 1965, might be still seen as an extension of liberal principles towards libertarianism; but it was equally likely to turn in an anti-liberal or positively illiberal direction, in versions of Marxist-Leninism. The lack of any truly anarchist core to the NL made this increasingly likely.

The fact that pluralism was a secondary feature of American society was suddenly used as a justification of its further elimination – in part to 'reveal' the totalitarian nature of that system. The manipulation of needs by vested interests was to be met by manipulation of needs by revolutionary organizers. It boiled down to something little less sophisticated – even in Marcusian language – than a political 'eye for an eye'. It produced a form of mirror-image of dominant system ethics; violence to be met with violence, intolerance (or pseudo tolerance) with intolerance; and manipulation with manipulation. That the NL should make this turnabout on questions of methodological principle, was partly due to frustration and the internal changes and external events already described, but on this specific issue it must also be attributed to the growing influence of a single thinker – Herbert Marcuse.

Marcuse always finds his place in any definition of the NL, and yet there are real questions as to whether he should be included at all. He came late on the scene as far as the Movement was concerned; to some extent his relationship with it was an artificial one, a marriage arranged by the media. His ambiguous, often contradictory, and always elusive writings, in so far as they were read in the Movement before 1967, were largely read because the media, both established and alternative, began to identify him as a 'NL theorist'. In fact one of the few groups to openly acknowledge his influence were the Situationists. [61]

When Marcuse was elevated in 1968 to the status of Movement Prophet, it was largely because the NL was already in crisis, and because, since 1966 his writing had struck common chords with certain leadership sections of the movement. Thus at this point Marcuse acted as a translator of actual Movement experience and to the degree to which the NL, particularly in its period of ideological anguish, invoked him as a source of reinforcement, and the degree to which his writing diverges so sharply from that of the ancestral Left, he becomes one of its theorists; he, after all, could see the link between NL politics and cultural revolution.

But, though Marcuse acted as an interpreter, selecting and filtering many movement values and ideas, he rarely contributed to its ideological development in any initiatory way. Only on the issue of the tolerance of dissent, was his role that of initiator and prime influence; in 1966 Marcuse made a number of anti-liberal attacks which challenged the existing NL's attitude to 'freedom'. He justified his support for left-wing intolerance in terms of the 'phoney' freedoms under capitalism.[62]

Liberalism's valid principles have been undermined, according to Marcuse's analysis, by the actual development of capitalism. Individual liberties promised and proclaimed by capitalism in power, are frustrated as competition and individualism give way to corporatism and monopoly. Liberalism maintains a safety valve tolerance, but fails to combat the rise of fascism and instead turns against socialism. Liberalism then evolves into fascism itself, ultimately abandoning even the pretence of freedom and liberty. But in America and the contemporary West, this evolution is perceived as far more subtle than in Weimar Germany; it is a 'creeping totalitarianism' that manipulates tolerance in order to prevent criticism of the intolerable (nuclear weapons, genocide, imperial exploitation, police and racial oppression, etc.).

Thus Marcuse's argument was used by the NL to justify its own growing proclivity towards intolerance, impatience, and violence. Marcuse in turn at first endorsed these developments even when they turned as much towards internal movement intolerance of dissent as towards intolerance of the intolerable outside the movement. Ironically it was an Old Left group (the Du Bois clubs) that took on the mantle of main defender of 'free speech' against the NL, when it argued 'the only way to fight ideas is with better ideas', rather than with their suppression.[63]

Marcuse was not the only NL spokesman to talk of fascism and totalitarianism in America; Mills had implied it; Hayden had made it explicit; Staughton Lynd talked of 'a twilight zone between democratically elected authority and something accurately called Fascism'.[64] SDS had from the outset claimed that corporate liberalism 'no longer *was* liberalism in its true sense'.

Nor was Marcuse new in seeing a 'clear and present danger' e.g. a drift into fascism justifying emergency action. Indeed the British nuclear disarmament movement had seen such a danger in nuclear weapons, feeling them to be intolerable and using similar arguments to justify mass illegal action. The argument of the Committee of 100 had been that an emergency situation did not allow people to 'tolerate' a system of mass slaughter, or its defence. The difference was that in all these cases, such emergency or crisis was not used to justify the suspension of internal liberty, or of the need for dialogue or the repression of individual dissenters. In the case of nuclear weapons the intolerance was morally rooted – dialogue continued even with those who made the weapons or maintained the delivery systems; but not so with the draft boards and arms manufacturers, or defence researchers of the later 1960s.[65]

It was but a short step from here to the acceptance of Marcuse's view that 'Law and order is always and everywhere the law and order which protects the established hierarchy'; thus a 'liberating tolerance' withdraws the privilege of tolerance from all those on the Right who are 'objectively' reactionary. From Marcuse too comes the principle of manichean polarization; everyone and everything which was not 'for' the 'revolution' (however defined) must be against it, and must not be tolerated; 'he who disagrees with me is objectively counter-revolutionary.' The effect was to reinforce a reawakening sectarian spirit on the Left, that was fundamentally novel and alien to the NL in all its previous growth, to make the rapprochement with Stalinism more imminent, and to further encourage manipulative styles of leadership.[66]

As far as the NL's theoretical and strategic lacuna was concerned, the fatal gap in Marcuse's thought was still the lack of a connection between the existentially derived belief in personally authenticating political action, and the non-repressive civilization that was to be achieved by it. The particular irony of this was Marcuse's own utopianism in many other spheres. Echoing Goodman, he had in fact accused liberalism of having lost, or abandoned, 'Utopia', and of failing to develop theories which could 'link the present with the future'.

Yet in his writings on tolerance and violence, Marcuse had himself moved to the point where the means-ends chain was broken at the level of ethics and methods. Whilst fighting 'fire with fire', it was enough for utopias to operate at the ideational level; it was sufficient apparently to imagine alternatives, rather than currently build or experiment with them. Whilst self-creation is, according to Marcuse, necessary, institutional creation can be largely ignored or postponed. This becomes part of Marcuse's overall pessimism about change within the present system or even growing out of it; he reinforces a politics of despair, an existentialist posture – rather than a political rebellion, and his analysis could be used to justify (like Sartre's) a conspiratorial élite strategy of subversion – a weird combination of elements that is to some extent exemplified in Weatherman. Marcuse's is a utopianism but without the incremental, practical, cell-building characteristics of the utopian socialist tradition.[67]

The NL responded to Marcuse in its impatience and lack of analysis; it agreed with him that many aspects of Western society were intolerable, but it made the mistake of personalizing this intolerance and introducing it into its own life and growth. The result was not effective 'intolerance' (of Dow Chemical or the CIA – although it reinforced the militancy of confrontations like these) but the growth of bans and expulsions, censorship and proscriptions – as well as heckling and harassment and even physical assault of individuals. Both internally and externally such actions plagued the movement in the years after 1968, and were typified by the 'expulsion' of the Maoist-dominated wing of SDS in 1969, or the enunciation of 'correct' positions by the score of splinters which resulted from this decision. As Dave Wellman argues: 'The object of their frustration has been the movement rather than the source of its problems.'[68]

Harrington, attacking this new élitism and authoritarianism in the NL, warned that those breaking up meetings would provide soon a rationale for the disruption or prevention of their own, and that is exactly what occurred. Similarly Marcuse's impact on the British movement, from the LSE events of 1966–7[69] up until the NUS decision of 1972 (to disrupt or prevent right-wing meetings) was dire indeed; not only were lectures interrupted, but lecturers were physically attacked. Suppression or heckling of deviant views became a dominant trend and obsession of student leftism, a token of its growing bankruptcy.

As NL disruption tended towards physical intimidation and the advocacy of physical violence against opponents, the comparison with the fascists' tactics was predictably employed by more conservative critics. This, together with the stress on the NL's 'anti-intellectualism' and 'anti-liberalism', helped create an even more distorted, but by this stage not entirely undeserved public image; this analogy, based on the anti-tolerance and irrationalism of the later NL years, had somewhat more credibility than similar attacks had done in the mid-1960s. Such attitudes represented an extreme extension of the opposition to liberalism, in which an amalgam of activism, cult of violence, rationalized intolerance, together with actual Stalinist remnants, were welded by the guilt and frustration of the middle-class young, into the final explosions of the movement.

Emasculation by the media

The effect of the predominant media version of the NL was to bring generations of young people into the movement through images and symbols which were inauthentic versions of it. People were recruited on the basis of highly slanted or commercialized interpretations of both the NL and the counter-culture; the orientation to personalities was far stronger in the media and poster business than in the Movement itself (though the alternative press tended to imitate and reinforce this trait).

The press and mass circulation magazines glamorized and distorted so that the expectations of the recruits of the later 1960s were formed not so much by Movement actions and publications, as by these alien images. The effect was to over-select those components in the Movement (cult of personality, cult of violence, 'urban guerillaism', street-fighting, etc.) that most fitted these inherited stereotypes. Even Bobby Seale accused the media of sensationalizing the Panthers and thus leading to an unwanted recruitment of members on a false basis. The Movement even adapted to fit these externally derived expectations – ones largely manufactured by those who wished to exploit it.[70]

The consequent distortions and sensationalism led to misinterpretations even by potential allies and friends. For example the press and TV inevitably focused on the most bizarre and experimental aspects of the embryonic counter-culture; in fact the 'summer of love' of 1966 was largely a media invention, reinforced by current pop songs.[71] But in the context of the mid-1960s, many political radicals were prepared to accept this media version of the counter-culture even though rejecting established versions of the Vietnam war and almost everything else. Such artificial misunderstandings had also a great deal to do with the delayed fusion of counter-culture and NL.

From the outset the Movement's cult of certain commercial films may provide also a clue to its impending capitulation to symbols and images alien to its experience. The actual effects of established film on the Movement are difficult to assess, and may well have had an enervating effect, as well as reinforcing the tendency towards revolutionary gesture; but it seems likely that they helped in determining existing trends in the Movement, independent of analysis or experience.[72]

The Movement's relationship with the media was always both ambiguous and ambivalent. The established press was usually inaccurate, destructive and often viciously unfair; sometimes it would ignore, often dismiss, usually sensationalize, sometimes exaggerate, sometimes underestimate, movement activities; it would inevitably seek to personalize the leadership – to find and create a 'star'. It would even trivialize or co-opt issues or values, emphasize (or even invent as in the case of 'ban-the-bomb') slogans rather than arguments. It tended to turn everything the Movement did into fashion or fad: a slogan for a badge or button. Yet, conversely, without its attention and publicity, the Movement would probably not have grown.

In the late 1950s and early 1960s, the key problem had been more one of media-silence – the breakthrough into regular attention came only after the beginnings of the student movement, the Vietnam war and the escalation of tactics. Before that, any access to the media represented a way out of isolation.[73] In the early 1960s, as Bertrand Russell had been the first to admit, civil disobedience was in part chosen as a tactic to offset media boycott of the issue. Equally violence was encouraged by the fact that it made the front pages whereas other methods did not.[74]

In the atmosphere of the early 1960s in Britain and America the use of civil disobedience seemed a dramatic innovation, and obtained widespread coverage. But by 1968, civil disobedience too seemed tame – action had to be violent as well as illegal, to be sensational enough to gain mass publicity.

Wherever a tactic was repeated it tended to gain decreasing publicity and this proved to have a disastrously distortive effect on Movement methods. Even arrest of civil rights and peace demonstrators after a while became commonplace and therefore less newsworthy. The press always highlighted the most violent and rowdy elements in demonstrations, as Peter Hain noted in the media coverage of the British STST actions; only disruptive events drew banner headlines.

As it was, even in nonviolent confrontations it was the scuffles and incidents which were stressed by the media. As one organizer complained, 'we have to be violent to get on the news screens'.[75] Such attitudes encouraged the manufacturing of 'pseudo events' for the press. In Germany, in much the same fashion, the Springer press combined its repressive attitudes, with an exaggerated publicizing of the radical bombings of the Baader-Meinhof gang.

With the media breakthrough of 1964–5, SDS began consistently to orient its direct action to the media. To some extent this was an exhilarating change, it made the Movement conscious of its potential – but it also tended to overemphasize leadership and gimickry. There was a strong element of narcissism among many Left militants – in Berkeley a number of radical activists and leaders were seduced by film producers into appearing as themselves and reproducing their actions for posterity;[76] the effect was both sensational and trivial.

The rise and growth away from the NL of the black power movement, culminating in the Panthers, illustrates well these problems associated with the media. In much the same way as the peace movement, the earlier civil rights movement had depended on national media coverage for its rapid growth.[77] Ninety per cent of all Negro families by the early 1960s, had a TV set; they could watch the actions of fellow blacks and white racists and police, and see and hear their black leaders. The news of demonstrations was thus spread widely and rapidly through the black community (reinforced by a growing black community press) and after 1960, helped spark a genuinely mass-based movement. In turn, the Black Panthers and Carmichael also depended crucially on media build-up.

But in terms of race tension, the white press hardly helped: exaggeration and scare-stories even typified the *New York Times* which 'discovered' the 'Harlem Blood Brothers' (a 'band of dedicated Negro assassins'). The sensationalized coverage of demonstrations and violence fanned the flames of hostility and suspicion. Subsequent expressions of solidarity by producers and broadcasters were listened to sceptically. Even Stokeley Carmichael, shortly to be totally seduced by the media, condemned the white press for 'defining black power'.

Yet none of these rebuffs and protestations was sufficient insulation for the movement, for there was, in addition to these sentiments, a phenomenon that has been termed 'ressentiment' – a certain grudging need for the whites and the bourgeoisie and their press as a scapegoat for protest. Radicals expressed this symbiotic dependency on the

Establishment's press and TV as their sounding board by eagerly scanning the media for coverage, and reinforcement.

However, the confidence of many radicals in the ability of the black movement to articulate the strategy of black power, was rudely undermined by the manner of the concept's birth and the publicity-seeking of its main protagonists; launched on behalf of the media and carried on by Carmichael's charismatic speaking tours of 1966 and 1967, these tours and the press conferences and TV shows associated with them, grew very distant from the organizational emphasis and anti-personality cultism of SNCC's original participatory democracy.

Carmichael's contempt for many or most in his audience was often unconcealed; he rarely engaged in dialogue or listened to opponents or questioners. The tours also made Carmichael rich – the tag 'TV Starmichael' stuck; his $100,000 mansion seemed a far cry from the humility of Mississippi Freedom Summer, and the blue workshirt and dungarees.[78] In an article 'Media as Enemy', the black left-wing journalist Julius Lester expressed the view that Carmichael's position as leader derived not from his relationship with the Movement and his involvement with the rank and file, but from 'his rhetoric and aggressive image on which the media voraciously gorged itself'. Since he no longer used the media to address himself to black people, 'Slowly the rhetoric and aggressive image began to devour both SNCC and Carmichael. The rhetoric replaced programme, the image replaced organizing.'[79]

As Newfield remarked:

This paradox of radical ideas creating celebrities could be an insidious process. It is hard to nurse your anger if you are getting $2,000 to spell it out on national television and it is hard to think creatively or to organize effectively, if you are deluged with a stream of speaking engagements, interviews and symposia. The danger of becoming performers subsidized to goose a decadent middle class is a real one for the New Left.[80]

Lester saw this over-orientation to the media as a major failure for the black movement; through media, the Panthers, like Carmichael, had become a force but mainly on the basis of 'image, rhetoric and Cleaver'. The BPP, with their military organization, uniforms, weapons and exhibitionist publicity, displaying a bravura calculated to appeal to both established and alternative media, soon displaced previous cult figures. But Lester argued:

The black radical movement [was] repeating itself. The media extracts personalities from its ranks and gives them enough publicity to make them 'leaders'. These 'leaders' get caught up in the glamour of their own image . . . a point of diminishing returns is soon reached and the movement comes to a stop while it yet appears in motion. The enemy is alerted by the glare of publicity and redirects the energy released. He takes the rhetoric and bends it to his ends.

Much the same could be said to be true of the white NL after 1967.

Carmichael was not the first, nor the only, black cult figure to be taken up by the white media; Robert Williams before him, Malcolm-X both before his death and after, LeRoi Jones who first sought its attention,[81] Rap Brown and the Panther leaders – especially Huey Newton, Bobby Seale and Eldridge Cleaver – and later George Jackson and Angela Davis, all became news-commodities for a spell.[82] LeRoi Jones was carried along by rhetoric and media attention, and at the end of the decade, Cleaver was very quickly co-opted on to the editorial board of *Ramparts Magazine*.[83]

Movement analysis of the media, from Mills to Marcuse, had continually warned of these snares, and stressed its corrupting role. For Marcuse, the tokenism of liberal tolerance allowed carefully managed dissent to act as a safety valve through a minority press or occasional gestures in the major communications organs. But the main feature of the new oppression was its new techniques of domination without direct coercion; the manipulation of popular consciousness, the perversion of human needs, the granting of empty choices and bi-partisan politics were largely the work of the means of mass communications – a means to which radicals had only token access.

Part of the mass media's ambiguity was rooted in the NL's conviction that it was 'not open to rational or moral arguments' which contrasted with the populist faith in the discernment of masses.[84] This created contradictory attitudes to the overwhelming power of the media in manipulating mass consciousness, yet the real ability of the NL to speak directly to 'the people' with a degree of optimism in the existence of a viable popular culture. The media represented a short-cut in organizing and communication, moreover, that was hard to renounce.

The influence of Marshall McLuhan's media writing on the movement was a diffuse and oblique one; it persuaded people of the critical role of visual communication, yet did not indicate how it could or should be used effectively by an opposition. Inspired in part by his message, the Yippees, and similar groups outside America, were probably more successful than Carmichael or the Panthers in using the media in a self-conscious way.

Jerry Rubin, in particular, was constantly orienting the movement into publicity-getting stunts and happenings; the confrontations at the Pentagon and in Chicago were dominated by these elements, including the pig as presidential candidate. Using the media, Rubin had publicized the Chicago events for over a year and the aim was to share all the publicity attendant on a big national party convention – and to that extent it worked, though a happier confrontation was probably envisaged. As a result, established journalists and media people were certainly alienated from the Establishment by the attacks on them by the Chicago police.

But in general, like the black movement, white radicals had grave difficulties in situating themselves in relation to the established media, and as long as the Movement or the counter-culture had not become a separate society, it had to deal with the effects of the established communications and restrain its more extroverted public relations men.

There were basically three approaches by which such a situation could be met – to use the media as it was, in the belief that all publicity was useful and that some of the message would 'get through'; to create a wholesale alternative communication system; or to work from within, to establish enclaves of sympathetic press and TV people in existing communications systems.

The first option was the most loudly rejected as impossible, and yet the most widely used; not only black militants and Yippees, but a whole range of Movement people, attempted to use the media just as it was. The effect was exactly as many of them predicted, the Movement became a victim, and eventually almost a creature, of the media. For several years, after 1967, the media would use almost anything about the Movement that was novel and was news, and the effect was disastrous for the solid base of organizing and ideas upon which the NL had been built, and depended. The Movement belatedly recognized the meaning of Lester's warning:

No matter how easy it may seem, one cannot use the media to one's own ends. Whatever gains are made are ultimately illusory. In present day America, the media can be nothing but an enemy of the revolution. And it definitely cannot be used as a substitute for revolutionary analysis, theory, programme, and strategy.

The second route, 'do-it-yourself', develops mainly as an aspect of the counter-culture: by 1968–9, it *did* seem to offer some real alternatives to established communications, at least at the level of community press. The early underground papers were marked by an 'a-political non-involvement',[85] but the development of the anti-war movement gave a new meaning and potency to challenges to established versions of the war. This was underlined abroad by the role of underground media during the Czech resistance; clandestine press and free radio even in the most oppressive circumstances were able to reach vast audiences, countering Russian distortion and misrepresentation. Established reportage could be subverted by such counter-institutions. In America this consciousness brought into being a number of co-ordinating and federative bodies to link the various innovations. By 1968, many were linked by the Underground Press Syndicate (UPS), Communications Services (1967) and the Liberation News Service (LNS).[86]

In America there were over 400 alternative papers with a circulation estimated at its height to be between 500,000 and two million. Many established some form of economic autonomy – free of most of the usual commercial pressures – though burdened with countless others. Supported by the street people and radical communities,[87] this decentralized independent character gave the underground press a staying power denied to many other counter-institutions, and indeed it survived at least the collapse of other large sections of the movement in 1969–70.

But the alternative press had no real counterparts in terms of other media.[88] The development of movement theatre was essentially a minority phenomenon on the fringes of the Movement.[89] Movement film also had a limited growth.[90] Only in the field of music was there a renewed independent and rapid expansion, and this too was subject to commercial exploitation, through the need to use established media (TV, radio, press, etc.), as well as agencies and professional management, recording studios, etc.; symptomatic of this, the growing commercialization of black music and black radio stations, was converting culture into commodity; objects to be packaged, promoted and sold.

One theme in the alternative papers was the hypocrisy of richer rock musicians espousing the philosophy of 'free' and the inconsistencies of protest themes and excessive profits. But the underground press was itself not without similar growing contradictions,[91] yet the financial plight of many of them was dire – unlike the established press, printing, sales and circulation were uncertain and street sellers and other distributors were often harassed by police and local residents. Production was often disrupted by police raids, unreliable printers, financial crises, assaults and court cases. There was a constant turnover of staff – some were arrested and even jailed – and costly legal battles and fines were a further drain on resources.

This instability, coupled with the inefficiency of UPS and the lack of the mainstream media's dependable news sources and distribution networks, was compounded by the debasement of Movement language; the repetitive and shrill tone of the papers steadily lost meaning and effect. Moreover, the financial crisis led many of them to depend on sexploitation and sex-advertising as a main source of revenue and sales.

Thus the changes in the alternative press are linked to, and are themselves important symptoms and portents of, the impending Movement crisis; the shift that gathers momentum after 1967 involves a more strident, more commercial, more cynical, more sensationalist approach, reflecting an increasing sexism and cultism and often a crisis in the internal relationships amongst those producing and distributing the papers.[92]

The limitations in the developments of alternative media had a good deal to do with reinforcing the third option: 'boring from within'. There was a belief that radicals could get and hold jobs within the professions, including press and TV journalism.[93]

'The mere fact that the Left had no adequate access to the media of mass communication' (Marcuse) was such a major obstacle that any sort of foothold offered hope. From the start this view was encouraged by a certain amount of favourable reportage of the NL by younger radical journalists.

Gitlin urged that the Movement demand equal access to the communications technology – not because the mass media could be humanized, but because it could be used. But the virtual blackout of the post-SDS demonstrations and bombings of May 1970, the failure to publicize continued anti-war organizing, desertion and draft-resistance after 1969, suggested the limitations of such an approach. The NL as a newsworthy seam had been 'worked out'. But against this the revelations of Ellsberg and later Watergate, suggested a new attitude amongst younger journalists, and the changed context in which the media operated in the seventies.

The music dies

If any evidence was needed for the strong links and overlap between the counter-culture and the 'political' NL, it would lie in the fact of their parallel development and crisis in the later 1960s. In some ways, it is their very fusion after 1967 which creates a common crisis; in their relationship to the media, in the crisis of the counter-institutions, in the tendency towards violence and greater authoritarianism, towards the politics of gesture and symbol, the developments are almost indistinguishable. The loss of vision, of utopian ideals, is perhaps more marked and decisive in the NL's political organizations, and the disintegration more sudden and complete: in the counter-culture, change is less decisive, more complex.

By 1967, this cultural base is clearly in search of a NL politics to extend and justify it. Equally the NL is constantly looking for a cultural milieu and critique. The continuing tension between the politicoes and the hippies of the first years (1965–7) diminishes, as with the Diggers, the street people, the Provos, Situationists and Yippees – and perhaps even the Weathermen – various syntheses are achieved. In the American student subculture, the hip and the radical become less distinguishable in a common personalism and emphasis on praxis and life-style. When the mass of students at Berkeley in 1966, at the end of an ostensibly political strike, had gathered in a bizarre but joyful rendering of the 'Yellow Submarine', the marriage seemed to be consummated.

As the gap between hippies and activists closes, other NL ideas and projects, that emerge to some extent outside the counter-culture, grow towards it. Rubin's mayoral candidacy in Berkeley was on a hip/NL platform; political theatre, both in San Francisco and in New York, becomes a line of communication between the political and cultural wings of the movement; both Situationists and Yippees, in parallel efforts, stressed the theatrical and spectacular elements of action which were most difficult to co-opt[94] and expressed the often bizarre range of influences on the hippy-political alliance.

Founded late in 1967, the Yippees[95] became, after Paris, an all-American Situationism combining elements of 'provo,' pop-art, theatre of the absurd, and political shock tactics which followed Marcuse in emphasizing cultural alienation as much as political critique; its extra-political orientation brought as many people to Chicago in 1968, and to other confrontations, as did straight political or peace organizations. In fact, many of the components of the Yippee spectacles were reminiscent of Ginsberg's proposals to the VDC several years before, though with an added edge and abrasiveness.[96] These ingredients re-appeared at the Pentagon: with the plan to levitate and exorcize it, the flowers placed in the National Guard weapons, and in similar manifestations at Chicago and during the People's Park confrontations.

The initial tension between the hippies and the radicals, such as it was, has often been portrayed in terms of a difference between 'changing one's head' and 'changing the system'. To 'live the Revolution', theorists such as Brown, Marcuse and others agreed, a change of 'consciousness' was critical; the salience of such change made it prior to other sorts of change, a reversal of the Marxian chronology and, in Brown's writing, a loss of concern in the structural change to follow.[97]

In 1970, Charles Reich placed himself on the side of changing consciousness (the individual's) before or in lieu of changing structure, and his popularization of certain alternative society themes and NL critiques was a bestseller in 1970–1.[98]

This often artificial dichotomy between personal and institutional change had meaning only at the extremes. There were those who believed that self-change was vital and that political change would, or might, follow. There were others who insisted, as vehemently, that structural change was paramount; without it nobody would or could change, and that change at the individual level would inevitably follow.

In fact such polar positions were adopted by few in either the NL or the counter-culture; the 'acid freak' and the structural-leftist were stereotypes around which this contrived debate revolved. Certainly, as the emphasis on the creation of institutions grew both within NL and counter-culture, the tension somewhat dissolved and these stilted arguments lost relevance. But as has been discussed, whether such dis-affiliation and opposition could become social revolt rather than merely a tolerated withdrawal or deviance, was a key issue depending on the extent and breadth of movement along various dimensions, and the salience of the normative challenge to established patterns as well as the degree of stress in the larger society.

Various contradictions in the hip ethos – introvert and extrovert, aggressive and nonviolent, strident and soft[99] – emerged clearly in the cultural enclaves of the mid-1960s; these communities suffered badly from the image-making boost given by the media to the small hip-locales of 1965; expansion was far too sudden and rapid; these communities might have coped with a smaller, slower increase in numbers, but in 1966 and 1967, the probable summer growth was of tens of thousands monthly. Predictably, the psychedelic and hip utopias could not bear the strain; the numbers wanting to use the community resources broke them. After 1967, the communal experiments in free food, medical aid, and music of the Panhandle and Provo Park, dwindled.[100] The hip communities found it very difficult to deal with these developments, and they were transformed within months into anomic ghettoes.

Chester Anderson's bitter attack (through his Underground Press Syndicate) censured the proselytizing underground media quite as much as the established press and television for causing this immigration. Calling them 'Uncle Tim's Children', Chester Anderson condemned those who had over-advertised the psychedelic community, accusing especially the hip-merchants and drug pedlars, but also blaming Leary's 'acid' cult, and Kesey's 'tripping'.

By this time, with home-grown versions of 'provo' evolving independently towards Yippee, the American communities were losing both some of the celebratory and carefree aspects of the early phase, as well as their political utopianism.

An obvious symptom of this is in the changing attitude to 'free'. The early development of the counter-culture, reaching its peak in the years 1965 and 1966, is marked both by a genuine property asceticism and a strong desire to simplify living, with an intensified dependence on surplus and used goods and materials and an attempt to increase the employment of cashless exchanges through counter-institutions like free stores; the circulation of resources outside the economy and the production of objects for barter was one mode of opting out of much consumer culture.

But the notion of voluntarism and selflessness was suffering too many reverses; the concept of 'free' was translated into the much less selfless and utopian philosophy of 'rip-off'. The change from the Diggers to Abbie Hoffman and the Yippees is not just from 'giving' to 'taking'; it is the translation of 'freedom' into theft – as against 'cashlessness', production, and cooperation. If it is not given, then it must be seized: the post-scarcity ethic has become more aggressive and individualistic, less antagonistic to commodity, and it marks an important cultural watershed.

As the cult of 'free' and cashlessness was translated into a philosophy of rip-off and theft, new common links were forged with the hustlers and the property-focused (yet in another sense anti-property) criminality of a traditional kind. This was extended into the idea that even personal theft is somehow a blow against the capitalist and property system.[101]

This change from a basically moralistic stance was reinforced by the marginality which the hip communities shared in common with other groups. These fringe communities juxtaposed innocence and depravity, the pure and the vicious, the hippy and the criminal, in a unique and novel way. There were, however, very real points of social and cultural interchange and contact.[102] In the first Weatherman statement, it was argued:

The laws against marijuana mean that millions of us are outlaws long before we actually split. Guns and grass are united in the youth underground.[103]

Nevertheless, the relationship between the outsiders of the counter-culture and the genuinely criminal sub-community was an uneasy one; part of the problem of the hip-ghettoes was that by the late 1960s, they had become a refuge of criminals of a more traditional sort, and the rejection of property on principled grounds, tended to be replaced by the 'culture of thieves', where the accumulation and sale of other people's property became one of the major subcultural pastimes.

The overlap between the politically radical and the traditionally criminal was particularly unclear in groups like the Muslims and the Panthers, both of whom in fact recruited criminals (in the non-political sense) to their ranks.[104] Both recruited disproportionate numbers of ex-prisoners, junkies and racketeers, though these typically renounced their past; however, the Panthers' image as gun-toting, uniformed, and glamorous, also attracted many criminal elements in the ghetto; some to use the party as a front for rackets and continued crime. Radicals would often insist that this was a secular salvation for those who would give a political edge to their crimes, and that in fact political bank robbery could become a service to the revolution, a tradition carried on by the Symbionese Liberation Army (SLA). But there was of course an ambiguity in this criminality, which often operated as much against the radical and the black communities as against the system of capitalism.

This overlap between the counter-culture and the revolutionary groups and the criminal subculture is another component which the NL shares with the tradition of anarchism. Anarchism too, had found it difficult to distinguish between its principled rejection of the 'criminal' structures of the state and capitalism or unprincipled opposition to those structures; did the former exclude the type of rebellion practised by the outcasts and those driven to acts labelled 'criminal' by the state? For the state itself, such distinctions were hardly likely to be perceived – especially by those who defined the whole subculture as deviant.[105]

The period after 1969 is for the counter-culture a period in which intensified rage and amoralism are combined with a mounting nostalgia and sense of loss,[106] and the counterpoint between these elements is partly responsible for the flight from the urban communities and the increasing popularity of spiritual rather than political escapism and fantasy. The search for transcendence that characterizes the widespread drug-cults and religious revivalisms of the late 1960s, partly reflects the decline of organized religion in the Western industrial countries. Most marked in predominantly Protestant cultures like Britain and the USA, this had already been seen as creating a spiritual vacuum in which religious needs may be partly displaced into politics.

These crises proved particularly acute for the young whites from the middle-class family from which the NL mainly recruited. As Mills had put it: 'The absence of any order of belief has left them [the white-collar class] morally defenceless as individuals and politically impotent as a group.' The flight of their children to the NL or the hippy ghettoes can be explained not least in terms of a central crisis of values.

The organizational disintegration of the Movement after the fragmentation of SDS, the wave of assassinations, the Chicago confrontations, Nixon's election (1968) and re-election (1972), the relative success of the property developments in breaking up the living environment of the alternative communities (e.g. People's Park), as well as the crisis of the Haight-Ashbury, are all significant ingredients causing a flight from the cities. But some of the movement activists who joined this migration still insisted on rationalizing it as a preface to 'guerilla offensives' based in the countryside; although there is no evidence that anything like this either occurred or was seriously prepared for.

Such escape (often from politics itself) increasingly marked the tendency to withdraw into genuine meditative religions or into a pseudo-mysticism, both often associated with drug experience. The search for the bizarre and the occult accompanied the Jesus-freak phenomenon, new Christian sects and revivals, drug cults, and the exploration of exotic and esoteric religions. Buddhism, Zen in particular, had had an impact on the counter-culture from the days of the Beats, and the writing of Watts and Snyder.[107]

The role of mysticism and drugs had also of course been a part of the counter-culture from the outset; Mailer maintained that there had been an even deeper identification between the 1960s' white 'hipster' and the hip culture of drugs, jazz and Negro youth; the rejection of the dominant society by the Beats of the 1950s and particularly by figures like Leary and Alpert, Ginsberg, Watts, Snyder or even Norman Brown, was sustained later through papers like the *Oracle* and the *East Village Other*; these developed the emphasis on transvaluational experiences, potentially linked to hallucinatory drugs or schizophrenia (Laing).

Such trends partly have to do with the explicit rejection of 'positivist' natural science and the accompanying definitions of rationality, objectivity, and 'value neutrality' which had become associated with a social and global 'balance-of-terror status-quo'. Like previous anti-rationalists, the counter-culture, and the anti-psychiatrist 'revolts against reason', since reason is employed in the service of the irrational and the unreasonable for purposes of brainwashing or adjustment, or justifying nuclear deterrence.

Although these tendencies intensified Movement problems, they could not be simply dismissed as irrelevant escapism. Some of what happened, like the cult of Tolkien, Cockaign or various Maharishis, more clearly was, but the NL, active politically, did little consciously to fill the vast spiritual vacuum and even among the activists there were felt needs for moves along this dimension; indeed Rennie Davis provides the outstanding example of a shift of a veteran of a decade of SDS activism and Chicago into the retinue of a guru.[108] Thus the quest for spiritual alternatives continued through psychedelic exploration and Christian revivalism as well as the millennial, apocalyptic and spiritualized politics of the late NL splinters.

At its most profound, the quest for non-Western solutions, whether through oriental religions, mystical experience, drug-induced vision, or a variety of transcendental cults, represented what Gary Snyder called a rejection of the 'Western Judeo-Christian tradition' (including Marxism) which had led society to moral bankruptcy. As such it represented an important complement to the ideological quest of the NL, with its trans-nationalism and its radical critique of Western values and societal relationships. But it was only *rarely* this; more typically it was as spurious as many other later NL postures of a more political kind; it was often a transient fad, a gimmick, a superficial cul-de-sac of interest, and the drop-out into it was frequently an easy option for those unwilling to make more serious commitments.

But the nostalgia and sense of loss that drove many to seek these solutions, probably represented in part remorse for the loss of the earlier vision of the counter-culture and the new radicalism (and to some extent, that illusory memory of the summers of love or the first 'be-ins'). This, together with a growing romanticism, is reflected in the reaction to these changes in the music. There was always a nihilist and destructive element in the counter-culture, partly derived from Dada and Surrealism, that was first clearly expressed in the cult of auto-destructive art and 'destruction in art'. Yet despite the marked tendencies in rock music towards violence, it is easy to exaggerate the death of the counter-culture, and the crisis it experiences in these years. The Woodstock Festival, in complete contrast to Altamont, emphasized many of the same values as the 'summer of love': indeed the idealistic and non-idealistic components had co-existed in the counter-culture throughout; only the press created the total contrast between 'summer of love' and later degeneration.

The film *Easy Rider* was taken by many as an allegory of the Movement and the counter-culture, because it portrayed an uncertain and escapist journey ending in violence and disaster. Along the way many of the problems – sexism, male chauvinism, commercialism, exploitation through drugs, the illusory trip, the playing with weapons, the fear and experience of violent repression – all of which accompanied the late history of the NL, were portrayed. Whether self-consciously or not, the problems of personality-cult and fantasy in the American movement were highlighted.

Alongside the sense of freedom and exhilaration, there was the paranoia and anxiety of those who felt themselves strangers in their own lands, and a feeling of claustrophobia that fed on itself. Here were rebels and outcasts driven to exploit 'their own' people (symbolized in the film by the commune dwellers). Yet here also was the one hopeful element; the inhabitants of the commune were idealized as the 'real' people, creating anew through their work. In contrast, the anti-heroes were merely 'heads' or 'trippers' and, as one of them commented in what might be taken to be an epitaph for the Movement, they 'blew it'.

17. Picking up the Threads

Reconnections

It is perfectly understandable why the NL was pronounced dead even by its own supporters and sympathizers during the early seventies. To those who had not been involved in the Movement and who had accepted a received image of it after 1967, clearly most of the well-publicized aspects of that NL were breaking up or disappearing. Black power, Weatherman, SDS and the anti-war movement, were all receding, especially in so far as big demonstrations were concerned.[1] On the other hand, many projects which had very strong relationships with the NL continued and even flourished. One undoubted and lasting result of the NL, as April Carter points out, was that direct – even illegal – action had become 'normal' by the 1970s.

Women's Liberation is the clearest example of continuity – by turning back to the concern with intimate associations of power and inequality, it appeared to open up new paths of growth, including alternatives to the family, often related to participation and democracy. In projects such as food cooperatives, day-care centres, rent strikes, as well as in personal relationships, a communally oriented movement and alternative life-styles continued to thrive and so too did the critique of established disciplines and professions: in addition, the continuing resistance to the state at many levels of industrialized societies and a more generalized anti-war consciousness, as well as the growing ecological awareness, became more closely linked.

Moreover, locally based actions, including People's Park or Free School projects, which appear to synthesize these new concerns and awarenesses with the concerns and methods of the mainstream NL of the mid-1960s, seemed to point forward to a new phase of development.

Although predictably shunned or even attacked by the NL militants in the context of May 1969, these confrontations display a classic fusion of movement ideas and methods with the orientation of the alternative society towards environmental awareness.

The People's Park revolt in Berkeley represented an alliance of street people and students, outside the organization of the 'Old' or 'New' Lefts (the latter by this time equally obsessed with internal factionalism) and used imaginative direct actions to try to regain possession over decisions that affected them. Whilst it was attacked by some local radicals and socialist militants, this campaign in fact embodied both utopian vision and an assault on the capitalist principle of private property; the collective action and cooperative work employed in trying to implement this vision, links People's Park to the earlier community organizing projects: using nonviolence, stressing participation, and embodying counter-institutional approaches, it picked up the threads.

Where it differs from them perhaps, is both in its more anti-technological tone, and in the fact that the Park itself grew out of the growing autonomy of a specific radical community, and the reaction of the authorities to this. Emerging at the end of 1968, it initially shared some elements with the Columbia University struggle; just as at Columbia a Harlem landlord in his construction project on hitherto public park land, clashed with both students and local residents, the University of California too owned a great deal of the land upon which the Berkeley 'scene' had developed. Radicals and street people in trying to protect some often very attractive wooden houses, including student dwellings, free stores, and shops patronized by the hip community against the legal order and the bulldozer, were fired into taking direct action. On a number of occasions these had already provoked sporadic bombings and burnings; bulldozers used in clearing the housing had been bombed, and on occasions half-constructed blocks replacing the older housing were burnt to the ground.

The People's Park issue itself was merely a further stage in this ongoing battle; but because of the appeal of the ecologically related direct action, which transformed one of the plots near Telegraph Avenue[2] into an attractive and needed park with trees and flowers, the whole community became galvanized into the defence of its environment.

Much of this type of activity thus did not die with the major NL organizations; do-it-yourself politics with a local focus was, during the 1970s, even more widespread; campaigns against urban renewal, road-schemes and demolitions, as well as Shelter, welfare rights and claimants' fights – or even Workers' Cooperatives – represented the spread of the same ethic as that underpinning inter-racial organizing of oppressed or alienated groups, which had characterized the early NL projects. In England, in the mid- and late-1960s in areas such as St Anne's, Nottingham, in Scotland Road in Liverpool, in the Golborne area of Notting Hill, the emphasis on 'letting the people decide' institutionalized in free schools, craft centres and neighbourhood councils had spread. In America community anti-draft projects at the local level often represented much the same impulse; so did community-based peace centres and GI coffee houses.[3]

Also in England, more militant but in the same vein, were the squatting campaigns and rent and anti-eviction fights, gypsy actions and later claimants' unions, all developing under anarchist influence. It is here that the survival of very many minor, somewhat inchoate, libertarian projects, activities and ideas after the break-up of the organizational NL, may suggest that the latter's disasters represent short-term Movement reversals disguising a longer-term social trend.

Moreover, these projects are all symptomatic of continuities with an earlier NL; as their localism, spontaneity and decentralism keeps its momentum, so in the British context does the revival of Welsh and Scottish Nationalism, which using direct-action tactics as well as parliamentary ones, seemed to be influenced by NL ideas of community and devolution of power.[4] Indeed, it is not even impossible to envisage the eventual re-creation of Movement organizations similar to the SDS of 1965. There still appears a chance that a movement will take up where it had left off, picking up many of the threads like participatory democracy, community projects, counter-institutions – even non-violence – that were jettisoned in a period of crisis.

In Europe, the Kabouter movement of 1970 was even more strongly wedded than the Provos had been to an alternative society strategy: 'out of the sub-culture of an existing order', it announced, 'an alternative society is growing'. Indeed, many utopian elements had survived the bad years after 1967 and 1968, and with the collapse of SDS, there are signs of a recovery which ranges over sociological concerns, rural communalism, sex-role liberation and radical education projects. In the same period the most notable example of the 'pure' counter-institution to survive is the commune – both urban and rural – which began to establish itself, particularly in America, as a vital and exemplary living unit in an 'alternative society'. Politically, the communes, more often than not, expressed a desire to control the affairs of an immediate community, as well as the right to be left alone by the state.[5]

In addition, a growth of many local community papers and small-presses somewhat compensated for the beginning of the decline of the national 'underground press' proper; even this latter process was considerably delayed in comparison with the collapse of the organizational NL.[6] Moreover, the death of the counter-culture, or at least its malaise, was not necessarily occurring outside the Anglo-American context, as the late flowering of the Kabouter phenomenon in Holland showed. But as they announced, a change of course was needed:

It is the end of the underground, of protest, of demonstrations; from this moment we spend our energy on the construction of an anti-authoritarian society.[7]

A key difficulty in studying political movements is gauging the contrary tendencies that may well be operating at the same time; for example, there is the easily discernible tendency, already described, for the NL to move towards more authoritarian solutions and indeed even a return to Stalinism, apparently completing the circle begun in the early 1950s.

But there is also, in the larger context, persuasive indication of a longer-term libertarian tendency within which this authoritarian resurgence is a subsidiary, perhaps temporary, trend. The second phase of the Anarchist revival in the 1970s, is in fact partly the result of people moving out of the factionalism, sectarianism and ideological disputes of organizations like VSC and SDS, or the various Old Left culs-de-sac.

It is true that some of the Anarchist groups of this period themselves retain a distinctly sectarian Old Left flavour[8] and doctrinaire stance, just as some of the 'New Marxist' groups attempt to move away from these; nevertheless, in its general eclectic and flexible character, the anarchism of the 1970s still appears to be a major successor to the NL of the mid-1960s.

It is noticeable for example, that by the 1970s, even the key figures in popularizing authoritarian approaches in the NL are beginning to speak of withered states, of full self-government, of alternative institutions, and an 'end to politics'; not so very far from a libertarian utopia. [9] There is an implicit reaffirmation of the counter-institutional strategies of the NL, an elaboration of life-style change; Laing, and even Sartre, began to talk the language of 'alternatives'.

The neglected utopian aspect of the Movement in its re-development in the 1970s represents yet another confirmation of the thesis that the NL represents a continuity with the traditions of libertarian Socialism, and Anarchist thought. The core idea of creating the new society within the womb of the old, became more and more explicit during the period of centrifugality and diversification after 1970.

The principle that there should be a continuity between the revolutionary movement and a new society links the communes and affinity groups of these years with utopian Socialist ideas of the past in a more self-conscious fashion.[10]

Moreover, as was argued previously, the year 1968 did not signal the disappearance of nonviolence from the movement, as many commentators had predicted. In the West (even within many of the events of that year), certain nonviolent strands are retained; after 1968, a number of nonviolent projects, in addition to the Resistance, survive alongside the various violent ventures – the SDS splinters and the black militant groups.

This subsidiary tendency continued quietly, without always advertising itself: and in England, although nonviolent direct action had been presumed to have gone out of favour with the decline of CND, the Seventies Tour campaign revived militant civil disobedience effectively and was in fact far more like its predecessor than at first appeared.

In America the major radical project continuing through these years which avoided any seduction into violent rhetoric or means, the strike of rural workers in central California,[11] like the Poor People's coalition, suggested that in organizing the poor and migrant workers, it was still possible to draw effectively from the armoury of unarmed resistance, whether or not 'pure' nonviolence was used. Significantly many students again endorsed these campaigns and continued to relate to them by active involvement, boycotts, and support activities.

Nonviolent in essence, if not always in language, a number of projects also obeyed Carmichael's advice to preach nonviolence to the white middle class,[12] not least amongst the drop-out communities. Most significant of all, on campus, anti-militarism continued to be linked to draft-opposition and in the years after 1968–72, the mantle of much of the earlier Movement had passed to the Resistance,[13] more than to any other group. The Resistance, with its emphasis on individual responsibility and personal basis of political action, continued to invoke the long anarchist-pacifist tradition and expressed it in the return of draft cards and the willingness to go to jail. As Harris argued:

The most elaborate bureaucracy for selective service in the world does not function without people such as you and me, willing to sign our lives over to that system. Without you and me, it's nothing. . . . American totalitarianism is . . . participatory. When you carry a draft card, I think you become one more link in a whole chain of death and oppression on people's lives around the world.[14]

Through its integrity and morally founded actions, the Resistance won a widespread identification amongst young Americans, even amongst those who chose other methods, such as the 150,000 who emigrated;[15] in the 1970s public opinion shifted drastically against the Selective Service system, but the years after 1968 are also years of prosecution and jail – and more than 2,000 were given prison sentences, and more than 10,000 draft cards were publicly burnt or turned in;[16] this style and spirit in the Resistance passed on into other local actions.

The unwillingness to accept the conveyor belt of the career, linked the drop-out from the university to those who refused automatic military service; indeed, Mario Savio's remarks might be translated into the speech of a draft resister:

and you've got to indicate to the people who run it, to the people who own it that unless you are free, the machine will be prevented from working at all.

Such sentiments were at the basis of the Resistance; non-cooperation was rooted in the belief that the operation of the war machine, like the education machine, had become 'so odious, it makes you so sick at heart that you cannot take part, you cannot even tacitly take part'.

Such attitudes emerge again in the revelations of the American anti-war movement; the nature of states' activities, ultimately publicized by such renegades as Ellsberg, and previously guessed at by the anti-war groups, could not be documented until the consensus cracked far enough for major sections of the national press to become involved. The CIA defectors, the soldiers of conscience, the bureaucrats with second thoughts, helped fill out the true contours of America's South East Asian involvement, as well as Nixon's administrative techniques.

Despite the extraordinary lacuna of pacifist theories of modern conflict, there was also a tendency to return to both a more libertarian, and more fully pacifist position on war. Particularly in the Resistance and in the GI organizing[17] during the last three years of American presence there is evidence of a return to opposition to war as such, with a recognition of the role of the state as a major focus of resistance (as opposed to anti-imperialism). The Praesidio sit-downs, the GI organizations and the forces' papers, grew largely independent of any existing NL groupings; a 25 per cent leap in desertion figures coincided with these projects and the Veterans' protests of spring 1969.[18]

Even on campus, the continuing protests against napalm (Dow Chemicals), the ROTC programmes or defence research contracts, tended to stress individual complicity in the war-machine and militarism in general, rather than just the specific deployment of the machine by an 'imperialist class' in South East Asia. The turn away from SDS's anti-imperialist militancy marks the occasions for the revival of civil disobedience after 1970, in massive demonstrations in Washington, and elsewhere. This change is also exemplified in the Catonsville Nine's assault on the draft records at a board office in a Maryland town and the destruction of some files by napalm that they had made themselves, and the blood-staining of others. A militant, if a-theoretical pacifism has returned to the offensive, and such sabotage was specifically limited to property.[19]

The appearance of priests and nuns on demonstrations, the activism of the Berrigans or the Berkeley Free Church and Chavez, the inspiration of figures like Camara or revolutionary guerilla priests like Camillo Torres[20] are signs that the late 1960s and 1970s are years of a new radical Christianity: the Christian-Marxist dialogue, and a relative secularization of religion, makes possible its rapprochement with non-religious radicalism and even non-Christian traditions and political activism.

Against this, both the movements for sex-role liberation and the commune movement had to some extent to rediscover nonviolence by refusing to project on to others private ills, though these had a social substance. Thus by the 1970s, anger and compassion seem to be relocated within the arena of personal oppression, rather than, for good or ill, in Vietnam or a distant ghetto. Passionate involvement in vicarious killing, or the rationalization of others' crimes, becomes again less central to radicalism.

Perhaps against the dominant trends, communal living, hippy

nonviolence and to a lesser degree Women's Liberation, carried forward a non-aggressive cultural ideal, institutionalized in various 'gentle' days and happenings. Significantly, even in their confrontations with police, national guard, landlords and straight bigots, the hip-communities that survived, although often affected by the violent responses of the alternative press, students and street people, showed that they had not entirely abandoned their gentle techniques amidst the shower of stones, bottles and the destructive paraphernalia of 'trashing'.

In turn, during People's Park, even students and street people showed flexibility, and as has been noted in Holland, the Kabouters moved even further towards a nonviolent strategy than had the Provos.[21] Thus, despite the brief general turn to violence, as Lens had argued, NL strategy would continue to be

generally nonviolent, if only because the enemy has a huge weapons superiority, and because in a society where most grievances are not economic, reliance must be placed on appeals to conscience.[22]

It is also significant that the Movement was best able to maintain its fragile identity, most likely to regain a sense of itself after the crisis years of 1968 and 1969, when it returned to the 'politics of self'. The re-emphasis in the early 1970s, as a decade earlier, is on individual self-discovery; the stress on an experiential sense of oppression, whether in relation to Women's Liberation, anti-psychiatry or draft-resistance, again becomes paramount.

This attempted repossession of self-life, the connection of private ills and public issues, that had also characterized the fledgling NL, did not mean an unawareness of overtly political oppression. The draft-resistance movement, in particular, expressed the realization of an integration of concerns; the politics of resistance to state impositions on the individual may be at many levels; the personal, the communal – in terms of alternative living environments – and the trans-national – in terms of confrontation with the war and the US Selective Service laws as an external force.

It is the importance of experience as opposed to theory that is central to the politics of new life-styles: the experiential politics of sex-roles, including the Gay Liberation movement, links radical approaches to loving and living, as well as child rearing, which are best expressed in the commune-affinity group movements. This in turn suggested the ways in which structural and environmental awareness might be recreated in terms of individual response.

The politics of living environments, ecological radicalism and conservationist action became interwoven with life-style revolt, a critique of industrialism and capitalism, and the persistence of communal alternatives; the claims of an apparently insane world are criticized from the standpoint of those often defined as deviant, if not 'mad'.

Whilst the 'politics of experience' in Laing's version may be specified in terms of the opposition to a 'psychiatry of adjustment', it has implications beyond this refusal of 'normality' versus 'madness'; for post-scarcity radicals too, the pathology of the system is seen as intimately related to the discontents of the individual.[23] In the politics of anti-psychiatry, the rejection of conformity and of the absurdity of growing up (Laing takes up similar positions to Goodman on this), may still point to 'revolution as a solution'.

But to many commentators, the NL, because of such shifts, and others they discerned in the counter-culture, was judged to be becoming a less overtly political movement. During the period of the Cambodian invasion and the war in Bangladesh, it seemed to indicate that the rump of the NL had already lost any orientation towards confronting world-political issues; the fall of Saigon tended to affirm this unconcern.

Whilst in its own terms, the movement remained political mainly in its confrontations with the issues of everyday life, for the media, the political critics and even some movement theorists, the recession in confrontation and issue-orientation, subsequently clearly exemplified in a lack of a NL response to the Watergate affair, or the new Middle East crises, betokened an introversion, a dropping out from 'real politics', an a-political retrenchment or withdrawal.

Such an interpretation seemed confirmed too by the exodus from urban environments such as the East Village, Berkeley or Haight-Ashbury, to rural communities. This had begun as early as 1966, but only gathered momentum in the period from 1969 onwards; it was an expression of frustration not only with urban life, but with developments within the Movement itself, and disillusion with certain 'political' strategies. Once again the question was repeated: 'Can the more purely cultural aspects of the NL be tolerated, repressively, while the political face is crushed?'[24]

Sexism and liberation

It may be significant that the most deeply seated, and least recognized attitude of the NL – its sexism – was the issue that spawned the most important of the movements to survive its demise; Women's Liberation and the other sex-role focused movements. WL arose as a sort of antibody in the movement, and it was forced outside the organizational confines of the NL as it existed in 1966–7 simply because it was almost impossible to make headway on the problem from within.

Indeed there is substantial evidence that sexism grew more virulent as the Movement entered its years of crisis and is intertwined with the descent into posturing, machismo, authoritarianism and violence. Male chauvinism was rarely dealt with successfully by anyone in the Movement even when accepted as an issue at all. The term 'sexism' is one of the very last additions to the NL's vocabulary. It was also the very last problem of 'selfhood' faced by activists or theorists. The failure to recognize and deal with it at an early stage is a symptom of a core-weakness in which the other degenerations were rooted. The women's movement survived the NL organizationally because a radical consciousness itself had highlighted rather than solved the problems of maleness – the Gay Liberation movements were inevitable by-products of the same crisis.

Nevertheless, one must trace the actual birth of Women's Liberation to activities and debates within the Resistance wing of SDS; the issue emerging as an implied criticism of the male-dominated NL movements like SDS. And WL as a movement initially took its themes[25] from the NL as a whole; although for the first two or three years, primarily an American phenomenon, WL's influence eventually spread to Britain and other European countries after 1969.

There it takes its own forms and character; usually less radical, militant and flamboyant than the transatlantic model which it claimed to follow. In these years, Women's Liberation was initially ridiculed from Movement platforms as 'pussy power',[26] although eventually in the white movement this stance was sharply reversed after 1969, and *male chauvinism* in turn was attacked from the platform and shouted down from the floor. But the position of women in the NL generally, in the view of many, had actually deteriorated from 1965 to 1969.

Such heightened oppression was recognized as early as 1965 in the workshop set up by SDS to investigate the problem. In 1967 an SDS Women's caucus fought strong opposition to pass a resolution on their situation. The tendencies of SDS towards more assertive public speaking instead of informal workshops, large rallies in place of small meetings, formal caucus-ridden sessions in place of informal coopera-tive gatherings, all worked *against* women in the Movement.

The growing machismo of movement symbolism (some of which, like the clenched fist and the rifle, was absorbed by the women's movement) depicted this growth of male imagery. For SDS, as for the counter-culture, such supremacy was glamorized in a set of male heroes, from rock stars to black leaders and Third World guerillas; the sexism of the rock culture was not criticized but imitated. The sexism of black power was accepted. The sexual machismo and stereo-typing of the Cuban revolution was, until the eruption of the women's movement, beyond criticism. Even GLF initially involved itself in the Venceremos brigade.

The growth of a women's movement was also partly provoked by the negative experiences of white women in the civil rights movement before 1965.[27] Certainly there is later a strong element of 'machismo', a stress on virility and maleness in both black power and the Black Panthers, expressed in the speeches and writings of Carmichael and Cleaver, that sometimes bursts into open sexism. Black power and the groups associated with it were overwhelmingly male, in a way which distinguishes them from the civil rights groups in which women had played prominent roles, reflecting their hitherto relatively high status in the black community; yet most black power groups ridiculed Women's Liberation.

The consciousness of the racial, sexual intertwining and the sexual stereotyping of black people, as well as the relatively strong matriarchal system of the ghetto, meant that the young developed a virility symbolism and associations of machismo that were quite divorced from any real life strategy of social power; these had, in other words, a deep laden psychic implication.[28]

Undoubtedly the image of black power 'flowing from the muzzle of a gun' was closely linked with the NL's own cult of machismo, and the growing sexism of the black movement. For example, the achievement of manhood, and the idea of 'getting guns', are continually interspersed in the writing of Cleaver and other militant celebrities: 'we shall have our manhood' by 'becoming armed'.

But this link was equally true of sections of the white NL. The guerilla mystique 'is the incarnation of virility in speech, action and dress', which is 'expressed by bravado, courage and ruthlessness' (Horowltz). The Latin American cult of 'machismo' was typified by the Cuban Barbudos, the 'bearded warriors' who spearheaded Castro's takeover. Their battle-fatigues, big cigars, and brandishing of weapons, as well as profoundly patriarchal attitudes to women – as domestics and nurses – was not unattractive to many American movement males. It was a posture of domination that went unchallenged, at least until the NL developed its own critique of the Cuban revolution,[29] and it had strong parallels with the felt 'crisis of black manhood'.

The inherited political traditions of the Left, which included this male leadership and iconography and a subordinate role for females, did not long go unchallenged. The critique was extended to the male chauvinism not only of the Cuban revolutionary movement (and others), but to the statements of Castro and Guevara, and Cuban social structure.[30] More particularly, criticism was aimed at the black movement which, from Carmichael to Cleaver, had gone through a particularly vicious period of blatant male chauvinism and sexist pronouncements presumably in an attempt to compensate for the 'emasculation' that was being blamed on white society.[31]

In strong parallels to the black movement's relationship to white values, Movement women found considerable difficulty in adjusting to a new scale of values which suddenly made male qualities and priorities less valid, and therefore less worthy of imitation or emulation. For many women, to become 'free' still was, apparently, mainly an aspiration to become more male, just as liberation of blacks was perceived sometimes as taking on the methods and aspirations of whites. Thus in order to achieve an identity, just as blacks had opted for exclusion in seeking their autonomy from whites, women, understandably, now moved towards their own separatism – and a solution was sought in the exclusion of males.

Yet even in the area of sexism itself, Women's Liberation's confusion could not be better exemplified than in its adoption of many male symbols of aggression; the weapon, hitherto a symbol associated with a male black or Vietcong, is portrayed now in the hands of women; their militarization is identified by some leaders as liberation,[32] and the acquired tool of violence is subsequently flourished with bravado as women appear in military or guerilla garb or roles. Some WL groups, e.g. in Britain, even adopted as their symbol the clenched fists and other traditional instruments of masculine aggression[33] derived from the male NL.

Particularly in England, these tendencies continue to be associated with the new Marxist, or Old Left Socialist, wing of WL; and typify the degree to which the movement remained influenced, if no longer controlled, by male-dominated Left groups and ideologies. The relationship with males – the question of female separatism – and the problem of relating to Marxism, the socialist sects, and the NL, are central, even obsessive, problems for these groups and much of the early debate centres on them.

The most ambiguous women's group in relation to these dilemmas were the 'Weatherwomen'. Having failed to make a clear break with the SDS tradition, they straddled the divide between WL and the late political NL producing in the process the first major woman leader to emerge in the NL (Bernardine Dohrn); they criticized WL for both its separatism and lack of revolutionary ideology, yet they also courageously used WL arguments within SDS and other groups and in a context of rampant sexism. In response, 'Weatherwomen' were widely criticized by Women's groups for their involvement in the 'macho' style of political aggression and in street-fighting.

Despite the prominent role of feminist arguments amongst Weatherwomen, O'Brien is probably correct in the assertion that the military model and discipline they imposed on themselves was ultimately 'based on masculine versions of strength and toughness',[34] though its adoption can be in part explained by the difficult conflict in roles forced on Weatherwomen. Bernardine Dohrn and the leading women in the group played a significant analytical role with their writing and speeches, sharpening the debate around revolutionary feminism and its relation with Marxism and revolutionary ideologies of the Left generally. But critiques of Weatherwomen, as well as the 'Bread and Roses' statement, attacked their anti-separatist position: 'The illusion of strength when you run hand in hand with your oppressors' (Morgan), or the adoption of violent machismo styles in order to 'compete as equals'.[35]

Whilst it suggested deep ideological confusion, overall this extreme identification with the aggressor was not typical of Women's Liberation as a movement, and even less of the Gay movement. At various points,

Women's Liberation was analysed both as distinguishing itself from other movements of class struggle, and as a trans-national one. It transcended national boundaries, it would be organized by no nation against another; and it varied from culture to culture, or group to group, rather than from nation to nation. What women had in common came to seem more important than what divided them through class or geopolitical boundaries; whilst this seemed equally true of the young, or students of cultural and ethnic minorities in the advanced societies, the sexual division cut deeper into basic relationships once given political emphasis. Like the generational conflict, it cut right across existing groups, both political and social, bringing to bear its critique within the relationships of the family, of the local SDS chapter, and of the male chauvinism embedded in radical, not least Marxist, ideology.

The failure of SDS to seriously adapt to the feminist impulse was noted during 1968 by erstwhile women activists:

We were still the movement secretaries . . . the shit-workers, we served the food, prepared the mailings . . . earth mothers and sex-objects . . . dependent on the male elite for direction and definition.[36]

Separatist tendencies amongst women in SDS grew stronger in 1968 as its machismo style became more pronounced; it was only the clutch of militant women left in SDS in 1969 who formed Weatherwomen; those attached to PL took an openly anti-feminist line in SDS.[37] Thus in part it was the failure of the women's movement to radically alter SDS that forced it to create its own independent movement and organizations.

By 1969, these existed outside the various NL fragments (all still male dominated),[38] and grew rapidly. Women's Liberation, as the last major movement of an NL constituency, thus evolved dramatically in the years following 1968. Although, as O'Brien has shown, the women's movement derived most of its early impetus and its recruits from women already active in the NL in the mid- and later-1960s,[39] and its leadership from those women drawn from SDS, it soon became a national phenomenon quite outside and beyond the confines of the NL itself, and increasingly distant from it. Yet this evolution cannot be understood except in the context of the NL's crisis and decline, and WL's emergence in the aftermath of its collapse, as a major – if by now somewhat isolated – force.

In many other spheres than sexism, the problems of the women's movement continued to be the same ones that had plagued SDS and SNCC, not least because it took its ideological and organizational cues from formations like them. That is why the role of factions associated with male-dominated socialist sects created deep tensions (as equally did the role of gay women's factions). Both of these attempted to put an indelible stamp on the movement, but to some extent, its very loose, decentralized nature, reminiscent of the earlier NL, served as a partial safeguard. Like the rest of the NL, WL, as a movement, tended to fall apart whenever the attempt was made to put a Leninist straitjacket on it organizationally, or introduce Marxian dogmatics ideologically.

Given these problematic relationships, it is understandable that many feminists, stressing personal liberation, denied that the women's movement was part of the NL at all. In so doing, they revealed their ignorance not only of the origins of their own movement, but of the origins and character of the NL itself. It is significant that those more concerned with their own oppression and with small-group experiential politics or PD (all condemned by Dohrn and other Weatherwomen) were in reality returning to the SDS style of pre-1966, and with it to an earlier emphasis on personal liberation and 'consciousness-raising'.

Thus the women's movement always carried with it the marks of its own birth and a strong continuity with the early NL – and even elements from its later growth; initially both movements sprang from individual and personalist concerns, using expressive and spontaneous techniques, including direct action, to highlight grievances.

Given the degeneration by 1969 of many of those aspects of the NL's identity most closely linked to WL, including the more participatory and egalitarian impulses, WL's rejection of the radical movement is understandable. But in its exploration of the political implications of relationships, in its construction of alternatives – day-care centres, play-groups, women's advice centres, women's communes, free schools and alternative women's papers – WL carries through the mainstream work of the NL, and represents an extension of its identity.

But, both in America and Britain, the women's movement developed in addition to its socialist and feminist wings (by no means a clearcut division) two major strategic perspectives: the one concerned with pragmatic demands – pressure for reforms, on issues such as abortion, contraception, discriminatory hiring, equal pay and conditions, nursery education and divorce – the other concerned with the cultural and identity-creating dimensions of transformation focused on self-awareness and more total 'revolutionary' demands by women on a 'patriarchal' society. These two perspectives, not always separated in practice, never simply coincide with the socialist/feminist tension, not least because, like the rest of the radical movement, WL, amorphous and disorganized, is often hostile to theory.

Moreover, this growth represents a further extension of the NL's concern with personal development that linked it to the principles of PD, the closing gap between theory and practice, and the experiential humanism, which had been typical of the early years. Through women's consciousness as a group, these same impulses were synthesized into a thorough-going critique of all facets of the current political and cultural movements; for example, in the context of the commune movement, it brought into sharper focus the problems of the traditional sex-based division of labour and child-rearing roles. In education, the family, politics and work, even on violence and aggression, basic assumptions and orientations were challenged and reversed – including, sometimes, the structure of power in these institutions, and especially Movement organizations, especially the sex-related division of labour.

In the view of some NL commentators, the emergence of this consciousness was the most spectacular example of the transformation of individual concerns into social and political issues in the whole development of the Movement. There was a growing awareness in some of the literature of American feminism that power, violence, inequality and aggression were profoundly inter-related;[40] that politics did indeed begin at home in the most archetypal relationships of male and female, both in themselves and as role models for children, and moreover, in the parental relationship as determined by the former. The realization that women even more than men, do not 'live their own lives or fulfil their own needs' was growing, just as it had grown amongst other groups – especially blacks. This explains the degree to which women identified with theoretical challenges to the 'adjustment-philosophy' of any oppressed group to its situation, or its attempted 'self-definition' *through* an alien or oppressor group.[41]

The attack on the assumptions of basic experiences, such as family life and child-rearing, implicit in sex-role liberation – and the challenge to inherited differentiations of task that this led to – were intimately related to the radical post-Freudian or 'anti-psychiatry' approach to the family in the West, its inadequacies and even demise. Both political psychologists like Sampson, and writers like Laing and Cooper, had located basic problems of power and oppression in the family institution, and their writing finds considerable resonance in the pronouncements and growing literature of Women's Liberation.[42] Inevitably many Freudian assumptions, especially about the sexual division of labour and a father-centred family psychology, were attacked and discarded.[43]

This synthesis of movement scepticism of ordinary institutions, together with the anti-psychiatrists' predictions of a 'death of the family' and a drift towards various types of alternative living situations, was intended to re-open new possibilities of change, not least in transforming the immediate institutions such as the family, the school or the clinic. Radical sociologists had long held that the nuclear family, reduced to an almost skeletal form, had become an acquisitive unit, individuated and colonized by organizations. It no longer provided the group life in an urban setting that the traditional community and extended kinship had offered. Child-rearing now urgently demanded a new set of institutions: for example, schools organically linked with a neighbourhood and parents, rather than impersonal, alienated and spatially distanced 'institutions': above all, a community that could 'look after its own' from the 'cradle to the grave', and redistribute the workload involved.

Many social experiments were now consciously related to actual changes in the division of labour, especially those involving sex roles[44] or the sex-role socialization of children. They could clearly act as partial replacements for the threatened or weakened family institution, and release women for other activities.

To some elements in the sex-role movements it was seen to be as necessary for liberation to transcend the patriarchal Marx, as Freud; the work of Fromm, Reich, Marcuse, Goodman and now Laing in particular, opened up modes of revision that would relate to the personal sense of oppression felt by sexual 'minorities'. While to some extent each of these still represented fusions by male theorists of elements of Marx and Freud, by attacking capitalism and authoritarian and conservative elements in the bourgeois family that Freud had taken for granted, they also went beyond both in rejecting the necessity of at least surplus repression.[45]

In Marcuse's view, the transformation to a 'natural order of freedom' had to resolve psychic tensions; in so far as sexuality (and the perverted forms of eroticism that emerged in repressive society)[46] is based on social counter-points it must be dissolved, and a 'new eroticism' discovered. This presumed, amongst other things, a potential equality between human beings that would demand the transformation or abolition of current sexuality (the inescapable corollary of WL).[47]

In this area, that of sexual expression and sexual identity, there develop deep tensions and splits in the counter-culture. The revolt against sexual repression and 'Puritan' mores was clearly a substantial component in the growth of the culture, yet this faced in several directions. For some, sexual liberation implied mainly *licence*, for others a transformation of sexuality, and there were certainly some in the counter-culture who attacked the emphasis on, and nature of, Western genital-sexuality *per se* and urged its transcendence. As with previous generations of radicals, it was soon discovered that any attack on bourgeois sexual norms, wherever grounded, appears to strike near the quick of society.

Yet had a more conscious integration of 'sexual freedom' with the NL's political critique been made earlier (as hinted in Reich's *Sex-Pol*) the attack might have been less prone to co-optation into a mere exploitative and trivial pornography (e.g. in the underground press). In fact it was the alternative press *itself* that tended to lead the way in promoting a sexist commercialism, even when it had begun to proclaim a sympathy with WL.

Within the evolution of the counter-culture, the sado-masochistic basis of much eroticism and sexuality in authoritarian social contexts is highlighted in this period, both through its *resolution* in androgynous, sexless or 'a-sexual' attitudes and roles in the counter-culture, or equally in its caricature and expressive exaggerations in music and the underground press.[48] Both the androgynous renunciation of the sado-masochistic form of sexual relationship that was favoured by many feminists (and indeed by many in the Gay Liberation movement), and the excessive imagery of the underground, attacked the basis of much inherited pornography and thus might be accepted as an ally.

But this alliance presumed that bourgeois sexuality was rooted in a restrained and limited, but nevertheless real, form of sado-masochism from which all but the most perverse could be rescued, by its caricature or satire. In England, *Oz*, for example, turned itself over to images of sexual mutilation, extravagant obscenity and the theatre-of-cruelty which was explicitly sexual, but anti-erotic; rationalized as an attack on the whole bourgeois edifice of sexual prudery, repression and hypocrisy, it revealed itself as just as much symptomatic of these same sicknesses.

Thus, the adoption by RYM and the Weatherpeople of a sexist and sadistic murderer (Manson) as hero[49] in his setting on the fringe of the counter-culture, led to a conclusion expressed by some revolutionary and anti-male feminists, that women, like blacks and peasants, would have to make their own revolutions.[50] Robin Morgan, in 'Goodbye to all that', her extended attack on male chauvinism in the NL – especially in SDS and Weatherman – ridiculed the 'theory of free sexuality' but actual practice of 'free sex on demand for males', warning against the adoption of sexual 'experimentation' that turned out to be 'exploitation'. Though the *degree* of male dominance in the NL and the alternative society before 1969, was *highlighted* in these clashes, the actual dominance of males prevailed in many areas, not least the underground press; this was partly, not least, because women and Gays organized themselves separately.

In part, these critical weaknesses in the whole movement, first highlighted by Women's Liberation, can be attributed to a failure in ideas; in part for example, a misunderstanding of Marcuse's attitudes to sexual liberation, and of his argument for the 'free development of libido against the constraints of the bourgeois work-ethic' (wrongly taken as an endorsement of sexual freedom). In fact, Marcuse too warned against the alienated release of frustrated sexuality; when he declared that a release 'within the dominion of (existing) institutions' would bear the 'marks of its suppression', he might well have been referring to the explosion of suppressed sexuality that characterized the alternative press;[51] or equally, when he talked of its 'hideous' manifestations. Moreover Marcuse clearly stressed that he was not talking about genital-centred sexuality but a broadening eroticism, both of which had to some extent been characteristics of the underground.[52]

The breakdown of sexual stereotypes, implicit in the hippy sub-cultures, had been a necessary precondition of the development of movements based on release from the cult of male-dominance. Indeed this breakdown was continuous with the sex-role liberation of both women and gay people; the re-awakened interest in the work of Reich and Fromm coincided with a more widespread awareness of sexual power and violence as the psycho-sexual counterparts of political domination and submission; these become a central cultural theme in the late 1960s.

As a result, it was possible for each sex-role movement to cautiously reapproach nonviolence, since much masculinity and aggression were now seen as largely extraneous and symbolic; the Gay movement in particular shared with the counter-culture the desire to destroy the emphasis on polar sexualities. Masculinity, it was proposed, can be defined without the cult of dominance and virility, just as femininity can be defined free of subordination and passivity.

Sexual liberation thus may become politically significant, but only alongside WL and as part of the general movement of the counter-culture. However, when isolated, the move towards 'permissiveness' merely became, as Marcuse warned, a token expression – a safety valve. In the optimistic (masculine) viewpoint of the early NL, two concerns of the movement, sexual liberation and political freedom, appeared to be merged since 'political domination' and 'sexual repression' (as Reich and others had argued considerably earlier) were seen to be 'of a piece'. But as the movement develops, these inadequate definitions of freedom and sexuality are shown up by both the Women's and Commune movements, and mark the crises in SDS.

It is ironic that first the black movement, and then sections of the white NL moved, as has been seen, in a quite different direction in this period: by both rejecting the effeminacy of the counter-culture and re-emphasizing male supremacy and the subordination of women, they revealed that the enterprise was both more complex and more perilous than had appeared. Gitlin, in particular, emphasizes the degree to which Movement relationships were then re-examined in the light of the self-revelations of male chauvinism brought on by this period of crisis.

Post-scarcity radicalism

The shifts in the movement of the 1970s were also accelerated by the development of a new sociological and philosophical appraisal of post-industrial society.[53] It is centred on the realization that, as Marcuse put it, 'the rationality of domination' had progressed 'to a point where it threatens to invalidate its own foundations'. Repression in post-scarcity society was based on the need to 'reaffirm the rationality of domination more effectively than before'. 'Post-scarcity consciousness', movement writers argued, on the other hand 'totally negates the established order and calls for a total alternative'.[54]

Three main currents of change had been detected by Schön as associated with the dissolution of the existing order; the imbalance between public and private (the product-based consumer society); the disillusion with the identification of progress with technology; and the emergence of hitherto subordinated constituencies, especially the young. For Bookchin and other post-scarcity Anarchists (as for Sartre and Marcuse), the key to dismantling bourgeois culture still lay in the conjuncture of youth opposition and cultural revolt. A post-scarcity identity, although an 'unprecedented' one, was the only possibility, in Gitlin's view, for any NL which would survive; only such a stance could have saved organizations like SDS, which had seemed to finally turn away from it. So far this identity had come closest in the experiments of the hippies – their

attempt to unravel society from within; destroying the rationale, undermining the legitimacy, the social ethic which is the moral cement which holds the whole fabric together.[55]

For in industrial society, scarcity can no longer be used to justify belt-tightening, self-repressive work and leisure, postponed satisfactions, and nineteenth-century styles of sexuality, regimentation and discipline. The portents of change first represented in the early dropouts, the Beats and the hippies, become, in Gitlin's words

an insurgent politics, taking off from an experimental culture and embodying the social values of love, co-operation, and decentral energy.[56]

Gitlin's NL and post-scarcity utopia is instructive, in being nearer to the timeless social commonwealth of William Morris than to the pre- and post-revolutionary development of new social forces that Marx or Lenin had described. Stressing fraternal interdependence and individual independence together, the role of direct democracy is still seen as fundamental. Alternatives which make values explicit 'must be lived by the movement' in order to make possible changes 'which the movement of post-scarcity does not know how to make and cannot make alone.' This stress on life-style, including voluntary poverty and the overall cultural condition of existence, in part represents the return to emphases in the earlier (not least English) NL and the English Anarchists.

Carl Oglesby argued that the essentially post-industrial revolution embodied most fully in the hip-communities, portends the 'historically most advanced development for socialist consciousness'. Whilst Oglesby was dubious whether existing alternatives linked to popular culture represented a full subversion of 'commodity fetishism', the consumption pattern of the alternative community was extremely limited in comparison with that of the American middle class. For radicals in a society producing and consuming as much as 35 per cent of the world's manufactured goods, such a move towards rejection of affluence and consumption might still seem bizarre. Many asked if it was possible.

Wellman,[57] like Gitlin, argued it had

to work toward the elimination of the sources of [their own] privilege without killing the dream to which [their] privileged position gave birth;

(such were the contradictions of 'post-scarcity'). Moreover, amongst the NL's ancillary constituencies, only parts of the middle class concerned with conservation and environmental issues took such opposition to consumer-values to their heart. Amongst blacks, the rejection of the consumer society was ambiguously expressed by recurrent looting in the ghetto uprisings; black materialism remained a peculiarly complex and symbolic phenomenon; notably in the black bourgeoisie it represented a continuing repression of cultural spontaneity.

In the development of these critiques of post-scarcity society, the role of mass-education is seen as paramount. The indoctrination of students or children into the bourgeois values of obedience becomes central to the advanced economy, and thus, it is speculated, confrontation with the university may yet become confrontation with its patron, the state. In this analysis, the university bureaucracy, almost a perfect embodiment of organizational liberalism, was fully integrated into the corporate structure of the state; its scientists were engaged in government projects, including military scientific research. At Berkeley, its agronomists were tightly integrated with the agrobusiness of California,[58] and the Radiation Laboratory and the Livermore (H-bomb research) Institute carried on the preparations for nuclear holocaust.[59]

One of the results of the peace movement revival of the 1950s and 1960s, as well as the student and black power movements, was a change in university curricula and research orientations,[60] including deepened interest in peace studies and non-military or civilian defence, that emerged directly from the nuclear pacifism of the early NL. Afro-American or black studies, Women-focused courses, and student-oriented 'participant education', experimental colleges and curricula were further examples of the same development. In England, the Hornsey Art College sit-in was linked with new experiments in art education which were repeated elsewhere after 1968. But 'growing up absurd' and 'compulsory miseducation' involved other institutions besides the university; in the 1970s primary attention is turned to the intermediary institutions, the family and the school as socializing instruments. Under the influence of writers like Goodman, A. S. Neill, Holt and latterly Illich, the idea of free schools begins to develop rapidly.[61] Many of them, run by voluntary help, related themselves to remedial social action in the local community. Socialist groups began to organize amongst teachers, to include curricula demands in state schools.

There was, however, as considerable a division over 'post-scarcity' ideas amongst Anarchists, as amongst the NL generally. From confidence in a centralized cybernated utopia, to a belief in a simplified decentralized 'intermediate' technology, the range of reactions to post-scarcity possibilities was enormous. On the whole, modern technology was seen as supportive of the interlinked processes of Statism, industrialism and modern war, if not fundamentally integrated with them.

Marcuse, like Mills, had stressed the loss of control, as a central component of alienation:

labour is work for an apparatus which [men] do not control which operates as an independent power to which men must submit if they want to live.

The repossession of politics and work demands participant power and a controllable technology. Only in this repossession could craft revive: a non-routinized, non-robotized work. Moreover, a political control, which did not imply technological control, was clearly limited if not meaningless. As Ellul argued, there could be 'no human autonomy in the face of technical autonomy', and the need for a humanized technology, intermediate in scale, decentralized in structure, was a clear counterpart to the demand for political direction.

The deliberate transformation of technology would be one of the first crucial tasks confronting the movement for participatory democracy.

Whilst there was general agreement with the view, already articulated by Goodman, Sartre and Marcuse, that the problems of advanced society were linked to artificial needs rather than necessity, there was a division between optimistic and pessimistic predictions of technologically advanced solutions. Part of the concern of Anarchists was to appraise which part of technology could be used in non-authoritarian ways; the practical applications of new techniques to solve basic problems.

Post-scarcity theory posed problems which had not been understood, let alone dealt with by the Old Left. For all the various revisions of Marxist theory during the period of the NL, there remained an unwillingness amongst most Marxists of whatever variety, to abandon the apparatus of industrial power as a means to progressive change.[62] There was a refusal to recognize that the loss of human control it implied, was part of the 'organized irresponsibility' and 'drift' of the juggernaut state condemned by Mills; in the most bleak interpretation, that of Ellul,[63] 'technique prevails over the human being'; but a whole range of theorists were no longer willing to give technology the benefit of the doubt; collectivization and the forms of industrialization implicit in Third World Communist change (even in China) continued to be viewed with a sceptical ambivalence, but mainly with the belief that this was only a more subtle way of reproducing the same 'progressive' transformation, that first capitalism, then Stalinism had achieved.[64]

Amongst Anarchist options, the most popular was close to Goodman's original belief in a technological decentralization of an intermediate kind, linked to a critique of useless and degrading work. The faith in small-scale living units which could be relatively self-sufficient, held that mankind could largely bypass this problem. But there was a growing tension between many 'Luddites' in the counter-culture, the intermediate technologists and those (like Leary) who were basically optimistic about the possibilities of technological advancement in terms of decentralism, leisure, decision-making or participation. But the latter's idea of a non-oppressive, and *advanced* participatory technology, was rejected by those who felt that such technique would always be the master of the technician, and would continue to imply an end to craft; but there remained a middle position.

The radical revolt against technology represented in part the search for an alternative to a crackpot positivistic rationality and the technical 'operationalism' associated with it. Opposition to the defoliating, computerized, American war-machine in Vietnam highlighted the contrasts between the so-called 'advanced' and 'backward' sectors of technology, the impact of 'civilization' on a rural culture, and the depersonalization of mechanized killing.

Weatherman's attempt to damage the 'war-machine' by direct violence against military installations, betokens not only its own move towards anarchistic disruption, but a Luddite impulse as well. In many quarters, opposition to the war was in part generated by opposition to the symbols of destructive, bureaucratic technology, which was polluting globally in the name of peace. Marcuse's analysis of the political and ideological domination that is implicit in science and technology, gives intellectual weight to what had been sometimes written off as romantic 'machine-breaking'.

The search for repossession pointed naturally towards the utopian solutions of Fromm and Goodman; industrial devolution on a manageable scale rooted in small relatively autonomous communities had a deep attraction for the urban discontented, already concerned about the urban environment and pollution. Elements of the progressive middle class began early in the 1960s to concern themselves with such problems as ecology and such solutions as intermediate technology. Moreover, in this search for alternative technology and in part as an extension of worker control, the NL came slowly to express a deeper realization of the profound problems associated with industrialized, mechanized production and life 'whatever the regime under which it lives'.[65] Whilst the counter-culture first introduced an anti-industrialist as well as anti-capitalist 'Luddism' to the Movement, the logic of the political NL, of participatory democracy, workers' control, decentralization and identification with peasant people, and the 'world's oppressed' generally, led there also; there is a definite synthesis of such concerns by the early 1970s.

A clear example is found in the communal wing of the 'alternative society'; increasingly stressful of ecologically sound life-styles during the 1960s, it had been focusing on consumption and production, and emphasizing the decentral principle for ecological as well as political reasons. It criticized Marxism and other left traditions for treating the planet as an exploitable resource, with the positivist assumption that nature is subordinate to man. The need for a planetary sensibility (which in turn they often linked to population campaigns, and WL's calls for 'contraception and abortion on demand') became the single most popular radical theme by 1971.[66]

New groups like Friends of the Earth emerged; and even the peace movement took on new dimensions in its 'Greenpeace' and 'Survival' groups and committees. The sense of a lost symbiosis with the environment created a renewed respect for communes and communities closer to the soil and seasonal cycle. This sentiment especially reinforced or renewed solidarity with minority and peasant peoples, threatened tribes, or exploited folk communities which retained this symbiosis, and were already identified as a dimension of NL's trans-national consciousness.

These shifts in awareness and attitude are betrayed not least in a growing global concern that had been precipitated in no small degree by the impact of external developments like the ever-present threat of nuclear devastation in every part of the world. This consciousness also reflects the growing realization of the finite limits of resources; the implications of the space race and the obvious depredations of industrial man on his planetary environment. It is an awareness both carried and reinforced by the counter-culture; to a large extent the so-called ecology and conservation movements also arise outside both the NL and the counter-culture. But the former takes up themes in the movement's deepest crisis, during the People's Park, and, in the 1970s, in the Greenpeace movement, that had already been developed particularly by CND and by the counter-culture.

With renewed threat of a Third World War, 'species interest' and 'individual interest' were finally brought together again by the growing awareness of potential environmental (including nuclear) catastrophe, at least amongst many Western radicals. In this period, human survival was seen to be at issue for both conservationists and nuclear disarmers alike; the epitaph to mankind used on the early CND marches, and written on a large model of a dinosaur, now seemed to ring even more true: 'Too much armour, too little brain, now he's extinct.' Acquisition of nuclear arms by India, underground testing by America in Amchitka, and Britain in New Mexico, by Russia in Nova Zemlya, as well as the atmospheric testing by the Chinese at Lop Nor, and by the French in the Pacific, latterly at Mururoa atoll – constantly reminded the world of this reality, after a decade of forgetfulness.

Echoes of the anti-war activities of the 1950s were also found in nonviolence, kept alive in the later 1960s and 1970s by trans-national projects relating to the less ideological national conflicts in Biafra and Bangladesh. Operation Omega exemplified in particular the boundary transcending and defying actions that had characterized the earlier projects;[67] and the Greenpeace voyages into testing zones concretize an even stronger and more direct link backwards with the origins of the NL, to the anti-nuclear protests and individual direct-action attempts of the later 1950s.

If People's Park represents the impact of ecological action at the communal level, these Greenpeace voyages represent its implementation at the trans-national one, and in relation to the peace movement. Greenpeace marches and projects in the early 1970s, opposing the nuclear test series by the Americans, French and the Chinese (and also against the continuing Vietnam war) are a direct echo of the voyages of an earlier period such as Everyman; and of CND, which began the popular concern with pollution in its publicizing of the problems of radiation. But the original anti-nuclear organizations of the 1950s and 1960s were, by the 1970s, largely dead or beyond revival – even by a dreamed of influx of new energy and talent.[68]

Among radicals there is still widespread belief, held on largely rationalistic grounds, that sooner or later, accidentally or by design, in a pre-emptive or surprise attack – in crisis or in retaliation – nuclear weapons will inevitably be used; if such use is limited, a mass movement against nuclear weapons may still revive, and if it does, particularly as a response to some limited or accidental use of nuclear warheads, then it will clearly bypass, flowing over and beyond, any existing structures and organizations – just as the anti-nuclear movement itself at its birth bypassed or absorbed its predecessors.[69]

As Roszak insisted:

We are a civilization sunk in unshakeable commitment to genocide, gambling madly with the universal extermination of our species. And how viciously we ravish our sense of humanity to pretend, even for a day, that such horror can be accepted as 'normal', as 'necessary'!

By bringing together a global environmental concern with the political tradition of the NL and the moral and nonviolent protest of the peace movement, 'post-scarcity rebellion' may yet represent the foundations of a future major revival. Even the struggles against what for the early NL was the greatest symbol of man's alienation and self-destructive capacity, nuclear weapons, cannot, any more than any other aspect of NL activity, necessarily be written off, or considered ended, merely because of the crisis, decline or disappearance of those organizations which at a certain historical moment captured or represented these concerns.

But where the Movement which develops outside these organizational expressions is changing, as a result of over a decade of NL activity, is in seeing the programmatic necessity and theoretical reality of more definite links between practical change at the level of the individual and group, and structural change at the level of trans-national or universal power systems and societal organization, especially in relation to the nation state.

As *Anarchy* had put it in earlier days:

We cannot oppose nuclear war without addressing ourselves to the causes of war. We cannot advocate nonviolence without considering the cause of all violence. We cannot resist the defence policy of the government without coming up against the problem of the allocation of power in society as a whole.

Appendix: Leninism, Militarism, and Peasant Revolution

The contribution of Leninism, foreshadowed in nineteenth-century revolutionary theory, represents a major disjuncture with Marx's own thought. Lenin's view of revolution, though in part derived from the imagery of 1789, did not sit easily with Marx's own overall view of the historical process. Marx was mainly concerned with describing epochal developments and the emergence of new social forces, leading to a new social order. Lenin was more concerned with a pragmatic strategy for revolutionary élite. Climactic events and the use of force had their place in Marx's scheme merely as the 'midwife' of changes which were occurring anyway. These were not confused with the changes themselves, nor did Marx favour induced or premature birth. In addition, Marx's was a majoritarian theory of popularly based change, not a theory of sudden action by a vanguard – the role of the party was to reflect this mass base, rather than create it. Finally, Marx showed real ambivalence about state power, about its retention or abolition, and about its use for a long-term proletarian dictatorship. In these respects at least his views often seemed nearer Anarchism than to the later developments of 'Marxism' and 'Leninism'.

V. I. Lenin, emphasizing will and organization, the role of ideology, mobilization and violence in altering the course of history, increasingly defined change in terms of a resolute, trained minority which would take control of the state, as a prelude to social transformation. This scenario of conscious action, leading to change wrought from the top by the captured state apparatus, had its roots in ideas of conspiratorial coup d'état associated with figures such as the nineteenth-century eccentric, Blanqui; Anarchists like Bakunin had also flirted with ideas of conspiracy as a means of dismantling the state. But Lenin transformed the notions in practice by linking them to his theory of the party, harnessing the more wild ideas of violent putsch to a systematic ideological preparation of revolutionary leadership and its strategy of takeover. Thus the party could act as a state in miniature, preparing the way for a centralized core in the revolutionary replacement of the old regime. It would use the coercive monopoly of state power for a range of purposes, but primarily, extensive and rapid industrialization. This model of élite organization proved the most potent tool for Leninist revolutionaries in mobilizing and manipulating large masses of people, both before and after the seizure of state power.

In this theory, it has been argued previously, the immediate criterion of success is the effective seizure of, and maintenance of, state power. Thus, twentieth-century revolutions have been mainly about power in nation states, in a world of nation states; as Trotsky argued, to ensure their military survival, the maintenance of boundaries becomes a first priority. Typically, revolutions have also been 'state building' – creating, reinforcing, and expanding the power of the central apparatus. To perform these appointed tasks requires an even greater concentration of power, and thus revolutionary regimes provide examples of 'the least withered state apparatuses in the world'. Ideological criteria of success become secondary; 'There are', writes one critic of contemporary revolution, 'no Marxist political leaders whose revolutionary pretensions are matched by their post-revolutionary performance.' Egalitarian utopias have little relevance to the goals of rapid industrialization, military expansion, or the increasing power of the state. Typically, the subsequent criteria of success adopted by mainstream Marxism are largely economistic ones, using indications of material growth (i.e. output) as the measure of achievement of revolutionary aims. The long-term political or cultural implications of revolution, including the costs of violence and the organizational results of military takeover, are absent from Marxist cost-accounting. Yet it may be argued that these connections between pre-revolutionary aspirations, the revolutionary seizure of the state, and the nature of change subsequently, are not entirely lost on the populations which experience them.

With the theory of Mao, and the practice of the Chinese 'People's War', the vanguard leadership role of the party was shifted decisively from the mobilization of workers to the mobilization of peasants. Peasants had played a far more critical part in the Russian revolution than could be admitted in Leninist theory; they had also played a determining if negative role in the French revolutions and acted as a dominant agency of the Mexican revolutionary struggles. In China the mass-base of the peasants 'once again', in Barrington Moore's view, 'furnished the main driving force behind the victory of a party dedicated to achieving, through relentless terror, a supposedly inevitable phase of history in which the peasantry would cease to exist.' The more vicious forms of repression in the Chinese experience were related to the imposition of the proletarian dictatorship and industrialization on a rural society, via three major institutions – the army, the party, and eventually the state. These classic forms of central power, three facets of the monopoly of coercion, were as external and alien to peasant society as urbanism itself.

To the peasantry, the rural culture represents the 'real' world, the natural society. The society imposed from outside by revolutionary élites is unnatural. The changes implemented by the agents of the state or party, the police, the officials, or the military recruiters, constructs an unreal society, alien, artificial, distorting the accepted order of life. On specific issues, these urban cadres in a pre-revolutionary situation undoubtedly win peasants to their cause, but in so far as such cadres begin to create their own 'alternative' structures, these take on an increasingly unnatural and threatening character that eventually necessitates the use of force or threat of it. Basically, the élites and bureaucrats from the towns depend on skills in organization and propaganda, but where these are ineffective, terror is introduced. A further factor in precipitating these excesses is the attempt to make the revolution 'permanent' – to use Trotsky's term: to maintain mobilization of persons and resources, by an artificially sustained tension and crisis.

The aim of rapid industrialization represents, in large part, the aspirations of national, often Western-oriented, élite groups to 'catch up'. In this, as in a whole range of confining conditions, the West has helped to limit the options open to these élites (including indeed the degree to which they can 'catch up'). But in the technocratic rationalistic orientation of such leaderships, in the role of a narrow nationalism, in the tendency towards centralization, and in the single-minded manipulation of the peasantry by depersonalized structures as well as (however unrealistic) the aspiration to create a centralized industrial state, some liberation struggles seem amongst the foremost to honour Stalin by imitation. Thus, either way, the inevitable destruction of peasant society was accepted; in addition, the Statism and bureaucracy of socialist control were not analysed in terms of their technological substructure by supporters or critics of such change.

Other have argued that the state and centralization, as well as the militarization of society, were not the necessary accompaniments of all types of industrialization, but only the rapid, extensive and heavy forms of industrialism characteristic of the West, or Russia, Japan and now possibly China. Third World theorists were even asking whether the developing world need pass through the industrialization experience; how limited, how selective, how decentralist, how organic or revolutionary could it be? Could Marx's dream of a leap from backwardness of the rural communes (the 'mir' which Lenin opposed and Stalin had helped destroy by collectivization) to Communism, be finally realized? Not all rural revolutionary movements had been centred around the need for industrialization; indeed peasant rebellion was often anti-industrial. The land revolution of the Gandhians, sceptical of modernization, offered an alternative. A tentative answer was suggested by the fact that where military revolution had been avoided, social transformation was less likely to be identified with heavy industry.

A significant component of Maoism, in comparison even with Leninism, is its greater emphasis on violence and militarism, on the revolutionary nature of protracted war, and the use of armed struggle as itself a means of social transformation, giving power, purpose and control to the revolutionary party. Extensive armed organization is not a phenomenon that can arise from peasant society; it too is imposed from outside by urban-trained military organizers, who may also play political roles. It is not always easy to persuade peasants to fight voluntarily and peasant armies are prone to high desertion rates. The people's war itself also encourages the mobilization of material resources to supply and equip the struggle and enhances the development of transport and communications. Trotsky himself had emphasized the importance of military organization for the entrenchment of the revolution, but had not gone so far beyond Lenin in emphasizing the primacy of military revolution. It is not an exaggeration to say that whilst for Marx power grew out of the organized strength of the working class, translated by Lenin into the power of the highly organized revolutionary party mobilizing mass support, for Lin Piao and for Mao, it did indeed 'spring from the barrels of guns', whether or not prior peasant support existed.

Such a process conforms more to the language of élites and masses than of classes; as Oppenheimer observes, the war of liberation throws up the party of nationalism 'dominated by men uprooted, dedicated, semi-educated and ruthless'. The expanded role of violence in the Maoist model thus may enable the redefinition of revolutionary élites as primarily military élites. The peasantry contributes men and food for the anti-colonial war, but find themselves, if they survive their exploitation, as often as not cannon-fodder and forced labour, under a new yoke imposed by their 'liberators'. The totalitarian structure of mass revolutions may thus be reproduced in miniature in the guerilla movements of the Third World.

Yet, to a greater or lesser degree, all wars of national liberation are engaged in similar process, however different their context. Far from the romantic image of the decentralized, spontaneous reactions of oppressed peasants, these wars mobilize and centralize resources and manpower, creating hierarchical communications systems and top-down political structures. They aspire to the technocratic, their ideology is ostensibly rationalistic, their weaponry is modern, and their structures depersonalized. They are fundamentally nationalist, developing an army with a nationalist anti-colonial ideology; where possible such movements are simultaneously engaging in the task of statebuilding, national unification and territorial consolidation. These tasks, coordinated by the administrative bureaucracy and the modern monolithic mass party, support this mobilization, and are implicitly or explicitly linked to modernization. The wars themselves liberate the forces of change including, ultimately, industrialization geared to military expansion. Together, the whole process seeks to find its underpinning in heavy industry, supplying the technological means of centralization and militarization which helps destroy the peasants. It is war itself, as an essential component, even a trigger of this process, that helps achieve such organizational goals.

Notes

Preface

1 See 'The childhood disease of "leftism" in Communism' (from Lenin's *Collected Works*, vol. 25), Lawrence & Wishart, 1947, and in E. H. Carr, *The Bolshevik Revolution*, Penguin, 1966, vol. 3, pp. 181–6.

Introduction

1 Throughout I have found myself forced to use terms like 'Right', 'Left' and 'New Left' because of their widespread and common-usage connotations: nevertheless any idea of single or simple left–right continuum is quite distortive and inappropriate.

2 This was a view expressed by many movement activists and theorists; see especially Staughton Lynd and Tom Hayden, e.g. Lynd in P. Long, *The New Left*, Porter Sargent, 1969, p. 2, and a SNCC statement (see p. 61) insisted on 'writing our own histories'.

3 Elinor Langer, 'Notes for Next Time', *Working Papers for a New Society*, vol. 1, no. 3, 1973, p. 60.

4 M. Teodori, *The New Left*, Cape, 1970, p. 73 and see chapter 1.

5 James O'Brien, *A History of the New Left, 1960–68*, New England Free Press, 1969, p. 26 (see Lynd's comments in Introduction to Long, op. cit., p. 8).

6 I have stressed these in relation to the NL crisis; of course the earlier events (Suez, Hungary, Pacific Testing, Cuba, Algeria, Sharpeville), and China (Cultural Revolution) were important as factors engendering NL growth.

7 J. O'Brien, 'Beyond Reminiscence, the New Left in History', *Radical America*, vol. 6, no. 4, 1972, p. 12.

8 E.g. see James Weinstein, 'The Left, Old and New', *Socialist Revolution*, July/August 1972, and Peter Clecak, *Radical Paradoxes*, Harper & Row, 1973, pp. 1–43, for discussions in relation to the American NL.

9 M. Bookchin, 'Spontaneity and Organisation', *Liberation*, March 1972, p. 8.

10 See select bibliography on pp. 477–9.

11 See C. W. Mills, 'Letter to the New Left' in Long, op. cit.; this helped popularize the term in Britain rather earlier than in America, where the terms 'Movement' or 'radical' remained in vogue in the early 1960s. Though the phrase had been used of French left-splinters a few years earlier.

12 Mills, ibid.

13 On these selections from earlier traditions: Lasch, Weinstein, Lynd and Lens, amongst other American historians, helped present an alternative radical-socialist tradition (e.g. S. Lynd's *Nonviolence in America*, Bobbs-Merrill, 1966; S. Lens, *Radicalism in America*, Apollo Books, 1969; C. Lasch, *The New Radicalism in America*, Alfred Knopf, 1965).

14 E.g. James Weinstein, *The Decline of Socialism in America, 1912–25*, Vintage, Random House, 1965.

15 Indeed there is little organizational continuity between the first and second phases of the English NL, and that latter phase was as derivative as it was ephemeral.

16 Quoted from *Peace News* by David Widgery, *The Left in Britain, 1956–68*, Penguin, 1976, p. 131.

1. Convergence and breakthrough

1 Reflecting a pre-Cold War convergence during the Second World War, the sociological concept of 'convergence' focuses on the similarity of these blocs, their structures, aims and assumptions, rather than on any 'ideologically' constructed or stressed divergences: from one standpoint this is a counterpart of the thesis (also prevalent in the late 1950s) that such ideological division generally was in decline anyway. See later discussion.

2 The revival of interest in Simone Weil's critiques dating from the late 1930s and encouraged by Dwight MacDonald and his post-1945 review *Politics* in the USA was significant of this tendency; the impact of Camus's tortured, political evolution was another indicator.

3 Especially *Universities and Left Review* (*ULR*) and the *New Reasoner* in Britain, and their counterpart, *Studies on the Left*, in the USA.

4 James Weinstein, 'The Left, Old and New' in *Socialist Revolution*, July/August 1972, p. 40.

5 In Britain in this period, a Prime Minister (Macmillan) presented the period of Tory rule as one of unity and class-collaboration; 'we are all more or less planners now', a remark quoted by an American political sociologist with approval: see S. M. Lipset, *Political Man*, Heinemann, 1960.

6 The NL, whilst it rejected this framework, and was critical of most consensus sociology, in some ways accepted and reflected elements or versions of it. Partly in reaction to such a sociology (or building on ideas of convergence, bureaucracy or alienation), the remarkable fact is that the dominant sociology to which they reacted was sustained to a very significant degree in America by apostate leftists, including many ex-Marxists: Lewis Feuer, Philip Selznick, Seymour Lipset, Nathan Glazer, Lewis Coser, Daniel Bell, are all examples of

this biographical similarity. See Coser's contribution to Leopold Labedz's *Revisionism*, Praeger, 1962. The concept they celebrated most eagerly was what they saw as an 'end of total ideology' as the 'practical' problems of industrialism were solved.

7 For a general appraisal, see Alvin Gouldner, *The Coming Crisis of Western Sociology*, Heinemann, 1971.

Parsons, Shils, Almond, Dahl, Kornhauser, Lipset, Bendix, Kerr and Siegel, Arendt, Riesman, Feuer, Hoffer, Glazer, Bell, Smelser and Selznick are names closely associated with this 'school'; with some exceptions, they also became early critics of the New Left.

8 'Dogmatism, authoritarianism and bureaucracy were identified as fundamental flaws of all Old Left groupings as well as features of the society the new leftists were rebelling against.' Dick Flacks, 'Making History v Making Life: Dilemmas of an American Left', *Working Papers for a New Society*, Summer 1974, p. 64.

9 Mills, 'Letter to the New Left', in P. Long, *The New Left*.

10 T. Roszak, *The Making of a Counter Culture*, Faber, 1970, p. 100. For British Anarchist views on 'Convergence', see D. E. Apter and J. Joll (eds), *Anarchism Today*, Macmillan, 1971, pp. 88 and 91.

11 As Engels had long ago warned (in 1890), factory production everywhere created a 'veritable despotism' that was 'independent of all social organization'. It had its own logic of domination.

12 'Port Huron Statement' in M. Teodori, *The New Left* and T. Hayden in P. Jacobs and S. Landau, *The New Radicals*.

See discussion, chapter 7.

13 B. Moore, 'Revolution in America', *New York Review of Books*, 30 January 1969 and S. Lynd in P. Long, *The New Left*, p. 2. See also subsequent discussion (chapter 7).

14 Marx had occasionally been interpreted as a technological determinist, but the proposition that ruling groups were instruments of their own technology went far beyond any previous Marxist position in the twentieth century.

15 Barrington Moore amplified aspects of this perspective on a comparative basis (cf. B. Moore, *Social Origins of Dictatorship and Democracy*, Beacon Press, 1966).

More generally, a convergent language was developed through 'political sociology', that could describe in common features of Russia, Britain and the USA: 'élite', 'bureaucracy', 'ideology', 'industrial society'. Given the military context of the Cold War blocs, it is significant that concepts such as 'mobilization' depicted a process that was analogous to (and included) state mobilization for war; i.e. ever more resources, men, loyalties and energies tapped by the central apparatus of the war-machine.

16 See Carl Oglesby, 'Decade Ready for a Dustbin', reprinted in M. Goodman, *Movement Toward a New America*, Knopf, Pilgrim Press, 1970, pp. 737–45.

17 A Trotskyist or 'libertarian Marxist' variant was provided in the early 1950s, e.g. Tony Cliff's analysis of Russia. Later a component in the growth of the International Socialist Group (IS), it identified Russia as 'State capitalist'.

18 Simone Weil, *Oppression and Liberty*, Routledge & Kegan Paul, 1958, pp. 5ff., reinforced this view: 'The bureaucratic and military machine, constituted, in Marx's eyes, the real obstacle in the way of a continuous march towards socialism through the simple accumulation of progressive reforms.'

19 *Solidarity* magazine was influential in the Committee of 100's development, especially its anarcho-syndicalist wing.

20 See, e.g. Simone Weil, op. cit., and J. Ellul, *Technological Society*, Vintage Books, 1967.

21 There was more than a hint in the writings of Mills and Marcuse that the USA itself was subject to a subtle and creeping totalitarianism, and Norman Mailer had talked about America's 'totalitarian fabric'; it was a theme taken up by NL spokesmen, especially Hayden.

22 See H. Arendt, *Origins of Totalitarianism*, Beacon Press, 1958. It was also a theme developed by Horkheimer in Germany. Some Marxists, especially Sartre, became obsessed with the comparison – or rather differentiation – of such regimes, laying the foundations for a 'double-standard' morality of politics deployed again, on mass atrocities in the Vietnam war. Sartre still retained a distinction between 'progressive' and 'reactionary' and a notion of 'historical rationality', that, however perversely, Russia continued to embody.

23 Both Orwell's *1984* and the revived allegories of Kafka were seen as ideologically neutral regimes, like those of other fictional anti-utopias (e.g. Huxley's).

24 Indeed, like so many other ideas of this school, it rebounded: if indeed these regimes were so similar, why were Western 'democratic' powers supporting allied police regimes in the name of freedom (even in the Western alliances, e.g. Spain, Portugal, South Africa, Cuba (before 1959), Haiti, South Vietnam, Greece and Turkey), but were prepared to blast the supposedly similar regimes of Eastern Europe off the face of the earth in a nuclear exchange?

25 Though for a critique from nearer the NL see R. Blackburn's view of convergence in *Student Power*, eds A. Cockburn and R. Blackburn, Penguin, 1969, pp. 175–6 and 193.

26 Whether that of the proletariat or that of the bourgeoisie. See Simone Weil, op. cit.

27 Non-Marxist sociology (even the radical sociology of Mills) hardly dealt with the historical and structural development of centralized bureaucratic nation-states.

28 The Weberian analysis of general bureaucratization, for long seen as a conservative analysis, and a pessimistic one when applied to socialism, had only been fleetingly revived by errant Trotskyites like Burnham, in the late 1930s and early 1940s. It was then taken up both by mainstream American sociologists and by dissident Communists; by Berle and Means in the USA; in the 1950s by sociologists like Selznick; the Yugoslav dissident, Djilas; and subsequently purveyed by figures like Raymond Aron; it was a commonplace of social theory by the 1960s (e.g. Bendix's work).

29 Miliband synthesized a Marxian view of the state 'in capitalist

society' with a Millsian power élite model; a perspective limited to what form and character the state takes, rather than posing the anarchist question, *'whether'* state or not. See n. 30, chapter 2.

30 This was the slogan at the entrance of the Brize Norton SAC/USAF nuclear bomber base near Witney, Oxon., scene of some early sit-ins and marches in the British nuclear disarmament movement (1958–60).

31 Initial opposition to military ventures, both East and West, was often planned and led by students and teachers.

32 In so far as these identifications were with *national revolutions* they did not break out of state-centred orientations into a genuine trans-nationalism.

33 E.g. in NATO, despite differences over foreign adventures.

34 New Leftists visited the whole string of socialist regimes, especially Algeria, Cuba and Vietnam in the 1960s; some of the latter-day editors of NLR even set out on the unlikely pilgrimage to Enver Hoxha's Albania. There was also the growing interest in African Socialism, not least the Tanzanian experiment.

35 Similar processes occurred in the development of industrialism or urbanism, or central state power, wherever it occurred, regardless of the ideology or character of economic distribution.

36 Todd Gitlin, "The Dynamics of the New Left', *Motive*, October/November 1970, p. 47.

37 H. Marcuse makes this plea in his address, 'The Old Model Won't Do', to SDS in New York, in 1968. See M. Teodori (ed.), *The New Left*, Cape, 1970, p. 471.

38 Simone Weil had struck at the problem of language on the Left in a classic passage, on the 'newspeak' concept of 'workers' state' (Weil, op. cit.):

> To call a state a 'Workers' State when you go on to explain that each worker in it is put economically and politically at the complete disposal of a bureaucratic caste sounds like a bad joke.
>
> As for the 'deformations' . . . of a state all of whose characteristics are exactly the reverse of those theoretically associated with a workers' state . . . the distinction between the pathological and the normal has no theoretical validity (Weil, op. cit.).

39 See Murray Bookchin, *Post Scarcity Anarchism*, Ramparts Press, 1971, and articles in *Liberation*, 1969/70.

40 See G. Thayer, *The Farther Shores of Politics*, New York, 1967. See also Marcuse in Teodori, op. cit. The Beat poets, Corso, Ginsberg, Ferlinghetti, and others like Kerouac, made an important contribution in breaking this consensus.

41 Shared by Beat poets and existential humanists – the detached philosophical intellects – as well as many early activists.

42 On occasions, Maoism has been put forward as a further candidate, but it does not fit. Maoism as an option appeared later, although its ingredients were all available in 1960; a bizarre synthesis of disparate and contradictory elements, it was able to make an impact on the NL because of its opportunism and eclectic character; combining

Stalinism and libertarian rhetoric, Statism and apparent decentralism, militarism and ostensible peasant communitarianism, both a belief and a scepticism of industrialism, it was multi-faceted enough to suit any interpretation. On the other hand, the commitment of its devotees suggested that this was nearer to a 'total ideology' than any of the other revivals, certainly than Trotskyism and Anarchism from which it superficially drew. (See Albert, *What is to be Undone*, Porter Sargent, 1975.)

43 For the character of this re-emergence see Colin Ward, *Anarchy in Action*, Harper & Row, 1974, which draws from the *Anarchy* magazine he edited in the early 1960s in England.

44 Revisionists like Lukacs and later Marcuse, neo-Freudians like Fromm, and libertarian radicals like Mills, each contributed to this. The alienation theme emerges again in Charles Reich's bestseller, *The Greening of America*, Penguin, 1972.

   A good example of the reduction of even critical concepts to operationalized trivia is the 'end-of-ideology' use of alienation and anomie. (See John Horton, 'The Dehumanisation of Alienation and Anomie' in *British Journal of Sociology*, vol. 14/15, 1964. See p. 138.)

45 In *One-Dimensional Man* (Beacon Press, 1964,) Marcuse links his neo-Freudian notion of 'repression' (*Eros and Civilisation*, Vintage, 1962) with the Marxian 'alienation' which 'reduces man to a status of a thing'. (He had summarized it earlier in his *Reason and Revolution*, Beacon Press, 1960.) Like Marcuse, Fromm also sought this synthesis of alienation and Freudian theory. See his *Marx's Concept of Man*, Ungar, 1961, Introd., pp. 1–8, 43–58, 93–110.

46 T. B. Bottomore, *Critics of Society*, Allen & Unwin, 1967, pp. 74 ff.

47 E.g. Marcuse, Camus, Weil, and some Anarchists and revisionist Marxists.

48 Who all hinted that nuclear weapons represent exactly the alien, uncontrolled 'monsters' that threaten to destroy their creators.

49 Here again figures such as MacDonald, Camus, Goodman and Mills stand out, but see fuller discussion below.

50 For example, E. P. Thompson emphasized the role of cultural and consumer exploitation as relevant as that at the point of production – and as relevant to political consciousness; Raymond Williams focused on a latent collectivist alternative to bourgeois values. See Thompson in *Socialist Register*, 1965, and discussion in chapter 8.

51 Its initial concern with a cultural sociology of the working class parallels the emerging American analysis of racism and black culture.

   Another innovation linked to the English NL was a new populist historiography, soon paralleled across the Atlantic (see Jesse Lemisch: 'Towards a Democratic History', *Radical Education Project*, February 1967).

52 Cf. Alan Haber, *The End of Ideology as Ideology*, SDS pamphlet, partially reprinted in F. Lindenfeld, *Reader in Political Sociology*, Minerva, 1968, p. 555, and also in *Our Generation Against Nuclear War*, Vol. 4, no. 3, 1964.

53 The group around *Liberation* linked civil rights, the New Left, and and the Vietnam War Movement with a tradition formed in the nonviolent revolutionary groups of 1945, in which Dellinger had been involved. Utopian and wildly ambitious as their schemes seem in retrospect, these represented one of the earliest foundations of the NL. See L. Wittner, *Rebels Against War*, Columbia University Press, 1969.

54 'Triple Revolution' statement printed in *Liberation*, April 1964.

55 As far as the initial libertarian development of the NL, especially in America, was concerned, the anarcho-pacifist editions of *Liberation* were prophetic in proclaiming in 1956 that this would be the politics of the future.

56 See, for example, the sociological emphases of *Studies on the Left*, *ULR* and *NLR*.

57 See Gouldner, op. cit., *passim*.

58 Bakunin's critique of the tyranny of categories might well have been the watchword of the new libertarian sociology of the 1960s in its attack on such concepts as function and role and system.

59 In Britain, though tactically underplayed for fear of academic reprisals, this role of sociologists was much more marked in the second 'borrowed' phase of the British NL between 1967–9.
   On the NL and sociology see Gouldner, op. cit., esp. pp. 1–15.

60 Perhaps subsequently expressed best in the growing use of the *New York Review of Books*, but also in a range of other periodicals (see Mills, in Long, op. cit., pp. 14 ff.), not least *Studies on the Left*.

61 Although 'pluralism' as a term had been co-opted by conservative sociology and political theory, these ideas re-echoed the socialist-pluralism of an earlier period. Even Marcuse, a more authoritarian NL theorist, at one point advocated a plural administration to replace a 'total' one.

62 Undeniably this elasticity of social organization gave radicals some common ground with those sections of the laissez-faire Right, opposing State tyranny and arguing for free choice and community control. Despite common ground with conservative pluralism, Mills was deeply critical of the survival of laissez-faire and entrepreneurial ideologies into corporate capitalist society (see further remarks in chapter 3).

63 Clecak (op. cit.) denies Mills's utopianism, because of his strong realistic, pragmatic tendency, but the other part of Mills's work is his 'contrast-concept' of political freedom.

64 Perhaps we should say Thompson's Marxist tradition. See E. P. Thompson, 'Open Letter to Kolakowski', *Socialist Register*, Merlin Press, 1972.
   For Thompson as for Kolakowski it appears there were ultimately only two sides: East or West, Marxist or Capitalist, the Communist parties or the Congress of Cultural Freedom; the belief in a third – or other possibilities – is jettisoned in these stark polarized alternatives.

2. The New Left: a core identity

1 In his letter of 1960 (reprinted in P. Long, *The New Left*). As an example of personal links between the movements in 1958 (two years after the Montgomery boycott), Bayard Rustin, black civil rights activist, later to organize the Washington sit-ins of 1960 and the huge Civil Rights March of 1963, addressed the start of the first Aldermaston March in London's Trafalgar Square.

2 Convinced of the madness of nuclear war, Fromm treated the bomb as a symptom of an overwhelming social psychological disorder (see his *Sane Society*, Rinehart, 1955); he named and helped start SANE and later the 'councils for correspondence' to offset the 'perversion of basic human drives' by propaganda. In England CND's newspaper took the name 'Sanity' (1962).

3 Thus SNCC began with the second great landmark of the integration movement (the first had been Rosa Park's occupation of the wrong seat in a Montgomery bus in 1955 which precipitated King's leadership of the boycott and SCLC).

   After these first SNCC sit-ins, within two weeks there were sit-ins in fifteen cities in five Southern States. J. O'Brien (*History of the New Left, 1960–1968*, p. 3) cites an estimated 50,000 participants in the first year's sit-ins in 100 cities (1960), before the freedom rides of 1961. For these see M. Cohen and D. Hale, in *The New Student Left*, p. 57; Kahn, 'The Significance of the First Freedom Rides' and 'The First Freedom Rides' (CORE) in P. Mayer, *Pacifist Conscience*, Penguin, 1966, pp. 363–85. For SNCC sit-ins, see T. Hayden, 'SNCC in Action' in Cohen and Hale, op. cit., p. 51, and M. Proudfoot, *Diary of a Sit-in*, College and University Press, 1964.

4 At the onset of FSM, as if to recognize the spread of direct action, SDS published its *Organisers' Handbook* by Clark Kissinger (Autumn, 1964). For the new breed of organizers, see Cohen and Hale, op. cit., *passim*. See also S. M. Lipset and S. Wolin, *The Berkeley Student Revolt*, Anchor, 1965.

5 Led by Joan Baez, singing the Civil Rights anthem, 'We shall overcome', the administration building was occupied with a largely spontaneous, but neat organization, reminiscent of an Aldermaston March; once within, the 'Free University of California' was proclaimed, and the NL had entered its major phase of growth. See Lipset and Wolin, op. cit.

6 In the same way, the comradely feeling of the FSM was contrasted with the sense of alienation and atomization prevalent in the anonymous corporation of the university. The contingent proliferation of corporatist bureaucracy had a lot to do with the spontaneity and comprehensiveness of the response that confronted it. See H. Jacobs, 'Populist Students and Corporate Society', *International Socialist Journal*, Feb. 1967. On these connections, 'a corporation amongst many', see also O'Brien, op. cit., p. 10.

7 I.e. at Berkeley, Michigan, Wisconsin, Chicago and Columbia.

8 For example, Al Haber and Tom Hayden at Michigan were developing similar orientations. Nevertheless, the militancy of Berkeley

surprised not only staff and students, but many radicals as well. Roszak (then editor of *Peace News*) refused a 'scoop' on FSM through sheer disbelief. See Hal Draper, *FSM: The New Left Uprising*, Grove Press, 1965.

9 Despite its origins CND's spring festival, symbolizing a youthful 'love of life' as much as a hatred of nuclear weapons, was recognized grudgingly in the title 'March for Life' (and the 'trad' jazz band was moved up to the front of this Easter celebration officially).

The first big circulation nuclear disarmament paper came from the Youth CND, *Youth Against the Bomb*, and YCND grew not through, but in spite of, the adult campaign.

10 The foremost of the younger SNCC leaders were: John Lewis, Julian Bond, Robert Moses (Paris), Ivanhoe Donaldson, James Foreman and Charlie Cobb. See H. Zinn, *SNCC: The New Abolitionists*, Beacon Press, 1964. Payne in Cohen and Hale, op. cit., p. 68, and R. Coles, 'Nonviolent Youth in the South' in E. H. Erikson, *Challenge of Youth*, Doubleday, New York, 1965. J. Finn, *Protest, Pacifism and Politics*, had interviews with these figures.

11 Of the school and university students, young professionals and Radical Christians becoming peace and civil rights workers, few were over thirty.

12 Stuart Hall, editor of *ULR/NLR* (1958–61) writing (1969) on hippy developments in America, remarked on both visual similarity to the 'raggle-taggle scrag-end of an Aldermaston march', and a fusion of expressive and activist styles that linked the two phenomena (the connection probably goes even deeper than that): 'The Hippies, an American Moment', pp. 170–202.

13 Lewis Feuer, *The Conflict of Generations*, Heinemann, 1970, and Kenneth Keniston, 'Youth and Dissent', in Erikson, *The Challenge of Youth*, from widely differing standpoints, sought the origins of the movement in generational conflict and revolt, rather than these more political experiences of the NL *helping* to create a generational culture, as is argued here.

14 Jeff Nuttall indicates in his review of the *Bomb Culture*, Paladin, 1970, that this fundamental integration of political and life-style rebellion springs from the shaping experience of Aldermaston and beyond: a response to an overall political-cultural milieu, and the ambiguous relationship with the culture of Americana and consumerism, to which Allen Ginsberg's 'best minds of my generation destroyed by madness, starving, hysterical, naked' had reacted earlier in similar forms.

15 Theodore Roszak's *Making of a Counter-Culture*. Roszak's is the fullest analysis in terms of cultural confrontation, p. 47.

16 Ibid.

17 The founding of the CNVA (Committee for Nonviolent Action) and the DAC (Direct Action Committee) in America and Britain in 1957, the revival of CORE in the field of de-segregation actions (previously an adjunct of pacifist groups), and the active groups around *Peace News* and its editor Hugh Brock in England, and around *Liberation* in America, are the organizational base of this

growth. See also Hunter and O'Brien, 'Reading about the New Left', pp. 76–7.

The radical pacifist weekly *Peace News* attracted many anti-militarists, nuclear pacifists and libertarian direct actionists in the years after 1957. By 1960, it was a substantial influence on both CND and the Committee of 100. (*Peace News* split from the traditional Pacifist PPU in 1957.)

18 Led by Pat Arrowsmith, April Carter, Michael Randle, Laurens Otter, Will Warren and others, organized a 3-year series of courage-ous actions: at Swaffham, North Pickenham, Foulness, Harrington and other sites – laying the basis for the (1961) Committee of 100. There were similar US actions at the Mead Inter-Continental Ballistic Missile (ICBM) base and other sites, led by Muste, from 1957–60; altogether some seventy-five such actions took place, accompanied by appeals to workers on the sites (see L. Wittner, *Rebels Against War*, ch. 9).

19 Amongst them were Muste (with links to FOR (Fellowship of Reconciliation)), Rustin and Farmer (of CORE), and Jim Peck, all still close to *Liberation* in the late 1950s (see Peck's *Freedom Ride* pamphlet, WRL; excerpts in *Nonviolent Direct Action*, eds Paul Hare, H. Bulmberg, Corpus Books, 1968.

At the SCLC conference of 1961 advocates of a nonviolent army of 8,000 members envisaged a jail-filling campaign in the deep south, of an uncompromising kind that would restructure those areas of black majorities – to take power from the white minorities.

20 Thus taking up Richard Gregg's idea of 'moral jiu jitsu'. See Gene Sharp, *Politics of Nonviolent Action*, Porter Sargent, 1974.

21 In a nonviolent Anarchist tradition direct action was mostly limited to personal example, and the creation of model institutions and ways of living. In Gandhi, and in other radical pacifist writers, the activist approaches came much closer; whilst paying his respects to the Anarchist tradition, and Tolstoi's individualist resistance, he stressed collective nonviolence.

22 See Lynd, Introduction to Long, op. cit.; and C. W. Mills in I. L. Horowitz (ed.), *Power, Politics and People*, Ballantine Books, 1963, p. 247.

23 The Harris Poll, in 1964, found that 40 per cent (representing several million black people) had participated in some form of protest: picket line, sit-in, sit-down, march, vigil or boycott (more than a quarter claimed to have boycotted). See W. Brink and L. Harris, *The Negro Revolution in America*, Simon & Schuster, 1964, p. 203.

24 As O'Brien remarks (in Hunter and O'Brien, op. cit., p. 77), the pacifist 'tradition of personal witness' exemplified in these acts, 'had a larger influence on the NL than is generally recognized'. In turn it reflected the impact of other traditions abroad.

As well as Gandhi's followers, e.g. Vinoba Bhave, Danilo Dolci's direct actions in Sicily, which gathered momentum at the end of 1955, were undoubtedly influential.

25 S. Lynd's anthology, *Nonviolence in America*, Bobbs-Merrill, 1966, documents this tradition, placing the new movement within it.

26 Muste himself cited as his inspiration an extraordinary variety of sources: Marx, Trotsky, Thoreau, Gandhi, Christ; he had been a Baptist minister, and, in the 1930s, the foremost Trotskyist labour organizer. He countered Communist Party influence on the Left, as he did conservative Niebuhrian influence in the Christian church. By the 1950s he had resumed a radical anarcho-pacifist stance, and, at the age of eighty, was still participating in projects; fasting, climbing AEC fences in Nevada, blocking the New York military induction centre, and participating in demonstrations both outside and inside the Pentagon. The Civil Defence demonstrations in New York in 1960–1 were the closest parallel to the Committee of 100, and were led by 'A.J.'.

27 Such a campaign, though foreshadowed in 1967, at the Pentagon, was not to develop until 1969–70 on a mass scale.

28 The Buddhist examples of self-immolation subsequently found their counterparts in three American suicides, Norman Morrison, Alice Herz and Roger La Porte, who had an enormous impact outside the West. This form of protest eventually spread to issues other than Vietnam, as instanced by Palach's suicide in Prague (January 1969).

29 In Europe a remarkable symptom of the massive increase in anti-militarist disaffiliation was the rise in numbers of conscientious objectors choosing other means of refusing military service. (After 1963 this was especially marked in the German army.)

30 Even before the American NL's growth this anti-nationalistic tendency was given expression in Norman Mailer's remark that 'people should not believe in countries and patriotism'. I have explored this problem of the national parameter – both in the peace movement and the radical tradition generally – in my 'Nation State and War Resistance' (Ph.D. thesis, University of California, Berkeley).

31 The concept of 'trans-nationalism' (e.g. groups relating across political frontiers), subsequently contrasted with 'left international-ism' (see below) popularized by Quaker activist and theorist George Lakey in the late 1960s, and by a number of peace researchers, began to take the interest of political scientists in the 1970s.

32 For example, Staughton Lynd emphasizes common links between international student revolt and American forerunners (in Long, op. cit.). On the growth of a subsequent student 'trans-nationalism', see C. Oglesby, *The New Left Reader*, pp. 274 ff., and in Cohen and Hale, op. cit.

33 Other trans-national aspects of the nuclear pacifist movement were international voyages and marches (most are described in *Peace News* articles: see December 1972, for a survey of these). The San Francisco–Moscow, Delhi–Peking and Quebec–Guantonamo walks were paralleled by Harold Steele's attempt of 1957 and the *Phoenix* and the *Golden Rule*, and later *Everyman* voyages. CNVA's appeals for peace in the Soviet Union were followed by a series of actions by the Committee of 100 demonstrators in Russia. Such direct-action unilateralism was a further reason for Soviet coolness to the Western nuclear disarmament movement; it came far too close to home.

R. V. Sampson, *Psychology of Power*, Vintage, 1968, remarks on this and participated in such actions, which were repeated again in August 1968 after the Czech invasion.

34 *ULR* adopted some similar positions (1958–60) in England.

Muste was eager to integrate these various ideas of Third Camp with those of social theorists (Mills, Arendt, Marcuse and Fromm) and political moralists (e.g. Camus). See Hentoff, *Peace Agitator*, Macmillan, 1963, and Muste's *Collected Essays*, ed. Hentoff, *Liberation*, 1968.

On Unilateralism see: April Carter, ed., *Unilateral Disarmament: Its Theory and Policy*, Housmans, 1965.

35 SPU, set up in 1959, represented the first impact of either NL or peace issues in many American universities and was important as an organizational stepping-stone in the rebirth of student radicalism and the formation of student left parties such as SLATE at Berkeley, POLIT at Chicago, 'Voice' at Michigan and 'Action' at Columbia.

In 1961, 3000–8000 SPU members demonstrated at both the Pentagon and the Soviet Embassy (Washington) against resumed testing. In February 1962, 8000 protested at the White House: SPU also attacked the fall-out shelter programme as making nuclear war more likely by creating illusions of reduced casualties (see O'Brien, op. cit., pp. 4–5).

By the early 1960s, SPU had several thousand members, and was closely linked with the youth group of the Socialist Party (YPSL). Its counterpart in Britain was the combined Universities CND (CUCaND).

36 During the later 1960s *Peace News* (*PN*) came closer to the counter-culture, and alternative society approaches.

37 Joan Baez's, 'With God on Our Side', Bob Dylan's, 'Blowing in the Wind', soon took their place alongside the repertoire of civil rights songs.

38 Norman O. Brown, debate with Marcuse in *Commentary*, February/March 1967.

39 Indeed, many of the best examples of embryonic non-military defence have been against such moves: labour strikes and a wide range of non-cooperation campaigns have defeated them. See A. Roberts, *Civilian Resistance as a Natural Defence*, Penguin, 1967.

On Czechoslovakia see also discussion in chapter 11 of present work.

The occasional view of some Direct Actionists (e.g. The Committee of 100) that they might constitute the embryo of a nonviolent defence force was of course wildly ambitious.

40 I.e. CORE, SNCC and King's SCLC (Southern Christian Leadership Conference). See CORE and SNCC statements of principle in Lynd, op. cit., p. 396, and Charles Jones, 'SNCC: Nonviolence and Revolution', in *New University Thought*, September/October 1963, Chicago.

41 Even the more conservative NAACP (National Association for the Advancement of Colored People) came to accept nonviolence and direct action; and the Urban League, reformist and non-activist, had

some of its leaders arrested. See Langston Hughes, *Fight for Freedom*, Berkeley, Medallion, 1962, chapter 6.

42 See also LeRone Bennett, *Confrontation: Black and White*, Penguin, 1965, chapter VII and subsequent discussion of this ambivalent and problematic stance.

43 Although one study implies this: see Inge Bell on *CORE and the Strategy of Nonviolence*, Random House, 1968. For discussion of the term 'nonviolence of the weak', see chapter 7, part 1, of this book.

44 'Port Huron Statement', 1962 (see M. Teodori, *The New Left*, pp. 163–72).

45 His attack on the guillotine first widely quoted in America in the protest campaigns to prevent Chessman's execution in 1960 and subsequently to oppose capital punishment both in Britain and in the USA was published in the San Franciscan Beat literary magazine, *Evergreen Review* in 1960.

On Sidney Silverman's campaign in this period in Britain, gaining success in 1955–7, see P. Duff, *Left, Left, Left*, Alison & Busby, 1971, pp. 101–13. NB also Camus's essay 'Neither Victims nor Executioners' in P. Goodman (ed.), *Seeds of Liberation*, Braziller, 1964.

46 Camus's gentleness was contrasted with the intemperate Sartre whose stream of almost fanatical polemic could be identified with by sections of the later NL as it turned away from Camus at the end of the decade (see discussion of Sartre by François Bondy in M. Cranston (ed.), *The New Left*, p. 51).

47 See chapter 12 and Zinn, op. cit., *passim*. Also J. Newfield, *A Prophetic Minority*, chapters 4–6.

48 The title of one of his most significant essays (reprinted in *Drawing the Line*, Random House, 1962).

49 Quoted in O'Brien, op. cit., p. 9. For Savio's nonviolence see his role in 'The Free Speech and Civil Rights Movement' (*News and Letters Pamphlet*, July 1965) – Savio was chairman of the SNCC group at Berkeley at the time of FSM.

50 Roszak, op. cit., pp. 47–9 (echoing Laing) defines technocracy as 'That social form in which an industrial society reaches a peak of its organisational integration.'

51 Advocating nonviolent non-cooperation, from a Tolstoian Anarchist standpoint, the radical moralism of Sampson's work was probably more in tune with the early mainstream of the NL than most commentators or critics would admit.

52 See Teodori, op. cit., p. 40.

53 Irving Howe, quoted from *Partisan Review*, Summer 1965, p. 38. See also his 'New Styles of Leftism' in *Dissent*, April 1965, p. 299.

54 This need was a key element of Marcuse's stance, although without the emphasis on moralism. See A. J. Muste, *Essays* (ed. Hentoff), and on language, M. Goodman, op. cit., Introduction, p. ix.

55 See Muste, in Lynd collection, op. cit.

56 A naval weapons station, north of Berkeley, supplying SE Asia.

57 Similar arguments were deployed (with less success) in America. The CNVA vigil at Fort Detrick CBW (Chemical and Biological

Warfare) base (1959–61) tried to emphasize the 'great suffering and nameless torture' 'being prepared for countless men, women and children in our own country and other lands', cited in Wittner, op. cit., p. 262.

58 On the margins of the NL, pacifist anarchism continued to be deployed in exemplary moral confrontation with the nihilism of nuclear war. Denouncing its strategic subordination of ethics, Sampson blamed the autonomy of a power-seeking politics; although his represented a lonely voice articulating a continuing nonconformist sense of outrage, it punctuated the prevalent 'liberal' defence consensus; during the CND years, this consensus on the nuclear issue remained, in Britain at least, an unstable one. Much of the moralism of these appeals against nuclear war passed on into the Vietnam war opposition – first in the USA, then in Europe.

59 This is in complete contrast to the Marxist and Leninist figures from the continent (e.g. Gramsci, Lukacs, Sartre, Althusser) taken up by *NLR* and promoted after 1963. Peter Sedgewick, in Widgery, op. cit., p. 31, and Alan Lovell, 'Direct Action', *NLR*, 1961.

60 He is probably referring to the movement's misunderstanding or exaggeration of Camus's *personal* commitment and the extent of his activist response against the established order. See Oglesby in M. Goodman, op. cit.

61 For example, *L'Homme révolté* was taken to be simply an Anarchist book about the degeneration of revolution, and the pamphlet 'Neither Victims nor Executioners' (in P. Goodman, op. cit., p. 24), taken to be a straightforward Pacifist statement. Finally, the degree of theoretical political commitment was also widely exaggerated, just as the ambiguities of Camus's political writing were overlooked.

62 He failed even to ally with the 'New Left' groups (e.g. Bourdet's) or the anti-war resistance of French youth, finding both deeply compromised in their relationship to the authoritarian violence of the Algerian Left. Ultimately, capitalism was a lesser evil for Camus than totalitarian rule and that was the main reason for critics calling him a liberal.

63 It is central as well to writers like Ronald Sampson in England.

64 A theoretical strain, neglected here, the psycho-analytic and neo-Freudian (echoed in Goodman's mélange of Reichian psychiatry and existentialist commitment). The social psychology of Fromm, Laing and Sampson and other writers, is a recurrent theme in the NL at this stage.

65 For example, drawing in part on the Quaker notion of the inner light, and on American tradition of several centuries, Muste's thought and action were rooted, like King's, in a notion of the inward search, which links them to militant young activists.

66 Tom Hayden in *Participatory Democracy*, ed T. E. Cook and P. N. Morgan, Canfield Press, 1971.

67 Andrew Kopkind, one of the liveliest of the NL journalists, captured this mood (*New York Review of Books*, 28 September 1967):
    the responsibility of the intellectual is the same as that of the street organiser, the draft resister, the Digger; to talk to people not

about them. The important literature now is the underground press, the speeches of Malcolm, the works of Fanon, the songs of the Rolling Stones and Aretha Franklin. The rest all sounds like the Moynihan report and the *Time* essay, explaining everything, understanding nothing, changing no-one.

68 As well as Lynd, Rustin, Dellinger, Fruchter, Landau, McReynolds, Goodman, Muste, Hayden, were influential both as writers and activists.

69 Amongst some influential theorists (Mills and Camus, and subsequently Marcuse and Sartre), political participation did not take publicly activist forms.

70 Individual nonviolent acts like those of Rosa Parks, James Meredith, Jim Peck, Medgar Evers, Mario Savio, Bob Parris, Harold Steele, Albert Bigelow, Pat Arrowsmith and Michael Scott, put a stamp on these years in Britain and the USA.

71 Noam Chomsky in *Dissenting Academy*, ed. T. Roszak (Penguin, 1967), p. 227.

72 A theme in Fromm and Marcuse; and a quest generated by Camus and Mills.

73 Port Huron Statement, in Teodori, op. cit.

74 Marcuse believes most of this repression (socially 'surplus repression') represents not the necessary control of uncivilized instincts, but a mode of social domination. Radical transformation becomes the best solution to personal problems caused by this repression. Not quite the simple formula that the counter-culture took it to be; but such anti-repressive psychological views were argued by an English Anarchist, Alex Comfort, *Authority and Delinquency in the Modern State*, Routledge & Kegan Paul, 1950

75 Marcuse in Teodori, op. cit., p. 469.

76 Ibid.

77 The phrase 'new man' suggests the lack of any consciousness of sexism in language at this stage of the movement and was widely employed in movement literature.

78 Lynd in Teodori, op. cit., p. 197.

79 E.g. of Freud and of Marx, in particular.

80 Or for that matter of a Sartre or a Reich, who had the added disadvantage for this period of speaking from within a European intellectual heritage.

81 See remarks on this in P. Clecak, *Radical Paradoxes*, and in chapter 7.

82 But within its common ground with movement thought in the early 1960s, tendencies in Marcuse's thought become exaggerated, reinforcing those elements in the movement that lead on to the crises of 1968 and after.

83 Assembled by Tom Hayden, whilst still a student at Michigan, in 1961–2.

84 *Liberation* (1956 New York); *Universities and Left Review* (1957), *New Reasoner* (1957) merged, in 1960, into *New Left Review* (UK); *Studies on the Left* (1959); *New University* (Oxford, 1960), *New University Thought* (Chicago, 1959), *Root and Branch* (California,

1960), *Anarchy* (London, 1961), and to a lesser extent, around existing journals such as *Dissent* and *New Politics*; *Freedom* and *Peace News* which became independent, and *Partisan Review*, or *Evergreen*. *Win* was founded later.

85 As the concern of the *ULR* and pre-1961 *NLR* with 'quality of life' problems declined, the theme was taken up by *Anarchy*, concentrating after 1962 on practical but utopian alternatives, anarchist programmes around specific issues.

86 See Hunter and O'Brien, op. cit. Amongst bestselling paperbacks of the 1950s that reached the first generation of New Leftists: Riesman's *Lonely Crowd*, White's *Organisation Man*, Fromm's *Sane Society* and, what O'Brien calls 'Goodman's prophetic masterpiece', *Growing up Absurd* were among the most important.

87 As well as the Port Huron Statement, and Al Haber's *End of Ideology as Ideology*, these included Paul Potter's *Intellectual as an Agent of Social Change*, Paul Booth's *Strategy for University Reform*, Carl Davidson's *Student Syndicalism*, Hayden's *Student Social Action*, Staughton Lynd's *Participatory Democracy, and the New Radicals*, and speeches and pamphlets by Dick Flacks, Nick Egleson, Clark Kissinger, Bob Ross and Todd Gitlin. The first official SDS statement after Port Huron was 'America and the New Era' (1963), in Teodori, op. cit., p. 172.

88 In England the editors of *ULR* – Hall, Williams and Thompson – came close to playing this role in the years 1958–62 – but they promptly abandoned it, when they split with *NLR*.

89 Newfield, op. cit., p. 20. Later, the much more limited concept of 'liberation' would predominate, but in the movement's optimistic and heady beginnings, the aspiration was for nothing less than a new order. For a discussion of 'freedom' and 'liberation', see H. Arendt, *On Revolution*, Viking Press, 1965, final section.

90 Even the militant M2M produced a paper called *Free Student*, and the Maoists proper had one called *Freedom* (see Teodori, op. cit.). M2M (May Second Movement) was a Maoist-Castroite group close to PL.

91 A view (Lasch) which included previous radical literary-political figures.

92 In its very first year, even before the missions to poor communities and early SDS projects had begun, a group of SDS activists were involved in the strike of miners in Hazard, Kentucky.

93 See chapter 7 of this book, and Lynd in Long, op. cit.

94 For example, the debates about nonviolence and participatory democracy were far more situationally specific in SDS than in the English context.

95 See discussion in chapter 7.

96 See Joyce Kornbluh, *Rebel Voices: an IWW Anthology*, University of Michigan Press, 1964.

97 Also influential was Sorel's syndicalist philosophy (see below); and NB the Preface to this book for Lenin's response.

98 Carl Oglesby, later SDS President, op. cit., p. 14.

99 Lynd's populism and non-cooperation as well as his academic work

can be seen in the context of his family and Quaker background. See P. Brock, *Pacifism in the 20th Century*, Van Nostrand, 1970, pp. 249–60, and the interview in J. Finn, *Protest, Pacifism, and Politics*, pp. 223–45.

100 Earlier Anarchists in their quarrel with Marx, had argued that one could never expect an egalitarian and a free society to emerge from an authoritarian organization. See Irving Horowitz's conclusion to *The Anarchists*, Dell, 1964.

101 On this repudiation see Teodori, op. cit., p. 40. See also N. Birnbaum in J. Nagel, *Student Power*, Merlin Press, 1969, pp. 148–9.

102 Or 'sex-role' liberation movements as they are more properly termed.

103 Expressed in the satirical songs and humour of the Free Speech Movement of 1964 (see pp. 308, 353). In the following year, Ken Kesey's 'merry pranksters' immediately foreshadowed the counter-culture's growth in San Francisco. Subsequently, R. D. Laing, who pursued these themes in his *Divided Self* (Penguin, 1970), reinforced the confidence of those who had chosen such political expressiveness. A 'new style of revolutionary politics . . . people doing things for themselves'. Robin Blackburn, quoted by Stafford in D. E. Apter and J. Joll, *Anarchism Today*, Macmillan, 1971, p. 89.

104 Similar strains even run through Fanon's writing (see Cook and Morgan op. cit., pp. 69–84 or F. Fanon, *Wretched of the Earth*, Grove Press, 1963).

105 On participation and control, see C. G. Benello and D. Roussopoulos, *The Case for Participatory Democracy*, Grossman, 1971 and Hayden in I. Howe, *The Radical Papers*, Anchor, 1966, pp. 363–77.

106 Mills, and R. V. Sampson in England, urged the connection between *personal* issues and *public* power, stressing the further idea (also developed by Marcuse) of a continuity and analogy between psychological and political inequality and alienation.

107 Many of the same issues became the basis of a direct-action oriented community politics in England in the same period. NB also Fruchter's film (on Newark), *Troublemakers*.

108 It was natural that the white organizers should begin to move into their own grassroots projects, such as those in Cleveland, Chicago and Newark. See Rothstein, 'ERAP: Evolution of the Organisers' in *Radical America*, March 1968, also in Teodori, op. cit.

109 In New Haven, Baltimore, Boston and Oakland and subsequently outside the USA. In England *ULR* was involved in community action as early as 1958, in Notting Hill. See George Clark on the tenants' associations in R. Benewick and T. Smith (eds), *Direct Action and Democratic Politics*, Allen & Unwin, 1972.

110 Raymond Williams, Conclusion to *Culture and Society*, Chatto & Windus, 1958. See also Campaign Caravan Workshops brochures containing a visionary fusion of NL ideas and community action projects; inspired by George Clark and employing other ex-CND personnel; it proved premature in the British context.

111 Encouraged by Colin Ward's *Anarchy* (1960–70) and Theodore Roszak's editorship of *Peace News* in the mid-1960s.

112 M. Oppenheimer, 'Sociology of P.D.', in H. P. Dreitzel, *Recent Sociology*, Macmillan, 1969, discusses these components.
113 Carl Davidson in Teodori, op. cit. and C. Oglesby, Introduction to *New Left Reader*. See also Benello and Roussopoulos, op. cit., pp. 3–9 and 270–83, and Cook and Morgan, op. cit., pp. 1–41 and 134–43.
114 Clearly, as Sartre, referring to Yugoslav worker self-management, pointed out, decentralization 'becomes meaningless as long as there is a centralized political organization in the hands of a privileged group.' (C. Oglesby, 'Decade Ready for a Dustbin', accepts this as inevitable.)
115 Blackburn quoted by Stafford in Apter and Joll, op. cit., p. 98, and see Marcuse, 'Old Model' in Teodori, op. cit., pp. 469 ff.

The German NL looked back to Syndicalist ideas and the workers' councils of the German revolutionary experience (1918) (see Hunnius, *Student Revolts: The New Left in West Germany*, War Resisters International, June 1968).

The Worker-Council tradition also contributed to the development of the ideas of P.D. See Hunnius in Benello and Roussopoulos, op. cit.
116 While most of the nuclear disarmament movement had remained rigid and formalistic, the meetings of the Committee and other CND off-shoots such as George Clark's Campaign Caravans, exemplified an English version of participatory democracy. In contrast see Ritchie Calder's description of CND's structure and leadership, and see also Duff, op. cit., p. 221, and in chapter 4 below.
117 Though in part it was responsible for this decline (see later).
118 See Cook and Morgan, op. cit.
119 See CNVA bulletin, August 1965, report by a participant.
120 See M. Oppenheimer, *Urban Guerrilla*, Penguin, 1970.
121 And the dream of instituting some sort of Syndicalist system such as delegates mandated from functional bodies, primarily occupational groups.
122 See Benello and Roussopoulos, op. cit., *passim* and especially M. Oppenheimer's 'Limitations of Socialism', p. 270.
123 SDS produced a pamphlet on this specific theme, and on 'organizing-out' of situations.
124 In many cases, it is only fair to say that even in SDS, this occurred *before* people started claiming it for themselves. Eventually this was a key source of the birth of Women's Liberation as a movement, see pp. 368 ff.
125 The nearest any single grouping came to embodying this essence was probably SDS in the years 1965 and 1966.

By the mid-1960s, SDS was moving towards the abolition of its central offices, presidency and vice-presidency, and moving towards the Field Secretary idea of the 1967–8 period. Unlike the previous experience of the peace movement, the splits resulting from this democratization were minimal. See Kirkpatrick Sale, *History of SDS*.

3. A new radicalism

1 J. Newfield, *Prophetic Minority*, Signet Books, 1966.
2 In the 1970 BBC Reith lectures, Donald Schön, an organization analyst, detected in this form of organization, a symptom of what he called the decline of the 'stable state'; his description is as good as any, of the structure of the movement and in describing how SDS actually operated in the years 1964–8. See *Listener*, 10 and 17 December 1970.
3 Schön, op. cit., describes the way the model works: 'The movement is then as much from periphery to periphery, from point to point on the periphery, as it is from centre to periphery.' Both Marcuse and M. Teodori (*The New Left*, pp. 53–4 and pp. 469 ff.) describe SDS and SNCC in terms remarkably similar to Schön; see Marcuse, 'Old Model' in Teodori, pp. 472 ff.: 'not a large centralized and coordinated movement, but local and regional political action against specific grievances – riots, ghetto rebellions and so on, that is to say, certainly mass movement.'
4 Marcuse, ibid., 'local activities, small groups . . . highly flexible and autonomous'.
5 Such as Berkeley's VDC (Vietnam Day Committee); active 1965–6; (perhaps the first of significance) a broad coalition at the start, it included SDS, Pacifists, Trotskyists, left-liberals, Communist Party members, unaffiliated anarchists, Bay area poets (including Ginsberg), Independent Socialists, Student Activists, street people, academics and professionals. Also active at the outset were various occupationally based groups against the war (clergy, etc.).
6 Involving especially mothers of young children, unable to attend evening meetings or travel to demonstrations; the most significant of these groups, 'Women Strike for Peace', was active in the early 1960s.
7 The march of 1958, initiated by the DAC (closely associated with *Peace News*), although CND was chary of it at first, confirmed alliances between various elements, including Christian groups (some already represented in the CND executive), unattached professionals, journalists, scientists, students, intellectuals, and members of the cultural avant-garde.
8 See M. Cohen and D. Hale, *The New Student Left*, on Berkeley (FSM), p. 237. As S. Hall, 'The Hippies: An American Moment', observes (p. 174) the most successful students often went through a rejection experience of the academic rat-race, dropping out into the counter-communities to form what Hall calls 'an informal community of scholars'.
9 In so far as these labels are at all useful in describing the individual heterodoxies of SDS members! (See T. Hayden in I. Howe, *The Radical Papers*, pp. 362–77 on SDS in 1963–6.)
10 'The new left's diversity and decentralism is one of its greatest strengths and should be supported and aided in every way.' Editors of *Studies on the Left* (Aronowitz, Baxandall, Genovese, Weinstein and Kramer) Spring 1965 (replying to Hayden, Fruchter and Cheuse).

11 Schön, op. cit., and Teodori, op. cit., Introd.
12 E.g. itinerant socialist organizers of early twentieth-century North America and Mexico or nineteenth-century Spain and Russia. In the spirit of the *Obrera Consciente* of nineteenth-century Spanish Anarchists, or the Wobbly 'hoboes' of 1910. (See Sid Lens, *Radicalism in America*, on these analogies.)
13 These perhaps also reflected a renewal of the cultural tradition of 'bums' in the USA, ever 'On the Road', celebrated by the Beat writers and folk singers.
14 Schön, op. cit. E.g. Hayden, Rothstein, Booth, Davis, Wittman, Shero and others most clearly fit this description in their SDS travels.
15 See S. Lynd in P. Long (ed.), *The New Left*, p. 10. K. Kenniston, in *The Young Radicals*, Harcourt Brace Jovanovitch, 1968, stresses their ability to engage in face-to-face direct and open relationships.
16 S. Lynd article 'Bicameralism from below' reprinted in T. E. Cook and P. M. Morgan, *Participatory Democracy*. See also Tom Hayden, 'Movement on Trial', ibid., p. 43 and *Ramparts* (July 1970).
17 See Julius Lester's *Revolutionary Notes*, Institute for the Study of Nonviolence, Palo Alto, January 1970, p. 3.
18 T. Hayden, 'Movement on Trial', p. 44.
19 A number of other writers made this analogy with the migration of Russian populist students (Narodniks) to the peasant communities (1860): they combined near mystical faith in the common people, with an urge to organize the masses through direct participation. (See also L. Feuer, *Conflict of Generations*.) Regardless of this parallel, the remarkable success of COFO's call for over 800 volunteers for Mississippi Summer, was based on a similar ethos.
20 Just 'As the Russian radical movement grew from Tolstoyism and the Narodnik's concern to dress simply, speak truth and "go to the people".' In 'The New Radicals and Participatory Democracy', Teodori, op. cit., p. 229.
21 E.g. close to the ideas of the Catholic Worker group in New York from which Michael Harrington's analysis of America's poor originally emerged in his widely read and quoted *The Other America*, Penguin, 1962. Having been a member of the CW cooperative in the Bowery, he was deeply influenced by its spiritual and political mentor, Dorothy Day.
22 Tom Kahn (a critic of the NL) in 'The Problem of the New Left' in *Commentary*, July 1966.
23 See discussion in P. Worsley, *The Third World*, Weidenfeld & Nicolson, 1967.
24 Such range and variation in NL images of the Third World and peasant cultures revealed distinct differences and interpretations and involved a variety of political meanings that held some fatal ambiguities. See chapter 9 and Appendix on peasant revolution.
25 See S. Lens in C. G. Benello and D. Roussopoulos, *The Case for Participatory Democracy*. Cuba, China, and Algeria were looked at with interest; less distant from NL practice and ideas were the

innovative communitarian-socialisms (Tanzania) or the Indian Gramdan 'land revolution' tactics of Vinoba. Although some elements of spontaneity and mass participation in the 'cultural revolution' seemed to echo movement experiences, many attempts to stress such parallels with China were propagandistic and disputed by sceptics.

26 I.e. not just the most advanced elements of the working class, but all oppressed, isolated, alienated or marginal groups.

27 In any discussion of the development of the theory of counter-institutions, these names are linked (Hayden was a founder of SDS), credited with elaborating and articulating the strategy; they differ substantially in emphasis and style, and their roles differed in practice, but they both made more abstract concepts (Fromm's, Goodman's, Mills's – or even Marcuse's) applicable in practice. See Hayden in Cook and Morgan, op. cit., pp. 43–8 and Lynd pp. 143–7.

28 For discussion of Participatory Democracy (PD) and Community Control see Introductions to Benello and Roussopoulos, pp. 3–9 (op. cit.) and to Cook and Morgan (op. cit.) pp. 1–41.

29 R. Blackburn, echoing Marcuse, quoted in Stafford in D. E. Apter and J. Joll, *Anarchism Today*, p. 89.

30 See G. Sorel, *Reflections on Violence*, Collier Books, 1961, and R. K. Merton, *Social Theory and Social Structure*, 'The Self-Fulfilling Prophecy', Free Press, 1964, chapter 11.

31 Mills strongly criticized the laissez-faire ethos emphasizing individual competition, initiative and achievement and profoundly mystifying the actual nature of mid-twentieth-century USA.

32 See C. W. Mills, *White Collar*, Oxford University Press, 1951, D. Riesman, *The Lonely Crowd*, Yale University Press, 1950, and W. White, *The Organisation Man*, Doubleday, 1956.

33 Fromm (e.g. in *The Sane Society*), far more clearly and radically than Riesman, linked this view to a critique of capitalism.

34 With Laing and other later writers, Fromm emphasized the crisis of selfhood and stresses its links with other individual symptoms of social malaise; e.g. boredom, insecurity, homicide, mental sickness and alcoholism. Subsequent events suggest that the analysis has some bearing on the fate of the Movement.

35 Following Kropotkin, Goodman remained an evolutionist, his utopianism not backward-looking, even if seeking to revive lost elements or earlier stages (still latent in society) to meet present needs.

36 Later this was to become an ideal of the commune movement of the later 1960s; but through Lynd it provided more general inspiration to the counter-institutional strategies of the NL at this earlier stage.

Lynd's anarchist communitarianism developed as a result of practical experience (a decade of communal living in the Bruderhof community) (see Cook and Morgan, op. cit., pp. 134–43).

37 See Roszak's discussion of Goodman in *Counter Culture* and *Dissenting Academy*.

38 *Anarchy* magazine (founded in 1961) was devoted to exactly these kinds of concerns and projects: practical, community-based, evolutionary, decentralist and technologically aware.

39 See discussion below (chapter 16) and in *Cultural Studies*, 7–8, Birmingham, Summer 1975 (9–73).
40 See article by Roussopoulos, in Benello and Roussopoulos, op. cit.
41 See A. Rigby, *Alternative Realities*, Routledge & Kegan Paul, 1974.
42 Already emphasized by the Catholic Workers and carried into the South by civil rights workers.
43 In America the influence of cultural and political 'deviance'; the poets (Ginsberg, Ferlinghetti and Patchen *et al.*); the small papers and magazines and other projects (Krassner's *The Realist*, the *Village Voice* and Arnoni's *Minority of One*, the *Evergreen Review* and the City Lights Bookshop); lone literary voices (Mailer, Trocchi); the humour of Lenny Bruce; together with the black jazz subculture, already constituted a considerable cultural 'underground' in the early 1960s.
44 This development, traced in England to the 'raggle taggle scrag-end' of an Aldermaston march, by Stuart Hall (a founder editor of *ULR/ NLR*) clearly linked up with the Beats in the USA. (See Hall, p. 196, in J. Nagel, *Student Power* and Fred Davis's 'The Hippies', *Transaction*, December 1967.)
45 But when Hall argues (ibid.) that 'Hippies start to construct within the womb of pre-revolutionary society. . . . What the activists plan and organise for', he does less than justice to the projects of the political NL (also see Julius Lester in *Revolutionary Notes*).
46 On a Socialist search for 'non-alienated' technology, see André Gorz, in C. Oglesby, *The New Left Reader*, pp. 41 ff.
47 On Alternative Society Strategies see, e.g. Cook and Morgan, op. cit., pp. 206–10 and Berke, *Counter Culture*.
48 Marcuse, op. cit. It is possible to glean from this writing, affirmation of the need to concretize 'possibility' of social change, i.e. in such a way as to make *ideas* widely understandable and enabling the manifestations of these ideas to be easily copied.
49 Hayden, 'Movement on Trial' in Cook and Morgan, op. cit., p. 45.
50 Hall in Nagel, op. cit.
51 Hall in ibid., p. 199 and see P. Berger and T. Luckmann, *The Social Construction of Reality*, Anchor, 1967.
52 In the counter-societies of the Haight, Berkeley and the East Village, free stores, free buses, free food and free festivals were variations on the 'free' theme. 'Free Schools' appear later.
53 The Diggers, a most dramatically political group, translated Provo ideas and methods into the American context; inspired by 'Emmett Grogan', they emphasized in a far more principled way than their Yippee successors, the innovations of cashlessness. (These were also less in evidence in the second phase of the Dutch experience.)
54 Davis, op. cit. E.g. these 'deviant meanings' were expressed in such theatrical actions as the distribution of free dollar bills in New York's stock exchange (1967).
55 'Politicoes' was the term used by 'hippies' of activists within this coalition (and vice versa).
56 It also bore the legend: 'last night we celebrated the growing fusion of head, heart and hands; of hippies and activists; and our joy and

confidence in our ability to care for and take care of ourselves and what is ours.' It expressed 'a trust in the future' and a 'longing for a place fit to live in' and the aim of creating 'the space needed' to build freedom. See Mike Rossman's 'Barefoot in a Marshmallow World', *Ramparts*, January 1966, and his miscellaneous writings on this period.

57 E.g. Berkeley, Cambridge (Mass.) Ann Arbor, Madison; some, like the East Village in New York, or the Haight-Ashbury, developed apart from major universities, with greater 'hippy' and lesser political emphasis.

58 Also John Hopkins's and Peter Jenner's Notting Hill Free School and community festivals; the Golbourne community council was a subsequent development in this context.

59 See Hayden in Cook and Morgan, op. cit., pp. 43–8.

60 Lens notes the strong resemblance of this synthesis to the utopian and socialist movements of the early nineteenth-century or the beginnings of syndicalism: these too had emphasized the growth of radical alternatives – communities, cooperatives and unions. See S. Lens, 'Road to Power and Beyond' (Benello and Roussopoulos, op. cit., pp. 300–16) and in his *Radicalism in America*.

61 The Dutch Anarchists used the phrase 'inside reality, but beyond its limits', to discuss their tactics – often focused on the day-to-day needs of ordinary people. 'Provo' who began their activities in Amsterdam in 1965 and were active until May 1967 also employed the concept of a 'counter-society'. See Apter and Joll, op. cit., pp. 164–80.

62 See later discussion on NL views of revolution (chapter 12).

63 SNCC statement quoted in George Feaver, 'Black Power' in M. Cranston, *New Left*, Bodley Head, 1970, pp. 139–75.

64 This was enormously influential on first-generation cultural revolt – the Beats or 'hipsters' (see N. Mailer, *The White Negro*, City Lights Bookshop, 1957). Then once contact was made both in New York and Paris with black writing (such as Fanon's) a fusion of blackness, poetry and revolt was confirmed and interchange of music, theatre and cultural rebellion took place.

65 Free university and free school movements both owe a great deal to Goodman's attack on 'compulsory mis-education', the absurdity of conformist socialization and his call for a 'community-based education'. On the birth of the Free U's, see Sol Stern in Teodori, op. cit., pp. 156–8.

66 On the demand for, and vision of, alternative education, and Free Universities, see J. Berke, *Counter Culture*, pp. 216–81.

67 The movement in the USA grew only slowly at first alongside and out of the growing dissatisfaction with the cybernated indoctrination of multi-universities; but after 1966 became trans-national in scope, and communal in orientation.

68 See chapter 4 for a fuller discussion of this.

69 See Teodori, op. cit., sections 8, 9 and 10, pp. 38–54. On the disillusion with liberalism of NL recruits in the early 1960s see Elinor Langer's perceptive piece, op. cit., p. 60.

70 But see R. Flacks's remarks in 'Making History versus Making Life', on the longer-term implications of this background and this 'conversion' (i.e. through guilt and compassion).
71 Teodori, op. cit., pp. 36–7.

4. After reformism: the dilemmas of extra-parliamentarism

1 For an early discussion of this political disenchantment in England by a sociologist active in the movement, see John Rex, 'The sociology of CND', *War and Peace* (CND quarterly), Jan. 1963.
2 It followed, 'that the moral imperative, the normative principle of love, operated only tangentially, and superficially on political institutions and struggles.'

'How much do you have to give away before you can be practically effective, until finally there isn't anything to give any more.'

See A. J. Muste, 'On Holy Disobedience' in *Nonviolence in America* (ed. Lynd), and *Collected Essays* (ed. Hentoff).

Mills also encouraged a de-mystification of the electoral system, but from a realist standpoint (*Power Elite*, Oxford University Press, 1956, chapter 13) (see later discussion).
3 This was the 'Student League for Industrial Democracy' (SLID) (the youth section of 'LID'). See Clarke Kissinger, 'From SLID to Resistance', *New Left Notes*, July 1968.
4 In the USA, the division with Bayard Rustin, Robert Gilmore, Irving Howe, Michael Harrington, Tom Kahn, Robert Pickus, James Farmer and to some extent, King himself, became open (by 1963). In Britain, however, Norman Birnbaum argues that the reverse occurred – a drift of left-social-democrats away from Labour Reformism helped the NL. See 'Great Britain: The Reactive Revolt' in *Towards a Critical Sociology*, Oxford University Press, 1971, p. 320.
5 On the concept of 'exclusionism' see Alan Haber in M. Teodori, *The New Left*, pp. 218 ff. On the blanket usage of the term anti-communist by the NL to include a wide range of critics see P. Clecak, *Radical Paradoxes*, pp. 16–18 and p. 304 (n3).
6 Rejected as late as an SDS conference in 1965. See S. M. Lipset, 'Student Opposition in USA' in *Government and Opposition*, April 1966, p. 362. In an SDS referendum on civil disobedience at this time, 56 per cent were *against* it.
7 One form of justification for extra-legal action both with respect to the Bomb and Vietnam, was that no popular endorsement or democratic mandate for government policy existed; in England, for example, Atlee had endorsed an A-Bomb programme secretly and his successors never sought electoral support; similarly, the war in SE Asia was 'undeclared'.
8 On the NL's revulsion from traditional politics see p. 412 of L. Feuer, *Conflict of Generations* and p. 63 in Marcuse, *Essay on Liberation*, Boston, 1969.

These changes in attitude can be detected, in particular, in relation to civil disobedience.

9 On this see Gene Sharp, *Civil Disobedience in a Democracy*, Peace News Reprint, 1961.

10 A number of episodic liberal reform movements had proved over many years to be culs-de-sac rarely achieving gains of substance.

11 A number of commentators have commented on the anti-political tone, of the early years of CND, as a reaction to the bipartisanship, closure and bureaucratic party structure that had eliminated the nuclear issue from public or electoral debate. E.g. see Frank Myers, 'British peace politics: 1957–1962; the CND and the Committee of 100', Ph.D., Columbia University, unpublished, 1965 (see pp. 103, 116 and 328–30). For the US Peace Movement see Roy Finch 'The New Peace Movement' in *Dissent*, Winter and Spring, 1963.

12 In much the same way 'Academic freedom' had presumed an inactive acquiescence – an end of ideological politics, and conformity and apathy. On most campuses (until FSM) this was a safe assumption.

13 The state's use of civil defence illusions as an organ of deceptive propaganda to imply the limited nature of nuclear wars was graphically subverted by Peter Watkins's documentation of the effects of nuclear attack (*The War Game*). This film was, after public and parliamentary outcry, shown on a limited basis, but never appeared for a mass television audience as intended.

14 See chapter 14 on 'repression'.

15 The view of Canon Collins, CND Chairman, February 1958.

16 And indeed was opposed by figures such as A. J. P. Taylor, who were bemused by the growth of a mass-politics around their élitist project.

17 The issues of 'unilateralism' and civil disobedience were never issues in SANE, since the distinction between it and CNVA was much more marked than in the CND/Committee of 100 relationship; nuclear pacifism and nonviolent action (dominant in CND's early days) were not part of SANE's platform, even though Fromm himself associated with both ideas.

18 Wilson, Kennedy in the USA (and at first LBJ himself). The disillusion in Britain began soon after the election of Wilson as PM, and intensified as his defence and foreign policies developed; it was equally marked in America after LBJ – supported by moderates on a peace and anti-Goldwater ticket – escalated the Vietnam war. Ironically, the Kennedy era had helped create an ambience in which the early New Left could thrive; many of those later to be associated with militant opposition to policies initiated by him, wept at the news of his death. One of the first overall critiques of 'Kennedy-liberalism' was in June 1965 when SDS's convention document ('America and the New Era') was published.

19 Which the Bank Leak of 1955 and other public scandals seemed to confirm. Michael Lipton comments on the 'aimlessness' of political life, the lack of long-term thought which reinforced public rejection of the party system (see *Labour's Last Chance*, Penguin, 1967, p. 18).

20 The first TV election of 1955 was followed by the mass political advertising campaigns of 1959 in Britain.

21 See my article 'CND: the Foolish Virgins', *New University*, 1961. So-called 'apathy' revealed in declining electoral votes, smaller political meetings and party memberships, is compounded by political satire on the one hand (*Private Eye* or *The Realist*) and bi-partisanship on the other (on this see Birnbaum, op. cit., p. 303). But was this withdrawal a-political? In fact popular passivity has often coincided with a growth of minority direct action as a correlate of bureau-cratization (see April Carter, *Direct Action and Liberal Democracy*, Routledge & Kegan Paul, 1973).

22 See Teodori, op. cit., p. 46.

23 For a different view of CND that associates it with a New Left revolt within the Labour Party (The Victory for Socialism group: VFS) opposing reformism and labourism and linking itself to *ULR/NLR*: 1956–61, see N. Birnbaum, 'Britain the reactive revolt', in *Towards a Critical Sociology*, pp. 320 ff.

24 Paul Potter's and Carl Oglesby's speeches on successive Washington demonstrations were key moments in this shift; see Elinor Langer's discussion of their statements (pp. 60–1, in her article, 'Notes for Next Time,' *Working Papers for a New Society*, Fall 1973).

25 SDS was influential in generating teach-in movements in the spring of 1965, both at Michigan and Berkeley and elsewhere.

26 E.g. see views of Hayden, Oglesby, Mills and Marcuse discussed below.

27 The usage of the terms 'parliamentarism'/'Extra-parliamentarism' is inexact. 'Electoralism' or 'party-system' would be more apt – especially for the USA – but the former terms have an accretion of specific meaning in over a century of Socialist usage in debates (especially in Europe) which passed into sociological writing.

The term 'extra-parliamentarism', as a broad NL phenomenon, is used here to cover political activity outside formal party/representa-tive systems of government, especially that of a non-institutionalized kind. It usually implies a demoting, or delegitimation, of established (national) government and legislative or administrative change as well.

28 This is the analysis of David Marquand, 'The Decline of CND', *Socialist Commentary*, January 1965, who generally misunderstands the complexity of the anti-nuclear movement.

29 One can hardly underestimate the significance of the fact that at the very moment of the apparent triumph of a parliamentary tactic, the major civil disobedience campaign was launched.

30 As one method of doing this the NL journals helped create groups (NL clubs and CND branches) aligned to its ideas and tactics (but these were not always so ready to shift into the Labour Party *en bloc*).

31 The document 'Steps Towards Peace' was produced by this ten-dency in 1963.

As this incrementalist proposal showed, watering down a popular movement's principles in order to gain 'political influence' is often counter-productive. See also my article 'Foolish Virgins', op. cit.

32 See R. Miliband, *Parliamentary Socialism*, Merlin, 1964, who

emphasizes the conflict between a 'constitutional' and a 'direct action' wing.

33 Such a pledge was to be implemented by Gaitskell's front group, the 'Campaign for Democratic Socialism' (in which Dick Taverne was active). CND's case, including positive non-alignment, had hardly got a hearing at Scarborough and was subsequently subordinated to infighting.

34 For example, an early poll showed 15 per cent of Conservative voters supporting unilateral nuclear disarmament. On the social composition of CND, see Frank Parkin, *Middle Class Radicalism*, Manchester University Press, 1968.

35 For the view of someone deeply implicated in CND strategy who nevertheless became increasingly sceptical and critical of the leadership, see P. Duff, *Left, Left, Left*, esp. pp. 163–4, 197 ff., 221 ff.

36 The alienation from politics is perhaps a clue or explanation for the poor showing of CND during the 1959 election – when it failed to assert an independent political presence. See D. Butler and R. Rose, *British General Election of 1959*, Nuffield Election Studies, London, 1960.

37 See the articles and speeches in D. Boulton, *Voices in the Crowd*, Peter Owen, 1963 (this title is somewhat ironic since most of the contributors are CND leaders!).

38 The tacit adherence to the LP strategy became more or less open in the CND newspaper *Sanity* from 1963 onwards, although as a central issue in the party it really only survived until 1962.

39 The Labour Party 'as it was' and a Labour Government 'as it would be' was unlikely to implement unilateralism. See N. Walter, 'Damned Fools in Utopia', *New Left Review*, 1962.

40 The Labour Party's administrative HQ in London.

41 Illustrated by the fact that the Left campaign to implement the Scarborough decision (the 'Appeal for Unity') was run on the dry, narrow (and in retrospect, largely irrelevant) issues of party-constitution and authority of conference decisions.

42 A number of previously sympathetic 'Left' Labour MPs refused to stand for CND's EC during the pre-election year of 1963 – unwilling to rock the boat under Wilson's leadership.

43 Stuart Christie's disillusion occurred whilst a youth member of CND in Glasgow; see S. Christie and A. Meltzer, *The Floodgates of Anarchy*, Kahn & Averill, 1970.

44 Especially large numbers left in the year after Wilson's election in 1964, including subsequently, Peggy Duff, General Secretary of CND (specifically on the issue of Labour's attitude to the Greek coup but as a cumulation of disenchantment).

45 CND could not even prevent a fifth nuclear Polaris submarine being immediately added to the British fleet by the new Wilson government.

46 Peace candidates were sponsored by groups like Pax in Boston or 'Voters for Peace' in Chicago and paralleled INDEC in Britain and the campaigns for specific Left-Labour MPs; there were 32

independent peace candidates in the USA in 1962, the most prominent being Noel Day and, in Massachusetts, the Congressional campaign of H. Stuart Hughes.

47 As April Carter (op. cit.) puts it, CND could not yet claim that constitutional methods had been tried and failed; yet it had both canvassing teams and volunteer workers in certain areas, superior to those of any of the three major political parties, and mass public support by autumn 1961. A good by-election opportunity (at Orpington) soon after this was missed and the delay was costly.

48 INDEC represented a substantial proportion of CND opinion but was pathetically cautious and belated – and predictably failed.

49 With movement support, but not necessarily official CND backing, so as not to embarrass Labour Party members (who risked proscription).

50 At first only at selected local by-elections, with local support, and where no other candidate supported nuclear disarmament. One or two respectable campaigns were waged, the most successful being in Bromley, and that of Michael Craft at Twickenham. The experiment ended with Richard Gott's disaster at the Hull by-election in 1964. See Duff's account and explanation, op. cit., p. 197.

51 The main focus of all these small groups and parties (with the possible exception of the SNP) was mainly extra-parliamentary in this period, and they shared with the NL as an extra-parliamentary phenomenon at least a tactical scepticism of Westminster.

52 May Day Manifesto, 1967, pp. 111–43 in C. Oglesby, *New Left Reader*.

53 A. J. P. Taylor, the historian, noted that these constituted some of the biggest in British political history, a view confirmed reluctantly by the press and other critics.

54 Russell argued that law-abiding methods alone would not promote a movement capable of changing government policy thus begging the question of extra-legal acts.

55 For the Committee of 100's view of these tactics see P. Cadogan in R. Benewick and T. Smith (eds), *Direct Action and Democratic Politics*, and (more guarded) G. Clark, *Second Wind*, pamphlet, 1962. Both *Solidarity* and *Peace News* kept up an attack on CND's leadership throughout the years after its first pronouncements of spring 1958.

56 Nuclear armed submarines (Polaris) arrived in Scotland's Holy Loch on 18 February 1961. The CND leadership in a post-Scarborough paralysis, almost entirely failed to respond. The Committee of 100 and other *ad hoc* groups actively demonstrated against it: on that day over 4,000 sat down against it, the rank and file of CND campaigned against it; Scots marched in force; Unions voted against it; francs-tireurs paddled canoes out to the ships; this anti-Polaris campaign was the nearest to major political success that CND ever got, yet it never really had the full backing of its officialdom and a massive shift of loyalty and respect away from the CND leadership followed. See accounts in Duff, op. cit., pp. 163–4 and C. Driver, *The Disarmers*, Hodder & Stoughton, 1964, chapter 5.

57 In spite of this public opinion polls still showed 55 per cent opposed

to nuclear testing, and even a clear majority against an independent deterrent; these could be used to justify extra-legal acts; on the other hand, opposition to the American bases was never much above 30 per cent and the majoritarian argument was weaker on this point as on straight unilateralism.

58 One poll showed 49 per cent of CND supporters either favouring civil disobedience or participating in it.

59 The Young Liberals' new-found radicalism dates from this period, as one libertarian strand of the peace movement became a dominant tendency in the YLs, emphasizing participatory democracy as opposed to the reformist parliamentarism of the adult Liberal Party. Its invocation of 'anarcho-syndicalist' traditions and 'community politics' places it as near as any other British group at this time to the early SDS and it later (1967) influenced the Radical Student Alliance (RSA).

60 Only with the confrontation with the State (which began at the Ministry of Defence in February 1961) did the movement begin to make a partial breach in the conspiracy of silence that had surrounded it since 1957.

61 Colin Ward in D. Apter and J. Joll, *Anarchism Today*, p. 92.

62 Denmark alone, amongst these countries with substantial nuclear pacifist movements, seemed to show the least sign of extra-parliamentarism, perhaps reflecting both its multiple party system, and its strong communal traditions; German extra-parliamentarism is discussed later.

63 In Hayden's words:
The emphasis in the movement on letting the people decide on decentralised decision making, on refusing alliances with top leaders, stems from the need to create a personal and group identity that can survive both the temptations and the crippling effects of this society. *The Radical Papers*, ed. I. Howe, p. 362 *passim*.

64 Lynd in Teodori, op. cit., p. 197.

65 Marcuse, op. cit. Such a view is reminiscent of Sorel's attack on the practitioners of bourgeois parliamentarism and his syndicalist advocacy of moving outside the existing structures and frames. Above all, Sorel had emphasized the need to insulate the movement from the blandishments of bourgeois culture, especially from the snares of election and office-holding.

66 Except for temporarily boosting income for a few people, this entire reformist trend has weakened the poor under the pretence of helping them and strengthened white rule under the slogan of curbing private enterprise (Hayden, op. cit.).

67 Those who had been excluded, have often created their own 'rights and duties' systems of democratic participation; the British working class produced a fully developed set of institutions. See my 'Prometheans and Troglodytes: The English Working Class and the Dialectics of Incorporation', *Berkeley Journal of Sociology*, 1967. Excerpts in P. Worsley, *Problems of Modern Society*, Penguin, 1972.

68 The Newark Community Union Project (see Teodori, op. cit.,

pp. 133–6) was dominated by Hayden, most ideological of the activists; NCUP became the most influential, well publicized, and by 1963, most important of the projects.

69 Lynd, 'Coalition Politics or Nonviolent Revolution', in Teodori, op. cit., pp. 197–202.

70 Hayden, op. cit.

71 Tom Kahn: 'The Problem of the New Left', *Commentary*, July 1966.

72 On the attempt to build alliances – particularly with the growing white–Negro population of students and hippies, and with other ethnic minorities such as Puerto Ricans and Mexican Americans – see following chapter.

73 S. Lynd, *Coalition Politics*.

74 See Teodori, op. cit., pp. 100–2.

75 See H. Zinn, *SNCC: The New Abolitionists*, and J. Newfield, *Prophetic Minority*, p. 71 *passim* (ch. 5) and see later discussion of the turn towards armed tactics in chapter 12.

76 Two-thirds of one of Harris Poll's black sample were 'alienated from the political system'; education did not remove this lack of identification with dominant institutional structures. This was not an alienation from all organization or political activity but from white majority politics; Harris found equally wide distrust of legislation on civil rights.

77 E.g. after George Wallace's big votes in 1963 and 1964.

78 Revealed in the 1964 Dawson–Rayner contest in Chicago, where educational issues were at stake.

79 The Mississippi Freedom Democratic Party (MFDP), created in 1964 outside established Democratic Party Machines and the State Registration systems (both white fiefs), registered voters, held conventions and sent delegates to claim seats nationally; rejecting a seating compromise, it challenged the validity of white delegations. The problem for MFDP's challenge to the Democratic Party was that by acting 'tactically' it left confusion amongst the rank and file as to whether the state-registration system and Dixiecrat machine-politics were finally rejected, or only temporarily 'by-passed'. MFDP was thus never clearly a 'counter-institutional' strategy; Zinn's hope that SNCC could work both within and against traditional politics was a vain one – particularly because it lacked any coherently mobilized base in the community.

80 The SNCC workers, and the 64 delegates they had selected and brought along in 1966, had at best little more relationship with the rest of the 800,000 Mississippians than an NLF officer, and his picked cadres, with the 'whole of the Vietnamese peasantry', or 'people' (see Newfield, op. cit.). The gap between leaders and led remained. The Lowndes County Freedom Organization of 1966 was offered as a more clearcut 'third-party' option, but outside the frame of white politics.

81 COFO came unstuck because of the role of its big personalities (King, Farmer, Wilkins and Rustin), which came to a head (Selma, 1965) when SNCC criticized King in particular, for arriving at decisions without consultation.

82 The SNCC-initiated voter-registration drives started in 1961 and reached a peak in 1964. At the outset only 1 in 10 of the potential black voters in Mississippi was eligible – through registration – to vote. With considerable debate about working 'inside' or 'outside' the electoral system, SNCC, poised on the margins, hedged its bets by registering voters who might – or might not – operate within the Democratic Party framework.

83 Moses and Foreman on one side: King and Rustin on the other.

84 See R. Lowenthal, 'Unreason and Revolution' in *Encounter*, 1966.

85 By and large these independent ventures were judged to be relative failures merely in terms of low votes. When 'Dove' candidates were elected they rarely (like CND's Labour champions) spoke out strongly on issues.

86 Those of Bond and the MFDP in 1965, which may be seen as a definite turning point.

87 In addition those of the Young Liberals of 1966–7 in Britain have some NL aspects, but were largely non-electoral.

88 Of which Scheer was a member (for a critique of the Campaign see Dave Wellman and Buddy Stein in *Studies on the Left*, January/February 1967, and in Teodori, op. cit.).

89 An editor of *Studies on the Left*, James Weinstein, stood in a similar campaign in New York.

90 For all this, the convention represented the potential for a broad coalition; over 370 organizations were (at least on paper) represented there.

91 A groundswell of support for McCarthy occurred in spring 1968.

92 On the *Guardian* see Munck, 'The Guardian: From Old to New Left', *Radical America*, vol. 2, no. 2, March 1969.

93 I.e. at least an equivalent number to the 1968 'non-voters', amongst the other 50 per cent or so of adults who did not vote. Sometimes as little as only 65 per cent of the actually registered USA electorate voted (and even those registered represent only about two thirds of the whole adult population, excluding for example many non-registered blacks in the South).

94 Minority candidates (including the Peace and Freedom Party) lacked media attention at this stage.

95 On European and Latin American precedents for student syndicalism see Widgery, op. cit., p. 308.

96 The label was first used in this connection by Carl Davidson, Vice-President of SDS, in an influential pamphlet (see excerpt in Teodori, op. cit., p. 323).

97 'Only this sort of organisation allows for decentralisation and direct participation of students', ibid. The particular issue around which Davidson stressed the need for such a syndicalism was that of grades related to the Vietnam war. Since these were a basis for student draft classification, the tactic was to call for their abolition.

98 Georges Sorel's attack on the a-moral decadence of the bourgeoisie and its political structures, finds a clear resonance in the student movement. Even Sorel's more problematic belief in the basic contrast between manual producers and intellectual workers, and his

versions of counter-institutions' direct democracy, workers' control and rejection of bureaucracy and oligarchy clearly parallel NL theories and critiques (see fuller discussion in chapter 7).

Put on their reading lists (possibly as a cautionary exemplification of the 'irrational in politics') many students and activists probably first came across Sorel's ideas in sociology courses (see R. Lowenthal, 'Unreason and Revolution').

99 'Extra Parliamentary Opposition' on the European student activism, see Dutschke in Oglesby, op. cit., p. 243, and Oglesby, in ibid., p. 274.

100 'Sozialistischer Deutscher Studentenbund', not to be confused with the American organization of similar initials; W. German SDS had an explicitly Marxist heritage but was at the time still affiliated to the SDP – the adult party though deeply critical of its reformism. See G. Hunnius, *Student Revolts.*

101 Ibid.

102 See Cook and Morgan, op. cit., chapter 6 *passim.*

103 On extra-parliamentarism in UK and Europe generally, see Tom Fawthrop in Tariq Ali, *New Revolutionaries: Left Opposition*, Peter Owen, 1969, pp. 54 ff.

104 The phrase is from André Gorz, 'Strategy for Labour', in Oglesby, op. cit.

105 T. H. Marshall hints at the inner contradictions of 'Citizenship' and 'Social Class' in *Class, Citizenship and Social Development*, Anchor, 1965, chapter 4.

106 The TUs through the Labour Party, by entering these institutions to secure immediate social gains for themselves, had inevitably weakened their claim to greater representativeness for their own organizations.

See Miliband, op. cit. Here too a parallel with the experiences of the Civil Rights Movement is clear enough (see above).

107 See Widgery, op. cit., chapters 4 and 6 (intros and documents).

108 As a secondary citizenship system before the entry into the Labour Party, the working-class movement had remained preponderantly democratic and often radical. Certainly it was less oligarchic and centralized than the subsequent development of the Labour and Communist parties (see my article, 'Prometheans and Troglodytes').

109 The term was even used by 'leftist' Barbara Castle as a term of abuse for opponents of her Incomes Policy. On newer perspectives on Workers' Control see A. Gorz in Oglesby, op. cit., p. 41 and the writings of Ken Coates of the IWC.

110 Quite unlike the CGT/CP attitude. Ironically, up to the post-1921 Comintern hegemony, reflecting the influence of the Russian dominated CP, the CGT had been profoundly Syndicalist in outlook (a view that long survived 1917). See F. Ridley, *Revolutionary Syndicalism in France*, Cambridge University Press, 1971.

111 For Geismar's statement see H. Bourges (ed.), *Student Revolt – The Activists Speak*, Jonathan Cape, 1968, p. 60.

112 See S. Hall in J. Nagel, *Student Power*, p. 196 and Julius Lester, *Revolutionary Notes.*

113 See R. Van Duyn, *The Wise Kabouter*, Duckworth, 1972 (mostly on Kropotkin).
114 Roszak, *Counter Culture*, p. 87.
115 See Lynd in Teodori, op. cit., p. 88.
116 Marcuse, 'Old Model'.
117 See Teodori, op. cit., p. 45 and see debate in *Studies on the Left*, 1966, Aronson, Weinstein, Genovese.
118 See Lerner in Apter and Joll, op. cit., *passim*, and also Zinn in op. cit., p. 67.
119 In Long, op. cit.
120 See April Carter's *Political Theory of Anarchism*, Routledge & Kegan Paul, 1971.
121 E.g. later Daniel Ellsberg proved a prime example.
122 David Harris quoted in M. Lerner, in Apter and Joll, op. cit., pp. 47–9. See also K. Boulding's essay 'The Impact of the Draft on the legitimacy of the National State' in M. Goodman, *Movement Towards a New America*.
123 In Ginsberg's poem 'Howl'.
124 Yet, how and where to decentralize was critical, as the issue of 'states-rights' showed: the decisions made at the Cuba Missile Crisis of 1962 seemed to confirm Mills's analysis of enormously irresponsible and concentrated power on the critical life and death decisions of the age; ex post facto consultation again typified the Gulf of Tonkin incident, and the incursion into Cambodia.
125 Mills, *Power Elite*.
126 H. Marcuse in *Critique of Pure Tolerance*, ed R. P. Wolff, Beacon Press, 1965, p. 81 *passim*. Also Mills, op. cit. (chapter 13 on the Mass Society).
127 NB. The notion of Bachrach and Baratz of the 'mobilisation of bias'. See also Shinya Ono's article in *Studies on the Left*, 1965, on bourgeois pluralism. (Ono later supported 'Weatherman'.)
128 But on the new developing tone of Europe's extra-parliamentary opposition in the late 1960s, see Tom Fawthrop in T. Ali (ed.), op. cit., pp. 54 ff.
129 See H. Marcuse, *Essay on Liberation*, p. 64.
130 The words of a critic of the NL, L. Feuer, *The Conflict of Generations*, p. 411.
131 R. Miliband, *State in Capitalist Society*, Weidenfeld & Nicolson, 1969.

5. The problem of agency

1 For Mills, this survived as a purely 'romantic faith'. See C. W. Mills in *Power, Politics and People*, ed I. L. Horowitz, p. 256. In any case, as socialists such as Nicolaus showed, the productive or manufacturing classes formed a diminishing sector of society, thus creating a crisis in Marxist predictions of revolution by way of any working class.
2 Mills admitted there were levels of power and stratification of sorts, but not in class terms; his book *The New Men of Power*, published in the late 1940s, had been a detailed analysis of the co-optation,

incorporation, and embourgeoisement of America's labour *leader-ship*. Subsequently, Mills tended to focus on such categories as white-collar workers, black people, women at home, students and intellectuals, rather than industrial producers.

3 Whilst blacks may not have reached a social consciousness similar to that of the British working class, nevertheless 'objective economic situation' (given racial definition and the development of a culture-community) could lead in similar directions. Stereotypes of a grim, stoical, determined traditional British working class and the careless, noisy, apathetic Negro may conceal a basic similarity in two group communities. The main differences are relative to the size of the two 'minorities' (the Negro in the USA constitutes 10 per cent, the British working class perhaps 75 per cent of the total) and the degree of political and economic organization – blacks lacked their own mass-based trades unions and political parties, both long advanced in Britain. Black Americans were far more aliens within the American systems, than working people were in Britain.

4 See *Anarchism Today*, eds D. E. Apter and J. Joll, and T. Kahn 'Problem of the New Left' in *Commentary*, July 1966.

5 This is stressed by the contributors and selections in Widgery's collection.

6 It is commonly estimated that up to one third of English working people consistently voted Conservative in the 1950s and 1960s. See Mackenzie and Silver, *Angels in Marble*, Heinemann, 1968.

7 This bore out the reports of CND canvassers who always found heaviest resistance in old working-class areas. Thus except among the under 20s, CND support was predominantly middle class; constituting at times over 25 per cent of the electorate, it was only very partially represented by the leftward portion of the Labour vote. See Frank Parkin, *Middle Class Radicalism*.

8 Tom Kahn, op. cit., and H. Marcuse in M. Teodori, *The New Left*. On the subsequent search for 'Agency' see M. Cohen and D. Hale, *The New Student Left*, p. 175 (Hayden).

9 As he demonstrates with the 'feudal remnants', the peasants, the lumpen-proletariat, the professionals, bureaucrats, and guild-workers.

10 Ralf Dahrendorf introduces the notion of multiple and newly emergent power-relationships independent of classical 'class' divisions in his book *Class and Class Conflict in Industrial Society*, Routledge & Kegan Paul, 1963. In his view such a plurality of dominance/submission relations, would prevent 'synchronized' conflict. New Left theory disagreed.

11 This was a point that Kornhauser, a theorist of *mass* politics, stressed.

12 Peter Worsley's book, *Third World*, introduces a discussion of the role of the lumpen-proletariat and the great mass of unemployed or unemployables of the Third World. This, and the impact of Fanon, foreshadows the late NL's belief in what Gitlin called 'an alliance of the useless' ('The Dynamics of the New Left', *Motive*, p. 44, 1970), the drop-out colonies and the poor in America, with their Third World counterparts. Another variation on this theme was the fear

expressed in 'America and the New Era' of mass unemployment among the young.

13 Lynd, 'The New Radicals and Participatory Democracy' in Teodori, op. cit., p. 228.

14 Harrington's writing was influential (even though he became an early critic of the movement).

15 Marcuse in Teodori, op. cit., p. 471. Most organized lower-class opposition of the 1960s, from the welfare recipient movements of the early 1960s to the Mexican-American land movements later, bore, however, decreasing resemblance to traditional working-class activity.

16 The 'invisible poor' described in M. Harrington's *The Other America.*

17 There was a good deal of ambiguity in S. M. Miller's prediction that the 'desegregation issue' would emerge 'as a social class issue affecting all lower-class persons, and not only as a racial issue affecting Negroes alone' unless one excluded lower-class whites, chief enthusiasts for segregation. There may be some parallels with the Irish in nineteenth-century industrial England.

18 Nevertheless, black projects such as SNCC's were able, within limits, to transcend these limitations; moreover common work, play, and suffering assisted the creation of the most distinctive subculture in America, with an emotionalism, spirituality, sensuality and lack of repression lacking in the dominant culture.

19 The atomization of indigenous African cultures, the forcible implantation of white values and corrupt white culture forms, was combined with a self-image derived from nineteenth-century white stereotypes of the 'Negro'. The 'cat' culture (described by Finestone) was an escapist, and thus normatively deviant, make-believe retreatism from reality, and much ghetto culture was a mixture of all these elements: white assimilationist conformity (especially in consumer habits), Afro-Americanism, and a great deal of the old a-political plantation life-style, as well as the retreat-escape-and-self-destruction syndrome (through narcotics, crime, 'hustling' and 'kicks'). See article by Finestone, 'Cats, Kicks and Color' in Raymond Mack's *Race, Class and Power*, American Book Company, 1963, p. 254.

20 See David Lockwood's article on integration, function, and racial pluralism. In his view both Black Power and civil rights take on a different complexion ('Some Notes on the Concepts of Race and Plural Society', *British Sociological Association*, 1969) despite Afro-Americanism, despite the problematical Herskovitz hypothesis, despite plays like *Blues for Mr Charlie* or *Dutchman*.

21 The value-system may structure aspirations for some strata which cannot be realistically met by the system, thus intensifying actual conflict: *The American Dilemma* of Myrdal's classic study is in essence a contradiction between proclaimed national standards and ideals and actual material and social conditions.

22 See John Rex, *Key Problems of Sociological Theory*, Routledge & Kegan Paul, 1961. Rex, South African by background, actively involved in the British NL, made a number of important contributions

as a sociologist to the development of fresh perspectives on race, conflict, and the peace movement.

23 A global, mass, economic exploitation of coloured peoples is to some extent preceded by a racial differentiation and definition. Race is not purely and simply, as some Marxists argue, an excuse for, or ex post facto justification of, oppression; rather than a member of the in-group, the choice is of an alien group to exploit. Any initial power relationship thus proves definitionally critical since the continuing relationship elaborates the ideology of this as (racial) dominance and submission. Subsequently the self-fulfilling prophecy mechanism sustains the relationship. Thus the economic role of racially defined groups reinforces their 'social' definition as 'inferior'.

24 Both socially and often geographically. Besides, the cultural difference (despite the often remarked folk-music overlap) was always quite distinctive. Certainly in the Southern states, the poor whites would see themselves as having far more in common with a white bourgeoisie, than with Negroes. On the other hand, poor white communities had regionally distinctive subcultures that separated them.

25 This perspective was already implicit in Student Syndicalism as it emerged in 1966 (see Calvert in Teodori, op. cit., p. 412).

26 Ibid. As against this, Lynd's 'populist' position tended to support or fuse with the more Marxist (and more extreme) standpoint whereby, as Gitlin puts it, 'students or déclassé intellectuals . . . are strictly appendages of real social forces (either the 'vanguard' or the 'tail' of the really real), thus representing only a 'class-appendage' or 'class-substitute'. T. Gitlin, 'Dynamics of the NL', op. cit.

27 Rudd, quoted in Oglesby, op. cit., p. 296 (see also p. 297).

28 See Calvert and Nieman, op. cit., and R. Flacks, *Youth and Social Change*, Markham, 1971.

29 Nevertheless, something which marked the Weatherman episode; see below ch. 13, pp. 275 ff.

30 The idea of a 'new working class' had in fact been foreshadowed in the Port Huron Statement and of course in sociological re-appraisals of stratification in the West. In the new system, youth appeared less integrated than the working class (Rowntree's thesis), see Teodori, op. cit., p. 418.

31 There are odd but distinct parallels here between Mills and Marcuse.

32 See for examples Lipset's 'Student Opposition in the USA' in *Government and Opposition*, 2, 1966, pp. 351–74.

33 Ibid. and see Teodori, op. cit., sections 11 and 16.

34 A figure which did not include drop-outs of various sorts; if one adds to the seven million, the over twenty million secondary or high-school students, one had a considerable constituency indeed.

35 With the lengthening number of years that students were spending at university, the old situation of an élite educational system focused on undergraduates (as in Britain), was transformed.

36 Perhaps the highest for the post-graduates spending many of their working years in universities.

37 The firing of a President of the University of California for liberal

policies – although he had fought strenuously against the student movement – is a clear example.

38 Savio used the phrase in the FSM: see bibliography, p. 30, in J. O'Brien, *History of The New Left 1960–68*, and also p. 9 of same article. Keniston and Feuer's 'generational' approaches were bypassed in the article by Rowntree, 'Youth as a Class', in Teodori, op. cit., p. 418. See also Mike Klonsky, 'Towards a revolutionary youth movement', *SDS National Council*, 1968, and Flacks, op. cit., ch. 4.

39 And as McReynolds remarked, 'the New Left is full of hostility for the adult world', *Liberation*, 1965.

40 S. M. Miller took up the theory in the early 1960s, but he was one of the few sociologists to do so.

41 Marcuse in Teodori, p. 371.

42 For a discussion of the concept in the English context, see Widgery, op. cit.

43 Rudd, quoted in H. Jacobs, op. cit.

44 Ostensibly Marcuse provided a Hegelian-Marxist approach to American society, yet many of these values, translated into Marcusian idiom, were derived not from Hegel or Marx (or Freud), but from Movement experience, and perspectives already formulated by it.

6. Black movements in crisis

1 This was increasingly true of black minorities elsewhere (e.g. Caribbean immigrants in England, or Africans in France).

2 In fact several West Indians took leadership roles in the American and British movements.

3 At first, there was only Liberia; or there were the dreams of a black state in America itself; or there was a belief in a new-found state, or a return to Africa. Despite diplomatic visits from various African leaders, the civil rights movement, partly because of its own fragmentation, established no links with specific African nations. Indeed, some tension became apparent between African and black-American styles and orientations (though the latter's trans-national character predominated). See H. Isaacs, *The New World of Negro Americans*, Compass, Viking, 1963.

4 For example Garvey's mass-based movement of the 1930s had stressed blackness, and preached Negro cooperation and secession.

5 One Harris poll found support for both standing at over 90 per cent.

6 SCLC at least represented a bridge between the two wings.

7 Their paper, *Muhammed Speaks*, nevertheless often reported civil rights activity favourably.

8 CORE accepted 'Black Power' at its 1966 convention, confirming its two-year commitment to urban projects.

9 The positive side of the slogan, in so far as it emerged in Carmichael's speeches, articles and interviews (see interview in *Peace News*, 29 July 1966) was in large part that which derived from the nature of SNCC. See J. Newfield, 'The Rebirth of a Movement', in *A Prophetic Minority*.

10 Carmichael's opponent, John Lewis, was ousted because of his

willingness to attend a White House Civil Rights Conference (on his own initiative and not as an SNCC representative) in 1966. John Lewis also endorsed the Kennedy administration's attempted enforcement of civil rights laws, though he criticized it bitterly on other counts (see above).

11 SNCC's autonomous political arm in Alabama.

12 On Black Power 1966 see M. Cohen and D. Hale, *The New Student Left*, pp. 79–120.

13 It can be argued that it had progressed already to the urban areas of the southern and border states.

14 See P. Goodman's article on 'Racial Spite', *New York Review of Books*, 1967.

15 Vincent Harding, 'Black Radicalism; the road from Montgomery' in Alfred Young (ed.), *Dissent: Explorations in the History of American Radicalism*, Northern Illinois Press, 1968, pp. 319–54, see especially pp. 325 ff.

Stage-managed by a white, Jerry Rubin, in the Greek theatre, this event revealed that even in the nonviolent movement, younger more militant leaders had emerged, ready to match Carmichael or Ron Karenga in vehement rhetoric.

16 For Black Power at the grassroots, see Cohen and Hale, op. cit., pp. 109–20 (on Carmichael) and pp. 79–97 (on Snick) and pp. 97–109 (on Whites in the movement).

17 From this viewpoint, the civil rights movement never spoke to the fundamental problem of poverty, nor to the cultural and identity problem. It is not even true (as Carmichael at one point suggested), that it spoke to the problem of blackness, except in the negative sense of an 'equality of opportunity' with poor whites. As one SNCC leader said 'When we've won the right to sit at your lunch counters – we are not sure that we will want to anyway.' Similarly, James Baldwin wrote: 'Actually we don't want your daughters – we just want to get you off our backs.' It was this realization that provoked the deepest crises in the black movement. See C. Silbermann, *Crisis in Black and White*, Vintage, Random House, 1964, chapters 5 and 6.

18 Harold Cruse, *The Crisis of the Negro Intellectual*, Morrow, 1957.

19 Roszak, op. cit.

20 See S. Carmichael, 'What We Want', *New York Review of Books*, 26 September 1966. See also S. Carmichael and Hamilton, *Black Power: the Politics of Liberation in America*, Vintage, 1967, and C. Lasch, *Agony of American Radicalism*, Penguin, 1973.

21 See David Lockwood, 'Some notes on the Concepts of Race and Plural Society', paper presented to the British Sociological Association Conference, 1969. And the *New York Times*, 23 August 1968, where Carmichael reportedly equated black *power* with black *violence*, citing this as a cause of his split with SNCC.

22 Indeed Carmichael elsewhere, rather paradoxically, answers that shame may be a revolutionary emotion; initial surprise amongst whites was replaced by a new identification with black people and, eventually, a willingness to withdraw from civil rights groups

gracefully. On whites in the movement see C. Levy, *Voluntary Servitude: Whites in the Black Movement*, Appleton, 1968.

23 See later discussion of the media's role, pp. 346ff.

24 F. Fanon, in *Wretched of the Earth*, stressed this point. Indeed many of these regimes *were* admired, like the Muslims, for their aggressive 'self-discipline'.

25 Attacks on the universality of racism tended to emphasize the deep sexual undertones of white–black relationships: rape, mutilation, castration, guilt and desire, suppressed sadism and masochism – not least the figurative emasculation of the black male – were stressed both at the level of cultural description in drama and fiction and historical subordination, political and cultural. See C. Hernton *Sex and Racism in America*, Grove Press, 1966.

26 Moynihan report, reprinted in M. Rainwater and W. Yancey, *The Moynihan Report and the Politics of Controversy*, MIT, Cambridge, Mass., 1967.

27 Though the counter-culture took several years to recognize it, the black groups did so fairly quickly.

28 On cultural self-denial see Raymond Williams and others who have suggested something of the same in working-class self-negation in England (i.e. the sense that 'bourgeois is better').

29 See I. Howe, 'New Styles of Leftism' in *Dissent*, April 1965. Some New Leftists would accept some of this, but still ask whether this kind of culture, these kinds of aspirations, were worth campaigning for, or risking one's life on behalf of.

30 Quoted from O'Brien, op. cit., p. 13. See Bayard Rustin in I. Howe, *Radical Papers*.

31 As it became clear that housing and job shortages were not solved by integration alone, reformist leaders, especially Rustin, pushed the idea of an economic 'package' deal for blacks, especially housing and jobs. CORE backed this demand with economic sanctions, in the belief that such reforms, equally relating to the north, might be less easily granted than civil rights concessions, or integration: indeed some believed that this would break the last links with northern liberals.

32 The first models of Black Power derived from the south in those areas – especially in Mississippi – where blacks were a numerical majority (though not usually, until after the registration drives – an electoral one) presenting the possibility of autonomous black political bases. Moreover, in a number of central cities, including Washington DC, black people had become, or were fast becoming, numerical majorities. As a result, some Negroes claimed that the census was actually wrong and that there were in fact more blacks than whites in the country as a whole! For all this, one must note the failure of registered black majorities, in many cases, to take control of local communities, even where they were predominant.

33 See S. Carmichael, 'What We Want'.

34 The BPP said that this 'pessimism' reflected the experience of SNCC, and Cleaver responded: 'A black racism is as bad as a white racism . . . we don't accept the analysis that we're doomed because

we're in a minority'; to which came the further rejoinder from Lester:
'Cleaver is yet another black victim of white radical politics. A hero
in the white, but not the black community.' See Julius Lester,
Cleaver, Carmichael and Black Liberation.
35 Peace and Freedom Party, q.v.
36 Seale and Newton recognized the problem of recruiting 'young
bloods' keen to exhibit their para-military powers.
37 Quoted in April Carter, *Direct Action and Liberal Democracy*, p. 85.

7. In search of ideology

1 Sidney Lens, 'The Road to Power and Beyond', see p. 300 in
   C. Benello and D. Roussopoulos, *Participatory Democracy.*
2 Port Huron Statement reprinted in M. Teodori, *The New Left.*
3 Just as the relative emptiness of the British angry young man
   phenomenon of Wilson, Amis, and Osborne was not immediately
   recognized, the ideological implications of Bell's thesis was not
   fully comprehended either.
4 In any case, only Maoism was to approach anything like a resurgence
   of the total dogma and commitment of classic Left ideology.
5 See T. B. Bottomore, *Critics of Society.*
6 B. Moore, see essay 'Revolution in America', *New York Review of
   Books*, January 1969. In order to try and establish an identity
   distinct from Liberalism, and yet not Marxist, Movement writers
   reserved some of their strongest polemic for those just across the
   dividing line in either direction.
7 Noted by David McReynolds, *Liberation*, August 1965.
8 Charles Reich, *The Greening of America*, Penguin, 1972; see also
   Mike Rossman, 'Barefoot in a Marshmallow World', in P. Jacobs
   and S. Landau, *The New Radicals*, p. 211.
9 Egleson quoted by G. Thayer, *British Political Fringe*, p. 410. SDS
   leaders, especially Oglesby and Egleson, stressed this 'vacuum of
   ideology'.
10 Kirkpatrick Sale, *History of SDS.*
11 Elinor Langer, 'Notes for Next Time', *Working Papers for a New
   Society.*
12 Sale, op. cit., p. 337.
13 Despite subsequent efforts to save the 'new working-class' theories
   in the fall of 1968 (by Calvert and others), an increasingly simplistic
   and reductionist Marxist formula became prevalent. Klonsky's
   judgment was typical: 'capitalism is *the* system which is at the root
   of man's oppression.'
14 A. Kopkind, 'They'd Rather be Left', *New York Review of Books*,
   September 1967. Embedded in this tradition moreover, is that of
   utopian socialism, an idea proclaimed again by Todd Gitlin's
   post-scarcity manifesto: 'The Dynamics of the New Left', *Motive*,
   October 1970.
15 C. Lasch, *Agony of American Radicalism.* Lynd especially, because
   of his constant and restless concern with genuinely Movement
   theory: a theory, 'a language and a history that emerges from the

movement itself, and is not implanted from outside its own action and experience.' Lynd described this as 'guerilla' theory and history. See Introduction and pp. 61ff.

16 Sale, op. cit., p. 390.

17 See P. Clecak, *Radical Paradoxes* and M. Albert, *What is to be Undone*. See for my usage of the term 'revisionism' in L. Labedz (ed.), *Revisionism*, Praeger, 1962.

18 See Appleman Williams in Benello and Roussopoulos, op. cit. and Zinn in P. Long, *The New Left*, pp. 56–9.

19 See J. Cleaver in *Minority of One*, December 1967. The nonviolent wing of the movement was equally eclectic; for example, Gandhian nonviolence and village communitarianism, Yugoslav worker self-management, Cuban moral incentive in terms of the whole community were elements in the highly varied inspiration of *Liberation*'s transnational themes: but in general the *practice* of each was more significant than its theory; see Lens in Benello and Roussopoulos, op. cit.

20 See Todd Gitlin, op. cit., p. 48; see also Lasch, op. cit.

21 See, e.g. Lasch, op. cit. Both strong critics like Cranston, and partial sympathizers like Roszak, talk of the NL's 'Anarchism'. Several commentators, including Howard Zinn, use the term 'anarchist' as well as the term 'anti-authoritarian', to describe it. So does Oglesby (as a synonym for Anarchist or Libertarian). On Dutschke's 'radical anti-authoritarianism', see D. Apter and J. Joll, *Anarchism Today*. Oglesby seems to use the term 'anti-authoritarian' to describe the Movement – rather than 'libertarian', in an attempt to come to terms with the fact that 'authoritarian' revolution may be supported if it opposes a technologically superior authoritarianism. See C. Oglesby, 'Decade Ready for the Dustbin' in M. Goodman, *Movement Toward a New America*.

22 Zinn in Long, op. cit.

23 See Daniel Cohn-Bendit, *Obsolete Communism: The Left Wing Alternative*, who, however, denied that his anarchism was filtered through Marcuse: 'Some people have tried to force Marcuse on us as a mentor; that is a joke. None of us have read Marcuse.' Daniel Cohn-Bendit quoted in H. Bourges (ed.), *The Student Revolt – The Activists Speak*, Library Press, 1971, p. 78.

24 See M. Cranston, *The New Left*, on Marcuse's 'anarchist Marxist' stance. This label was due not so much to his political critique as to his psychological writing, particularly his *Eros and Civilization* of 1955 in which, starting from Freud's notion that 'civilization has progressed as organised domination', Marcuse conceives, against Freud, of the removal of repressive forces. See also Bruce Brown, *Marx, Freud and the Revolution of Everyday Life*.

25 See Mitchell Goodman, op. cit., Introduction.

26 Lasch describes the white NL as 'sharing with the black power, the language of romantic anarchism'. Lasch, op. cit.

27 Oglesby, in M. Goodman, op. cit. A writer who summarizes this early and strange synthesis of anarchism with cultural and generational revolt is Nuttall in his account of the English counter-culture

after CND, *Bomb Culture*. Even the Beats had had a similar libertarian political component in their rejection of established structures;
the poet Rexroth had talked of the state as 'a social lie'.

28 The degree to which the anarcho-pacifist, direct-action perspective
could still be allowed within the orbit of a semi-Marxist magazine
is exemplified by Alan Lovell's article on direct action in the early
issue of *New Left Review*, March 1961.

29 See Colin Ward, *Anarchy* 1, 1961.

30 The resurgence of anarchist analysis and prescription, was attended
by a good deal of academic interest, but of course neither, in any
sense, filled a vacuum that could only be occupied by a revived
anarchist political style and praxis. Indeed, the real foundations of
an anarchist social theory had its basis not so much in the academic
sphere (e.g. the post-Mills 'new Sociology') or even in the writing
of movement theorists (e.g. Lynd or Hayden) but in the direct
experience of projects and actions.

31 See Apter and Joll, op. cit., *passim* and Woodcock, 'Anarchism
Revisited', *Encounter*, 1969.

32 In one place only did an organized Anarchist movement clearly
remain. In Uruguay and Argentina it retained a popular and
industrial base, and an activist orientation, that survived long
enough to overlap with the new libertarian outbursts of the 1960s,
ibid.

33 See Apter and Joll, op. cit.; Apter, 'The Old Anarchism and the
New'. Joll, 'Anarchism – a Living Tradition'.

34 This emerges in Fruchter's film *Troublemakers* (on Newark) for
example.

35 Geoffrey Ostergaard, *Anarchy* magazine, 1964 and T. Gitlin, 'The
Dynamics of the New Left'.

36 From about 1870 onwards, this was the major issue dividing
Anarchists and Marxists. Anarchism's development had mirrored
the rise of the modern state, just as other socialisms, particularly
the Marxist version, confronted the development of capitalism.
Each in turn were protest movements, at the outset reactions to
conditions, which were related both in their critiques and their
practice. Yet for the Anarchist and the Syndicalist, not merely the
capitalist nature, or 'class-basis' of state oppression was attacked,
but its very structure, operations and functions. Libertarians were
convinced that the abolition of class rule in no way guaranteed the
necessity of statelessness; structural elements and class functions of
the state were largely independent and modern war could also be
used as a justification for further mobilization of individual energies
and communal resources on behalf of the state, or for industrialization: it was partly because of the underpinning of these equations
by modern science and technology that anarchism became
increasingly sceptical of both. War had equally as much, or more, to
do with the 'necessity' of the state and its nature, as capitalism.
(Socialism, like Fascism or Liberal Democracy, had demanded its
military tribute, both in men and money.)

37 See discussion below and in M. Useem.

38 Especially through the writing of Bookchin (see final chapter) and in the pages of *Liberation*.

39 Thus many of the 'false starts' of the English NL can be attributed to its understandable wish to re-vitalize working-class movements and parties in relation to reinvigorated socialist theory and language.

40 See John Horton, 'Dehumanization of Alienation and Anomie', pp. 14–15. See also discussion in chapter 1, notes 44, 55, pp. 19, 20.

41 Partly influenced by W. A. Williams, a Marxian historian, Chicago's *New University Thought*, and *Root and Branch* from California's Bay area, were much less 'Marxist' in the traditional sense, drawing more Millsian conclusions than Marxian about American society.

42 Hayden, its main author, was initially undoubtedly no Marxist.

43 Both writers, in revolt against the categories of Marxism and sociology, thus recognize that people's aspirations may have been valid in terms of their own experience – including the 'revolutionary conspiracies' and 'communitarian ideals' of the historic working class that Thompson describes: though particularly focused on the working class, this approach was better termed *Marxian* than 'Marxist'. (Thompson talks of Marxism as 'tradition'.)

44 Alvin Gouldner makes similar points in his 'The Metaphoricality of Marxism and the Context-Freeing Grammar of Socialism', *Theory and Society*, Winter 1974.

45 See Julius Lester, *Revolutionary Notes*, p. 3 and Lasch, op. cit.; also chapter 5 above.

46 Cruse maintained that many leaders of the black movement remained throughout this period and despite this rhetoric 'disoriented prisoners of white leftists, no matter how militant they sound': H. Cruse, *Crisis of the Negro Intellectual*.

47 The opponents of the advances of Marxism within the movement found an unlikely and unexpected ally in Carmichael (J. Lester, *Revolutionary Notes*, p. 116), who accused the Black Panther Party of becoming 'dogmatic' in its 'newly acquired ideology'. This ideology (Marxist–Leninism) led 'all those who disagree with the party line' to be 'lumped into the same category and labelled cultural nationalists and reactionary pigs'.

48 On Panthers see in Cook and Morgan, op. cit., pp. 428–31. The Panthers set themselves up as a 'vanguard party'; after the 1969 purge, the party confirmed its strict Marxist–Leninist position in association with a tight Old Left party discipline, following a debate over whether racism was a product of capitalism, or preceded it: 'Whether racism now has an independent existence, and whether it can exist in any economic system (including socialism)', i.e. could the destruction of capitalism mean the automatic destruction of racism? See Julius Lester, *Cleaver, Carmichael and the Politics of Black Liberation, passim*.

49 See chapter 15 and Clecak's discussion, op. cit.; Sweezy's brand of anti-capitalism at first represented the Communist Party tradition, whereas Deutscher's (and later Mandel's) was closer to Trotskyism. Their influence was largely indirect; by the 1960s its

implicit authoritarianism was disguised or blunted. Herbert
Aptheker's AIMS (American Institute for Marxist Studies) carried
on the tradition of an old Marxism, from an earlier era, almost
alone. See P. Baran, *Monopoly Capital*, Monthly Review Press,
1966.

50 Zinn's argument to the Marxian-leaning segment of NL leadership of
the late 1960s (in Long, op. cit.) is strategically astute. It reasons from
within the Marxian framework towards a libertarian position, in
contrast to Bookchin's somewhat crude head-on confrontation in
'Listen Marxist', in M. Bookchin, *Post-Scarcity Anarchism*.

51 The British NL, in particular, debated the degree of centralization in
Yugoslavian experience and its relevance in judging nationalized
industries. See K. Coates and T. Topham, *The New Unionism:
The Case for Workers' Control*, Hillary House, 1973 and in Cook and
Morgan, op. cit.

52 Daniel Guerin is one writer who represents this attempt most clearly.
See his *L'Anarchisme*, Gallimard, Paris, 1965.

53 Syndicalism represents a major bridge between Marxism and
Anarchism, because though it tends to reject the use of political
parties and the state, it does identify with the working class and with
the idea of the emergence of dynamic social forces in society.
Syndicalists are more voluntarist than most Marxists, but less
libertarian than most pure Anarchists, since they envisage definite
organization, even if it was only the loose and decentralized organization of the IWW or other unions, or of the soviets, councils,
communes and sections of the past.

54 In this period, even the IS in Britain in their opposition to the
Incomes Policy, were attacked for Syndicalist tendencies and
Widgery's IS-oriented anthology confirms the openings in this
direction. ('The Left in Britain'.)

55 There is an anarchism which has little to do with socialism in its
collectivist sense, just as there is a socialism which is authoritarian
and statist, but the historical overlap is far more considerable than
many Marxists (after Marx) and Anarchists were prepared to admit;
the mainstream of Anarchism had been consistently anti-capitalist.
Its impact on liberalism surfaced in the somewhat bizarre
adherence of the Young Liberal leadership to 'anarcho-syndicalism'
in the later 1960s in Britain.

56 The interpretation of these concepts and the dialogue and tension
in much of Marx's work was denied by those, like Hal Draper (*Two
Souls of Socialism*, Independent Socialist Club, Berkeley, 1965), who
argued that this divergence was only manifested in the developments
of the socialist *movements*, states and parties.

57 In fact, as writers on Marx and the International have argued,
Marx was far closer to Bakunin and the libertarianism of the
Commune than he was to many of the authoritarian Marxists and
later Leninist movements, and certainly less authoritarian than
Engels; thus Bakunin, at times, thought of himself as a 'Marxist' of
sorts, despite his quarrels with Marx.

8. The New Left in Britain: 1956–70

1 Sedgewick dates this first and false start of the 'fertilising, founding New Left' as lasting only from spring 1957 to summer 1961. See Sedgewick in D. Widgery, *The Left in Britain*, p. 131 and p. 22.

2 See Widgery in ibid.

3 See for example letters in *The Times* from Peter Cadogan and others of 26 August 1969 (responding to Ernst Fischer's article on 'The New Left' as defined in this book). Right-wing critiques in England shared their definition of the NL with these radicals.

4 In any case, as Marx had already pointed out in the 1870s, American labour movement institutions had never been as extensive or solidary as the English trades unions, because of racial, ethnic, religious, and regional differences and divisions.

5 See April Carter, *Direct Action and Liberal Democracy.*

6 The International Socialists originated in 1951 after a split with other Trotskyites on the issue of support for North Korea and its allies.

7 10,000 communists had left the CP between 1956 and 1958, including many intellectuals active in this phase.

8 Norman Birnbaum, *Towards a Critical Sociology*, p. 320. On the other hand, it does not so easily explain the coincidental libertarian and Trotskyist revivals.

9 At the end of CND's first major meeting, it was *ULR* elements who led a spontaneous march and sit-down to Downing Street (February 1958).

10 Quoted in Widgery, op. cit., p. 131. See E. P. Thompson, 'The New Left', *New Reasoner*, Summer 1959.

11 For comments on this merger see 'The Two New Lefts' by P. Sedgewick reprinted in Widgery, op. cit., chapter 3 and pp. 509–11.

12 Thompson talks about his own attempt to 'rehabilitate the utopian energies within the socialist tradition'; 'Letter to Kolakowski', *Socialist Register*, Merlin Press, 1973, p. 1.

13 Birnbaum, op. cit., p. 321; Sedgewick takes a different view however.

14 For example, such publications were probably far less influential than bestseller paperback editions of books like W. Whyte's *The Organisation Man* 1956, D. Riesman's *Lonely Crowd* 1950, or Packard's *Status Seekers* 1957 or even Fromm's books. Norman Birnbaum, op. cit., emphasizes synthesis of such a variety of elements from the USA with continental traditions.

15 For A. Gramsci's concept of 'organic intellectuals' see *Modern Prince*, Lawrence & Wishart, 1957, which became popular somewhat later. Cf. Gwyn Williams, 'Gramsci's Concept of Hegemony', *Journal of the History of Ideas*, October 1960, p. 586.

16 As Widgery puts it, 'The *NLR*'s super-Marxism was uncontaminated by suggestions as to what Marxists might actually do', op. cit., p. 512.

17 Peggy Duff, *Left, Left, Left*; E. P. Thompson, 'The New Left'.

18 The papers of the Left were no substitute; the paper that claimed to lead the anti-bomb movement, the Bevanite *Tribune*, initiated the disastrous compromise move (1961) on the Crossman–Padley 'bait'.

CND's monthly newspaper *Sanity* with a largish circulation (of about 40,000 by 1962) remained a pretty lifeless affair.

19 CND, after 1962, put heavy emphasis on publication and research, with substantial resources spent on specialist correspondence, pressure and study groups; all of these activities were very much influenced by NL intellectuals, and also by those concerned with strategic ('defence') arguments. On the poor reception accorded to 'Steps', see *Sanity*, May 1964.

20 This was especially true of various *NLR* apologetics for Third World authoritarianism (not only Blackburn and Anderson, but also Hall, Worsley, and Fruchter indulged in such exercises). Thompson, on the other hand, emphasized his 'frontal critique of Stalinism'.

21 As well as these successive departures from the editorial group, Pearson and Taylor had left; Prince and Lovell were by now working for *Peace News* and all the other libertarians had also gone.

22 Some of its editors became involved in new English Marxist–Leninist factions.

23 This decline in numbers was reflected in further departures from the editorial group into Trotskyite groups or to create new publications. 'With the organisational passing of the old new left, whatever was distinctive in its ideas has perished also', see Sedgewick (1964), 'Two New Lefts', in Widgery, 1976, p. 145.

24 The phrase is E. P. Thompson's in his critique of the *NLR* group; see for example 'Peculiarities of the English' in *Socialist Register*, Merlin Press, 1965.

25 The emergence of the magazine edited by Ben Brewster, *Theoretical Praxis*, was an offshoot which took these tendencies to their extremity.

26 Widgery, op. cit., p. 47.

27 *NLR* did also foreshadow and reflect the growth in Third World identifications during the 1960s.

28 See Widgery, op. cit., p. 24, and P. Duff, *Left, Left, Left*.

29 The Student Peace Union ended in 1964; SANE and WSP survived longer, but in a reduced role.

30 Just as the civil rights movement had similarly been replaced by its own self-induced internal opposition.

31 Initially, they even opposed the Aldermaston March, on the grounds that it was 'direct action' (inspired by the DAC) which might alienate respectable support. See Duff, op. cit.

32 A. J. P. Taylor, Kingsley Martin, Victor Gollancz, J. B. Priestley, Donald Soper, Stephen King-Hall, Blackett, Collins and many others.

33 For example, it could no longer be put in the same category as the anti-hanging lobby of 1957, even at the outset.

34 A graduated, incrementalist disarmament programme, including nuclear free zones.

35 NATO was first fully rejected in the 1960 CND conference.

36 The search for a 'national mission' was never far from slogans like 'Britain must lead'; thwarted great-power aspirations did not leave even internationalists untouched.

37 Of course, the Committee of 100 *was* involved in the 'Spies for Peace' revelations on the 1963 Aldermaston March, when the government plans for RSGs were first publicized. Subsequently local Committees demonstrated at every one of these RSGs around the country.

38 By this stage many of the 'big name' sponsors of the Committee had resigned, and it was unable to predict people's willingness to refuse to be 'bound over' (i.e. to renounce further illegal actions) or to actually block runways at USAF/RAF air bases to prevent or delay bombers taking off. Thus, both the strategy of 'filling the jails' and of *effective* direct action, were unrealistic.

39 CND's 'Festival of Life' (1970) revealed a belated urge to put on beads and bells and ape the youth culture CND had itself helped spawn a decade earlier, a temptation easily resisted until the end of the 1960s; this last and opportunistic bid to recapture a lost youth and innocence, and form an alliance with the counter-culture, was a half-hearted attempt and despite a number of peace festivals, they came too late to revive CND.

40 Other peace groups did not gain much ground either and only the 'Stop the Seventies Tour' (STST) seemed to take up some of the 'slack' created by CND's decline, building on the anti-apartheid agitation after Sharpeville.

41 Though less so outside London, where a more non-aligned stance was predominant.

42 The way in which British demonstrations operated increasingly in a vacuum, divorced from popular awareness, was already illustrated in 1963 when actions against the Greek royal visit were unsuccessfully linked with radical or peace movement causes.

43 See also Tom Hayden, *Student Social Action* (1962); SDS reprint, 1966.

44 Though of course ex-Communists did, as some resigned on the issue.

45 Indeed the Communist *Daily Worker* attacked rather than supported CND policy in its first years. Writing in 1962, Birnbaum (op. cit.) was able to dismiss CP influences as worthy of little attention (p. 330) (but see also articles by Linzie and others in *Peace News*, 18 May 1962 *et al.*).

46 At least one Trotskyite group defended a concept of 'the workers' bomb'.

47 CND's newspaper *Sanity* circulation reached a peak in 1962/3 and then declined as its Eastern alignments became more marked and its anti-Americanism more pronounced.

48 See previous discussion in chapter 4.

49 See article, J. Linzie, 'Communists in CND' in *Peace News* and N. Glazer, 'The Peace Movement in America' in *Commentary*, 1961, p. 288.

50 The CPUSA actually supported the invasion.

51 The subject of Old Left influence in, and on, the NL is returned to in chapter 15.

52 By now even its events (such as the Festival of Life, etc. – see above) were in part inspired by an inept opportunism.

53 The small NALSO (Labour students) was more Trotskyist than NL in character though the two appeared to overlap briefly in 1960.

54 There is a hiatus between NALSO and the Radical Student Alliance of 1966. On the late emergence of such a movement in Britain, see Widgery, op. cit., p. 308.

55 George Clark was himself influenced by the SDS community projects which he visited in 1964. See his article 'Remember your Humanity' in R. Benewick and T. Smith (eds), *Direct Action and Democratic Politics*.

56 Sedgewick notes how the English NL failed to *cumulate* between CND and the VSC, and also points out the Marxist revolutionary leadership of the latter without for one moment considering that the two are related: that the moral and political differences are perhaps a key explanation for this lack of cumulation (though a *New Society* survey found that 60 per cent of all VSC marchers *had* been involved in CND). See Widgery, op. cit., pp. 20 ff.

57 Following NALSO, and the RSA, it was the RSSF which set the base for Marxist influence on the students' unions after 1970.

58 Oglesby's mistaken analysis of the Essex demonstrations gives the show away; as far as he interprets it in terms of the American NL's later development, it has more in common with Berkeley 1966.

59 On LSE see Colin Crouch, *The Student Revolt*, Bodley Head, 1970 and Tom Fawthrop, Tom Nairn and David Triesman, 'Three Student Risings', in Oglesby, op. cit., p. 274.

60 Sedgewick in Widgery, op. cit., p. 20.

61 Though some continuing echoes are found in the *Socialist Register* or 'Marxist Education' groups.

62 The International Marxist Group, though less wedded to the working class than IS, assumed a more central role for it in the 'British Revolution' (see Tariq Ali's *The Coming British Revolution*, Cape, 1972) than its eclectic and opportunistic rhetoric suggested.

63 The *Red Mole* later became the *Red Weekly*: note also the IS theoretical magazine *International Socialism* (founded on a broader coalition basis in 1960, before turning into a 'house organ' later).

64 By 1974, the NUS was dominated by Communists and Trotskyites at the upper levels. The belated influence of 'Student Syndicalism' hit Britain in the 1970s, where bread-and-butter issues became predominant and replaced 'heroic altruism and abstraction'; though 'student *power*' demands *had* characterized the 1968–9 occupations.

65 See Widgery, op. cit., p. 31:

> a long definite and traceable genealogy of anti-capitalist policies, and prescriptions for industry, running from the early Utopian Socialists through the Marxists and the Industrial Unionists and Syndicalists into the Guild socialists, lately banded around the Trotskyite and academic left and the IWC (Institute for Workers' Control).

66 On the IWC Conference of 1969 see report in *Peace News* and John Durham's commentary. For a theoretical statement see André Gorz, 'Strategy for Labour' in Oglesby, op. cit., p. 41.

67 The takeovers at Plessey, UCS (Clyde), and Fischer-Bendix

continued the proliferation of factory-occupations; it was estimated that 200 occupations took place between 1969 and 1970 and over 100 between 1971 and 1974.

9. Vietnam and alignment

1 On the NL's development of a trans-national orientation see chapter 2. Also paper on Muste by J. A. Robinson, *Alternative Peace Strategy*, Committee for Peace Research in History, USA 1969. (Reprinted in C. Chatfield, *Peace Movements in America*, Schocken, 1973.)

2 This was far more pronounced than in A. J. Muste's version.

3 Birnbaum argues in 'Great Britain: The Reactive Revolt', *Towards a Critical Sociology*, that the role of Britain in CND's 'positive neutralism' was a Socialist version of the imperialist attitudes to the Third World (p. 319) even though it included an idealization of such states. (See also Peter Worsley, *The Third World*.) Once the move towards European integration was underway, such independent postures had less appeal as an alternative foreign policy.

4 This suspicion is confirmed retrospectively by remarks in the 'May Day Manifesto' reprinted in Oglesby, p. 135.

5 Other magazines, like *New Politics* and *Dissent* in America, were openly hostile to Russia.

6 Even Widgery's (op. cit.) claim that the 1956 Suez demonstrations were predominantly 'working class' certainly lacks evidence; they appeared to be an assembly of Labour Party workers, CP members, *New Statesman* readers and a scatter of students and teachers – the majority middle class, middle aged and 'respectable' (despite clashes with the police).

7 I have discussed this at greater length in my study 'Nation State and War Resistance' Ph.D., Berkeley.

8 This was a small VDC rally organized by SWP YSA and took place a year after the first major teach-in.

9 See Oglesby, op. cit., Introduction, pp. 10 ff. In this view nationalism is thus seen as a stage in the growth of 'inter-nationalism', just as socialism leads on to communism. But see also Isaac Deutscher in *Liberation* (interview) and quoted in Oglesby, op. cit., p. 10.

10 This idea was popularized by Lin Piao from whom M2M, active in 1964-6, drew its 'inter-nationalism'. See his *Long Live the Victory of the People's War*, Foreign Language Publishing House, Peking, 1965.

11 George Lakey, a young American Quaker, helped popularize the concept both in his actions and writings, e.g. *Strategy for Nonviolent Revolution* (pamphlet), Housmans, 1970.

12 Thus many discussions of 'peasant nationalism' are misplaced (see Appendix).

13 When peasant ideology *is* linked to a conception of territory, it is either in terms of the village itself and a local region, or a vague pan-'ism' (pan-Africanism, pan-Slavism, etc.) rather than more familiar forms of nationalism.

14 See Debray's usage of this term in his *Revolution in the Revolution*.
15 See Fanon quoted in Coser, 'Myths of Peasant Revolution' in *Continuities in the Study of Social Change* and also Howe, *The Radical Papers*; cf. also Barbara Deming, *Revolution and Equilibrium*, *Liberation* reprint, 1968.
16 Of course scepticism of industrial progress was by no means universal in the NL. It was often argued that forced industrialism, the nation-state, military defence and the process of building them, were the political and structural imperatives of our time, and thus could not be avoided by the developing world. But the existence of 'moral imperatives' (over and against self-interested materialism of capitalism) were the kind of straws some in the NL clutched at.
17 *New Left Review*, 9 May 1961.
18 See Appendix, and my pamphlet on *War, National Liberation and the State*, Christian Action, 1969. Many other critiques of these wars have been made, besides the structural ones – i.e. that they are too costly in terms of destruction and human suffering, that they 'complement' the oppressive techniques of the imperialist powers by meeting them on their own ground; it is, however, their structural character which is most relevant to the NL's support for them, and indeed to theories such as Fanon's.
19 See Dellinger in *Seeds of Liberation*, P. Goodman (ed.), p. 201.
20 Lipset actually compares the Castroite movement with the NL in America, because of its youth and innovation. See S. Lipset, 'Student Opposition in the USA' in *Government and Opposition*, p. 357. Despite its proximity, the IRA was unable to offer the same inspiration to the British Left in the 1970s.
21 E.g. in the Port Huron Statement.
22 As well as A. J. Muste, Dellinger, Lynd and McReynolds, the *Liberation* group also involved Paul Goodman, Barbara Deming, Sid Lens, Nat Hentoff, Mulford Sibley and (until 1966) Bayard Rustin, who were all more sceptical of the Cuban and Vietnamese revolutions. It also maintained contact with older socialists like Fromm, Norman Thomas, and Irving Howe; as well as with the younger Leftists from SDS, like Tom Hayden. McReynolds, initially critical of communism and totalitarianism, was pragmatic and even reformist (he once lined up with Rustin) yet seems to have shifted the most sharply on these issues.
23 See S. Lynd in J. Finn (ed.), *Protest, Pacifism and Politics*, p. 223. Presumably implying that he would not absolutely condemn either. See also Lynd's letter to *Liberation* about the War Crimes Tribunal. As an example of the propagandistic role of 'Medical Aid', see the *Newsletter* of the British Medical Aid for Vietnam group.
24 Nevertheless, SDS's utter naïveté about the war at this stage is symbolized by a song about 'Strategic Hamlets' (written by Al Haber's wife in 1965): 'Before I'll be fenced in, I'll vote for Ho Chi Minh and go home to the north and be free' (cited in K. Sale, *History of SDS*, p. 178).
25 Since 1945, pacifism has undoubtedly found itself profoundly compromised by successive wars of liberation, faced by the armed

strategies of the FLN in Algeria, of Castro and Guevara, the Biafran and other African military struggles, Bangladesh, the Palestinian guerillas and the IRA in Northern Ireland, etc. In this last case the arguments around the 'British Withdrawal' campaign run somewhat parallel to those on the Vietnam issue, i.e. simple withdrawal vs. ceasefire and negotiated withdrawal.

26 Daniel Berrigan and the FOR both strongly identified with the Buddhists but only at a late stage did this become widespread in the peace movement (Adam Roberts had advocated this even in the early 1960s in the pages of *Peace News*).

27 See Thich Nhat Hanh *et al.* and other Buddhist writers on this exclusion: *Peace News Fellowship* and also in *Le Lotus* (their overseas peace newsletter). McReynolds both supported their exclusion and opposed even a temporary ceasefire to enable humanitarian tasks to be performed.

28 See my 'Wars of Liberation and the State', *Peace News*, 1969. The common justification was often that armed methods were only used when all other channels had been tried and found blocked, justifying support for violent methods and goals for the Third World (tacitly or more directly by practical help) that would be rejected outright in working for changes in advanced industrial societies. This was Sweezy's position in particular (see P. Clecak, *Radical Paradoxes*, p. 323) after 1965.

29 See SNCC/SDS statement on NLF in Sale, op. cit. In adopting such a strong stance, SDS was probably marginally influenced by the formation of M2M on an anti-imperialist, pro-Chinese, pro-Cuban (Maoist-Castroite) ticket in 1964.

30 An exception was Gail Kelly of the SPU – 'Who are the Viet Cong?', *Peace News*, 1966.

31 See Clecak's remarks, op. cit., pp. 304–5, and T. Kahn, 'The Problem of the New Left, *Commentary*, 1966.

32 See Chapter 1.

33 The evidence suggests that Ho was, after 1968, much more effective in deceiving the Western NL than Vietnam's peasantry about the nature of the war. The propaganda from Hanoi and its allies certainly played a role in the earlier development of the movement against the American presence, e.g. 1964–6.

34 As I argued elsewhere at the time 'War, National Liberation and the State',

> The war is being sustained by two rather large coalitions of groups of Vietnamese 'people' fighting against each other with outside help, and with a third rather larger group (mainly peasants) indifferent to the outcome or preferring neither. There is a relationship between leaders and led to be examined, and a reality which is much more complicated than the formula: struggle between the *people of Vietnam* and the American government.
> Such a formula clearly begs the question of the identification of the NLF with the 'people of Vietnam' (a slogan not a description).

35 In understanding the emergence of this Manichean choice, it is worth recognizing that most NL activists do not seem to have

known that other popular options even existed, because of the degree to which the establishment and the Old Left alike presented the war as a simple military struggle between two sides. But one of the more sinister elements in the Vietnam tragedy was that this essentially *third force* option was not even allowed to enter radical debate between 1965 and 1968. Here again those libertarian pacifists, aware of the Buddhist struggle against Diem, and of the continuing size of the Buddhist movement, have something to explain. In new contexts, largely unaware of its nature and the immense difficulties of developing strategies that were appropriate or realistic, the radical pacifist wing of the NL still had few justifications for this apostasy.

36 M. Oppenheimer, *Urban Guerrilla*, p. 39 and I. Howe, *The Radical Papers*, p. 322. The NL was correct in so far as, like other peasants in other revolutions and wars, some Vietnamese were persuaded to support the intermediate aims of the revolutionary élites. But building a centralized, industrial state – the implied objective of new leadership groups – is not the preference of any peasant people; indeed it amounts to conscious self-elimination in fact (certainly in a cultural if not physical sense). Vietnam, a traditionally fragmented society whose disparate groups had shown little support for central authority of any kind, initially supported this decentralist impulse which worked strongly in favour of opposition groups like the Communists, who were seen to be opposing Saigon. The war thus grew on a decentralist basis in alliance with regional and ethnic groups, but this support became decreasingly voluntary as the NLF and later the PRG began to construct its own system of authority – including eventually an alternative central authority – in the countryside. See also Bob Potter, 'Vietnam: Whose Victory?', *Solidarity*, 1973, for a somewhat belated libertarian socialist analysis.

37 See Potter, ibid., on Ho's close links with Stalinism.

38 See Bernard Fall, *The Two Vietnams*, Pall Mall Press, 1965.

39 In the early stages of the second Vietnam war there was some evidence that weapons used by the NLF (as distinct from the divisions from North Vietnam) were American, captured from the Saigon army. This gradually changed, however, as Chinese and Russian support increased, and supplies from the North intensified.

40 Oppenheimer, op. cit., and Roszak, op. cit., p. 77; cf. also Thich Nhat Hanh, *The Lotus in the Sea of Fire*, SCM, 1967. Since these are revolutions that liberate the forces of modernity, the mobilization and organization of men and resources, and the centralization of control in a context of nationalism and technological development linked to military action, they must be imposed from outside – by conquest, by the transformation of feudalism, the intervention of state or urban-trained revolutionary cadres – working as military organizers (see Appendix). Recent history argues that such patterns cannot create or sustain political orders of freedom.

41 The term 'Vietnam war' rather than 'peace' or 'anti-war' is appropriately used to describe the movement of the later 1960s, since these other terms only accurately describe the majority of the movement

before 1967 – after that only the draft-resistance and pacifist organizations fit such labels. In 1967, the VSC in England was, for example, in effect, a *'pro-war'* organization – favouring not ceasefires or settlements but further intensified military 'struggles' against 'imperialism' everywhere (very much the mood of 1968–9).

42 Typical of this argument, which fails to take seriously the influence of Giap's 'protracted-war' theory in the DRVN leadership even before Dien Bien Phu, is the view of NLF militarism as the violence of the last resort, e.g. see Fall, op. cit., chapter 15. This was Malcolm Caldwell's position whilst chairman of CND in this period. But the disciplined ranks of the Viet Minh and later the Viet Cong armies, were structures imported externally to peasant cultures. Various hierarchies of struggle – the combat parties, cadres, terrorist structures, guerilla or peoples' militias like the political arm of the war, the provisional Revolutionary Government and the central bureaucracies – arose and were officered from outside the peasantry itself; it is hard to persuade peasants to fight, or stay fighting for long in such a process (as is implied by Cabral, 'Liberation of Guinea', *Monthly Review*, 1972; B. Davidson, *Liberation of Guinea*, Penguin, 1967; and E. Wolf, *Peasant Wars in the 20th Century*, Faber, 1969).

43 Even the native student movement was to some extent activated by US students, for example at the LSE; see P. Hoch and V. Schoenbach, *LSE: The Natives are Restless*, Sheed & Ward, 1969.

44 N. Birnbaum (*Towards a Critical Sociology*) notes that a 'curious idealization of colonial liberation leaders and movements' had long characterized the Labour Left, and the analogy between Republican Spain and North Vietnam, however inept, had a powerful appeal among them in these years. Of course it should be added that in the earlier period many of these Third World freedom movements (India, Ghana, Tanzania, etc.) were non-military ones – even in Southern Africa.

45 Sedgewick linked this 'third world indiscriminacy' to the NL's domestic eclecticism. See his article 'The Two New Lefts' reprinted in Widgery, op. cit., p. 143.

46 In addition marchers were equally surprised to be offered as their official Easter badge (for over ten years this was usually a version of the peace symbol), a portrait of the same lady. Significantly perhaps, CND's national office was left with most of the badges on its hands: the attempt to match the VSC had been a flop.

47 Referring to the purges of Vietnamese Trotskyists in the 1930s and 1940s; see Fall, op. cit.

48 On this anti-Americanism see J. J. Revel, *Without Marx or Jesus*, MacGibbon and Kee, 1972, especially ch. 11.

49 Excessive black fatalities in war zones and apparent over-representation of blacks in the armed forces generally, lent further weight to these negative feelings, even though a military career was still perceived as a channel of upward mobility for blacks.

50 Tony Cliff and Paul Cardan are two of those associated with developments in this critique of 'State capitalism'.

51 On this see Castro, quoted in the *Guardian* (London), 30 July 1973:

'we do not understand the strange theory which refers to two imperialisms.'

52 SDS's early belief in the domino theory was expressed in its call for the 1965 Washington demonstration (see Sale, op. cit., p. 181). However, this was reversed in 1966.

53 Gitlin had, like Howe, argued (in 'The Dynamics of the New Left', *Motive*, October 1970, p. 50) that the 'idea that post-scarcity possibilities rest' on the 'looting of the rest of the world' was 'to some extent exaggerated'.

54 Several critics stressed corporatism, rather than imperialism, as the key concept and it had been widely argued that the export of capital was in any case less important after the 1930s; see, J. Strachey, *The End of Empire*, Praeger, 1964.

55 See Hal Jacobs, *Weatherman*, Ramparts, 1970, for a discussion of the term.

56 Though SDS had earlier accepted it (see above and in Sale, op. cit.).

57 In 'Decade Ready for a Dustbin', op. cit.

58 E.g. one of the difficulties of exploiting opposition to nuclear weapons and CBW on an *anti-imperialist* basis was its moral ambiguity – thus the attempt at justification of 'anti-imperialist' H-Bombs (e.g. China's) or North Vietnam's napalm, etc., was significantly rare. However the 'workers' bomb' thesis gained some credence amongst Trotskyists in the late 1950s, as a form of opposition to CND's moralism.

59 N. Egleson, 'Anguish and Politics' speech to SDS reprinted in *New England Free Press*, October 1965. See also Gitlin, op. cit., on what he calls 'packaged revolution'.

60 C. Lasch, *Agony of American Radicalism*, p. 152.

61 See New American Movement, *Manifesto*, 1970.

62 See chapter 5 above.

63 Gitlin in Hal Jacobs, op. cit., p. 107. Leading sections of SDS 'chose the path of least resistance, defining their emergence almost wholly in terms of the liberation of others'.

64 J. Weinstein, 'The Left, Old and New', *Socialist Revolution*, pp. 52–3 and see Appendix.

65 Sartre endorsing Fanon rather than Marcuse, places his hopes in the Third World (see chapter 4 above).

66 'Instead of learning what was relevant, while carefully recognising the differences between a revolution in a peasant society and a revolution in an advanced industrial society, many sections of the movement have attempted to mechanically transplant the messages of the third world to this country' (New American Movement, *Manifesto*).

67 Julius Lester, *Revolutionary Notes*, reprinted by the Institute for the Study of Nonviolence, p. 4.

68 See previous discussion (chapter 3) and H. Arendt's discussion in her *On Revolution, passim*.

69 See J. Weinstein, 'The Left, Old and New', and T. Gitlin, 'The Dynamics of the New Left'. The 'imperialist war crime' and 'revolutionary heroism' thus may describe the butchering of the

same family – now or later; in the 'revolutionary morality', advocated by Madame Binh – the justification of all that furthers the ends
of the revolutionary leadership, creates the 'double standard', a
morality of means judged by an end-product.

10. SDS in flux

1 Even by 1966, Etzioni cites a figure of 4 per cent of all American
college students (i.e. out of nearly 5 million), as 'supporting' the NL,
though only 8000 were members of SDS by 1966. This estimate is
qualified, if not disputed, by Lipset who argues that this figure
(e.g. of 200,000) exaggerated the size of this constituency in 1966. Of
course, this was by no means in the period of the NL's greatest
growth, and for this period these would not be excessive figures.
This dramatic growth in SDS by 1968 was exemplified by the 600
attending a national council meeting, normally a much smaller
gathering, but now larger than previous conferences. See also
figures given in K. Sale, *History of SDS.*

2 Through the 1960s the 'northern student movement' had cooperated
with SDS, and the Southern Student Organizing Committee founded
in 1964, worked with both SDS and SNCC in the south.

3 See p. 408 in L. Feuer, *The Conflict of Generations,* and T. Cook and
P. Morgan, Introduction to *Participatory Democracy* which surveys
the (inadequate) development of themes of participatory democracy.
See also the analysis in a pamphlet by M. Oppenheimer, 'Sociology
of Participatory Democracy' reprinted in H. P. Dreitzel, *Recent
Sociology,* p. 88.

4 Most clearly shown in accounts of Columbia (1968), but already
noticeable in Berkeley by 1966.

5 During 1965, SDS grew from 35 chapters to over 100 in the 3 months
April–June, and to over 180 by Christmas: the main reason for this
was its role in the first major Vietnam war protests of April and
subsequently. But the timing of its plans to hold the April demonstration was largely fortuitous: the SDS decision was taken without
foreknowledge in December 1964, and thus by luck it outflanked
the whole of the peace movement. In 1964 there had been only
16,000 US 'advisers' in Vietnam, and though armed infiltration
from the North was expanding rapidly, no one had predicted the
massive US escalation which was heralded by the beginning of
routine bombing raids on the North in February 1965.

6 The watershed was the SDS 'grassroots' conference of 1966. See
T. Hayden in I. Howe, *The Radical Papers,* pp. 362–77. Paul Potter
in fact stressed that community organizing was the best way to
change 'the system' responsible for the war (see his Vietnam speech
of April 1965 at Washington, reprinted by SDS and in M. Teodori,
The New Left). See also Carl Wittman on the Chester project in
M. Cohen and D. Hale, *The New Student Left.*

7 Nor did the teachers' union gain recognition and it lost the right to
strike. Ronald Reagan vociferously opposed negotiations and the
administration would not even agree that governmental agencies

should be denied special privileges unavailable to other off-campus groups.

8 Although SDS earlier had an argument with its sponsor (LID) over the issue of civil disobedience, and the question came to a head again on the issue of draft-resistance.

9 After their exclusions from civil rights groups some whites joined the 'Northern Student Movement' – others 'Friends of SNCC' – but all remained close in spirit to the black movement. Some ERAP organizers were also later thrown out, and by 1967 even in the North, whites could no longer organize blacks; by 1968 even poor whites were rejecting the evolutionary organizing styles of the Movement.

10 When it came to black power, no one in the NL wanted to risk being called destructive. Yet the lack of a critique of the potentially negative aspects of one man's interpretation (Carmichael's, with all its ambivalence and contradiction, was the one that predominated) was a remarkable commentary on SDS's relationships with other groups, even at this stage.

11 See J. O'Brien, *History of the New Left, 1960–68*, p. 26.

12 ERAP, under director Rennie Davis, still had 200 volunteers in 1965; but see Carl Davidson, *Student Syndicalism*, SDS pamphlet 1966 (excerpt in Teodori, op. cit.).

13 They 'organised themselves out of projects' – in this sense the analogy with Russian populism, the young Narodniks who had been thrown out of peasant villages, does not hold. See Feuer, op. cit., and on Russia, A. Yarmolinsky, *Road to Revolution*, Collier, London, 1957. Also see F. Venturi, *Roots of Revolution*, Grossett, NY, 1966.

14 The MDS, formed in 1967 following a Radicals in the Professions conference, also led to the later 'New University Conference'. It foreshadowed further developments in the 1970s (such as the New American Movement).

15 Jim Jacobs, 'SDS: Between Reform and Revolution' in *Nation*, 10 June 1968, and Anne Gordon, 'Conventional SDS' in *Connections*, 1–22 July 1968.

16 The plaintive appeals of the NO fell on deaf ears: 'It is not principled to pack meetings in order to manipulate acceptance of a line, or to tie up valuable time discussing issues that the collective does not wish to discuss' (Bob Pardun quoted in Sale, op. cit., p. 465). See also Milstein, 'New vs. Left in SDS' in Cook and Morgan, op. cit.

17 Or 'contestation' as the Parisian students termed it.

18 See Sale, op. cit., for the reasons. The June SDS convention had only narrowly voted against participation at Chicago, although many SDS veterans were involved in planning the event. This vote undoubtedly reflected PL's influence, and their hostility to groups like the Yippees, who were involved in the mobilization.

19 See Sale, op. cit., pp. 473–5. This development was accelerated by the organization of radical street gangs among Chicago youth – an off-shoot of the 'Join' project. See also H. Jacobs, *Weatherman*.

20 The plight of various minorities in Labour (e.g. rural workers); the

bureaucratic nature of the unions and American Federation of Labour – Council of Industrial Organizations (AFL-CIO); the economics of full employment and the quality of work; all still offered issues around which to organize workers in all areas of production.

21 See Sale, op. cit.
22 See chapter 7 for background to debates on ideology *vis-à-vis* PL. On leadership problems in SDS, see Richie Rothstein in P. Long, *The New Left*, pp. 272–89, and also ch. 15, part 4.
23 PL numbered (at the SDS 1969 conference) less than 500 delegates (a third); hard-core National Office support, judging by the first walk-out led by Dohrn, stood at around only 200 (see estimates in Sale, op. cit.) though its unofficial gatherings drew two to three times that number. The rest of the 1500 (i.e. between 400 and 800 were probably uncommitted or alienated by both. For accounts of this SDS conference of 1968, see Milstein in Cook and Morgan, op. cit., pp. 199–205 and C. Benello and D. Roussopoulos, *The Case for Participatory Democracy*, p. 321, as well as in Sale.
24 See the Anarchist pamphlet, *Students for a Stalinist Society* reprinted by Freedom Press, not dated.
25 See T. Gitlin, 'Dynamics of the New Left', *Motive*, October 1970.
26 Afterwards Klonsky himself was to form and lead a separate though ephemeral faction (RYM II).
27 Lynd quoted in Sale, op. cit., launches an attack on national officers for 'vanguardism, meaningless rhetoric and empty sloganising'. Mark Rudd defended minority action by the left; 'vanguardism' is, he claimed, 'justified', 'because it is based on a better understanding than everyone else'. See also Michael Schneider, 'Vanguard, Vanguard whose got the Vanguard', in *Liberation*, May and August 1972.
28 Emerging mainly from RYM I, the chronicle of Weatherman has a separate character and deserves separate attention (see discussion in chapter 13).
29 See Sale, op. cit., p. 496, *passim*.
30 See G. Calvert and C. Nieman excerpt in Teodori, op. cit., p. 140, and in *A Disrupted History*, Vintage, 1971.

11. Annus mirabilis: 1968

1 In Europe, the activities in Amsterdam and the Free University of Berlin after 1965, Strasbourg in 1966, Frankfurt, Nanterre and the London School of Economics in 1967. See J. Berke, *Counter Culture*, pp. 196–205, 212–82.
2 Moreover in Holland, Italy and Sweden, as well as in Canada.
3 See J. O'Brien, *History of the New Left, 1960–68*.
4 For Edgar Morin's *Le Monde* quotations and Marcuse on Parisian 'organised spontaneity', see the articles reprinted in *Peace News*, 28 June 1968.
5 Stop the Draft Week was described as an 'anarchist party'.
6 The name of the Yippees' nominee (a pig) for the presidency at the Democratic Convention in Chicago.

7 On the 'unknown' Tet offensive, see Thich Nhat Hanh, *Lotus in a Sea of Fire*, and Vietnamese Buddhist newsletters and Douglas Pike's *Massacre at Hue* (a US government publication, but substantially documented).

8 See Bo Wirmark's pamphlet, *The Buddhists in Vietnam*, War Resisters, 1974; and Thich Nhat Hanh, op. cit. The growing refugee and orphan problem, intensified by Tet, was a major focus of Buddhist humanitarian social work.

9 Barbara Deming, *Revolution and Equilibrium*.

10 This was most clearly so in the open-housing marches in Chicago (Cicero).

11 See *Peace News* articles (19 April 1968) and previous interviews with King (April 1968).

12 Daniel Bell, quoted in J. Avorn, *Up Against the Ivy Wall*, Atheneum, 1968.

13 Dotson Rader in Cook and Morgan, op. cit., pp. 335–40. But see also Mark Rudd in C. Oglesby, *New Left Reader*, p. 290.

14 See A. Quattrocchi and T. Nairn, *The Beginning of the End*, Panther, 1968.

15 Apter and Joll, op. cit. See also on the Sorbonne, Oglesby, op. cit., p. 267.

16 Quoted in T. Roszak, *Counter Culture*, p. 22.

17 The 22 March movement was a coalition, which included some Maoists and 'anarcho-Maoists'. See Quattrocchi and Nairn, *The Beginning of the End*, and Hervé Bourges (ed.), *The Student Revolt*, Cape, 1968, pp. 67–80, 86, 129–38; and also in D. Cohn-Bendit, *Obsolete Communism*.

18 The major solution offered in May 1968 was that of workers' councils, another antidote was 'self-management'; many looked back to the pre-war French occupations or the events in Turin in 1920 when both solutions had been fused in the factory occupations there. Nevertheless, many of the factory occupations in France 1968 were *non*-participant and controlled by the CGT.

19 Against the charge of counter-revolution, the city displayed a neon sign (later shot to pieces by Russian tanks): 'City searched, not one counter-revolutionary found'; see Mnacko, *The Seventh Night*, Dent, 1969.

20 Violent resistance, which the Russians had expected and might have preferred, would have been singularly inappropriate. Armed struggle is one sure prophylaxis against effective political communication. See Adam Roberts (with Philip Windsor), *Czechoslovakia 1968*, Institute of Strategic Studies, 1969.

21 Even in preventing nuclear conflict, such communication is an essential component of non-military defence, e.g. see S. King-Hall, *Defence in the Nuclear Age*, Gollancz, 1958.

22 *Survey*, October 1968, pp. 3–6.

23 In Chicago, millions of TV viewers saw Mayor Daley's police force (which until recently had had Ku Klux Klan members) run amok in the streets. See Walker Commission Report: 'Violence in the Streets'.

24 G. Lakey in his *Strategy for a Living Revolution*, Grossman, 1973, remarks on this.

25 In a strange and never easily explained transition from PL to Yippee activism Rubin had become both the impresario and provocateur extraordinary of the confrontation wing of the movement. It was he also who had launched the call to levitate the Pentagon, and stage-managed the first Black Power assembly at Berkeley (1966).

12. Turn towards violence

1 Nonviolent direct action spread to over 200 cities involving tens of thousands of demonstrators, many of whom went to jail; see W. H. Burns, *Voices of Negro Protest*, Oxford University Press, 1963, p. 59, and Charles Jones, 'SNCC, Nonviolence and Revolution', *New University Thought*, September 1963.

2 Bayard Rustin, 'From Protest to Politics', in Howe (ed.), *Radical Papers*, p. 347; see also William Miller, *Nonviolence*, Allen & Unwin, 1964, p. 83, for SCLC discussions at this time.

3 See Julius Lester, *Cleaver, Carmichael and the Politics of Black Liberation*.

4 See *Commentary*, June 1960, and Rustin, op. cit. Also H. Zinn on *SNCC: The New Abolitionists*.

5 See King in Lynd, *Nonviolence in America*. It is interesting that King himself cites awareness of African liberation movements as one cause of this feeling. See also H. Isaacs, *The New World of Negro Americans*.

6 E.g. Hain and the STST in Britain (see Carter, *Direct Action and Liberal Democracy* and Hain in R. Benewick and T. Smith, *Direct Action and Democratic Politics*).

7 Unlike the peace groups, at crucial moments, these movements did cooperate together (e.g. in Chicago and New York for the boycotts of segregated schools when the CCCO Federation in Chicago and the new COFO organized jointly the 'Freedom Summer' in Mississippi).

8 See Colin Crouch on the LSE violence and its background in *The Student Revolt*.

9 Men like Bayard Rustin and James Farmer of CORE, and Martin Luther King, still able to instil ideas of nonviolence and able to sustain a nationwide organization committed to it, were influential enough to carry a major section of the community with them.

10 For a discussion of the emergence of such alternative strategies and the debates over them, see chapter 13, pp. 266–75.

11 And perhaps themselves.

12 In three and a half years it registered nearly half a million new black voters in the South and elected scores of new representatives; this and the return of a number of black representatives occurred both before and after the Birmingham Campaign of 1963 and the civil rights legislation of that year.

13 Examined in detail in chapter 13.

14 Violence in the later 1960s stemmed almost solely from the volatile

and detached male strata of unemployed and desperate urban blacks. See T. Hayden, *Rebellion in Newark, Official Violence and Ghetto Response*, Random House, 1967.

15 J. O'Brien, *History of the New Left, 1960–68*.

16 E.g. see reports in the weekly *Guardian* (USA).

17 In the early growth of the movement, Sartre was of no importance, but as the mood altered, both Fanon and Sartre, influential on one another, came to the fore. Sartre's view that man may recreate himself through violence, echoed and reinforced Fanon's belief in violent catharsis. (See introduction to F. Fanon's *Wretched of the Earth*.) Sartre's writing is far more reminiscent of some Fascist writing than that of Sorel, whom he so gratuitously condemns.

18 'Violence' it had been argued 'requires generally the transformation of the target, be it a human being or a community of people, into a depersonalised object of hate' (Port Huron Statement, reprinted in M. Teodori, *The New Left*).

19 As Carmichael said of the new black recruits: 'It is the young bloods who contain especially the hatred Che speaks of.'

20 Similar Old Left arguments had been deployed during the Spanish Civil War, and later during the Korean and Algerian wars.

21 Gerassi's more extreme rhetoric of 'the Revolutionary Contingent' was confronted by both Laing and Goodman; see *Dialectics of Liberation*, Penguin, 1968. Carmichael endorsed Guevara's stress on the need for 'hatred as an element of the struggle, relentless hatred of the enemy that impels us over and beyond the natural limitations of man, and transforms us into effective, violent, selected and cold killing machines', see *Dialectics of Liberation*, p. 162 (quoted by Carmichael from *Venceremos* Gerassi (ed.)).

22 See D. McReynolds, *We Have Been Invaded by the 21st Century*, Praeger, 1970, p. 107.

23 This handful being mostly radical pacifists writing in *Liberation* and *Win* in America (like Barbara Deming, Goodman and Lynd) and the editors and some contributors to *Peace News* in Britain.

24 Ironically, the first edition of A. Roberts's book, *The Strategy of Civilian Defence – Nonviolent Resistance to Aggression*, Faber, 1967, was published just before the Czech actions against the Soviet invasion. Apparently quite uninfluenced by this school of thought, they nevertheless exemplified many of the theories and methods put forward in the book. Many similar tactics had however been used in Budapest (1956).

25 See Roberts and Windsor, *Czechoslovakia 1968*, and Mnacko, *The Seventh Night*. For a NL response see McReynolds, op. cit., pp. 49–56.

26 To give an extreme, but concrete, example from the Czech experience: one could hardly expect to successfully 'fraternize' with the enemy troops at one end of the street, whilst comrades were hurling molotov cocktails at them from the other. See Andrew Mack's paper presented to IPRA conference, 1969 at Karlovy Vary, and his *War Without Weapons* (with Anders Boserup), Pinter, 1974.

27 On this, see Gerry Hunnius, *Student Revolts in Western Europe*.

Symbolic acts of violence against property or objects were permitted, but violence against persons was not tolerated.

28 Though professedly violent and anti-integrationist, Black Muslims actually encouraged civil rights work through their paper *Muhammed Speaks*, which carried less of the inflammatory reporting of white thuggery, lynch pictures, or calls to violent reprisals, than one would expect, and indeed many photos of nonviolent actions; even Malcolm-X worked closely with civil rights groups in 1963–4; his speech 'Ballots or bullets' came with his break with the Muslims.

29 The idea of a white backlash was promoted in particular by *Newsweek* magazine. See also M. Oppenheimer, *Urban Guerrilla*, and below.

30 See later discussion of 'Repression and the NL'.

31 Except in the later freelance writing of Julius Lester (in the *Guardian* and elsewhere), there was not even a hint of a critique of political violence, and much of the rhetoric such as that of Carmichael, Cleaver and LeRoi Jones, who announced that black people may 'cut off the heads of the slave-masters to achieve their manhood', was not even explicitly political. Indeed the term 'racism in reverse' could now be accurately used of Jones's proclaimed belief in the slaughter of whites.

32 This escalation, the racial arms race and the use of military language is perhaps part of the tragedy of American radicalism. Even its anti-nuclear (but non-unilateralist) peace movement had never fully challenged this rhetoric of deterrence, and the balance of power. See Bookchin's critique of this.

33 Oppenheimer: 'For the young ghetto black, para-military posturing may soon replace the juvenile fighting gang as his way of finding the masculinity denied him by white society' (*Urban Guerrilla*, p. 55).

34 On black militarism, see George Jackson, *Blood in My Eye*, Bantam, 1972, e.g. pp. 152 ff.

35 See the debate on the issue in the *New York Review of Books*, 1967–8.

36 Similar arguments had been used against anti-militarist critics and COs in the wars against Germany.

37 Oppenheimer, op. cit., p. 138.

38 See for example, Truman Nelson's introduction to Robert Williams, *Negroes with Guns*, Marzani & Munzell, 1962. The armed equality of blacks with whites is claimed as a 'basic right'.

39 Julius Lester, *Revolutionary Notes*, p. 10, confesses that 'all of us who have used the rhetoric of violence have helped to convince others to commit their lives'. In Lester's judgment, the black movement became a violent movement *because* of its rhetoric. Even Malcolm-X, who had ridiculed nonviolence, later claimed that he advocated violence *not* to bring it about, but because it was the only thing America understood.

40 *Liberation*, 1970.

41 Howe, four years earlier. See also reply by Lynd to Howe in *Dissent*, 1965, p. 324. Howe used the term 'kami-kazi radicalism' at this time.

42 Lester, op. cit. Oppenheimer makes the same observation about relations between the BPP, the ghetto and the police.

43 What made them more *dramatic* was the extensive use of tear gas, adding noise and smoke to the confusion.

44 Both were also interpreted as challenges to the Berkeley power structure, and in both cases the police came out in force to contain crowds of only about 500–1000 on Berkeley's Telegraph Avenue. But in 1966, despite some police violence and counter-attacks against them when they tried to clear the street, the situation was never truly out of control; there was a political leadership – in addition to the YSA – which made sure there was a tactical retreat from the sidewalks; few arrests were made, and though somewhat threatened by the political militants, police discipline held. Except by the police and city manager, the incident was largely forgotten.

45 From which they recruited many new members.

46 In Berkeley, the 'Avenue' changed as much again in 1966–8 as in 1964–6; more hippies, more 'crime', more drugs, more runaways, more people.

47 They were supported by the underground press (the *Berkeley Barb, San Francisco Express-Times, Movement* and the *Barricade*) which tended towards both anarchist and Castroite perspectives.

48 The new mood indicated by SDS's adoption of a 'working-class' symbol of the clenched fist (in *New Left Notes*, etc.) was in fact derived from a general identification with left-militancy and solidarity (e.g. as in working-class politics in a period of the popular front and military struggle in Spain, in the 1930s which had been especially associated with the CPs).

49 Even Carl Davidson announced, 'Police violence does not go unanswered any more.'

50 Increasingly publicized by the media.

51 Sidney Lens, *Radicalism in America*.

52 US News and World Reports figures quoted (as estimates) in *Communism and the New Left*.

53 At the end of the 1960s, instruments were wielded as weapons, or smashed, and lyrics predominated that were violent, sexist, even nihilist.

54 This was revealed particularly in the performances of The Who and the Stones; it was a mood reinforced both in some of the musical papers like *Rolling Stone*, and in *Oz* and other underground papers. Increasingly this was also true of many Movement newspapers – though there were notable exceptions (*Win* in the USA and *Peace News* in England). See P. Stansill and D. Marowitz (eds), *BAMN: Outlaw Manifestoes*, Penguin, 1971, for documents of this phase.

55 Violence in sport, for example, or the fashionable representation of rocketry in terms not of its East–West killing potential, but of the technological achievement and the space race: see my article 'The Culture of Rockets', *Sanity*, May 1963.

56 Lester, op. cit., p. 473.

57 SDS National Council resolution, 1968 (cited in K. Sale, *History of SDS*).

58 See Oppenheimer, op. cit. For the Jewish analogy and 'gas chambers,' see Carmichael's articles and speeches, a theme taken up

by Cleaver, Newton and Seale as well as many white leaders, and the underground press.
59 See chapter 14.
60 Helicopters were increasingly used, for example.
61 Lester, op. cit., above.
62 See ibid. and, on the revival of nonviolence, Lynd and Calvert in C. Benello and D. Roussopoulos, *The Case for Participatory Democracy*; also J. O'Brien, *History of the New Left* and J. Weinstein, 'The Left, Old and New'. Lakey, however, in *Strategy for Living Revolution*, argues that the nonviolent option had never been as subordinate as the media has represented it.
63 Weinstein, ibid. The latter remained predominantly the case in the Western countries, despite the increasing readiness of the state to physically repress.

13. Revolution and the New Left

1 As Zinn points out, the term 'revolution' appears even in SNCC's earlier statements, *SNCC: The New Abolitionists*, pp. 7–13. But see also Calvert in C. Benello and D. Roussopoulos, *The Case for Participatory Democracy*, who observes this change in 1966 in the white movement.
2 And the phrase 'negro revolution' was used of the civil rights movement.
3 See I. L. Horowitz, *Radicalism and the Revolt against Reason*, Routledge & Kegan Paul, 1961.
4 Baran and Sweezy's contributions are analysed in P. Clecak, *Radical Paradoxes*.
5 *New York Review of Books*, 1969.
6 In the same way the category 'Communist revolution' came to have little meaning either (see chapter 1).
7 M. Oppenheimer, *Urban Guerrilla*, p. 43; see also Appendix.
8 See J. Dunn, *Modern Revolutions*, Cambridge University Press, 1972, p. 19. Cf. also my review of Dunn 'The Person not the Gun', *Peace News*, March 1972.
9 See Appendix.
10 See E. Wolf, *Peasant Wars in the Twentieth Century*, and Barrington Moore, *Social Origins of Dictatorship and Democracy*. Peasant villages could provide a base, as had Zapata's, for revolution in Mexico, and it was a model that was to some extent co-opted by Mao's revolution, in its strategy of rural base areas, but this was basically incompatible with any 'bolshevik' imagery of revolution (i.e. to a large extent Zapata's revolution derived from, and was not imposed on, the villages of Morelos). However primitive their aspirations, the Levellers and Diggers of seventeenth-century England, the Anabaptist millenarians, and even Fourierist experiments, all pointed to parallel and alternative decentralist scenarios.
11 Just as the Chinese Communists had looked back to the Russians and Marxism, and the Russians had to the French revolution; see B. Moore, 'Revolution in America', *New York Review of Books*, 1969.

12 Though naturally the French uprising of 1968 invoked French revolutionary traditions from 1789 onwards – looking back especially to the Paris Commune of 1871; see C. Tilly, 'Reflections on the Revolution in Paris', *Social Problems*, no. 12, 1964.

13 See Wolin on Lenin in *Politics and Vision*, Little Brown, 1960, chapter 10. Also see M. Buber, *Paths in Utopia*, Beacon, 1958; and J. Lester, *Revolutionary Notes*.

14 On Ideology see chapter 7.

15 J. Weinstein, 'The Left, Old and New', *Socialist Revolution*, July 1972.

16 Todd Gitlin in Hal Jacobs, *Weatherman*, p. 107.

17 See the New American Movement, *Manifesto*. Note also the double standards of the War Crimes Tribunal, who refused to entertain evidence that challenged this image.

18 See R. Lowenthal, 'Unreason and Revolution' in *Encounter*, 1966. The linkage of revolution to militarism and war in the twentieth century is certainly a direct one – both in the sense that revolutions have involved, or been related to both internal (civil) and external wars (military defeats, conquest, etc.).

19 Oppenheimer, op. cit., p. 48.

20 Moore, op. cit.

21 Ibid.
   The movement towards a distinct form of community might easily become and remain distinct, but only in trivial ways, such as dress, eating habits, tastes, in art and music . . . perhaps even sexual practices where deviance now scarcely threatens the status quo. The result would be to leave the new forms of social life as tourist attractions that don't change anything. The surrounding society could proceed serenely in its normal path of growing investment in destruction.

22 See also C. Reich, *The Greening of America*, p. 253, on difficulties of contemporary revolution against the 'machine state'. 'How can those who oppose organisation and the machine expect to win a fight where the field of battle is power?' Like other liberal sympathizers, Reich argued that 'new values' and 'consciousness-raising' was the key.

23 Nick Egleson, 'Anguish and Politics'. Egleson, a former national SDS president, made this speech at the time that the revolutionary vogue was spreading.

24 John Arden in *Peace News*. In Britain the VSC/IMG/RSSF/Black Dwarf/Red Mole/grouping, was most closely associated with this tendency.

25 Egleson, op. cit.

26 Moore, op. cit. See also Dunn, op. cit.

27 Oppenheimer, op. cit.

28 There is little evidence to support this prediction – though it is possible to surmise that the extensive campaign of bombings of 1968–70 was based on service expertise, and could not have been the work entirely of student amateurs.

29 'Internal colonialism' – an analogy partly drawn from Fanon, and

denoting an institutionalized racism rather than individual prejudice; it involved a fierce critique of paternalist welfare programmes.

30 Cleaver in *Ramparts*, 1968 (quoted in Oppenheimer, op. cit.).

31 E.g. especially those in Indo-China, Algeria and Cuba.

32 See above and C. Lasch, *Agony of American Radicals*, also Robert Williams, *Negroes with Guns*.

33 On the role of PL and others at Hazard, Kentucky, my main informant was one non-PL activist who took explosives and guns to Hazard (but see also p. 100 in Luce, op. cit., and transcripts of subsequent trials).

34 Before Harlem, PL announced its revolution: 'There is no lawful government in this country. Only a revolution will establish one' (Fred Jerome, ed. of *Challenge* in 1964).

35 On the background to the Harlem riots, and armed defence, see Bill Epton's fantasies in Luce, *The New Left*, p. 42, 18 July speech in Harlem (1964) which immediately preceded the riots.

36 In encouraging violence, Jerome argued: 'Let us not run and let us not pray – let us fight back', and said of the Harlem riots: 'If this is civil rebellion, let us make the most of it' (op. cit.).

37 Quoted from Robert Williams, "The Crusader' in Luce, op. cit., p. 58.

38 This subtle transition in Carmichael's speeches from *predicting* urban guerilla outbursts to *advocacy* can be detected in 1967.

39 'Men are now appearing in the ghettoes who might turn the energy of the riot into more organised and continuous revolutionary direction'. See T. Hayden, *Rebellion in Newark*.

40 See Lasch, op. cit. After Robert Williams initiated 'The cult of armed defence as revolutionary action', King, Rustin and Farmer still argued that as a mediating and negotiating force, to prevent chaos and repressive violence, the leadership of black movement must maintain constant contact with whites.

41 In Goodman's view (see article 'Racial Spite', *New York Review of Books*), the Watts riots were part blackmail, part insurrection, part despair – the need to be noticed. The paradox was the sense of being a *majority* unnoticed, a revolt less against internal colonialism than invisibility and class-hypocrisy, which 'ignored racial identity'.

42 See Kenneth Clark on the ghettoes in S. Engleman, *Violence in the Streets*, Duckworth, p. 288.

43 Even the radical white militancy, though on a smaller scale, was, after 1969, mostly self-hurting.

44 Oppenheimer, op. cit.

45 Ibid.

46 See Appleman Williams in C. Benello and D. Roussopoulos, *The Case for Participatory Democracy*.

47 The Tupamaros came perhaps closest of any genuine urban-guerilla groups to NL ideology.

48 See Conor Cruise O'Brien quoted in Carter, *Direct Action in a Liberal Democracy*, p. 106.

49 The IRA had, of course, little or nothing in common with the NL as a movement, and thus is not comparable with the groups previously discussed in this context.

50 H. Marcuse, 'The Old Model Won't Do' in M. Teodori, *The New Left*.
51 Paul Goodman, 'Causerie at the Military Industrial Complex', *New York Review of Books*, 23 November 1967.
52 Robert Williams quoted from the *Crusader* in Luce, op. cit., p. 58.
53 Oppenheimer, op. cit.
54 T. Roszak, *The Making of a Counter Culture*, p. 7.
55 See Roussopoulos, 'The Urban Commune' in Benello and Roussopoulos, op. cit., and also Moore, op. cit.
56 'I think that for the first time there is a chance, a possibility of a non-catastrophic revolution', D. Cohn-Bendit quoted in H. Bourges (ed.), *The Student Revolt – The Activists Speak*.
57 Moore, op. cit.
58 Especially Goodman, Lynd, Muste and Deming.
59 Though Barbara Deming (*Revolution and Equilibrium*), George Lakey, and others raised the issue, and my pamphlet was a further attempt to do so. (*War, National Liberation and the State*.)
60 D. Schön in *Listener*, December 1970.
61 Norman O. Brown stressed the progression from 'politics to life – and therefore revolution as creation; resurrection; resistance – instead of progress. Change was changing people's heads rather than transforming reality'. Reply to Marcuse in *Commentary*, March 1967.
62 Though Camus's view perhaps had been closer to Brown's. But when Sartre stresses the inherently doomed nature of the Russian regime, he remarks that its deterioration was *implicit in its development*. Because of this he warned of the dangers of bureaucratic degeneration of revolution, even in a Western context.
63 Moore, op. cit., p. 372.
64 Cf. Chalmers Johnson, *Revolutionary Change*, Little, Brown, 1966.
65 See interview with Ellsberg, *Rolling Stone*, 8 November 1973.
66 Clearly the availability in any collapse of society, of such alternative centres of organization, as the anarcho-syndicalists had envisaged, might offset the terroristic and centralizing dangers of such a situation, and might draw to themselves loyalties and involvements previously imbricated into the old order.
67 The major weapon of the Eastern European workers against Stalinism was the general strike.
68 'Alongside the customary structure of authority, parallel bodies – organs of dual power arise' (see S. Lynd, 'Bi-cameralism from below', in Teodori, op. cit., p. 484) and in P. Goodman, *Seeds of Liberation*, p. 67. This recurring image of dual power is found in the Utopian Socialists, the Paris Commune, Rosa Luxemburg's soldiers' and workers' councils, the Russian soviets, including Kronstadt and Petrograd, American 'Wobblies', French syndicalism and even the early Kibbutzim. It even appears in more deterministic fashion in Marxism's pre-revolutionary relational forms (socially determined rather than created by pre-revolutionary action).
69 M. Buber, *Paths in Utopia*, p. 13.
70 Dave Dellinger had been associated with this concept since the 1940s (see Lawrence Wittner, *Rebels Against War*). Direct action, civil

disobedience, strikes, sabotage, seizure of public property, local control of the means of production by workers on the job, were advocated, as well as the development of cooperatives as opposed to nationalization. Violence and war were condemned as counter-revolutionary. John Lewis reaffirmed this approach in his Washington speech of 1963. In the 1970s, the main theoretical contribution was Gene Sharp's encyclopaedic survey, *Politics of Nonviolent Action*, and *Peace News* in England adopted a more explicitly nonviolent revolutionary posture.

71 See Sharp, ibid., 1975.

72 Carl Oglesby, 'Decade Ready for the Dustbin' in M. Goodman, *The Movement Toward a New America*.

73 T. Gitlin's 'The Dynamics of the New Left', *Motive*, October 1970.

74 M. Bookchin, 'On Spontaneity and Organization', *Liberation*, 1972, see also Todd Gitlin, op. cit.

75 See Weinstein in Jacobs, op. cit., p. 391.

76 The relationship between music and political change is obscure, nevertheless the cultural impact of many songs, e.g. those of Dylan, Beatles and Stones or such films as *Bonnie and Clyde* and *The Battle of Algiers*, seem to have had an elective affinity with movement developments.

77 In France the 'Enragés' offer further parallels in 1968.

78 21 May 1970: in Jacobs (ed.), op. cit., pp. 509–10, Weatherbureau statement. A useful summary of the Weatherman experience is contained in Stuart Daniels, 'The Weathermen', *Government and Opposition*, 1974.

79 See Sale, op. cit., p. 428. Weatherman was in fact influenced by a group which had already been active in opposition to PL previously, not initially inside SDS, but *in* the M2M – largely run by PL.

80 See David Horowitz, 'Revolutionary Kharma versus Revolutionary Politics', *Ramparts*, 1971.

81 See Jacobs, op. cit. The overwhelming tide of support (especially amongst white radicals) for violence which, by 1968 had swept the civil rights, black, student, and even peace movements, must also be seen as a response to this contained outrage over Vietnam. In response to escalation, the further capitulation to militarist and authoritarian identification in Vietnam was reflected in the style, methods, theories and practice of the new élites in SDS (of whom Rudd, Ayers and Jones were major spokesmen).

82 See N. Egleson, 'Organizing American Movements', occasional publication of the New England Free Press.

83 See Jacobs, op. cit., statement 'New Morning, Changing Weather' and Ginsberg's Comments, *Partisan Review*, 3, 1971, p. 304.

84 Though in addition, there were continuing attempts to link these issues to Women's Liberation.

85 See Jacobs, op. cit.

86 But both Ginsberg and Dellinger remarked on how tiny Weatherman violence really was in comparison with State (e.g. military) violence.

87 Perhaps foreshadowing Weatherman's 'war-effort': there was,

however, another viewpoint in SDS, that was sceptical of the ability of Movement terror (e.g. against military installations) to sufficiently disrupt the US war-machine to cause any real setbacks to US Vietnam policy; indeed it was understood that this might be used to justify greater efforts at home and abroad to repress threats from the Left. It is possible that the Anarchist historical tradition – both in Europe and America (e.g. Berkman, Most, the Haymarket affair and other bombings of the late nineteenth century) was also a minor influence on both Weatherman and other 'radical bombers' in this period.

88 *Psychology Today*, February 1971.

89 The RYM I group was viewed as the closest to anarchism at the 1969 conference of SDS in Chicago.

90 See I. Howe, 'New Style of Leftism' in *Dissent*, on kami-kazi radicalism.

91 Amongst blacks and white radicals, motivations cited for violence, including manhood and identity crises, assertiveness, fear, catharsis and spiritual-cleansing, were examined. But for a sympathetic view, see K. Keniston, 'Youth, Change and Violence', in *Daedalus*, 1967, and Jacobs, op. cit.

92 See Weinstein in Jacobs, op. cit., p. 392.

93 Berrigan saw Weatherman as having its origins in *nonviolence*!

94 See 'New Morning, Changing Weather' in Jacobs, op. cit. and account in Sale, op. cit.

95 Jacobs, op. cit.

14. Provocation: response and repression

1 Or 'contestation' as it was termed in France, May 1968 (M22). This term was more prevalent in Europe.

2 As the Columbia leader remarked: 'Confrontation politics puts the enemy up against the wall and forces him to define himself' – Mark Rudd, 'University in Revolt' in Jerry Avorn, *Up Against the Ivy Wall*, p. 100.

3 C. Oglesby, 'Decade Ready for a Dustbin' in Mitchell Goodman, *The Movement Toward a New America*.

4 Yet although this idea of self-transformation had often accompanied action on behalf of others, paradoxically internal repression and alien or external identification (with the Black Panthers or the NLF) had grown and reached their peak together.

5 Oglesby, op. cit. The anarcho-hippy paper *RAT*, edited by Jeff Shero in New York, had as its aim (1968) 'To get people onto the street' and to politicize the Chicago confrontation and its aftermath as a major theme. 'Stop-the-Draft-Week' was described by one of the leaders as an 'anarchist party'.

6 As occurred in the Haight-Ashbury riots of 1968, clashes in New York's Lower East Side, and Boston street-fighting: there was in fact a general and widespread movement on to the streets in this period.

7 GI coffee-house 'peace centres' became a focus for such dissent.

8 C. Lasch, *The Agony of American Radicalism.*

9 Ibid.: 'An unconscious and merely disruptive left will not survive the police state.' SDS lack of strategy in the view of one commentator led to 'an unattractive form of goal displacement in which disruption (the means) becomes an end in itself', David Osher, 'Roar Lion Roar', in *Win* magazine, 15 June 1969.

10 Julius Lester, *Revolutionary Notes.*

11 'While the experience of police brutality may lead those involved and those sympathetic to them, to look with new eyes at political authority, it will not necessarily have that effect on the majority', April Carter, *Direct Action and Liberal Democracy*, p. 129.

12 Bookchin attacks 'The utter stupidity of the American "Left" during the late sixties in projecting a mindless "politics of polarisation" and thereby wantonly humiliating so many middle class elements who were prepared to listen and to learn can hardly be criticised too strongly', Murray Bookchin, 'Spontaneity and Organisation' in *Liberation*, March 1972, p. 8.

13 Carter, op. cit.: 'The SDS strategy of showing the middle class the true oppressive nature of our society is mistaken because it threatens them.' Such confrontation 'cannot convert those who have not altered their consciousness – it only makes them more rigid', Charles Reich, *The Greening of America*, p. 246.

14 For his attack on Mary McCarthy's position, see Lasch, op. cit. On the other hand, in the 1960s, America's free-world role still sat awkwardly with the denial of basic liberties to black southerners, and its contempt for such freedoms in allied states.

15 M. Oppenheimer, *Urban Guerrilla.* 'It is not enough to speak of brutality', Gitlin argued, 'this is counter-revolution', T. Gitlin, 'Dynamics of the New Left', *Motive* magazine, October/November 1970, p. 52.

16 It is true that the failure of the Left to take movements on the Right, including those of Hitler and Mussolini, seriously enough and early enough, fatally weakened its ability to deal with them. There too, the Right had won a solid lower-class and lower-middle-class base and neutralized local authorities. But there too, by pushing ideological and cultural polarization to extremes, encouraging confrontation and street-fighting with revolution in view, the Left abandoned its liberal, centrist, and social democratic allies. It succeeded only in presenting a suitable rationale for a reactionary backlash movement, such as Wallace's support, which was disproportionately from America's white union members and the poor.

17 Hal Jacobs, *Weatherman.*

18 SDS is criticized by Charles Reich for this vision of class struggle which 'would engage in a hopeless head-on fight against the state and against people who could be their allies instead of their seeming enemies'. This was frontal assault rather than cultural subversion.

19 The backlash in the South, even though referred to as a 'last ditch stand', was extremely powerfully organized.

20 Lasch, op. cit. In Charles Reich's words: 'The law turns lawless' (*The Greening of America*).

21 Although the former was usually seen by the Right as merely another version of the latter.

22 Oppenheimer, op. cit.

23 Kitson's scenario was followed by a number of private counter-revolutionary proposals, including that of Colonel Stirling; on his plans for a special corps, as well as actual preparations by other private groups, see *Peace News*, special issue, 1974 'Rumbled'.

24 And new agencies and institutes set up to deal with its threat.

25 See Kerner Commission, Report of the National Advisory Commission on Civil Disorders, Bantam, 1968.

26 These observations are based on my own unpublished personal research on Berkeley street confrontations 1966–8, also for the 'Law and Society' project (director Rodney Stark), 1968.

27 Certainly the CPUSA had been hounded in the 1950s and the HUAC hearings kept the myth alive.

28 Arrests of students were often both violent and selective with staff and students used as informers in both British and American universities.

29 Indeed one of the first real signs of an awakening American movement was the 1960 San Francisco HUAC demonstration up to 8000 strong and many of them from Berkeley; see D. Horowitz, *Student*, Ballantine Books, 1962 for a description of the pre-FSM period. But the growth can be traced from the founding of SLATE in 1957, through protests against compulsory ROTC and Fred Moore's lonely hunger strike, 1959, the protest against Chessman's execution, 1959, more anti-ROTC actions, 1960–1, to the protests against HUAC from 1960 onwards.

30 But see chapter on the repression of the New Left in Alan Wolfe, *The Seamy Side of Democracy: Repression in America*, McKay, 1974.

31 See later discussion on Media and the New Left.

32 At Berkeley, the blame for much of the media's false information was subsequently placed on Kerr's press office. One opponent of the FSM, ex-senator William Knowland, owner of the *Oakland Tribune* (and other discriminatory hiring enterprises) had already been a target of civil rights activity.

33 Examples included: that the students were led by outside agitators, (49 per cent Maoist-Castroites(!)) and were 'non-students' – Kerr was forced to retract a further charge of vandalism. See Hal Draper, *Berkeley Student Revolt*, Black Cat Books, 1964. (Much of the work of denigration was done on the administration's behalf, however, by a number of sociology professors including Lipset, Glazer and Feuer; the latter insisted that the FSM was an elaboration of collective Oedipal revolt, in addition the students 'hadn't washed'.) In fact the movement was also an outrage to their cherished consensus theories; of the three, Lipset had the grace later to retract many of his observations. See Feuer's *New Leader* articles in 1964–5, and his *Conflict of Generations*.

34 Rudi Dutschke emerged as a leader of this campaign to 'terrorize' the Springer machine.

35 Both by non-reporting and direct censorship, as in the banning of Peter Watkins's film, *The War Game*, CND was also attacked not only officially, but by HM opposition: it was claimed that apologetic appeals for civil defence emanated from a party not conspiring to repress as much as siding with quietism, and an acquiescent parliament, against an increasingly 'awkward' controversy, safer ignored.

36 See P. Cadogan in R. Benewick, *Direct Action and Democratic Politics*, p. 171.

37 See R. Kasinsky on draft resisters in Canada.

38 The Chicago march and Festival were banned initially on the grounds of traffic congestion. In England the nuclear disarmers often faced prohibition from public squares and poster sites, or found public halls always 'booked', a form of harassment by police and local authorities that was difficult to deal with: it took months of haggling to agree a route for the Aldermaston March each year.

39 Including Genovese, Lynd, Marcuse and Angela Davis – or the Dick Atkinson affair in England. Blackburn and others were fired from the LSE, and in many cases activists on both sides of the Atlantic were not re-hired.

40 In Britain the main attacks on the student movement came later in the 1960s – for example those of Edward Short when Secretary of State.

41 See M. Cohen and D. Hale, *The New Student Left*, Introduction. From the paternalism and benevolence of an earlier administration, the attitude soon changed after FSM.

42 'Escalating the rents, tearing down cheap housing and replacing it with hotels, convention centres and university buildings', see Hayden, 'On Trial' in T. Cook and P. Morgan, *Participatory Democracy*. This was exemplified in problems of underground press; police raids on offices of underground papers and harassment of sellers and distributors by police and local residents. 'Politicians declare a "crime wave" (dope) and double the police patrols.' See Wolin and Schaar reprinted in *Peace News*.

43 See Alan Wolfe, *The Seamy Side of American Democracy*; however evidence for *significant* roles for the FBI and other agencies (as informers, provocateurs, etc.) in the NL, is scanty before the fall of 1968.

44 Kirkpatrick Sale, op. cit., pp. 500–1. Predictably, it was at this time that Nixon accused the students of 'chipping away at the fragile structure of ordered liberty'(!).

45 Sale, ibid., pp. 550–5. 'The movement is divided, confused, and deeply depressed and the forces of death are everywhere', Reich, op. cit., p. 326. See also Sale's afterword in *Win*, 21 June 1973: 'The New Left: What's Left?'

46 It is estimated that a similar number of Panthers died in this same period, most as a result of police attacks, see K. Sale, *History of SDS*.

15. The New Left and the Old

1 D. Flacks, 'Making History v. Making Life'.
2 Todd Gitlin, 'Dynamics of the New Left', *Motive*, November 1970.
3 Mills, contemptuous of the Marxist sects, stressed the enormity of US power, the existence of formal freedom and democracy, and the lacuna of organized Communism'. See also, L. Coser, 'USA Marxists at Bay', in L. Labedz, *Revisionism*, p. 351.
4 The struggle in SANE over Communist membership began in 1960 when Dodd first threatened to expose Communists in SANE, and lasted until 1962 when Student SANE disaffiliated and disbanded after refusing to exclude Communists and 'totalitarian' elements. A number of developments, such as SPU, SDS's non-exclusionism clause and the *Minority of One Magazine* date from this experience. See N. Glazer, 'The Peace Movement in America', *Commentary*, 1961, pp. 288–96.
5 This then left the field open to the YPSL-dominated SPU.
6 Undoubtedly the issue of non-exclusionism reflected the importance and tactical success of the CP-dominated anti-HUAC campaign. The CP effectively used the civil liberties theme in the 1950s after McCarthy; this counter-attack included the injustice of Chessman's trial, the Rosenberg and Hiss convictions and other causes célèbres.
7 Quoted in P. Jacobs and S. Landau, *The New Radicals*, Random House, 1966.
8 Ibid. Du Bois, founded first as a local west coast youth front in 1961, was extended into a national organization by the CP in 1964.
9 Op. cit.
10 Left liberals were of course ready to envisage a limited 'peace-keeping' role for US armed forces abroad (and indeed in the Deep South or Watts) just as the CPUSA supported Russia's armed intervention, and policing of its satellites. The social democrats were largely pragmatic about whose violence they supported, when and where.
11 See Michael Munk in *Radical America*.
12 Or Christian ones, for that matter.
13 See T. Kahn, 'The Problem of the New Left', LID reprint from *Commentary*, 1966, p. 1.
14 Irving Howe, 'New Styles of Leftism', *Dissent*, p. 316. See also my statement, 'On Military Revolution' presented to the War Resisters' International Conference, August 1972 (in *Peace News*, August 1972) and L. Coser's 'Myths of Peasant Revolution', *Continuities in the Studies of Social Change*.
15 Quoted in D. Apter and J. Joll, *Anarchism Today*, section on the Provos.
16 Norman Fruchter's valuable film about the Newark project, *Trouble-makers*, depicted typical activity: organized protests for such things as street crossings and traffic lights, better refuse collection and schools; and against police brutality, tenement repairs, welfare payments; but the film is also a classic document of that element of 'romantic defeatism' in the movement.

17 Howe, op. cit. Subsequently and retrospectively some NL activists agreed.
18 This argument was repeated by Eric Hobsbawm in a *New Society* article in 1969, advocating puritanism in sex, dress and behaviour for genuine revolutionaries.
19 In Britain, the later New Left editors adopted a view that, in an immediate sense, their life-style was irrelevant: contrasting with the sober and self-denying character – even respectability – of Old Left groups, this was by no means voluntary poverty.
20 Howe, op. cit., pp. 304–7. See also S. Lynd, Introduction to P. Long, *The New Left*.
21 Such Marcusian themes of 'de-totalization' are taken up by both Gitlin and Oglesby at the end of the decade; see Andrew Rigby's writings.
22 See Brown's reply to Marcuse, in *Commentary*, March 1967, p. 83.
23 But see Bruce Brown's comments in *Marx, Freud and the Critique of Everyday Life*, Monthly Review Press, 1963, Chapter 1, esp. pp. 21–31.
24 T. Bottomore, *Critics of Society*, p. 73.
25 Flacks, op. cit., p. 64. NB also Thompson in the Kolakowski letter, who defines his 'revisionism' in terms of 'the radiating problems of historical determinism on the one hand and of agency, moral choice and individual responsibility on the other' (*Socialist Register*, 1973, p. 1).
26 See Elinor Langer, 'Notes for Next Time', *Working Papers for a New Society*, 1973.
27 On libertarian Marxism, see previous discussion (on ideology, chapter 7 above), and D. Guerin, *L'Anarchisme*.
28 Ibid.
29 James Weinstein, 'The Left, Old and New' in *Socialist Revolution*, p. 40.
30 Ibid.
31 Charles Reich's 'Consciousness II' was a summary of this, see his *The Greening of America*.
32 Reich's 'Consciousness III', ibid. See David Horowitz's critique of Reich in 'Beyond the Valley of the Heads', *Ramparts*, 1970.
33 Hal Jacobs, *Weatherman*.
34 Lynd, Introduction to Long, op. cit.
35 See J. Weinstein, 'The Left, Old and New', pp. 40–59.
36 Ibid.
37 This should be compared with the 1,500 at the SDS conference of 1969, see Sale, op. cit. YSA membership (Sale's estimate) was 10,000 by 1970 – with at least 20,000 in its 'Student Movement'. At its Cleveland conference, the 3,500 delegates reveal the extent to which YSA was the beneficiary of SDS demise during the fall of 1969.
38 Analysed in the subsequent section.
39 Sidney Lens, *Radicalism in America*, p. 365.
40 'Student mobilisation', successor of the 'National "Mobe"', organized the 1968 April strike – which clashed with SDS's abortive

'Ten days of resistance', and indeed overshadowed it, see Sale, op. cit., and Jacobs, op. cit.

41 This was formed, in turn, out of the NCAWR (National Committee Against War and Racism).

42 See B. Schwartz, 'Modernisation and the Maoist Vision: Some Reflections on Chinese Communist Goals' in *Dissent*, vol. 12, no. 4, autumn 1965; see also I. Howe, 'New Styles in Leftism'.

43 Like Fanon, Maoism also purveyed the concept of such revolution being imported from the countryside into the towns (e.g. Lin Piao).

44 See Philip Luce, *New Left*, and A. Adelson, *SDS, a Profile*, Scribner, 1972 (the PL account of its New Left fronts).

45 Ibid. The name Progressive Labor was probably derived from A. J. Muste's largely Trotskyite old organization of the 1930s, Progressive Labor Action. In fact PL was not the working-class body it claimed to be (see articles in Krassner's *Realist* magazine).

46 See Luce, op. cit.

47 Robert Williams quoted in Luce, ibid. See also Howe, op. cit., pp. 302–3, quoting *Monthly Review* (editorial), December 1964.

48 Possibly influenced by this, a number of SDS members joined with PL cadres in Berkeley to picket the Russian ambassador, Rogachev. The rest of Berkeley SDS was mobilized in time to counter these pickets in strength, and to indicate that the Third World War was not yet part of SDS's programme. But coming as early as this in SDS, it was a portent of things to come, and of PL's rising influence.

49 Like the indiscriminate use of the term 'fascist', or 'imperialist', it began to lose all meaning.

50 C. W. Mills, 'Letter to the New Left' in *Power, Politics and People*, ed. I. L. Horowitz.

51 Including by Klonsky himself (see Sale, op. cit., pp. 520–1).

52 See P. Clecak, *Radical Paradoxes*.

53 And indeed endorsed the highly revisionist Italian CP.

54 On PL discourse, see Luce, op. cit. and Weinstein, op. cit., pp. 51–3. Gitlin talks of PL's 'top-down organisation and imagery of authoritarian revolution' in this period, op. cit., p. 48.

55 Eventually these events raised again basic issues of organization, analysed in *Liberation* magazine. See for example May and August 1972 issues and articles by Schneider on Vanguards and Cadres.

56 See C. Oglesby, 'Decade Ready for a Dustbin', in M. Goodman, op. cit.

57 Kirkpatrick Sale, op. cit., fully documents the role of PL in SDS including their bids for power, their rigid repetitious Marxism, self-righteousness and caucusing – but he is fair enough to show also that on the whole PL operated in a less hysterical and temperamental manner than the RYM groupings.

58 PL formed its own organization with the title SDS. See Alan Adelson's poor account from the Maoist's own standpoint, *SDS, a Profile*.

59 See Sale's verdict on PL/SDS, op. cit., p. 656, and the Adelson account, op. cit.

60 Julius Lester, *Revolutionary Notes*, p. 4, and Howe, op. cit.

61 H. Jacobs, op. cit.
62 The one possible exception being the RUM (Revolutionary Union Movement) in San Francisco.

16. A crisis of identity

1 See pp. 49–54, 189–91, and C. Oglesby, 'Decade Ready for a Dustbin' in M. Goodman, *The Movement Toward a New America*, and N. Birnbaum in J. Nagel, *Student Power*.
2 D. Schön, 'The End of the Stable State', *Listener*, December 1970.
3 Ibid.
4 Nancy Graham in 'Participation in Mass Movements' in a UNESCO seminar paper (August 1968) on status inconsistencies, who cited evidence on SNCC/CORE. The young militant black leaders of CORE and SNCC etc. came from lower-middle-class families characterized by such status anxiety, reflecting mobility and social disruption.
5 K. Sale, *History of SDS*, remarks on SDS's lack of any unified political identity after 1968 compared even with a certain 'loose identity' achieved in earlier periods.
6 'Insensible to the unique constellation of possibilities that stared it in the face, the "left" simply fed its guilt and insecurities about itself' (M. Bookchin, 'Spontaneity and Organisation', *Liberation*, 1972).
7 Call to December 1965 SDS conference quoted in T. Kahn, 'The Problem of the New Left', *Commentary*, 1966. See also Dave Wellman, 'A Post-Scarcity Radical is something to be', *Motive*, April 1971, p. 27.
8 See Julius Lester, 'Media as Enemy', *San Francisco Express Times*, November 1968.
9 It seems likely that, as with the other figures, some conservative critics may have foisted Marcuse on the Movement, not perhaps so much because he often *does* seem to echo NL sentiments, but because they found him an easy target, and through him, attacked the Movement's intolerance and violence.
10 See N. Egleson, *Anguish and Politics*, pp. 3–4.
11 Bookchin condemns the 'insane politics', 'mindless mimickry' and 'systematic alienation from all the authentic radicalizing forces in US society', op. cit., p. 8.
12 Both Howe's article, 'New Styles of Leftism', *Dissent*, and Maurice Cranston's book on *The New Left* are good examples of this. See also R. Lowenthal, 'Unreason and Revolution', *Encounter*, 1969.
13 See discussion in previous chapter.
14 Charles Reich, *The Greening of America*.
15 Writing in 1972 (*Beyond Reminiscence: the New Left in History*).
16 See Roussopoulos in Introduction to C. Benello and D. Roussopoulos, *The Case for Participatory Democracy*, p. 5.
   Gitlin too focuses finally on these 'internal deformations and diseases'. 'The roots lie in the marrow: arrogance, elitism, competitiveness, machismo, guilt – the replications of (inherited) patterns of domination and mystification.'

17 Noted by S. Lens in 'Road to Power and Beyond', in ibid., p. 313.
18 See S. Lynd in P. Long, *The New Left.*
19 Greg Calvert, 1967. 'A liberal fights for someone else's liberation: a radical fights for his own.'
20 The same too could be said for Women's Liberation, see chapter 17.
21 On the break-up of the American movement, see O'Brien, op. cit.; J. Weinstein, 'The Left, Old and New', *Socialist Revolution*; J. Lester, 'Cleaver, Carmichael and the Politics of Black Liberation,' and Sale, op. cit., and K. Sale, 'New Left, What's Left?', *Win*, 1972.
22 'It left the field and faded away', J. Schaar, 'Power and Purity', *American Review*, 19, p. 153.
23 Though one can disagree with his estimate of what these internal weaknesses actually were.
24 It should be noted, however, that Marcuse's position was strongly reinforced and paralleled by remarkably similar writing by Sartre in this period. Like Marcuse, Sartre had abandoned the traditional faith in the organized working class, replaced with the cult of revolutionary violence, combined with new dogma and a double-standard moralism.
25 The Critical University in Berlin, the Anti-University of London and the Experimental University in Amsterdam were more traditional in structure and more doctrinaire in tone than American counterparts. In some cases top-down lecturing was introduced and the small group-cooperation model abandoned. See J. Berke, *Counter Culture.*
26 This included their educational work.
27 See Hayden in T. Cook and P. Morgan, *Participatory Democracy*, 'On Trial' and in I. Howe, *The Radical Papers*. These positions are similar to Gorz's concept of 'non-reformist reforms', 'Strategy for Labour', in C. Oglesby, *The New Left Reader.*
28 See H. Zinn, *SNCC: The New Abolitionists.*
29 See Lynd, 'Bicameralism from Below' in Cook and Morgan, op. cit.
30 Food conspiracies or Co-ops, survived much longer than most alternatives.
31 This issue was raised very much by the writing of Ivan Illich.
32 See Schön, op. cit. An alternative strategy was what Dave Wellman entitled 'The Long March through many American Institutions' (see his response to Gitlin (*Motive*, 1970), 'A Post-Scarcity Radical is something to be').
33 Barrington Moore's article 'Revolution in America', *New York Review of Books.*
34 Kenneth Keniston quoted in C. Lasch, *Agony of American Radicalism*, p. 174.
35 D. Schön in *Listener*, 24 December 1970 and M. Oppenheimer, *Urban Guerrilla.*
36 Moore, op. cit. It was mainly Hayden increasingly arguing for such 'free territories'. See 'On Trial' in Cook and Morgan, op. cit.
37 Hayden, op. cit. and see also J. Dunn, *Modern Revolutions*. In my article 'The Dialectics of Incorporation' (on working-class culture), *Berkeley Journal of Sociology*, 1967, I develop the argument that

this nineteenth-century culture did succeed to some extent in achieving such insulation.

38 Barrington Moore, 'Revolution in America'.

39 Quoted in Kahn, op. cit. Amongst Movement figures, McReynolds attacked SDS's 'participatory democracy' as phoney as early as the 1965 Vietnam march (see *Liberation*, August 1965 and Weinstein, op. cit., p. 59).

40 The technocratic systems theories' use for such a network model should have warned the NL against an over-emphasis on *form* rather than on content: particularly as corporate 'human relations' experts were turning to the T-group and sensitivity training, closely parallel with participatory democracy. Whether adoption of such a model is compatible with authoritarian and repressive ends is another question.

41 S. M. Lipset, 'Student Opposition', op. cit.

42 It was at one such celebrated meeting that Ginsberg introduced his hip-demonstration proposal which only failed by a handful of votes (see Teodori, *The New Left*).

43 Lipset, op. cit.

44 To be fair it was those organizations like SDS which were experimenting with PD who first became aware of these problems, including those related to women.

45 See L. Feuer, *Conflict of Generations*, p. 408 and Introduction to Cook and Morgan, op. cit. See also Kahn, op. cit., p. 8.

46 M. Oppenheimer in P. Dreitzel, *Recent Sociology*.

47 Feuer, op. cit., p. 410 and see also Martin Oppenheimer, 'Sociology of Participatory Democracy' in Benello and Roussopoulos, op. cit. A number of critics (including Nancy Graham, op. cit.) argue that it is *not* the oppressed who participate.

48 These original ideals are summarized by Massimo Teodori, op. cit., pp. 50–7, 'The individual shares in these social decisions determining the quality and direction of his life; that society be organised to encourage independence in men.' See also chapter 3 above.

49 See Kahn, op. cit. The crisis and demise of Syndicalism had been partly rooted in these organizational problems; see I. Howe, 'New Styles of Leftism', pp. 313–14 and Lens, op. cit.

50 T. Gitlin, 'The Dynamics of the New Left', *Motive*, 1970.

51 See in Teodori, op. cit. The editors of *Studies on the Left* like those of the *National Guardian* felt differently however.

52 H. Marcuse, 'The Old Model Won't Do' in Teodori, op. cit.

53 NB Schön, op. cit.

54 See K. Keniston, *The Young Radicals*.

55 Anarchists, social democrats, liberals, or other 'unreliable' members of SDS were not informed of meetings; see *Freedom* pamphlet, 1969, no. 2, James Cain (ed.), 'Students for a Stalinist Society', p. 11, reprinted from *Anarchos*; this was as true at the LSE as in SDS – see P. Hoch and V. Schoenbach *LSE: The Natives are Restless*, p. 14, and J. Avorn on Columbia in *Up Against the Ivy Wall*.

56 Greg Calvert and Carol Nieman, *A Disrupted History*, p. 140. Indeed in Gitlin's view 'the Left's sectarianism' may have given

liberalism a new lease of life – as exemplified in the anti-war movement after the Moratorium of 1969, Gitlin, op. cit., p. 60.
57 See Widgery, *The Left in Britain: 1956–68*, p. 57.
58 See *Culture and Society*, final chapter.
59 As April Carter observes 'if liberal freedoms and the associated
values of individualism, rationality, and tolerance are simply a
historical product of capitalist society, then they may be discarded
under socialism', *Direct Action and Liberal Democracy*, p. 119. This
author differentiates three NL positions:
1. civil liberties have existed but are now eroded or limited;
2. civil liberties still exist but are rendered ineffective;
3. civil liberties do not genuinely exist in this system but act as a
distraction from its actual repression.
In practice these are not as clearcut and probably the NL held all
these positions, at times simultaneously.
60 See Raymond Williams in final section of *Culture and Society*.
61 See D. Apter and J. Joll, *Anarchism Today*. SDS constantly shifted
in its attitude to him. For an instance of this ambivalence see Dohrn's
introduction to Marcuse's speech at the *Guardian* dinner and the
subsequent controversy (reported in Sale, op. cit., summarized in
Teodori, op. cit.).
62 Alasdair MacIntyre (who had barely renounced his Trotskyite
associations) attacked Marcuse for élitism and irrationalism from an
essentially liberal standpoint. Yet Marcuse's own expressed
preference for a liberal administration and the rule of law and
relative endorsement of two concepts (pluralism and convergence
theory) from the mainstream of 'liberal' social science, compounded
the ambiguity of his position.
63 There was a good deal of hypocrisy in this stance; since the opening
Du Bois convention it had been an entirely managed and monolithic
affair, with suppression of any dissenting (i.e. non-CP) factions.
E.g. see P. Luce, *New Left*, McKay, 1966.
64 See Lynd in Teodori, op. cit. and Hayden's 'a sort of pseudo-fascism'.
65 Though there were isolated attempts to communicate to such groups,
mainly by liberal pacifists (e.g. visits to arms firms).
66 On its effects in England see Hoch and Schoenbach, op. cit., p. 203
and in Colin Crouch, *The Student Revolt*.
67 Whilst in some sense it returns to pre-Marxian idealist utopias it
never embodies the communitarian notions which had preceded the
Marx–Engels diatribes against Owen, Fourier and Proudhon.
68 Wellman, op. cit.
69 See above. At LSE a Professor Day was assaulted because he refused
to lecture on Northern Ireland in an Economics class. Such actions
were endorsed by the main radical chroniclers of LSE unrest (Hoch
and Schoenbach, op. cit., p. 141). True to form, the British confrontationist experience, which is foreshadowed in CND, but really
only dates from 1967, dragged on for several years in episodic
fashion, increasingly aimed at right-wing minority groups: attempts
to break up small neo-fascist marches, or meetings, were encouraged
by the Marxist splinters, for example.

70 For example, systematic street confrontations were undoubtedly influenced partly by media-coverage of violent Japanese student clashes with police; indeed training in 'Japanese techniques' was given at Chicago.

71 The previous summer and fall (1965) in San Francisco were in many ways more novel and more innovative, but were not publicized.

72 As well as the socialist-realist and anti-war films of the 1960s (mainly British), commercial films including *Battle of Algiers, Bonnie and Clyde, Zabriskie Point, Easy Rider*, had great appeal within the movement.

73 The NL particularly liked to view itself in the media-mirror, it was collectively and individually vain: the fact that these were distorting mirrors was ignored.

74 See Carter, op. cit.

75 1970, quoted in ibid., p. 77. See also Clark Kissinger's *Organisers' Handbook*, Fall 1964.

76 Antonioni's *Zabriskie Point* was merely one of several more obvious examples, cf. also *The Strawberry Statement* and other ephemera.

77 The television coverage in particular was a key factor.

78 His marriage to Miriam Makeba confirmed his place amongst the NL stars favoured by the media; other such movement-media marriages included those of Tom Hayden and Jane Fonda, and David Harris and Joan Baez, though in both latter cases, the partners managed to combine their media roles with activism, as Marlon Brando, Vanessa Redgrave, and others, also did.

79 Julius Lester, op. cit., p. 2.

80 Jack Newfield, *Prophetic Minority*, p. 157.

81 Jones moved from a theatrical media-oriented guerilla-theatre towards actual advocacy and fringe involvement in urban guerillaism. Publicly the distinctions became inevitably blurred – art and reality fused.

82 Williams's broadcasts from Cuba are the first of a series of flamboyant media gestures by such figures.

83 *Ramparts* – a glossy production situated uneasily between the alternative and the established press, found a niche exploiting movement news as a saleable item, and briefly held a very large circulation.

84 See Norman Birnbaum, 'The Reactive Revolt', *Towards a Critical Sociology*.

85 Amongst the precursors of the Underground Press should be noted the *Village Voice* (1955) and the *Realist* (1958). *Village Voice*, first ancestor of underground papers, became too staid by the mid-1960s when the first of the new papers emerged: *LA Free Press* and the *East Village Other*, soon followed by the *Berkeley Barb* (1965).

86 UPS was loose-knit and idealistic; LNS more leftist and 'engaged'. For surveys see: Roger Lewis, *Outlaws of America*, Penguin, 1972, and R. Glessing, *The Underground Press in America*, Indiana, 1971.

87 Some papers instituted forms of workers' control and many had a reciprocal relationship with the street communities in terms of distribution.

88 Independent (i.e. non-commercial) free radio had a limited growth,

beyond the scattering of liberal and radical radio stations that already existed such as the Pacifica Chain. There was no development of alternative TV. Most of the current so-called free radio in Britain and Europe was in fact commercial – this was much less true in America, see Berke, op. cit. An early issue of *Anarchy* dealt with the possibilities in Britain.

89 Perhaps the most significant contribution was made by the small theatre and mime groups: San Francisco Mime Troup, Bread and Puppet (New York), Agitprop, Black Theatre and Street or Guerilla Theatre, as well as Julian Beck's 'Living Theatre' group.

90 A number of Movement films were also made – about community organizing, the peace movement and the black community – but the best came early in the NL's history: free cinema in England, and Fruchter *et al.* for SDS; a left-wing film outfit (Newsreel) was established, but this too, due to an ambivalence about commercial film production, remained a marginal development. The most ambitious attempt (on the Vietnam movement) was Jerry Stoll's *Sons and Daughters*.

91 Though hardly matching the wealth of rock groups, and indeed few papers making even a profit.

92 E.g. the split in the *Berkeley Barb*.

93 There remained a faith that certain films, books, articles, etc. of radical content, could still find their way largely uncensored through the established system. The articles of Andrew Kopkind, Nick van Hoffman, Nat Hentoff, Howard Zinn, Jack Newfield, Paul Jacobs and Herb Caen, most of them people active on the fringes of the movement were highly regarded. There was a twilight zone of magazines and publishers between the Establishment and the alternative – a spectrum which stretched from *Playboy*, *New Republic* and *Nation*, through the *New York Review of Books*, to *Ramparts*, and a scatter of Left-liberal and glossy magazines interspersed between them. Note also Wechster's film *Medium Cool* (Chicago, 1968).

94 Fusions of Surrealism, Zen and other oriental influences, Dada, Situationism, ecology, anarcho-pacifism made these efforts *ad hoc* and widely utopian at the outset; but they created a style which spread. See Peter Stansil and D. Z. Mairowitz, *BAMN: Outlaw Manifestoes*, which also documents the crisis in the counter-culture.

95 Youth International Party.

96 In 1965, Allen Ginsberg proposed to the VDC a march-spectacle involving flowers, music, flags, crosses, mass calisthenics, the incantation of Three Blind Mice and other mantras, sweets and paper haloes for the Hell's Angels and police (see Teodori, op. cit.).

97 However, Marcuse claimed that whilst he (Marcuse) puts the onus of change on social structure rather than on the individual (i.e. closer to Marxism), Brown, like Fromm, placed too much emphasis on personal transformation.

98 See Reich's discussion of the Alternative Society in *The Greening of America*, p. 24 and *passim*.

99 For example see Gitlin, op. cit., p. 45 and S. Hall, 'The Hippies: An American Moment', in J. Nagel, *Student Power*.

100 The Diggers ceased giving free food in 1967 when The Free Stores closed and groups such as Country Joe and the Fish ceased giving their free concerts. See Howard in Cook and Morgan, op. cit., pp. 206–10.
101 This was encouraged by such writing as that of Abbie Hoffman and Jerry Rubin, *Steal this Book* and *Do it*, etc.
102 Even the soft drugs (grass and acid) of the hippies and the hard drugs of the black and the white addicts, often derived from the same pushers.
103 First Weatherman communiqué: see H. Jacobs, *Weatherman*. This link between criminality and political radicalism represents another parallel with historic Anarchism, which recruited from the underworld and demi-monde.
104 The IRA attracted and recruited similar elements during its post-1970 offensive.
105 SDS figures such as Bernardine Dohrn and Cameron Bishop appeared on FBI lists of most-wanted criminals. David Harris of the 'Resistance' described the position of the criminal in America as 'the most honorable position'; but there is a real distinction between these types of criminality in the ways in which they are 'criminal'.
106 This is very much reflected in much of the retrospective literature on the NL, e.g. E. Langer, 'Notes for Next Time', Dotson Rader, *I ain't marching anymore* and Paul Potter, *A Name for Ourselves*, Little, Brown, 1971. As Jeff Lustig remarks, they turn Mills on his head: 'turning public issues into private problems'.
107 Its links with the Movement were not necessarily only meditative or 'escapist'; its belief in nonviolence and counter-creativity of course placed it extremely close to some forms of earlier movement activism, and the incredible examples of 'love in action' of the Buddhists of South Vietnam in their increasingly political third-way struggle made a delayed but eventual impact on America's radical consciousness. See Thich Nhat Hanh's *Love in Action*, FOR, 1969 (pamphlet).
108 See Sale's comments in *Win*, 1973.

17. Picking up the threads

1 There was a brief swansong with the invasion of Cambodia (1970) – but the reaction to Cambodia, although extensive, could not be compared in numbers, militancy or organization with the major confrontation of 1967–9.
2 Scheduled as a car-park.
3 See T. Hayden, SDS Pamphlet, 'Student Social Action', in M. Teodori, *The New Left*. GI coffee houses near army bases after 1969 were a focus of the growth of GI organizing in this period and a source of anti-war literature and newspapers. Other types of peace centres flourished elsewhere.
4 For the theoretical implications of Welsh, Scottish and Irish nationalism see M. Hechter, *Internal Colonialism*, Routledge & Kegan Paul, 1975.

5 See Andrew Rigby, *Alternative Realities*. Also D. Roussopoulos on 'Urban Communes' in C. G. Benello and D. Roussopoulos, *The Case for Participatory Democracy*.

6 The numerical and circulation decline of the alternative press is not marked until after 1970 (and is by no means complete at time of writing). See J. O'Brien, *Beyond Reminiscence*, pp. 40–1.

7 See D. E. Apter and J. Joll, *Anarchism Today*, section on the 'Kabouters'.

8 Ibid.

9 See discussion of Marcuse above (chapter 15).

10 To Owenism, Tolstoian communism or the early Kibbutzim, but also to aspects of anarcho-syndicalism discussed previously; in England 'Alternative Socialism' groups emerged in the 1970s.

11 The success of first the grape strike led by Cesar Chavez in the San Joaquin valley, the formation of a new union, and the waging of successive nonviolent struggles by Chicano farm workers were clear and notable triumphs for explicitly Gandhian techniques, which received increasingly widespread publicity and support after 1970, though the Movement received a number of subsequent rebuffs.

12 'Let them preach nonviolence in the white community' – such groups as the Institute for the Study of Nonviolence moved from middle-class Carmel to a small white urban suburb (Palo Alto).

13 And to the leadership of Lynd, Calvert, Harris, Lennie Heller and Steve Hamilton (ex-PL).

14 David Harris in 'Hard Love and Participatory Totalitarianism', Institute for the Study of Nonviolence, 1970.

15 See Devi Prasad, *They Love it or Leave it*, WRI, 1969. The numbers of deserters as well as numbers of draft resisters were continually underestimated (see *War Resistance*, vol. 2, no. 27, 1968, 'American Deserters'), not least the scores of thousands who emigrated, about half of them to Canada. About 10,000 who stayed in America were prosecuted. Over 7 years, total resisters may have reached the million mark if official COs are included in the figures running at about 30,000 per year as well as non-registrants, deserters, and those who went underground.

16 In April 1967, 150 cards were burnt, in October 1,400, in the following April 2,000. Even right-wing young groups opposed the draft. The return of cards continued after 1968. See Staughton Lynd, 'The Movement: a New Beginning' in Benello and Roussopoulos, op. cit., and M. Ferber and S. Lynd, *The Resistance*, Beacon, Boston, 1971.

17 The first climax of the resistance with a mass draft card return was in October 1967; the last mass return of this period was in April 1968.

18 Organizations in the armed forces during 1969 included the American Services Union and 'Movement for a Democratic Military'; each had their own newspapers. The Vietnam Veterans played an increasingly prominent role (returning medals, etc.).

19 Sabotage as a specific tactic (i.e. destroying draft files) had less chance, it was argued, of escalating into para-militarism or endangering life.

20 Their views and actions were promoted in radical Christian magazines such as *Slant* and the *Catonsville Roadrunner* in England.

21 Like the Kabouters, hippy nonviolence had been predicated on an unwillingness to respond to the violence of authoritarian structures in kind; somewhat parallel to the Gandhian principle of moral jujitsu, the idea was to throw the 'man' off balance.

22 For Sidney Lens's remarks on the New Left attitude to violence, see his 'Road to Power and Beyond' in Benello and Roussopoulos, op. cit., p. 312 and in *Radicalism in America*.

23 The ideas of Erich Fromm and Mills in this connection find resonance with the more creative ventures of the 1970s (Mills's private ills as public issues link with the 'politics of everyday life').

24 T. Gitlin, 'The Dynamics of the New Left', *Motive*, p. 60.

25 Before it split off from SDS, Women's Workshops were established by Naomi Weisstein, Heather Booth and others at the Des Moines and Chicago meetings of Resistance in August and December 1966. See article by Munaker, Goldfield and Weisstein in P. Long, *The New Left*, p. 326.

26 The term 'pussy power' was originally used by the black power-groups in ridiculing Women's Liberation. It was also used in SDS as late as the SDS conference of 1969.

27 See Casey Hayden's remarks in *Liberation* (and those of Jane Stembridge).

28 See C. Hernton, *Sex and Racism in America*, Grove Press, New York, 1966.

29 See I. L. Horowitz quoted in M. Oppenheimer, *Urban Guerrilla*, p. 54, and Robin Morgan, 'Goodbye to All That' reprinted in Leslie Tanner (ed.), *Voices from Women's Liberation*, Signet, 1970.

30 See Juliet Mitchell, *Woman's Estate*, Penguin, 1970, and the 'Bread and Roses' collective statement, printed in Hal Jacobs, op. cit.

31 For the background see Calvin Hernton, op. cit.

32 Though presumably Israeli women's military role was on the whole now less laudable.

33 As has been seen the image, already adopted by SDS, was the clenched fist. But smashing through what traditionally was the circular womb symbol it was an odd symbol for the new feminism and was symptomatic of WL's uneasy overlap with the NL in general, and SDS in particular.

34 By adopting this style and model, Bernardine Dohrn's leadership was in many ways a disastrous one both for SDS and the Women's Movement. See O'Brien, op. cit., p. 38. The Weatherwomen, although widely criticized for their implication in the 'macho' style of aggression, played a significant catalytic role sharpening the debate around revolutionary feminism. Bernardine Dohrn, although one of the first major NL leaders to be a woman, was one of its most problematic.

35 See Morgan in Tanner, op. cit.

36 Naomi Weisstein and others in Long, op. cit., p. 326. Yet Dohrn still attacked such separatist positions as 'bourgeois, chauvinist and lacking consciousness'!

37 See Long, op. cit.
38 See K. Sale, *History of SDS*.
39 O'Brien, op. cit., p. 35.
40 Emphasized by Robin Morgan in 'Goodbye to All That' and in Kate Millett's *Sexual Politics*. Ronald Sampson's book *Equality and Power*, published in 1965 (Heinemann) had linked issues as disparate as Women's Liberation and nuclear weapons in so far as they exemplified a link between the nature of inter-personal domination and submission and the problems of international power. C. W. Mills's 'Darling Little Slaves' in *Power, Politics and People*, Horowitz (ed.), showed a prophetic awareness of some of these issues.
41 Such challenges, especially those of R. D. Laing, often took psychic or psychiatric adjustment as a starting point (as Fanon, also a psychiatrist, did).
42 Especially Kate Millett and Shulamith Firestone, and later Juliet Mitchell. Fromm had foreshadowed the critique of the social-psychological crisis of the 'death of the family' which becomes the central focus of Laing, Cooper and others a decade later, and then an orienting standpoint of the new Feminism. See also Mills's 'Darling Little Slaves'.
43 There were some feminist defences of Freud however.
44 Such as pre-school playgroups, communal child-rearing and free schools (NB Everett Reimers writing on their role).
45 Freudian theory had been especially conservative in its rejection of the idea of a natural order of freedom, and its belief in the necessity of repressive male-ordered civilization, to contain both destructive urges and libertarian excess. Such ideas had in the past, been subordinating, inducing acceptance of a male-centred sexuality, because of these assumptions about human nature, especially their pessimistic psycho-sexual assumption, dominated by – mostly male – violence and aggression.
46 And reflected in the degenerations of the counter-culture.
47 I.e., since this sexuality derives its major appeal from that inequality (e.g. power, aggression, cruelty and its sadistic/masochistic consequences). See H. Marcuse, *Eros and Civilization*.
48 It is significant that whether 'pastiche' or real, the extremely sadistic or morbid images of the alternative press and underground literature of the early 1970s were often heralded as an attack on exploitative sexuality.
49 The music paper *Rolling Stone* dwelt on the details of the murder of the pregnant Sharon Tate, ripped open by Manson's female followers on his orders, without any comment, analysis or critique, condemning or dissociating from the act.
50 Robin Morgan, op. cit., 'Goodbye to the dream that being in the leadership collective will get you anything but gonorrhea'. 'Know what they call a Weatherwoman? A heavy cunt. Know what they call a hip revolutionary woman? A groovy cunt. Know what they call a radical militant feminist? A crazy cunt. America is the land of free choice. Take your pick of titles.'

51 The former he would see as a dangerous and fraudulent co-optation (and commercializing) of an objectified aspect of sexuality, a process that incidentally tended to reinforce male–female stereotypes against the arguments of WL and against the actual tendency for the hippy counter-culture to play down overt sex-role differences.

52 Whilst widely canvassed in these years, an alternative 'androgynous' eroticism was often a matter of style rather than either the actual attitude change or libidinal transformations envisaged in Marcuse's theory, or any approach to that 'abolition of genital organisation' about which Norman O. Brown speculated.

53 Based on the earlier work of critics like Mills and Marcuse, Goodman and Fromm, the new sociology as has been suggested already had a great deal in common with Anarchist standpoints, though the confluence was largely unconscious. The NL sociology of Mills had moved first in the direction of a revisionist Marxist sociology, but there were already signs of libertarian emphases. In Mills's pupils, like Horowitz, this is accentuated and in the 'Movement sociology' of Lynd, Gitlin and Oppenheimer, etc., it points towards the Anarchist reappraisals of Bookchin and others.

54 Gitlin, op. cit.

55 Stuart Hall in J. Nagel, *Student Power*; arguing a priori that the cultural challenge has become critical in post-industrial society, Hall uses a neo-Marxian analysis that parallels Marcuse, to emphasize the paramount role of ideas-production as against the material base. See also H. Marcuse, 'Socialism in the Developed Countries', *International Sociology Journal*, 2, 1965.

56 Gitlin, op. cit.

57 D. Wellman, 'A Post-Scarcity Radical is Something to be', *Motive*, p. 27.

58 Against which the movement of Chavez and the Mexican workers was beginning to develop.

59 California was now the largest war-material producing state; with hundreds of government contracts and training schemes (many in priority defence areas).

60 The emergence of an academic peace research movement, much of it divorced from the activist peace movement, leant towards incremental social engineering solutions; some of it was reformist, and some of it was dubiously related to 'peace' at all. (See my 'Peace Research and the Peace Movement', *Agora*, Fall, 1964.) But with the impact of Vietnam, and the NL, it became significantly radicalized by the early 1970s.

61 From the first scatter of projects in the 1960s, hundreds of experiments are launched, including the mini-schools, neighbourhood or black schools, and schools rooted in decentralized communities as advocated by these theorists.

62 B. Moore, 'Revolution in America', *New York Review of Books*.

63 J. Ellul, *Technological Society*.

64 The development of the conservationist ethos after 1970, merely strengthened this attitude (NB parallel stress on food/diets).

65 T. B. Bottomore, *Critics of Society*.

66 Books such as Charles Reich's *The Greening of America* helped add this ecological dimension to liberal politics.

67 Formed in 1969 when transporting aid directly but illegally across the borders of occupied Bangladesh; it later became involved in aiding Namibia.

68 As a group that helped initiate environmental concern through its original actions against atmospheric testing and radio-active pollution, CND at least lived to see the nuclear issue revived, largely through the efforts of groups like Greenpeace. But part of the problem was the nuclear disarmament groups' fear of being absorbed into the conservation issue, so cooperation was often minimal.

69 And indeed as the civil rights movement and NL had done.

Select Bibliography

Collections and documents

The New Left is fortunately documented by a number of excellent collections, the best of which I have listed below:

APTER, DAVID E. and JOLL, JAMES (eds), *Anarchism Today* (Macmillan, London, 1971).

BENELLO, C. GEORGE and ROUSSOPOULOS, DIMITRIOS (eds), *The Case for Participatory Democracy* (Grossman, New York, 1971).

COHEN, MITCHELL and HALE, DENIS (eds), *The New Student Left* (Beacon Press, Boston, 1966).

COOK, TERENCE E. and MORGAN, PATRICK M. (eds), *Participatory Democracy* (Harper & Row, New York, 1971).

FINN, JAMES (ed.), *Protest: Pacifism and Politics* (Vintage Books, New York, 1968).

GOODMAN, MITCHELL (ed.), *The Movement Toward a New America* (Pilgrim Press, Philadelphia, 1970).

GOODMAN, PAUL (ed.), *Seeds of Liberation* (George Braziller, New York, 1964).

JACOBS, PAUL and LANDAU, SAUL (eds), *The New Radicals* (Random House, New York, 1966).

LONG, PRISCILLA (ed.), *The New Left* (Porter Sargent, Boston, 1969).

TEODORI, MASSIMO (ed.), *The New Left* (Jonathan Cape, London, 1970).

Bibliographies

Exhaustive bibliographies can be found in Cook and Morgan, Finn, Long, Teodori (see above); and Roszak (see below). See also 'Reading about the New Left' by Allen Hunter and James O'Brien in *Socialist Revolution*, 1972, and in D. Widgery, *The Left in Britain: 1956–68* (Penguin, Harmondsworth, 1976), pp. 506–14, 522–30 and 534.

Other useful books that help define the period:

CARTER, A., *Direct Action and Liberal Democracy* (Routledge & Kegan Paul, London, 1973).

COHN-BENDIT, D., *Obsolete Communism: The Left Wing Alternative* (Penguin, Harmondsworth, 1969).
DELLINGER, D., *Revolutionary Nonviolence* (Anchor Books, New York, 1971).
DELLINGER, D., *More Power Than We Know* (Doubleday, 1975).
OPPENHEIMER, M., *Urban Guerrilla* (Penguin, Harmondsworth, 1969).

Journals

Throughout the period the magazines and papers that are the best guide are:

In America:
Liberation
Win
New Left Notes (up to 1969)
Studies on the Left (ceased publication in 1967)

In Britain:
Universities and Left Review and *New Left Review* (up to 1963)
Anarchy (up to 1970)
Peace News
Socialist Register (1964 onwards)
Solidarity

Introductory surveys

Adequate analysis and description is more elusive and is better for the earlier New Left. See:

CLECAK, PETER, Preface and chapters 1, 2, and 7 of *Radical Paradoxes* (Harper & Row, New York, 1973).
JACOBS, PAUL and LANDAU, SAUL, Introduction to *The New Radicals* (Penguin, Harmondsworth, 1967).
LYND, STAUGHTON, Introduction to *The New Left*, (ed.) Priscilla Long (Porter Sargent, Boston, 1969).
NEWFIELD, JACK, *Prophetic Minority*, Signet Books, 1966.
O'BRIEN, J., *History of the New Left, 1960–68* (New England Free Press, Boston, 1968) – pamphlet.
OGLESBY, CARL, Introduction to *The New Left Reader*, (ed.) Carl Oglesby (Grove Press, New York, 1969).
OGLESBY, CARL, 'Decade Ready for a Dustbin', in *The Movement Toward a New America*, (ed.) Mitchell Goodman (Pilgrim Press, Philadelphia, 1970).
TEODORI, MASSIMO, Introductory section of *The New Left*, (ed.) Massimo Teodori (Jonathan Cape, London, 1970).

On Britain

WIDGERY, D., *The Left in Britain: 1956–68* (Penguin, Harmondsworth, 1976). Very much with an 'International Socialist' slant, but has some interesting introductory sections.

On SDS

JACOB, H. *Weatherman* (Ramparts Press 1970).
SALE, KIRKPATRICK, *History of SDS* (Random House, New York, 1971), is both exhaustive and largely dependable.

On the 'Counter Culture'

BERKE, J., *Counter Culture* (Owen, 1969).
HALL, STUART, 'The Hippies: An American "Moment" in Student Power', ed. Julian Nagel (Merlin Press, London, 1969).
NUTTALL, JEFF, *Bomb Culture* (Paladin, London, 1970).
ROSZAK, THEODORE, *The Making of a Counter Culture* (Faber & Faber, London, 1970).

Other works cited extensively

BENEWICK, R. and SMITH, T., *Direct Action and Democratic Politics* (Allen & Unwin, London, 1972).
DUFF, P., *Left, Left, Left* (Alison & Busby, 1971).
GITLIN, T., 'The Dynamics of the New Left', *Motive*, October/November, 1970.
HOWE, I., *The Radical Papers* (Anchor Books, New York, 1966).
KAHN, T., 'The Problem of the New Left', *Commentary*, July 1966.
LASCH, C., *Agony of American Radicalism* (Penguin, Harmondsworth, 1973).
LENS, S., *Radicalism in America* (Apollo Books, 1969)
LESTER, J., *Revolutionary Notes* (Institute for Study of Nonviolence, 1970).
REICH, C., *The Greening of America* (Penguin, Harmondsworth, 1972).
WEINSTEIN, J., 'The Left, Old and New', *Socialist Revolution*, July/August 1972.
ZINN, H., *SNCC: The New Abolitionists* (Beacon Press, Boston, 1964).

Index

Abernathy, Ralph, 35
AFL-CIO, *see* American Federation of Labor
agency, 3, 99–113
Al Fatah, 251
Albania, 16
Aldermaston marches, 1, 24, 28–9, 37, 49, 58, 64, 75–6, 146, 150–1, 154, 180, 245
Algeria, 16, 151, 166–9, 188, 257, 260, 279–80
Ali, Tariq, 4, 160
alienation, 11–12, 19–21, 76, 131–2, 142, 210, 216, 218, 354, 379
Alpert, Richard, 357
Altamont Music Festival, 250
alternative institutions, *see* counter institutions
Althusser, Louis, 147
'America and the New Era', 132
American Federation of Labor/ Council of Industrial Organizations (AFL-CIO), 100
American New Left, 1–2, 5–6, 17, 56, 131, 138
Amsterdam, 93, 205
anarchism, 9, 18–19, 23, 30, 33–4, 47, 52, 58, 77, 91, 95, 127, 134–7, 141–3, 197, 237, 255, 273, 298, 332, 356
anarchist/s, 9, 13–14, 30, 52, 62, 88, 94, 100, 103, 133–43, 154, 157, 160, 161, 181–2, 200–1, 216, 220, 256, 269, 271, 279–80, 379–80; British, 11, 13, 77, 135, 145, 172, 379
Anarchy, 77, 135, 383
Anderson, Chester, 355
'Angry Brigade', 279–80
anti-imperialism, 2, 69, 329, 365
anti-psychiatry, 234, 357, 366, 373
arms race, nuclear, 7, 11–12, 153
Arrowsmith, Pat, 30
Atlanta Democratic Convention, 84
Auschwitz, 20
Ayers, Bill, 202

Baader-Meinhof group, 280, 348
Bailey, Ron, 158
Bakunin, M., 4, 103–4, 134, 385
Baldwin, James, 114–15, 117, 121
Baran, Paul, 140
Bardacke, Frank, 330
Barnett, Ross, 293
Batista, President, 278
Battle of Algiers (film), 279
Bay of Pigs, 169
BCPV, *see* British Campaign for Peace in Vietnam
Beats, 34, 54, 135, 357, 377
Bell, Daniel, 213
Berke, Joseph, 234
Berkeley, 6, 26–7, 32, 49, 53, 60–1, 89–90, 110, 119, 190, 196, 199, 207, 211, 215, 220, 238, 245–6, 289, 291–2, 295, 306, 308, 326, 337, 342, 353, 367, 378
Berkeley Draft Information Committee, 32
Berkeley Free Church, 249, 365
Berlin, 74, 76, 205, 220; steelworkers, 16
Berrigan, Daniel, 32, 171
the Berrigans, 271, 365
Binh, Mme T., 180
'Birchers', 287
Birmingham (Alabama), 25, 116, 225–6, 228
Birnbaum, Norman, 146, 324
black culture, 105–7, 124
Black Dwarf, 159, 161
black movement, 61, 139, 226–7, 231, 238–9, 260–4, 328–9, 349–50, 378
Black Muslims, 55, 105, 114, 117, 123, 127–8, 238, 356
black nationalism, 82, 87, 114–15, 118, 199–200, 320
Black Panthers, Black Panther Party (BPP), 84–7, 118, 126–9, 133–4, 139, 186, 193, 200–1, 206, 240–1, 243–4, 250, 260, 262–5, 268, 275, 279, 282, 288, 293, 297, 303, 316, 320, 327, 331, 346–50, 356, 368

Black Power, 2–3, 54, 56, 61–2, 81, 108, 115–16, 125, 226, 229, 241, 243, 262, 306, 331, 340, 349, 357
black self-defence, 118, 243–4
Black September, 250, 260, 282
Blackburn, Robin, 160
Blanqui, Auguste, 385
Bond, Julian, 84–5, 87, 225
Bookchin, Murray (alias Lewis Herber), 4, 133, 377
Booth, Paul, 43
Bottomore, T. B., 19–20, 130
Boumédienne, Houari, 316
BPC, *see* British Peace Committee
BPP, *see* Black Panthers
British Campaign for Peace in Vietnam (BCPV), 179
British Peace Committee (BPC), 156
Brown, Norman O., 4, 34, 92–3, 270, 307, 354, 357
Brown, Rap, 128, 215, 241, 262, 326, 350
Buber, Martin, 36
Budapest (Hungarian Revolution, 1956), 16, 219–20
Buddhists, Vietnamese, 207, 281

Calvert, Greg, 43, 108–9, 192, 247, 254, 276, 329–30, 341–2
Camara, Bishop Dom Helder, 365
Cambodia, 15, 185
Campaign for Nuclear Disarmament (CND), 3, 6, 16, 26, 29, 37, 42, 49, 52, 55, 63, 66–8, 70–7, 85, 101, 135, 144, 146–59, 179–81, 219, 226, 265, 292, 298–9, 322, 381–2
Camus, Albert, 22, 35–8, 41–3, 46, 134, 136, 138–9, 169, 172, 230–3, 270, 280, 302, 309, 333
Canada, 32, 78
Carmichael, Stokeley, 4, 29, 41, 49, 87, 104 5, 115, 117 26, 128, 183, 192, 211, 215, 226–7, 231–4, 239–43, 247, 262, 276, 278, 283, 302–3, 325–6, 331, 348–50, 364, 368–9
Carter, April, 145, 288, 360
Castle, Barbara, 69
Castro, Fidel, 40 1, 182, 184, 188, 220, 255, 258, 312, 230, 369
Castroism, 169, 255
Catonsville Nine, 365
Central Intelligence Agency (CIA), 192, 212, 267, 345, 365
CGT, *see* Confédération Générale du Travail
Chardin, Teilhard de, 33
Chavez, Cesar, *see* Grape Strike
Chessman, Caryl, 291
Chicago, 196, 198–9, 203, 229, 240, 341, 354; Battle of, *see* Democratic Convention, Chicago, 1968, demonstrations; Conspiracy Trial, 252, 279–80

China, 9, 14, 16, 165–7, 175, 177, 183, 185, 187, 216, 256–8, 260, 315, 317, 379
Chomsky, Noam, 179
Christie, Stuart, 73
CIA, *see* Central Intelligence Agency
civil disobedience, 29–32, 196, 265, 291, 294, 347–8
Civil Rights Act (1964), 82, 115, 295
Civil Rights Association (CRA), 265–6
Civil Rights Movement, 2–3, 28, 31, 63, 80, 82, 106, 116, 148, 227–30, 240, 245, 248, 265, 291, 295, 324, 328, 348
Clark, George, 60, 158, 341
Cleaver, Eldridge, 87, 114, 124, 127–9, 243, 262, 275, 278, 326, 349–50, 368–9
CND, *see* Campaign for Nuclear Disarmament
CNVA, *see* Committee for Nonviolent Action
Cobb, Charles, 120
Coffin, Tristram, 294
COFO, *see* Council of Federated Organizations
Cohen, M., 5
Cohn-Bendit, Daniel, 4, 31, 41, 134, 216, 269
Cold War, 8, 10, 13, 14 15, 23, 138, 143, 151, 153–4, 156
Cole, G. D. H., 161
Collins, Canon John, 151
Columbia, 4, 196
Columbia University rebellion, 189, 196, 199, 206–8, 212–15, 275, 291, 361
Committee for Nonviolent Action (CNVA), 30, 34, 293
Committee for Sane Nuclear Policy (SANE), 24, 66, 74, 148, 152–3, 298–300
Committee of 100, 1, 73–7, 95, 134–5, 146, 148, 151, 153–5, 158, 160, 226, 291–3, 340, 344
Communications Services, 351
Communist Party (Britain) (CPGB), 8–9, 70, 79, 145–7, 153–7, 160
Communist Party (France) (PCF), 147, 217
Communist Party (Soviet Union) (CPSU), 9, 13
Communist Party (USA) (CPUSA), 8, 87, 150, 239, 298–302, 317
community organizing/action, 2–3, 56, 132, 155, 158
Confédération Générale du Travail (CGT), 217
confrontation, 244–53, 257, 283–6
confrontationism tactics, 283, 286, 290

Congress of Racial Equality (CORE), 82, 116, 118, 127, 212, 225, 228, 230, 238, 241, 330, 335
Connor, Bull, 284, 293
conscienceism, 131
convergence, theories of, 10, 12–15, 21
Cooper, David, 234, 373
CORE, *see* Congress of Racial Equality
Cornell University, 249
Council of Federated Organizations (COFO), 84, 228
counter culture, 2–4, 7, 17, 19, 37, 54, 58–63, 92, 111, 123, 135, 152, 160, 235, 237–8, 250, 271, 275, 304–7, 323, 331–6, 347, 351, 353–9, 367, 374–6
counter institutions, 48–9, 54, 59, 61–3, 65, 132, 137, 235, 238, 272, 305, 326–7, 329, 331–6, 352–5
CPGB, *see* Communist Party (Britain)
CPSU, *see* Communist Party (Soviet Union)
CPUSA, *see* Communist Party (USA)
CRA, *see* Civil Rights Association
'Crossman-Padley' (compromise document, 1960), 71
Cruse, Harold, 121
Cuba, 8–9, 15–16, 33, 152–4, 166, 169–70, 175, 188, 195, 201, 216, 239, 256–8, 260, 278, 304, 315
Czechoslovakia, Russian invasion, 1968, 4, 7, 16, 156, 206–8, 218–20, 235–6, 273, 351

DAC, *see* Direct Action Committee
Dada, 135, 216
Daley, Richard J. (Mayor of Chicago), 88, 208, 221, 284
Davidson, Carl, 43, 48, 108–9, 247, 330
Davis, Angela, 350
Davis, Rennie, 358
Deacons (for Defense and Justice), 127, 229, 238, 241, 243–4
Debray, Régis, 4, 41, 166–8, 187, 232, 248, 251, 255, 257–60, 278, 326
Dellinger, David, 31, 39, 43, 169–70, 172, 179, 248, 300, 341
Democratic Convention, Atlanta, 84
Democratic Convention, Chicago, 1968, 86–7; demonstrations, 88, 196, 206–8, 215, 218, 221–2, 248, 264, 275, 284–6, 350, 357
Democratic Party, 67, 79, 83–6, 88, 208, 287
Detroit, 211, 252, 264
Deutscher, Isaac, 139, 164–5
Dewey, John, 304
Dialectics of Liberation Conference, Roundhouse, London, 1967, 234, 263
Diem, President, 178, 278

Diggers, 135, 253, 353, 355
direct action, 2, 77, 136, 145, 222, 224, 226, 327, 248, 360–1
Direct Action Committee (UK) (DAC), 49, 51
Djilas, Milovan, 12
Dodd, Thomas, 298
Dodge Revolutionary Union Movement (DRUM), 105
Dohrn, Bernardine, 4, 202, 276, 281, 341, 370, 372
Dominican Republic, 15
Donaldson, Ivanhoe, 120, 225
Dow Chemical Company, 248, 345, 365
draft: card burnings, 32, 133; emigration, 294; resistance, 2, 32, 39, 55, 95, 273, 292, 294, 342
DRUM, *see* Dodge Revolutionary Union Movement
DRVN, *see* North Vietnam
Du Bois Clubs of America, 87, 139, 298, 300, 306, 309, 313, 344
Dubček, Alexander, 218
Duff, Peggy, 148–9
'Duragraha', 224–5, 228, 239
Dutschke, Rudi, 4, 91, 291
Dylan, Bob, 275

East Village Other (EVO), 357
Easy Rider (film), 358
Economic Research and Action Project (ERAP), 47, 51, 58, 78
Egleson, Nick, 43, 131, 258
Ellsberg, Daniel, 271, 353, 365
Ellul, Jacques, 12, 379
Engels, F., 142
English New Left, 1, 2, 5–6, 9, 17, 47–8, 55, 139–40
Eniwetok nuclear test zone, 33
Epton, Bill, 114, 230, 261, 318
ERAP, *see* Economic Research and Action Project
Evers, Medgar, 31, 224
'Everyman', voyage of, 33
EVO, *see* East Village Other
extra-parliamentarianism, 3, 56, 59, 63, 66–98, 135, 159

Fanon, Franz, 41–3, 49, 54, 103, 115, 121, 123, 140, 166–7, 175, 183, 187, 232, 243, 255, 257–8, 260, 315, 326, 338
Fanonist, 168
Farmer, James, 118, 239, 263
Federal Bureau of Investigation (FBI), 8, 267, 295
Ferber, Michael K., 32
Flacks, Richard, 43
FLN, *see* Front de Libération National
FOE, *see* Friends of the Earth
Foreman, James, 120, 128, 241
France, *see* Communist Party (France); Nanterre; Paris

Frankfurt School, 147
Frazier, Franklin, 239
free cinema, 146
free radio, 137
'free' schools, 43, 137, 335, 378
Free Speech Movement (FSM) (Berkeley), 1–2, 16, 26–7, 35–6, 43, 49, 51–2, 56, 60, 89–90, 109–10, 134, 137, 190, 245, 337
Free Student, 316
free universities, 27, 43, 52, 59, 90, 316, 332, 335
Freedman, Professor, 241
Freedom, 135
Freedom Democratic Party, *see* Mississippi Freedom Democratic Party
freedom rides, 3, 38
Freedom Summers, 26, 43, 193, 225, 239, 288, 349
Freud, S., 374
Friends of the Earth (FOE), 381
Fromm, Erich, 19–20, 23, 24–5, 35, 38, 41–3, 57, 230, 307, 374, 376, 380
Front de Libération National (Algeria), 168–9, 257, 279
FSM, *see* Free Speech Movement

Gaitskell, Hugh, 68, 72–3, 150, 152, 156
Galbraith, J. K., 140
Gandhi, Mohandas K., 31, 35, 55, 133, 219, 223–4, 227–8, 233, 237, 239, 273, 387
Gay Liberation movement, 366, 368, 370, 375–6
Geismar, Alain, 92
Gerassi, John, 196, 234, 258, 263, 326
ghetto (USA), 105, 108, 117, 124–5, 203, 211, 227, 238, 244, 258–65, 326, 369, 378; culture, 93, 105, 243
Giap, General, 168, 257, 278
Gilbert, Dave, 108
Ginsberg, Allan, 95, 354
Gitlin, Todd, 46, 94, 133, 188, 200, 241, 254, 256, 298, 323, 339, 343, 353, 376, 278
Glazer, Nathan, 124
Golden Rule, voyage of, 33
Goldwater, Barry, 82–3, 239, 287
'Good Soldier Schweik', The, 219
Goodman, Mitchell, 134, 294
Goodman, Paul, 20, 23, 31, 35, 36, 40–3, 45, 46, 57, 58, 62–3, 118, 134, 214, 231, 234, 257, 263, 267, 307, 345, 367, 374, 378–80
Gramsci, Antonio, 42
Grape Strike, California (United Farmworkers), 207, 239, 363–4
Grass, Günther, 220
Gray, Jesse, 230, 261
Greece, 151
'Greenpeace', 153, 381–2

Greensborough (North Carolina), 25, 43, 224
Grosvenor Square demonstrations, 159, 226, 273
Guardian (New York), 88, 303
guerilla: theory, 245, 258; warfare, 2, 112, 168, 178, 209, 241, 243–4, 248, 257–8, 326, 331; *see also* urban guerilla tactics
guerillas, Palestinian, 250, 265
Guevara, Ernesto 'Che', 4, 40–1, 133, 175, 184, 187–8, 204, 209–10, 215, 232, 234, 248, 255, 258–9, 315, 320, 326, 369

Haber, Al, 43, 66
Haight-Ashbury (San Francisco), 124, 357, 367
Hain, Peter, 348
Hale, D., 5
Hall, Stuart, 147, 307
Hanoi, 173–4, 177, 181; *see also* North Vietnam
Harlem, 45, 82, 212, 230, 240, 261, 315
Harpers magazine, 325
Harrington, Michael, 42, 80, 103, 140, 346
Harris, David, 32, 96, 134, 271
Hayden, Tom, 23, 35, 39–41, 43, 45, 47, 54, 56, 59, 69, 78–80, 103, 105, 169–70, 179, 191, 221, 232, 235, 244, 247–8, 262, 267, 271, 275, 284, 295, 300, 330, 333, 335, 338, 340, 344
Hazard (Kentucky), 261
Herber, Lewis, *see* Bookchin, Murray
Hershey, General, 95
Hilliard, David, 127
hippies, 34, 54, 58, 88, 93, 124, 237, 246, 253, 365, 377
Hiroshima, 20
Ho Chi Minh, 133, 159, 176, 179–80, 182, 187–8, 218, 220, 234, 256–9, 315
Hoffman, Abbie, 326, 355
Holt, John, 378
Homme Revolté, L', 38
Horowitz, David, 276, 369
House Unamerican Activities Committee (HUAC), 291, 298–9
Howe, Irving, 80, 140, 275, 281, 303, 305–6, 326
HUAC, *see* House Unamerican Activities Committee
Hughes, Stuart, 85
Humphrey, Hubert, 68, 88–9, 285
Hungary, 9, 16, 139; *see also* Budapest
Hus, Jan, 219

IDA, *see* Institute of Defense Analysis
ideology, 3, 9–11, 16–17, 21–2, 36, 39, 44–5, 48, 130–43, 288; *see also* New Left ideology

Illich, Ivan, 378
IMG, *see* International Marxist Group
Independent Nuclear Disarmament Election Committee (INDEC), 74
Independent Socialists (USA), 87, 139
India, 166
Indo-China, *see* Vietnam
Industrial Workers of the World (IWW), *see* 'Wobblies'
Institute for Policy Studies (IPS), 87
Institute for Workers' Control (IWC), 161
Institute of Defense Analysis (IDA), 212–14
integration/ism, 114–20, 124–6, 227
International Marxist Group (IMG), 139, 160–2, 311
International Socialists (IS), 75, 139, 145, 160–2, 311
IPS, *see* Institute for Policy Studies
Irish Republican Army (IRA), 182, 251, 260, 264, 266, 279–80
IS, *see* International Socialists
IWC, *see* Institute for Workers' Control
IWW, *see* 'Wobblies'

Jackson, George, 350
Jacobs, Hal, 277–8, 319
Jacobs, Paul, 5, 87–8, 200, 301
Japan, 78, 183–4
Jeunesse Communiste Révolutionnaire (JCR), 311
John Birch Society, *see* 'Birchers'
Johnson, President Lyndon B., 86, 179, 205–6, 212, 329
Jones, Le Roi, 114–15, 117, 215, 239, 262, 278, 350

Kabouter Movement, 93, 135, 235, 366
Kahn, Tom, 80, 101, 174, 339
Katzenbach, Attorney General, 291
Keniston, Kenneth, 53, 334, 341
Kennedy, President John F., 68–9, 82, 86, 89, 228–9, 250
Kennedy, Robert, 86, 88, 208, 295
Kerr, Clark, 90, 292, 295
Kesey, Ken, 355
King, Martin Luther, 29–31, 35–6, 39, 82, 87, 115–16, 118, 126, 206–7, 210–12, 223–31, 233, 237, 239, 241, 261, 263, 315
Kirk, President, Columbia University, 215
Kissinger, Clark, 43
Kitson, Brigadier, 289
Klonsky, Mike, 202, 248, 252, 279, 318, 323
Kopkind, Andrew D., 132
Kronstadt, 133
Kropotkin, Peter, 58

Khrushchev, Nikita, 317

Labour-left, 75, 92, 147, 149, 154, 180
Labour Party (British), 5, 52, 63, 68–77, 91–2, 140, 145–8; Scarborough conference, *see* Scarborough; tactic, 146–7, 155
Laing, R. D., 4, 25, 39, 234, 363, 367, 373–4
Lakey, George, 248, 273
Landau, Saul, 5, 301
Langer, Elinor, 2
Laos, 185
Lasch, Christopher, 106, 132, 186, 221, 241, 260, 281, 284, 286, 289, 322
League for Industrial Democracy (LID), 300
Leary, Timothy, 124, 355, 357, 380
Lenin, V. I., 133, 140, 256, 306, 319, 377, 385, 387–8
Leningrad, *see* Petrograd
Leninism, 42, 182, 216, 254–5; *see also* Marxism-Leninism
Leninist, 94, 147, 162, 168, 184, 187, 202, 246, 256, 300, 339
Lens, Sidney, 130, 248–9, 366
Lester, Julius, 139, 188, 224, 250, 269, 278, 285, 308, 349, 351
Lévi-Strauss, Claude, 147
Lewis, John, 82, 118, 120, 225
liberalism, 2, 3, 8, 10–11, 13, 16, 18–19, 21–2, 66–70, 103, 106, 118, 130, 141, 143, 221, 283–4, 288, 333, 342–6, 378
Liberation (magazine and group), 12–13, 21, 30–1, 33–4, 42, 169–70, 182, 269, 272
Liberation News Service (LNS), 351
LID, *see* League for Industrial Democracy
Liebknecht, Karl, 91
Ligt, Bart de, 273
Lin Piao, 166, 183, 388
Lipset, S. M., 306, 337
Liu Shao-Chi, 318
LNS, *see* Liberation News Service
Lodge, Henry Cabot, 179
London School of Economics (LSE), 159, 205, 207, 226, 291, 342, 346
Los Angeles (LA) Free Press, 43
Lowndes County Freedom Organization, 84–5, 118, 120
LSE, *see* London School of Economics
'Luddites', 380
Lukács, G., 42
Lumumba, Patrice, 133
Luxemburg, Rosa, 42, 91, 133, 216
Lynd, Staughton, 23, 31, 34, 39–40, 43–6, 47, 54, 56, 58, 69, 75, 78, 82, 96, 103, 169–74, 177, 192, 202, 244, 272, 300, 329–30, 333, 344

McCarthy, Eugene, 86, 88–9, 198, 206, 208, 221, 331
McCarthy, Joseph, 5, 15, 290–1, 299; McCarthyism, 287, 296
McCarthy, Mary, 182, 286
Macdonald, Dwight, 5
McGovern, George, 86, 89, 331
McKissick, Floyd, 241
McLuhan, Marshall, 350
McReynolds, David, 169–70, 172, 179, 182, 234
Mailer, Norman, 5, 357
Malatesta, Enrico, 46
Malcolm-X, 41, 85, 114–17, 127–8, 133, 187, 215, 225, 230, 239, 243–4, 303, 312, 326, 350
male chauvinism, 358, 367–71
Mandel, Ernest, 139, 141
Mann, Eric, 214
Manson, Charles, and 'family', 250, 375
Mao Tse-Tung, 4, 133, 166, 168, 187–8, 209, 215, 243, 250, 258–9, 386, 388
Maoism, 140, 166, 200, 255, 261
Maoist, 52, 160–1, 165, 173, 175, 180, 185, 200, 229, 247, 277, 300, 319–20, 346
March Twenty-Second Movement (M22M), 134, 216
Marcuse, Herbert, 4, 10, 17, 19–20, 25, 40–3, 51, 59, 79, 91, 93–4, 96–8, 99–101, 103–4, 112–13, 133–4, 139, 175, 187, 200, 203, 207, 227–8, 231–2, 234, 250, 252–3, 267–8, 271–2, 274, 280, 283–5, 307, 320, 322, 325–7, 331–2, 338–40, 343–6, 350, 352, 374–7, 379–80
Martin, Barnaby, 158
Marx, Karl, 12, 19–20, 99, 102, 104, 133, 138, 140–2, 195, 215, 255, 374, 377, 385, 387–8
Marxism, 3, 5, 8–14, 20–3, 24, 47, 91, 103, 130–3, 134, 138–43, 144, 147, 203, 219, 232, 254–6, 269, 274, 298, 319, 332, 338, 354, 381; Soviet, 10, 23, 139
Marxism-Leninism, 127, 133, 139–40, 182, 185, 188, 197, 202, 246, 261, 306, 330; see also Leninism
Marxist, 16–18, 39, 42–3, 47, 99, 103, 108, 112, 130–3, 136, 138–9, 142–3, 148, 166, 168, 185, 195, 254–6, 266, 269, 299–300, 304, 306, 332, 340–1, 379
Marxist humanism, 9, 19, 138
'mass society' theory, 57
Max, Steve, 191
May Day Manifesto, 1967, 75, 146, 148, 160, 342
May 2nd Movement (M2M), 185, 300–1, 315–16, 321

MDS, see Movement for a Democratic Society
media, the, 9, 20, 93, 126, 137, 153, 159, 212, 219, 230, 240, 243, 245, 267, 277, 292–3, 324–5, 343, 346–54, 367
Memphis, 206–7, 210–12, 230, 237
Menderes, Adnan, 110
Meredith, James, 31, 224, 226
'Meredith March', the, 117, 119
Merseyside, 45
MFDP, see Mississippi Freedom Democratic Party
Michels, Roberto, 49, 133
militarism, 20–1, 385–9
Mill, J. S., 304
Miller, David, 32
Mills, C. Wright, 5, 7, 10–11, 14, 20, 23, 24–5, 31, 38, 41–3, 45, 46–8, 57, 85, 96–7, 99, 103, 109, 112, 131–2, 139, 144, 169, 276, 318, 333, 344, 350, 357, 379
Minutemen, 242, 265, 287
Mississippi, 26, 43, 45, 47, 53, 64, 79, 82, 288, 293
Mississippi Freedom Democratic Party (MFDP), 43, 83–4, 86, 333
Mobutu, General, 123
Montgomery: Bus Boycott, 1955, 43, 224; March, 229; see also Selma-Montgomery March, 1965
Moore, Barrington, jnr, 11, 130, 143, 255, 258, 269, 270, 334, 336, 386
Moore, Fred, 32
Morgan, Robin, 370, 375
Morin, Edgar, 207
Morris, William, 37, 377
Morrison, Norman, 32
Moses, Bob, 31, 35, 83, 120
Mouvement du 22 Mars, see March 22nd Movement
Movement for a Democratic Society (MDS), 109
movement theory, 1, 44
Moynihan Report, 124
Muskie, Edmund, 86
Muslims, see Black Muslims
Muste, A. J., 12, 20, 24, 30–1, 33, 35–9, 43, 45–6, 66, 85, 96, 169–71, 179, 231
Myrdal, Gunnar, 124–5

NAACP, see National Association for the Advancement of Colored People
NAM, see New American Movement
Nanterre, 291; see also Paris
National Association for the Advancement of Colored People (NAACP), 82, 115–17, 129, 224, 239, 300
National Conference for New Politics (NCNP), 80, 87–8
National Convention of the Left, 1969, 160

National Coordinating Committee to End the War in Vietnam, 170, 312
National Democratic Party Convention, 1968, *see* Democratic Convention, Chicago
National Guard, 238, 283, 289, 297
National Liberation Front (Algeria), *see* Front de Libération National
National Liberation Front (Vietnam), 165, 171–9, 185–6, 195, 200–1, 206, 208–10, 233, 237, 241, 250, 257, 260, 276–7, 279, 300, 320
national liberation movements, 165–7, 173–5, 183, 187
National Mobilization Committee to End the War in Vietnam, 194, 221, 330
National Peace Action Coalition (NAPC), 313
National Union of Students (NUS), 161, 346
nationalism, 164–6, 182–3, 362, *see also* black nationalism
NATO, *see* North Atlantic Treaty Organization
Nazism, 13
NCNP, *see* National Conference for New Politics
NCUP, *see* Newark Community Union Project
Nechaev, Sergei G., 134
Neill, A. S., 378
Neiman, Carol, 108, 342
New American Movement (NAM), 187, 194
New Left ideology, 17–18, 130–43
New Left movements, 1, 35–43; *see also* American New Left; English New Left
New Left Notes, 195, 200, 203, 251
New Left Review (*NLR*), 70, 135, 144–8, 330
New Left theory, 6–7, 38–41, 59, 322
'New Politics Conference', *see* National Conference for New Politics
New Reasoner, 52, 139, 144, 146
'new working-class' theories, 108–13, 132
New York Times, 241, 348
Newark Black Power Conference, 1967, 124
Newark Community Union Project (NCUP), 80, 105, 305; *see also* Economic Research and Action Project; Hayden, Tom
Newark Rebellion, 262, 330
Newfield, Jack, 4, 51, 84, 349
Newsweek, 167, 325
Newton, Huey P., 126–9, 187, 204, 244, 350
Nicolaus, Martin, 139
Niemöller, Martin, 90

Nixon, President Richard M., 89, 208, 286–7, 296, 357
Nkrumah, Kwame, 123
NLF, *see* National Liberation Front (Vietnam)
NLR, see New Left Review
non-alignment, *see* positive neutralism
nonviolence, 2, 82, 116, 118–19, 207–8, 210–11, 218–19, 221, 223–41, 246, 249, 253, 259–61, 265, 273, 304, 327–8, 361, 365, 376, 382–3
North Atlantic Treaty Organization (NATO), 150, 155–6, 219
North Vietnam, 170, 175–6, 178–9, 184–5, 206, 209, 233, 237; *see also* Giap, General; Hanoi; Vietnam
NPAC, *see* National Peace Action Coalition
nuclear arms race, 7, 11–12, 153
nuclear deterrence, 156; *see also* Campaign for Nuclear Disarmament; Committee of 100
nuclear disarmament, *see* Campaign for Nuclear Disarmamant; Committee of 100
NUS, *see* National Union of Students
Nuttall, Jeff, 29

Oakland Induction Centre, 32, 245–6, 249
O'Brien, James, 2, 197, 230, 275, 279, 314, 328, 331, 339, 370–1
Oglesby, Carl, 12, 36–7, 43, 108, 112, 123, 135, 164–5, 178, 185, 216, 256, 269, 274, 283–4, 309, 319, 322–3, 324, 329–30, 339, 377
Ohnesorg, Benno, 291
Old Left, 2–3, 9, 18, 44, 53–4, 58, 78, 93, 133, 139–40, 157–60, 167, 170, 188, 189, 199–200, 220, 230–1, 249, 256–7, 264, 269, 280, 290, 298–323, 330–1, 336–7, 342, 344, 361, 379
Oppenheimer, Martin, 49, 241, 245, 252, 255, 258, 263, 268, 289, 335, 337, 388
Oracle (San Francisco), 357
Oswald, Lee Harvey, 242
Owen, Robert, 161
Oz, 375

pacifism, 11, 15, 30–5, 52, 168–74, 185, 237, 273, 365, 378
Palach, Jan, 281
Palestinian guerillas, 250, 265
parallel institutions, *see* counter institutions
Paris, May 1968 events, 7, 91, 134, 136, 141, 205–7, 215–16, 220, 248, 266, 312
Parks, Rosa, 224
Parris, Bob, 225
participation, 53

participatory democracy (PD), 2–3, 28, 31, 45, 46–50, 54, 79, 81, 91–2, 96, 123, 132, 163, 189–90, 214, 218, 302, 311, 325, 329–30, 336–41, 372, 379
PCF, *see* Communist Party (France)
PD, *see* participatory democracy
Peace and Freedom Party (PFP), 87–8
peace movement, 2–3, 11, 31, 34, 49, 71–2, 135, 152–3, 292–4, 328–9, 378
Peace News (*PN*), 135
peaceful co-existence, 155–6
peasant communes, 133, 387
Pentagon: confrontation, October, 1967, 205, 221, 245–7, 350; demonstrations, 1965, 1966, 1967, 196, 354
People's Park, 4, 237, 290, 295, 354, 357, 360–1, 366, 381
'Pepsi generation', 29, 118, 302
Petrograd, 133
PFP, *see* Peace and Freedom Party
Phoenix, voyage of, 33
Picasso, Pablo, 15
Pigs, Bay of, 169
PL, *see* Progressive Labor
pluralism, 10, 22 3
PN, see Peace News
Poland, 16
police and repression, 86, 88, 208, 213–15, 221, 224–7, 235, 239–42, 244–6, 250, 261, 283–97; *see also* provocation tactics
'police state', 284–6
polycentrism, 16, 218
Poor People's Coalition, March and Campaign, Resurrection City, 1968, 80, 207, 210, 230, 237
Port Chicago: anti-war vigil, 1965–8, 293
Port Huron Statement (SDS), 35, 42, 47–8, 57, 65, 69, 130, 132, 138, 231
positive neutralism, 3, 15, 33, 163–4
'post-scarcity', 17, 133, 367, 377–81
Potter, Paul, 43, 335
Powell, Enoch, 164, 287
press, underground, *see* underground press
PRG, *see* Provisional Revolutionary Government (Vietnam)
Progressive Labor (PL), 112, 128, 132–3, 139–40, 185, 192, 194–202, 214, 229–30, 245, 252, 260–2, 279–80, 300–1, 303–6, 309, 315–20; *see also* Students for a Democratic Society: alliance with Progressive Labor
proletariat, 99–101, 103, 160, 259, 343; black, 104–7; *see also* working class
Proudhon, P., 91
Provisional Revolutionary Government (Vietnam) (PRG), 233

provocation tactics, 283–97
Provos, 7, 46, 60, 93, 135, 291, 366

Rader, Dotson, 214
Radford, Jim, 158
radical populism, 132
Radical Students' Alliance (RSA), 159, 161
Ramparts magazine, 86, 350
Reagan, Ronald, 288, 291
Red Mole, 159–60
reformism, 65, 79, 82, 150, 155, 227
Regional Seats of Government (RSGs), 95, 151
Reich, Charles, 131, 354
Reich, Wilhelm, 4, 42, 133, 374, 376
repression, *see* Marcuse, Herbert; police and repression
repressive tolerance, 342
Reserve Officers Training Corps (ROTC), 192, 252, 365
Resistance, the, 95, 134, 157, 294, 311, 330
Reuther, Walter, 66, 100
revisionism, 138–43
Revolutionary Socialist Students' Federation (RSSF), 159, 161
Revolutionary Youth Movement (RYM), 140, 198–9, 251, 375; RYM I, 134, 201–2, 278, 330; RYM II, 201–2, 252, 279, 321
Riesman, David, 81
Roberts, Adam, 64
Rosenbergs, the, 290
Ross, Bob, 66, 319
Rossman, Mike, 60
Roszak, Theodore, 121, 135, 382
ROTC, *see* Reserve Officers Training Corps
RSA, *see* Radical Student's Alliance
RSGs, *see* Regional Seats of Government
RSSF, *see* Revolutionary Socialist Student's Federation
Rubin, Jerry, 4, 222, 326, 350, 353
Rudd, Mark, 4, 108, 112–13, 196–7, 202, 208, 211–15, 278
Rumania, 16
Russell, Bertrand, 39, 76, 151, 347
Russia, 9, 11, 13–16, 23, 135, 137, 154, 156, 176–7, 255–6, 298, 315
Rustin, Bayard, 80, 104, 106, 118, 125, 140, 174, 224, 232, 263
RYM, *see* Revolutionary Youth Movement

Sacco and Vanzetti case, 290
Sale, Kirkpatrick, 52, 132, 200, 203, 247, 275, 342
SALT, *see* Strategic Arms Limitation Talks
Sampson, Ronald, 36, 373
Samuel, Ralph, 147

San Francisco *Oracle, see Oracle*
SANE, *see* Committee for Sane Nuclear Policy
Sartre, J.-P., 4, 42, 138–9, 147–8, 167, 175, 187, 216, 231–3, 255, 270, 279–80, 284, 317–18, 326, 338, 345, 377, 379
'Satyagraha', 223, 228, 239
Savio, Mario, 4, 26–7, 35, 39, 308, 364
Scarborough Labour Party Conference, 1960, 71–3, 76
Schaar, J., 331
Scheer, Robert, 86
Schön, Donald, 53, 102, 324, 334, 377
SCLC, *see* Southern Christian Leadership Conference
SDS, *see* Sozialistischer Deutscher Studentenbund (German SDS); Students for a Democratic Society (SDS)
SDS/PL, *see* Students for a Democratic Society: alliance with Progressive Labor
Seale, Bobby, 126–9, 346, 350
Sedgwick, Peter, 161
Selective Service (SS) System, 192, 248
self-defence, 226–7, 235, 238–42, 252, 292; *see also* black self-defence
Selma-Montgomery March, 1965, 1, 25, 117
sex roles, liberation from, 366, 372, 376
sexism, 352, 358, 367–76
Sharp, Gene, 273
Shero, Jeff, 191
Sirhan, Sirhan, 250
Situationists, 7, 135, 142, 216–17, 343, 353–4
SLA, *see* Symbionese Liberation Army
SLATE (Berkeley), 190
SLL, *see* Socialist Labour League
SNCC, *see* Student Nonviolent Coordinating Committee
Snyder, Gary, 357–8
Social Democrats, 66–8, 140
socialism, 11–12, 15, 18–21, 23, 99, 134, 140–1, 344
Socialist Labour League (SLL), 154
Socialist Student League, *see* Sozialistischer Deutscher Studentenbund
Socialist Worker, 160
Socialist Workers' Party (SWP), 170, 301
Solidarity (magazine and group), 11–13, 135
Sorbonne, 49, 216–17, 341
Sorel, Georges, 42, 57, 85, 90, 139, 255
South Vietnam, 172, 177, 205, 233; *see also* National Liberation Front (Vietnam); Vietnam
Southern Christian Leadership Conference (SCLC), 82, 116, 224, 229
Soviet Union, *see* Marxism, Soviet; Russia
Sozialistischer Deutscher Studentenbund (German SDS), 90, 134, 216, 220, 238, 291
Spain, 135
Spartacists, 301
Spender, Stephen, 214
spiritual/religious revival, 356–9
Spock, Dr Benjamin, 32, 87, 201, 271, 294
Spontaneists, 216
Spring Mobilization Committee, 170, 313
Springer Press (Hamburg), 292–3
SPU, *see* Student Peace Union
squatters (squatting campaign), 134, 158, 162
Stalin, Joseph, 387
Stalinism, 3, 8–9, 13, 15, 18, 23, 143, 147, 154, 174, 216, 233, 257, 299, 310, 317–19, 326, 345, 379
Stalinist, 5, 22, 140, 180, 187–8, 201, 218, 256, 267, 274, 299, 346
STDW, *see* Stop the Draft Week
'Steps Towards Peace' (document), 146, 150
Stevenson, Adlai, 69, 86
Stockholm Peace Appeal, 154
Stone, I. F., 243
Stop-It Committee, 179
Stop the Draft Week (STDW), 196, 214, 221, 245–9, 276, 330, 342
Stop the Seventies Tour Campaign, 1969–70 (STST), 158
Strategic Arms Limitation Talks (SALT), 153
street theatre, 222
Strong, Chancellor William, 90
STST, *see* Stop the Seventies Tour Campaign, 1969–70
student activism/activists, 6, 11, 22, 146, 212
Student Mobilization Committee (Student Mobe), 314
Student Nonviolent Coordinating Committee (SNCC), 1, 3, 5, 24–6, 28–9, 31–2, 36, 43, 46–53, 56, 58, 61–3, 66, 82–5, 87, 103, 115–20, 123, 126–9, 134, 157, 174, 193–4, 202, 224–6, 228, 230–1, 238–41, 243–4, 246, 251, 254, 301, 303, 310, 329–30, 340, 349, 371
Student Peace Union (SPU), 34, 66, 148, 152, 190, 299
Student Power, 158
Student Strike for Peace Committee, 313
student strikes/action, 108–11, 205
'student syndicalism', 89–90, 108–9, 132, 330
students as a class, 110–13, 205

Students for a Democratic Society (SDS), 3–5, 21, 23, 27, 29, 31–2, 34–6, 42–4, 46–53, 56, 58, 66, 69–70, 78, 80, 83, 86, 88, 94, 100–1, 103, 107–9, 112, 130–2, 134, 144, 159, 170, 174, 176, 185–204, 208, 212–15, 218, 220–1, 231–2, 238, 244, 246–9, 251–2, 257–9, 271, 275, 278–9, 284–5, 291, 296, 299–306, 309–15, 318–22, 324–6, 329–31, 333, 335–6, 339–42, 344, 346, 348, 357–8, 360, 362–3, 365, 368, 370–1, 376–7; alliance with Progressive Labor (SDS/PL), 112, 195, 207; community projects, 2, 24; *see also* Port Huron Statement
Studies on the Left, 94, 138, 164
Suez, 15, 150, 164
Surrealism, 216
'Survival', 381
Sweezy, Paul, 140, 255, 317–18
SWP, *see* Socialist Workers' Party
Symbionese Liberation Army (SLA), 356
syndicalism, 5, 77, 80–1, 89–92, 97–8, 108–9, 132, 136, 140, 330, 332
Synghman Rhee, 110

Temps Modernes, 147
Teodori, Massimo, 2, 51, 339
Test Ban Treaty (partial), 152–3
Tet Offensive (Vietnam), 173, 177–8, 181, 197, 206–10, 250, 264
Thailand, 185
Thieu, President, 173, 210
'Third Camp', 33–4, 55, 163
Third World, 103, 133, 158–9, 163–4, 179, 183–4, 186–7, 256, 258–9, 379
Thomas, Norman, 85
Thompson, E. P., 6, 23, 54, 74, 79, 101, 139, 145, 147, 319
Thompson, Mayor of Jackson, Mississippi, 239
Thoreau, Henry David, 31, 97
Time, 325
Tito, Titoism, 141, 256
tolerance, 232–3, 292, 329, 341–6, 350
Tolkien, J. R., 358
Tolstoi, L., 136
Torres, Camillo, 365
totalitarianism, 13, 15–16, 20, 22, 174, 233, 343–4, 364
trades unions, 80, 91–2, 265, 273–4
Tribune, 52
Trotsky, L., 14, 42, 216, 386–8
Trotskyism, 13, 18–19, 141, 165, 255
Trotskyist, 23, 87, 141, 147, 154–5, 160, 172, 181, 190, 200, 256, 280, 298, 300–1
Tshombe, M., 123
TTP, *see* Turn Towards Peace
Tupamaros, 134, 260, 276
Turn Towards Peace (TTP), 300

UFW, *see* United Farmworkers Union
Ulbricht, Walter, 273
ULR, *see* Universities and Left Review
underground press, 17, 160–1, 223, 250, 352, 375
Underground Press Syndicate (UPS), 351
unilateralism, 33, 71–4, 77, 144, 146, 149, 156
United Farmworkers Union (UFW), 207, 237, 365
United Nations, 15, 115
United States, 5–7, 12, 15–16, 140
Universities and Left Review (ULR), 42, 52, 70, 139, 144–7, 160–1
UPS, *see* Underground Press Syndicate
urban guerilla tactics, 217, 243, 259–68, 327
Urban League, 116–17
USSR, *see* Russia

Vaneigem, Raoul, 207, 216
VDC, *see* Vietnam Day Committee
Vietnam, 4, 15, 16, 31–2, 55, 68–9, 100, 103, 112, 148, 153, 156, 158, 164, 168–9, 172, 175, 179, 188, 201, 228, 233–4, 236, 256–7, 284, 304, 341, 347, 380; *see also* Hanoi; North Vietnam; South Vietnam; Tet Offensive (Vietnam)
Vietnam Day Committee (VDC), 32, 51, 60, 86, 246, 289–90, 304, 313
Vietnam March, October 1968, 266
Vietnam Solidarity Committee Campaign (VSC) (Britain), 4, 152, 159–60, 206, 313; *see also* Grosvenor Square demonstrations
Vietnam war movement, 2–3, 6–7, 31, 53, 69, 80, 95, 150, 184, 191, 206, 312–13, 328–30
Vietnam Week, 313
VSC, *see* Vietnam Solidarity Committee Campaign

Wallace, Governor George, 83, 88, 100, 221, 239, 287–8
Walter, Nicholas, 72
War Resisters' International (WRI), 34
Warsaw Pact, 156
Washington: demonstrations, 237, 365; march of March 1963, 82, 221; march of April 1965, 69, 75
Waskow, Arthur, 87
Watergate, 353, 367
Watts, Alan, 357
Watts riots (Los Angeles), 114, 122, 126, 211, 227, 229, 240, 242–4, 252
Weathermen, 134, 201–3, 248, 251–2, 256, 262, 268, 275–82, 288, 296, 322, 326, 341, 345, 353, 356, 360, 375, 380

Weatherpeople, 140, 221, 244, 250, 288, 375
Weatherwomen, 370–2
Weber, Max, 14, 133
Weil, Simone, 42
Weinberg, Jack, 26
Weinstein, James, 9, 108, 187, 253, 256, 322
Weissman, Steve, 96, 330, 341
Wellman, Dave, 346, 378
White Citizens, 287
Williams, Raymond, 101, 139, 147, 342
Williams, Robert, 225, 229, 239, 261–2, 267, 312, 317, 350
Williams, William Appleman, 5
Wilson, Des, 158
Wilson, Harold, 68–9, 74, 150, 152, 159, 179
Win, 273
'Wobblies' (IWW), 31, 44, 94, 332
Women Strike for Peace (WSP), 53, 148
Women's Liberation, 199, 333, 337, 360, 366–76
Woodstock Festival, 277, 358
Worker-Student Alliance (WSA), 198, 201–2, 319
workers' control, 11, 21, 48, 58, 136, 140–1, 158, 161, 216–17, 380

workers' councils, 217
working class, 11, 54, 99–101, 104, 138–9, 149, 162, 197–9; culture, 21, 145; *see also* proletariat
World Council of Peace, 154
WRI, *see* War Resisters' International
WSA, *see* Worker-Student Alliance
WSP, *see* Women Strike for Peace

YCL, *see* Young Communist League
Yippees, 88, 124, 135, 208, 221–2, 235, 250, 253, 275, 277, 280, 288, 320, 350–1, 353–4
York, Dick, 249
Young, Andrew, 211
Young Communist League (YCL), 157
Young Liberals, 75
Young People's Socialist League (YPSL), 299, 301
Young Socialist Alliance (YSA), 141, 200, 245, 300–1, 309, 312–14
YPSL, *see* Young People's Socialist League
YSA, *see* Young Socialist Alliance
Yugoslavia and workers' control, 16, 140, 161

Zinn, Howard, 45, 83, 94, 133, 173, 327